Family Records,

or

GENEALOGIES
OF THE
FIRST SETTLERS
OF PASSAIC VALLEY
(And Vicinity)

⁙❦Ⅱ❧⁙

BY
JOHN LITTELL

CLEARFIELD

Reprinted for
Clearfield Company, Inc. by
Genealogical Publishing Co., Inc.
Baltimore, Maryland
2002

Originally published: Feltville, New Jersey, 1852
Reprinted: Genealogical Publishing Co., Inc.
Baltimore: 1976, 1981
Reprinted from a volume in the collection
of the New Jersey State Library
Library of Congress Catalogue Card Number 76-348
International Standard Book Number 0-8063-0713-7
Made in the United States of America

FAMILY RECORDS,

OR

GENEALOGIES

OF THE

FIRST SETTLERS

OF

PASSAIC VALLEY

(AND VICINITY,)

ABOVE CHATHAM.

BY

JOHN LITTELL.

1852.

PREFACE.

It is an interesting object of curiosity to most men to search into the origin of their own families, to trace their descents, and to collect the history of the individuals who compose them. However remote in time or consanguinity, it is natural to believe that we inherit from our fathers their mental and physical peculiarities, though modified by circumstances. We enter affectionately into their concerns, and rejoice in their honors or prosperity, and are personally grieved by their misconduct or misfortunes.

These sentiments are undoubtedly founded in the innate and best feelings of the human heart, which delights in multiplying and extending the ties that bind us to our fellow creatures. The love of our kindred is the first degree of expansion of the heart in its progress towards universal benevolence. The history of states is but a history of families.

To satisfy this curiosity, in some measure, has been my aim in collecting the materials for the genealogies in this publication. Much pains have been taken to obtain correct information respecting families. Wherever family records could be obtained, they have been used; but in most cases no such record could be had. I therefore had to depend on the memory of some one or more of the family, and in consequence, no doubt, many errors may be found; but I hope for the most part the names are correct. With the exception of one or two, every family may be traced back to some branch that lived in Passaic Valley previous to the year 1800.

I have now submitted to the public, and especially those whose families or ancestors are named, the labors of some seven years, hoping that some, at least, will be pleased to learn something more of their ancestors and connections than they would otherwise have known.

JOHN LITTELL.

Passaic Valley, New Providence, April, 1852.

ERRATA.

Page 10, line 3. for David read Daniel.

17,   22, for Mary Lindsley, daughter of Joseph, read Nancy Lindsley, daughter of Matthew G. Lindsley.

17,   37, for Mary, read Nancy.

19,   15, for Silas read Sineas.

19,   17, for Zina read Silas.

31,   bottom line, for Eusace read Eunice.

32,   Heading, for Baldwin read Ball.

32,   12, for Wats read Watts.

32,   80, for Boll read Ball.

36,   Strike out 5th Generation.

42,   Heading, for Jacob read William.

43,   do.   do.   do.

44,   Heading, for William Bedell, son of John, read Henry Bedell.

45,   21, for daughter read daughters.

45,   39, for John S. Bradford read John S. Bedford.

47,   29, for Elizabeth B. Tickenor read Elijah B. Tichenor.

43,   13, for Tickenor read Tichenor.

50,   7, for his read her.

54,   45, for Larney read Laney.

57,   8, for Jonathan read Thomas.

60,   13, for Herbet read Herbert.

60,   27, for Naphtoli read Naphtali.

61,   14, Strike out 3d after Parsons.

63,   Heading, for George read John.

64,   35, for Payer read Poyer.

67,   3 from bottom, for time read times.

71,   40, insert 3 before children.

72,   Heading, for William read Robert.

73,   do.   for William read Hugh.

73,   4 from bottom, for Mehateble read Mehetabel.

74,   13, for grand-daughter read grand-father.

85,   45, for William 1st read William 3d.

86,   8, for William 1st read William 3d.

101,   bottom line, strike out son of John 3d.

102,   12, insert He at the end of the line.

102,   24, strike out double ll.

105,   2 & 3 include (son of Stephen Crane.)

103, 109, 15, 34, in the parenthesis, for Julia read Julia Anne.

112,   6, for son read daughter.

113,   29, for nine read ten.

117,   25, strike out a at the end of the line.

128,   36, for Morace read Moreau.

129,   29, for Joseph read Joshua.

134,   19, strike out will.

134,   31, for Labina read Lebbius.

136,   38, for returned read removed.

136,   39, begin the line with a capital I.

139,   19, for Polly read Patty Allen.

Page 149, line 7, strike out, and died young.
 151, 24, for Illinois read Victor, Wéstern N. Y.
 151, 7 from bottom, for a daughter read Esther.
 151, 2 from bottom for 4th read 14th.
 155, 44, for Marth read Martha.
 156, 41, for Swan read Swain.
 164, 30, for Michigan read Yates Co., N. Y.
 169, 9, insert 7th before son of Joseph.
 173, 24, for Sarah Hand read Sarah Anne Hand.
 175, 4, & 5, for Reed, in each line read Reeve.
 187, 20, for Daniel Hole read Charles Hole, Jun.
 215, for Zachariah Sickle read Zachariah Van Sickle, and so
    of his children.
 224, Heading, for John Littell read Benjamin Littell.
 249, 19, for 49 read 29.
 264, 29. for six read eight.
 283, 11, for 794, read 1794.
 302, Heading, for Capt. Jonathan Mulford read John Noe.
 303, 9, for David read Daniel Hart.
 306, 9 from bottom, for 848 read 1848.
 307, 8 from bottom, for brrham read Abraham.
 326, Hannah, Rhoda, Mary, Ezra, William and Eliza Pot-
    ter were children of Maxwell Potter and sisters and bro-
    thers of Benjamin Potter, son of Maxwell.
 326, 5, for Maxwell read Samuel Maxwell.
 326, 2 from bottom, for Levi read Maxwell.
 331, 4. for Louisa read Levisa.
 342, 19, read died after who.
 353, Heading, for James read Matthias.
 356, 18, strike out see Lamb.
 369, 13, for Zebra read Sebra.
 383, 21, read, 2. Mary Terry married Ephraim Bryant, of
    Plainfield ; 3. Caleb Conklin went to Missouri, and
    married there.
 383, 24, for 7. Caroline, read 8. Cornelia.
 388, 34, read Miles for Mills, and Valley for Vally.
 389, 5, read Jacob I. for Jacob T.
 390, 20, read Rachel for Hannah, and first line above Rachel,
    insert 3. Polly married Benjamin Moore ; bottom line
    read Larzalier for Lavzalier.
 394, 11 & 12, read Genung for Genning.
 395, 10, read 4. Juliette for 2. Juliette.
 398, 38, read Ithamar for Ithaman.
 411, 11 from bottom read Goltra for Gottra twice.
 412, 11, read 2d Gen. for 1st Gen.
 426, 36, read Israel for Isaac.
 470, 28, read Mercy for Mary.
 471, 32, add "and had a daughter Miranda."

GENEALOGIES

OF THE

FIRST SETTLERS OF PASSAIC VALLEY,

&c. &c. &c.

JONATHAN ALLEN.

JONATHAN ALLEN owned one hundred acres, No. 28 of the Elizabethtown lots, surveyed above the first mountain, on which Daniel Allen and Joseph Allen afterwards lived, who were probably his sons.

DANIEL ALLEN married Nancy Halsey, near Elizabethtown, and had children:

1. David, who married Jane Pasnet, and lived at Paterson.
2. John, who married at Pompton, and lived and died there.
3. Elizabeth married Jonathan Parsons, son of William Parsons, and died 4th July, 1844; Mr. Parsons died 9th September, 1821, at 57 years. (*See Parsons.*)

JOSEPH ALLEN, (brother of Daniel,) married Lydia Potter, daughter of Col. Samuel Potter, and had children:

1. Bethuel, who married, in Ohio, Clara Gee, and had a son, John; when his wife died, and he married the widow Polly Scott, daughter of John Dean, of Springfield, N. J., and had another son.
2. Phebe married David Clark, son of Stephanus Clark, Sen., in Ohio.
3. Jemima, married in Ohio.
4. Chloe.
5. Moses, died a young man, unmarried.

Lydia, the wife of Joseph Allen, died 10th Feb. 1799, aged 42 years, after which he went to Ohio, to his children, and died there.

NOTE.—I know of no connection between this family and Joseph Allen, Jun , which follows.

JOSEPH ALLEN, Jun.

JOSEPH ALLEN, Jun:, married Sarah Willcockse, daughter of Peter Willcockse, Sen. (The family now spell the name Willcox.) He drew No. 113 of the Elizabethtown lots surveyed above the first mountain, about one mile east of the Mount Bethel Church, but lived in Washington Valley, between the mountains. They had children :

1. David, who married Mary Camp, daughter of Aaron Camp, son of John Camp, (or Johannes Vancampen,) of Passaic Valley.

2. Peter, married Mary Marshall, daughter of James Marshall, of Washington Valley.

3. Gideon, married, 19th August, 1787, Susannah Cory, daughter of Elder Daniel Cory, of Longhill.

4. William married 10th March, 1790, Nancy Marshall, sister of Peter's wife.

5. Philip, married Betsey Clark, daughter of Elias Clark, who lived on Stony Hill.

6. Henry, twin to Philip, married Phebe Clark, daughter of James Clark.

7. Patty, who married Joseph Doty, [See Doty.]

8. Sarah married Jonathan Ruckman, [See Ruckman.]

DAVID ALLEN, (1st child of Joseph, Jun.,) and Mary Camp, daughter of Aaron, had children:

1. Sarah, who married John Blackford, son of Benjamin Blackford, of Piscataway, and went to Readstone.

2. Jemima, married 31st May, 1785, Joseph Cole, Jun., son of Joseph, of Scotch Plains. (See Cole.)

3. Phebe, married Jacob Allen, son of Joseph Allen, and went to Cincinnati.

4. Polly, married Levi Parker, son of Isaac Parker, and went to the Lakes, N. Y.

5. Amy, married Richard Roff, son of Richard. (See Roff.)

6. Betsey, married Thomas Willet, son of Jonathan Willet, of Stony Hill Valley.

7. John, (the Colonel) married Betsey Cole, daughter of Master William Cole, of Scotch Plains ; she died without children, and he went to the west and married there.

8. Joseph, married Hannah Willet, daughter of Jonathan Willet, above named.

9. Rachel, married Aaron Scudder, son of George Scudder, and went to the Lakes, New York.

10. Martha, married William Sherwood, of Connecticut.

11. David Allen, Jun. married Susan Townley, daughter of Matthias, son of James Townley.

12. Aaron, married at Pittsburg, and went to Ohio.

13. Squier, married Hannah Cory, daughter of Parkhurst Cory, of Stony Hill Valley, and died without children.

JOSEPH ALLEN, (8th child of David Allen) and Hannah Willet, went to French Creek, and had children :
1. Camp, is unmarried.
2. John, who married Esther Hall, and went to French Creek, Penn.
3. Bradford, married——Line, daughter of -Amos Line.
4. Betsey, who died at about the age of 6 years.

DAVID ALLEN, (11th son of David Allen,) and Susan Townley, lived in Washington Valley, and had children:
1. Aaron, who married Maria Stead, daughter of Thomas Stead, and had children, 1st, Sophia Elizabeth.
2. Sarah Anne married Israel Moore, 21st February, 1849, son of Moses Moore, and had children,1st, David Allen Moore.
3. Elias, married Elizabeth Caroline Spencer, 28th February, 1849, daughter of James L. Spencer, and had children, 1st, Cornelia.
4. David, 3rd.
5. John.
6. Mary.

PETER ALLEN, (2d child of Joseph Allen, Jun.) and Mary Marshall, had children.
1. Rhoda, who married William Ross, son of Ezra Ross, of Long Hill.
2. Noah, who married Phebe Jennings.
3. Peter, who married Phebe Johnson, of Albany.
4. Anne married Levi Gould, of New York, —— have no children.
5. Deborah, married David Buckley, of Connecticut ; have no children:
6. Betsey, married William Randall, of Scotch Plains, and have children · 1. Philip Randall ; 2. Elizabeth Randall, who married Ebenezer Cooper ; 3. Harriet Randall.
7. Mary Anne, married James Beatty, of Staten Island.

GIDEON ALLEN, (3rd son of Joseph Allen, Jun.) and Susannah Cory, had children.
1. Daniel, who married Hetty Tucker, daughter of Joseph Tucker, son of John.
2. Henry married Esther Achor, daughter of Philip Achor, of Scotch Plains.
3. Patty.
4. Phebe, married Lines Tucker, son of Joseph Tucker, son of John.

5. Fanny, married William Jennings, son of Benjamin Jennings, of Mount Bethel.

6. Lydia married, 1st, Joseph Hamilton; 2d, William Tallman.

7. Sarah, married Henry Moore, son of Henry. (*See Moore.*)

DANIEL ALLEN, (son of Gideon,) and Hetty Tucker, had children :

1. Rosetta, who married her cousin Ephraim Achor, son of Philip.

2. Israel Cory, married Anne Titus, daughter of William.

3. John married Anne, ——— of New-York.

4. Gideon.

5. Aristedes Heustis.

WILLIAM ALLEN, (4th son of Joseph Allen, Jun.) and Nancy Marshall, had children :

1. Marsh, who married Mary Willcox, daughter of Daniel. [*See Willcox.*]

2. Betsey, married David D. Smalley, son of David, Esq. (*See Smalley.*)

3. Sally, married Moses Stiles, of Morris County.

4. Polly, married, 1st, Mr. Woodruff, but had no children by him. 2d, Frederick Dell, 20th July, 1843.

5. Jane, married Isaac Clark, son of Abraham, of Westfield.

6. William, married Huldah Cole, daughter of Amos, of Scotch Plains.

HENRY ALWARD.

HENRY ALWARD came from England, married Miss Compton; lived between Liberty Corner and Basking Ridge, near the mill now owned by Matthias Woodard, and had children:

1. David, who went to French Creek.
2. John. } **HENRY ALWARD, Jun.**
3. Henry, Jun., who married Mary Cox, and had children:
1. John, who married—and had children, Henry, and two others.
2. Samuel married Caty King, sister of John King, of Liberty Corner.
3. Benjamin married Sarah Ayers, daughter of Elisha Ayers, and sister of Major John Ayers, of Basking Ridge.
4. Sarah married Daniel Hampton, whose father lived where John Steele did.
5. Mary married, 1st, Mr. Vankirk—2d, Cornelius Tunison, of Washington Valley.
6. Mercy married Ephraim Martin, son of Col. —— Martin.
7. Henry, 3d, married Osee Pennington, daughter of Jonathan Pennington.
8. William married Elizabeth Cross, daughter of William.

SAMUEL ALWARD, (2d child of Henry Alward, Jun.,) and Caty King, had children:
1. Mark.
2. Mary, who married John Pope, Jun., son of John Pope.
3. David.
4. Henry married —— —— lived at Succasuna Plains.
5. Sally married John Mizener, of Peapack.
6. Samuel, Jun., who went to the Lakes, New-York, and married there.
7. Betsey married Mr. Brown, of Monmouth Co.
8. Charlotte went to Michigan.

BENJAMIN ALWARD, (3d child of Henry Alward, Jun.) and Sarah Ayers, had children:
1. Elisha, who died at 27 years (by the kick of a horse) unmarried.
2. Mary, married Joseph Ruckman, son of Jonathan Ruckman. (*See Ruckman.*)
3. Jane married John Yeatman, an Englishman, and went to Philadelphia; they had no children.
4. Hannah married Nathan Ruckman, brother of Joseph. (*See Ruckman.*)

5. Benjamin, Jun., married Lydia Coddington, daughter of Benjamin Coddington.

6. Sarah, married Jonas Bird, son of George Bird, of Mount Bethel.

7. Esther, (twin to Sarah,) married Stephen Lawrence, son of William Lawrence, of Schoolies Mountain.

8. William, married Phebe Lyon, daughter of Ebenezer Lyon, and went to French Creek, Penn.

9. Elizabeth married Benjamin Boylan, son of Dr. James Boylan, of Vealtown.

10. Anne married Samuel Carman, of French Creek, Penn., and lived there.

11. Stephen married Miss —— Pool, of Schoolies Mountain.

12. Daniel married Mary Miller, daughter of Smith Miller.

13. Phebe, twin to Daniel, married John Kinsey, of Amboy, and live there.

SARAH ALWARD, (4th child of Henry Alward, Jun.,) and Daniel Hampton, had children :

1. John Hampton, who married, as his 2d wife, Miss —— Bloodgood.

2. Mary Hampton married Mr. —— Jackson.

3. Henry Hampton married Miss —— Edgar.

4. Dr. William Hampton married Eliza Leddel, daughter of Dr. William Leddel, of Mendham.

5. Penina Hampton did not marry.

6. Dr. Reuel Hampton.

MARY ALWARD, (5th child of Henry Alward, Jun.,) and Cornelius Tunison, had children :

1. Henry Tunison, who married Miss —— Casner.

2. Elizabeth Tunison married John Bakeman.

3. Nelly Tunison married John Bray, of New Brunswick.

4. Hannah Tunison married Jephtha Mundy; lives at Middle Brook.

MERCY ALWARD, (6th child of Henry Alward, Jun.,) and Ephraim Martin, had children :

1. Patty Martin, who married Samuel Stites, son of Isaac Stites, of Mount Bethel, and went to Illinois, and had 14 children.

2. Mary Martin married Mr. —— Scudder.

3. Betsey Martin married —— ——

4. Richard Martin   lives near Rahway ——

HENRY ALWARD, (7th child of Henry Alward, Jun., and Osee Pennington, had children :

4th Generation. 1. Jonathan, who married Deborah Burrows, daughter of Waters Burrows, of New Providence.

2. Mary married Goin McCoy, son of James McCoy, of Basking Ridge.

3. Anne married Jonathan Hand, son of Jonathan Hand, of Basking Ridge. (*See Hand.*)

4. Osee.

5. William married Miss —— Allen, of Peapack.

6. Henry, 4th, married Fanny Guerin, and soon died.

7. Jacob married and soon died.

8. Joseph married Matilda Doty, daughter of David, son of Zeb.

9. Betsey married, 1st, John Ryerson; 2d, Mr. Barman.

WILLIAM ALWARD, (8th child of Henry Alward, Jun.) and Eliza Cross removed to the Lakes, New York, and had children:

1. Phebe.

2. Sarah.

3. Nathaniel.

4. Jerusha

5. William.

6. Squier.

7. Jarvis.

BENJAMIN ALWARD, Jun. (5th child of Benjamin Alward,) and Lydia Coddington, had children:

5th Generation. 1. Hugh, who went to Illinois.

2. Esther, who married John Phillips, of Newark.

3. Sarah, who went to Illinois.

4. Jackson, who went to Illinois.

SARAH ALWARD, (6th child of Bejamin Alward,) and Jonas Bird, went to the Lakes, New York, and had children:

1. Esther Bird, who died at about 18 years, unmarried.

2. George Bird, who died at about 16 years.

3. Phebe Bird.

4. Silas Bird.

5. Sarah Bird.

ESTHER ALWARD, (7th child of Benjamin Alward,) and Stephen Lawrence, had children:

1. Mary Lawrence, who married Stephen Coleman.

2. William Lawrence, married Miss Coleman, sister of Stephen.

3. Sarah Lawrence, married William Walk.

4. John Lawrence, married Miss —— Pool.

5. Benjamin Lawrence,

6. Sylvester Lawrence.

7. Amanda Lawrence, married her cousin Benjamin Alward, son of David.

8. Elizabeth Lawrence, died at about 12 years.

9. Stephen Lawrence, Jun.

10. Jane Lawrence.

ELIZABETH ALWARD, (9th child of Benjamin Alward,) and Benjamin Boylan, had children .

1. Anne Boylan, who died at about 22 years, unmarried.

2. Sarah Boylan, married William Hoff.

3. John Boylan, —— lives in Newark.

4. William Boylan, —— lives in Brooklyn, N. Y.

5. James Boylan, —— lives in Newark.

STEPHEN ALWARD, (11th child of Benjamin Alward,) and his wife, Miss Pool, had children :

1. Sarah.

2. Esther.

3. Benjamin.

DANIEL ALWARD, (12th child of Benjamin Alward,) and Mary Miller, had children:

1. Benjamin, who married his cousin Amanda Lawrence, daughter of Stephen Lawrence,

2. Moses Miller married Sarah Drake, daughter of Abraham J. Drake, son of William, of Schoolies Mountain.

3. Elizabeth.

4. Elisha, born 29th April, 1826 — married, 31st August, 1847, to Rachel Drake, daughter of the above-named William Drake.

5. Daniel, Jun.

6. William.

7. Esther.

8. Smith Miller.

9. Rachel.

PHEBE ALWARD, (13th child of Benjamin Alward,) and John Kinsey, of Amboy, had children:

1. Daniel Kinsey.

2. Sarah Kinsey.

3: Esther Kinsey.

4. Wesley Kinsey.

JONATHAN ALWARD, (1st child of Henry Alward, 3d,) and Deborah Burrows, had children:

1. Edward, who died, — September, 1834, aged 25 years.

2. Jonathan Pennington, born 21st July, 1812,—graduated at

5th Generation.

Princeton College, — studied Theology, became a Presbyterian Minister, — married Catherine Fredenburg, daughter of the Rev. Mr. Fredenburg, of Somerville. They went to WesternAfrica, as Missionaries. He died there in April, 1841, and she returned home.

3. Osee.

4. Waters Burrows married his cousin, Mary Frances Burrows, daughter of the Rev. Waters Burrows.

5. Francis, who died in 1845, aged 25 years.

6. Eliza Anne, who died in her 9th year.

7. Joseph, born July 4th, 1828, is preparing for the ministry.

JAMES ANDERSON.

JAMES ANDERSON, married, 14th September, 1766, Lydia Badgley, and had a son, Badgley Anderson. His wife Lydia then died, and he married Polly, the widow of Richard Shaw, and had two other children :

2. Robert, who married Nancy Moore, daughter of Isaac Moore.

3. Betsey, married David Clark, son of Elias Clark, sen. [*See Clark.*]

BADGLEY ANDERSON had three children:

1. John.

2. Israel.

3. —— a daughter who married Mr. Benward.

ROBERT ANDERSON and Nancy Moore had children :

1.

2.

3.

4. Elizabeth.

5.

6.

7.

NOTE.—RICHARD SHAW had children :

1. Lewis Shaw, who married Phebe Willis, daughter of William Willis.

2. Sally Shaw, who married William Brown, son of John Brown, Sen.

JOHN, JAMES AND GEORGE BADGLEY.

These three brothers, together with their three sisters, Phebe, Sarah, and Betsey, came over from Long Island, to Elizabethtown. George settled in Elizabethtown. He had a daughter, Nancy, who married John Brown, and removed to Stonyhill, [see Brown.] John and James, with their three sisters, came up and settled in the Valley between the 1st and 2nd Mountains, in the year 1736-7. When Joseph Morse, the Elizabethtown Surveyor, was surveying this region, he surveyed for John and James Badgley, a tract of 400 acres of land, between the mountains lying along Blue Brook, and extending South to the top of the first mountain. John Badgley had one son, John Badgley, Junior, whose wife's name was Effa.

JAMES BADGLEY had four children :
1. James, Jun., whose wife's name was Sarah.
2. Joseph, married Betsey Scudder, sister of Benjamin Scudder, below Springfield.
3. Anthony married Anne Woodruff.
4. Robert, married Rachel Vreland.

PHEBE BADGLEY married Peter Willcockse, Senior. [See Willcockse.]

SARAH BADGLEY married Joseph Doty, Senior. [See Doty.]

BETSEY BADGLEY married Uriah Hedges, Senior. [See Hedges.]

JAMES BADGLEY, Jun., and Sarah, his wife, had children :
1. James, 3rd.
2. Joseph, 2nd.
3. Lydia.
4. Sarah.
5. Rhoda.

JOSEPH BADGLEY, 2nd, (2nd child of James Badgley,) and Betsey Scudder, had children :
1. Timothy.
2. Moses, who married Susannah — and had two children.
3. George.
4. Nancy.
5. Hannah.

ANTHONY BADGLEY, (3rd child of James Badgley,) and Anna Woodruff, had children :
1. Jonathan, who married, 1st Lydia Scudder ; 2nd, Hannah Searing, daughter of Noah Searing.
2. Noah.
3. Anthony, 2nd, married Abigail Hedges, daughter of Uriah Hedges.

4. Samuel, married Polly Frazee, daughter of Henry Frazee.
5. Jenny married Barna Hole. [See Hole.]
6. Nancy, married Maxwell Frazee, son of Henry Frazee, [See Frazee.]

ROBERT BADGLEY, (4th child of James Badgley,) and Rachel Vreland, had children :
1. Enoch, who married Sally Simson, daughter of John Simson, 2nd, and had a daughter, Sarah, who died 23rd April, 1784.
2. Robert, Junior.
3. William married, 19th June, 1796, Betsey Frazee.
4. Hannah, married Joseph Scudder.

MOSES BADGLEY, son of Joseph, son of James Badgley, Jun., married Susannah, —— and had children:
1. Sarah, who married Calvin Parker, 11th June, 1788, son of Benjamin Parker, of Longhill, and had an only son, Moses B. Parker, who died unmarried.
2. Peggy, who married, 1st June, 1793, William P. Doty, son of Anthony, Senior, [See Doty.] Mrs. Susannah Badgley died 25th December, 1799, aged 49 years, and Mr. Badgley married, as his 2nd wife, Nancy, the widow of Thomas Oakley. They lived on Longhill. Another Moses Badgley married, 20th September, 1795, Anna, the widow of Samuel Miller, and daughter of John Simson, Junior, and went to Ohio.

JONATHAN BADGLEY, (1st son of Anthony, the 3rd son of James Badgley,) and Lydia Scudder, lived on North side of the 2nd Mountain, and had children :
1. Ahijah, who married Betsey Willcox, daughter of Noah Willcox, Senior.
2. Stephen married Catherine Denman, daughter of Joseph Denman, of Springfield.
3. Noah, who died unmarried.
4. John S. married Hannah Sturges, daughter of Benjamin Sturges, of Green Village.
5. Polly, married David C. Hand, son of Nehemiah Hand, and had no children.
6. Nancy married Thomas Seward, of Springfield, and died in about six months.
7. Jane, married Samuel Ball, son of Garner Ball; he died, and she married Mr. Travers. By his 2nd wife, Hannah Searing, he had other children.
8. Aaron, —— who went to Canada.
9. Nancy who went to Canada, and married there.
10. Jacob, who died young.
11. Jonathan.
12. Noah, 2nd.
13. Sarah, who died young.

ANTHONY BADGLEY, Junior, (3rd son of Anthony, 3rd son of James Badgley,) and Abigail Hedges, lived on the North side of the first mountain, where his son Samuel now lives, and had children :

1. Jemima, who married Jacob Price, son of Rice Price. [*See Price.*]

2. Samuel, who was born 1st December, 1793, married Betsey Reeve, daughter of Elias Reeve, of Springfield.

3. Anthony, 3rd, married Hannah, widow of William Raddin, and daughter of Elias Clark, and had no children.

4. Phebe, married John R. Clark, son of Stephen Clark.

5. David, married Harriet Wilkison, daughter of Nathan Wilkison.

6. Mary, married George Brown, son of William Brown, son of John, and had no children.

7. Dayton, married Sarah Lyon, daughter of John Lyon, son of Ebenezer.

8. Hetty, married Benjamin Sturges, son of Benjamin Sturges, of Green Village, and had no children.

9. Abigail, born May, 1811, married Moses Reeve, born July, 1809, son of Watts Reeve, of Springfield.

JEMIMA BADGLEY, (daughter of Anthony Badgley, Jun.,) and Jacob Price, removed to Western New York, and had an only child, Phebe Price, who married ――― and soon died.

SAMUEL BADGLEY, (2nd child of Anthony Badgley, Jun.) and Betsey Reeve, had children ·

1. Charles.
2. Caroline.
3. Ann Eliza.
4. John Milton.

PHEBE BADGLEY, (4th child of Anthony Badgley, Junior,) and John R. Clark, lived on the South side of 1st Mountain, and had children :

1. Susan Clark, who married Brooks Roll, son of James, son of Brooks Roll.

2. Abigail Clark, who died at about 17 years, unmarried.

3. Lucilla Clark, married William Woodruff, son of Daniel Woodruff.

4. Hetty Clark.

DAVID BADGLEY, (5th child of Anthony Badgley, Junior,) and Harriet Wilkison, lived at N. P. Village and had children:

1. Samuel, who married Hetty Hanford, daughter of Simeon Hanford, and grand-daughter of Isaac Simson, [*See Simson.*]

2. Elizabeth, married, September 23rd, 1849, William G. Marsh, son of Isaac Marsh and Catherine Griffin.

3. Amos.
4. Lyman.
5. William Hanley.

DAYTON BADGLEY, (7th child of Anthony Badgley, Junior,) and Sarah Lyon, had children :

1. Mary, born April, 1836.
2. Ellen, who died at about 7 years.
3. Margaret.
4. Isabella died 5th September, 1848, in youth.
5. Eugene.
6. Eliza.
7. Harriet Meeker.
8. James.

ABIGAIL BADGLEY, (9th child of Anthony Badgley, Junior,) and Moses Reeve, had children :

1. James W. Reeve, born November, 1833.
2. Mary Elizabeth Reeve, born April, 1836.
3. Hester Anne Reeve, born 2nd June, 1838.
4. Benjamin Franklin Reeve, born March, 1847.
5. George B. Dallas Reeve, born December, 1844.
6. Sarah Jane Reeve, born 23rd March, 1850.

SAMUEL BADGLEY, (4th son of Anthony Badgley,) and Polly Frazee, lived between the 1st and 2nd Mountains, and had children :

1. Aaron, who married Betsey Force, daughter of Samuel Force. They both soon died, and left a son, Aaron, who died at about 16 years.
2. Moses Frazee, married Sally Wilkison, daughter of Nathan Wilkison; he soon died; he left a daughter, Lydia, who married, and went to Ohio, and soon died.
3. Henry, married, 1st, Phebe Sturges, daughter of Benjamin Sturges, of Green Village. 2d. Sarah Gillam, daughter of James Gillam; he died December, 1844.
4. Huma married Ezekiel Clark, son of Stephen Clark, of Westfield.
5. Sarah, married William Price, son of Rice Price, [*See Price.*]
6. Lydia, who died in 1818, aged 19 years.
7. Anne, married Jesse Cahoon, from West Jersey; they had no children.
8. Maxwell, married Sally Parker, daughter Calvin Parker, and had no children.
9. Jacob Foster, born 2nd February, 1808, married Anne Brown, born 26th April, 1812, daughter of William Brown.

HENRY BADGLEY, (3rd child of Samuel,) and Phebe Sturges, had children :

1. Mary.
2. Samuel.
3. Lavina.
4. Caroline.
5. Benjamin.

6. Phebe.

By his 2nd wife, Sarah Gillam, he had no children.

HUMA BADGLEY, (4th child of Samuel Badgley,) and Ezekiel Clark, lived in Westfield, and had children:

1. Maria Clark, who married Joseph P. Hays.
2. Silas Clark, married Lucretia Haines.
3. Eliza Clark, married John Heaton.
4. Anne Clark, married Jesse Heaton, brother of John.
5. Sarah Clark, married James Agens.
6. William Clark, married Anne Pink, of Brooklyn.
7. Charlotte Clark, married Elias Angleman.
8. Samuel Clark.
9. Charles Clark.

JACOB F. BADGLEY, (9th child of Samuel Badgley,) and Anne Brown, lived where his father did, and had children:

1. Moses, born 21st January, 1833.
2. George Brown, born 19th August, 1835.
3. Henry, born 26th November, 1837.
4. John, born 14th June, 1840.
5. Lydia Anne, born 26th October, 1842.
6. Samuel, born 8th March, 1845.
7. Crook Vancleve, born 15th June, 1847.
8. Mary, born 2nd June, 1849.

ABNER BAILEY.

ABNER BAILEY was a hatter. He came from Connecticut, and bought a house and a small tract of land of Jeremiah Clark, and lived on it, (where the widow Polly Day now lives.) He married, 1st, Margret, — she died 15th March, 1793, and he married, 2nd, the widow Sarah, — a sister of Philip Cochran, of New York. Mr. Bailey died January, 10, 1810, without children, and his widow Sarah, married, 23rd September, 1811, Thomas Baldwin, son of Nathan, of Union, as her second husband; he died by accidentally falling from a wagon, (*See Baldwin*,) and she died April 18th, 1835, aged 72 years. Mr. Bailey, left no heirs, in New Jersey.

JONATHAN BAILEY.

JONATHAN BAILEY lived at New Vernon, Morris County. He married Rachel Osborn, daughter of John Osborn, Sen., and had one son, Samuel, who lived in Passaic Valley, where Benjamin Hand now lives, [*See Osborn.*]

Samuel Bailey, married Sally Tappen, daughter of James Tappen, [*See Dunham.*] He was a Captain of the Militia, and died May, 1824, aged 52 years. They had children:

3rd Generation.

1. Jonathan, who married Abigail Beach, daughter of John Beach.
2. Samuel married Mary Lindsley, daughter of Joseph Lindsley, son of Major Lindsley, of Morristown.
3. Esther married, 6th July, 1820, Squire Manning, son of James, son of Isaac Manning, of Plainfield, and had an only daughter, Sarah, who married William T. Brokaw, son of Cornelius, of Plainfield. Mrs. Esther Manning died September, 1840, and Mr. Manning married Mary Stevens, daughter of John Stevens, of Newfoundland, New Jersey, and died 19th December, 1850.

JONATHAN BAILEY, son of Captain Samuel Bailey, and Abigail Beach, lived in Newark, and had children:

4th Generation.

1. Silas, who married Mary Haddon, daughter of Benjamin Haddon, of New York, and had children: 1. Theodore, 2. Reynolds.
2. Henry, who married, 24th December, 1850, Elizabeth A. Reuck, of Newark.

SAMUEL BAILEY, Jun., son of Captain Samuel Bailey, and Mary Lindsley, lived in Morristown, and had children:

1. William Francis.
2. Sarah Kirtland.
3. George Edgar.
4. Theodore Frelinghuysen.

SARAH MANNING, (daughter of Squire Manning,) and William T. Brokaw, had children:

1. Joel Terry Brokaw, born 11th December, 1845.
2. George Brokaw, born 20th May, 1849.

THOMAS BAKER.

THOMAS BAKER emigrated from England, and settled on
Long Island, and from thence he removed to Connecticut Farms,
(now Union,) and there died.

THOMAS BAKER, Jun., his son, married Hannah Thompson,
sister of Thomas Thompson, on Rahway River, in Union, and
removed to Passaic Valley, in New Providence, and bought of
John Blanchard, of Elizabethtown, in March, 1738–9, 40 acres,
part of lot No. 50,—and in 1761 he bought of William Maxwell
lot No. 26, of 99 acres, lying west of Jacob Bedell's land, and
bounded north by the river, and west by Johonis' Camp, afterwards
owned by Richard Scudder. He also bought of Joseph Rolph and
John Ocheltree lot No. 57, lying south of No. 50, and extending
south to the Stony Hill Road, and sold part of lot No. 57 to William Baker, and 35 acres, adjoining Jacob Bedell, to Jonathan
Mulford, for his son Cornelius Mulford, who lived on it many years,
till he died. William Crane, who married the grand-daughter
of Cornelius Mulford, now lives on it. Peter Hill owns 48 acres,
and John Littell, the remaining 15 acres, of Lot No. 26.

THOMAS BAKER, Junior, and Hannah Thompson, had children: 1st. Thomas Baker, 3d who married, 19th March, 1769, Hannah
Howel. He married a 2d wife, (I have not learned her name.) He also
married for his 3d wife, January, 1785, the widow, Martha Line, a
sister of Benjamin Bedell; his children are not known; he died March
6th, 1787.

2. William Baker, who married Rachel Valentine, daughter of
Richard Valentine.

3. Daniel Baker, married, 24th December, 1766, Abigail
Hendricks, of Westfield, and died 15th January, 1776.

4. Nathan, who died April, 1788.

5. Sarah married, 23rd July, 1769, William Littell, son of Andrew
Littell, and went to Sussex, New Jersey, [*See Littell.*]

6. Elizabeth married, 1st, William Maxwell, son of John Maxwell,
Senior, [*See Maxwell,*] 2nd, Obadiah Valentine, son of Richard
Valentine, [*See Valentine.*]

WILLIAM BAKER, son of Thomas Baker, Junior, and Rachel
Valentine, had children :

1. Thomas, baptized 25th December, 1763.

2. Abner, baptized 21st, June, 1767.

3. John.

4. Hannah, who died 29th January, 1784.

His living children went to Ohio, — and are not known here. He
died 4th July, 1787. His widow died in April, 1790.

THOMAS BAKER. 19

DANIEL BAKER, son of Thomas Baker, Junior, and Abigial Hendricks, had children :
1. Aaron, who married, 14th December, 1793, his cousin Hannah Maxwell, daughter of William Maxwell.
2. Daniel Baker, Junior, who married ——— ——— in Western Pennsylvania, and went to Ohio.
3. Hannah, married Joseph Rutan, son of Abraham Rutan, of Long Hill, [See Rutan.]

AARON BAKER, son of Daniel Baker, Senior, and Hannah Maxwell, removed to Dayton Ohio, and had children :
1. Betsey, who married Moses Simpson, son of Alexander Simpson, of Dayton, [See Simpson.]
2. David, married, 1st, Sophia Vancleve, daughter of Benjamin Vancleve, of Dayton; 2nd, Sophia Sourbray.
3. Silas, who died a young man, uumarried, in New Providence, New Jersey.
4. Zina, also died a young man, unmarried.
Aaron Baker, was a Justice of the Peace, in Dayton. His wife, Hannah, died December, 1818, and he married, 2nd, in Dayton, Mary Nolan, who died December, 1819, and he married, 3rd, Sally, widow of David Valentine, and daughter of Benjamin Day, Esq. She died 1833, and he married, 4th, Eve Wright, formerly of New York. He had children only by his first wife.

Note.—I have not traced any blood kin between Thomas Baker, 1st, and Henry Baker, 1st.

HENRY BAKER.

HENRY BAKER, 1st, lived half a mile from Westfield church, towards Springfield. He married Phebe Hedges, of Long Island. They had children :
1. Daniel, 1st, born 3rd June, 1753, and died 2nd September, 1788. He married Margaret Osborn, born 14th July, 1760.
2. William, who married Jemima Woodruff, daughter of Thomas Woodruff, Esq.
3. Jonathan, I. married, 1st, Keziah Clark ; 2nd, Charity Clark, sisters, daughters of Jesse Clark, Esq.
4. Jeremiah, married, 4th March, 1798, Mary King. They lived at Dover, Morris county. He was born 28th August, 1770. She was born 9th June, 1778.
5. Phebe married Ziba Ludlow, of Berkshire Valley, Morris county.
6. Henry, Jun. who married. ——— ———

DANIEL BAKER.

DANIEL BAKER, (1st child of Henry Baker, 1st,) and Margaret, Osborn, had children :
1. MARY, born 25th June, 1780, and married Ezekiel De Camp, son of Moses and Sarah De Camp.
2. Phebe Hedges, born 25th September, 1782, — married John Marsh, of Westfield.

3. Margaret, born 14th April, 1784, married William Britton, of M dison, Morris County. [*See Britton.*]

4. David, born 11th June, 1780, married Cynthia Briggs, of Albany, and died 7th September, 1832.

5. Daniel, 2nd, who died, aged one and a half years.

6. Elizabeth, born 2nd August, 1789, married Abraham Britton, brother of William, [*See Britton.*]

7. Daniel, Junior, born 28th December, 1790, married.—— ——

8. Hedges, born 12th August, 1792, married Charlotte K. Crane, daughter of Benjamin Crane, 3rd, and died in April, 1831, aged 39 years and 4 months.

9. Prudence, born 12th April, 1794, and died 26th January, 1823. She married Moses Lee, son of Thomas Lee ; lived at Willow Grove, near Rahway.

10. Cyrus, born 20th December, 1795, went to Darien, Georgia, and married Jane Eliza Donnely, and died there in February, 1831.

11. Henry, born 18th December, 1797, married Mary Anne Radley, daughter of John Radley.

12. Hannah, born 20th March, 1800, married Ephraim Clark, (tanner,) of Westfield, as his 2nd wife.

13. Elihu, born 3rd July, 1802, married Joanna and Charlotte Carter, sisters, daughters of Lewis Carter, of Madison, Morris Co. He lives in Middletown, Monmouth county; is cashier of the bank there.

14. Electa, born 28th September, 1804, married, 1st, Aaron Woodruff, son of Noah Woodruff, had no children ; married, 2nd, Benjamin Crane, stone-cutter, son of Benjamin, Crane, 3rd; lives at Paterson, [*See Crane.*]

MARY BAKER, (1st child of Daniel Baker,) and Ezekiel De Camp, had children :

1. Phebe De Camp, who married Mr. —— Hand, son of Ellis.
2. Hannah De Camp, who married Mr. —— Hand, brother of Phebe's husband.
3. David De Camp.
4. Hiram De Camp.
5. Walter De Camp.
6. Hervy De Camp.
7. John De Camp.
8. Joseph De Camp.
9. Margaret De Camp.
10. Mary De Camp.
11. Sarah De Camp.
12. Moses De Camp.
13. Job De Camp.

PHEBE HEDGES BAKER, (2d child of Daniel Baker,) and John Marsh, had children:
1. Thomas Marsh.
2. Mary Marsh.
3. Anne Marsh, who married Mr. —— Covert, of Seneca Co., New York.

4. Margaret Marsh.
5. Daniel Marsh.

4th Generation.

HEDGES BAKER, (8th child of Daniel Baker,) and Charlotte
K. Crane, had children:
1. Margaret, who married Lansing Whitehead.
2. Daniel, married Elizabeth Holt.
3. John.
4. Elizabeth.
5. Francis.

PRUDENCE BAKER, (9th child of Daniel Baker,) and Moses
Lee, had children :
1. Mary Lee.
2. Elizabeth Britton Lee, who married Philip Miller.

CYRUS BAKER, (10th child of Daniel Baker,) and Jane E.
Donnely, had children :
1. Daniel William.
2. Cyrus Osborn, died in Darien, Georgia.

HENRY BAKER, (11th child of Daniel Baker,) and Mary
Anne Radley, had children:
1. Courtland Radley, who married Caroline Van Pelt, who
died, leaving a daughter about two years old.
2. David, who was killed by lightning, in Ohio, in 1847, aged
24 years.
3. Elihu.
4. Anne Martin married Amos Miller, son of Jacob Miller.
5. Henry.

HANNAH BAKER, (12th child of Daniel,) and Ephraim Clark,
had children :

1. Cyrus Osborn Clark.	NOTE.—Ephraim Clark,
2. Daniel Clark.	by his 1st wife, Phebe, had
3. Phebe Clark.	children :
4. Margaret Clark.	1. Edwin.
5. Mary Britton Clark.	2. James.
6. Catherine Clark.	3. Hervy.
7. Ephraim Newton Clark.	4. Anne.

ELIHU BAKER, (13th child of Daniel Baker,) and Joanna
Carter, had children :
1. Nancy Carter.
2. William Morris.
3. Lewis Carter.
4. Alfred Britton.
5. Margaret. And by his 2d wife, Charlotte Carter, had,
6. Joanna.

WILLIAM BAKER.

WILLIAM BAKER, (2d son of Henry Baker,) and Jemima Woodruff, had children :

1. Henry, who married Hannah Ross, daughter of James Ross, Esq.
2. William, Jun., married Jane Thompson, daughter of Moses, son of Hezekiah Thompson.
3. Nancy Woodruff, who died at 15 years.
4. Jeremiah, who died at 25 years, unmarried.
5. Jacob married his cousin, Anna Maria Britton, daughter of Colonel William Britton, of Madison.
6. Mary Hedges married Christopher Cory, son of Benjamin.
7. Phebe married Augustus V. H. Webb.

HENRY BAKER, (1st child of William Baker,) and Hannah Ross, had children :

1. James Ross, who died September, 1820, aged about 12 years.
2. William T. married Elizabeth Anne Miller, daughter of Abner Miller, and had children : 1st, Catherine, born——1839 ; 2nd, Elizabeth.
3. Sarah Eliza married William Radford, of New York, and had children : 1. William Henry Radford ; 2. James Radford ; 3. Edwin Radford.
4. James Ross, 2d, married Catherine Mundy, and had children : 1st, Eliza Ranford Ross.
5. Phebe Webb, married John Squire, 3rd, a son of John Squire, Jun., and had a child, James Wade Squire.

WILLIAM BAKER, Jun., (2d child of William Baker,) and Jane Thompson, had children :
1. Nancy Woodruff.
2 Moses Thompson, who married Maria Pollard, of Parcipany, Morris County.
3. William, 3d, married Anne Eliza Baker, daughter of Matthias Baker.
4. James Augustus married Clarissa ———
5. Jeremiah married his cousin, Elizabeth Cebra Webb, daughter of Augustus V. H. Webb.
6. Esther Anjoline married Thomas Hathaway.
7. Mary married Benjamin Crane ; (not of the Westfield Cranes.)
8. Aaron.
9. Sarah Jane.
10. Ferdinand.

JACOB BAKER, (5th child of William Baker,) and Anna Maria Britton, had children :
1. William.
2. Margaretta.
3. James Hervy.
Mr. Jacob Baker died. ——— ————

MARY H. BAKER, (6th child of William Baker,) and Christopher Cory, live in Indiana, and had children :
1. William Cory.
2. James Richards Cory.
3. Mary Cory.

PHEBE BAKER, (7th child of William Baker,) and Augustus V. H. Webb, had children :
1. Elizabeth Cebra Webb, who married her cousin, Jeremiah Baker, son of William Baker, Jun.
2. Augustus Webb.
3. Mary Webb.
4. William Henry Webb.

JONATHAN I. BAKER.

JONATHAN I. BAKER, (3d son of Henry Baker, 1st) and Keziah Clark, had children :
1. Charity, who married William Cory, son of Joseph Cory.
2. Gitty, married Job Clark, ———— of Rahway.
3. Jesse Clark, married Betsey Thompson, daughter of Hezekiah Thompson.
4. Harriet married John Squire, Jun., son of John Squier.
5. Mary married Ezra Drake, as his 2d wife, son of Noah Drake.

CHARITY BAKER, (daughter of Jonathan I. Baker,) and William Cory, had children :
1. Hezekiah Cory, who died at 18 years.
2. Levi Cory.
3. Margaret Cory.
4. Mary Cory, who died at 18 years.
5. Abby Cory married Washington Pierson, son of Moses.
6. Joseph Cory, who died at about 2 years.
7. Jonathan Cory, who died at about 10 years.
8. Sarah Cory.

GITTY BAKER, (2d daughter of Jonathan I. Baker,) and Job Clark, had children :
1. Elizabeth Clark.
2. Harriet Clark.
3. Mary Clark.
4. Martha Clark.
5. Keziah Clark.

JESSE C. BAKER, (3d child of Jonathan I. Baker,) died September, 1832. His wife, Betsey Thompson, died September, 1840. They had children :
1. Amelia, who married Dr. John Williamson, of Union Township.
2. Phebe married William Earl, son of Robert Earl, of Union.
3. Jonathan.
4. David.
5. Elizabeth.

HARRIET BAKER, (4th child of Jonathan I. Baker,) and John Squier, Jun., had children:

1. Mary Squier, who married James Wade, son of James W. Wade, Esq., of Union Township.
2. John Squier, 3d, married Phebe Webb Baker, daughter of Henry, son of William Baker, and had a child, James Wade Squier.
3. Caleb Squier.
4. Hannah Squier.
5. Jonathan Baker Squier.

MARY BAKER, (5th child of Jonathan I. Baker,) and Ezra Drake, had children:

1. Mary Williams Drake.
2. Jonathan Drake.
3. George Drake.

JEREMIAH BAKER.

JEREMIAH BAKER, (4th child of Henry Baker,) and Mary King, had children:

1. Andrew, born 5th April, 1799, married Nancy Hurd, 16th October, 1823.
2. Henry, born 29th April, 1801, is unmarried.
3. Elizabeth, born 18th September, 1803, married, 28th December, 1822, James B. Carle.
4. William H., born 3d January, 1806, married, 13th June, 1848, Clarissa Dell.
5. Nancy W., born 24th May, 1808, married, 17th November, 1836, William Henry Spencer, (as his 2d wife,) son of William Spencer, Esq., of Chatham. [*See Spencer.*]
6. Mary King, born 24th August, 1809, married, 26th June, 1834, Silas S. Palmer.
7. Phebe, born 28th November, 1815, married 28th November, 1838, John Dehart, of Parcipany.
8. Margaret, born 29th October, 1818, married, 20th July, 1845, John Butterworth.

ANDREW BAKER, (1st child of Jeremiah Baker,) and Nancy Hurd, had children:

1. Jeremiah.
2. Emily, who married ——— Byram, and had a child, William Henry.
3. Adeline.
4. Adolphus.
5. Henry.
6. Anne Eliza.
7. Nancy Louisa.

ELIZABETH BAKER, (3d child of Jeremiah Baker,) and James B. Carle, had children:

1. Mary Carle.

2. Margaret Carle.
3. Jane Carle.
4. William Carle.
5. James Carle.
6. Frederick Carle.
7. Salina Carle.
8. Lucy Carle.

WILLIAM H. BAKER, (4th child of Jeremiah Baker,) and
Clarissa Dell, had
1.

MARY K. BAKER, (6th child of Jeremiah Baker,) and Silas
S. Palmer, had children :
1. Jeremiah Palmer.
2. Seely Palmer.
3. Henry Palmer.

PHEBE H. BAKER, (7th child of Jeremiah Baker,) and
John Dehart, had children :
1. Mary Jane Dehart.
2. John Dehart.
3. Winfield Scot Dehart.

MARGARET BAKER, (8th child of Jeremiah Baker,) and John
Butterworth, had children :
1. Hudson Butterworth.

PHEBE BAKER, (5th child of Henry Baker, 1st,) and Ziba
Ludlow, had children :
1. Mary Ludlow, who married Thomas Tone, and both died.
2. Henry Ludlow!
3. Daniel Ludlow.
4. Phebe Ludlow.
5. Hedges Ludlow.
6. Ziba Ludlow, Jun.

JOHN BALDWIN.

JOHN BALDWIN, ―――― ―――― had children ;

1. Capt. Enos Baldwin, who lived in Livingston Township, and married,

1st, Phebe Williams, and had three children.

2nd, Sarah Woodruff, and three other children

3rd, widow Phebe Tucker, by whom he had no children.

4th, widow Prudence Mulford, and had no children :

2. Nathan Baldwin, married Elizabeth, widow of Jerry Ball, and daughter of Jeremiah Hart, as his 2nd wife. By his 1st wife he had a son, Lewis, who married Anny Hart, his father's 2nd wife's sister.

3. Ezekiel Baldwin, ―――― who was father of Gabriel Baldwin.

4. Molly Baldwin, who married Mr. Wade, of Union.

5. Jemima Baldwin, married Colonel Samuel Potter, [*See Potter.*]

6. Phebe Baldwin, married Mr. Ogden.

CAPT. ENOS BALDWIN.

CAPT. ENOS BALDWIN, (son of John Baldwin,) had children :

1. Phebe, who married Matthias Denman, of Springfield.

2. Martha, married George Townley, son of Effingham. [*See Townley.*]

3. Esther, married Nicholas Parcels, on W. O. Ridge, Springfield.

4. Samuel, married Lucy Fairchild.

5. Sally, married David Brainard Dickerson, son of Philemon, [*See Dickerson.*]

6. David, married Elizabeth Reeve, daughter of Captain Isaac Reeve.

7. A daughter who married James Morehouse, son of David, the 26th November, 1788, and had a son, Baldwin, when she died, and Mr. Morehouse married Polly Potter, daughter of John Potter, of New Providence. [*See Potter.*]

PHEBE BALDWIN, (1st child of Captain Enos Baldwin,) and Matthias Denman, lived in Springfield, and had children :

1. Sally Denman, who married William Parcel ; had no children.

2. Samuel Denman, ―――― ―――― lived and died in Philadelphia.

3. Aaron Denman, married ―――― ―――― Mulford.

4. Elizabeth Denman, married Colonel Abraham K. Wooley, son of Colonel Abraham Wooley, of Springfield.

5. David Denman, married Miss Lyon, daughter of Elijah Lyon.

6. Phebe Denman, married Oliver Wade, son of Jonas Wade, Esq.

7. Mary Denman, married, 1st, Mr. Tenbrook ; 2nd, Charles Atwater.

8. Charlotte Denman, married Rodney Wilber, Esq., of Newark.

ESTHER BALDWIN, (3d child of Captain Enos Baldwin,) and Nicholas Parcel, had children :

1. Mary Parcel, who married Nathaniel Squier, son of John, of Livingston.

2. Smith Parcel married Miss Lewis, sister of Lawrence Lewis.

3. Enos Parcel married Caty Smith, of Springfield.

4. Patty Parcel married Stephen Edwards, —— of Livingston.

TWINS. { 5. Nicholas Parcel married Mary Anne Lyon.
{ 6. Esther Parcel married Smith Denman, son of Jacob.

SAMUEL BALDWIN, (4th child of Captain Enos Baldwin,) and Lucy Fairchild, had children:
1. Sally W., who married Bern Foster.
2. Mary married William Brewster, son of John.
3. Elizabeth married Abraham Cook, son of Epaphrus, of Livingston.
4. Rhoda.
5. John married, 1st, Phebe Camel; 2d, Jane, the widow of Dr. Camp.
6. Hannah married John Steinbreck.
7. Matthias.
8. Martha.
9. Charlotte.

DAVID BALDWIN, (6th child of Captain Enos Baldwin,) and Elizabeth Reeve, had children:
1. Isaac, who married Mary Roll, daughter of Brooks Roll, [See Roll.]
2. Moses married Elizabeth Ball, daughter of Enoch Ball.
3. Lydia married Jacob Morehouse, son of Benjamin, who was half brother of Enos Littell's wife.
4. Aaron married Anna Gould, daughter of Samuel, of Caldwell.
5. Nancy married, 1st, Zophar Canfield; 2d, Andrew Ayers, son of Samuel, of Ulster county, New York.
6. Enos, who died at 23 years, unmarried.
7. Catherine married, 1st, Abraham French, son of Robert; 2, Andrew Miller Camp.

TWINS. { 8. William married Margaret Dean, daughter of Daniel Dean, of Springfield.
{ 9. Mary married William Littell, son of Enos;— had no children.

10. Abner married Hannah Day, daughter of Charles Thompson Day, son of Thaddeus.
11. David married Elizabeth Carnes, of Pennsylvania, and went to Michigan.
12. Harriet married Leander Tyson.

ISAAC BALDWIN, (1st child of David Baldwin,) and Mary Roll, had children:
1. Julia Anne, who married William Gouldy.
2. Cornelia A. married Stephen M. Littell, son of Enos. [See Littell.]
3. James Augustus married Catherine Brown, of Newark.
4. Elizabeth married Mr. Styer, in Ohio.
5. Mary married Henry Anderson.
6. Lydia.

MOSES BALDWIN, (2d child of David Baldwin,) and Elizabeth Ball, had children:
1. John, who married Sabina Doty, daughter of Captain Aaron Doty.
2. Joanna married Dennis Smith, of Newark.
3. Hervy Dayton.

LYDIA BALDWIN, (3d child of David,) and Jacob Morehouse, had children:
1. Hervy Williams Morehouse, who married Julietta Baldwin.
2. Aaron Baldwin Morehouse married Elizabeth Gould, daughter of Richard.
3. William Sanford Morehouse married Mary Emily Davison.
4. David Baldwin Morehouse.

AARON BALDWIN, (4th child of David,) and Anna Gould, lived in Newark, and had children:
1. Harriet, who married Moses Searing.
2. Lewis Broadwell married Amanda Ogden.
3. Milton (is a Doctor,) married Aveline King; — lives in Newark.
4. Martha Louisa married George Hall.

NANCY BALDWIN, (5th child of David,) and Zophar Canfield, had children:
1. Enos B. Canfield, who married Julia Costar Benjamin.
2. Jane Canfield, who died at 16 years; and by her 2d husband, Andrew Ayers, had children:
3. Catherine Victoria Ayers.
4. Jane Ayers.

CATHERINE BALDWIN, (7th child of David,) and Abraham French, had children:
1. Abraham Morris French; and by Andrew M. Camp, had
2. Harriet Elizabeth Camp, who died at 4 years of age.

WILLIAM BALDWIN, (8th child of David,) and Margaret Dean, had children:
1. Jacob Henry.

ABNER BALDWIN, (10th child of David,) and Hannah Day, had children:
1. Aaron.
2. Mary Elizabeth.
3. Theodore.
4. Charles Thompson.
5. Lydia, who died at about 2 years.
6. Abner, who died at about 2 years.
7. James.

DAVID BALDWIN, (11th child of David,) and Elizabeth Carnes, had children : 1. Margaret : 2. George Martin ; 3. Sarah Anne ; 4. Charles ; 5. Elias Reeve ; 6. William.

HARRIET BALDWIN, (12th child of David,) and Leander Tyson, had children :¨ 1. David Alexander Tyson ; 2. Lewis Baldwin Tyson; 3. Mary Elizabeth Tyson ; 4. William Courtland Tyson.

NATHAN BALDWIN.

NATHAN BALDWIN, (2d son of John Baldwin, 1st,) had children :
1. Thomas married, 1st, ——; 2d, 23d September, 1811, Elizabeth, the widow of Abner Bailey.
2. Ethan.
3. John.
4. Ezra, who married Abigail Clark, daughter of Elder John Clark. [See Clark.]

EZRA BALDWIN, (son of Nathan,) and Abigail Clark, lived near Cheapside, and had children :
1. Phebe, who married Joseph T. Hardy, and removed to Ohio,
2. Sally married Matthias Swaim.
3. Stephen married Hannah Morehouse.
4. Esther married Ebenezer Morehouse.
5. Abigail married Benjamin Morehouse, brother of Stephen's wife.
6. Mary married John Davison, son of John.
7. Daniel married Catherine Meeker.

STEPHEN BALDWIN, (3d child of Ezra,) and Hannah More-house, had children :
1. Phebe, who married Jacob Reeve, son of Elias.
2. John Clark married Phebe Roff.
3. Lewis married Sally Parcel, daughter of Thomas.
4. Mary married Joseph Horton Reeve, brother of Phebe's husband.
5. Ezra married Martha Burtis, daughter of Abraham, of Brooklyn.
6. Abigail married Aaron Day, son of Joseph, son of Thaddeus.
7. Hannah Maria.
8. Lydia married Samuel Bailey, son of Samuel, of Springfield.
9. Sarah.

JOHN CLARK BALDWIN, (2d child of Stephen,) and Phebe Roff, had children :
1. Emily Clark Baldwin.
2. Sarah Elizabeth Baldwin.
3. Abby Maria Baldwin.
4. Stephen Clark Baldwin.

GABRIEL BALDWIN.

GABRIEL BALDWIN, (son of Ezekiel,) removed from Connecticut Farms to Longhill, North of New-Providence Church. He married Rachel Littell, daughter of John or Henry Littell. She died 30th October, 1794, aged 63 years. He died ——, aged 86 years. They had children :

1. Mary, who married Nehemiah Osborn. [*See Osborn.*]
2. Samuel married, 13th March, 1794, Johannah Squier, daughter of Ellis Squier, went to Ohio, and had children : 1. Squier, who married Sally Crowel, daughter of Samuel, of Dayton, Ohio ; 2. Amos married Miss —— Tucker, near Hamilton, Ohio, and died soon after ; 3. Sarah married Uriah Sawyer, in Ohio, a Yankee.
3. Susan married Nathan Halsey, of Parcipany, and had children : 1. Alfred Halsey; 2. John Halsey; 3. Albert Halsey, who died young ; 4. Nancy Halsey, who married Abner Bonnel, son of Ichabod Bonnel, of Chatham ; 5. Arabella Halsey married Joel Bonnel, brother of Alva ; 6. Susan Halsey married, 1st, Richard Vaus ; 2d, she married —— —— ; 7. Rachel Halsey, twin to Susan, married Charles Pool, an Englishman, and had children : 1. Elizabeth Pool, born 1st July, 1843 ; 2. John Halsey Pool ; 3. Dwight Pool.
4. Nancy married Daniel S. Wood, Jun., son of Captain Daniel S. Wood. [*See Wood.*]
5. David married two sisters, Phebe and Polly Brant, daughters of David Brant, and by Phebe Brant had one child : 1. Ellis D., who married Jane Todd, daughter of William, son of James Todd, whose wife, Jane Martin, was daughter of Alexander Martin, of Longhill. And by Polly Brant had children: 2. Samuel, who married Mary Coddington, daughter of John Coddington, and grand-daughter of Samuel Parsons ; 3. Asa married Emeline Wilkison, daughter of Nathan Wilkison.

ELLIS D. BALDWIN, (son of David, son of Gabriel,) and Jane Todd, had children :
1. David.
2. Catherine.
3. John.
4. Emily.

SAMUEL BALDWIN, (son of David,) and Mary Coddington, had children :
1. Phebe.
2. Sarah Anne.
3. John.

ASA BALDWIN, (son of David,) and Emeline Wilkison, had children :
1. William.
2. Caroline.
3. David.
4. Mary Elizabeth.

EDWARD BALL.

EDWARD BALL lived in Newark—was Sheriff of the county
of Essex in 1693. In 1678, Edward Ball and Daniel Dod were appointed to run the Northern line of the town of Newark from Passaic River to the Mountain. He had a son, Thomas, and also a
daughter, Abagail. She married Daniel Harrison, who died 1st
December, 1738, aged 77 years. His son, Thomas Ball, had nine
sons.

DAVID BALL, who lived in Rahway, had a son, Stephen
Ball, who was spitefully hung by the British refugees at Bergen
Point, 29th January, 1781, in consequence of his activity and
daring as a partizan patriot, leaving a widow, two daughters, and a
son, Ezekiel Ball, Jun., who removed to Middletown, Ohio, and
was a Justice of the Peace, Judge of the Court, and Post-master
there, many years.

EZEKIEL BALL, Esq., of Middletown, Ohio, had children :
1. Stephen, who was a Captain in the Militia, in 1805.
2. Abigail, who married Matthew Nichols.
3. Polly married Abraham Squier, son of William, son of Benjamin Squier, of Westfield.
4. Hannah.
Among the nine sons of Thomas Ball, son of Edward, probably
were,
1. Timothy Ball, who lived in Rahway, and had a son, Stephen,
and two daughters.
2. Tusken Ball, of Middleville, who built Tusken Hall there.
3. Nathaniel Ball, of Connecticut Farms.
4. Dr. Stephen Ball, whose daughter was the wife of Hobart
Littell, of Newark.
5. Edward Ball, of Clinton, who married Esther Mulford, daughter of Captain Jonathan Mulford, of New Providence.
6. Joseph Ball, who married Phebe Hand, daughter of William
Hand, of Livingston, [See Hand,] and whose daughter, Mary,
married Robert Cauldwell, son of William Cauldwell, of Passaic
Valley, and went to Ohio. [See Cauldwell.]

NATHANIEL BALL lived at Connecticut Farms, near where
the tavern is now kept, on the turnpike. He —— —— had
children :
1. Phebe, who married Jacob Jennings, of Passaic Valley,
Morris County. [See Jennings.]
2. Rhoda, who married Patrick Crilley, an Irishman, of Connecticut Farms, now Union, and had children : 1. John Crilley;
2. Moses Crilley; 3. Sarah; 4. Esther; 5. Martha Crilley; 6.
Betsey Crilley; 7. Elias Crilley; 8. David Crilley.
3. Rebecca married Mr. —— Loyd, of Camptown, now Clinton.
4. James married Eusice Meeker, of Connecticut Farms.

5. Salome married Solomon Line, of Sodom—went to Redstone, Penn.

6. Esther married John Mulford, son of Job, [*See Job Mulford.*]

7. Aaron married, 1st, Patty Wade, daughter of Captain Henry Wade, of Union; 2d, Hannah Willis, daughter of Nathaniel, of Springfield.

8. Nehemiah married Esther Sallee, sister of John Sallee, and had children: 1. Betsey; 2. Elihu; 3. Nathaniel; 4. Puah and Esther, twins; 6. Sineas; 7. James.

9. Pauh married John Sallee, and removed to Trenton, Ohio.

10. Davis married Miss —— Hetfield.

11. Eunice, married Doct. Wats Bonnel, of Union.

JAMES BALL, (4th child of Nathaniel,) and Eunice Meeker, had children:

1. Rhoda, who married Jacob Stookey, and had chidren: 1. Stephen, who died at about 16 years; 2. Eunice; who married —— ——; 3 David, marrried, 1st, Betsey Howard; 2. Sophia Rittenhouse; 4. Abby, who went to New-York, and married there. 5. Aaron Stookey, who married and lived in New-York.

2. David, who married Abby Wade, daughter of Caleb Wade, and lived at the Turnpike gate, in Union, and had children:

1. Eliza, who married Jotham Brown, son of Henry, and died leaving three children: 1. James Brown, 2. Abby Brown, 3. Caleb Brown.

2. Jane, married John Potter, son of Benjamin son of John, [*See Potter.*]

3. Phebe, married John Burnet, son of Daniel, son of Matthias Burnet, and had children: 1. Anna Burnet, 2. Caroline Burnet.

4. James, married Jane Burnet, daughter of Capt. Jonathan Burnet, and had children: 1. William Merton Boll.

5. Samuel, married Caroline Willcox, daughter of Noah Willcox, son of Noah, and had children: 1. Emma Ball.

AARON BALL, Esq., (6th child of Nathaniel,) and Patty Wade, had children:

1. Polly, who married Abner Meeker.

2. Aaron, married, 1. Betsey Willcox, son of John Willcox, 2. Betsey Woodruff.

3. Henry, married, 1st, Hannah Conklin, daughter of Benjamin Conklin, of Union; 2nd, Sarah Mullock, daughter of William, of Mount Hope, Orange county, New-York.

4. Phebe married John Hallock, Jun., son of John, of Orange county, New-York. He was Judge of the County Court, and member of Congress. By his 2d wife, Hannah Willis, Aaron Ball, Esq., had children:

5. Harriet, who married Stephen Bonnel, son of Abraham, of Plainfield.

6. Nancy married Joseph Shotwell. Live in Rahway.

7. John, who went to Mexico when a young man, and married there, and had two children, and died there in June, 1845.

POLLY BALL, (1st child of Aaron, Ball, Esq.,) and Abner
Meeker, had children :

6th Gen.   1. Martha Meeker, who married Turner Frazee, son of George,
of Westfield.

2. Rachel Meeker, married James Ireland, an Englishman.

3. Aaron Ball Meeker, married Hannah Frazee, sister of Turner,
and had children: 1. Anne Judson Meeker; 2. George D. Board-
man Meeker; 3. Harriet Newel Meeker.

4. Mary Meeker, married William Woodruff, of Elizabethtown.

5. Henry Wade Meeker, married Julia Clendenen, daughter of
George.

6. Obed Meeker, married ———.

7. Ezekiel Meeker, married ———.

8. Henry Meeker, married ———.

NOTE. — Abner Meeker, and all his children, except Aaron Ball Meeker, removed to Ohio, and lived in the vicinity of Franklin, Warren county.

MAJOR AARON BALL, (2d child of Aaron Ball, Esq.,) lived
at Westfield, and by his first wife, Betsey Willcox, had an only
child, Henry, who married Betsey Woodruff, daughter of Asa, of
Westfield.

HENRY BALL, (3d child of Aaron Ball, Esq.,) is a Baptist
Minister, — lives in Sussex county, and by his 1st wife, Hannah
Conklin, had four children: 1. Newton ; 2. Newton, 2d ; 3. Mary;
4. William Vanhorn, who all died, and his wife died.

By his 2nd wife, Sarah, Rev. Henry Ball had children: 5.
Thomas Jefferson, who also died young; 6. John; 7. Clarissa
Jane ; 8. Elizabeth; 9. Hannah, who died young; 10. Harriet;
11. Julia ; 12. Phebe ; 13. Martha.

PHEBE BALL, (4th child of Aaron Ball, Esq.,) and John
Hallock, Esq., had children :

1. Dewitt Hallock; 2. Charlotte Hallock; 3. Sanford Hallock.

HARRIET BALL, (5th child of Aaron Ball, Esq.,) and Stephen
Bonnel, had children:

1. Eliza Bonnel, who married J. A. Wood ;—live in Jefferson
County, New York; 2. John Bonnel; 3. Julia Bonnel; 4. William
Henry Bonnel.

NANCY BALL, (6th child of Aaron Ball, Esq.,) and Joseph
Shotwell, live in Rahway, and had children:

1. Gustavus Shotwell; 2. Harriet Shotwell ; 3. Henry Shotwell ;
4. John Shotwell.

TIMOTHY BALL.

TIMOTHY BALL, (probably one of the nine sons of Thomas)
married and had children :

1. John, who married, 1st, Miss ——— Crane, and had chil-
dren: 1. Calvin; 2. Luther ; 3. Rachel. John married, 2d,
Miss ——— Fairchild, and had other children: 4. John ; 5. David; 6.
Daniel ; 7. Uzel.

D

2. Uzel Ball, son of Timothy, married Abigail Burnet ———,
and had children:

1. Enoch, who married Joanna Lyon, daughter of Daniel.
2. Jonathan married Phebe Headley, daughter of Cary, and had
an only son, Uzel.
3. Noah married Fanny Edwards, daughter of Aaron.
4. Lafayette married Phebe Parker, daughter of Joseph, and
had an only son, Andrew.
5. Rachel married James Hogan, and had children, Ira and
Rachel Hogan.
6. Rhoda married William Johnson.
7. Mariah married Daniel Parker, brother of Phebe.

ENOCH BALL, (son of Uzel,) and Abigail Burnet, had children:

1. Calvin, who died at 21 years, unmarried.
2. Abby, who married Josiah Durand, son of Briant.
3. Betsey married Moses Baldwin.
4. Jonathan married, 1st, Jane Condit, daughter of Jared; 2d,
Peery Stevenson.
5. Mahala married John Gildersleeve, son of Joseph.
6. Randolph married Hannah Stevenson.
7. Mary married William Hollinn, son of Jacob.

NOAH BALL, (son of Uzel, son of Timothy Ball,) and Fanny
Edwards, had children:
1. Charles, who married Emeline Hand, and had children: 1.
Henrietta; 2. Thomas; 3. Fanny Jane; 4. Juliette; 5. Salina;
6. Susan; 7. Theodore; 8. Noah; 9. Catherine.
2. Susan married Albert R. Meeker.
3. Mariah married Thomas A. Reeve, son of Walter S. Reeve.
4. Marcus Lafayette married Pamela Durand, daughter of
Henry.
5. Jane married Nathaniel Burt.
6. Daniel Freeman married Catherine Alexander, daughter of
John.
7. Caroline married James S. Brady.
8. Harriet.
9. Emeline married John Gardner, son of Daniel.

RHODA BALL, (daughter of Uzel,) and William Johnson,
had children:
1. Hervy Johnson; 2. Susan Johnson; 3. Mariah Johnson;
4. Eliza Johnson; 5. Alexander Johnson; 6. Alonzo Johnson;
7. Charles Johnson; 8. Jephtha Johnson.

MARIAH BALL, (daughter of Uzel,) and Daniel Parker, had
children: 1. Uzel Parker; 2. Caroline Parker; 3. Abby Parker;
4. Mary Anne Parker; 5. Harriet Parker, 6. Daniel Parker; 7.
Joseph Parker; 8. Almira Parker; 9. Albert Parker.

SAMUEL BEACH.

SAMUEL BEACH lived near Jeffersonville, in Union Township. Married ——, and had children :

1. David, who married ——, and removed to the Lakes, N. Y.
2. John married Jerusha Bunnel, daughter of David Bunnel, (whose wife was Elizabeth Jones, of Union.)
3. Ebenezer married in Washington City, and settled in New York, and had children : 1. Maria ; 2. James ; 3. Joanna ; 4. William.
4. Susan married Isaac Miller, of New Vernon, and had children: 1. Mary, who married Farrand Cochran, of New Vernon ; 2. Betsey married Isaac Riggs ;. 3. Isaac ; 4. Phebe.
5. Elias married Hannah Headley, of Union, and removed to the Lakes.
6. Samuel married in Washington, settled in New York, and died there. Had children: 1. Susan; 2. Eliza ; 3. Julia ; 4. Harriet; 5. Patty.
7. Hannah married Stephen Harris, and went to Redstone, Penn.
8. Patty married Mr. —— Evarts.
9. Phebe married David Dean, of Springfield, and had children :
1. Elias Dean, who married his cousin, Hannah Dean, daughter of Jacob, above Springfield.
2. Jerusha Dean married Smith Lyon.
3. Hannah Dean married Joseph Smith, son of William, son of Walter, of Springfield.
4. Aaron Dean married Abby Crane, daughter of Samuel Crane, of Springfield.
5. Isaac Dean married ——, of Newark.
6. Harriet Dean married John Smith, son of William, son Walter Smith.
7. John Dean married —— Crane, only daughter of David Crane, Esq., of Newark.

JOHN BEACH, (2nd son of Samuel Beach,) and Jerusha Bunnel, lived on Stony Hill, south of Thomas O. Scudder's, and subsequently removed to Springfield. He was born 12th May, 1757. She was born 17th January, 1764. They had children :
1. James, born 7th March, 1782, and married, 1st, Ann McGinnis, of Newark ; 2d. Catherine Allen, of Newark. He then removed to Lexington, Kentucky ,and married there, 3d, Betsey Ellis ; 4. Mildred Garniss, cousin of Joseph's 2d wife.
2. Joanna, born 12th February, 1784, and died in infancy.
3. Susan, born 15th May, 1785, who married Jacob G. Broadwell, son of Hezekiah. [*See Broadwell.*]
4. William, born 7th August, 1787, married Susan Sovercool ; lives in Newton, Sussex county.
5. Joseph, born 15th April, 1790, married, 5th October, 1814, 1st, Rebecca Hoaglin, daughter of Martin Hoaglin. She was born 29th June, 1795, in Kentucky—she died 17th February,

1821. He married, 2d, the widow Catherine Wallace, 29th Sept. 1822, daughter of Thomas Garniss, of New York. She was born 25th April, 1790, was cousin of James' 4th wife.

   6. Jabez, born 22d June, 1792, married Maria Tillou, daughter of John Tillou.

   7. Samuel, born 3d January, 1795, married, 1st, Phebe Mitchel; 2d, Elizabeth Van Pelt, in Kentucky; 3d, ——— in Kentucky.

   8. John, born 12th August, 1797, married, 1st, Mary McCollum; 2d, Abigail McCollum, sisters, daughters of Aaron McCollum, of Sussex, near Newton. His 2d wife died 2d February, 1850, without children.

   9. Abigail, born 18th May, 1800, married Jonathan, son of Capt. Samuel Bailey. [*See Bailey.*]

JAMES BEACH, (son of John) by his 1st wife, Anne, had seven sons—all died young but one, William, who married his cousin, Eliza J. Broadwell, daughter of Jacob G. Broadwell. By his 2d wife, 3 children; but one living. 2. Elisha married Elizabeth Winters, of Newton. By his 3d wife, two living—3. Thomas, 4. Lucy. By his 4th wife, Mildred, one—5. Joseph.

WILLIAM BEACH, (4th child of John Beach,) and Susan Sovercool, had children:

   1. Anne Margaret Sovercool, who married Thomas H. Shafer, son of Isaac Shafer, of Newton, and had children; 1. Louisa Anne Shafer; 2. Susan Elizabeth Beach Shafer.

   2. Alfred.

   3. Hannah married John H. Lyon, son of Stephen Lyon, of Basking Ridge, and had children: 1. Emma Louisa Lyon—died at two or three years; 2. Anna Lyon; 3. William James Lyon.

WILLIAM MELANCTON BEACH, (4th son of William, son of John,) married Catherine Roy, son of Stephen, of Sussex, and had children: 1. Sarah Lucilla.

   5. John Sovercool, who went to St. Louis, Missouri.

   6. Jacob Coursen.

   7. Joseph Greer.

JOSEPH BEACH, (5th child of John Beach,) and his 1st wife, Rebecca Hoaglin, had children:

   1. Joan H., born 25th July, 1815, and died 13th Feb. 1817.

   2. Mary Evelina, born 11th August, 1817, and died 13th May, 1819.

   3. James Martin, born 2d August, 1819, married Malinda Slitfield, and had a son, Joseph, born 8th February, 1841. And by his 2d wife, Catherine, had children:

   4. Lillis Ferrier, born 11th February, 1824, and died 25th February, 1824.

   5. Thos. Garniss, born 16th Aug. 1825—died 25th Aug., 1826.

   6. Thomas Garniss, 2d, born 12th December, 1827, died 14th October, 1829.

   7. Catherine Garniss, born 16th January, 1829, died 16th August, 1829.

JABEZ BEACH, (6th child of John Beach,) and Maria Tillou, had children :
1. Harriet; 2. Caroline ; 3. Mary; 4. Jerusha; 5. Mariah Catherine.

SAMUEL BEACH, (7th child of John Beach,) and Phebe Mitchell, his 2d wife, had children :
1. John William ; 2. Margaret Jerusha.

JOHN BEACH, (8th child of John, son of Samuel,) and Mary McCollom, had children :
1. Sylvester, who married Mary Catherine Havens, of Marksborough, and went to Illinois.
2. Ithamar married Mary Elizabeth Bross, daughter of Peter Bross, of Hamburg, Sussex Co., and had a child, Jerusha Anne.

BEBOUT.

The father of the Bebout family came from Holland, and married Mary Miller, sister of the Rev. Benjamin Miller, Baptist minister at Scotch Plains. They had two sons, John and Peter.
John lived near Vealtown, in Somerset County, and early removed to the west.

PETER BEBOUT married, December 1st, 1767, Sarah Jewel, and had a son, Ebenzer, who also removed to the west.
Peter Bebout, married, 2d, Sarah Darling, half-sister of William Parrot, Sen., and had other children :
2. Peter Bebout, Jun.
3. William married, 1st, Martha Tingley ; 2d. Hannah Ogden, of Hanover, Morris county.
4. Christian, who died at about 18 years of age.
5. Abigail married Isaac Potter, son of Colonel Samuel. [*See Potter.*]
6. Mary married John Osborn, son of John Osborn. [*See Osborn.*]
7. Martha married, 12th November, 1786, 1st, John Bedell, son of Jacob, [*See Bedell,*] 2d, Luther Jones. [*See Jones,*]
8. Lewis, who died at about 15 years.
9. Stephen married Sally Cory, daughter of Elder Daniel Cory.
10. Nancy married, 1st, Simeon Dunn; 2d, Elisha Coriell, by Green Brook.
Peter Bebout, Sen., died 13th January, or 23d August, 1784; the statements differ.
William Bebout died 20th February, 1820, aged 70 years.
His widow, Hannah, died 5th September, 1828, aged 72 years.
John Bedell (husband of Martha) died 1st June, 1788.
Martha died 18th May, 1847, aged 80 years.
Stephen died ―― ――.
Sally, wife of Stephen, died 5th July, 1843.
The family has lived on the north side of Long Hill, now nearly a century.

WILLIAM BEBOUT, (3d son of Peter Bebout,) by his first wife
had no children. By his 2d wife, Hannah, he had one daughter,
Sally, who married Joseph Crane, son of Joseph. [*See Crane.*]

STEPHEN BEBOUT, (8th child of Peter,) and Sally Cory,
had children :
1. Peter, who married Abigail Potter, daughter of Samuel, son
of Caleb Potter.
2. Israel, born 30th October, 1799, married, 4th June, 1843,
Mary Crane, daughter of Norris.
3. Daniel Cory, who died a young man.
4. Julia married Benjamin Crane, son of Norris. [*See Crane.*]
5. Sineus married Louisa Mundy, of Bridgetown ; lives at Plainfield.
6. William married Phebe Anne Martin, daughter of Richard,
of Plainfield.
7. Susan.

4th Generation.

PETER BEBOUT, (1st son of Stephen Bebout,) and Abigail
Potter, had children :
1. Joel Thompson ; 2. Elizabeth Potter ; 3. Mary Potter.
Peter's wife, Abigail, died 22d October, 1847, aged 49½ years.

ISRAEL BEBOUT, (2d son of Stephen Bebout,) and Mary
Crane, had children :
1. Helen Todd.
SINEUS BEBOUT, (5th child of Stephen,) and Louisa Mundy,
had children :
1. Sydney ; 2. Sarah ; 3. Sylvester ; 4. Emma Louisa ; 5.
Stephen.

5th Generation.

WILLIAM BEBOUT, (6th child of Stephen,) had children : 1.
Almira ; 2. Martha.

BENJAMIN BEDELL.

BENJAMIN BEDELL, lived in the house where Capt. Abner Stites, lately lived, and kept a tavern there in the time of the Revolutionary War.

He married Sarah Herriman, of Elizabethtown, and had children :-

1. Mary, who was baptized 19th August, 1764.

2. Benjamin, baptized 27th December, 1769, and both died young.

3. Nathan, who married Ruth Morrell, daughter of Robert Morrell.

4. Susannah married, 1st, Jonathan Elmer, son of Rev. Jonathan Elmer ; 2d. James Hedges, 13th April, 1788, son of Uriah Hedges, Jun.; 3. Daniel Cochran, of Green Village.

5. Timothy married, 2d March, 1789, Chloe Hedges, daughter of Uriah Hedges, Jun.

6. Abigail, who was blind—she died at Basking Ridge in 1846, unmarried.

Benjamin Bedell, sold his farm in New Providence to Capt. Abner Stites, and bought another at Basking Ridge, but died 13th December, 1793, before removing there.

In the spring of 1794, the family removed to Basking Ridge. Timothy subsequently sold the farm, and removed to western Pennsylvania, and the widow and her daughter, Abigail, lived and died at Basking Ridge.

Nathan Bedell died 1st December, 1793.

Susannah Cochran died 7th October, 1822, aged 63 years.

Timothy's wife, Chloe, died 3d August, 1793, aged 22 years.

NATHAN BEDELL, (son of Benjamin Bedell,) and Ruth Morrell, had children :

1. Sarah, who married Stephen Sutton, son of Uriah, of Basking Ridge.

2. Benjamin married on Long Island, and had a son, John.

3. Mary, who died unmarried.

4. Robert Morrell married Keziah Goble, daughter of Timothy Goble, of Jockey Hollow.

5. James Harper married Nancy Allen, daughter of Zachariah, of Scotch Plains.

6. Betsey married Gould Silliman, of Long Island.

SARAH BEDELL, (daughter of Nathan,) and Stephen Sutton, had children :

1. Catherine Sutton, who married Pierson Howel, who lives in Newark.

2. Ruth Sutton married, 1st, Benjamin Cook. 2d. Pierson Howel, above-named, as his 2d wife.

3. Eliza Sutton married. —— ——

4. Uriah Sutton.

ROBERT M. BEDELL, (son of Nathan,) and Keziah Goble, lived at Basking Ridge, and had children:

1. Sarah, who married Lawrence Blue, of Somerville, and had a daughter, Harriet Blue.
2. William, who died at 14 years of age.
3. Betsey married Amos McIntire, and had children : 1. Harriet; 2. Jane ; 3. Eliza ; 4. Sarah McIntire.
4. Hervy, who died at 16 years of age.
5. Jane married William Strang, on Staten Island, and have, children : 1. Robert Strang, and others.
6. Robert Finley.
7. Rebecca married James Cross ;—live in Brooklyn.
8. Harriet married, 18th January, 1850, Winant B. Morrell, of Brooklyn.
9. Ruth.

Robert M. Bedell's wife, Keziah, died, and he married a 2d wife, and lives in Brooklyn.

SUSANNAH BEDELL, (4th child of Benjamin,) and Jonathan Elmer, had an only child :

I. Philemon Elmer, who married, 1. Nancy Potter, daughter of Isaac; 2. Catherine Jones. And by her 2d husband, (James Hedges,) had children :
2. Mary, who married Daniel Frost, of Green Village.
3. Sarah, married Thomas Kinnan, son of Thomas.
5. Margaret married John Sturges, of Green Village.

MARY HEDGES, (daughter of James,) and Daniel Frost, had children :

1. Jedediah Sherred Frost, who married Eliza Jane Bruen, daughter of Benjamin Bruen, of Madison, and had children :
1. Charles Bruen Frost; 2. Francis Caroline Frost; 3. Hervy Benjamin Frost ; 4. Eliza Josephine Frost.
2. William Frost.
3. Ezekiel Frost, who died a young man, unmarried.
4. Hannah Frost, who married Isaac S. Miller, son of Isaac, of New Vernon, and had children : 1. Mahlon M. Miller; 2. Phebe Crowel Miller ; 3. Susan Miller; 4. Luke Sturges Miller ; 5. Mary Jane Miller.
5. Hervy Frost.
6. Charles Frost.
7. Jane Frost, who married Nicholas Johnston, in Ohio.

NOTE. — William, Hervy, Charles, and Jane Frost, went to Ohio, and married there. Their mother went with them, and also married there.

NOTE. — I know of no connection between Benjamin Bedell, and John Bedell.

JOHN BEDELL.

JOHN BEDELL, Sen., had a son, John Bedell, Jun., who was an Elder in the church, in Turkey. He lived where Isaac Crane now does, in Morris county, and owned 100 acres of land, No. 24, (Addition) of the Elizabethtown Survey, and also 114 acres, No. 20, (Addition) lying North in the next tier of lots, extending into the Great Swamp.

There was also an Elder Jacob Bedell.

ELDER JOHN BEDELL, married Susannah, Valentine, and had children :

1. Jacob, who married Eleanor, or Aula, Powers, and was also an Elder in the church.
2. William, married Esther Littell, daughter of David, Sen.
3. Martha, married Elder Daniel Cory, of Longhill.
4. Susannah.
5. Mary, married Henry Gray.

Old Mrs Bedell, widow of Elder Jacob Bedell, died 9th September, 1773,

John Bedell Sen., died 2d January, 1768.

Elder John Bedell, died December, 1763.

Jacob Bedell, son of Elder John, died 16th June, 1777, aged 51 years; his widow, Aula, married Capt. Jonathan Mulford, and died about 1803.

JACOB BEDELL, inherited half the above named Lots, Nos. 24 and 20, and owned also 120 acres in Essex county, on the opposite side of the River, 100 acres of which is still owned and occupied by his grand-daughter, Catherine, the wife of Philemon Elmer, son of Jonathan.

JACOB BEDELL, and Eleanor Powers, had children :

1. Eleanor, who married Samuel Rutan, son of Abraham, [*See Rutan.*]
2. Abraham, married Polly Osborn, daughter of John, Sen.
3. John, 3d, married Martha Bebout, daughter of Peter, Sen.

ABRAHAM BEDELL, (1st son of Jacob Bedell,) sold out his lands here, and removed, in April, 1800, with John Maxwell, and William Littell, to Sussex county.

Abraham Bedell, and his wife, Polly Osborn, had children :

1. Betsey, who died young.
2. Sally, who married, 25th December, 1797, Lewis Meeker, of Union ; went to Seneca county, New-York.
3. Locky, married Henry Crampton, and went to Ohio.
4. Caty, married John Meeker Littell, son of William, above named.
5. Jacob, married ———— ————; lives Newark.
6. John, married Abby Campfield, of Newark; was drowned in the North River.

7. Abraham, married Sally Edwards, —— ——lived in Newark.
8. William married Mary Mackerley, of Sussex, and had a child.
1. Abraham Howel.

SALLY BEDELL,(1st daughter of Abraham,)and Lewis Meeker
had children:

6th Generation.

1. Abraham Meeker.
2. John Meeker, who died at about 22 years, unmarried.
3. Jacob Meeker, married. —— ——
4. Clarissa Meeker.
5. Jane Meeker.
6. Rhoda Meeker.
7. Matilda Meeker.
8. Emeline Meeker.

JOHN BEDELL, son of Jacob, inherited his father's farm of 120
acres, in Essex county. He and his wife, Martha, had but one
daughter, Catherine, born 4th December, 1787, and married in
June, 1806, Erastus Jones, son of Luther Jones, from Connecticut.
Her father died 1st June, 1788, aged 24 years, and she inherited
the farm, except about 20 acres, which her father sold to Nathaniel
Littell, Esq.

5th Generation.

Catherine Bedell, and Erastus Jones, had several daughters, who
all died young except one, Mary Mulford Jones, who married Isaac
L. Willcox, and had children:

1. Caroline Jones Willcox.
2. Erastus Jones Willcox.

WILLIAM BEDELL.

WILLIAM BEDELL, (son of John, Jun.) inherited the half of
the before named lots, 24 and 20, and lived where his father did. He
and his wife Esther Littell, had children :

4th Generation.

1. Susannah, who married Jonathan Davis.
2. Phebe, married, 1st, Charles Johnson, son of Uzel Johnson, on
Longhill, [See Johnson;] 2d, Caleb Mulford, son of Job Mulford ;
[See Job Mulford.]
3. Lydia, married, 7th August, 1787, Elijah Davis, brother of
Susannah's husband.
4. Mary, married, 13th March, 1785, Daniel Hole, son of Charles,
as his 2d wife.
5. James, married, 5th October, 1791, Nancy Oakley, sister of
Polly, wife of John Abel.
William Bedell, sold out his lands in October, 1792, to his brother-
in-law, Nathaniel Littell, and with his son-in-law, and son, and their
families, removed to a section of land that he purchased for $250,
of Daniel Thompson, between the two Miami Rivers, in Warren
county, Ohio, where they all settled.

SUSANNAH BEDELL, (1st child of William,) and Jonathan
Davis, had children :

1. William Davis, who married Sarah Lamb, daughter of Colonel Joseph Lamb ; they both joined the Shaking Quakers, among whom he died ; she is with them yet.

2. John Davis, married Elizabeth Serrin, and removed to Texas.

3. Mary Davis, went to the Shakers, where she continues.

4. Huldah Davis, who married John Monger.

5. Hester Davis, married Joseph Q. Lamb, son of Col. Joseph Lamb, [See Lamb.]

PHEBE BEDELL, (daughter of William,) and Charles Johnson, had children :

1. Betsey Johnson, who married Boaz Murphy, in Ohio.

2. Charles Johnson, married Betsey Trembly.

Mr. Johnson died, and she married Caleb Mulford, as his 2d wife. Mr. Mulford, by his two wives, had children :

1. Jacob Mulford, married Jane Hole, daughter of John.

2. Rebecca Mulford, married Elias Littell, son of Ephraim, son of Andrew, [See Littell.]

3. William Mulford, married Martha Meek.

4. Job Mulford, married Mary Dudley.

LYDIA BEDELL, (daughter of William,) and Elijah Davis, had children :

3. Esther Davis, Jonathan Davis, and Elijah Davis, who all went to the Shakers, and are lost.

MARY BEDELL, (daughter of William,) and Daniel Hole, had children :

1. Phebe Hole, who married Daniel Clark, son of Daniel, a Baptist Preacher.

2. Esther Hole, married David Bowers.

3. Stephen Hole, married Miss —— Eddy.

4. Catherine Hole.

5. Aaron Hole.

6. Mary Hole.

7. Elizabeth Hole.

JAMES BEDELL, and Nancy Oakley, had children :

1. John, who married Nancy Enyart.

2. William.

3. Esther.

I know of no connection between Benjamin, John and Henry Bedell.

HENRY BEDELL·

HENRY BEDELL, lived in Passaic Valley; his 1st wife's name was Sutton, by whom he had two children :

1. John, who married Deborah Mulford, daughter of Capt. Jonathan Mulford.

2. Henry, Jun., went to Sussex, married and raised a family

there.   The first wife of Henry Bedell, Sen., died, and he married
a 2d wife, in the southern part of New Jersey, and soon after removed to the State of Georgia; — settled and died there, leaving
three other children :
    3. Chester, who married in Georgia ; — had no children.
    4. Jacob, married in Georgia, and had a son, Henry.
    5. Phebe, married ; — nothing is known here of her children.
    Henry Bedell, Jun., went to Sussex ; married and raised a
family there. I have learned nothing of them.

JOHN BEDELL, (1st child of Henry Bedell,) and Deborah
Mulford, lived by the Spring at the then called Bedell's Bridge,
(now called Littell's,) and had children :
    1. Isaac, who married Mary Kinnan, daughter of Thomas
Kinnan, Sen.
    2. Stephen, married Phebe Drake, and lived in Sussex, where
his father did, and had eight children:
    3. Ezekiel, married ——— , and died, leaving two children.
    4. Mary, married Martin Vandyke. Mary died, and Mr. Vandyke
married Ezekiel Bedell's widow.
    5. Esther, married Jacob Crossman.
    John Bedell, with his family, except his son Isaac, removed to
Sussex county, near the Delaware River ; — he died there.
    Isaac Bedell, lived on Long Hill, where Samuel Stanbury formerly
lived, and had ten children; four of which died in infancy ; — the
other six were, 1. John Kinnan ; 2. Sarah ; 3. Deborah ; 4. Isaac ;
5. Mary ; and 6. Chester.   Deborah died in youth, and Chester
died in childhood.
    Isaac Bedell, removed to Mendham, where his wife died, Sub-
sequently, he with three of his children removed to Athens, Ohio,
where he died.
    Sarah married Ezekiel Day, of Mendham, and went to Athens
with their father, and subsequently to Illnois, and had children :
1. Mary ; 2. Phebe ; 3. Sarah.
    Isaac, married Harriet Martin, daughter of Isaac Martin, of Mend-
ham, and also went to Athens, and settled in that vicinity, and had
children : 1. Mary ; 2. Sarah.
    Mary also went to Athens with her father.

JOHN K. BEDELL, (son of Isaac, Sen.,) married Hannah
Jones, near New Vernon, and lives there, and had ten children :
    1. Chester, who married Amy North, of Long Island, and had
children : 1. William Forrester ; 2. Levi North, who died
young ; 3. John Chester, who also died young ; 4. Mary Elizabeth.
    2. Phebe married Daniel Oliver, of Water street, Mendham,
and had children : 1. Mary Irena ; 2. Chester.
    3. Deborah.
    4. Sherrod, who died young.
    5. William.
    6. Mary married Daniel Smith ;—lives in New York.
    7. Sarah ; 8. Abigail ; 9. John, who died young ; 10. Isaac.

TIMOTHY BEDFORD.

TIMOTHY BEDFORD, whose wife was Rachel ———, had children :

1. Hnnnah, who married Ezekiel Stillwell; — lived in Sussex.
2. Sarah, married William Willis.
3. Stephen married Lydia Drake, daughter of William Drake, of Piscataway.

STEPHEN BEDFORD, son of Timothy, and Lydia Drake, had children :

1. Timothy, who married Catherine McCarty, daughter of Jacob, of Chatham.
2. Andrew, who died young.
3. William Drake, married, 1st, Asenath Swain, daughter of Richard, near Hobart's Hill ; 2. Hannah, widow of Mahlon Simson, and daughter of Mr. Le Hommedeau, of Warren county.
4. Charlotte, married Benjamin Lyon, of South Orange.
5. Rachel and Lydia, twins, who died in infancy.
6. Aaron, married Ruth Whitehead, of Short Hills.
7. Polly, married John Tyson, an Englishman ; lived in Chatham.
8. John Simson, married 1st, Catherine Jennings, 13th December, 1822 ; she died 6th July, 1836 ; 2d. Joanna Jennings, daughter of David Jennings.

WILLIAM D. BEDFORD, (son of Stephen,) and Asenath Swain, had children :

1. Betsey, who married William Effner, of Hacketstown.
2. Lydia married Isaac Hadden, of South Orange.
3. Charles Nelson married Sarah Johnson, of Stanhope.
4. Stephen Oliver.
5. Mary married John Drew, of Short Hills, in Springfield Township.
6. Harriet married Squier Day, son of Zacheus, 17th Dec. 1745.
7. William Jackson.
8. Emeline, (twin to Abby, who died.)
9. Sarah.
By his 2d wife, Hannah, whom he married, 23d August, 1842, had children: 10. Elmira ; 11. Frank Day ; 12. Isabel ; 13. Lydia Anne.
His wife, Asenath, died 1st June, 1840, aged 49 years.

JOHN S. BRADFORD, (son of Stephen,) and Catherine Jennings, had children :

1. Phebe, who married Benjamin Parker, son of Calvin. [*See Parker.*]
2. Elizabeth married Joseph Chamberlain.
3. Albert ; 4. Daniel ; 5. John ; 6. David ; and by his 2d wife, Joanna Jennings, he had, 7. Mary Catherine.

NATHANIEL BONNEL.

NATHANIEL BONNEL, 1st, came from Long Island to Elizabethtown—was one of the first company of the " Elizabethtown Associates," and from thence he removed to Passaic River, above Chatham, and there settled. He married Hannah Miller, of Westfield, and had children :

2d Generation.

1. Benjamin (Esq.) who married Rachel Van Winkle.
2. Nathaniel (Capt.) married, 1st, Elizabeth Allen ; 2d, in 1775, Mary Simpson.
3. John married Sarah Carter.
4. Sarah married Samuel Roberts.
5. Betsey married Capt. Isaac Ward.
6. Abigail married Mr. Gardner.
7. Mary married Elijah Woodruff.

BENJAMIN BONNEL, Esq., (son of Nathaniel, 1st,) and Rachel Van Winkle, had children :

3d Generation.

1. Jane, who married Abner Brown, 21st July, 1763.
2. Joanna married Matthias Woodruff, 2d January, 1764.
3. Benjamin, 2d, (bellows-maker,) married Hannah Ward, daughter of David.
4. Nathaniel married, 19th February, 1772, Sibbe Howel, and had children : 1. Calvin ; 2. Luther ; 3. Elijah ; 4. Lockey.
5. Samuel married Betsey Crane, and had children : 1. Jane ; 2. Lewis.
6. John (a tailor,) married Nancy Day, daughter of Stephen Day, Esq.
7. Aaron married, 29th May, 1785, Rachel Clark.
8. Paul married, 28th December, 1783, Mary Parsons, daughter of William, Jun., and had children : Elizabeth, Abigail, &c., and went to Ohio.
9. Rachel married, 13th March, 1783, Major Luke Miller, of Bottle Hill.
10. Sarah married Jacob Searing Parsons, son of William, Jun., [See Parsons.]
11. Abigail married Jonathan Johnson, son of Stephen Johnson. [See Stephen Day.]
12. Rhoda married Calvin Morrell, 17th May, 1787, son of Jacob, of Chatham, and went to Ohio.
13. Polly married Stephen Day, Jun., brother of John's wife.
Benjamin Bonnel, Esq., was a Justice of the Peace, and an Elder in the Presbyterian Church here. He was drowned in the winter of 1800, by the upsetting of a ferry-boat, in New York Bay, when several persons of this Valley were lost.

BENJAMIN BONNEL, 2d, (3d child of Benjamin, Esq.) and Hannah Ward, had children :

4th Gen.

1. Enos, who married Rachel Ball.
2. Matthias married Sally Ward, daughter of Ichabod, son of David.

3. Sarah married Enos B. Townley, son of George. [*See Townley.*]

4. Phebe married Dr. Amos King, of Chatham, son of Stephen King, of Orange County, New York.

5. Prussia married Bonnel Brant, of Chatham.

ENOS BONNEL, (son of Benjamin, 2d,) and Rachel Ball, had children :

1. Jane.

2. Charlotte, who married Paul Lum, son of Israel Lum, Esq., had no children.

3. Elam W. married Tacy Howel, daughter of David, of Madison.

4. Benjamin, 3d, married Sarah De Camp, daughter of Moses, of Caldwell.

5. Alfred married Henrietta Cooper, daughter of John G. Cooper, Esq.

6. Matilda married Jotham Brant.

7. Harriet married Jared Hathaway, of Morristown.

8. John married Miss Stagg, of Elizabethtown.

9. Almira married Talbert Butler, of Staten Island.

10. Mary married, and soon after died.

11. Eliza married Mr. Baker, of Staten Island.

MATTHIAS BONNEL, (son of Benjamin, 2d,) and Sally Ward, had children :

1. Louisa, who married Albert Leonard, of Connecticut.

2. Moses Ward married Elizabeth Hunt, daughter of James, of New York.

3. Joanna Day, who died 30th January, 1850, in her 38th year.

4. Enos married Phebe Anne Gardner, of Newark.

5. Jane married Elizabeth B. Tickenor, daughter of William, of Clinton.

PHEBE BONNEL, (daughter of Benjamin, 2d,) and Dr. King, had children :

1. Prussia King, who married Franklin Day, son of Moses, and had children: 1. Charlotte Day, who died at 24 years, unmarried; 2. Sylvanus Day, who married Clarissa Fenner; 3. Hannah Maria Day; 4. Almira Day, who died at 18 years, unmarried; 5. Matilda Day; 6. Harriet Day; 7. Benjamin Franklin Day; 8. Calvin Day.

2. Almira King, married, 1st, Hartman De Gray, and had children: 1. Jane Agusta De Gray; 2. Amelia De Gray.

She married, 2d, Daniel Witter. Live in New York.

PRUSSIA BONNEL, (daughter of Benjamin, 2d,) and Bonnel Brant, had children :

1. Laura Adaline Brant, who died at 18 years.

2. Sofronia Brant married Mr. Scofield, and died at 22 years.

3. Benjamin Brant married in Penn., and lives in Philadelphia.

5th Generation.

4. Lavenda Josephine Brant, lives at Sam'l Robert's.
5. Elliet Constantine Brant, lives in Newark.
6. Margaretta died at about 17 years.
7. Sarah died at about 2 years.

JOHN BONNEL, tailor, (6th son of Benjamin Bonnel, Esq.,) and Nancy Day, had children:

1. Joanna, who married, as his 2d wife, Capt. Brooks, near Honesdale, Penn.
2. Barna married Lucy Brooks, daughter of Capt. Brooks.
3. Polly married Mr. Wood.
4. Stephen.
5. Julia married, 9th August, 1816, Rev. John M. Babbit, of Mendham.

BARNA BONNEL, (son of tailor John,) and Lucy Brooks, had children:

1. Joan Minerva, who married Charles E. Lum, son of David B., of Union, and had children: 1. Isabel Alathea Lum, born March, 1847; 2. Jane Bruen married Ira O. Tickenor, son of Josiah, of Clinton; 3. Mary Frances; 4. Elijah Day.

CAPT. NATHANIEL, (2d son of Nathaniel Bonnel, 1st,) was born 1731;—died July, 1809; he lived where his grand-son, Daniel L. Bonnel, now lives. By his first wife, Elizabeth Allen, he had children:

1. Abigail, born July, 1754,—married, September, 1755, Jacob Minthorn.
2. Nathaniel, 3d, born June, 1756, married, 1783, Martha Crane, daughter of Isaac.
3. Caleb Gilbert, born November, 1758, married his cousin, Joanna Woodruff, daughter of Elijah. He died 2d May, 1834, aged 76 years. She died 17th December, 1846.
4. Phebe, born May, 1761, married William Johnson, son of Uzel. [*See Johnson.*]
5. Jane, born April, 1763, married Samuel Crane, son of Joseph. [*See Crane.*]
6. Jonathan, born March, 1765, and died young.
7. Jacob, born May, 1767, was a clock-maker, married Margaret Crane.
8. Elizabeth, born August, 1769 — married, 29th July, 1787, Gabriel Friend. Capt. Bonnel's wife, Elizabeth, died 20th April, 1774, and he married, 24th November, 1775, Mary Simpson, daughter of Alexander, and had children.
9. William, who died young,
10. Nancy, born July, 1778, married her cousin, Sylvanus Bonnel, son of John. [*See S. Bonnel.*]
11. Chloe, born December, 1779, married Abraham Samson, son of David. [*See Samson.*]
12. William, 2d, born January, 1783—married, 25th December, 1806, Sally Doty, daughter of James.
13. Enoch, born 5th October, 1785, is unmarried;—lives with William.

NATHANIEL BONNEL, 3d, (2d child of Capt. Nathaniel Bonnel,) and Martha Crane, had children :

1. Philemon, born 29th March, 1785, married, 26th January, 1806, Rachael Noe, daughter of John.

2. Huldah, born 1st September, 1787, married, 1st, Timothy D. Pettit, son of Capt. Benjamin. [*See Pettit.*] Had an only son, Timothy D. 2d, she married David Noe, son of John. [*See Noe.*]

3. Jonathan Crane, born 29th September, 1790 — married, 2d November, 1814, Phebe Ward, daughter of Ichabod, son of David.

4. Mary, born 29th February, 1792—married, 9th January, 1813, Charles Day, son of Moses, and had an only daughter, Elizabeth Day, and Mr. Day died.

5. Jane, born 3d July, 1795, married her cousin, John M. Stites, son of Capt. Abner. [*See Stites.*]

6. Elizabeth, born 11th February, 1797 — married Matthias Osborn, son of Nehemiah. [*See Osborn.*]

7. Sarah, born 17th February, 1799, married James T. Lennington, and went to Ohio.

8. Maline Miller, born 22d July, 1802—married Elizabeth D. Walker, of New York.

Nathaniel Bonnel, 3d, died 15th April, 1814. His widow died 20th June, 1846. Maline M. Bonnel sailed for California, 17th July, 1849, and died of cholera, at sea, the next day.

PHILEMON BONNEL, (1st child of Nathaniel, 3d,) and Rachael Noe, had children :

1. Huldah, who married Sylvester Crane, son of John. [*See Crane.*]

2. Mary Noe married Ashbel A. Tomkins, son of Joseph. [*See Tomkins.*]

3. Ellis married, 1st, 11th November, 1835, Betsey Day Potter, daughter of Major Jotham, and had children : 1. Ellis ; 2. Phebe Pettit ; 3. Rachel Noe ; 4. Jotham Potter.

Ellis Bonnel's wife, Betsey, died 7th June, 1843, aged 31 years, and he married her cousin, Charlotte Potter Osborn, daughter of Stephen B., and had other children : 5. Betsey Pettit ; 6. Hannah Burnet.

4. Nathaniel, 4th.

5. Martha Crane married, 3d December, 1845, John Noe, son of Frazee, son of Lewis, and died 11th May, 1849, without children.

6. John Noe.

7. Maline.

8. Sally Doty married, 13th February, 1847, Isaac L. Wood, son of Daniel S. [*See Wood.*]

JONATHAN C. BONNEL, (3d child of Nathaniel, 3d,) and Phebe Ward, had children :

1. Mahetabel, born 8th December, 1816, married William Littell, son of John Littell, Esq. [*See Littell.*]

E

2. Julia, born 1st January, 1819, married, 27th April, 1836, Dr. John S. Smith, son of Abner Smith, of Long Hill. Dr. Smith died 16th August, 1841, without children.
3. Harriet.
4. Charity Frost.
5. Emeline.
6. Jonathan.
7. David Ward.

SARAH BONNEL, (7th child of Nathaniel Bonnel, 3d,) and James Lennington, had children :
1. William Lennington.
2. Thomas Scott Lennington.
3. Nathaniel Bonnel Lennington, twin to Thomas S.
4. Martha Jane Lennington.

MALINE M. BONNEL, (8th child of Nathaniel Bonnel, 3d,) and Elizabeth D. Walker, had children :
1. Helen R., born 4th February, 1836.
2. Martha C., born 30th May, 1839.

JOHN BONNEL.

JOHN BONNEL, (3d son of Nathaniel Bonnel, 1st,) and Sarah Carter, had children :
1. James, born 10th October, 1758, married Rosa Burnet; lived by the Franklin Mill.
2. Nancy, born 4th September, 1760, married William Day, son of Stephen, Esq. [See Day.]
3. Jonathan, born 12th May, 1763, married, 10th August, 1783, Mary Burnet, sister of Rosa.
4. Israel, born 24th May, 1765, married Fanny Hand.
5. Joanna, born 20th October, 1767, married Moses Day, son of Paul. [See Paul Day.]
6. Hannah, born 9th September, 1770, and died young.
7. Sylvanus, born 28th February, 1773, married his cousin, Nancy Bonnel, daughter of Capt. Nathaniel.
8. Eleanor, born 21st January, 1776, married Matthias Ward, son of Capt. Enos, of Chatham. [See Ward.]
9. David, born 5th September, 1778, and died at 18 years, by the fall of a tree, in the Great Swamp.
10. Sally, born 28th July, 1781—married Ezekiel Sayre, born 1st February, 1774, and died 20th January, 1850. He lived where his wife's father did, near Passaic River, by the brook, near the line between New Providence and Springfield.
11. Caty, born 1st February, 1784, and died in infancy.

JAMES BONNEL, (1st child of John, son of Nathaniel, 1st,) and Rosa Burnet, had children :
1. Stephen Carter, who married Sally Simpson, daughter of Isaac Simpson.

2. Electa married Abraham Walker, son of Asher, and died, leaving a daughter, Electa Walker, who married Dr. John L. Munn, son of Dr. J. B. Munn, of Chatham.

3. Elias married Caty Simpson, daughter of Isaac Simpson.

4. Hannah married Stephen Parcel, had a son, John Parcel, and removed to the west.

5. Nancy, who went to the west with Hannah, and died.

6. David married Sally Day, his cousin, daughter of Sally Bonnel, daughter of John.

7. Mahlon, twin to David, married Sally Oliver, daughter of Capt. Oliver, of New Vernon.

STEPHEN C. BONNEL, (son of James, son of John,) and Sally Simpson, had children:

1. Catherine, who married Nathan Foster, son of Stephen, of Union, and had children: 1. Sarah Bonnel Foster; 2. Susan Foster.

2. James M., born 13th August, 1809, and died 1848, unmarried.

3. Elias, born 9th July, 1811, and died 1836, unmarried.

4. Nancy, born 16th May, 1813, married, 15th August, 1832, William Andrews, from Ireland, and had children: 1. Thomas Andrews; 2. Stephen Bonnel Andrews.

5. Electa, born 4th July, 1816—married, 24th October, 1835, James Helm, and had a son, Elias Bonnel Helm, and died 28th February, 1837.

6. Stephen Carter, born 7th June, 1818, and died 21st September, 1820.

7. Hannah Parcel Bonnel, born 1st September, 1821, and married, 3d June, 1838, David N. Ruckman, son of Nathan. [*See Ruckman.*]

(margin: 5th Generation.)

ELIAS BONNEL, (son of James, son of John,) and Caty Simpson, had children:

1. Edwin, who married Eliza Scofield, of Connecticut.

2. Caroline married Thomas Smith, of New York.

3. Rhoda married Francis Doremus.

4. Elias Freeman married Maria Tashier.

DAVID BONNEL, (son of James, son of John,) and Sally Day, had children:

1. Harriet, who married Benjamin Wade.

MAHLON BONNEL, (son of James, son of John,) and Sally Oliver, had children:

1. Joanna, who married Henry Lytle, of New York. 2. David, who married —— ——; 3. John; 4. Henry; 5. Sarah; 6. Salina; 7. Mahlon; 8. Cornelia.

JONATHAN BONNEL, (3d child of John Bonnel, son of
Nathaniel, 1st,) and Mary Burnet, had children :
  1. Matilda, who married Alexander Bruen, son of Joseph,
and had children :
  1. Serenus Bruen, who married a daughter of David
   Burnet.
  2. Jonathan Bruen married Sally Muchmore, daughter
   of Stephen.
  3. Harriet Bruen married Mr. Knapp, from Connecticut.
  4. Albert Bruen married —— ———. Live in Chester,
   Morris County.
  5. John Bruen married —— ———, in Newark.
  6. Charlotte Bruen married —— ———.
  7. Hervy Bruen.
  2. Ichabod, who married Sally Parcel, daughter of Thomas,
and had a child, Mary Bonnel, who married John Helm, of
Basking Ridge.
  3. Joel, who married Arabella Halsey, of Hanover, and
had children :
  1. Albert Bonnel married a daughter of Carter Bruen,
   of Madison.
  2. Mary Anne Bonnel married Mr. ——, from Conn.
  3. Joel Bonnel, Jun., married —— Meeker, daughter
   of John Meeker.
  4. —— ——.
  5. Francis.
  4. Alva, who married Nancy Halsey, sister of Joel Bonnel's wife, had children :
  1. Halsey Bonnel, who married—— ——, in Newark.
  2. Marcus Bonnel married Miss —— Lacy, of Elizabethtown.
  3. Elizabeth Bonnel, not married.
  4. Joel Bonnel married —— ——.
  5. Sylvanus Bonnel married —— ——.
  6. John Bonnel.
  5. John went to the west, and was drowned.

ISRAEL BONNEL, (4th child of John Bonnel, son of
Nathaniel, 1st,) and Fanny Hand, had children :
  1. Harriet, who married Lewis Freeman, near Green
Village, and had children :
  1. Lewis Freeman ; 2. Francis Freeman ; 3. Sarah Freeman ; 4. a son ; 5. a daughter.
  2. Sarah.
  3. Lewis married ——, and left his wife, and went to Iowa.

SYLVANUS BONNEL, (7th child of John, son of
Nathaniel, 1st,) and Nancy Bonnel, lived at Springfield, and
had children :

1. Eliza, who married George Sayre, son of Nathan, of Elizabethtown. Live at Madison, (he is a merchant there,) and had children: 1. Sylvanus Sayre; 2. Edward Sayre; 3. Theodore Sayre, who died in infancy.

2. Calvin married Julianna ——, from Philadelphia, and had children; 1. William; 2. Nancy; 3. ——; 4. —— ——

3. Hervy married —— ——, in Iowa.

4. John.

5. Charlotte married Abner Stites, of Springfield, son of Abner Stites, of New Providence.

6. Sylvanus.

7. Nancy.

8. William.

All these, except Eliza and Charlotte, went to Iowa, and settled there.

SALLY BONNEL, (daughter of John,) and Ezekiel Sayre, had children:

1. Sally Day, who married her cousin, David Bonnel, son of James, and had an only child, Harriet, who married Benjamin Wade.

2. Electa Sayre, who married Stephen Bower, son of Daniel, and had children: 1. George Bower; 2. Laura Bower; 3. Catherine Bower; 4. Franklin Miller Bower; 5. a son.

3. Catherine Sayre, who died at 35 years, unmarried.

4. David Sayre, married Mary Spencer, daughter of Samuel, son of William, and had children: 1. Frederick Sayre; 2. —— ——; 3. —— ——.

5. John Edgar Sayre.

6. Lewis Sayre. Lives at St. Louis, Missouri.

SOLOMON BOYLE.

SOLOMON BOYLE, emigrated from Ireland, and married a French girl in this country. He purchased of East Jersey Proprietors, 600 acres of land, (west of and adjoining the Berkley tract,) a long piece between that tract and Passaic River, separated from the Berkley tract by a line running from the river, due North crossing Long Hill, to the river again. He lived where William Boyle now lives, and had children:

1. John, who married Hannah Frazee.

2. Solomon, Jun., born February, 1734–5, and married Margaret Hull.

3. Benjamin, who died unmarried.

4. William.

5. Bobert, who resided in New-York.

6. Joseph, who married Caty Cross, daughter of Robert Cross.

7. Jane, married Joseph Dalrimple, of Succasunna Plains.

8. Sarah, married Joseph Doty.

9. Lynche, married John Cooper, son of Daniel, 1st. [*See Cooper.*]

10. Polly, married Daniel Munroe.

JOHN BOYLE, (1st child Solomon, 1st,) built a grist-mill, saw-mill, and forge, at the fall where the river passes through Long Hill, the site now occupied by Dunn's Mills. He and his wife, Hannah Frazee, had children:

1. Jonathan.
2. Lynche.
3. Sally.
4. Patty.
5. John, who married Betsey Runyon.

SOLOMON BOYLE, Jun., (son of Solomon, 1st,) and Margaret Hull, had children:

1. Agnes, who married Stafford Wilson, from Ireland. [*See Wilson.*]
2. Susan, married Allen Simpson.
3. Elizabeth, married David Moore, son of Isaac. [*See Moore.*]
4. Jane, is unmarried, —— lives with her brother Col. Solomon.
5. Solomon, 3d, (Col.) married Elizabeth Pierson, daughter of Jonathan, and grand-daughter of Col. Cornelius Ludlow.
6. William, (Doct.) married Maria Lafferty.
7. Sarah, who died young.
8. Anne married Jacob Larzalier, and went to near Cayuga Lake, New-York.

COL. SOLOMON BOYLE, (5th child of Solomon, Jun.,) and Elizabeth Pierson, lived on Long Hill, on the original tract of 600 acres, and had an only child:

1. Mahetabel Day, who married Jo hnTunis, son of Daniel, of New Vernon; had children: 1. Phebe Elizabeth Tunis; 2. Sydney Adolphus Tunis; 3. William Lindsley Tunis; 4. John Sineus Tunis.

DR. WILLIAM BOYLE, (6th child of Solomon, Jun.,) and Maria Lafferty, had children:

1. William, who married Hannah Anderson, daughter of George Esq., of Vealtown.
2. Anna Maria, married Dr. James Howard Hutchins, of Brooklyn, New-York.
3. Adaline, married Albert H. Osborn, son of David L. Osborn, of Brooklyn, who was son of Nehemiah Osborn, of this Valley.

JOSEPH BOYLE, (6th child of Solomon Boyle, 1st,) and Caty Cross, lived south of Long Hill, on the 600 acre tract, near the river, and had children:

1. Robert, who married, 1st, his cousin Polly Cross, daughter of William; 2. Larny Appleman, daughter of David, of Washington Valley.

2. Polly, who died young.

3. William, married his cousin Nancy Cross, sister of Robert's wife, and had an only son, Augustus Alexander Boyle.

4. Susan, married Peter Cooper, son of Daniel Cooper, Esq. [*See Cooper.*]

5. Patty, married Williams Miller, son of Jonathan, near and North of Liberty Corner.

6. Solomon, married Harriet Parcel, daughter of Captain John Parcel, of Liberty Corner, and had an only child, John Ferdinand Boyle, who married Lydia Anne R. Annin, daughter of William C. Annin.

7. Alexander, who went to Cuba, (West Indies,) and never returned.

ROBERT BOYLE, (eldest child of Joseph, son of Solomon,) and Polly Cross, had children : 1. Cathrine ; 2. Joseph ; 3. Sarah Anne.

4. William Cross Boyle, who married Mary Aletta Annin, daughter of William C. Annin, of Liberty Corner, and went to Jeffersonville, Illinois, in 1848.   Robert Boyle's wife, Polly, then died, and by his 2d wife Lany, had other children :

5. David, who died at about 7 years ; 6. Mary L. ; 7. Elizabeth ; 8. Martha.

WILLIAM BRITTIN.

WILLIAM BRITTIN'S wife's name was Sarah —— ; she died 29th December, 1787.   They had children :

1. William, Jun., who married Mary Pierson, daughter of John, of Lyons Farms.

2. Jacob, who married Elizabeth Van Sickle, 3d March, 1774, whose mother was sister of Thomas Thompson, of Springfield ; also was sister of Elizabeth, wife of William Cauldwell.   [*See Thompson & Cauldwell.*]

3. Joseph married Elizabeth Ward, daughter of Cooper Ward, of Hanover, Morris county.

4. John married, 5th June, 1772, Phebe Pettit, daughter of Benjamin Pettit, Jun.

WILLIAM BRITTIN, Jun., (son of William, Sen.,) and Mary Pierson, had children :

1. Mary, who died young.

2. Abbey, who married Joseph Green, and had no children.

3. Vashti married Jeremiah C. Garthwaite, of Elizabethtown.

4. William, 3d, married Freelove Lewis, of Long Island.

5. Fanny married Elias Thompson, son of Jonathan, of Madison.

6. Elihu married, 1st, Mary Price, daughter of Thomas, of Elizabethtown; 2. Albina Ralston, daughter of William, son of John, of Mendham.

VASHTI BRITTIN, (3d child of William, Jun.,) and Jeremiah C. Garthwaite, had children:

4th Generation.

1. William Garthwaite, who married, 1st, Elmira Parker; 2d, Abba Ward, daughter of Dr. Ward, of Newark.

2. Abba Garthwaite married Albert Pierson, of Piersonville, Morris county.

3. Samuel Garthwaite married Mary Damon, of Elizabethtown.

4. Mary Carthwaite married Ira Pierson, brother of Albert.

5. Anne Garthwaite married Henry Geiger, of Elizabethtown. Live in Newark.

6. Jeremiah C. Garthwaite, Jun., married Caroline Darcy, daughter of Dr. J. Darcy.

7. Elizabeth Garthwaite married Joseph Wheeler, of Newark.

8. Thomas Garthwaite married Margaret Brittin, daughter of Colonel William, of Madison.

9. John Rudd Garthwaite, who was killed by the explosion of a steamboat, on the Mississippi river.

WILLIAM BRITTIN, 3d, (4th child of William, Jun.,) and Freelove Lewis, lived on Long Island, and had children:
1. William, 4th; 2. Maria; 3. Caroline; 4. John Pierson; 5. Lewis; 6. Mary: 7. Joseph Dayton; 8. Lavina; 9. Jane Eliza.

FANNY BRITTIN, (5th child of William, Jun.,) and Elias Thompson, lived at Madison, and had children:
1. Abby Thompson, who married Joseph P. Tucker, son of Charles.

2. William Thompson married Miss —— Marsh.

3. Mary Thompson married Jonathan Crane, son of Isaac, of Madison.

4. Jonathan Thompson, married Bethia Clarkson.

5. Phebe Thompson married Edgar Smith, son of James, of Woodbury.

6. Abel Thompson, who died a young man.

7. Jane Thompson married Mr. Freeman, of Rahway.

COLONEL ELIHU BRITTIN, (6th child of William Brittin, Jun.,) born 1778, and died 9th November, 1849, in his 71st year. He lived in Elizabethtown, and by his 1st wife, Mary Price, had children:

1. Henry, who married Eliza McBride, daughter of Hugh, of Tarrytown, New York, and had children: 1. Mary Frances; 2. Lavina; 3. Henrietta; 4. James; 5. George; 6. Jeannette, (twin to George.)

2. Julia, who married Amos Vreeland, and had children: 1. Mary Vreeland, who married William Smith; 2. Henry Vreeland.

3. Henrietta married William P. Mulford, son of Jonathan, of Pluckemin, and had children: 1. Elizabeth Mulford; 2. George Mulford; 3. Emeline Mulford; 4. Francis Mulford; 5. Lavina Mulford; 6. Mary Mulford; 7. Julia Mulford.

4. Maria, who married John Silvers, son of Noah, of Rahway, and had children:

1. Mary Malvina Silvers, who married Rev. William V. Wycoff, and had children: 1. HelenMaria Wycoff.

2. Elihu Brittin Silvers; 3. John Silvers.

5. John Pierson Brittin married Sarah Fay, daughter of —— ——, of Cazenovia, New York, and had a daughter, Gertrude Fay Brittin. He died at about 36 years.

6. Emeline, who married Abraham C. Squier, son of Recompence Squier, of Rahway, and had children: 1. Mary Esther Squier; 2. Jonathan Squier; 3. William Henry Squier. And by his 2d wife, Albina Ralston, Colonel Brittin had other children: 7. Mary Helen; 8. Luna.

JACOB BRITTIN, (2d son of William Brittin, 1st,) lived on Longhill, and owned 100 acres of land, No. 23 (addition,) of the Elizabethtown survey, and also part of No. 27, extending south to the river.

He and his wife, Elizabeth Van Sickle, had children:

1. Theodocia, who married Miller Walker, son of Asher. [*See Walker.*]

2. William, born 8th February, 1778, and married Margaret Baker, daughter of Daniel, of Westfield. He was Col. of the Militia—Judge of the County Court, and was a member of the Legislature several years, and also member of Council, from Morris county.

3. Abraham, born 20th February, 1780; married Elizabeth Baker, sister of William's wife.

William and Abraham were merchants in Madison many years.

4. Isaac married Abby Ludlow, daughter of Benjamin, of Westfield; he also lived at Madison.

5. Sally married Caleb Boss, son of Joseph, of Longhill. They both died leaving no children.

Jacob Brittin died 18th August, 1784, and his widow Elizabeth, married Jonathan Miller, of Westfield, who lived with her at Longhill till she died, 15th July, 1795, aged 41 years.

Mr. Miller married again a Miss Hedges, of Long Island, and died of asthma, 30th July, 1802, aged 41 years.

COL. WILLIAM BRITTIN, (2d child of Jacob Brittin,) and Margaret Barker, had children :

1. Sylvester, born 5th February, 1802, married Pamela, widow of Dr. Henry G. Elmer, and daughter of Gabriel Johnson, Esq., — both died without children :

2. Eliza Van Sickle, born 4th June, 1804, married William Woodruff, son of Flavel, and had children.
    1. Mary ElizabethWoodruff ; 2. Sophia Woodruff.

3. Anna Maria, born 16th August, 1806, married Jacob Baker, son of William, brother of Daniel, [*See Baker.*]

4. Hervy, born August, 1809, and died a young man.

5. Mary, born ——, 1812, married Apollos M. Elmer, son of Doct. Moses, and had a daughter, Elizabeth, who became deaf in youth. Mrs. Elmer died 9th April,1836, aged 24 years.

6. William Jackson, married Helen Maria Howel, daughter of Ezra Howel, of East Madison, and had children :
    1. William Ezra.   2. Edwin Ludlow.

7. Isabella.

ABRAHAM BRITTIN (3d child of Jacob,) and Elizabeth Baker, had children :

1. Edwin, who married Rosina Black, of Arkansas.   He died 27th Sebtember, 1847, at his father's, and left children :
    1. Fanny Elizabeth.
    2. Abraham Ludlow.
    3. William Isaac.
    4. Ford.

2. Alfred Bishop, born 1st October, 1814, is an engineer.

3. Margaret Osborn, born 11th June, 1819, married Jacob Thomas Garthwaite, son of Jeremiah C., of Elizabethtown ; — lives in Newark, and had children : 1. Elizabeth Brittin Garthwaite ; 2. Mary Turner Garthwaite, who died at about three years eight months.

4. Mary Walker, married Joseph P. Turner, of Alabama, and lived there and had children : 1 Rossina Brittin Turner ; 2. Fredrick Brittin Turner ; 3. Edwin Brittin Turner.

ISAAC BRITTIN, (4th child of Sacob,) and Abby Ludlow, had but one child :

1. Benjamin Ludlow, who went to Washington, Arkansas.

JOSEPH BRITTIN, (3d son of William, 1st) lived at Schenectady, New-York.   He and Elizabeth Ward had children :

1. Jacob.

3d Generation.

2. William, who died a young man.
3. Maria, who married Asa Sprague, of Connecticut.
4. Eliza, married Dr. Dunlap, of Schenectady.
5. Sarah.
6. Samuel.
7. Lydia.
8. Joseph.

JOHN BRITTIN, (4th son of William Brittin,) lived in Sussex.
He and his wife, Phebe Pettit, had children :
1. Pettit, who married ———, lived in Sussex.
2. Betsey, who married James Primrose, ——— lived in Sussex.

WILLIAM BROADWELL.

WILLIAM BROADWELL, Sen., drew lot No. 13, of the Elizabethtown Survey, and probably built the house upon it by the
brook where the Parsons family afterwards lived. He also drew
lot No. 18, South of No. 13, where Isaiah Meeker subsequently
lived ; he had children :

1. William Jun., married Mary ———, who died 23 September,
1757, aged 32 years. He had a daughter, Jane, who married her
cousin Moses Broadwell, son of Josiah Broadwell, Esq.

David, married Mary Howel, 25th November, 1767; she died 9th
April, 1769, aged 21 years. William Broadwell, Sen., died in
1746, aged 64 years ; his head-stone is of the oldest date of any in
the Presbyterian grave-yard. William Broadwell and Josiah
Broadwell, Esq., were of the Committee, in 1757, to confer with
the Rev. Jonathan Elmer, respecting his settlement as a minister of
the Presbyterian church, in New Providence.

3d Generation.

WILLIAM BROADWELL, Jun., and Mary ———, had children :
1. William, 3d, who died 5th May, 1761, in his 6th year.
2. Jane, who married her cousin Moses Broadwell, son of Josiah,
Esq.

JOSIAH BROADWELL, Esq., lived on lot No. 18, and had
children :
SONS. — Samuel, who married Miss Lindsley, and went to Ken-
tucky.
Hezekiah, who married Abigail Green, daughter of Rev. Jacob
Green, of Hanover, and sister of the Rev. Ashbel Green, D.D.
LLD. — late of Philadelphia, who was born 6th July, 1762, and
died 19th May, 1848.
Simeon, married Rachel Lindsley, sister of Samuel's wife, and
went to Dayton, Ohio. Jacob married Jane ———, of Metuchen.
Moses married his cousin, Jane Broadwell, daughter of William.
DAUGHTERS. — Polly, or Hannah, married William Darling, and
lived where Isaac Meeker does.
Esther, married, 1st, John Mills Frost; 2d, Ichabod Ward.
[See *Ward.*] She died 29th April, 1835, aged 81 years.

4th Generation.

HEZEKIAH BROADWELL, son of Josiah, Esq., and Abigail Green, had children:

1. James, married and had children :
   1. Charles, who is a Printer in Cincinnati.   2. —— ——
   3. Jane, who married in Cincinnati.
2. Jacob Green Broadwell, was born 4th April, 1780, and married Susan Beach, daughter of John, son of Samuel.
3. Abby, who died unmarried.

POLLY, (or HANNAH,) BROADWELL, (daughter of Josiah, Esq.,) and William Darling, had children :
Thomas Darling, who married Betsey McComb, of Newark, had children:
1. Herbet Darling.
2. Lewis Darling.
3. Thomas Darling, Jun.
4. Mary Darling, married Silas Lindsley, Jun., son of Silas, Esq. of Spring Valley.
5. Edgar Darling.
6. James Good Darling, married Martha Wilson, daughter of Charles Wilson, and Meriam High, daughter of Jacob.
7. Augustus Darling.
8. Isaac Darling, married Laura Seigler, of Bloomfield, and lived in Newark.

SIMEON BROADWELL, (son of Josiah Esq.,) and Rachel Lindsley, lived in Dayton, Ohio, and had children :
1. Silas ; 2. Ephraim ; 3. Josiah; 4. Lewis.
1. Silas, who married, 1st, Sally Byram, daughter of Naphtoli, of Morristown ; 2d. Anne Byram, (his first wife's sister, and had no children by her,) and had children :
   1. Ebenezer Byram Broadwell, who married ——, in Dayton.
   2. Mary, who married Joseph Plunket——, of Dayton.
   3. Simeon married ——; 4. Josiah married Ella Cutter, of Cincinnati; 5. Anne, married George Joycelin ; 6. Amy ; 7. Susan ; 8. Silas.
2. Ephraim, married Jane Gardener, daughter of Benjamin Gardener and Sarah Thompson. [See Thompson.]
3. Josiah, married 1. —— ; 2. —— ; 3. ——.
4. Lewis, married Nancy Valentine, daughter of David, son of Obadiah, and lives on St. Mary's River, Ohio.

JACOB G. BROADWELL, (2d son of Hezekiah,) and Susan Beach, had children :
1. Wickliff Green, who was born 9th April, 1840, and married Joanna Sayre, daughter of Nathan, of Elizabethtown ; had no children.
2. Hannah W., born 28th July, 1805, married, 22d December, 1821, Samuel Parsons, 5th son of —— ——
3. John B., born 10th November, 1807, who died at 9 months.
4. Jerusha B., born 24th January, 1809, died at 20 months.

5. William B., born 13th June, 1811, married Mary Ann Miller, daughter of Isaac Miller, of Newark.

6. Joanna H., born 26th January, 1814.

7. Eliza Jones, born 1st August, 1816 ; died at 3.years.

8. James Beach, born 22d March, 1818, died at 18 months.

9. Eliza Jones, 2d, born 4th February, 1820, married, 19th June, 1840, her cousin William Beach, son of James, and lived in Kentucky.

10. John Beach, 2d, born 11th March, 1822.

11. Jacob Green, born 1st October, 1825, married, 10th June, 1846, Eliza Anderson, daughter of James Anderson, of Newark.

HANNAH W. BROADWELL, and Samuel Parsons, had children :

1. Margaret Parsons, 3d, who died at 17 years, unmarried.

2. William Henry Parsons.

3. Samuel Parsons.

4. Charles Parsons, died at about 2 years.

5. Mary Eliza Parsons, died at about one year.

6. Wickliff Parsons.

7. Mary Anne Eliza Parsons.

8. Richard Parsons.

9. Albert Parsons.

WILLIAM B. BROADWELL, and Mary Anne Miller, had children : 1. George Broadwell ; 2. ——— ——— ; 3. Ira Green ; 4. Lillis, born 25th December, 1849.

ELIZA J. BROADWELL, and William Beach, had children, who all died but Anna McGinnis Beach.

Jacob G. Broadwell, and Eliza Anderson, had children .

1. William Henry, born 11th April, 1847 ; 2. James Anderson, born 25th September, 1849.

GEORGE BROWN.

GEORGE BROWN, (son of Andrew Brown,) lived on Stony Hill, where John W. Hand now lives. His wife's name was Elizabeth Martin, of Woodbridge. She died, 6th August, 1777, aged 25 years ; and he married ——— Wood, a sister of Samuel Wood, of Dayton, and also a sister of Esther, the wife of Jonathan Totten. He had children :

1. Thompson, who married Patty Wade, daughter of Andrew, of Morris County, whose wife was Rachel Osborn, daughter of John.

2. Noah, who died at about 22 years.

3. Elizabeth, who married, 15th March, 1796, Lewis Badgley, and removed to Paterson.

Thompson Brown removed to Westfield, and owned a large distilling establishment there. He left his wife and children there, and went to Ohio. He had children :

1. Andrew Wade, born 2d September, 1811, and married
Elizabeth Douglas, daughter of Jesse V. Douglas, and lives in
Springfield Township, at Sayre's Bridge, over Rahway River.
2. Mary marrried John Keith, in Ohio, and had children:
   1. Martha Keith; 2. Andrew Keith.

ANDREW W. BROWN, and Elizabeth Douglas, had children:
   1. Thompson, born 14th March, 1834.
   2. Mary, born 9th October, 1835.
   3. Caroline, born 4th June, 1837.
   4. George, born 24th June, 1839.
   5. Eliza Jane, born 15th March, 1841.
   6. Sarah Anne, born 12th February, 1843.
Thompson Brown died November, 1842.
Patty, his wife, died ——, 1842, aged 63 years.
Elizabeth, wife of A. W. Brown, died 1846.

JOHN BROWN.

JOHN BROWN came from England to Elizabethtown, and
married Nancy Badgley, daughter of George Badgley.
He removed to Stony Hill, on the Pettit place, and afterwards
bought the place where his grandson now lives, where Samuel
Johnson formerly lived.   They had children:
1. Rachel, who married Henry Hueston, and lived at Bellville,
and had children:
   1. Jane Hueston, who married Israel Simpson, son of John.
     [See Simpson.]
   2. John Hueston, who died at 19 years.
2. James, who married Mary Lyon, daughter of Ebenezer, of
Stony Hill.
3. William married Sarah Shaw, daughter of Richard.
4. Nancy married Allen Doty, son of Elder Joseph Doty. [See
Doty.]
5. Sally married William Simpson, son of John. [See Simpson.]
6. Polly married Thaddeus Titus, and went to Paterson.

JAMES BROWN, (son of John,) and Mary Lyon, had children:
1. John, born March, 1799, who married Elizabeth Radley,
daughter of John, of Westfield.
2. Aaron married —— ——, in New York, and went to French
Creek, Penn.
3. Sally married William Mulligan; live on Stony Hill.
4. Nancy married William Koyer, of Paterson, and live there.
5. Maria, who died at 18 years, unmarried.
6. Henry married Locky Moore, daughter of Isaac B., of Warren Township.
7. Peter married Sarah Hemmingway, an English girl.

JOHN BROWN, (son of James,) and Elizabeth Radley, had
children :
1. Fanny.
2. Mary Anne, born 1822.
3. Jonathan M. Willcox, who died at 9 months ; 4. Eliza died at
12 months ; 5. James ; 6. Maria ; 7. John Lyon ; 8. Eliza Jane,
born 1832.

SALLY BROWN, (3d child of James, son of John,) and
William Mulligan, had children .
1. John Mulligan ; 2. Mary Mulligan ; 3. Jane Mulligan ; 4.
William Ellis Mullegan ; 5. George Henry Mullegan.

NANCY BROWN, (4th child of James, son of John,) and
William Koyer, had children :
1. James Koyer ; 2. William Koyer ; 3. Henry Koyer ; 4.
Maria Koyer ; 5. Sarah Jane Koyer ; 6. Peter Koyer.

HENRY BROWN, (6th child of James, son of John,) and
Locky Moore, had children :
1. Mary ; 2. Albert ; 3. Margaret ; 4. William ; 5. Isaac ; 6.
Jeremiah.

PETER BROWN, (7th child of James, son of John,) and
Sarah Hemmingway, had children ;
1. John Lever ; 2. Margaret ; 3. Hetty ; 4. Charlotte, 5.
Thomas ; 6. William.

WILLIAM BROWN, (3d child of John,) became insane, and
is in the Ney Jersey Insane Asylum, at Trenton.
He and Sarah Shaw, had children :
1. Polly, who married Israel B. Long, son of John ; lived where
Richard Valentine did. [See Long.] Died March 10th, 1851.
2. George married Polly Badgley, daughter of Anthony, Jun. ;
have no children.
3. Anne married Jacob F. Badgley, son of Samuel. [See
Badgley.]
4. Hetty married Henry Price, son of William, son of Rice
Price. [See Price.]
5. John married Anjoline Irvin, daughter of John W. Foster, of
Westfield, and has children : 1. Amanda Merwin ; 2. ———.

POLLY BROWN, (6th child of John Brown,) and Thaddeus
Titus, had children :
1. Cornelius Titus, who married his cousin, 1st, Sally Doty,
daughter of Allen, son of Joseph, and had children : 1. Lorenzo
Titus ; 2. Cornelius Titus, Jun. ; and by his 2d wife, Maria, (an
Irish girl,) had other children : 3. John
2. Henry Titus married, 1st, Eliza Post, of Paterson ; 2d, Mary
Jane Box ; has no children.

3. Jane Titus married Willard Fisk, son of Russel Fisk, and had children: 1. Amanda Fisk; 2. Russel Fisk; 3. Mary Jane Fisk.
4. Rachel Titus married Christian Overnier, and had children: 1. Cornelius Overnier.
5. Mary Titus, who died at 6 years of age.
6. Thompson Titus married Anne Lowrey, and had children: 1. Henry Titus; 2. Sarah Titus; 3. Thompson Titus, Jun.

WATERS BURROWS

WATERS BURROWS, married Frances Meeker, (daughter of James, son of Robert Meeker.) They removed from Elizabethtown, and lived where Stephen Day does, and had children:
1. Hannah, who married David Jones; lived where Jonathan Totten does.
2. Stephen, who went to Cincinnati, Ohio. He died of cholera in 1850.
3. Nancy went to Cincinnati with Stephen.
4. James went to western New York.
5. Aaron went to western New York.
6. David went to Cincinnati,—has three sons in Iowa, John, David, and ——, and Frances and Mary Anne, in Newark, N. J.
7. Mary married Josiah Wilkison. She died 30th April, and he died May 1st, 1838.
8. Deborah married Jonathan Alward (son of Henry, 3d,) of Basking Ridge. [See Alward.]
9. Waters, Jun., (Rev.) married Margaret Wood, daughter of Captain Daniel S. Wood.
Mr. Waters Burrows died 5th July, 1815, aged 69 years.

REV. WATERS BURROWS is a minister of the Methodist Episcopal Church. He and Margaret Wood had children:
1. Sarah Anne, who married Abraham Parrot, son of Squier. [See Parrot.] 2. Mary Frances; 3. Samuel; 4. Waters, 3d.

MARY BURROWS, (7th child of Waters Burrows,) and Josiah Wilkison, had children:
1. James M. Wilkison married Eliza Payer, of Warren county, and lives there.
2. Stephen Burrows Wilkison married Drusilla Young, daughter of Stephen, of East Madison.
3. Mary Burrows Wilkison married Daniel Y. Harrison, of Newark, and went to Cincinnati.
4. Elias Riggs Wilkison married Charlotte F. Davis, daughter of Isaac L., of Elizabethtown.
5. Eleazer B. Wilkison married Hannah Anne Dickerson, of Sussex.

MARY BURROWS, (daughter of Waters,) and Josiah Wilkison, had children :
1. James M. Wilkeson, (son of Josiah,) and Elizabeth Poyer, of Warren county, had children:
  1. Josiah, who died at one year.
  2. Abiathar, who died at one year.
  3. Jonathan A., who died at 4 years old.
  4. Samuel, born 1826.
  5. Isaac Newton, who died at 7 years old.
  6. John Newton, born 1829.
  7. Elias Riggs, born 1832.
  8. Charlotte Anne Poyer, born 1835.
  9. Mary Margaret Burrows, born 1837.
  10. Malvina Young, born 1840.
  11. James Jaquet, born 1843.

NAPHTALI BYRAM.

NAPHTALI BYRAM lived at Morristown. He married Amy Hedges, and had children :
1. Abigail, who married her cousin, Byram Ayers, son of Elias Ayers. They removed to Lexington, Prebble county, Ohio.
2. Amy married Samuel Halliday, of Newburg, New York. He lived at Morristown, and was Sheriff of Morris county several years.
3. Ebenezer married Mary Littell, daughter of Nathaniel, and went to Darke county, Ohio. [See Littell.]
4. Huldah married Loammi Moore, of Morristown; he was a merchant.
5. Susan, who died, aged about 50 years, unmarried.
6. Silas Condit married Nancy Brown, daughter of Daniel, of Madison; (she was sister of Caleb Dickerson's wife;) he went to Dayton, Ohio.
7. Sally married Silas Broadwell, son of Simeon. [See Broadwell.]
8. Anne married the same Silas Broadwell, and had no children; she was confined to her bed about seven years, at Morristown. by disease, and subsequently went to Dayton, Ohio, and married.

ABIGAIL BYRAM, (1st child of Naphtali Byram,) and Byram Ayers, have children:
1. Mary Ayers, who married John Cummings, of Lexington, Prebble county.
2. Phebe Ayers, not married in 1850.
3. Amy Ayers married Jacob Westerfield, of Lexington, son of Samuel.
4. Huldah Anne Ayers married John Miller, of Lexington.
5. James Ayers married —— ——.

AMY BYRAM, (2d child of Naphtali,) and Samuel Halliday, had children :

F

1. Betsey Halliday.
2. David Halliday is a Presbyterian minister at Peekskill, N. Y
3. James Richards Halliday.

HULDAH BYRAM, (4th child of Naphtali,) and Loammi Moore, had children :
1. Byram Moore married in Virginia, and lives there.
2. Sally Anne Moore married Silas Pierson, son of Benjamin. above Madison ; lives at Mercersburgh, Penn., and keeps a high school.
3. Susan Moore married —— Baldwin, of Orange, and lives there.
4. Abigail Moore went to her sister's, at Mercersburgh.
5. Phebe Moore also went to Mercersburgh.
6. William Moore went to Cincinnati, and married there, and keeps a book-store.
7. Eliza Moore also went to Mercersburgh.

SILAS CONDIT BYRAM, (6th child of Naphtali,) and Nancy Brown, had children :
1. Ebenezer, who married Sarah Hand, daughter of Aaron Hand, of Basking Ridge, and had children : 1. Aaron Milton; 2. Eliza; 3. Delia; 4. Silas; 5. Albert Barnes; 6. Hannah; 7. William Byram.
2. Amy married Eli Tomkins ——; lives at Orange, N. J.
3. Henry married Anna Searing, of Spring Valley, Morris county, New Jersey, and has children : 1. Sarah Anne; 2. Susan; 3. Henry.
4. Mary married her cousin, Nathaniel L. Byram, son of Ebenezer. They both died, and left one child, Harriet Byram, who lives with her relative, the Rev. David Halliday, of Peekskill, New York.
5. David married Delia Bishop ;—lives in Monmouth Co., N. J.
6. Jonas, who went on a whaling voyage, and never returned.
7. Frances married ——, at Succasunna Plains, and went to Illinois.
8. Silas Pierson.
Silas C. Byram and his wife both died, and are buried at Dayton.

JOHANNES VANCAMPEN.

JOHANNES VANCAMPEN, (in English called John Camp,) owned 300 or 400 acres of land, lots No. 50, 51, 52, of the Elizabethtown lots, adjoining Passaic River, west of Littell's lot, where he lives. He lived on lot No. 55, south of Mulford's bridge, by the brook. He probably exchanged lot No. 50 with John Blanchard, for lot No. 55. He lived on No. 55, and Blanchard subsequently sold 40 acres of No. 50 to Thomas Baker, in 1738. About half his 300 acres were sold (100 acres of which was subsequently owned by Richard Scudder, now owned by John Littell.) The remainder was inherited by his son, Aaron Camp, who lived where his father did. Aaron Camp died 8th December, 1788, and his farm was divided among his children. Aaron Camp married, 1st, ——, 2d, Hannah Clark, daughter of Daniel.

Aaron Camp, by his 1st wife, had children :

1. Mary, who married David Allen, son of Joseph Allen, Jun., of Washington Valley. [*See Allen.*]

2. Aaron, Jun., married, 22d April, 1771, Ketura Clark, daughter of Daniel, and sister of his father's 2d wife, and lived in Caldwell, near the Little Falls.

3. Moses married, 1787, Martha Rutan, daughter of Abraham, of Longhill, and removed to Pennsylvania.

4. Job married, 7th January, 1790, Mary Tucker, daughter of John, of Stonyhill, and went to western Pennsylvania, and from thence to Ohio.

5. John married, 8th November, 1789, Rachel Sayre ; and by his 2d wife, Hannah Clark, Aaron Camp had other children: 6. Lot; 7. Sally ; 8. Amy; 9. Theodocia.

Aaron Camp died, and his widow married Deacon William Connet.

(margin: 3d Generation.)

THOMAS CARLE

THOMAS CARLE lived on Long Island, and had two sons : Jona ; Jacob.

Jona Carle sold, in the year 1729, to Benjamin Pettit, of New Rochelle, in the State of New York, 105 acres of land adjoining Passaic River, and yet in the Pettit family.

In the deed, from John Blanchard for the Church Parsonage lot, Jacob Carle is said to adjoin it on the west ; therefore it would seem that Jocob Carle and Jona Carle owned from the Parsonage lot up the river, to about the middle of the Pettit farm, and that Jacob sold the remainder to Elnathan Cory, who subsequently owned it.

Jacob Carle removed to the farm now owned by John Worth, on the north of Dead River. He then bought 500 acres, the one-fourth part of the Berkley Tract of 2000 acres, north of Passaic River, on which his grandson, Daniel Carle, now lives.

Jacob Carle married Rebecca Stites, daughter of William Stites, and had children :

1. John, who married Providence Layton, sister of Capt. Peter Layton. (Providence and Peter Layton's mother was sister of Richard Runyon, Sen.

2. Sarah, who married Bedient Baird, who lived where Clark Squier does.

3. Jonas, who married Anna Cooper, daughter of Daniel Cooper, 1st.

John Carle, son of Jacob Carle, lived on Long Hill, on the 500 Acre Tract, which was divided between him and his brother Jonas. He was a Justice of the Peace, a Judge of the Court and several time, a member of the Legislature of the State, and in 1783, was a member of the Privy Council.

JOHN CARLE, Esq., (son of Jacob,) and Providence Layton, had children :

1. Jemima, who married, 22d April, 1771, Samuel Hayden, and went, after the war, to Canada.
2. John, married Lydia Perrine,and he became a Presbyterian minister.
3. Sally, married Alexander Kirkpatrick, son of David. [*See Kirkpatrick.*]

JONAS CARLE, (son of Jacob,) lived where his father did, and Anna Cooper, had children :

1. Betsey, who married James Vail, son of Isaac Vail, who was brother of Daniel Vail, Sen. [*See Vail.*]
2. Jacob, who died a young man, unmarried.
3. Elijah, who died in youth.
4. Anne is unmarried, and lives with her brother Daniel.
5. Timothy, who died at 19 years of age, unmarried.
6. Daniel is unmarried, and lives on the farm his father owned.
7. Sally, married Ebenezer Williams, son of John. [*See Williams.*]
8. Lydia, married the same Ebenezer Williams. They live near the cross-roads, one mile east of Basking Bridge.

JAMES CAULDWELL.

JAMES CAULDWELL, with his wife Mary, emigrated from Ireland, about the year 1732, when his son William was six years old, and settled on Long Hill, on lot,No. 30, addition of the Elzabeth-town lots, which it appears he drew.

From tradition among the families, it would seem, and I am led to believe, that James Cauldwell's wife was Mary Gaston, sister of the father of Hugh Gaston, of Peapack,

Hugh Gaston, was brother of Capt. William Logan's wife, and probably also brother of the wife of Thomas Kirkpatrick, at Liberty Corner. His children called him Uncle Hugh Gaston, and Mr. Gaston, Mrs. Logan, and the old Kirkpatrck family claimed kin to the Cauldwell family.

JAMES CAULDWELL, had children:

1. William, who married Elizabeth Thompson, sister of Thomas, of Springfield.
2. Robert, who married ———— ————, and died, leaving three daughters, Sarah, Mary and Elizabeth.
3. Hugh, who married Jane Parker, his cousin; lived on Long Hill.
4. Abraham, married Catherine Hill; lived in Orange Co, New-York.
5 James, married Peggy ————, lived near Goshen, Orange Co.
6. John, who died unmarried.
7. Jennet, married Mr. —— Miller.
8. Sarah, married Isaac Roll, son of John. [*See Roll.*]

WILLIAM CAULDWELL, (1st child of James,)and Elizabeth Thompson, owned, and lived on lot No. 17, (addition,) adjoining Passaic River, in Morris County, immediately below Johnson's Bridge. They had children:

1. Aaron, born 7th Jan. 1752, and died unmarried.
2. James, born 23d Sept. 1753, married his cousin Elizabeth Cauldwell, daughter of James.
3. John, born 23d August, 1755, married Hannah Rutan, daughter of Abraham.
4. Mary, born 14th Feb. 1757, married Nathaiel Littell, son of David. [*See Littell.*]
5. Moses, born 30th Oct. 1758, and died unmarried.
6. Sarah, born 3d May, 1760, married, 26th March, 1787, Isarel Cory, son of Elder Daniel. [*See Cory.*]
7. Robert, born 13th Sept. 1762, married Mary Ball, born 25th Aug. 1763, daughter of Joseph.
8. Elizabeth, born 9th June, 1764, married, 8th May, 1788, Alexander Simpson, son of John. [*See Simpson.*]
9. Dan, born 28th Jan. 1766, married 8th May, 1788, Rachel Potter, daughter of Amos, son of Daniel.
10. Abraham, born 5th Sept. 1768, married, 14th June, 1791, Elizabeth Rutan, daughter of Abraham.

NOTE.—William Cauldwell, died in 1799, aged 73 years. His wife, Elizabeth, died 20th March, 1794, aged 65 years.

John Cauldwell, died 10th Sept. 1801, aged 46. His wife, Hannah, died, 3d June, 1797, aged 36 years. William Cauldwell, and his son John, were elders in the church here.

JAMES CAULDWELL, (2d child of William,) and Elizabeth, his wife, lived in New York, and had children.
1. Jane, who married. 2. John 3. Thomas.

JOHN CAULDWELL, (3d child of William,) lived where his father did. He and his wife Hannah Rutan had children:
1. Rachel, who died 16th Aug. 1784, aged 10 months.
2. John, who married Electa Hand, daughter of Benjamin, of Long Hill.
3. Abraham Rutan, married, 1. Electa Johson, 26th April, 1815, daughter of Gabriel, Esq. 2. Aquilla Berry, daughter of Judge Berry, of Urbana.
4. Hugh, born 15th May, 1790, married, 28th July, 1811, Abigail Gibbs, born 24th Oct. 1793, daughter of Joseph Gibbs, of Elizabethtown, and lived there.
5. Peter Rutan, married Levinah Fitch; lived in Urbana, Ohio.
6. Robert M. married his cousin Betsey Cauldwell, daughter of Abraham.
7. Jerry, married, 5th Nov. 1793, Mary Eliza Boyer; all these but Rachel and Hugh went to the State of Ohio.

JOHN CAULDWELL, (son of John, son of William,) and Electa Hand lived in ———, Ohio, and had children:

1. Abraham. who married. —— 2. Hannah, married 1.——
Rutan, 2. —— Mars. 3. Azel, married Jane Stewart ; lives near
Hill Grove, Darke Co., and had children; 1. Dennis ; 2. John; 3.
James Mc Nab ; 4. Electa ; 5. Martha; 6. Catherine ; 4. Ludlow,
married ; 5. —— ——, who died in infancy ; 6. Phebe, married
—— ——; 7. Mary ; 8. John, 3d ; 9. Peter.

ABRAHAM R. COLWELL, (so he spells his name) son of
John, son of William, By his first wife, Electa Johnson, had children :
1. Maria Johnson, who married Dr. Wilson Everet, a printer.
2. William Johnson, who married Jane Ward.
And by his 2nd wife, Aquilla Berry, had other children :
    3. Charles ; 4. Eliza ; 5. Mary ; 6. Girden ; 7. Benjamin ;
    8. John.

HUGH CAULDWELL, (3d son of John, son of William,) and
Abigail Gibbs had children :
1. Jane, born 25th Oct. 1812, married, 4th November, 1838,
Daniel Trembly, son of John, of Rahway ; lived in Elizabethtown,
and had children :
    1. William Trembly. 2. Anna Meeker Trembly. 3. John
    Joseph Trembly. 4. Jane Trembly.
2. Robert, born 5th November, 1816, married, 16th, May, 1841
Julia Anne. Marsh, daughter of Gideon Marsh, of Westfield, live in
Elizabethtown, and have children :
    1. Freeman. 2. George.
3. Hannah Maria, born 25th December, 1818, and died 25th
April, 1838.
4. William McDowel, born 12th May, 1821, and died 8th May,
1839.
5. Elizabeth, born 7th January, 1823, and died 9th August, 1824
Hugh Cauldwell died 14th November, 1822, in Elizabethtown.

PETER R. COLWELL, (son of John,) and Levinah Fitch had
children ;
1. James, born 8th June, 1817, married, 18th Sept. 1844, to
Sidney Lawrence, and died 25th Sept. 1844. 2. Robert, R. born
24th Oct. 1819. 3. Lavinah. 4. Mary Jane, born 11th August,
1823, married 5th Nov. 1843, Milo Chatfield, and died 25th Sept.
1845. 5. William Vance, born 13th Jan. 1826. 6. Anne Maria,
born 23d Dec. 1828, and died 1st Sept. 1829. 7. Elizabeth
Electa, twin to Anne Maria, died 21st Sept. 1845. 8. Calvin
Fletcher, born 26th Feb. 1831 ; 9. Philander ; 10. Olivia ; 11.
Rebecca ; 12. Fanny.
Peter R. Colwell died 16th November, 1847.

ROBERT M. COLWELL, (son of John,) and Betsey Cauldwell,
his wife, had children :

1. Luther Littell, born 1st December, 1818, and died at about 19 years. 2. Eliza Jane. 3. Abraham. 4. Hannah, who died at about 16 years ; 5. Jonathan Chaplain ; 6. Enos ; 7. David.
Robert M. Colwell, died in the spring of 1840, in the field alone, supposed by the bursting of a blood vessel.
JERRY COLWELL, son of John, and Mary E. Boyer, had children :
1. Wallace ; 2. William ; 3. Jerry, born January, 1832, and died.
Jerry Colwell, son of John, was kicked by a horse on the head which broke his scull, and resulted in his death after about two and a half months. He died 24th May, 1832.

ROBERT CAULDWELL, (7th child of William,) removed to Butler county, Ohio, lived there many years, and subsequently removed to near Covington, Indiana.
Robert Cauldwell, and his wife Mary Ball, had children :
1. Joseph, born 7th November, 1795, married Nancy Reynolds, and had children :
   1. Mary Jane ; 2. Eleanor ; 3. Robert ; 4. Franklin ; 5. Joseph ; 6. Amzi.
2. Aaron, born 16th August, 1797, and died at about 22 years, unmarried.
3. Rachel, born 20th February, 1799, and died at 7 or 8 years of age.
4. Elizabeth, born 24th, January, 1801.
5. Hannah, married S. S. Moody, and had children :
   1. Mary Moody ; 2. Robert Moody ; 3. Matilda Moody; 4. Elizabeth Moody ; 5. Ulysses Moody ; 6. Nathaniel Moody.
6. Margaret, married James Elder, and had children :
   1. Marietta Elder ; 2. John Boyd Elder ; 3. Robert Elder ; 4. Abraham Colwell Elder ; 5. Pamela Elder ; 6. Eleanor Elder.
7. Jane, married, 1st, Anthony Dancer, and had children :
   1. Eliza Dancer ; 2. Mary Elizabeth Dancer, and by her 2d, husband, John Hayden, had other children; 3. Robert Hayden ; 4. Lorena Hayden.
8. Mary, married William Thompson, and had children :
   1. Aaron Thompson; 2. Levi Thompson ; 3. Mary Thompson; 4. Margaret Thompson ; 5. Robert Thompson ; 6. Lucinda Thompson.
9. Hugh, married Martha M. Galloway, and had children :
10. Abraham, married, for his third wife, Elmira Boo, and had children : 1. William ; 2. Ellen ; 3. Christian.
11. William married —— ——.
12. James, married Mahala Patson.

DAN CAULDWELL, (9th child of William,) and Rachel Potter, lived on the same section of land with Robert, and had children :
1. Polly, who married David Johnson, son of Uzel Johnson, of Long Hill.
2. Betsey, married Josiah Carter.

3. Nancy, was drowned in the Little Miami River.
4. William, married twice.
5. Catherine, married her cousin, Jerry Cauldwell, son of Abraham.
6. John.
7. Sally, married Hugh Stevenson.
8. Charlotte, married Mr. Stone, and soon after died.
9. James, married Lydia Anne Hilyer.
10. Rachel, died a young woman.

ABRAHAM CAULDWELL, (10th child of William,) and Elizabeth Rutan, lived on the same section of land with Robert and Dan, and had children :

1. Joseph, who married, 1st Ibbe Linn ; 2. Betsey, the widow of Mr. Stewart, and daughter of Mr. Thompson, and by Ibbe Linn, had children :

    1. William, who married a Miss —— Stewart.
    2. James Thompson.
    3. Ella Jane, who died at about 19 years.
    4. Catherine.

And by his 2d wife, Betsey Thompson, had children : 5. Freelove ; 6. Sarah Ellen ; 7. Minerva.

2. Jerry, who married his cousin Catherine Cauldwell, daughter of Dan.

3. Hannah, who married, and had one child, which died in infancy ; her husband died, and she married, 2d, Mr. —— Hulse, and had children :

    1. Elizabeth Hulse, who married James Denise.

4. Betsey married her cousin, Robert M. Cauldwell, son of John, and had 7 children : [See Robert M., son of John.]

ROBERT CAULDWELL, (2d son of James Cauldwell,) married —— ——, and had children :
1. Sarah.
2. Mary.
3. Elizabeth, married, 1st, Mr. Woodruff, and had a son, Joel Woodruff, who died ; Mr. Woodruff then died, and she married, 2d, Jacob Denman, and had children :

    1. Elizabeth Denman, who married Stephen Muchmore, son of Samuel.
    2. Moses Denman, married Patty Morehouse, daughter of Isaac, of Cheapside.
    3. Aaron Denman, died at about 45 years, unmarried.
    4. Isaac Denman, went a ship-carpenter to sea, and never returned.
    5. Robert Denman, married Jane Miller, daughter of Major Luke Miller, of Madison.
    6. Hiram Denman, married Sally Hardy, daughter of Joseph T. Hardy, of Cheapside, lived on White Oak Ridge, and had an only son, Theodore.

7. Hetty Denman, married William Parcel, son of Thomas, of White Oak Ridge.
8. Smith Denman, married Esther Parcel, daughter of Nicholas, of do.

ELIZABETH DENMAN, (daughter of Jacob,) and Stephen Muchmore, had children :
1. Elizabeth Muchmore, who married Elias B. Sturges, son of Ebenezer Sturges, of Chatham, and had children :
  1. Harriet Sturges, who married Hervy Lum, son of Samuel.
  2. William Henry Sturges.
  3. Mary Elizabeth Sturges.
  4. Benjamin Smith Sturges.

2. Smith Muchmore, who married Mary Tucker, daughter of Elias Tucker, and had children :
  1. Elias Muchmore.
  2. Anne Elizabeth Muchmore.
  3. John Joseph Muchmore.
3. Hetty Muchmore.
4. Sarah Muchmore, married Jonathan Bruen, and had children : 1.Elizabeth Bruen ; 2. George Washington Bruen.
5. Joel Muchmore, married Elizabeth Bond, daughter of Nathaniel Bond, of Springfield, and had children : 1. Caroline Muchmore : 2. Eliza Muchmore ; 3. Frederick Muchmore.

MOSES DENMAN, (2d child of Jacob Denman, and Elizabeth Cauldwell,) and Patty Morehouse, had children : 1. Mary Denman ; 2. Isaac Denman, and then Moses Denman went to the Lake country, New-York.

ROBERT DENMAN, (5th child of Jacob Denman, and Elizabeth Cauldwell,) and Jane Miller, had children : 1. George Denman,; 2.Louisa Denman ; 3. Sarah Jane Denman ; 4. a daughter 5. Electa Denman.
Robert Denman then removed to Ohio.

HUGH CAULDWELL,(3d son of James Cauldwell,) and Jane Parker, lived where his father did, at the foot of Long Hill, where Abraham Parrot now lives.

NOTE. — Jane, the wife of Hugh Cauldwell, had a sister, Mary Parker, who married 24th January, 1787, James Stinson. Jane and Mary Parker's, father, was brother of John Parker, who married Betsey Pettit, daughter of Benjamin Pettit, Jun., James Parker, brother of John, went to New England, and settled.

HUGH CAULDWELL, and Jane Parker, had children :
1. John ; 2. James ; 3. Elizabeth ; 4. John, 2d ; 5. Sarah ; and 6. Jane. These all died young, except John, 2d, and Jane.
John, married Mahateble Day, daughter of Colonel Israel Day, and had children :
1. James, who married Martha High, daughter of Ephraim, son of Jacob, and went to Illinois.

2. Israel Day, married Catherine Hoagland, of New-York, and had chileren : 1. Frederick Ludlow, who died June, 1848, aged 10 years ; 2. Catherine ; 3. Jenette ; 4. Elizabeth ; 5. ———.

3. Elizabeth, born 1812, is unmarried.

4. Hugh, who went to St. Louis, Missouri ; — returned, and died in Newark.

5. William, who died in infancy.

6. Jenette, who died at 2½ years.

JANE CAULDWELL, (daughter of Hugh,) married Daniel Rutan, son of Joseph, son of Abraham, and had children :

1. Hugh, who died in Newark.

2. Hannah, who also died in Newark.

Daniel Rutan lived where his father and grand-daughter had lived ; he died 6th February, 1820, aged 28 years, and his widow, Jane, removed to Newark, where both her children died, and she died 2d February, 1849, in Newark, aged 61 years.

ABRAHAM CAULDWELL, (4th son of James,) and Catherine Hill, in Orange county, New-York, had children ;

1. Nathaniel, who married Miss Crawford, daughter of Jennet Miller.

2. John.

3. Abraham.

4. James.

5. Sally.

6. Susan.

JAMES CAULDWELL, (5th child of James,) and Peggy ——, of Orange county, New-York, had children :

1. Thomas.

2. James, 3d.

3. Elizabeth, who married her cousin, James Cauldwell, son of William.

4, Sally, married James Young.

5. Mary, married Zach. Young, nephew of James.

6. Temperance.

JENNET CAULDWELL, (daughter of James,) and Mr. —— Miller, had children :

1. John Miller, who married Charity Rutan, daughter of Abraham, and had a son, James, who lived near New Vernon.

2. Samuel Miller, married Abigail Roll, daughter of John Roll,2d. and had children : 1. Rachel Miller ; 2. Abigail Miller.

Samuel Miller's wife, Abigail, died 20th March, 1788, and he was killed, 4th July, 1793, by the upsetting of a wagon loaded with stone.

3. Abraham Miller.

4. Jennet Miller, married Mr. Crawford, father of the wife of Nathaniel Cauldwwell, son of Abraham.

5. James Miller.

DANIEL CLARK.

DANIEL CLARK, by his 1st wife, had children :
1. John, who lived and died at Rockaway, Morris County.
2. Daniel, who married ——; was a Baptist preacher.
3. Sarah, who married John Doty, son of Joseph Doty, 1st. [*See Doty,*] Daniel Clark's 1st wife then died, and he married, 2d, Miss Shipman, and had other children:
4. Stephanus, who married, 28th May, 1776, Keziah Doty, daughter of George, and removed to the State of Ohio.
5. Jabez, who married Caty Sickle, daughter of Samuel Sickle.
6. Keturah married, 22d April, 1771, Aaron Camp, son of Aaron. [*See Camp.*]
7. Deborah, married Elias Runyon, son of Richard, 1st. [*See Runyon.*]
8. Abigail married Thomas Scudder, brother of Richard, who owned and lived on the Townley Farm. [*See Thomas Scudder.*]

STEPHANUS CLARK, (4th child of Daniel,) and Keziah Doty, had children :
1. Polly, who married Jeremiah H. Osborn, 3d March, 1795, as his 2d wife. [*See J. H. Osborn.*] 2. Israel ; 3. Elmer ; 4. Sally.

ELIAS CLARK.

ELIAS CLARK, came up from Rahway, and settled on Stony Hill, on No. 47, of the Elizabethtown lots.
He married Betsey Clark, daughter of Benjamin Clark, of Rahway, and had children:
1. Elias, who married Sarah Swain, daughter of Jacob.
2. Nancy married Philip Allen, son of Joseph. [*See Allen.*]
3. Betsey married 28th October, 1793, Enoch Sutton, son of William. [*See Sutton.*]
4. Ichabod married Phebe Badgley, and had a son :
    1. John who married, 18th Febuary, 1817, Susan Radden, daughter of Jeremy.
5. Sarah married David Stewart, son of William, and went to Ohio.
6. Mary Anne, who had a son, James C. Lyon, and married Henry Littell.
7. Lockey, married David Wilson, of Mount Bethel.
8. Hannah, married, 15th July, 1809, William Raddin, son of Jeremy, [*See Radden.*]
9. David married, 1st, Betsey Anderson, daughter of James ; 2d, Lockey, widow of Michael Long, and daughter of William Stewart.

ELIAS CLARK, (1st son of Elias,) and Sarah Swain, had children :
1. Benjaman, who went to Long Island.

2. Noah, married Harriet Smith, daughter of Thomas.
3. Betsey, married Ephriam Howard.
4. Stewart, went away unmarried.

DAIVD CLARK, (9th child of Elias Clark,) and Betsey
Anderson, had children :
  1. Nancy, who married Samuel Chamberlain, of Newark,
and had, 1st, Mary Rebecca, who died at about 4 years; 2d,
Jane Elizabeth; 3d, Phebe, who died at about 5 years.
  2. Elias married, 1st, Phebe Long, daughter of Michael;
2d, Caroline Doty, daughter of Henry, of Washington Valley,
and had children by his first wife : 1. Elizabeth ; 2. Samuel.
  3. Robert, born 6th April, 1818, married Sarah Wilson,
born 7th March, 1817, daughter of Benjamin, and had children : 1. Benjamin, born 26th June, 1839 ; 2. David, born 3d
December, 1840 ; 3. Elizabeth, born 2d December, 1842 ;
4. Phebe, born 3d Nov., 1844 ; 5. Stewart, 26th Feb., 1849.
  4. James married Hannah Mariah Doty, daughter of Henry.
  5. Mary Anne married Garret Pier, of Newark ; she died
30th August, 1849, and left children: 1. Jane Pier ; 2. Robert
Pier.
  6. Eliza married John Wilson, brother of Robert's wife,
and had children : 1. Isaac Wilson, who died at 2 years;
2. Mary Anne Wilson.

ISAAC CLARK.

ISAAC CLARK, lived near Johnson's Bridge, where
Samuel Duryee now lives. He died 8th November, 1784,
aged 72 years. His widow died 28th August, 1793. Isaac
Clark had children :
  1. Samuel, who married Chloe ——, and early removed
to the west.
  2. Ezekiel also early went to the west.
  3. Isaac, Jun., was the Blind Fiddler ; lived where Aaron
Johnson now lives. He married, 7th December, 1787, Rachel,
the widow of Andrew Wade, and daughter of John Osborn,
and had children : 1. John Osborn, who married Elizabeth
Sale, daughter of Daniel, son of Daniel Sale, of Elizabethtown.
  2. Ezekiel, who died in infancy.
  3. Polly married John Sullard, of Conn., and removed there.

JOHN CLARK

JOHN CLARK came from Long Island, and settled in
this place He was said to be no kin to Daniel, Elias, or
Isaac Clark, nor they to each other. He was an elder in the
church here. He lived where Matthias Osborn now lives,
and, by his first wife, had children :

1. Jeremiah, who married, 16th January, 1771, Hannah Roberts. He built the house and lived where the widow Polly Day lives. He sold it to Abner Bailey, and removed to the west.

2. Stephen, who also removed to the west.

3. Ketura married Mr. Roff, of Newark, and had children: 1. Aaron Roff; 2. Moses Roff; 3. Stephen Roff; 4. David Roff.

Elder Clark's wife then died, and he married Sarah, the widow of Jeremiah Hart, and had other children:

4. Samuel, born 9th December, 1752, married, 1st, Jane Osborn, daughter of John, who was born 25th November, 1756; 2d, Damaris Day, daughter of George.

5. John, born 12th September, 1754; married Sarah Doty, daughter of George, and removed to the Susquehanna River, Luzerne County, Pennsylvania.

6. Abigail, born 9th May, 1755, and married Ezra Baldwin, son of Nathan, son of John, of Union, and lived near Cheapside. [*See Ezra Baldwin.*]

7. Susannah, born 12th October, 1757, married Jacob Potter, son of Daniel, 2d. [*See Potter.*]

8. Sarah, born 9th January, 1759, married Amos Potter, Esq., brother of Jacob.

Elder John Clark died 12th May, 1794, aged 84 years.

His wife, Sarah, died 1st September, 1808, aged 91 years.

Sarah, wife of Amos Potter, died 15th January, 1796, aged 37 years.

Susannah, wife of Jacob Potter, died 23d March, 1841, aged 83½ years.

SAMUEL CLARK, (4th child of Elder John Clark,) lived where his father did, and was Judge of the Court of Common Pleas, and Justice of the Peace. He and his wife, Jane Osborn, had children:

1. Daniel Seely, born 12th August, 1773; married, 28th February, 1796, Sally Willcox, daughter of John, and died 22d February, 1843, nearly 70 years of age.

2. Eunice, born 5th December, 1775, and died a young woman, unmarried.

3. David C., born 15th March, 1777; married Susannah Condit, of Orange, and died 13th January, 1832.

4. Stephen, born 6th June, 1788, married Joanna Miller, daughter of Jacob, of Long Hill, and went with him to Butler County, Ohio.

5. Polly, born 14th August, 1782, married James Parcel, and went to Clark County, Illinois.

6. Sibbel, baptized 7th June, 1783, and died in infancy.

Samuel Clark's wife, Jane, died 17th November, 1791, aged 38 years, and he married, 1st September, 1792, Damaris Day, daughter of George, and had other chileren :

7. Abraham, who married Jennet Doty, daughter of James Doty, and had an only son, James Doty Clark.

8. Martha Day Clark, who died 16th February, 1827, aged 24 years, unmarried.

Samuel Clark, Esq., died 23d February, 1822, aged 71 years. His widow, Damaris, died 28th December, 1840.

DANIEL S. CLARK, Esq., (1st son of Samuel,) was a Justice of the Peace. He lived on his father's farm — was a merchant—and he and Sally Willcox had children :

1. William M., who married, 1st, Rachel Wood, daughter of Daniel S. Wood. Jun. ; 2d. Sally Wood, sister of his 1st wife.

2. Levi, who married, 1st, Eliza Crane, daughter of Joseph, 2d, Elizabeth Tucker, daughter of Moses, son of John.

3. Samuel married, 4th December, 1844, Mary Noe, daughter of David, son of John.

4. Daniel Seely, Jun., who went to Louisville, Kentucky, and married there.

5. Stephen, who also went to Kentucky.

6. Jane married Hervy Spencer, son of William Spencer, of Chatham. [*See Spencer.*]

7. Eliza married Henry Schureman, son of Thomas, Esq., of Hunterdon Co. She lives in New York.

8. Sarah married Mr. Myers, of New York, and went to St. Louis, Missouri.

9. Mary married Joseph Graham, of New York, and lives there.

WILLIAM M. CLARK, (1st child of Daniel S. Clark, Esq.,) lived in this valley, in Morris County; was a merchant, and was a Major in the Militia, and Justice of the Peace. He and his wife, Rachel, had children :

1. Mary ; 2. Anne Curry; 3. Hannah. And by his 2d wife, Sally, had other children : 4. Emeline.

LEVI CLARK, Esq., (2d child of Daniel S. Clark, Esq.,) was a Justice of the Peace—lived where his father did—and he and his wife, Eliza Crane, had children :

1. Jeremiah.

2. Joseph Crane, who died at 17 years.

3. John Wesley.

4. Sarah Elizabeth.

5. Charles Pitman.

6. Ira Crane.

7. Daniel Seely.
8. Abigail Morris.

His 1st wife, Eliza, died 24th October, 1834, aged 34 years ; and by his 2d wife, Elizabeth Tucker, he had other children : 9. Frances ; 10. Emeline.

SAMUEL CLARK, (3d child of Daniel S. Clark, Esq.,) lives in Newark. He and Mary Noe had children :
1. Arthur Berry ; 2. Samuel ; 3. Jane Noe.

DAVID C. CLARK, (3d child of Samuel Clark, Esq.,) and Susannah Condit, had children :
1. John D., who married Sally Miller, of Westfield.
2. Smith.
3. Jane married Jeremiah Crane, son of Jeremiah, son of Timothy, and had no children.
4. Polly, who died unmarried.
5. Phebe, who died 23d December, 1846, unmarried.

David C. Clark, died 13th January, 1832, aged 55 ; his wife died 26th February, 1841, aged 65 years.

STEPHEN CLARK, (4th child of Samuel Clark, Esq.,) and Joanna Miller, had children in Ohio :
1. Jonas P. who married ———, and had three sons and three daughters.
2. David C. married ———; had five sons and 1 daughter.
3. Jane married John Hamilton. She died March, 1834 without children.

Stephen Clark died, and his widow married Jacob Morris, and had children : 1. Mary Morris, who married William Jordan ; 2. Hannah Morris, who married Charles Porter.

Mr. Morris died about 1837, and she lives with Mr. Porter, in Vermilion County, Indiana.

POLLY CLARK, (5th child of Samuel Clark, Esq.,) and James Parcel, had children :
1. Jane Parcel, who married William Crawford, from Long Island, and had children. He died in 1840.

Twins. {
1. Royal F. Crawford, who is a Physician in Clinton Co., Indiana.
2. George W. Crawford, a Physician in Cole's Co., Illinois.

3. William lives in Clinton Co., Indiana.
4. Adaline married Stanley Cash ; lives in Clark Co., Illinois.

2. William Morris Parcel, born 1st April, 1803 ; had two wives and six children.

3. John Ira Parcel, born 5th October, 1805, had 2 wives and 8 children ; lives in Westfield, Clark Co., Illinois.

4. Lucinda married Philip Sliper ; lives in Clinton Co., Ind.

5. Margaret married Joseph G. Hayes ; has three sons and two daughters ; lives in Clinton Co.

JOHN CLARK, Jun., (5th child of Elder John Clark,) and Sarah Doty, had children :

1. Aaron, baptized 4th June, 1786, who married Thirza Gore, and had no children.

2. Philemon, who married Betsey Chandler.

3. George Doty, who married Deborah Osborn, daughter of J. H. Osborn.

4. Sebia Howel, who married David Doty, son of Joseph, 3.

5. Sally, who married John Osborn, son of Jonathan H. Osborn. [*See Osborn.*]

6. John, 3d, married Betsey Tompkins.

GEORGE DOTY CLARK, (3d son of John Clark, Jun.,) and Deborah Osborn, had children :

1. Sarah, who married, 1st, Salma Hyde ; 2d, —— ——.

2. Miriam married Mr. —— Dunham.

3. Jotham Potter married —— ——.

Mr. John Clark, Jun., and all his family, but Mrs. Sally, wife of John Osborn, lived in Luzerne Co., Penn.

Mr. G. Doty Clark died, and his widow, Deborah, married a Mr. Camel, and went to 'Ohio, but had no other children, and he died and left her a widow again.

WILLIAM COLE.

WILLIAM COLE lived by Green Brook, on the north side, in Somerset County.   His wife was Betsey Dennis. They had children :

1. William, who married Elizabeth Williamson. daughter of William Williamson of Plainfield.

2. James, who married Elizabeth Frazee.

3. Dennis, who died an aged man, unmarried.

4. Mary married Daniel Hand ; lived on the top of the First Mountain.

5. Elizabeth, married John Merril, of Staten Island.

6. Phebe, died an aged woman, unmarried.

WILLIAM COLE, (son of William Cole,) was a surveyor and school-master, and was known as "Master Cole." He and his wife, Elizabeth Williamson, lived where his father did, and had children :

1. Isaac, who went to North Carolina, and there married Betsey Blanchard, and died there.
2. Abigail, who married Jonathan Smith, near Springfield.
3. Joseph married Hannah Paine, daughter of John Paine, of Rahway.
4. Levi, who died at about 33 years, unmarried.
5. Catherine married Samuel Pound, son of Zachariah, of Plainfield.
6. Elias married, 1st, Jemima Tingley, daughter of Jacob Tingley, of Washington Valley ; 2d. Mary Mulford, daughter of Cornelius, of Passaic Valley.
7. Elizabeth married Colonel John Allen, son of David, of Washington Valley, and died without children.
8. Phebe married Daniel Shotwell, son of Jacob, of Scotch Plains. [*See Shotwell.*]

ISAAC COLE, (1st child of Master William Cole,) and Betsey Blanchard, in North Carolina, had children :
1. James, who married ——, and lived in Newbern, N. Carolina.
2. William, who died at about 8 years.

JOSEPH COLE, (3d child of Master William Cole,) and Hannah Paine, had but one son.
1. Freeman, who was a Justice of the Peace, and a Surveyor ; he married Hannah Drake, daughter of Nathaniel, of Plainfield.

ELIAS COLE, (6th child of Master William Cole,) and Jemima Tingley, had children :
1. Levi, who went to South Carolina, and died there at about 23 years.
2. William, who is a Doctor of Physic. He married Keren-happuc Vail, daughter of Alexander, son of Daniel, Sen., and had children : 1. Mary ; 2. Martha.
3. Jacob married Mary Anne Randolph, daughter of David, of Stonehouse Village, and had children : 1. Randolph; 2. Sarah Anne.
4. George, who died at about 6 or 7 years.
5. Silas married, 25th September, 1849, Jemima Shotwell, daughter of Daniel, and by his 2d wife, Mary Mulford, Elias Cole had children.
6. Mulford, who married Emeline D. Shotwell, daughter of Daniel, and had children: 1. Elias; 2. Phebe, born 19th February, 1849.
7. Mary married William Crane, 28th May, 1849, son of Isaac, of Long Hill, and had children : 1. Cornelius.

JAMES COLE, (2d child of William Cole, Sen.) and Elizabeth Frazee, had children:
1. Jemima, who married William Vail, son of Daniel.
2. Rachel married James Clark, of Rahway.

G

3. Betsey, who died at about 20 years.

4. Dennis (who was a printer by trade) married Catherine Van Deusen, of Newburgh, New-York.

5. David married Mary Miller, daughter of Benjamin Miller, of Scotch Plains.

DENNIS COLE, (son of James,) and Catherine Van Deusen, lived at Scotch Plains, and had children :

1. William, who married ———, in New-York.

2. Betsey married Elias Frost, son of ———, of Mine Brook, Somerset County, and died without children.

3. Maria married Mr. Crane, of Newark.

4. Abraham married ——— ———.

5. Susan married Mr. Stout.

Dennis Cole, Esq., was a member of the Legislature in 1829 and 1830 ; was a Justice of the Peace, and was much engaged in settling estates as Executor, Administrator, and other public business. He died 10th January, 1844.

DAVID COLE, (5th child of James Cole,) and Mary Miller, had children :

1. James, who married ——— ———.

2. Charlotte married Abraham Hutchings, son of Abraham Hutchings, of Springfield.   He is a grocer of Newark.

3. David married——— ; lives in Rahway.

JOSEPH COLE, brother of William Cole, Sen., had children :

1. Abraham.

2. Mary, who married Henry Line, son of Henry Line.

3. Sarah married Abraham Williams.

4. Patty married Benjamin, son of the Rev. Benjamin Miller, of Scotch Plains.

5. Jonathan married, 1st, Dorcas Wallen ; 2d, ———, widow of William Elstone.

6. Joseph married, 31st May, 1785, 1st, Jemima Allen, daughter of David, Sen., of Washington Valley ; 2d. Catherine Willet, daughter of Jonathan.

JOSEPH COLE, (6th child of Joseph Cole,) had children :

1. Frazee, who married Harriet Vail, daughter of Daniel, Sen.

2. Allen married Sally Badgley, daughter of Joseph, and had no children.

3. Sally married John Osborn, son of Deacon John Osborno Scotch Plains.

4. David married Polly Tucker, daughter of Moses, and had one daughter, Mary.

5. Phebe married Ezra Littell, son of Ebenezer, from Connecticut

6. Amos married Betsey Syland, daughter of Benjamin.

7. Aaron.

8. Isaac, who went to French Creek.

FRAZEE COLE, (son of Joseph,) and Harriet Vail, had children :

1. Mary, who married Job Squier, son of Jonathan, of Rahway, and had children :
   1. Jonathan Squier.
   2. Harriet Squier.
   3. Anne Squier.
   4. Mary Squier.
   5. Martha Squier.
   6. Frazee Squier.
   7. Lizzy Squier.
   8. Irene Squier.
   9. Jacob Squier.
   10. —— ——.
2. Jacob, who married Christian Crowel, of Rahway, and had children :
   1. William Squier Cole.
   2. Albert.
   3. Harriet.
   4. Edward, who died in infancy.

WILLIAM CONKLIN.

WILLIAM CONKLIN married Ruth Hedges, of Long Island, and removed from there to Basking Ridge, and had children :
1. Stephen, 1st, who married Deborah Dimon ; 2. William, 2d ; 3. Abraham ; 4. Isaac ; 5. Jacob ; 6. Thomas ; 7. Mary ; 8. Ruth.

STEPHEN CONKLIN, (1st son of William, 1st,) and Deborah Dimon, had children :
1. Climena, who married Josiah Ayers, son of Elisha Ayers, of Basking Ridge.
2. William, 3d, married Rebecca Whitaker, daughter of Jonathan, of Mine Brook.
3. Stephen, 2d, married Rachel Lindley, daughter of Benjamin Lindley, Esq., east of Morristown.
4. Ruth, 3d, married Stephen Whitaker, brother of Rebecca, of Mine Brook. (See *Whitaker*.)
5. Mary, 2d, married John Runyon, son of Richard, of Long Hill, and went to Ohio. (See *Runyon*.)
6. Isaac, 2d, married Comfort Pitney.
7. John married Phebe Mills.
8. Abraham married Jemima Lindley, daughter of Major Joseph Lindley, east of Morristown.
9. Deborah married John Seward, and went to Goshen, New-York.

CLIMENA CONKLIN, (1st child of Stephen Conklin,) and Josiah Ayers, had children :

1. Stephen Ayers, the celebrated itinerant Dr. Ayers, so eminently successful in curing the Cholera at Montreal, in 1832. He never married.

2. Deborah Ayers, who married Stephen Cave, shoe merchant, of New-York.

WILLIAM CONKLIN, 3d, (2d child of Stephen Conklin, 1st,) and Rebecca Whitaker, lived at Basking Ridge. He was a tanner and currier ; had a farm. and a tan-yard, and was a Justice of the Peace. He and his wife were members of the Presbyterian church there. They had children :

1. Phebe, born 29th Sept. 1779, and died aged 6 years.

2. Stephen, 3d, born 3d Feb. 1782, married, January, 1807, 1st, Sally Coriell, daughter of Elias, of Long Hill. He married, 2d, Catherine Tailor, 15th August, 1809, daughter of Willet Tailor, of Raritan.

3. Jonathan, born 28th October, 1783, married Apha Colie, daughter of Daniel, of Springfield.

4. Mary, born 7th October, 1785, married, 6th May, 1809, John Littell, son of Nathaniel, of New Providence, [See Nathaniel Littell.]

5. William, 4th, born 23d August, 1787, married Ketura Green, and had no children. He married, 2d, Cornelia, widow of Elias Sturges, and daughter of Thomas Goltra, near Liberty Corner.

6. Joseph, born 28th Nov. 1789, married Viletta Hampton, daughter of James, of Woodbridge.

7. Isaac, 3d, born 24th Jan. 1792, married Sarah Hall, daughter of Richard.

8. Nathaniel, born 5th March, 1794, married Emily Halsey Fitch, daughter of Col. Grant Fitch, of Newton, Sussex Co.

9. Sarah, born 2d Oct. 1796, married, in New-York, James S. Rose, and has a son, James Augustus Rose, who married Caroline Drake, daughter of Reuben Drake, near Woodbridge, who lives at Amboy, is a butcher, and has children :

1. Mary Margaret Rose ; 2. Anne Eliza Rose, born 17th Nov 1847.

William Conklin, Esq., died in a fit, in his bark-house, on the 14th February, 1803.

STEPHEN CONKLIN, (2d child of William Conklin, 3d, Esq,) lived where his father did, was a member and elder in the Presbyterian church, at Basking Ridge. He subsequently removed to Somerville, where he died 3d Nov. 1849. He and his wife Sally Coriell had a daughter :

1. Sarah, born 15th Dec. 1808, and married Thomas Layton, had a son, Theodore Layton, and died 23d Feb. 1842.

Stephen Conklin, by his 2d wife, Catherine Tailor, had other children :

2. Willet Tailor, born 6th October, 1810, who married Emeline Heath, 21st Dec. 1836, daughter of Daniel Heath, and had children :

1. William Wilson; 2. Catherine Jane; 3. John Tailor; 4. Stephen.

3. Jane, born 15th August, 1815, married John Littell, at the south branch of the Raritan River, Somerset County, and had children:
1. Margaret Sydam Littell.
2. Catherine Elizabeth Littell.
3. Mary Conklin Littell.

4. William, born 11th April, 1818, married Mary Toms, daughter of Charles Toms, Esq., of Somerville, and had children:
1. Harriet.
2. Albert.

5. John Tailor, born 25th Jan. 1821, married Elizabeth Higgins, daughter of Elias T. Higgins, of Rahway, and had children:
1. Nathaniel.

6. Nathaniel, born 20th Oct. 1823. He graduated at Rutgers' College, New Brunswick, and became a minister of the Dutch Reformed Church, and is preaching in Monmouth County. He married, 24th Oct. 1848, Elizabeth Woodruff, daughter of Archibald Woodruff, of Newark, and has children:
1. Catherine.

7. Mary Elizabeth, born 13th August, ——.

JONATHAN CONKLIN, (3d child of William Conklin, 3d,) and Apha Colie, had an only child:
1. Mary, born 9th Feb. 1803. He died September following.
Mary married, 31st, Dec. 1848, John Faulks, of Elizabethtown, an Englishman, who died 4th March, 1849.

WILLIAM CONKLIN, 4th, (5th child of William Conklin, 3d,) and Cornelia Goltra, had children:
1. William, 5th.
2. Mary Elizabeth.
3. James Alonzo.
4. Stephen, who died 9th July, 1849.
5. John Littell.
6. Sarah Agusta.
NOTE.—Mrs. Conklin, by her first husband, had one son, Elias Sturges.

JOSEPH CONKLIN, (6th child of William Conklin, 3d,) and Viletta Hampton, lived several years in New-York, and from thence removed to Woodbridge. He was an elder of the church there. They had children, besides two who died young:
1. Eliza Hampton, born 3d August, ——.
2. Joseph W., born 29th July, ——.
3. Margaret Anne, born 17th Nov., ——.
4. Nathaniel, born 19th Sept. 1832, ——.

ISAAC CONKLIN, 3d, (7th child of William, 1st,) lived at Basking Ridge; was a shoe manufacturer and farmer. He and Sarah Hall, had children:

1. Elisha Whitaker, born 2d August, 1819, and married, 27th March, 1843, Margaret Hibler, born 8th Feb. 1824, daughter, of Jacob Hibler, of Danville, Penn. He was a graduate of Princeton College; is now a bookseller in Danville.

2. Mary Elizabeth.

3. Emily Halsey, who died at about 16 years.

4. Oscar.

NATHANIEL CONKLIN, (8th child of William 1st,) graduated at Princeton College, and studied theology at the Princeton Seminary; became a minister of the gospel, preached some years in Sussex County, from there removed to Coshocton, Ohio; preached there; there his wife died, and he removed to Covington, Indiana; after preaching there several years, he returned, with his children, to New Jersey. He and his wife Emily H. Fitch had children :

1. Emily Halsey, born 30th July, ——.

2. Charles Fitch, born 9th August, ——.

3. Mary Littell, born 12th Jan. 1831, married, 12th Feb. 1850, Capt. Robert Evans, a member of the bar, son of Thomas J. Evans, of Covington, Indiana, and resides there.

4. Millecent Rebecca, born 2d May, ——.

5. Nathaniel Whitaker, born 21st December, 1835.

STEPHEN CONKLIN, 2d, (3d child of Stephen Conklin, 1st, son of William,) and Rachel Lindley, had children:

1. Sally, who married the Rev. Aaron Condit, Presbyterian minister, of Hanover, Morris County, as his 2d wife; she had no children.

2. Betsey, who never married. She was a milliner, and kept a milliner's store at Morristown. She brought up and educated several of the children of her brothers, Stephen and Benjamin.

3. Rachel, who died in youth.

4. Stephen, 3d, who married Abby Cook, daughter of James Cook, of Morristown. They lived in New-York, and had children.

 1. Elizabeth, who married in Illinois.

 2. Edgar married in Cincinnati, Ohio.

 3. Henry married in Ohio.

 4. James is a lawyer, married —— ——, and lives in Springfield, Illinois.

Stephen's wife, Abby, then died, and he married Margaret Dunlap, of Newburg, and removed to Illinois, and had several other children.

5. Benjamin married Mary Johnson, of New-York. He lived in New-York; was a grocer; and died there, leaving 4 children :

 1. Eliza, who married John Landen, of New-York, and died, leaving 2 children : 1. Marietta Landen; 2. Frederick Landen.

 2. Mary.

 3. Jane Kipp, who married Philip W. Crater, merchant at Morristown, and had children : 1. Margaret Elizabeth Crater.

 4. Henrietta.

ISAAC CONKLIN, 2d, (6th child of Stephen, son of William, and Comfort Pitney, had children.

1. Sally, who married Sineus Baker, of Littletown, Morris County, and had children : 1. Isaac Conklin Baker ; 2. Harriet Baker.
2. Damon, who married Sally Nevill, daughter of Charles Nevill, of Basking Ridge, and had children :

    1. John Nevill.
    2. Elizabeth, who married Abraham P. Jones, son of Edward of Newark, and had children : 1. Edward ; 2. John Nevill, who died 23d September, 1848, at 3 years.
    3. William.
    4. Charles married, 7th January, 1851, Lydia A. Bird.
    5. James.
    6. Frances.

    Mr. Damon Conklin died when on a visit to Rochester, New-York, in August, 1842. His family lives in Newark.

Note.— No relation exists between William and Joshua Conklin.

JOSHUA CONKLIN.

JOSHUA CONKLIN, lived at Williams Farms, near Elizabethtown. He had children :

1. Joseph, born 29th July, 1755, married Miss Crissy, sister of Moses, of Elizabethtown.
2. William, born 10th March, 1757, married, 6th March, 1780, Sarah Halsey, daughter of Joseph. [*See Halsey.*]
3. Joshua, Jun., born 3d May, 1759, married Polly Johnson, sister of John Johnson, New-York.
4. John, twin to Joshua, Jun., married Jerusha Haines.
5. Sarah, born 16th September, 1766, married John Mott.
6. Abigail, born 26th November, 1768, married Mr —— Pangborn, of Rahway, and by his 2d wife Joshua Conklin had children :
7. Benjamin, born 28th August, 1777, married Mary High, daughter of Jacob, of Sterling Valley.
8. Keziah Bonnel, born, 12th October, 1779, married Mr —— Garthwaite, of Elizabethtown.
9. Temperance, born 2d February, 1781, married John Totten, son of David. [*See Totten.*]

Mr. Conklin was accidentally killed by the fall of a tree in the great swamp.

JOSEPH CONKLIN, (1st child of Joshua,) and his wife, Miss —— Crissy, had children :
1. James ; 2. Joseph ; 3. Betsey ; 4. Phebe.

WILLIAM CONKLIN, (2d child of Joshua,) and Sarah Halsey, had children :

1. Sarah Halsey, born 16th June, 1781, married William Crane, brother of Captain Isaac Crane, of Chatham, and had four children, three of which died young; the other died at 19 years.
2. William Pierson, born 29th March, 1786, married Nancy Crane, daughter of Norris.
3. Ahijah, born 24th December, 1786, and died 24th Sept.; 1791.

4. Caleb, born 26th February, 1789, married Lucy Hoagland, and died 3d June, 1826;—left no child.

5. James, born 5th February, 1792, married, 1st, Susan Vredenburg, and had a daughter Susan ; 2d, Lucy French, daughter of Anderson. She had no child.

6. Ezekiel, born 24th December, 1797, married Polly Berry, daughter of Charles, of Long Island.

WILLIAM PIERSON CONKLIN, (2d child of William, son of Joshua,) and Nancy Crane, had children :

1. Sarah Anne, born June, 1811, married, 1829, John M. Dodd, who was born Jan, 1806, and had children:

    1. Louisa Dodd, born 15th August, 1829, died 2d February, 1835.

    2. Sarah Anne Dodd, born 4th July, 1832, and died 31st |Jan. 1835.

    3. John C. Dodd, born 18th June, 1834, died 5th February,

    4. Elizabeth W. Dodd, born 7th April, 1836.

    5. Anne Marsh Dodd, born 19th April, 1838.

    6, Helen M. Dodd, born 7th April, 1840.

2. Mary, born 13th June, 1823, and died July, 1823.

3. William, born 16th July, 1824, and died July, 1824.

EZEKIEL CONKLIN, (6th child of William,) and Polly Berry, had children: 1. William, who died at 18 years ; 2. George ; 3. Henry ; 4. John ; 5. Harriet ; 6. Charles.

Sarah, the wife of Joshua Conklin, died 17th May, 1770.

William Conklin, son of Joshua, died 20th January, 1806.

Sarah H., his wife, died 27th August, 1802:

William Pierson Conklin, son of William, died 15th September, 1835.

James Conklin, son of William, died 21st October, 1835.

Ezekiel Conklin, son of William, died 28th July, 1821.

Sarah Anne, wife of John M. Dodd, died 11th April, 1840.

JOSHUA CONKLIN, Jun., (3d child of Joshua Conklin,) and Polly Johnson, lived in Spring Valley, and had children:

1. John Johnson Conklin married Hannah ———, and had children :

    1. Joshua.

    2. Caleb married Margaret Williams, daughter of Abner, son of Noah, of Long Hill.

    3. William.

    4. Eveline.

    5. Mary, married ——— ———.

    6. Abigail married William Fairchild, of Morristown.

    7. Sarah, or Phebe.

2. Polly married Brooks Sayre, son of Isaac. [See Sayre.]

3. Phebe, is unmarried.

4. Benjamin Crane Conklin.

5. Abigail.

6. Betsey married Mr. Miller.

JOHN CONKLIN, and Jerusha Haines, had children:

1. Catherine, who married Isaac Conklin, son of Isaac, had a son who died in infancy.

2. John married Abby Woodruff; had but one son, who died at 18 years, in 1849.

3. Abby married William Garthwaite, son of Jeremiah, and had a son Isaac.

4. Hannah is unmarried; lives in Elizabethtown.

5. Mary married David Merril, of Staten Island; had no children.

SARAH CONKLIN, (5th child of Joshua,) and John Mott, had children:

1. Jeremiah Mott, who married Polly Hand, daughter of Benjamin. [*See Hand.*]

2. Sally Mott married Mr. Smithson.

3. Polly Mott married Mr. Smithson, (brothers.)

ABIGAIL CONKLIN, (6th child of Joshua,) and Mr. Pangborn. had children:

1. Sarah Pangborn, who married —— ——, and went to the Lakes.

2. William Pangborn went to the Lakes, and married there.

3. Isaac Pangborn went to New-Orleans, and died there unmarried.

BENJAMIN CONKLIN, (7th child of Joshua,) and Mary High, had children:

3rd Generation.

1. David, who married Lavina Pollard, daughter of Joshua, of Green Village, and had children: 1. Debby Jane; 2. Mary Elizabeth; 3. Benjamin Francis; 4. William; 5. Hannah Mariah.

2. Deborah married William B. Crane, son of Joseph, Jun., and had children: 1. Elias Crane, 2. Mulford Crane; 3. Jerusha Crane.

3. James D., went to Ohio, and married, and lives there.

4. William P. married Harriet Roberts, daughter of Samuel, and had children: 1. Sophia.

5. Anna, who died at 16 years.

6. Mary, who married James Weir, of Ohio.

HENRY CONNET.

HENRY CONNET died July 10th, 1761, aged 63 years. The widow Connet, mother of Deacon William Connet, died 31st Aug., 1771; they had children.

2d Generation.

1. William Connet lived opposite the Franklin Mill, and was a deacon and elder in the Presbyterian church, in New Providence. He married, 18th December, 1766, Sarah Rogers, and 2d, Mary, the widow of Aaron Decamp, 24th May, 1790.

2. John Connet married, 13th December, 1767, Rachel Allen,

3. Daniel Connet married, 26th November, 1769, Eleanor Woodruff.

4. Hannah Connet, who died, 14th May, 1764, unmarried.

DEACON WILLIAM CONNET, and Sarah Rogers, had children :

1. William Connet, Jun., who married, 25th April, 1791, Charity Bowers.

2. Jemima Connet, baptized 21st April, 1771 ; married, 10th April, 1793, Daniel Bowers.

3. Sally Connet married, 14th November, 1793, Phinehas Bowers,

4. Henry Connet married, and lived at Waterstreet, near Mendham, and had children :

    1. Lockey, who married Mr. Lindley, and went to Mount Auburn, Illinois.

    2. Mary married Charles Marsh ; lived at Morristown.

    3. Sarah.

    4. William, who went to Ohio, and died there.

    5. Ira, who married Phebe Runnels, and had children :

        1. George Minton ; 2. Sarah Wilson ; 3. Mary Elizabeth ; 4. Henry, who died unmarried ; 5. Samuel Runnels ; 6. Caroline ; 7. Louisa ; 8. Henrietta ; 9. Florentine.

DANIEL COOPER.

The parents of Daniel Cooper emigrated from Holland to New-York, in the year 1695. It is said that he was born at sea on their voyage, and that the father never arrived. He was born May 1st, 1695, and married, 17th April, 1726, Grace Runyon, lived in Piscataway, and removed to Passaic Valley, Morris County, in March, 1732. He bought lot No. 2, of the Berkeley tract, containing 500, acres, lying east of and adjoining the quarter owned by Jacob Carle. They had children :

1. Catherine, who was born January, 1728, and married Colonel Cornelius Ludlow.

2. Daniel Cooper, Jun., born 14th January, 1729, and died May, 1787.

3. Agnes, born 15th May, 1732.

4. Peter, born 11th February, 1735, died October, 1755.

5. John, born 20th August, 1738, died 31st March, 1778.

6. Benjamin, born 13th December, 1741, died December, 1794.

7. Rosannah, born 26th March, 1743, died —— ——.

8. George, born 20th August, 1745, died 20th September, 1801.

9. Providence, born 27th March, 1748, died February, 1798.

10. Anne, born 4th October, 1750, died 5th February, 1795.

Anne married Jonas Carle, son of Jacob. [See Carle.]

Daniel Cooper had six wives :

1. Grace Runyon, born January, 1706, and died November, 1755.

2. Jane Westbrook.

3. Grace Manning, died April, 1777.

4. Widow Fanny Jones, died January, 1787.

5. Barbara Margaret Gibbs, who died December, 1789.

6. Hannah Martin, widow of Colonel Ephraim Martin.

He died, 2d May, 1795, aged 100 years.

DANIEL COOPER, Jun., Esq, (son of Daniel, 1st,) married, 1st, Miss Conover; 2. Nancy Cross, daughter of the Rev. Mr. Cross. He lived in Passaic Valley, on the 500 acre tract of his father.

By his first wife he had a daughter, Catherine Cooper, who married her cousin, John Ludlow, of Long Hill, son of Colonel Cornelius Ludlow;

And by his 2d wife, Nancy Cross, had children:

3rd Generation.

2. Lydia, who married Samuel Annin.
3. Polly, who married Mr. ——— Crane.
4. Peter married Susan Boyle, daughter of Joseph, of Long Hill.
5. William went to Kentucky.
6. Doctor John, who settled at Easton, Pennsylvania.
7. Stephen married Mahetabel, widow of John Colwell, and daughter of Colonel Israel Day.
8. Anne married Alexander Richards, of Rahway.
9. Betsey married Henry Freeman, of Elizabethtown.
10. Sally married Capt. David Kirkpatrick, of Mine Brook, as his 2d wife.
11. Daniel, 3d, who went to Kentucky.
12. Joseph also went to Kentucky.

PETER COOPER, (4th child of Daniel Cooper, Jun.,) lived on Long Hill, on the 500 acre tract of his father. He and Susan Boyle had children:

4th Generation.

1. William, who married his cousin, Sally Anne Cooper, only child of Stephen Cooper and Mahetabel Day. And she, Sally Anne Cooper, died 25th October, 1846, without children: and he married ——— ———, daughter of Elias Brown, Esq., of Pluckemin.
2. Caty Anne, who married Abraham Dunn.
3. Joseph, who died in youth.
4. John, who also died in youth.
5. Alexander married, 31st December, 1849, Abby Parrot daughter of Squier Parrot.

JOHN COOPER, (5th child of Daniel Cooper, Sen.,) married Lynche Boyle, daughter of Solomon Boyle, 1st, and had children:

4th Generation.

1. Lynche, who married William Annin.
2. Susan married Squier Martin, son of Colonel Ephraim Martin.
3. Charity married Samuel Sayre, of Madison.
4. Daniel married Sally Manning.
5. Solomon, who lived and died on Long Hill, unmarried. He owned part of the 500 acre tract; he was an Elder in the Basking Ridge church.
6. Neaty married David Crane, of Union, in Essex County. They had no children.

BENJAMIN COOPER, (6th child of Daniel Cooper, Sen.,) married and had children:

1. Polly, who married, 1st, Mr. Cross, 2d, John Annin, as his 2d wife.

2. Caty married Amos Dayton, son of Jonathan, of Basking Ridge.

GEORGE COOPER, (8th child of Daniel Cooper, Sen.,) lived where his father and grandfather did. He married Margaret Lafferty, and had children :

1. Daniel C. Cooper, who went to Dayton, Ohio, and settled. He was the principal proprietor of the town. He was born 21st November, 1773 ; married Miss Green, in Ohio ; had several children ; and died, 13th July, 1818 ; and his wife and children have all died.

2. Bryan Lafferty Cooper, born 6th January, 1775, died 12th June, 1798, unmarried.

3. Mary Cooper, born 30th March, 1778, and died 27th Jan., 1794, unmarried.

4. John G. Cooper, born 24th March, 1780, and died 24th October, 1822, at 42 years and 7 months.

5. Fanny Cooper, born 20th November, 1782, and died 28th September, 1811, unmarried.

JOHN G. COOPER, Esq., (4th child of George Cooper, son of Daniel Cooper, Sen.,) lived in the valley where his father did. He married Eleanor Perrine, and had children :

1. George, who went to Michigan ; is Treasurer of that State.

2. John.

3. Harriet, who married Calvin Bonnel, son of Enos, son of Benjamin.

4. Catherine.

ELIAS CORIELL.

ELIAS CORIELL was son of Abraham Coriell, of Piscataway. Elias Coriell came up from Piscataway, and settled on Long Hill, on No. 1 of the Berkley tract, adjoining Solomon Boyle's tract. He married Sarah Runyon, daughter of Richard, and had children :

1. Jane, who married John Melick, son of David, of Peapack, and removed to Schoharie, New York.

2. Peter married Sally Lindley, of New Vernon.

3. David married Anna Squier, daughter of Thomas.

4. Anne married John Kirkpatrick, son of Thomas, of Liberty Corner. [See Kirkpatrick.]

5. Sally married Stephen Conklin, son of William, Esq., of Basking Ridge. [See Conklin.]

6. Lydia, twin to Sally, married Isaac Davis, of Plainfield, as 2d wife. She died, 29th September, 1846, leaving no children.

JANE CORIELL, (1st child of Elias Coriell) and John Melick, had children :

1. Elias C. Melick ; 2. Aaron Melick; 3. Peter Melick; 4. Sarah Melick; 5. Charlotte Melick; 6. Jane Melick; 7. Anne Melick.

PETER CORIELL, (2d child of Elias Coriell,) lived near Dead River, S. W. of the Stonehouse. He and Sally Lindley had children :

1. Elias, who accidentally got killed on board a ferry-boat coming from New York.

2. Philip married ——; lives in Dayton, Ohio.

3. David married Rachel Nesbitt, daughter of James, near Basking Ridge, and has children: 1. Peter, who went to Illinois; 2. James.

4. Richard married Abigail Squier, daughter of Ludlow, of Plainfield, and had children : 1. Elias ; 2. Anne Elizabeth.

5. Israel (Doctor) was killed by falling, or being dashed, from his sulkey in the road.

6. John, who died at home, unmarried.

7. Mary married Abraham King, son of John, near Liberty Corner, and had a child, Mary, and then died ; Mary King married Robert Cross Bullman, son of Joseph Bullman, of Warren Township, and went to Illinois.

Mrs. Peter Coriell died 29th March, 1849.

DAVID CORIELL, (3d child of Elias Coriell,) and Anna Squier, lived in Elizabethtown, and had children :

1. Augustus ; 2. Edwin ; 3. John ; 4. Helen ; 5. Rachel.

Mr. David Coriell died in Elizabethtown of a dreadful disease, with much the appearance of leprosy, and the widow and all the family removed to Dubuque, in Wisconsin, and the widow died there, on the 13th July, 1846, aged 60 years.

STEPHEN CORWIN.

STEPHEN CORWIN lived between the mountains near Feltville. He married Betsey Drew, daughter of George Drew of Springfield Township. They had children :

1. John, who married Betsey French, daughter of David French, Sen.

2. Polly, who died, aged about 30 years, unmarried.

3. Anne married Samuel Price, son of Rice Price. [*See Rice Price.*]

4. Abby married Cornelius Willcox, son of Noah Willcox, Sen. [*See Willcox.*]

5. Noah ; 6. Nathan ; 7. Isaac ; these three went to the Lakes, New York.

4th Generation.

His wife, Betsey, died, and he married the widow of Noah Willcox, Sen.

Nancy Corwin, a daughter of Stephen, married Jonas Frazee, son of Samuel Frazee and Sarah Littell, and went to Ohio. [*See Sarah Littell, 4th child of Benjamin.*]

ELDER BENJAMIN CORY.

BENJAMIN CORY lived west of Elizabethtown, towards Westfield. He was an elder in the 1st church of Elizabethtown. He married Hannah Mulford, sister of Thomas Mulford, of Elizabethtown, and had children:

1. Mulford, who married, 1st, Betsey Clark; 2d. Maria Conklin.
2. Polly, who married David Mulford, son of Jonathan Mulford, Jun., of New Providence. They both died, leaving no children:
3. Hannah, who married William Meeker, son of Moses Meeker.
4. Phebe married Ezekiel Miller.
5. Abigail married Joseph Hinds.

MULFORD CORY, (1st child of Elder Benjamin Cory,) with his first wife, Betsey Clark, lived near Union Village, Somerset County, and had children:

1. Jonathan, who died at nine weeks old, 15th January, 1792.
2. Charlotte, who died, September, 1802, aged 9 years.
3. Mary, who married Mr. Stedman.
4. Fanny, who married James H. Smith, son of Oliver Smith, of Elizabethtown.

His wife, Betsey, died 18th September, 1802, aged 31 years.

He then removed to near Elizabethtown, and married, 2d, Mariah Conklin, and had children.

5. Joseph, who married Mary M. Magie, daughter of Elder David Magie, of Elizabethtown.
6. Benjamin Crane, twin to Joseph, married Mary M. Crane, daughter of Job Crane, of Elizabethtown.
7. Aaron C. Cory, who died at about 19 years.

Mr. Mulford Cory died in 1814, aged 47 years.

Joseph and Benjamin Cory entered Princeton College together, and graduated at the same time. Studied theology; were licensed on the same day to preach the gospel, 1834; were both ordained at the same session of Presbytery, in April, 1835, Joseph over the congregation of New Vernon, Morris County, and Benjamin over the congregation at Perth Amboy, Middlesex County.

REV. JOSEPH CORY, (5th child of Mulford Cory, son of Elder Benjamin,) and Mary M. Magie, had children:
1. Joseph T., who died in infancy; 2. David Magie Cory.

REV. BENJAMIN CORY, (twin to Rev. Joseph Cory,) and Mary M. Crane, had children:
1. Julia; 2. Jane; 3. Mary; 4. Benjamin, who died in infancy; 5. Sarah.

HANNAH CORY, (3d child of Elder Benjamin Cory,) and William Meeker, had children:
1. Moses Meeker, who died at about 12 years.
2. Mary Meeker, who died at about 20 years, unmarried.
3. Hannah Meeker, who married Andrew Crane.
4. Jonathan Meeker.
5. Abby Meeker.
6. Anne Meeker, who died at about 20 years, unmarried.
7. Susan Meeker.

ABIGAIL CORY, (5th child of Elder Benjamin Cory, and Joseph Hinds, had children:
1. Elizabeth Hinds, who married James Mulford, son of Jonathan.
2. Phebe Hinds married Mr. ——— Clark.
3. Jennette Hinds.
4. Lydia Hinds married ——— ———.
5. Benjamin Hinds went to St. Louis, and married and died there.
6. Julia Hinds.

DANIEL CORY.

DANIEL CORY lived on the north side of Long Hill, where Israel Bebout, his grandson, now lives. He was an elder in the Presbyterian church in New Providence. He married Martha Bedell, daughter of John Bedell, Jun. She died 9th April, 1791, aged 54, and he died 26th June, 1815, aged 82 years. They had children:
1. Benjamin, who died in youth.
2. Susannah, who married Gideon Allen, son of Joseph, Jun. [See *Allen.*]
3. Israel married, 26th February, 1787, Sarah Cauldwell, daughter of William Cauldwell, son of James.
4. Sally married Stephen Bebout, son of Peter. She died 5th July, 1843. [See *Bebout.*]
5. Daniel, Jun., married Joanna Ludlow, daughter of Jacob Ludlow, of Westfield, whose wife was Phebe; who after his death married, 25th September, 1791, Elder Daniel Cory, for his 2d wife. [See *Obadiah Ludlow.*]

3d Generation.

ISRAEL CORY, (3d child of Elder Daniel Cory,) and Sarah Cauldwell, had children:

1. William, who married Rachel Toms.
2. Israel married ——— ———.
3. Electa died in youth; — was drowned in Simpson's mill-pond.
4. Betsey Cauldwell, baptized 15th April, 1792, and died young. William and Israel removed to western New-York, north of Auburn.

Israel Cory died, 25th November, 1792, aged 26 years.
His wife, Sarah, died a few years after.

DANIEL CORY, Jun., (5th child of Elder Daniel Cory,) and Joanna Ludlow, had children:

1. Ludlow, who married Sarah Kelly, in New-York. They had a daughter, Sarah, and his wife died, and he went to Vicksburg, Mississippi, and died there.
2. Benjamin, who married Hannah Cory, daughter of Noah Cory, of Scotch Plains, and had but one child, Albinos. Benjamin Cory died suddenly, in a fit, 26th Feb., 1849.
3. Martha married Joseph Parrot, son of Thomas Parrot, Esq. She had but one child:
    1. Phebe, who married Augustine Trowbridge, and had children: 1. Martha Jane; 2. Joanna: and Phebe died May 1st, 1847.

ELNATHAN CORY.

ELNATHAN CORY lived in a house near where now stands the house of the Rev. Waters Burrows. His wife's name was Hannah. He owned about 200 acres there, formerly owned by Jacob Carle, and also about 100 acres, No. 33, of the Elizabethtown lots, south of that tract.

He died the 8th October, 1766, aged 65 years.

His wife died 24th January, 1785. He left his lands to his five sons:

1. Ebenezer, who married, for a 2d wife, Mary or Molly Mills, of Westfield. He lived where his father did, and owned west of the parsonage lot. He died 14th April, 1784.
2. Jeremy, who owned next west of Ebenezer, and sold to Dr. Jacob Jennings, who built the "Red House," by the well, west of Nathan Elmer's present dwelling. Jeremy Cory married, 18th December, 1764, Mary Wood. She died 25th June, 1776. They lived in Morris County, where Luke Parsons now does, and had children:
    1. Daniel Cory; 2. Noah Cory; 3. Hannah Cory.
3. Thomas married Jane Roll, said to be sister of John

Roll, son of John, 1st. He lived where Mrs. Noe now lives, and had children: 1. Cate Cory; 2. Betsey Cory; 3. James Cory; 4. Mary Cory.

4. James lived where Jonathan M. Meeker now does. He married Patty Carter, of Chatham, and had children:

    1. Jacob Cory; 2. Luke Cory; 3. Simeon Cory.

5. Joseph lived in 1775, in a house that stood in William Kindell's orchard, south of Benjamin Pike's house. He married, 10th September, 1765, Phebe Simpson, a sister or daughter of old Alexander Simpson, and had children:

    1. Nathan Cory.

    2. Jacob Cory.

    3. Stephen Cory, who died 13th January, 1773.

    4. Elizabeth Cory, who died 15th January, 1773.

    5. Joseph Cory, Jun., married, 22d July, 1783, Martha Morehouse.

6. Job married, and had a son, David Parsons Cory, and went to the Mississippi.

EBENEZER CORY, (eldest son of Elnathan Cory,) and his 1st wife, Hannah, who died 25th October, 1763; had a daughter, Sarah, who married, 1st, John Johnson; 2d, David Martin: and by his 2d wife, Molly Mills, had children:

2. John, who married 15th June, 1774, Rebecca Raimond, and went with the militia to Ticonderoga, and there died.

3. Ebenezer, Jun., who died 20th December, 1772.

4. Elnathan married Sarah Walker, daughter of Richard and Sarah Walker.

5. Hannah married, 2d October, 1775, John Walker, son of Richard.

6. Samuel married Hannah Davis, sister of Jonathan and Elijah Davis, and had children: 1. Mary; 2. Hannah; 3. John Cory.

7. William, who died at 22 years.

8. George, born 15th September, 1772, married Rachel Price, born 20th March, 1771, daughter of Abraham Price.

9. Job.

10. Mary, who died 6th November, 1784.

GEORGE CORY, (8th child of Ebenezer,) and Rachel Price, had children:

1. Mary Anne, who married Lewis Osborn, son of John Osborn, Jun. [See Osborn.]

2. Locky married Daniel Oakley, son of Thomas. [See Oakley.]

3. Betsey married William M. Griffin, son of Isaac. [See Griffin.]

H

4. Benjamin married Eliza Willcox, daughter of Benjamin; has no children.

5. William, born 13th July, 1802, married Harriet Leforge, born 4th August, 1802, daughter of Abraham, of Somerset Co.

6. Polly married, 15th June, 1822, George Van Benscoten, of New York.

7. Sally married, 4th February, 1824, James C. Vaught, of New-York.

8. Hannah, born 20th October, 1810, married William Ryckbeck, of New York; had no children. He was killed by the upsetting of a locomotive engine.

9. Jane, who died in youth.

10. Abby married David Devoe, of New-York.

WILLIAM CORY, (son of George, son of Ebenezer,) and Harriet Leforge, had children:

1. Abraham Morrel, born 1st August, 1828; 2. Mary Elizabeth, born 31st August, 1835; 3. William Ryckbeck, born 8th April, 1837; 4. Apollos Elmer, born April ——.

POLLY CORY, (daughter of George,) and George Van Benscoten, had children:

1. Mary Jane Van Benscoten; 2. Sarah Van Benscoten; 3. Henry Van Benscoten; 4. John Van Benscoten; 5. George Van Benscoten; 6. Tunis Van Benscoten; 7. James Van Benscoten; 8. Martha Van Benscoten.

SALLY CORY, (daughter of George,) and James C. Vaught, had children:

1. George C. Vaught, born 19th July, 1828.

2. John William Vaught. Mrs. Vaught then died.

ABBY CORY, (daughter of George,) and David Devoe, had children:

1. Sarah Anne Devoe; 2. Theodore Devoe; 3. Almira Devoe; 4. Mary Louisa Devoe; 5. Leander Devoe; 6. Emmagene Devoe; 7. Adaline Devoe, born 11th April, 1840; 8. Matilda Devoe; 9. Sophia Devoe; 10. Lavenia, born 23d October, 1845.

ANDREW CRAIG.

ANDREW CRAIG lived in the township of Westfield. He was one of the 2d generation of the "Elizabethtown Associates," admitted in 1699, and many years an Alderman of the borough of Elizabeth. He married —— ——, and had children:

1. James, whose wife's name was Lydia.

2. Susannah, who married David Littell, son of Samuel. [*See David Littell.*] Alderman Craig may have had other children.

JAMES and LYDIA CRAIG had children :

1. Daniel, who married Miss —— Clark, sister of Richard, Clark, of Rahway.
2. James, Jun., married Mary Jennings, daughter of William, of Rahway.
3. Andrew married Miss —— Bailey.

DANIEL CRAIG, (son of James, 1st,) and Miss Clark, had children : 1. Isaac ; 2. Terril ; 3. Clark, and two or three others. He removed to Esopus, New-York, and settled there.

JAMES CRAIG, JUN., (son of James and Lydia Craig,) and Mary Jennings, had children :

1. Sally, who married William Robins, of Ohio.
2. James, 3d, who married Betsey Tucker, daughter of Amos, of Rahway.
3. William married Jane Roff, daughter of Nathaniel, of New-Providence.
4. Andrew, born 29th January, 1785, married Alsie Manning, born 20th August, 1784, daughter of Isaac, of Plainfield.
5. John married Sally Cooley, an English girl, and had children : 1. David Stewart Craig, and three others.

All this family, except Andrew, after their father's death, went to Ohio.

JAMES CRAIG, 3d, and Betsey Tucker, had children :

1. John, who married in Ohio.
2. William married —— ——, and died, leaving four children.
3. Phebe, who died at about six or seven years.

WILLIAM CRAIG, (3d child of James Craig, Jun.,) and Jane Roff, had children :

1. James.
2. —— Shipman.
3. Eliza.
4. Phebe.
5. Nathaniel.

ANDREW CRAIG, (4th child of James Craig, Jun.,) and Alsie Manning, lived where his father did, in Westfield, and had children :

1. John Manning Craig, born 26th August, 1809, went on a whaling voyage and died.
2. Margaret Craig, born 31st January, 1812, married Matthias Burnet, son of Matthias, of Union, and has one child, Mary Anne Burnet.
3. Isaac Clarkson Craig, born 11th February, 1815, married Lavenia Herdman, daughter of Aaron Herdman, of Newark, and had children : 1. Charles Edwin Craig ; 2. James Andrew Craig ; 3. Albert Kitchel Craig.

[margin: 3d Generation. 4th Generation. 5th Generation. 6th Gen.]

4. Alsie Anne Craig, born 16th August, 1817, married John
Jeroloman, of Bellville, and had children:
    1. Richard Manning Jerolomon.
    5. Mary Catherine Craig, born 9th May, 1820, married Obadiah
Kitchel, son of Jesse, of Obadiah Kitchel, of Hanover, Morris
County, and had children: 1. Silas Manning Kitchel; 2. Mary
Hopping Kitchel; 3. Alsie Craig Kitchel.
    6. Richard Merril Craig, born 28th January, 1825.

JASPER CRANE.

JASPER CRANE and four others, about the year 1644, removed from New Haven to East Haven, where he built a house,
and there his son Jasper was born, 2d April, 1651. He sold
out at East Haven, 7th September, 1651, and removed to Branford,
and from then ceto Newark.

JASPER CRANE, (son of Jasper,) was a representative from
the town of Newark, in the Legislature of New Jersey, in 1699,
and, indeed, the whole time of the administration of Lord Corn-
bury as Governor of the Province.
He was also a magistrate, and held other offices of trust.
He married Joanna Swain, daughter of Johannah and Samuel
Swain.
He died 16th March, 1712. His wife died in 1720, aged 69
years. They had children John, Azariah, and Jasper 3d.

John had children :	Azariah had children :	Jasper Crane, 3d, had children :
John.	Nathaniel.	Joseph Crane, Esq.
Daniel.	Azariah.	Jonathan Crane, Esq.
Jasper.	John.	Elihu.
Sarah.	Robert.	David.
	Mary Baldwin.	
	Jane Rule.	

The children of Joseph Crane, Esq., (son of Jasper, 3d,) were
Benjamin, Ezekiel, Isaac, Israel, Josiah, Joseph, Abigail, and
Joanna. Joanna married Samuel Congar, who died in 1752, and
left children: David; Jonathan; Stephen; and Samuel Congar.
Joanna subsequently married Joseph Camp, Esq., and had a
daughter, Joanna.
The children of Jonathan Crane, Esq., (son of Jasper, 3d, son of
Jasper, Jun.,) were Samuel, Caleb, Nehemiah, Elihu, John Treat,
and Margaret Johnson.
The children of Elihu Crane, (son of Jasper, 3d,) were Lewis,
Christopher, Charles, Elihu, Isaac, Hannah, and Phebe.
The children of David Crane, (son of Jasper, 3d,) were Jedediah
David, Joseph, Abigail Johnson, Phebe Lawrence, Mary Alling
Dorcas, and Sarah.
It is said that Azariah Crane married Mary Treat. Nathaniel
and Azariah Crane, sons of Deacon Azariah Crane, obtained a
large tract of land, at the foot of the mountain, called Crane Town,
now West Bloomfield.

STEPHEN CRANE.

STEPHEN CRANE, it is said, was the ancestor of the Cranes in and about Elizabethtown and Westfield. He was one of the first "Elizabethtown Associates," and had sons, John Crane and Jeremiah Crane, and perhaps Daniel Crane who was born 1673, and died 24th February, 1724. Jeremiah Crane was one of the 2d generation of Associates, admitted in 1699.

JOHN CRANE, 1st, (son of Stephen,) had sons John 2d, Joseph ; Matthias, Benjamin, Samuel; and daughters, Abigail, Esther, Sarah ; Rebecca, and Deborah.

JOHN CRANE, 2d, (son of John, 1st, son of Stephen,) had children :

1. John, 3d, who married, 1st, Huldah Grant ; 2d, Miss Bedell, of Westfield; 3d, a widow Force.

2. Stephen.

3. Jacob, who went to Canada, soon after the Revolutionary war.

4. Isaac, who married Mary Miller, daughter of John, and removed to Passaic Valley.

5. Joseph married Ruth Miller, sister of Isaac's wife, and came to Passaic Valley.

JOHN CRANE, 3d, and Huldah Grant, had children ;

1. Elijah, who married Miss Ross, daughter of David Ross, of Westfield.

2. John, 4th, married Phebe Ross, sister of Elijah's wife.

3. Sarah married Isaac Hendricks, of Westfield.

And by his 2d wife, who was sister of Jacob Bedell, of Westfield, he had,

4. Mary, who married Aaron Sayre, of Westfield.

By his 3d wife, the widow Force, he had no children.

ELIJAH CRANE, (son of John Crane, 3d,) and Miss Ross, had children :

1. Stephen, who married Miss Williams.

2. David, who married Miss Denman, daughter of Andrew Denman, of Westfield.

3. Huldah married William Miller.

STEPHEN CRANE, (son of Elijah,) and Miss Williams, had children :

1. John Marsh Crane ; 2. Williams Crane ; 3. Marsh Crane, who married Elias Potter, son of Major Jonathan Potter, of Union, and all went to Peoria, Illinois.

ISAAC CRANE, (son of John, 3d, son of John, 2d, son of John,

1st, son of Stephen,) removed from Westfield to Passaic Valley, purchased and lived on a tract of land of 178 acres, being lot No. 1, and part of lot No. 2, of Corsen's survey of Elizabethtown lots, above the first mountain lying south of Joseph Cory's farm. He and Mary Miller had children :

5th Generation.

1. Jonathan, who died 14th Dec. 1770.
2. Isaac Miller died 28th April, 1784.
3. Mary, who married Samuel Parsons, son of William. .[*See Parsons.*] She died 11th Nov. 1850, aged 89 years, 10 months. He died 25th Dec. 1822, aged 64 years.
4. Martha married 15th Jan. 1783, Nathaniel Bonnel, son of Capt. Nathaniel. [*See Bonnel.*] She died 30th June, 1846. He died 15th April, 1814, aged 58 years.
5. Huldah married 18th Feb. 1786. Capt. Abner Stites, son of Elijah. [*See Stites.*] She died 24th June, 1835, aged 71 years. He died 29th August, 1831, aged 68 years.
6. Sally married 4th Nov. 1792, Nathan Elmer, son of Rev. Jonathan Elmer. [*See Elmer.*] She died 19th July, 1838, aged 69 years.

JOSEPH CRANE, brother of Isaac, came up from Westfield, and purchased of Nathaniel Smith, in May, 1764, the Farm of 154 acres lying north of Isaac Crane's, and west of Benjamn Pettit's farm, and extending to the river. He married Ruth Miller, sister of his brother Isaac's wife, and had children, 7 sons, and 4 daughters :

1. Samuel, who married, 7th. Nov. 1792, Abby Roberts.
2. John married 23d Sept. 1792, Betsey Mulford, daughter of Jonathan, Jun.
3. Stephen married Esther Thomas, daughter of William, of Stony Hill, and went to Ohio.
4. Jonathan married Keziah Tappin, daughter of James Tappin, and went to Ohio.
5. Abner married, in Ohio, Huldah Robinson, daughter of John, from Westfield.
6. Joseph, Jun., married Sally Bebout, daughter of William ; lived on the Bebout farm.
7. Moses married, in Ohio, Susannah Dilts, of Warren County.
8. Joanna married William Valentine, son of Obadiah ; went to Redstone. [*See Valentine.*]
9. Annar married Benjamin Corrington, 13th Nov. 1782 ; went to Redstone.
10. Ruth married William Hole, 5th July, 1785, son of Charles ; went to Redstone. [*See Hole.*]
11. Betsey married, 1st May, 1794, Daniel Doty, son of John ; went to Middletown, Ohio. [*See Doty.*]
Joseph Crane was born 1741, and died 7th June, 1778, aged 37 years.
Ruth, the widow of Joseph Crane, went to Ohio, with her sons, and died, over 90 years of age.

JOSEPH CRANE, Jun., and Sally Bebout, had children:

1. William Bebout Crane, who married, 24th April, 1820, Deborah Conklin, daughter of Captain Benjamin Conklin, and had children: 1. Elias; 2. Mulford; and 3. Jerusha.

His wife, Deborah, then died, and he married, 2d, Nancy Potter, daughter of Samuel, son of Caleb, son of Colonel Samuel Potter, and had other children: 4. Elizabeth; 5. Hannah; 6. Sarah; 7. John; 8. Jacob.

William B. Crane removed to Ohio.

2. Eliza married Levi Clark, son of Daniel S. Clark, Esq. [*See Clark.*]

3. Ruth married Linus H. Stephens, son of Christopher. [*See Stevens.*]

4. Jacob, who, with all the young children, except Hannah, went to Ohio and Illinois.

5. Aretas married his cousin, a daughter of Daniel Doty, son of John. [*See Doty.*]

6. Hannah, who died at about 19 years, unmarried.

7. Ira.

8. Nancy.

9. Catherine married her cousin, Daniel Doty, son of Daniel, of Middletown, Ohio.

10. Joseph.

11. Sarah Wheeler.

Joseph Crane died 3d June, 1829, aged 58 years.

His wife, Sally, died 31st August, 1825, aged 47 years.

JOHN CRANE, (2d son of Joseph Crane,) and Betsey Mulford, lived on part of his father's farm, and had children:

1. Jonathan Mulford, who died a young man.

2. Elias, who went to Indiana, married, and died there.

3. Huldah married Levi Willcox, Jun., son of Levi, and went to Illinois. [*See Willcox.*]

4. Orpha married Dr. Erastus D. Crossfield, from New England, and went to Warren County, Ohio, and had an only child, John, Edgar Crossfield.

5. Deborah married Ezra Ludlow, son of Joseph; lived in Elizabethtown. [*See Ludlow.*]

6. Sylvester married Huldah Bonnel, daughter of Philemon; had three children; his wife died 13th Sept. 1835, aged 29 years. The children were Rachel, who died at 8 years and 6 months, John, and Elias. Sylvester went to Illinois, and took Elias, who soon died. John lives with his grandfather Philemon Bonnel. Sylvester was a lieutenant in the Mexican war.

7. Mary married Aaron H. Lanning, of Warren County. and had children: 1. Laura Burnet Lanning; 2. Orpha Jane Lanning; 3. John Joseph Lanning.

8. Daniel went to Indiana, and married Catherine Rogers.

9. **Harriet married Samuel G. Benedict, from Connecticut, —went to Illinois, where he died, and she removed to her sister Crossfield's, in Ohio.**

10. Elizabeth married Samuel T. Day, son of Stephen, and lives where her father did. [*See S. T. Day.*]

John Crane died 18th July, 1843, aged 79 years.

His wife, Betsey, died 9th March, 1828, aged 53 years.

JOHN CRANE, 4th, and Phebe Ross, had children :

1. Rebecca, who married Major Jotham Potter, son of John ; both died; left three children. [*See Potter.*]

2. John Grant Crane, married Sally Pierson, daughter of William, son of William, and had children : 1. John Davis Crane, who married Catherine Potter, daughter of William B. Potter : 2. William married ———, daughter of John Miller, of Westfield. 3. Elizabeth married Thomas Moore, son of Robert, of Woodbridge, and had children : 1. David Moore; 2 Robert Moore ; 3. John Moore ; 4. Israel Moore ; 5. Phebe Moore.

4. Phebe married Benjamin Potter, brother of Major Jotham. [*See Potter.*]

5. Elias, born 24th April, 1789, and married Esther Maxwell, daughter of John, lives in Union, and had children :

    1. John, who married Sarah Cutter, daughter of William Cutter, of Woodbridge.

    2. Mary Anne married Nathan Winans, son of Aaron, of Elizabethtown.

    3. Phebe married Silas Miller, son of Abraham, son of Abraham.

    4. Susan married Isaac Williams, of New-York, son of Matthias.

    5. Elias Maxwell Crane.

    6. Amzi Armstrong Crane.

6. Josiah married Electa Ross, daughter of John, of Union and lived where Col. Jacob Crane formerly did, and had children :

    1. Mary married Hampton Cutter, son of William Cutter above named.

    2. John Grant Crane married Abby Miller, daughter of John O. Miller, and lives on the old John Crane homestead.

    3. Anne Elizabeth, married Job Williams, son of Moses Williams, of Union.

    4. Josiah married Sarah Jane Miller, daughter of Jacob.

7. Huldah married John Potter, also a brother of Major Jotham, and had but one child, Mary Hannah Potter.

8. Sarah, who is unmarried.

SARAH CRANE, (3d child of John Crane 3d,) and Isaac Hendricks, had but one child, Huldah Hendricks, who married Aaron Pearce, son of Melvin, of Scotch Plains, and had children :

    1. Hendricks Pearce, who was a physician, and married a daughter of Enoch Miller.

    2. Felix Pearce.

    3. Melvin Pearce.

6th Generation. 7th Generation.

BENJAMIN CRANE.

BENJAMIN CRANE, (son of John, 1st,) son of Stephen Crane, married Esther Woodruff. She died 22d February, 1809, aged 98 years. They had children:

1. Benjamin Crane, 2d, who married Phebe Halsey, daughter of Joseph Halsey, who lived between Elizabethtown and Rahway.

2. Eleazer Crane, who married Susan Day, (5th child of Dayid Day, Esq.,) and died without children. [*See Day.*]

BENJAMIN CRANE, 2d, and Phebe Halsey, lived in Westfield, and had children :

1. Benjamin, 3d, born 29th November, 1761, married Sarah Thompson, daughter of Hezekiah.

2. Abigail, born 27th November, 1762, and died unmarried.

3. Norris, born 9th February, 1764, married Jane Dunham, daughter of John, Sen.

4. John, born 18th April, 1765.

5. Phebe, born 19th December, 1766, married John Johnson, wholesale grocer, New-York, as his 2d wife. She had no chlidren.

6. Sarah, born 12th April, 1771, married John Ogden, of Green Village, Morris County.

7. Abigail, 2d, born 17th September, 1774, and died young.

BENJAMIN CRANE, 3d, (son of Benjamin, 2d, son of Benjamin, 1st, son of John, son of Stephen Crane,) and Sarah Thompson, lived in Westfield, and had children :

1. John, who married Mary Clark, daughter of Robert, of Westfield.

2. Abigail married David Keyt, son of James.

3. Esther, who died at about 18 or 20 years, unmarried.

4. Hezekiah Thompson married, 1st, Amanda Osborn ; 2d, ——

5. Phebe married, 1st, Francis Randolph, son of Dr. Robert ; 2d, George R. King, of Warren County, and lived there.

6. Charlotte King married Hedges Baker, son of Daniel. [*See Baker.*]

7. Norris, who went to Cincinnati, Ohio, and married there.

8. Jacob Thompson went to Cincinnati, and died there at 35 years, unmarried.

9. Benjamin, 4th, married Electa Baker, as her 2d husband, daughter of Daniel.

10. David Johnson married Anne Eliza Roll, daughter of Isaac, son of John.

11. Moses Thompson married Eliza Scudder.

JOHN CRANE, (son of Benjamin, 3d,) and Mary Clark, had children: 1. Benjamin Franklin ; 2. Abigail ; 3. Betsey Anne.

ABIGAIL CRANE, daughter of Benjamin, 3d, and David Keyt, had children : 1. James Keyt ; 2. Anne Eliza Keyt.

5th Generation.

6th Generation.

7th Generation.

HEZEKIAH T. CRANE, (son of Benjamin, 3d,) and Amanda Osborn, had children: 1. John.

PHEBE CRANE, (daughter of Benjamin, 3d,) and Francis Randolph, had children : 1. Bennington Randolph ; 2. Sarah Anne Randolph married Samuel Clark.
And by George King, Phebe had three other children.

BENJAMIN CRANE, 4th, (son of Benjamin, 3d,) and Electa Baker, lived at Patterson, and had children :
1. Catherine Shelts, who died at 5 or 6 years.
2. Alfred Britton.
3. Margaret Baker.
4. Benjamin Hervy.
5. Sarah Thompson.
6. Joan.
7. Jane.
8. Electa, who died young.

DAVID J. CRANE, (son of Benjamin, 3d,) and Hannah Eliza Roll, had children :
1. James.
2. Jacob Thompson, who died at $2\frac{1}{2}$ years.
3. David Newton.
4. George King.
5. Isaac Roll.
6. John Hezekiah.
7. Benjamin Franklin, who died at two weeks old.

MOSES T. CRANE, (son of Benjamin, 3d,) and Eliza Scudder, had children:
1. Theodore Augustus.
2. Sarah Anne.

NORRIS CRANE, (son of Benjamin Crane, 2d,) and Jane Dunham, (born 13th May, 1765,) lived in Sterling Valley, and had children :

1. Nancy, born 29th September, 1790, and married William Pierson Conklin, son of William. He lived in New-York; his widow Nancy is blind; lives with her brother-in-law, Israel Bebout.

2. Isaac, born 25th October, 1792, and married Polly and Anne, two daughters of Thomas Parrot, Esq.

3. Sally, born 27th March, 1797, and married Peter Parrot, son of Thomas Parrot, Esq, [See Parrot.]

4. John, born 29th September, 1799, and married Abby Flatt, of New-York, and lives there.

5. Benjamin, born 16th April, 1802, and married 2d December, 1824, Julia Bebout, daughter of Stephen.

6. Albert, born 17th March, 1804, and married ——— ———, daughter of Anderson French, of Westfield.

7. Mary, born 16th March, 1807, and married Israel Bebout, son of Stephen. [*See Bebout,.*]
Norris Crane died 21st February, 1846.
Jane, his wife, died 23d June, 1848.

ISAAC CRANE, (son of Norris, son of Benjamin Crane, 2d,) and his 1st wife, Polly Parrot, had children:
1. Abraham, who married Margaret Ayers, daughter of Richard of Long Hill, and had children: 1. George Abraham and Margaret, twins; 2. Joanna; 3. Richard Henry; 4. William; 5. a son and daughter, twins.
2. William, born 30th January, 1820, married, 28th May, 1849, Mary Cole, daughter of Elias Cole, of Scotch Plains, and had children, 1. Cornelius.
3. Anne.
And by his 2d wife, Anne Parrot, he had other children:
4. Mary.
5. John Halsey.
6. Albert.
7. Isaac.

JOHN CRANE, (son of Norris,) and Abby Flatt, had children:
1. Phebe; 2. Norris; 3. Caroline; 4. Charlotte; 5. Hannah; 6. Benjamin Franklin.

BENJAMIN CRANE, (son of Norris,) and Julia Bebout, had children: 1. John Ogden; 2. Fanny; 3. Sarah.

ALBERT CRANE, (son of Norris,) and ——, had children:
1. Jane; 2. Lucy; 3. Mary; 4. George; 5. James.

STEPHEN CRANE.

STEPHEN CRANE, born 1709, and died July 1st, 1780, was probably son of Jeremiah, son of Stephen Crane, 1st. His wife's name was Phebe, who died 17th August, 1776, aged 62 years.
They had children:
1. Daniel, born 3d January, 1735.
2. Stephen, born 14th October, 1737. He was killed by a party of British soldiers, on their way to Connecticut Farms, when that place was burnt.
3. Elizabeth, born 10th March, 1740.
4. David, born 27th November, 1742, married, 21st November, 1762, Anne Sayre. She was born 23d May, 1742, and died 24th November, 1805. They had children: 1. David, born 7th Feb. 1772, and died 27th September, 1791; 2. Sarah, born 13th May, 1778, and died 16th September, 1778. He married, in 1806, Agnes or Neaty Cooper, daughter of John, son of Daniel Cooper, 1st, but had no children by her.
5. William, who entered the army, and accompanied General Montgomery to Quebec, and was severely wounded in the attack on that city. He became general of the militia after the war. He

married twice; his 2d wife was Abbe Miller, daughter of Benjamin; had 6 children.

6. Phebe, born 2d June, 1750.

7. Joseph, born 20th May, 1752; married, 1. Susannah Ross, who died 22d October, 1781, aged 32 years; 2. Margaret Van Vechten, of Somerville.

8. Jonathan, born 15th May, 1754.

9. Catherine, born 8th October, 1756.

GENERAL WILLIAM CRANE, (5th child of Stephen,) had children :

5th Generation.

1. William, who was commodore in the United States Navy. He died about 1844.

2. Ichabod B., a colonel in the United States Army, now in command at Governor's Island.

3. Joseph H. married Julia Elliot; lives in Dayton; is judge of the supreme court of Ohio.

4. Mariah, who lives with Joseph; is unmarried.

5. Joanna married John Magie, and died about 1818, leaving a daughter Julia Magie.

6. Phebe, who died about 1818, unmarried.

JOSEPH CRANE, (brother of General William Crane,) and Susannah Ross, had children :

6th Generation.

1. William, who married Sarah Townley, daughter of Richard. [*See Townley.*]

2. Susan married Henry Weaver, and went to Trenton, Butler County, Ohio. She died 22d January, 1851, aged 75 years.

3. Nancy married Abraham Van Sickle, and went to Trenton, Ohio, and by his 2d wife, Margaret, had children :

4. John, who married Sarah Conover, and lives in Hamilton, Ohio; is a major of militia.

5. David lives on the River St. Joseph's, Ohio.

6. —— Van Vechten.

7. Sally, who died unmarried.

8. Richard, who lives near David.

WILLIAM CRANE, Esq., (1st child of Joseph,) and Sarah Townley, had children :

1. David R. Crane who married Phebe Anne Hallam, daughter of Lewis Hallam of New-York.

2. Agnes married Rev. Curtis Tally, a methodist minister, and had a daughter, Helen Williams Tally.

3. Richard T. Crane, married Jane T. Dolebeer of Union, and had children : 1. Theodore T. Dolebeer; 2. Frederick T. Dolebeer.

4. Joseph W. Crane, married, 1st, Harriet J. Willcox, daughter of Ezekiel, and had a daughter, 1. Harriet Jemima Crane. His wife died, and he married, 2d, Emma S. Brookfield, daughter of Lewis P. Brookfield of Spring Valley, and had children : 2. Lewis W.; 3. Augustus.

. Jonathan T. Crane, who graduated at Princeton College, and became a methodist minister, is Principal of the "Pennington Male Seminary." He married Mary Helen Pe k, daughter of Rev. George Peck, D. D., of N. Y., and had a daughter, Mary Helen Peck.

SUSAN CRANE, and Henry Weaver, had children :
1. Nancy Weaver, who married Mr. Clawson.
2. William Weaver married Miss Clark.
3. John Weaver married Miss Bowman.
4. Polly Weaver married James Beard.
5. Samuel Weaver.
6. Eliza Weaver.
7. Clark Weaver.

NANCY CRANE, 3d child of Joseph, and Abraham Van Sickle had children :
1. Susan Van Sickle, who married, 1st, Mr. Long ;2d, Mr. Bailey : 3d, Mr. Brown.
2. Henry Van Sickle
3. Mariah Van Sickle.
4. Catherine Van Sickle.
5. Joseph Van Sickle.

7th Generation.

MAJOR JOHN CRANE, (4th child of Joseph,) and Sarah Conover, had children :
1. William, who married Rachel Crawford, and had children : 1. John ; 2. William.
2. Joel H. married Sarah Walker.
3. Margaret married H. M. Moore, and died.
4. Tryphena E. married Thomas Davis, and had children: 1. Charles Davis ; 2. Margaret Davis ; 3. Thomas Davis.
5. George W .   6. Mary.
7. Mariah E.   8. John C.
9. Jane C.   10. Joseph.

7th Generation.

JUDGE JOSEPH H. CRANE, (3d son of General Wm.,) and Julia Elliot had chidren :
1. Mariah, who married Doctor Clements, and had a son, Joseph Clements.
2. William.
3. Wilbra.
4. James.
5. Henrietta.
6. Joseph.
7. Clements.

6th Generation.

TIMOTHY CRANE* married Mary Congar, a sister of Designer Congar, who lived in a house which stood near where Dayton Badgley now lives.

Timothy Crane and Mary Congar lived in the house next to and east of Amos Morehouse. They had an only son Jeremiah, who married Joannah Cogswell, daughter of Nathaniel Cogswell, near Chatham, and had children: 1. Jeremiah, who married Jane O. Clark, daughter of David C. Clark, and had no children; 2. Designer Congar Crane, who married Mary Beach, daughter of Benjamin Beach, of Mendham, and died leaving two children:

1. Joanna Crane, who married Robert Hatch, of Newark.
2. Harriet.

DESIGNER CONGAR had children:

Polly Crane, baptized 19th January, 1785.

Anna Designer, baptized 13th April, 1786, as the daughter of the widow Congar.

So it seems that Designer Congar died between those two dates.

JOHN DAVIS.

JOHN DAVIS, was born 11th January, 1731, and died in the spring of 1760. He married Sarah Crane, born 9th January, 1728.

They had children:

2d Generation.

1. Anna, born 7th March, 1753, and married William Pierson, of Westfield.
2. John, born 29th December, 1754, and was killed at the battle of Springfield, in the Revolutionary war.
3. Jacob, born 6th February, 1758, and died 22d February, 1843; was an elder in the church at Westfield. He married Mary Littell, 2d child of Moses Littell and Abby Thompson. She was born 13th March, 1762, and died 21st October, 1823.

JACOB DAVIS, (son of John,) and Mary Littell, lived in Westfield, and had children:

3d Generation.

1. John, born 20th October, 1779, married Phebe Acken, daughter of Deacon Joseph Acken, of Westfield, and died 14th March, 1850.
2. Sarah, born 28th October, 1781, married Henry Hand, 15th child of Hezekiah. [*See Hand.*]

* I have not learned to what family Timothy Crane belonged.

NOTE.— Sarah, the widow of John Davis, married David Conkling, as his 2d wife, who was born 29th May, 1721. By his two wives, David Conkling had children:

1. Daniel Conkling, born 23d January, 1751.
2. Mary Conkling, born 27th January, 1755.
3. Hannah Conkling, born 14th February, 1757.
4. Sarah Conkling, born 30th March, 1759.
5. Abigail Conkling, born 13th December, 1761.
6. Samuel Conkling, born 21st July, 1765.
7. David Conkling, born 10th January, 1767.

The three or four last named may have been children of Sarah.

3. Betsey, born 29th January, 1784, married, 1st, Lewis Ludlow, son of Matthias, 2d, William Mulford, son of John.
4. Isaac Littell, born 10th October, 1788, and died 12th April, 1845. He married, 1st, Margaret Farrand, of Newark; 2d, Catherine, widow of George Price, and daughter of John N. Oliver, of Elizabethtown.
5. Jacob Davis, Jun., born 30th October, 1793, and died 22d May, 1817, unmarried.
6. Mary, born 5th April, 1796, married Isaac French, son of Robert, of Springfield.

JOHN DAVIS, (son of Jacob,) and Phebe Acken, had 7 children :
1. Joseph Acken Davis, who married his cousin, Mary Mulford, daughter of William, and had children :
  1. Phebe Ladoiska Davis.
  2. ———.
2. Mary Davis, who married David M. Woodruff, of Union, and had children:
  1. Hiram Washington Woodruff.
  2. James Woodruff.
  3. Jacob Woodruff.
  4. Wesley Woodruff.
  5. Mary Woodruff.
3. Rebecca Davis married Henry B. Faitout, of Union, and had children :
  1. Emma Faitout.
  2. James Faitout.
4. Betsey Davis married Benjamin Pierson, son of John D. Pierson, son of William Pierson, of Westfield, and had children:
  1. Mary Pierson.
5. Jacob Davis married Sarah Cory, daughter of Jonathan, son of Andrew Cory.
6. Thomas C. Davis is a merchant in Newark.
7. Sarah Anne Davis married Hervy Cory, son of Jonathan, and a brother of Jacob's wife.

SARAH DAVIS, (2d child of Jacob Davis and Mary Littell,) and Henry Hand, removed to Sandusky, Ohio, where he died, and she removed to a place below Peoria, Illinois, where she died. They had 11 children :
1. Abigail Hand, born 25th July, 1801, and married Mr. ——— Raymond.
2. Nancy Hand, born 8th August, 1803, married ——— ———.
3. Jacob Davis Hand, born 24th October, 1805, married — —.
4. Moses F. Hand, born 4th November, 1807, married — ———.
5. Mary Davis Hand, born 8th December, 1809.
6. Betsey Davis Hand, born 3d April, 1812, married ——— ———.
7. Rhoda Hand, born 27th August, 1814, married ——— ———.
8. Henry Hand, } twins, born 21st June, 1817, { married ———.
9. Sarah Hand, } { married ———.

10. Caroline Hand, born 21st March, 1820.

11. Catherine Hand, born 10th October, 1822.

BETSEY DAVIS, (3d child of Jacob Davis,) and Lewis Ludlow, had children :

1. Melancthon Ludlow, who died a young man, unmarried.

2. Benjamin Ludlow, who married Fanny Smalley, son of Abner, son of James, and had an only daughter, 1. Elizabeth Ludlow.

His wife, Fanny, then died, and left his daughter here with her grandfather Smalley, and went to Buffalo and married there.

3. Sarah Ludlow, who married, 1st, William Miller, son of Lewis Miller, of Westfield, and had a son :

　　1. Lewis Miller, who married Martha Hand, daughter of Matthias, son of Nehemiah.

She married, 2d, Caleb Miller, son of Nathaniel, of Springfield, and had, 2. Israel M. Miller; 3. Mary Miller.

She married, 3d, William Day, of Elizabethtown, an Englishman, and had, 4. Catherine Day; 5. William Day.

Lewis Ludlow, after having three children, died, and his widow, Betsey, married William Mulford, son of John. [See Mulford.]

ISAAC L. DAVIS, (4th child of Jacob Davis,) and Margaret Farrand, lived in Elizabethtown, and had children :

1. Charlotte, who married Elias Riggs Wilkison, son of Josiah. [See Burrows.]

2. Margaret, who married John Campbell, of New York.

Isaac L. Davis, by his 2d wife, Catherine Oliver, had children :

3. Sarah.

4. Henrietta married ——— ———.

MARY DAVIS, (6th child of Jacob Davis,) and Isaac French, lived at Westfield, and had children :

1. Robert French, born 24th September, 1814, married Phebe Mooney, daughter of James, and had children :

　　1. Mary Elizabeth French.

　　2. Isaac Halsey French.

　　3. Richard French.

　　4. James French.

　　5. Phebe French.

2. Catherine French, born 7th December, 1817, married William Woodruff, son of Benjamin, son of Robert Woodruff, whose wife was Mary, daughter of Andrew Denman, and had children :

　　1. William Alfred Woodruff.

3. Mary French, born 23d December, 1822, married Benjamin Woodruff, son of Benjamin, of Westfield. She died 16th August, 1847, and he died, leaving no children :

4. Jacob Davis French, twin to Mary, married Lydia Pierson, daughter of Moses Pierson, of Westfield.

GEORGE DAY.

GEORGE DAY lived on Long Island.

He had a son, George Day, who came to New Jersey, and lived on the north side of Long Hill, and east of Sterling Valley. It is believed that John, David and Joseph Day were also his sons.

GEORGE DAY, 2d, had a son, George Day, 3d, who died 8th September, 1803.

The wife of George Day, 3d, was Elizabeth ; she died 26th February, 1815, aged 79 years.   They had children:

1. Damaris, who married Samuel Clark, Esq. [*See Elder John Clark.*]

2. Martha married Abijah Wells ; she died 20th January, 1811, of apoplexy, aged 49 years.

3. Polly, who died in May, 1835, unmarried.

4. John, who married Polly Marsh, daughter of Joseph, and grand-daughter of John Osborn, Sen.

MARTHA DAY, (daughter of George Day, 3d,) and Abijah Wells, lived where her father did, and had children :

1. Elijah Day Wells, who married 18th June, 1823, Eizabeth Hud on, of Mendham.   He became a Presbyterian minister— preached at ——, in New York.

2. Charles Thompson Wells married and became a Methodist preacher.

JOHN DAY, (son of George Day, 3d,) and Polly Marsh, had children: 1. Charles; 2. George.

JOHN DAY, (said to be son of George Day,) of Long Island, had children : 1. Martin Day, who had a son Absalom.
      2. Nathaniel Day.

NATHANIEL DAY, (son of John Day,) had nine children :

1. Rachel, who married David Peppers.

2. Joseph married, 31st July, 1788, Patty Totten, daughter of Samuel Totten.

3. Hannah married John Graham, of New York, and had no children.

4. Zacheus married, 1st, Sally Locey ; 2d, Sarah Parcels.

5. Josiah married, 2d July, 1795, Dorcas Oakley, born 20th January, 1774, daughter of Thomas, and had no children.

6. Elijah married Polly Oakley, sister of Dorcas, and went to Ohio.

7. Israel married Polly Brant, and went to Ohio ; had several children.

8. Elizabeth married John Harrison ; had but one child, who died in infancy.

I

9. Mary married Jesse V. Douglass, and had children:
  1. Elizabeth, who married Andrew W. Brown, son of Thompson. [*See Brown.*]
  2. Jemima, who married Joseph W. Totten, son of Jonathan.
10. Sarah married Mr. Mills, and had but one son, Lewis Mills.

RACHEL DAY, (daughter of Nathaniel,) and David Peppers, had children:
  1. Polly Peppers, who married David Drew.
  2. Betsey Peppers married Stephen Drew, brother of David.
  3. Jane Peppers, who died at about 18 years, unmarried.
  4. Dorcas Peppers married her cousin, Joseph Day, son of Joseph, son of Nathaniel.

JOSEPH DAY, (2d child of Nathaniel,) and Patty Totten, had children:
  1. Nancy, who married Joshua Sturge, of Green Village.
  2. Rhoda married Simeon Reynolds.
  3. David married Sarah Green.
  4. Israel married Susan Radly, daughter of William.
  5. Aaron, who died at about 18 years.
  6. Josiah married Jenette Day, daughter of Moses, son of Paul Day.
  7. Joseph married his cousin, Dorcas Peppers, daughter of David.

ZACHEUS DAY, (4th child of Nathaniel,) and Sarah Locey, had children:
  1. Elijah married Anne Roff, daughter of Nathaniel, son of Richard, sen.
  2. Polly, who died at about 25 years
  3. Nathaniel died at about 30 years, of consumption.
  Zacheus Day, by his 2d wife, Sarah Parcels, had
  4. Betsey, who married Thomas Williams, lives in Newark, and had children: 1. Anne Williams; 2 George Williams; 3. Hervy Williams, who died young; 4. Emeline Williams; 5. Harriet Williams.
  5. Abby married Miller Derieu, of Madison, and had children: 1. Caroline Derieu; 2. John Derieu.
  6. Israel married Gracia Anne Blazier, daughter of George, of Basking Ridge: children, 1. Abigail; 2. Mary Elizabeth; 3. William; 4. George; 5. David.
  7. Squier married Emeline Bedford, daughter of William D., of New Providence, and had children: 1. Harriet.
  8. Stephen, who went to Ohio with Captain Benjamin Conklin.

ELIJAH DAY, (1st child of Zacheus,) and Anne Roff, lived in Sterling Valley, and had children:
  1. Nathaniel, who married Anne Elizabeth Browning.

2. Erastus married Gertrude Nesty, daughter of William, of Spring Valley.
3. Henry.
4. Mary.
5. Sarah.
6. Abby Anne.

ELIJAH DAY, (6th child of Nathaniel,) and Phebe Oakley, had children :
1. Stephen Snethen.
2. Elias Riggs.
3. Cyrus Bruen.
4. John G. Bergen.

DAVID DAY, ESQ.

DAVID DAY, Esq , (son of George Day, 1st.) owned a farm where Peter Hill, William Crane, and John Littell now live. He sold 50 acres to Jacob Bedell, on which John Littell and Mrs. Elmer now live.

He had five daughters, but no sons.

1. Abigail, who married William Maxwell, son of John Maxwell, of Westfield. (*See Maxwell.*)
2. Sarah married David Harrison ; lived in Cauldwell township.
3. Mary married Matthias Potter, son of Joseph. [*See Potter.*]
4. Jemima married,
    1st, Mr. Day.
    2d, Aaron Wade.
    3d, Mr. Kirkpatrick, who lived at Liberty Corner.
    4th, Rev. Mr. Kennedy, minister at Basking Ridge.
    5th, Jonathan Miller, Sen., of Basking Ridge.
5. Susan married, 1st, Eleazer Crane, of Elizabethtown, bro.her of Benjamin Crane, 2d ; 2d, Matthias Allen.

JOSEPH DAY, (son of George Day, 1st,) married Hannah Sargeant, and had children :
1. Jonathan.
2. Amos, who married Miss Magie.
3. Thomas.
4. Paul, who married, 1st, Elizabeth Thompson ; lived at Chatham ; 2d, Elizabeth Crane ; 3d, Patty Willcox, (of the family of George, at Elizabethtown,) who was the mother of Samuel Condit, of Chatham.
5. Stephen married, 1st, Damaris Foster ; 2d, Jemima, widow of Stephen Johnson, and daughter of Justice John Ogden, of Newark, and sister of Hannah, the wife of the Rev. James Cauldwell.
6. Sarah married Gershom Mott, and had children :
    1. Sarah Mott.
    2. Polly Mott, who married David Thompson.
7. Martha married, 1st, Samuel Lum, father of Israel Lum, Esq. ; 2d, Stephen Howel ; 3d, Mr. —— Carnes, of Mendham.
8. Susannah married, 1st, Mr. —— Darling ; 2d, Mr. ——

3d Generation.

Beach, of Rockaway, and had a daughter, Electa Beach, who married Mr. —— Jackson.

JONATHAN DAY, (son of Joseph, son of George, 1st,) of Long Island, had a son:

1. Daniel, who came to New Jersey, lived at Camptown, now Clinton, and had children:

1. Benjamin, who was a justice of the peace. He married, 1st, Elizabeth Darling, daughter of Thomas; 2d, Elizabeth Roberts, 19th July, 1770, daughter of Daniel Roberts, and sister of Samuel Roberts, Sen., and also sister of Phebe, the wife of Peter Davison.
2. Samuel.
3. Artemas.
4. Timothy married Mehetabel Merry, daughter of John.
5. Daniel, Jun., married.
6. Ezekiel.
7. Jeremiah.
8. Nehemiah.
9. Mary.
10. Keziah.
11. Hannah.
12. David.

BENJAMIN DAY, (1st child of Daniel, son of Jonathan, son of Joseph Day,) and Elizabeth Darling, had children:

1. Stephen, 1st.
2. John.
3. Moses.
4 Darling.
5. Abner.

His wife, Elizabeth Darling, then died, and he, by his 2d wife, Elizabeth Roberts, had other children:

6. Daniel, who married Nancy Morrell, daughter of Abraham, of Elizabethtown.
7. Stephen, 2d, born December, 1778, married, 1st, Sally Mulford, daughter of Cornelius; 2d, Elizabeth Wood, daughter of Captain Daniel S. Wood. He was a captain of the militia.
8. Abigail married, 1st, Jonathan Valentine, son of Obadiah; 2d, John Schureman. [*See Obadiah Valentine.*]
9. Sarah married, 1st, David Valentine, brother of Jonathan, 2d, Aaron Baker, Esq, of Dayton, Ohio.

Benjamin Day, Esq., died September, 1783, and his widow, Elizabeth Roberts, married Obadiah Valentine, as his 3d wife.

DANIEL DAY, (6th child of Benjamin Day Esq., and Nancy Morrell, had children:

5th Generation.
6th Generation.

1. Abraham Morrell.
2. Thomas, who went to Ohio.
3. Eliza.
He died August, 1845, aged 71 years.

CAPT. STEPHEN DAY, (7th child of Benjamin Day, Esq.,
son of Daniel, son of Jonathan, son of Joseph,) and Sally Mulford,
had but one son, Mulford, who married, 1st, Sarah Brookfield,
daughter of Job, of Spring Valley, and had children: 1. Harriet;
2d George Bangheart; 3. Phebe Anne. His wife Sarah then
died, and he married, 2d, Sarah Thompson, daughter of Elias, of
Bordentown, and had other children; 4th, Elias Thompson; 5th,
Rachel; 6th, Betsey; 7th, Benjamin; 8th, Mary Thompson.
Mulford Day died 26th June, 1851.
   2. Daniel, who died in 1805, aged 9 months.
   3. Benjamin, who married Mary Taylor, daughter of Moses, of
Bergen County, New Jersey, and had no children:
   4. Stephen married Rachel Brookfield, daughter of Job, half
sister of Mulford's first wife, and had children: 1. Elizabeth, who
died at about 2½ years; 2. Mulford Brookfield; 3. Daniel Davison.
   5. Peter Davison, married, 1st, Stella Elizabeth Reading, of
Sussex County, and had a son, Watson, who died young, and she
died, and he married, 2d, Jane Voorhies, of Mendham, and had
children: 2. Sarah Elizabeth; 3. Stella Jane; 4. Frances.
   6. Samuel Thomas married Elizabeth Crane, daughter of John,
nd had children: 1. Wilbor Fisk; 2. Waters Burrows; 3. Johna
Crane; 4. Benjamin; 5. Stephen Sylvester.
   7. Waters, who accidentally shot himself when a young man,
and died.
   8. Daniel W. married, 17th November, 1847, Caroline Parrot,
daughter of Squier, and had children: 1. Squier Parrot.
   9. Francis Asbury married, 16th November, 1847, Hannah D.
Hick, daughter of William, of New York, and had children: 1.
Sarah Elizabeth.
   10. William McKendry married, 28th September, 1847, Lydia
Anne Cole, daughter of Watson, of Trenton, and had children:
   1. Sarah Elizabeth; 2. Edwin Augustus.
   11. Edwin Augustus.

TIMOTHY DAY, (4th child of Daniel, son of Jonathan,
son of Joseph Day,) and Mehetabel Merry, lived at Chatham,
and had children:
   1. Israel, born 15th November. 1765, and married, 3d May,
1785, Elizabeth Ludlow, born 25th April, 1767, daughter of
Col Cornelius Ludlow, of Long Hill.
   2. Betsey married, 1st, Capt. Benjamin Pettit, 3d; [*see
Pettit;*] 2d, Amos Potter, Esq., son of Daniel, 2d. [*See Potter.*]

COL. ISRAEL DAY, (son of Timothy,) was a colonel of
cavalry, justice of the peace, commissioner of deeds, and elder

of the Presbyterian church in Chatham. He and Elizabeth
Ludlow had children :

    1. Benjamin Ludlow, who married Harriet Kipp, of New York,
and had children : 1. Margaret ; 2. Eliza ; 3. Helen Kipp, who
died 7th February, 1850, unmarried.

    2. Mehetabel married John Colwell, son of Hugh, of Long
Hill, and had children :

        1. James married Martha High, daughter of Ephraim, son of
        Jacob High.

        2. Hugh died a young man, unmarried.

        3. Israel Day married —— ——.

        4. Elizabeth is unmarried.

    Mr. Colwell then died, and she married Stephen Cooper, son of
Daniel, 2d, Esq., and had a daughter : ·

        5. Sally Anne, who married her cousin, William Cooper,
        son of Peter.

    3. Agnes, who married Doct. Elias Runyon, son of Elias, of
Long Hill ; had no children : live at New Market, Middlesex
county.

    AMOS DAY, (son of Joseph, son of George Day, 1st) and Miss
—— Magie, had children :

    1. Amos Day, Jun., who married, as his 2d wife, Patty
Denman ; 2. Isaac ; 3. Aaron ; 4. Sophia ; 5. Phebe ; 6. Polly.

    THOMAS DAY, (son of Joseph, son of George Day, 1st,)
married —— ——, and had children :

    1. Elizabeth, who married, 1st, Mr. Gibbon ; 2. Mr. Parkison.

    PAUL DAY, (4th child of Joseph, son of George Day, 1st,) and
Elizabeth Thompson, had children :

    1. Thaddeus, who married Susanna Parcel, daughter of Henry.

    2. Paul, Jun., who died young.

    3. Betsey married her cousin, Israel Lum, Esq , son of Samuel·

    4. Moses married Joanna Bonnel, daughter of John, son of
Nathaniel, 1st.

    5. Abigail married Philip Minthorn.

    6. Rachel married George Minthorn, brother of Philip.

    7. Matthias married Hannah Ward, daughter of Gen. Thomas
Ward, of Newark.

    8. Hannah married James Kitchel, son of the Hon. Aaron
Kitchel, of Morris county.

    THADDEUS DAY, (1st child of Paul Day,) and Susanna Parcel,
had children :

    1. Joseph, who married Polly Brown, and had children :

        1. David, who married Ellen Britton, daughter of Stephen ; live
        in Newark.

        2. Louisa married Smith Gold, above Morristown.

3. Aaron married Abigail Baldwin, daughter of Stephen, of Cheapside.

4. Caroline married Osborn Hedges, of Hanover.

5. Electa married Mr. Reeves, of Cheapside.

6. Hervy P. married Miss Baldwin, Cheapside.

7. Mary married Stephen Foster, of Rensellaer.

2. Catherine, who married Peter Dickerson, son of Philemon, 1st. [*See Dickerson.*]

3 Paul married, 1st, Amutal Ward, daughter of Capt. Enos Ward ; 2d. Sarah Pierson, daughter Gabriel Pierson, niece of his first wife. He had no children.

4. Charles Thompson married Polly Woolley, daughter of Jacob, of Springfield.

5. Henry Parcels Day was blind ; he died at about 30 years.

6. Electa married Benjamin Winget, son of Benjamin, of Madison, and had no children.

CHARLES THOMPSON DAY, (4th child of Thaddeus, son of Paul, son of Joseph Day,) and Polly Woolley, had children :

1. Jacob, who married ———.

2. Madison, twin to Jacob, died young.

3. Catherine.

4. Hannah married Abner Baldwin, son of David, of Cheapside. [*See Baldwin.*]

5. Hetty married Mr. Scofield, of Newark.

6. Mary married Mr. Appleton, of New York.

7. Sarah married Nehemiah Baldwin, of Newark, as his 2d wife.

8. Paul.

9. Henrietta.

10. Julianne.

BETSEY DAY, (3d child of Paul, son of Joseph Day,) and Israel Lum, Esq , had children :

1. Stephen Lum, who married ——— ——— and lives in Newark, and had children: 1. William Lum ; 2. John ; 3. Hannah ; 4. Margaret.

Israel Lum, Esq., by his 2d wife Patience Pierson, daughter of Benjamin Pierson, above Morristown, had children :

2. Benjamin Pierson Lum, who was a judge, and justice of the peace, and who married Temperance Muchmore, daughter of Samuel, of Madison, and has an only child, Benjamin Pierson Lum, Jun.

3. Israel Lum married Hetty Fairclo daughter of Isaiah, of Flanders, and had children : 1. Caroline Lum ; 2. Elizabeth Lum.

4. Paul Lum married Charlotte Bonnel, daughter of Enos ; had no children.

5. Samuel Lum married Amutal Genung, daughter of David.

6. Betsey Lum married Samuel Day, son of Amos, of Union, and brother of William Day, the butcher of Union.

7. Nancy Lum married William Kelly, son of Thomas Kelly.

Samuel Lum, (son of Israel Lum, Esq.,) and Amutal Genung, had children :

1. Charles Lum, who married Miss Muchmore, daughter of John T.
2. Hervy Lum married, 1st, Harriet Sturges ; 2. Miss Bruen, daughter of Ashbel.
3. Phebe Anne Lum.
4. Caroline Lum.

Betsey Lum, and Samuel Day, had an only son, 1. Israel Lum Day, who married —— ——, in Easton.

Nancy Lum, and William Kelly, had children :
　　1. Nelson Kelly ; 2. Hervy Kelly ; 3. Charles Kelly: 4. William Kelly, Jun.

MOSES DAY, (4th child of Paul, son of Joseph Day,) and Joanna Bonnel, had children :
　　1. Charles, who married Polly Bonnel, daughter of Nathaniel, 3d, and had a daughter, Elizabeth Day.
　　2. Betsey married Nathan Potter, son of Jacob Potter. [*See Potter.*]
　　3. Matthias, who went to Cincinnati, Ohio, and married, and had children : 1. Nemina ; 2. Sophia ; 3. Matthias, Jun.
　　4. Nancy lives in Newark.
　　5. Franklin married Prussia King, daughter of Doct. King and Prussia Bonnel.
　　6. Sylvanus went to Ohio.
　　7. Emulus went to Ohio.
　　8. Henry went to Ohio.
　　9. Jenette married Josiah Day, son of Joseph, son of Nathaniel Day.
　　10. Thaddeus, who died young.
　　11. William.

MATTHIAS DAY, (7th son of Paul, son of Joseph Day,) and Hannah Ward, lived in Newark, and had children :
　　1. Charles Thompson, who married Elizabeth Miller.
　　2. Matthias, Jun. married Henrietta Tenbrook, of New York.
　　3. William Ward married Eliza Canfield, daughter of Jabez, of Newark.
　　4. Sarah.

STEPHEN DAY, Esq., (5th son of Joseph, son of George Day, 1st,) and his 1st wife, Damaris Foster, had children:
　　1. Joanna, who married, 1st, Moses Lum, and had a daughter :
　　　　1. Mary, who married Doct. John C. Budd ; when Mr. Lum died, and she married Ichabod Ward, son of David Ward. [*See Ward.*]
　　2. Elizabeth, who died unmarried.
　　3. Elijah, born 24th January, 1757, and died unmarried.
　　4. William married Nancy Bonnel, daughter of John, and kept tavern at Chatham.
　　5. Nancy married (Tailor) John Bonnel, son of Benjamin, Esq. [*See Bonnel.*]

6. David died at Pittsburg, in 1794, unmarried. He went out in the New Jersey regiment, against the Whisky Boys.

7. Mary married Isaac Samson, son of David. [See Samson.]

8. Stephen, Jun., married Polly Bonnel, daughter of Benjamin, Esq, sister of Nancy's husband. By his 2d wife, Jemima, Stephen Day, Esq., had children:

9. Elijah, 2d, married Phebe Crane, daughter of John Crane, of Orange, and had a daughter Adaline, who married Charles Alling, of Newark, and had a child, and soon after died, and the child died.

10. Electa, who died in infancy.

11. David Ogden married Maria Stackhouse, daughter of Samuel, of Elizabethtown.

Mary Lum, (daughter of Moses Lum and Joanna Day,) and Doct. John C. Budd, had children:

1. Bern W. Budd, who married Catherine Reynolds, daughter of David, of Madison.

2. John S. Budd married Charlotte Ward, daughter of Aaron M., son Israel Ward.

3. Mary C. Budd married John Meeker, son of Daniel H., son of Isaiah Meeker. [See Meeker.]

4. Joanna Vashti Budd married, 1st, Parrot Reynolds, son of William; 2d, Noble Barry, from Ireland.

5. Jane C. Budd married Israel Dickerson, son of D. Brainard Dickerson. [See Dickerson.]

6. Vincent B. Budd married, 1st, Nancy Ward, daughter of John, son of David; 2. Jane Hancock, daughter of Rev. John Hancock.

7. Phebe Budd married, 1st, Edwin Tryon, son of Rowland Tryon, of Connecticut; 2d, Mr. Loundsbury, of Michigan, and lives there.

8. Susan A. Budd married Ambrose Bruen, son of Carter, of Madison.

Doct. Budd married, 2d, the widow Betsey Cobert, of New York, and had other children:

9. Eliza Budd, who married Stewart Marsh, son of John T. Marsh, of Rahway.

10. Sarah Budd married George Servin, and live in Elizabethtown, and had a daughter, Sarah Servin.

Bern W. Budd, (son of Doctor John C. Budd,) and Catherine Reynolds, had children:

1. Elizabeth R. Budd, who married Thomas Gallaudet, of New York, 2. David R. Budd; 3. Bern L. Budd; 4. Charles A. Budd.

John S. Budd, (2d child of Doctor Budd,) and Charlotte Ward, had children:

1. John C. Budd, who married Bridget Warren; 2. Thomas D. Budd; 3. Nancy A. Budd; 4. Sylvester I. Budd; 5. Stephen Boplan Bausabin Budd; 6. Caroline E. Budd; 7. Ellen Day Budd; 8. Ludlow Day Budd; 9. George S. Budd; 10. Mary E. Budd.

9. Joanna Vashti Budd, 4th ehild of Doct. Budd, had no living chid by Parrot Reynolds. By Noble Barry, she had only one daughter, Emma Barry.

Jane C. Budd, (5th child of Doctor Budd,) and Israel Dickerson, had children: 1. David B. Dickerso;n 2. Sarah A. Dickerson; 3. Bern W. Dickerson; 4. Caroline L. Dickerson.

Vincent Budd, (6th child of Doctor Budd,) and Nancy Ward had children: 1. Thomas Bond Budd; 2. Melissa Ward Budd. And by Jane Hancock had children: 3. Jane Hancock Budd; 4. Benjamin Ward Budd.

Phebe Budd, (7th child of Doctor Budd,) and Edwin Tyson, had children: 1. Charles Tyson; 2. Ambrose Tyson; 3. Caroline Tyson; 4. William Tyson; 5. Israel Tyson.

Susa'n A. Budd, (8th child of Doctor Budd,) and Ambrose Bruen, had children: 1. Lewis B. Bruen; 2. Caleb C. Bruen; 3. John C. Bruen.

Eliza Budd, (9th child of Doctor Budd,) and Stewart Marsh, had children: 1. Albert Marsh; 2. John Marsh.

CAPT. WLILIAM DAY, (4th child of Stephen Day, Esq.. son of Joseph,) and Nancy Bonnel, lived in Chatham, and had children:

1. Foster, who married Susan Smith, daughter of Doct. Peter Smith, of Chatham.

2. Sally married Henry Crane, son of Capt. John Crane, of Chatham.

3. Charlotte married Frederick Smith, of Chatham.

4. Lewis, who died a young man.

5. Calvin, who also died a young man.

6. Joanna married Ichabod Burnet, son of Daniel Burnet, of Madison.

5th Generation.

FOSTER DAY, (son of Captain William Day,). and Susan Smith, had children; 1. Lewis; 2. William Foster; 3. Richards.

6th Gen.

STEPHEN DAY, Jun., (8th child of Stephen Day, Esq., son of Joseph,) und Polly Bonnel, had children:

1. Jane, who married Moses Ward, son of Ichabod. [See Ward.]

2. Elias is a Presbyterian minister in Wayne county, Penn.

3. Mary married Mr. Ketchum, near Bethany, Wayne county.

4. Barna.

5. Edwin married Fidelia Gleason, of Connecticut.

6. Lewis married, and lived with his father in Wayne county, Pennyslvania.

5th Generation.

DAVID O. DAY, (11th child of Stephen Day, Esq., son of Joseph,) and Maria Stackhouse, had children:

1. Harriet is unmarried.

2. John Ogden Day married Emily Brown, 30th September, 1840, daughter of Jonathan, and had children:

     1. Eugene; 2. Webster; 3. Robert Baldwin.

5th Generation.

3. Flavel Woodruff, born 5th February, 1813, and died 12th September, 1815.

4. Hannah Maria, born 10th February, 1815, and died 30th October, 1831.

5. Flavel Woodruff. 2d, born 28th Nov. 1816, married Miss Reynolds, daughter of Samuel Reynolds, Esq., above Busking Ridge.

6. James Oliver.

NOTE—Jemima, the 2d wife of Stephen Day, Esq., had by her 1st husband, Stephen Johnson, two children :
1. Jonathan Johnson, who married Abigail Bonnel, daughter of Benjamin Bonnel, Esq.
2 Hannah Johnson, who is unmarried. She lives with David O. Day, and is nearly 80 years old.

MARTHA DAY, (7th child of Joseph, son of George Day, 1st,) and Samuel Lum, her first husband, had children: Israel Lum, who married Betsey Day, 3d child of Paul Day, [see Paul Day,] and had an only son, Stephen Lum, who married, lives in Newark, and had children: 1. William; 2. John; 3. Hannah; 4. Margaret.

After the death of Stephen Lum, she married, 2d, Stephen Howel, and had children :

4th Generation.

1. Luther Howel, who married Miss Young, of Whippany.
2. Calvin Howel married Polly Sayre, daughter of Ephraim, of Madison.
3. David Howel married Sally Burnet, daughter of Josiah.

Calvin Howel, (2d son of Stephen Howel and Martha Day,) and Polly Sayre, had children :

5th Generation.

1. Cornelia Howel, who married Philemon Dickerson, son of Peter. [See Dickerson.]
2. Rachel Howel married Samuel Hopping, son of Daniel, of East Madison.
3. Eliza Howel married Benjamin Cook, Jun., son of Benjamin of Madison, and had a son, Elias Cook, when Benjamin, Jun., died.
4. Martha Howel married Mathias F. Noe, son of John. [See Noe.]
5. Stephen Howel married Martha Way.
6. Ephraim Howel, who died at about 17 years.

PHILEMON DICKERSON.

PHILEMON DICKERSON lived at the east end of Sterling Valley, on the road to Morristown. He married Johannah Sweazy, above Morristown. He died 12th April, 1777, aged 38 years. His widow married Isaac Badgley. He had children:

1. David Brainard, who married Sally Baldwin, daughter of Capt. Enos Baldwin, of Cheapside, and lived there.
2. Peter married Catherine Day, daughter of Thaddeus, son of Paul.
3. Caleb married Matilda Brown, daughter of Daniel, of Madison.
4. Hannah married, 19th February, 1767, Lot Darling.
5. Philemon, Jun., who died, 5th August, 1776, aged 14 months.

DAVID BRAINARD DICKERSON, (1st son of Philemon,) and Sally Baldwin, had children:

1. Philemon, who married Hetty Paradise; lived in Springfield, and was a justice of the peace there.

2. Sarah married William Gibbs; had no children.

3. Mary, who died unmarried.

4. Israel married Caroline Budd, daughter of Doctor J. C. Budd. [*See Day and Budd.*]

PHILEMON DICKERSON, Esq., (son of D. Brainard,) and Hetty Paradise, had children:

1. William, who married Euphemia Kelly.

2. John married, 1st, widow Ellen Camp, and daughter of Isaac Roll, son of John Roll; 2. Mary Stackhouse.

3. Sarah Anne married Stephen Shafer.

4. Philemon, Jun., married Mary Roll, sister of John's first wife.

5. Wesley.

6. Julianne married Theodore Birt, son of Jacob, of Springfield.

PETER DICKERSON, (2d son of Philemon,) and Catherine Day, had children:

1. Philemon married, 1st, Cornelia Howel, daughter of Calvin; 2. Hannah, widow of Squier Badgley, and daughter of Benjamin Sturges.

2. Paul, who died aged 20 years.

PHILEMON DICKERSON, (son of Peter,) and Cornelia Howel, had children:

1. Calvin, who married, 1st, Mary Ulick, daughter of Adam, of Hackets Town, and had a daughter, Mary Catherine. His wife then died and he married; 2d, Miss Tester, of Sterling Valley.

2. Paul.

3. Mary Catherine, who died 22d July, 1841, aged 21 years.

4. Cornelia married, 15th May, 1845, Samuel Schureman, son of John McClasky Schureman, and went to Illinois.

5. Peter; 6. Eliza; 7. Sarah Anne; 8. Electa; 9. William Day; 10. Stephen; 11. Mary Catherine, 2d.

CALEB DICKERSON, (3d son of Philemon,) and Matilda Brown, had children:

1. Samuel, who married Mary Freeman, of Woodbridge.

2. Mary is unmarried.

3. Brainard married Mary Ridgeway, of Staten Island, and went to Ohio.

4. Caleb is unmarried.

5. David went to Tuscaloosa, and married there, Elizabeth Mallard.

6. Wesley went to Natchez, Mississippi, and married Elizabeth Wright, and died there.

7. Philemon married Catherine Griffin, daughter of William M.

8. Israel, who died young.

9. Caroline married David A. Harrison, son of Abraham, of Orange.

DANIEL DOD.

Capt. Robert Treat, John Curtis, Jasper Crane, and John Treat, were sent, in 1660, from Branford, Milford, and Guilford, in Connecticut, to view the country and lands in New Jersey. They returned and reported favorably, and were sent back with power to select a site for a town, and make a purchase. The result at that time was a purchase of the township of Newark, by its ancient boundaries.

The Indians called the town Passaic, but the inhabitants, called it Newark, after a town in England, from which the Rev. Mr. Pierson, their pastor, had come. Trumbull, the historian, says that Mr. Pierson, and almost his whole church and congregation, soon removed from Branford to Newark, and carried with them the church records. This removal took place some time previous to the 24th of June, 1667.

DANIEL DOD, Jun., eldest son of Daniel Dod, Sen., came to Newark, a minor, probably with the colony from Branford. He had a lot of land for his home lot in Newark, about Bridge Street, and northward.

His farm lands were on the hill west of the town. In the year 1678, Daniel Dod and Edward Ball were appointed to run the northern line of the town, from the Passaic to the Mountain. He was chosen deputy to the provincial assembly in 1692.

Of the three sons of Daniel Dod, Jun., viz. Daniel, 3d, Stephen, and John, Daniel, 3d, lived the longest, and died about 1766, being eighty years of age or upwards.

From 1721 to 1731, Daniel Dod, 3d, was filling the office of freeholder and surveyor; then living on his patrimony. In the year 1737, his brother John appears in the office of surveyor. In the year 1754, John's son John, then called John-3d, was appointed Assessor about the year 1762, the names of Isaac and Amos Dod begin to appear as town officers. Isaac was a captain, and at the beginning of the revolution was appointed justice of the peace, and continued to sustain that office till his death, in 1804. Amos Dod was also captain, and Caleb Dod major, in the same regiment.

DANIEL DOD, from England, married Mary ———, probably about the year 1646. He died in the winter of 1664–5. She died 26th May, 1657. They were both buried in Branford; they had children:

1. Mary, born 1647, and married Aaron Blachley, about 1664.
2. Daniel, Jun., born in 1649, or 1650.
3. Ebenezer, born 11th December, 1651, and died about 1675.
4. A daughter, born 29th March, 1653, died ——— ———.
5. Stephen, born 16th February, 1655, and died in Guilford, October, 1691, in his 37th year. He married, 18th May, 1678, Mary Stevens, and had children, Daniel and Stephen; his wife died previous to 1691.
6. Samuel, born 2d May, 1657. *His* family ran out in the female line.

7. Anne, who married Mr. Fowler.

DANIEL DOD, Jun , (son of Daniel, 1st,) had children :
1. Daniel, 3d, married Mary Alling, of Newark, and died at 80 years.
2. Stephen, 2d, married Phebe Harrison.
3. John married Miss Samson.
4. Dorcas married Mr. Ward, the ancestor of Zebina Ward, probably his grandfather.

DANIEL DOD, 3d, (son of Daniel Dod, Jun.,) and Mary Alling, had children :
1. Eunice, born 3d November, 1718, married David Baldwin, and had eight sons and two daughters, and died, 20th October, 1803, aged 85 years.
2. Sarah, born 18th December, 1720, and married ,Timothy Freeman, and had three sons and one daughter.
3. Thomas, born 7th January, 1723, married Sarah Newcombe. He died 8th September, 1815, aged 92 years, 8 months. She died 31st March, 1791, in her 68th year.
4. Daniel, 4th born 1st May, 1725, married, 1st, Jane Smith; 2d, the widow Martha Harrison. He died 1795, without children.
5. Isaac, born 8th July, 1728, married Jemima Williams, born 6th January, 1729. He died 19th August, 1804, aged 76 years. She died 25th July, 1810, aged 81 years.
6. Joseph, born 12th September, 1731, died 4th June, 1789, n his 58th year. He married, 1st, Mary Lindsley, who died 14ht Feb 1763, aged 29 years He married, 2d, Sarah Williams, who idied 2d, September, 1818, aged 76 years.
7. Moses, born 18th June, 1734, and died in youth.
8. Amos, born 15th September, 1737, and died 7th October, 1811, aged 74 years. He married Hannah Condit, who died 23d June, 1826, in her 68th year.
9. Caleb, born 26th May, 1740, and died in Cauldwell. He married Hannah Harrison.

THOMAS DOD, (3d child of Daniel Dod, 3d,) and Sarah Newcombe, had children :
1. Eunice, who married Joseph Crane, and died 20th Feb. 1822, aged 80 years.
2. Ezekiel married ——— ———, and had a daughter, Jemima.
3. Samuel married ——— ———, and had children :
1. Hannah; 2. Isaac; 3. David.
4 Nancy married Amos Tomkins.
5. Elias married Lydia Ward, and had children :
1. George; 2. Abraham; 3. Charlotte.
6. Daniel married ——— ———, and had children :
1. Robert ; 2. Nancy.
7. Enos married Mary Edo, and had children :
1. Jemima, born 24st October, 1776, married Samuel ,Dodd,

4th; 2. Aaron, born 19th October, 1779; 3. Sarah, born 2d Dec. 1782; 4. Samuel. born 6th March, 1787; 5. Jonas and Hannah, (twins,) born 28th March, 1792; 6. Jonas, born 6th Sept. 1796.

8. Jonathan married Eunice Smith, and had children:
    1. Hiram; 2. Phebe; 3. Thomas.
9. Thomas married Mary Hallam, and had children:
    1. John; 2. William.
10. Sarah married ——— ———.

ISAAC DODD, (5th child of Daniel Dod, 3d,) and Jemima Williams, had children:
1. Sarah, born 2d March, 1753, married, 1st Matthias Baldwin; 2. Aura King, and raised two sons and two daughters, and died 1838, aged 85 years.
2. Moses, who married Lois Crane.
3. Abijah, born 9th November, 1758, died September, 1837.
4. Abby, born 8th October, 1759, died 24th December, 1764.
5. Joanna, born 9th March, 1762, married Isaac Baldwin.
6. Abby, 2d, born 26th October, 1764, married Joseph Dodd, 3d.
7. Jephtha, born 17th May, 1767, died young.
8. Jairus, born 21st January, 1770, married 9th September, 1792, Sarah Davis.
9. Isaac, Jun., born 23d December, 1772. He married the widow Jane Smith, and died 8th September, 1806.

MOSES DODD, (2d child of Isaac,) was born 9th December, 1755, married, 3d July, 1775, Lois Crane, born 26th March, 17 54, and died 17th October, 1818; they had children:
1. Stephen, born 8th March, 1777, married, 1st Phebe Pierson, 29th November, 1799. She was born 25th August, 1776, and died 27th February, 1815. He married, 2d, Abigail Anne Law.

NOTE.—Stephen Dodd became a preacher of the gospel; was ordained 28th September, 1803; supplied two congregations seven years, in the town of Carmel, Dutchess county, N. Y. In October, 1810, he removed to the town of Waterbury, Connecticut, and became pastor of the Congregational church of Salem. He resigned that office in 1817, and, the 10th December, 1817, was installed pastor of the Congregational church in East Hanover, and was there still in 1839.

2. Hiram, 2d child of Moses, born 22d Nov. 1779, died 21st July, 1823. He married, 14th Feb. 1799, Julia Crane, and had children:
    1. Abel Jackson; 2. Christiana; 3. Fanny; 4. Mehetabel, who died 25th June, 1815, aged 12 years; 5. Moses; 6. Jairus; 7. Lois; 8. Stephen; 9. Lewis; 10. Margaret, who died young.
3. Abigail, born 20th January, 1782, married, 31st January, 1800, Jacob Ward, Jun.
4. Betsey, born 3d May, 1784, married, 15th October, 1803, Henry King.
5. Ira, born 22d June, 1786, married, 20th September, 1810, Anne Harrison.

6. Fanny, born 25th April, 1791, and married, 15th February, 1813, Rev. Humphry M. Perrine.

IRA DODD, (5th child of Moses,) and Anne Harrison, had children :
    1. Mary, who married Isaac Newton Dodd.
    2. Moses Woodruff, who is a bookseller in New York.
    3. Phebe.
    4. Amarintha.

ABIJAH DODD, (3d child of Isaac Dodd, married Mary Dodd, and had children :
    1. Jephtha married. 1st, Eunice Baldwin, and had children :
        1. Betsey ; 2. Mary. And by his 2d wife, Phebe Munn, had a daughter Jane.
    2. Cyrus married Mary King, and had a daughter Catherine.
    3. Rhoda.
    4. Lucy, who died young.
    5. Isaac married Catherine Canfield, and had children :
        1. Horace ; 2. Edwin.
    6. Joel married Betsey Harrison, and had children :
        1. Phebe ; 2. Mary ; 3. Jane ; 4. Cyrus ; 5. David.
    7. David.
    8. Morris.
    9. Abijah, Jun.
    10. Lucy, 2d, married Thomas Exley.

JAIRUS DODD, (8th child of Isaac Dodd, son of Daniel, 3d.) born 21st January, 1770, married, 9th September, 1792, Sarah Davis, and had children :
    1. Joanna, born 23d January, 1794 ; 2. William, born 6th June, 1795 ; 3. Abigail, born 4th June, 1797, 4. Isaac Davis, born 17th April, 1799 ; 5. Sarah, born April, 1801 ; 6. Ambrose, born 22d January, 1803 ; 7. Moses, born 20th March, 1805 ; 8. Mary, born 20th May, 1807 ; 9. John, born 4th June, 1809 ; 10. Nathaniel, born 13th October, 1811.

ISAAC DODD, Jun., (9th child of Isaac, son of Daniel, 3d,) and the widow Jane Smith, had children :
    1. Morace St. John, who died in infancy.
    2. Rollin Horace, who also died in infancy.
    3. Hannah, who married Caleb Davis.
    4. Lydia, who married Marquis D. Thomas.

JOSEPH DODD, (6th child of Daniel Dodd, 3d,) and Mary Lindsley, had children :
    1. Matthias, who married Sarah Munn.
    2. Ebenezer married Deborah Crane.

3. Rachel married Bethuel Munn.

4. Joseph. Jun , married Eunice Baldwin, born 5th March, 1763 ; she d ed in 1814.

5. Mary, twin to Joseph, Jun , born 10th October, 1760, married Aaron Williams.

Joseph Dodd, by his 2d wife, Sarah Williams, had other children :

6. Abigail, born 1769, and died 1st September, 1777, aged 8 years.

7. Amos.

8. Daniel.

9. Moses married Mary Smith.

10. Lydia married James Reynolds.

11. Abby married Samuel Crane.

12. Allen married Mary Osborn.

MATTHIAS DODD, (1st son of Joseph, son of Daniel, 3d,) and Sarah Munn, had children :

1. Jared, who went to sea, and was pressed into the British navy.

2. William was killed by lightning, 18th June, 1799, on Governor's Island, aged 20 years.

3. Rachel, at 20 years old, was drowned, together with her father and cousin Munn, at Coney Island, in 1800.

4. Lewis ; 5. Abby ; 6. Charlotte ; 7. Nancy ; 8. Mary ; 9. Bethuel.

EBENEZER DODD, (2d son of Joseph, son of Daniel, 3d,) and Deborah Crane, had children :

1. Betsey ; 2. Orra Buel ; 3 Mary ; 4. Nancy ; 5. Lois ; 6. Ebenezer. Jun. ; 7. Joseph Holloway ; 8. Joseph Horton ; 9. John ; 10. Valeria.

JOSEPH DODD, Jun., (3d child of Joseph, son of Daniel, 3d,) and Eunice Baldwin, had children :

1. Mary, born 27th March, 1786.

2. Sarah, born 11th September, 1788, died in 1813.

3. Joseph, 3d, born 12th September, 1790, married, in 1813, Nancy Clark.

4. Louisa, born 1st November, 1792.

5. Zophar Baldwin, born 28th October, 1794, married Jane Cochran, born 12th May, 1794.

6. Lydia, born 1st November, 1796.

7. Martha, born 27th November, 1798, and died in 1805.

8. William, born 28th February. 1801, and died in 1824.

9. Matthias, born 3d April, 1803, and died in 1805.

K

JOSEPH DODD, 3d, (3d son of Joseph Dodd, Jun.,) and Nancy Clark, had children :

1. Sarah ; 2. Amarintha ; 3. Caroline ; 4. Margaret ; 5. George ; 6. William ; 7. Eunice.

6th Gen.

ZOPHAR B. DODD, (5th child of Joseph Dodd, Jun., son of Joseph,) and Jane Cochran, had children :

1. Thomas Cochran, born 15th January, 1818.
2. Sarah Louisa, born 22d February, 1819.
3. Mary Jane, born 23d May, 1820.
4. Esther Caroline, born 19th December, 1821.
5. Edward Mills, born 22d June, 1824.
6. Esther Catherine, born 26th June, 1829.
7. Catherine Mariah, born 8th October, 1835.

6th Generation.

MOSES DODD, (9th child of Joseph 1st, son of Daniel, 3d,) and Mary Smith, had children :

1. Mary ; 2. Moses, Jun. ; 3. Edward ; 4. Jane.

ALLEN DODD, (11th child of Joseph, 1st, son of Daniel, 3d,) and Mary Osborn, had children :

1. Joseph, who died, 3d September, 1816, in his 5th year.
2. George ; 3. Daniel ; 4. Mary ; 5. Elizabeth.

AMOS DODD, (8th child of Daniel Dod, 3d,) and Hannah Condit, had children:

1. Isaac, born 27th June, 1763, married Polly James, who died 8th December, 1826, in her 68th year.
2. Eunice, born 2d June, 1765, married Joel Williams.
3. Mary, born 29th July, 1768, married John Condit.
4. Sarah, born 4th August, 1770, married Squier Baldwin, and died 25th November, 1832.
5. Elizabeth, born 28th February, 1773, and died 4th October, 1776.
6. Daniel, born 2d March, 1776, married Esther Ward.
7. Amos, Jun, born 4th October, 1781, married Polly Canfield.

ISAAC DODD, (1st son of Amos, 8th child of Daniel, 3d,) and Polly James, had children :

1. Betsey, who married Eleazer D. Ward.
2. Lucy married Jabez Cook.
3. Mariah.

DANIEL DODD, (6th child of Amos, 8th child of Daniel, 3d,) and Esther Ward, had children :

1. Phebe, who married Jacob K. Mead ; 2. Lewis ; 3. Josiah ; 4. Philetta ; 5. Abby ; 6. Isaac Newton ; 7. Sarah Anne ; 8. Augustus.

AMOS DODD, Jun., (7th child of of Amos, 8th child of Daniel, 3d,) and Polly Canfield, had children:
1. James Collard; 2. David Canfield; 3. Harriet Newel.

CALEB DODD, (9th child of Daniel Dod, 3d,) and Hannah Harrison, had children:
1. Rebecca, who married Joseph Patterson.
2. Elijah married Lois Williams, and had one son, Jabez, and four daughters. One of his daughters married William Scott, and another married the Rev. Mr. Thanhouse.
3. Caleb, Jun., married Polly Bates, and had children:
    1. Elijah; 2. Phebe; 3. Sarah; 4. Philemon; 5. Ezra Squiers.

STEPHEN DOD, 2d, (2d son of Daniel Dod, Jun., son of Daniel, 1st,) and Phebe Harrison, had children:
1. Nathaniel, who married Ruth Condit.
2. Silas married Hannah Smith.
3. Stephen, 3d, married Ruth Peck.
4. Joshua married Abigail Condit.
5. Phebe married Jonathan Williams.

4th Generation.

NATHANIEL DODD, (1st child of Stephen, 2d, son of Daniel, Jun.,) and Ruth Condit, had children:
1. Parmeneus, who married Jane Crane.
2. Matthew married Charlotte Martin, and died 20th April, 1826.
3. Mary married Daniel Condit.
4. Lydia.
5. Jane married Nathaniel Harrison.
6. Reuben married Lydia Dodd.
Reuben was drowned in the Narrows of New York Bay in 1802.

PARMENEUS DODD, (1st son of Nathaniel, son of Stephen, 2d,) and Jane Crane, had children:
1. Thaddeus; 2. Nathaniel; 3. Stephen; 4. Jephtha; 5. Daniel; 6. Matthew; 7. Albert; 8. Abner; 9. Reuben; 10. Isaac.

MATTHEW DODD, (2d son of Nathaniel, son of Stephen, 2d,) and Charlotte Martin, had children:
1. Jane; 2. Caroline, who died at two years.

REUBEN DODD, (6th child of Nathaniel, son of Stephen, 2d,) and Lydia Dodd, had children:
1. Zebina; 2. Nathaniel.

SILAS DOD, (2d child of Stephen Dod, 2d,) and Hannah Smith, had children:
1. Dorcas, who married Sophia Condit.
2. Jane married Amos Munn.

STEPHEN DODD, 3d, (3d child of Stephen Dod, 2d,) and Ruth Peck, had children :
1. Jemima ; 2. Phebe ; 3, Stephen, 4th; 4. Jeriah; 5. Abigail.

JOSHUA DODD, (4th child of Stephen Dod, 2d,) and Abigail Condit, had children :
1. Bethuel graduated at (Queen's now) Girard College New Brunswick, and became the pastor of the Presbyterian church at Whitesborough, New York, about 1794, and died 1799.
2. Nathaniel, who married Lucy Baldwin.
3. Phebe married Ichabod Harrison.
4. Betsey married Stephen Harrison.

NATHANIEL DODD, (2d child of Joshua Dodd,) and Lucy Baldwin, had children :
1. Bethuel ; 2. Matthias ; 3. Robert ; 4. Alvin ; 5. William.

JOHN DOD, (3d child of Daniel Dod, Jun.,) and Miss Samson, had children :
1. John, Jun., who married Jane Smith.
2. David married Sarah Harrison.
He died 31st March, 1817, aged 83. She died 12th March, 1827, aged 90 years.
3. Abigail married Job Crane.
4. Mary married David Chandler.
5. Phebe married Elihu Ward.
6. Elizabeth married John Peck.

JOHN DODD, Jun., (1st son of John, son of Daniel Dod, Jun.,) and Jane Smith, had children :
1. Hannah, who married Bethuel Ward.
2. Eleazer married Abigail Harrison.
3. Uzel married Phebe Freeman.
4. John, 3d, born 5th November, 1761, and died 5th Sept. 1826, aged 65 years. He was colonel of the militia, and commanded the detachment composing the Essex county regiment at Sandy Hook, in 1814, and subsequently became general. He married Abigail Dodd.
5. Linus, who married Betsey Pierson.

ELEAZAR DODD, (2d child of John Dodd, Jun,,) and Abigail Harrison, had children :
1. Hannah ; 2. Stephen ; 3. Abiel ; 4. Lydia.

UZEL DODD, (3d son of John Dodd, Jun., son of John,) and Phebe Freeman, had children :
1. Mary, who married Caleb Baldwin.

2 Samuel Morris, and his only son Samuel C., both died 21th October. 1831, by entering into an old cistern to cleanse it, and died, as was supposed, in consequence of bad air in it.
3. Amanda.
4. Lucinda.

GEN. JOHN DODD, (4th child of John Dodd, Jun.,) and Abigail Dodd, had children :
1. Jemima.
2. Jane, who married Joseph Rogers.
3. Joseph Smith graduated at Princeton College in 1813. He studied physic. and practised in Bloomfield and vicinity. He married Miss Grover, daughter of the Rev. Mr Grover, of Cauldwell.
He was state senator under the new constitution of New Jersey.
4. Amzi also graduated at Princeton. and engaged in the practice of the law. He was a member of council, and of the assembly of the state legislature. He died in 1838, unmarried.
5. Sarah married William Whelpley.
6. Charlotte married Hugh Randolph.
7. Phebe.
8. Louisa married Jesse Pitt, Esq.

Dr. JOSEPH S. DODD, (3d child of General John Dodd,) and Miss Grover, had children :
1. John.
2. Amzi, who graduated at Princeton.
3. Stephen Grover, who also graduated at Princeton.
4. A daughter.
And by his 2d wife Doct. Dodd had two children.

LINUS DODD, (5th son of John Dodd, Jun., son of John,) and Betsey Pierson, had children :
1. Acsah, who married Daniel D. Condit.
2. Calvin.

DAVID DODD, (2d son of John Dodd,) and Sarah Harrison, had children :
1. Polly, who married Abijah Dodd.
2. Zebina married Betsey Range.
3. Elizabeth, who died 21st August, 1794, aged 30 years.
4. David, Jun., married Lydia Ward.
5. Sarah.
6. Abby married John Baldwin.
7. Phebe.
8. Lydia married, 1st, Reuben Dodd ; 2d, John Baldwin.

ZEBINA DODD, (2d child of David, son of John,) and Betsey Range, had children :
1. Polly.

2. Lydia, who both died with consumption, unmarried.
3. Nancy, who married Mr. Meeker.
4. John Range.
5. Tyler.
6. Israel.

DAVID DODD, Jun., (4th child of David, son of John,) and Lydia Ward, had children:
1. Ezra ; 2. Mary ; 3. Chandler; 4. Reuben; 5. Joshua ; 6. Margaret; 7. Almira, who died 16th September, 1822.

STEPHEN DOD, (the 5th child of Daniel Dod, 1st,) married Mary Stevens, and settled in Guilford, Connecticut. They had children:

1. Daniel, who was born about 1679, and married Elizabeth ——————, at about 22 years. He removed to Newark, when he was about 27 years of age.

2. Samuel married Hannah Savage, of Middletown, Connecticut, 19th January, 1704. Their father Stephen had divided his lands in Guilford, by will, equally between Daniel and Samuel.

Daniel sold, and by will quit-claim dated May 3d, 1707, conveyed all his right and title to the lands and tenements left him by his father Stephen, to his brother Samuel, of Guilford ; most of these lands are in the possession of the descendants of Samuel Dod to this time (1839).

DANIEL DOD, (son of Stephen, son of Daniel Dod, 1st,) and his wife Elizabeth, had children:
1. Stephen, born 4th April, 1703, and married Deborah Brown.
2. John married Jemima Harrison.
3. Timothy married —— ——.

STEPHEN DODD, (son of Daniel, son of Stephen,) and Deborah Brown, had children:
1. Zebina, who married Mary Baldwin.
2. Thaddeus married Phebe Baldwin.
He graduated at Princeton College, and studied theology.
3. Daniel married Charity Freeman, and had children:
   1. Silas ; 2. Ithiel ; 3. Daniel.
4. Parmeneus married Patience Wright, and had children :
   1. Daniel ; 2. Mary ; 3. Ziba ; 4. Phebe ; 5. Stephen ; 6. Azubah ; 7. Sarah.
5. Uzel married Abigail Homan, and had an only child Martha; 6. Elizabeth ; 7. Keziah ; 8. Deborah ; 9. Sarah ; 10. Hannah ; 11. Abigail.

LEBBEUS DODD, (1st child of Stephen, son of Daniel,) and Mary Baldwin, had children :
1. Hannah ; 2. Eunice ; 3. Phebe ; 4. Stephen married Mehetabel Gould ; 5. Abner married Hannah Gould ; 6. Rachel ; 7. Mary ; 8. Daniel married Nancy Squier ; 9. Abigail ; 10. Elizabeth.

REV. THADDEUS DODD, (2d child of Stephen, son of Daniel,) graduated at Princeton College, in 1773, and settled in the gospel ministry in Western Pennsylvania. He and Phebe Baldwin had children :
1. Cephas; 2. Stephen; 3. Sarah.

STEPHEN DODD, (4th child of Lebbeus, son of Stephen,) lived in Newark; was a surveyor and judge of the court of common pleas in Essex county. He and Mehetabel Gould had children :
1. Mary.
2. Lebbeus.
3. John Gould.
4. Sarah Anne.
5. Charles.
9. William graduated at Princeton College in 1833, and is Professor of Mathematics in Center College, Kentucky.
7. Stephen.
8. Mehetabel.

ABNER DODD, (5th child of Lebbeus, son of Stephen,) was a mathematical instrument maker in Newark. He and Hannah Gould had children :
1. Horace ; 2. Susan; 3. Charles ; 4. Jacob; 5. Catherine ; 6. Abby Elizabeth married, 13th June, 1850, John W. Stryker.

DANIEL DODD, (8th child of Lebbeus, son of Stephen,) was a machinist. He made the machinery for a steamboat at Elizabethtown, New Jersey, and went towards New York to try it, when he with his assistants were blown up, and perished in the ruins. He, with his wife Nancy Squier, had children :
1. Ezra Kitchel.
2. Lewis Southard.
3. Caroline.
4. Susan.
5. Albert Baldwin (Rev.) graduated at Princeton College in 1822, and was Professor of Mathematics in that college till his death.
6. Mary.
7. Charles.
8. William graduated at Princeton College, and is a Presbyterian minister ; preaches at Port Richmond, near Philadelphia.

JOHN DODD, (son of Daniel, son of Stephen, son of Daniel, 1st,) and Jemima Harrison, had children :
1. Adonijah, who married Mary Ogden.
2. Mathias died unmarried.
3. James married Sarah Harrison.
4. Cody died unmarried.
5. Abel married Martha Osborn.
6. Jemima died unmarried.
7. Betsey died unmarried.

ADONIJAH DODD, (3d son of John, son of Daniel,) and Mary Ogden, had children :
1. Aaron ; 2. Catherine ; 3. Samuel ; 4. Matthew.

JAMES DODD, (son of John, son of Daniel,) and Sarah Harrison, had children :
1. Abraham ; 2. Phebe ; 3. Hannah ; 4. Naomi.

ABEL DODD, (5th child of John, son of Daniel,) and Martha Osborn, had children :
1. Jemima ; 2. Rachel ; 3. Polly ; 4. Phebe ; 5. John ; 6. William, who died in infancy ; 7th, William, 2d, who also died in infancy.

TIMOTHY DODD, (brother of John, and son of Daniel, son of Stephen,) married ———, and had children :
1. Jesse, who married Miss Perry, and had children :
  1, Joseph.
  2. A daughter, who married Mr. Riker.
2. Timothy, who died unmarried.
3. Phebe, who died unmarried.

SAMUEL DOD, (2d son of Stephen, son of Daniel, 1st,) and Hannah Savage, lived in Guilford, Connecticut, and had children : (NOTE.—Samuel died 24th May, 1757.)
1. Ebenezer, born 22d December, 1705, married, 1st, Sarah White, of Hadley, and died 19th May, 1782.
2. Samuel, Jun., born 28th February, 1707, and died 25th Aug. 1731, unmarried.
3. Hannah, born 25th July, 1712, married, 18th May, 1737, Thomas Burgis. They had two sons and three daughters ; one of the sons died in infancy. She (Hannah) died 26th July, 1795.
4. Sarah, born 24th April, 1715, married John Burgis. She (Sarah) died January, 1757. They had no children.
Ebenezer married, 31st August, 1737, Hannah Benton, his 2d wife, and for his 3d wife married, 22d April, 1741, Mary Evarts, and had a daughter Mary, born 10th January, 1742, and died within 20 days and ; the mother died 18th November, 1790

EBENEZER DOD, (son of Samuel, of Guilford, Connecticut,) and Sarah White, had children :
1. Sarah, who married Giles White, of Hadley.
2. Mary married Leumen Ward, of Guilford.
Both returned from Guilford many years since. The Dod family in Guilford, in the line of Samuel, is extinct.
In a town meeting at Newark, 13th February, 1679, Samuel Dod, (the 6th child of the English Daniel Dod, 1st,) of Branford, was admitted a citizen and a planter, and had his land assigned him on the hill at the north end of the town, since called Governor Place.
Subsequently he had new lands assigned him on the east side of his brother Daniel's land on Watsessing Place. He had a son,

1. Samuel, Jun., born about 1694, married Mary Pierson. He died 16th April, 1774, in his 78th year, she died in 1795, about June. They had children:

   1. Martha, born 20th May, 1731, and married Matthew Harrison.

   2. Mary, born 16th December, 1732.

   3. Hannah, born 18th December, 1734, married —— Smith.

   4. Samuel, 3d, born 11th January, 1736, married, 1st, Elizabeth Hinman: 2d, Sarah Baldwin ; and died of small-pox, in July, 1795.

   5. Aaron, born 13th January, 1738, and died 9th March, 1821, aged 83 years.

   6. Rebecca, born 5th Feb. 1740, married Samuel Fairchild.

   7. Keturah, born 26th July, 1744.

   8. Jemima, born 25th March, 1747, married Isaac Suverill.

SAMUEL DOD, 3d, (son of Samuel Dod, Jun.,) and Elizabeth Hinman, had children:

   1. Jonas, born 1762, and died 20th August, 1770, aged 8 years.

   2. Naomi, born 1764, and died 24th May, 1766.

   3. Abiathar, who married, 1st, Cornelia Cadmus; 2d, Sophia Cogswell ; 3d, Mary Bigelow.

And by his 2d wife, who died 14th October, 1819, he had,

   4. Elizabeth, who died 20th August, 1770, in her 2d year.

   5. Elizabeth, 2d, who died 13th June, 1790, aged 16 years.

   6. Samuel, 4th, who married Jemima Dodd.

   7. Abner married, 1st, Betsey Canfield ; 2d, Charlotte Walter, and died 17th January, 1833.

   8. Patty,

   9. Naomi, who married Joseph S. Ward.

ABIATHAR DODD, (3d child of Samuel Dod, 3d,) and his 1st wife, Cornelia Cadmus, had a daughter.

   1. Cornelia ; and by his 2d wife, Sophia Cogswell, had children :

   2. Christopher Cadmus Washington,

   3. Cornelius ; and by his 3d wife, Mary Bigelow, had,

   4. William.

SAMUEL DODD, 4th, (6th child of Samuel Dodd, 3d,) and Jemima Dodd, had children :

   1. Samuel, 5th.

   2. Sarah.

   3. Aaron, who married Sarah Nutman, who died 26th September, 1805, aged 60 years.

   4. Mary.

   5. Martha.

   6. Lorinda married Isaac King.

ABNER DODD, (7th child of Samuel Dodd, 3d,) and Betsey Canfield, had children :

1. Eliza ; 2. Abner ; 3. John ; 4. Anne ; and by his 2d wife, Charlotte Walter, Abner Dodd had,

5. Samuel ; 6. Charlotte.

AARON DODD, (3d child of Samuel Dodd, 4th,) and Sarah Nutman, had children :

1. Mary, who married the Rev. Amzi Armstrong, of Mendham.

2. Job, who died of cholera, 1834, aged 58 years.

3. Rebecca married Samuel Ingham.

4. Joanna, who died 27th September, 1815, aged 58 years.

5. Robert married Rebecca Randall, and had a daughter, who died of consumption.

6. George Adams, who died 6th February, 1812, in his 24th year.   The family of Aaron Dod is now extinct in the male line.

139

JOSEPH DOTY, 1st.

JOSEPH DOTY, 1st.

Joseph Doty came from the east end of Long Island, and owned part of lot No. 39 of the Elizabethtown lots, in Stony Hill Valley, on which he lived. He married Sarah Badgley, sister of John and James Badgley, and had children :

2d Generation.

1. Joseph, Jun., who died young.
2. George, who married Sibbe Howel.
3. John married, 1st, Sarah Potter, and 2d, Sarah Clark, daughter of Daniel Clark. [*See Daniel Clark.*]
4. Anthony married and had but one child,
    1. William Parsons Doty, who married, 1st June, 1793, Peggy Badgley, daughter of Moses, son of Joseph Badgley. [*See Badgley.*]
5. Elizabeth married Jeremy Ludlow, son of Jeremiah. [*See Ludlow.*] "Old Mr. Doty died 10th September, 1768," per Rev. Mr. Elmer's record.

GEORGE DOTY, (2d child of Joseph Doty, 1st), lived on Stony Hill, and owned a mill on the brook running down by Samuel M. Magie's and Israel Doty's. He and Sibbe Howel had children :

1. Joseph, 3d, who married Polly Allen, daughter of Joseph, Jun., of Washington Valley. [*See Allen.*]
2. George, Jun., married Nancy Cook.
3. David, who went to the lakes of New York, and married there.
4. Kezia married Stephanus Clark, son of Daniel Clark. [*See Daniel Clark.*]
5. Sarah married John Clark, Jun., son of Elder John Clark.

JOSEPH DOTY, 3d, (1st child of George,) lived where his grandfather, Joseph Doty, 1st, did. He and his wife, Patty Allen, had children :

3d Generation.

1. Anthony, who married Mary Willcox, daughter of Levi.
2. Allen married Nancy Brown, daughter of John.
3. David married Sibbe Clark, daughter of 'John, Jun., son of Elder John Clark.
4. Sarah married Aaron Oakley, son of Thomas. (*See Oakley.*)
5. Aaron (Capt.) married, 15th Dec. 1811, Betsey Hedges, daughter of Gilbert, and went to Luzerne county, Pennsylvania.
6. Sibbe is unmarried.
7. Mary married Jesse F. Pitts, son of George Pitts, of Orange county, New York.
8. Martha married, 24th January, 1824, Benjamin Weed, from Massachusetts.

ANTHONY DOTY, (1st son of Joseph Doty, 3d,) and Mary Willcox, had children :

4th Generation.

1. Rachel, who married William Boyland ; lived in Newark.
2. Betsey married John Winans Hand, son of Nehemiah and has no children.

ALLEN DOTY, (2d son of Joseph Doty, 3d,) and Nancy Brown, had children :

1. Anna, who married Benjamin Lacy, and had children:
    1. Moses Lacy ; 2. William Lacy.
2. Rachel, who married Ephraim Howard, and removed to the west.
3. Aaron married, 1st, Rachel Quackenbush ; 2d, Ellen Medan ; 3d, —— ——.
4. Ellen married, 1st, Samuel Vangesen, and had children:
    1, Mary Anne Vangesen; 2. William Vangesen; 3. Abby Vangesen.
Her husband then died, and she married Edward Brown, and had no children by him.
5. Squier.
6. Joseph.
7. William married Mary Simpson, daughter of William.
8. Sally married her cousin, Cornelius Titus, son of Thomas Titus, of Patterson, New Jersey.
9. Jane went to the west with her father, and married there.
10. Mary, and 11. Abraham.

CAPT AARON DOTY, (3d son of Joseph Doty, 3d,) and Betsey Hedges, had children:
1. Jane, who married Philetus Foster, born 2d October, 1810, son of Silas, of Chatham.
2. Phebe married Daniel Hedden, of Clinton.
3. Martha, born 1824, married, 1843, Smith Taylor, of Millville.
4. Sabina married John Baldwin, of Chatham, son of Moses, son of David.
5. Josiah.
6. George.

JANE DOTY, (daughter of Capt. Aaron, son of Joseph Doty, 3d,) and Philetus Foster, had children :
1. William, who married Hetty Clark, daughter of John R. Clark, on the first mountain.
2. Emily married Ambrose Mulford, of Green Village.
3. Sophia married Samuel Johnson, from Ireland.
4. Lucinda; 5. Phebe Anne; 6. Margaret; 7. Mary; 8. John; 9. Elizabeth; 10. Manning; 11. Edwin Foster.

5th Generation.

MARY DOTY, (7th child of Joseph Doty, 3d,) and Jesse F. Pitts, had children :
1. James Clark Pitts.
2. Theodore L. Pitts.

MARTHA DOTY, (8th child of Joseph Doty, 3d,) and Benjamin Weed, had children :
1. Ira Doty Weed; 2. Hannah Maria Weed; 3. Marcus Hervy Weed; 4. John Wesley Weed; 5. Gideon Allen Weed; 6. Mary Elizabeth Weed ; 7. Julia Anne Weed.

Joseph Doty, 3d, died 8th December, 1844, aged 93 years. His wife Patty, 13th April, 1820, 55 years. He was an elder in the Presbyterian church, from January, 1808, till he died.

4th Generation.

JOHN DOTY.

JOHN DOTY, (3d son of Joseph Doty, 1st,) and Sarah Potter, lived in Stony Hill Valley, near, but west of his father's house, and had children:

1. Chloe, who died 27th November, 1772, unmarried.
2. James, born 16th January, 1756, married, 29th September, 1788, Nancy Locey, daughter of Daniel Locey of Mendham.

John Doty's wife then died, and he married Sarah Clark, daughter of Daniel, and had children:

3. Daniel, born 23d March, 1765, and married, 1st, Elizabeth Potter, 2d, Betsey Crane, daughter of Joseph, and went to Middletown, Ohio, and settled there.
4. John Doty, Jun., married Phebe Cooper, of Hanover, and removed to Western New York, and from thence to Middletown, Ohio.
5. Zina went to Ohio, with his father and family, and married there.
6. Betsey married, 22d March, 1794, Stephanus Clark, Jun., and went to Ohio. [*See Stephanus Clark.*]
7. Jane went with her father to Ohio, and married Sam Clark, there.
8. Chloe, 2d, died 27th December, 1784.
9. Ketura, who died young.

JAMES DOTY, (2d child of John Doty,) and Nancy Locey, had children:

1. Sally, who married William Bonnel, son of Capt. Nathaniel. [*See Nathaniel Bonnel.*]
2. Betsey married James H. Pierson, son of Jacob Serring Pierson. [*See Parsons.*]
3. Israel, born 1st July, 1794, married, 1st, Sally Noe, daughter of John; 2d, Eliza Squier, widow of Joseph Squier, and daughter of Henry Mundy, of Rahway.
4. Phebe married Edward Hedges, son of Gilbert. [*See Hedges.*]
5. Jenette married Abraham Clark, son of Samuel Clark, Esq., and had an only child, James Doty Clark.

Mr. James Doty died 14th December, 1747, aged 90 years 11 months. Nancy, his wife, died 19th April, 1741, aged 74 years. Sally, their daughter, wife of William Bonnel, died 5th January, 1843, aged 54 years. Betsey, their daughter, wife of James H. Pierson, died 10th December, 1832, aged 42 years. Sally, wife of their son Israel Doty, died 3d October, 1828, aged 31 years.

ISRAEL DOTY, (3d child of James, son of John Doty,) and Sally Noe, had children:

1. James, who married Harriet Fairfield, of Boston, and live there, and had children: 1. James 2. Harriet.
2. John Noe Doughty.
3. Matthias married his cousin, Rachel Noe, daughter of Ellis Noe, and had children: 1. John Henry.
4. Israel, Jun.

DANIEL DOTY, (3d son of John, son of Joseph Doty, 1st,) married, 1st, Elizabeth Potter, eldest child of Amos, son of Daniel Potter, 1st. He married, 2d, Elizabeth Crane, daughter of Joseph Crane. He left home 10th September, 1790, on an exploring tour down the Ohio river, and landed at Cincinnati 23d October, following when there were but two log-houses in that city; one of them was occupied by Major Benjamin Stites, from the Scotch Plains, Essex county, New Jersey, the other was occupied by Capt. John S. Gano. St. Clair's defeat was on the 4th day of Nov. 1791. The Rev. Daniel Clark, from Pennsylvania, was the first minister of the gospel in that region. Daniel Doty had no living children by his first wife. He was born 23d March, 1765, and died 8th May, 1848. He returned from Ohio to New Jersey, and married, for his 2d wife, Elizabeth Crane, and again soon removed to Ohio, and purchased a large tract of land at and about Middletown, and settled upon it. He, with his wife, Elizabeth Crane, had children:

1. Joel, born in New Jersey 9th February, 1795, and was drowned in the Miami river at 11 years old.

2. Noah, born 6th May, 1796, in Ohio, and died in his 7th year.

3. John, born 15th December, 1797, and married Peggy Jewel, daughter of John, of Middletown.

4. Daniel, born 9th August, 1799, married, 1st, Molly Burges, daughter of Anthony. He married, 2d, Catherine Crane, daughter of Joseph, son of Joseph.

5. Betsey, born 16th January, 1801, married Ambrose Doty, son of George, son of George, and had children:
    1. Nancy, who died in Iowa, at 19 years; 2. Huldah; 3. ——.

6. Huldah, born 8th January, 1803, married John Williamson, and had children: 1. Daniel; 2. Hendrick died at about 19 years; 3. Joseph; 4. Ellen; 5. Elias; 6. William; 7. Mary Anne; 8. Sarah Jane; 9. Abner; 10. John Henry Williamson.

7. Orpha, born 8th June, 1804, married Thomas Van Tyle, and had children:
    1. Sarepta, who married Mr. Golden, and died at about 20 years, had no children.

8. Sarepta, born 16th February, 1806, married, 1st, James Jewel, brother of John's wife; 2d, Aretas Crane, son of Joseph Crane, son of Joseph, and had children: 1. John Jewel; 2. Albert Jewel; and by Aretas had, 3. Joseph; 4. Sarah; 5. William; 6. Elias.

9. Joseph, born 7th January, 1808, married Mary Vail, daughter of Samuel, son of Samuel, brother of Stephen Vail, the proprietor of Middletown, and had children: 1. Russel; 2. Gilbert; 3. Ruth Jane; 4. Zina; 5. Deborah; 6. Ellen.

10. James Mier, born 8th October, 1809, married Susan Anderson, and had children: 1. Joel; 2. Elizabeth; 3. Ruth Anne; 4. Elias; 5. Daniel; 6. Jerusha.

11. Jerusha, born 9th January, 1814, married Simeon Taylor, and had a son, George Taylor, when Mr. Taylor died.

12. Elias, born 23d June, 1815, and died in Iowa, at about 22 years. He married Pamelia Bogart, and had a son, Noah.

DANIEL DOTY, Jun., (son of Daniel,) and Mary Burge, had children :
1. Randolph, who died at 23 years ; 2. Mark ; 3. John. And by Catherine Crane had, 4. Aretas ; 5. George ; 6. Pitman ; 7. Sarah, who died at 4 years ; 8. Joseph; 9. Daniel.

JOHN DOTY, (4th child of John,) and Phebe Cooper, had children :
1. Electa.
2. Harriet.
3. John, 3d.

ZINA DOTY, (5th son of John Doty,) married Sarah Moore, daughter of Levi Moore, whose wife was Hannah Enyart, daughter of Benjamin, and brother of Rufus, [*see Daniel Thompson,*] and had children :
1. Electa, who died in infancy ; 2. James died at 10 years ; 3. Levi died at 14 months ; 4. John died at one year ; 5. Elizabeth married James Daugherty, and had children :
    1. Hannah Cevilla Daugherty ; 2. Aquilla Daugherty ; 3. Melissa Daugherty; 4. Sarah Daugherty ; 5. Harriet, Daugherty.
6. Mary married Robert Chapman, and had a son, Butler D. Chapman.
7. Hannah married Aquilla Daugherty, brother of James, and had children : 1. Electa Jane Daugherty ; 2. Sophronia Mariah Daugherty.
8. Noah is unmarried in 1851.
9. Sarah married William McNichols, and had children :
    1. Emma McNichols ; 2. Ellen McNichols.

BETSEY DOTY, (6th child of John Doty,) and Stephanus Clark, Jun., had children :
1. John Clark, who died at 19 years.
2. Jonathan Clark married Betsey Patten, and had a son, Samuel.
3. Zina married, 1st, Sarah Clendennen, and had a son, Valentine Clark.
4. Patty married Abraham Clark, son of Jabez, son of Daniel, and had children : 1. Nancy Clark, who married Mr. Freeman : 2. Daniel Clark ; 3. Catherine Clark ; 4. Stephanus Clark ; 5. Martha Clark ; 6. Washington Clark.
5. Abraham Doty.
6. Jotham Doty.
7. Elizabeth Doty.

JANE DOTY, (7th child of John Doty,) married Samuel Clark a relative of Stephanus; went to Illinois, and had children :
1. James Clark ; 2. Abby Clark ; 3. Sarah Clark, and others.

JOSHUA DOTY.

JOSHUA (Doty after a time written) DOUGHTY lived at or near the mill's at the west end of Long Hill. He married Sarah Boyle, 8th child of Solomon Boyle, 1st, and had children:

1. Solomon, who married Polly Pierson, daughter of Jonathan Pierson, whose wife was Agnes Ludlow, 2d child of Col. Cornelius Ludlow, of Long Hill. Solomon Doughty was first brigadier, then major-general, of militia.

2. Margaret married Joseph Bullman, and went to Ohio.

3. Susan, who died unmarried.

GEN. SOLOMON DOUGHTY, and Polly Pierson, had children:

1. Agnes, who married Doct. John D. Jackson, of Rockaway, Morris county.

2. Joshua married Susan Southard, daughter of Col. Isaac Southard, of Somerset. He is a merchant, and president of the Somerset County Bank.

3. Betsey Pierson, born 1803, married Doct. Charles H. Jackson. from Rockaway. She died 28th July, 1838, soon after she was married, and without children.

4. Sineus, who was born 1808, and died 20th October, 1832, unmarried.

5. Sarah Maria, born 13th July, 1814, and died 25th July, 1838, unmarried.

6. Eugene S, who married the widow Elizabeth Underdunk, at Somerville; he is a lumber-merchant there; he has children:
   1. Eugene.

DOCT. JOHN D. JACKSON, and Agnes Doughty, had children:

1. Edward E., who married Miss Osborn.

2. Charlotte married Mr. Robison, son of Collin Robison, Esq, of Morristown.

3. Mary married Mr. Chandler.

4. John Jackson, a physician in Rockaway.

5. Agnes.

6. Laura.

JOSHUA DOUGHTY, Esq., (son of Gen. Solomon Doughty,) and Susan Southard, had children:

1. Louisa; 2. Sarah; 3. Mary; 4. John Rolan; 5. Joshua; 6. Susan.

EDWARD DRAKE.

EDWARD DRAKE came from Piscataway and settled in Washington Valley.

He married Molly Vail, and had children :

1. Joseph, who went to the South and married there.
2. Jeremiah married, for a 2d wife, Elizabeth Wooden, sister of Ezra.
3. Andrew married Eunice Martin, daughter of Edward.
4. Mary married Mr. Vail.
5. Caty married Ebenezer Lyon, son of Peter Lyon, of Stony Hill. [*See Lyon*]
6. Sarah married William Littell, son of Andrew, and went to Sussex. [*See Andrew Littell.*]

2d Generation.

JEREMIAH DRAKE, (2d son of Edward,) and his first wife, had children :

1. Jeremiah Drake, Jun.
2. Joseph.
3. Betsey.
4. Mary.

Jeremiah Drake, by his 2d wife, Elizabeth Wooden, had children :

5. Peter, who went to Albany and married there.
6. Jacob married Rebecca Runyon, daughter of Ephraim, of Piscataway.
7. Joel married Phebe Noe, daughter of Lewis Noe, of Long Hill.
8. Rhoda.
9. Mary.
10. Edith married Washington Leason ; live on Long Hill.

ANDREW DRAKE, (3d son of Edward,) and Eunice Martin, had children :

1. Noah, who married Margaret Cole, daughter of Jonathan Cole.
2. Polly married Gideon Allen, Jun., son of Gideon, of Washington Valley.
3. Experience married Thomas Martin, son of Azariah Martin.
4. Martha married James Frazee, son of Jotham Frazee, Esq., of Scotch Plains.
5. Sarah married Samuel Seacore.
6. Piatt married Hannah Smalley, daughter of Daniel, son of David Smalley, Esq.

L

NOAH DRAKE, (son of Andrew, son of Edward,) and Margaret Cole, had children:

1. Ezra, who married, 1st, Polly Williams, daughter of Zophar Williams, of Passaic Valley, and had one daughter,
    1. Eliza Williams, who married Freeman Tucker. son of Lines. Ezra's wife died, and he married Polly Baker, daughter of Jonathan 1. and had children: 2. Mary Williams; 3. Jonathan Baker; 4 George Whitefield.

2. Dorcas married Jacob Shotwell, son of Ralph. [*See Shotwell.*]

3. Jonathan married Mariah Frazee, daughter of Maxwell, and had a daughter, Sarah Anne, when he died.

4. Humphrey Martin married Sarah Frazee, daughter of Maxwell, and had children: 1. Jonathan C; 2. Maxwell Frazee. His wife, Sarah, then died, and he married the widow Sally Young, and daughter of Philip Achor, and had children: 3 Margaret; 4. Eliza, and then removed to Michigan.

5. Randolph married Jane Randolph, daughter of Simeon, and had children: 1. Edward; 2. Margaret Anne; 3. Experience; 4. Simeon; 5. David.

6. Edward Drake, (son of Noah, son of Edward.) married Mary Waldron, daughter of Laffert Waldron, and had children: 1. Hannah Anne; 2. Jonathan; 3. Daniel; 4. Harriet; 5. George Washington.

7. William married Huma French, daughter of David French. Jun., and had children; 1. Matilda; 2. Noah; 3. David.

8. Nathaniel, born 22d July, 1815, married Sarah Tingley, born 11th Sept. 1815, daughter of Squire Tingley, and had children: 1. Emma, born 27th Sept. 1837; 2. Lucretia, born 13th October, 1839; 3 David, born 18th January, 1842; 4. Albert, born 7th August, 1846.

9. Eunice married James Drake, son of Elkanah, and had children: 1. Madison; 2. Anne Eliza; 3. James Drake.

10. Sarah married William Cornell, and had children:
    1. Thomas Lavender Cornell; 2. Mary Cornell.

11. Piatt married Julia Brant, daughter of David.

12. John Q. married Thirza S. Stewart, daughter of Wm. D. Stewart, Esq.

JAMES DUNHAM.

JAMES DUNHAM lived at Littell's Bridge, in Morris county, and owned a farm there of upwards of 60 acres He had brothers, John, David, and Joseph, and sisters, Abby and Polly: they were children of two mothers. He married the widow Sarah Hedges, who then had a daughter, Sarah Hedges, who died 7th Dec. 1820, aged 63 years, unmarried.

He had a son James, who died 5th May, 179), aged 25 years, unmarried, and a daughter Hannah, who died 9th July, 18*17*, aged 54 years, unmarried.

James Dunham, Sen., died 7th June, 1796. aged 75 years. His widow died 7th August, 1807, aged 71 years. When Sarah Hedges died, this family was extinct.

JOHN DUNHAM.

JOHN DUNHAM was half brother of James ; he married Keziah Marsh, daughter of Ephraim Marsh, and had children :

1. Nancy, who married James Tappen, and went to Ohio.
2. Hetty married Jacob High, son of John, of Westfield. [*See High*]
3. John, Jun., married, 1st, Sarah High, sister of Jacob ; 2d, Patty Smalley, daughter of David, Esq.
4. Jane, born 8th May, 1764, married Norris Crane, son of Benjamin. [*See Benjamin Crane.*]
5. Betsey married Samuel Potter, son of Caleb, son of Col. Samuel. [*See Potter.*]
6. Polly married Enos Meeker, of Connecticut Farms, now Union.
7. Phebe married, 14th February, 1796, Joseph Ogden Meeker, son of Jotham, of Plainfield.

NANCY DUNHAM, and James Tappen, had children:

1. Sally Tappen, who married, 3d March, 1795, Capt. Samuel Bailey. [*See Bailey*]
2. Keziah Tappen married Jonathan Crane, son of Joseph. [*See Crane.*]
3. Marsh Tappen, who died at about 18 years.
4. Samuel Tappen married Catherine Dyke, in Ohio.
5. Betsey Tappen married William Livingston, in Ohio.
6. Jane Tappen married Henry Rogers, of Plainfield, and went to Ohio.
7. Phebe Tappen married Thomas Smith, in Ohio.
8. Benjamin Tappen married Eliza Shaw, of Pennsylvania ; lived in Cincinnati, Ohio.
9. Isaac Tappen married Nelly Dunham, daughter of Doctor Dunham, of Indiana.
10. Susan Tappen married Peter P. Good, an Englishman ; live in New York, and have an only child, Pato Good.

JOHN DUNHAM, Jun., (son of John Dunham,) and Sarah High, had children :

1. Rachel, who married Christopher Stevens, son of John. [See Stevens]
2. Deborah married, 30th January, 1796, James Sayre, son of David ; live at Madison.
3. Keziah, born July, 1780, married, 20th June, 1807, Aaron Thompson, son of Thomas. [*See Thompson.*]

4. Joel married Eunice Baldwin, of Bloomfield, and lives there.

5 Fanny married Levi French, son of David French, Sen. [*See French*]

6. Ezra married Nancy Hobro, and went to the lakes, New York, and lives there.

7. William went to the lakes.

8. Sally married 22d November, 1822, George Miller, an Englishman.

9. John, 3d, married Phebe Anne Williams, daughter of Henderson Williams, of Westfield, and had a daughter Ellen, when his wife died.

John Dunham, Jun., married, 2d, Patty, daughter of David Smalley, Esq., and had a 10th child.

POLLY DUNHAM, (6th child of John Dunham,) and Enos Meeker, had children :

1. Phebe, who married Calvin Freeman.

2. Ephraim married Phebe ———.

3. Joseph married Electa Headley, daughter of Timothy.

4. Wheeler married Phebe Fox, daughter of John.

5. Enos.

PHEBE DUNHAM, (7th child of John Dunham,) and J. Ogden Meeker, had children :

1. Mary Meeker, who married John Squier, son of Aaron Squier, of Long Hill. [*See Squier.*]

2. Sarah Meeker married Ezra Hatfield, son of Daniel, of Westfield, and had children : 1. Ogden Meeker Hatfield ; 2. Phebe Meeker Hatfield ; 3. Harriet Hatfield ; 4. Rebecca Hatfield ; 5. Charlotte Hatfield ; 6. Sarah Hatfield ; 7. Mary Hatfield ; 8. —— Hatfield.

3. Anna Meeker married William Line, son of Isaiah, and had children : 1. Isaiah Line, who died at 22 years 2. Huldah Line married Michael McVay ; 3. Hannah Line married Anthony Farley, son of Anthony Farley, of Hunterdon ; 4. George Line ; 5 Sarah Line ; 6. Aaron Line ; 7. Amelia Line ; 8. Phebe Line [*See Line.*]

4 Rachel Meeker married Samuel Rutan, son of Joseph, of Long Hill, and had no children.

5. John Meeker married Margaret, daughter of Anthony Farley, of Hunterdon county, and had no children.

REV. JONATHAN ELMER.

REV. JONATHAN ELMER was born in Norwalk, Conn.' the 4th June, 1727. He married Amy Gale, near Goshen, Orange county, New York. He came to Turkey, and became the stated minister of the Presbyterian church and congregation the 1st of October, 1757, and was installed the 13th

November, 1765, and continued the pastor till the 14th Oct. 1793, when he was dismissed, and was never afterwards settled. He died 5th June, 1807, aged 80 years.; his wife Amy, died 24th July, 1812, aged 94 years. They had children:

1. Jonathan, born 15th July, 1750. married. 29th May, 1776, Susannah Bedell, daughter of Benjamin ; had a son Philemon, and a daughter Hannah, baptized 30th May, 1784, and died young ; and he died 29th March, 1784, aged 34 years.

2. Philemon, born 13th Sept 1752, became a physician and a surgeon in the army of the Revolution. He married, 1st, 13th Nov. 1774, Mary Marsh, and lived in Westfield ; 2d, Catherine Slack ; 3d, the widow of Charles Clark, Esq.

3. John, born 29th Sept. 1753, and died 14th May, 1764.

4. Moses Gale, born 26th September, 1757 ; he became a physician, and married, 2d December, 1792, Chloe Meeker, daughter of Matthias Meeker, of Morristown ; he lived where John T. Willcox now lives ; he died 31st May, 1835 ; his wife, Chloe, died 19th June, 1833, aged 60 years.

5. Sarah, born 11th August, 1760, and married, 4th April, 1779, Abraham Morrell, of Elizabethtown, who died 15th April, 1794, and she then married Thomas Lovell, merchant of New York.

6. Nathan, born 5th November, 1763, married, 4th Nov. 1792, Sarah Crane, daughter of Isaac.

NOTE.—The four first children were born at Florida, near Goshen, in the highlands of Orange county, N. York, and the two last in Turkey, or New Providence.

JONATHAN ELMER, son of Rev. Jonathan Elmer, and Susannah Bedell, had but two children: 1. Hannah, who married, 18th January, 1795, Thaddeus Thompson, and died in child-bed, with her first child ; 2. Philemon, who married Nancy Potter, daughter of Isaac, and had children :

1. Abigail Caroline, born 4th February, 1807, and died 20th July, 1807.

2. Jonathan Gale, born 13th August, 1808, and died 25th April, 1828, aged 20 years.

3. Abigail Caroline, 2d, born 5th January, 1810, and died 14th March, 1845, aged 35 years, unmarried.

4. Louisa, born 28th October, 1811, and died 21st January, 1829, aged 18 years, unmarried.

5. Potter Elmer, born 6th July, 1813, and went to Western Pennsylvania, and married, 8th March, 1839, Amy McFarlan.

6. Nancy, born 12th January, 1815, and died 27th July, 1836, aged 21 years, unmarried.

7. Philemon, born 14th January, 1817, and died a young man in Western Pennsylvania.

8. Simeon Dunn, born 2d December, 1818, and died 24th

February, 1835, aged 16 years.

9. Amy, born 27th November, 1820, and married 7th April, 1846, William C. Green, son of Calvin, of Madison, and had children: 1. William Elmer Green; 2. Sarah Caroline Green.

10. Israel, born 29th July, 1822. died 29th September, 1826.

11. Sarah Lovel, born 25th February, 1825, and died 8th July, 1850, aged 25 years.

Nancy, the wife of Philemon Elmer. died 31st December, 1831, aged 49 years, and he married Catherine, the widow of Erastus Jones.

DOCT. PHILEMON ELMER. (son of the Rev. Jonathan Elmer.) and Mary Marsh, had children:

1. Sally, who married Doct. Loree.

2. Polly married Doct Quimby, of Westfield, and died without children.

And by his 2d wife, Catherine Slack, Doct. Elmer had children:

3. Betsey married Ellis Potter, of New York, and had children: 1. Frank Potter; 2. Ellis Potter; 3. Edward Potter.

4. Caty married Aaron Coe, Esq, now of Westfield, and had children: 1. Philemon Elmer Coe, now an Episcopal minister; 2. Catherine Coe.

5. Nancy; 6. John; 7 Julia; 8. Caroline; 9. Stewart.

The five last named children of Doct. Philemon Elmer died unmarried.

DOCT. MOSES ELMER, (son of Rev. Jonathan Elmer,) and Chloe Meeker, had children:

1. Matthias Meeker, baptized 24th July, 1794, and died.

2 Henry G Elmer maried, 8th December, 1822, Pamelia Johnson. daughter of Gabriel Johnson, Esq., and died 11th February, 1824, aged 25 years.

3. William, who died unmarried.

4. Apollos Morrell married Mary Britton, daughter of Col. William Britton of Madison, and had one daughter,

1. Elizabeth. who has become deaf.

Mrs. A. M Elmer died in 1836, and he married, 12th April, 1838, Theodocia Morrell, daughter of Rev. Thomas Morrell, of Elizabethtown, and had children:

2. William Henry.

BENJAMIN ENYART.

BENJAMIN ENYART lived in Passaic Valley, between Alexander Kirkpatrick's and Benjamin Alward's, and had children :
1. Samuel.
2. Sarah, who married Timothy Thompson, son of Daniel.
3. David.
4. Rufus married Sally Thompson, daughter of Daniel, and sister of Timothy.
5. Rachel married Benjamin Thompson, brother of Daniel, as his 2d wife.
6. Susannah.
The family all removed to Ohio *about* the year 1800.

JAMES FINLEY.

JAMES FINLEY emigrated from Scotland ; he lived some years at Princeton, and last at Basking Ridge, where he died ; he had children :
1. James, who became a physician, and lived in Western New York.
2. Robert, who graduated at Princeton College ; studied theology, and was ordained and installed in the ministry at Basking Ridge. He married Esther Caldwell, the 5th child of the Rev. James Caldwell, of Revolutionary memory.
3. Anne, who married Charles Morford, of Prineton ; lived at Basking Ridge in 1810, and subsequently removed to Illinois.
4. Alexander was a carpenter and cabinet-maker ; lived at Basking Ridge. He married Susan Whitaker, eldest daughter of Stephen Wihtaker. [*See Whitaker.*]

REV. ROBERT FINLEY, (son of James,) and Esther Caldwell, had children :
1. Mary L. who married John R. Davison, only child of Peter Davison, of Basking Ridge.
2 Helen Smith married James Cammack ; lived in Georgia ; he died about 1846 ; had three children : 1. James Cammack ; 2. Thomas Cammack ; 3. Margaret Cammack. Two had died previous to his death.
3. James C., who became a preacher of the Methodist denomination ; married Margaret Smith, daughter of Doct. Smith, of Cincinnati, and had children : 1. Helen ; 2. William ; 3. a daughter.
4. Robert S married Julia Robins, of Kentucky ; lived at St. Louis, Missouri, several years ; edited the Liberia Advocate, five years at St. Louis, and removed thence to New York, and continues that publication. He is a Presbyterian minister, and was installed over the church at Metuchen, the 4th of November, 1850, by the presbytery of Elizabethtown ; he had no children.

b. Josiah was licensed to preach the gospel ; went to Liberia, Africa, as a missionary, and soon died there by violence.

6. Anne, who died at about 35 years, unmarried.

7. John married Miss Fox, of Mississippi ; both died, leaving one child, Mary Anne.

8. Susan married William Brown, Esq., a lawyer of Illinois ; had children : 1. Mary Brown : 2. Anne Brown.

9. Hannah married and lives in Illinois.

MARY L. FINLEY, and John R. Davison, had children :

1. Robert, who died at 23 years.
2. Anne Mariah.
3. John.
4. James, who died at 23 years.
5. Frederick Josiah.
6. Mary, who died at 20 years.
7. Helen, who died at 2 years.
8. William, who died at 4 years.
9. George, who died at 5 years.
10. Edward ; 11. Julia ; 12. Robert.

ANNE FINLEY, (daughter of James Finley, Sen.,) and Charles Morford, had children :

1. Margaret Morford.
2. Mary Anne Morford.
3. James Morford.

ALEXANDER FINLEY, (4th child of James Finley,) and Susan Whitaker, lived at Basking Ridge, and had children :

1. Anne, who married Elisha Whitaker, son of Samuel, of Newark. [*See Whitaker.*]
2. Hetty.
3. Robert, who married and went to Cincinnati.
4. Mariah married Samuel Hall, son of Richard ; lived in Newark. [*See Hall.*]
5. Eliza married Rev. David McKinney, D. D., lived in Pennsylvania ; has children living ; 1. Jane, who married Henry Floyd, has a son Thomas Floyd ; 2. Susan McKinney ; 3. Isaac McKinney, born Nov. 1828, is principal of the academy in Lafayette, East Alabama ; 4. Alexander ; 5. Anna McKinney married James Bailey, had one child, Anna Bailey, and died ; 6. William McKinney ; 7. David McKinney.
6. Sophia.
7. Jane, who died a young woman.
8. Susan married Elias Beam, of Newark, and died, leaving children : 1. Alexander Finley Beam ; 2. Julia Brownlee Beam ; 3. Frederick Betts Beam ; 4. Helen Amanda Beam
9. Alexander married Elizabeth, daughter of John Tuttle, of Newark, and went to St. Louis, Missouri, and had children : 1. Isaac

4th Generation.

Baldwin ; 2. Josephine lives with the Rev. R. S. Finley, of Metuchen, New Jersey ; 3. Anna Whitaker ; 4. John Tuttle.

10. Stephen Hervy.

11. Cornelia married Frederick Betts, of Pennsylvania.

12. Sarah.

13. Helen married Mr. Hurxthal; lives in Clearfield county, Pennsylvania.

NOTE.—The Rev. James Caldwell, the father of Esther, the wife of the Rev. Robert Finley, D. D., was shot by a soldier standing as a sentinel at Elizabethtown Point, the 24th November, 1781. (The sentinel was hung for the act.) He was a Presbyterian minister at Elizabethtown. His family resided at Connecticut Farms, (now Union.) His wife, Hannah, was shot, the 25th of June, 1780, by one of a party of British passing through that place to Springfield, leaving nine children, who were all taken up to Chatham, to the house of Stephen Day, Esq., whose wife was a sister of Mrs. Caldwell, where David O. Day now lives. [*See Stephen Day.*]

The nine children of Mr. Caldwell were,

1. Margaret, who married Isaac Canfield, of Morristown.

2. Hannah married James R. Smith, merchant, of New York.

3. John Edwards was taken by the Marquis Lafayette to France.

4. James B. was many years a judge of the court of Gloucester county, and died in Woodbury.

5. Esther married the Rev. Robert Finley, D. D., of Basking Ridge.

6. Josiah F. was many years in the Post Office department at Washington.

7. Elias was some years clerk of the United States Supreme Court.

8. Sarah married the Rev. John S. Vredenburg, many years pastor of the Reformed Dutch Church at Somerville.

9. Mariah married Robert S. Robertson, merchant, of New York.

DAVID FLINN.

DAVID FLINN lived where Elias Osborn, son of Stephen B. Osborn, now lives ; he married, 1st, —— ——, and had children :

1. Benjamin.

He married, 2d, Lydia, the widow of Andrew Prior, and daughter of David Littell, son of Samuel, and had children :

2. Stephen, who married Sally ——.

3. Lydia, who married, in Ohio, Edmund Buxton.

4. Susanna married John Miller. They and family went to the Shakers. Mrs. Flinn had, by her first husband, Andrew Prior, two sons, Andrew Prior, Jun., and Moses Prior, the latter of whom was killed by the Indians in the war of 1794. [*See Prior.*]

STEPHEN FLINN, (son of David,) had children :

1. Joanna, who married William Mills.

2. James married Sophronia Smith ; lives on Indian Hill, Hamilton county, Ohio.

3. David married Sally ——.

4. Vincent married Alla Robison ; lives near Dayton, Ohio.

5. Jesse married Henrietta Hammel ; have a son, John.

6. Moses ; 7. William, who died at 21 years.   And by his 2d wife Joanna, half sister of his first wife, had 8. Sarah, who died at about 18, and 9. Sabra, who died at 17 years.

JOSEPH FRAZEE.

JOSEPH FRAZEE was one of the eighty associates of Elizabethtown, who associated together for the purpose of managing,
settling, surveying, and disposing of the lands of the " Elizabeth
Town Grant," purchased of the Indians, a part of which, lying
above the first mountain, was surveyed, in the years 1736 and 1737,
into 100-acre lots, and distributed among the freeholders of Elizabethtown, by lot.

Joseph Frazee drew and owned two of those lots, Nos. 64 and 65,
lying in the valley at and about the Falls Mills, but not including
the mill site, (the mill site at the Falls having been taken up of the
proprietors before the survey was made, to the number of 25 acres,
by Daniel Cooper, of Morris county.)

Joseph Frazee had children :
1. Cornelius, who married Sarah Robins.
2. John married Hannah Willcox, daughter of Peter, Jr., 5th
December, 1764.
3. Henry married Sarah Maxwell, daughter of William Maxwell.

CORNELIUS FRAZEE, (son of Joseph Frazee,) and Sarah
Robins, had children :
1. Cornelius, Jun., who married, 1st, Sheba Hedges, daughter of
Benjamin Hedges ; 2d, Mary Tilyou, daughter of John Tilyou.
2. Betsey, who married William Badgley, son of Robert, son of
James, 1st.
3. Hannah, who went to the South, and married there.

CORNELIUS FRAZEE, Jun., (son of Cornelius,) and Sheba
Hedges, had children :
1. Polly, who married John D. Murphy, and had three children.
2. Sally married Abraham Hyat, and had one son.
And by his 2d wife, Mary Tilyou, he had children :
3. John, who died at 16 years of age.
4. Catherine, who is unmarried.
5. Moses, who married Susannah Hamilton, grand-daughter of
John Hamilton.

JOHN FRAZEE, (son of Joseph,) and Hannah Willcox, had
children :
1. Peter.
2. Noah.
After the death of John Frazee, the family removed to the
West.

HENRY FRAZEE, (son of Joseph,) and Sarah Maxwell, had
children :
1. Polly, who married Samuel Badgley, son of Anthony, 1st.
[See Badgley.]

4th Generation.

2. Maxwell, born 10th November, 1774, married Nancy Badgley, sister of Samuel. He married, 2d, Nancy, widow of Noah Cory, and daughter of Joseph Line ; had no children by her.

3. Moses married Susan Miller, daughter of Benjamin, of Scotch Plains.

4. Sally married Jacob Foster Stites, son of Isaiah, of Scotch Plains.

MAXWELL FRAZEE, (son of Henry, son of Joseph Frazee,) and Nancy Badgley, had children :

1. Henry, who died at 12 years.

2. Noah, born 31st August, 1799, married Betsey Squier, born 13th December, 1792, daughter of Aaron, of Long Hill.

3. Maria married Jonathan Drake, son of Noah, and had a daughter, 1. Sarah Anne Drake, when he died, and she married Jacob F. Randolph, son of John, as his 2d wife, and had children : 2. Abby E. Randolph.

4. Anne married James C. Lyon, (son of John,) as his 2d wife, and had no children.

5. Sally, (twin to Anne,) married Humphrey M. Drake, (son of Noah,) and had children :

5th Generation.

    1. Jonathan C. Drake.

    2. Maxwell F. Drake.

When she died, and he removed to Michigan.

6. Abby married the above-named Jacob F. Randolph, and had children :

    1. Mary M. Randolph ; 2. George W. Randolph.

When she died, and he married her sister, Maria, Jonathan Drake's widow.

7. Susan married Enoch Rino, and had but one daughter,

    1. Susan Rino.

NOAH FRAZEE, (son of Maxwell,) and Betsey Squier, had children :

1. Henry, born March, 1819, married Mary French, daughter of Willis, and had children : 1. George Willis ; 2. Sarah Elizabeth ; 3. Anne Augusta.

2. Aaron ; 3. Mary, who died at 12 years ; 4. Samuel, born 11th February, 1826 ; 5. Squier, born 1st December, 1827, married Catherine —— ; Anson, born 27th August, 1829 ; 7. John, born 25th November, 1832 ; 8. Anne, born 30th March, ——.

MOSES FRAZEE, (son of Henry,) and Susan Miller, had children :

1. Betsey, who married Abraham Nelson, who kept the tavern, in 1849–51, at Scotch Plains, and had children : 1. Julia Anne Curry Nelson ; 2. Marth Nelson ; 3. Loyd Nelson ; 4. —— ——.

2. Phebe married Aaron Drake, (son of Hugh Drake, and Hannah Littell, daughter of Jonathan Littell,) [see *Littell*,] and had children : 1. Delia Drake ; 2. Randolph Drake ; 3. Sarah Drake ; 4. Louisa Drake ; 5. Henry Drake.

ASA FRAZEE was son of Joseph Frazee, of Connecticut Farms. His children know not of any relation between them and the other Joseph Frazee. He married, 25th June, 1775, Sophia Littell, daughter of Andrew Littell. He lived on the north side of Sutton Hill (or 2d mountain) ; they had children:

2d Generation.

  1. Jemima, who married, 1st, Abner Tucker, son of Jacob Tucker ; [see *Tucker* ;] 2d, George Holley, of Perth Amboy, and had a son, 1. Philip Holley, and lived at Amboy.

  2. Sophia married Thomas Smith, of Connecticut Farms, lived where her father did, and had children:

    1. Asa Frazee Smith married Mary Anne ——.

    2. Joseph Smith married Miss Jennings, and lived in New York, and had children: 1. Silas Smith ; 2. Andrew Smith ; 3. Charles Smith.

    3. Margaret Smith married Thomas Wright, and had children : 1. Margaret Anne Wright ; 2. Susan Wright ; they lived in Williamsburgh, opposite New-York.

    4. Harriet Smith married Noah Clark, son of Elias Clark, Jun., and had children: 1. Smith Clark ; 2. Frazee Clark ; 3. Thomas Clark. Noah Clark then died, and she married John Bryson, of New-York.

    5. Thomas Smith married Lydia Eliza Hoffman, of Dutchess county, New-York ; lives on Long Island, and has children : 1. John W. Smith, born 27th August, 1828. 2. James Henry Smith. 3. Adelia Smith. 4. Charles Smith, born 25th July, 1835. 5. Mary Eliza Smith.

    6. George W. Smith married Phebe Jane Presley, and kept a large store of brooms, baskets, pails, &c., near Fulton Market, New York, and had children: 1. George H. Smith ; 2. Sarah Anne Smith ; 3. Mary Jane Smith; 4. Delia Smith ; 5. Emma Smith ; 6. William James Smith.

    7. Anne Eliza Smith married Timothy Murry, and had a son, 1. John Murry, who lived on Staten Island.

    8. James Smith, who died at 11 or 12 years.

    9. Servia Jane Smith, who married Thomas Cruger, and had a son, John Adolpha Asa C. Cruger.

  3. Betsey Frazee married John Curtis of Monmouth county ; lived where her father did, and had children :

    1. James Buckeliew, who married Eliza Swan, daughter of Benjamin. He removed to Zanesville, Ohio, and had children ; 1. Mary Curtis ; 2. John, who died at 1½ years ; 3. John, 2d, who died in infancy ; 4. Rebecca Curtis ; 5. Elizabeth Curtis ; 6. James Curtis ; 7. Catherine Curtis ; 8. Almira Curtis.

    2. William Curtis is unmarried.

3. Asa Frazee Curtis married Martha Smith, daughter of Jacamiah, son of Elijah Smith, of Long Hill, and had children:
1. Cornelia, who died 21st November, 1850, at three years.
2. Caroline, twin to Cornelia.

4. Jonathan Curtis married Hannah Angleman, of Plainfield, and had children: 1. Henrietta Curtis; 2. Alfred Berry Curtis.

5. David Curtis, born 8th November, 1820, married Catherine Long, daughter of Israel B. Long, and had children: 1. Mary Elizabeth Curtis; 2. Esaias Curtis; 3. Luthetter Curtis.

6. Eliza Curtis married Cornelius Williamson, son of John, of Somerset county, and had children: 1. Martha Elizabeth Williamson, born 12th May, 1835; 2. Jonathan Curtis Williamson; 3. Harriet Jane Williamson; 4. Abraham Parrot Williamson; 5. James Henry Williamson.

DAVID FRENCH.

DAVID FRENCH came from Connecticut Farms, now Union, and settled about one mile east of David Smalley's, Esq. He had a brother, John French, who lived where Thomas Conn now does, who sold out to Mr. Conn, and went to the lakes, New York. David French married, 30th May, 1776, Sarah Willcox, daughter of Will am, son of Peter Willcocks, Sen., and had children:

2d Generation.

1. Benjamin, who married Polly Collard, daughter of Benjamin Collard.

2. Polly married David Hays, of Westfield.

3. Willis married Hannah Hetfield, daughter of Moses, of Westfield.

4. Levi married Fanny Dunham, daughter of John, Jun., and went to the lakes.

5. Sally married James Williamson, of Monmouth county.

6. David, Jun., married, 2d November, 1809, Margaret Noe, daughter of Lewis N e.

7. Cornelius married Sally Winans, above Morristown, and went to the lakes.

8. Betsey married John Corwin, son of Stephen. [*See Corwin.*]

9. Phebe married Moses Moore, son of Isaac Moore. [*See Moore.*]

10. Nancy married Moses S. Littell, son of Master Benjamin Littell; went to the lakes. [*See Littell.*]

3d Generation.

WILLIS FRENCH, (son of David,) and Hannah Hetfield, had children:
1. Betsey is unmarried.

2. Sarah, who married Barzilla Ayers, lives in Elizabethtown, and has children: 1. Mary Elizabeth; 2. Moses Hetfield; 3. Hannah Frances.

3. Moses Hetfield married Betsey Cole, daughter of Freeman

Cole, Esq. [*see Parrot.*] owned the Stone Mill in Washington Valley, lives there, and has children: 1. Elias C.; 2. Adelia H.; 3. Agnes R. ——; 4. ——.

4. David A., who married Margaret Wood, daughter of Daniel S. Wood, Jun., and h s children: 1. Mary Eliza; 2. Barziila Ayers; 3. Rachel Anne; 4. William Theodore.

5. Mary married Henry, son of Noah Frazee. [*See Frazee.*]

DAVID FRENCH, (son of David,) and Margaret Noe, had children:

3d Generation.

1 Huma, who married William Drake, son of Noah. [*See Drake.*]

2. Phinehas married Mary Emeline Oswald, daughter of Henry, of New York, lives at Plainfield, owns or manages a grist-mill there, and had children: 1. Theodore; 2. Mary Elizabeth; 3. John Henry.

3. Lewis Noe, who died by accident, 6th January, 1849, unmarried.

4. Phebe married David Coulter, near Mount Bethel, Warren, Somerset county.

5. Harriet married Benjamin Lollard, near Mount Bethel.

6. Margaret married Frederick Bryant, of Hunterdon county.

7. Maria, (twin to Margaret).

8. Sally Anne.

9. Hetty Jane.

TIMOTHY GRIFFIN.

TIMOTHY GRIFFIN married Catherine Sayre, daughter of Isaac Sayre, of Springfield Township, and had children:

2d Generation.

1. Jane, who married, 1st, Francis Brown; 2d, Robert Sweetman
2. Thomas married Triphena Foster.
3. Patty married John Wheeler Foster, of Westfield.
4. Isaac married Betsey Musty, of Shrewsbury, Monmouth county.
5. Frazee died unmarried.
6. Betsey married Charles Graves.
7. Rachel married John Gray.
8. Prudence married, 1st, Charles Delaney; 2d, William R. Vigers, a Frenchman.
9. Mary married Peter Maverick, engraver, of New York.
10. Ephraim married Effa Simpson, daughter of John Simpson.
11. Timothy died unmarried.
12. William died in infancy.
13. William S. married in New York, and died leaving one child.

PATTY GRIFFIN, (daughter of Timothy,) and John W. Foster, had children:

3d Gen.

1. John Foster, who married Betsey Miller, lives in Westfield.
2. Miriam Foster married Matthias Hand, son of Nehemiah. [*See Hand.*]

3. Maria Foster married John M. Clark, son of John, of Westfield ; had no children.

4. Charles Foster married Sarah Cole, daughter of Joseph.

5. Eliza Foster married Mr. Murphy, of Connecticut, and lived there.

6. Martha Foster married Kinney McManners, son of Moses, of Westfield.

Patty, wife of John W. Foster, died, and he married Rhoda Price, daughter of Rice Price, and had children :

7. Susannah Foster, who married Martin Hulbert, son of Joshua, of Mendham.

8. Lavisa Foster married David Dunham, son of Amos, or Liberty Corner.

9. Marcus Foster, who died at ten months.

ISAAC GRIFFIN, (son of Timothy,) and Betsey Musty, had children :

1. William M., who married, 15th February, 1816, Betsey Cory, daughter of George Cory.

2. Catherine married, 28th December, 1822, Isaac Marsh, of Westfield, and had a son, William G. Marsh, who married, 23d September, 1849, Elizabeth Badgley, daughter of David, son of Anthony Badgley. Catherine Marsh died 8th November, 1850.

3. James.

4. Isaac married ———— in New York, and lives there.

EPHRAIM GRIFFIN, (son of Timothy,) and Effi Simpson, had children :

1. Frazee, who married ——— ———.

2. John.

3. Matilda married James Parmer, in New York.

4. Mary married Edward Childs, in New York.

5. Susannah married Mr. Sanford, in New York.

6. Timothy

7. Israel, who died in 1848, a young man, unmarried.

WILLIAM M. GRIFFIN, (son of Isaac, son of Timothy,) and Betsey Cory, had children :

1. Mary Anne, who married Philemon Dickerson, son of Caleb [See *Dickerson.*]

2. Elizabeth.

3. Catherine married Jonathan Hanford, son of Simeon.

4. William.

5. Abigail.

6. Lewis R.

7. Amanda L.

4th Generation.

JOHN HALL.

JOHN HALL lived near Basking Ridge, and had children:

1. John, Jun. He died unmarried at Basking Ridge, about 1845, an old man.

2. Richard, who married Elizabeth Roy, the widow of William Roy, and daughter of Eliphalet Whitaker.

NOTE.—William Roy was son of judge John Roy, of Basking Ridge, who also had a son, Joseph Roy, the father of Major Peter Roy, of Vealtown, now Bernardsville; married Nancy Rickey, daughter of Colonel Israel Rickey, who lived at the saw-mill on Passaic River, east of Basking Ridge.

NOTE.—Elizabeth Roy, and William Roy, had two children:
1. Hannah, who married Aaron Hand, son of Jonathan, of Basking Ridge.
2. William Roy, Jun., married Deborah Whitaker, daughter of Stephen, and lived in Yates county, New York.

3. Isaac Hall.

4. Jacob married Theodocia Fairchild.

5. Robert married Mary Hand, daughter of Jonathan, of Basking Ridge.

RICHARD HALL, (2d child of John Hall,) and Elizabeth Roy, had children:

1. Isaac, who married Betsey Strimple, daughter of ——— ; lives near Liberty Corner, and had children: 1. Jane; 2. Eliza; 3. Samuel; 4. William; 5. Platt; 6. Sarah; 7. John; 8. Catherine; 9. Helen; 10. Elisha.

2. Elipahlet Hall, (2d son of Richard, son of John, 1st,) married Electa Ward, daughter of Samuel C. Ward, of Bloomfield; lived there, and was a justice of the peace; they had children: 1. Sarah; 2. John; 3. Richard; 4. William; 5. George; 6. Catherine.

3. Platt, who died a young man, unmarried.

4. Ruth married Levi Dayton, son of Jonathan, of Basking Ridge, and had an only son, Elias H. Dayton, who married Huldah Conover, of Monmouth county, and had children: 1. Frank, who died in infancy; 2. Huldah.

5. Samuel married Mariah Finley, daughter of Alexander, of Basking Ridge; lived in Newark, and had children: 1. Elizabeth; 2. Alexander Finley; 3. Sophia; 4. Anne.

6. Catherine married Joel C. Homan, son of Thomas H., of Mendham; lived there, and had children:

1. Samuel Hall Homan, born 6th September, 1819, married Caroline Vance, daughter of Elias Vance, of Mendham, and had children: 1. Samuel Hall Homan; 2. Annie Mosely Homan; and died in August, 1847.

2. Melancthon Homan.

3. Elizabeth Sarah Homan, who died at four years.

4. Thomas Homan.

5. Elizabeth Sarah Johnson Homan.

6. Louisa Homan.

7. Sally married Isaac Conklin, son of William, Esq., of Basking Ridge. [*See Conklin.*]

8. Betsey married David Howel, of Mendham ; lived there, and had children : 1. Anna Mariah Howel ; 2. Amelia Howel ; 3. Elizabeth Howel ; 4. Charles Howel.

9. Miriam married John Drake, son of Daniel, of Mendham, and lived there, and had children ; 1. Sarah Drake ; 2. Aaron Drake ; 3. Caroline Drake.

10. John married Mary Alling, daughter of David, of Newark, and lived there ; had children : 1. David Alling ; 2. Antoinette ; 3. Louisa ; 4. Horace.

JACOB HALL, (4th child of John, 1st,) and Theodocia Fairchild, had children :

1. Jacob Burrows Hall, who married Rachel Hall, daughter of John, son of Richard, 1st, had children :

1. Charles Hall, D. D. a Presbyterian minister, and secretary of the A. H. M. S. of New York. He married Sarah Lawrence, of Geneseo, New York, sister of the wife of his uncle, Israel Hall, and had children : 1. Charles ; 2. James ; 3. Cornelia ; 4. Mary ; 5. Anne.

2. Sarah married George Carkner, of Michigan ; lived there.

3. Benjamin Hudson is an elder of the church, at Tecumseh, Lenawa county, Michigan.

4. Eliza married her cousin, Sherrod McKane, son of William.

5. Maria married Samuel L. Spafford ; lived at Tecumseh, Michigan.

6. Lewis Austin married Fanny Landen, daughter of Doctor Landen, of Michigan.

7. Sophia.

8. Rachel Catherine married Mr. Keith, of Monroe, Michigan, and lives there.

2. Phebe married William McKane, and had children :

1. Sherrod McKane married his cousin, Eliza Hall, daughter of Jacob B. Hall.

2. Mahlon McKane, twin to Sherrod.

3. John married Miss Howel.

4. Nancy married Mr. —— Baldwin, of Orange, New Jersey.

5. Theodocia married Mr. —— Bryan.

6. Abraham B. married Sally Hate, of Albany ; is a silversmith, in Geneva, New York, and had children :

1. Harriet, who married Truman P. Handy, cashier of the Commercial Bank, at Cleveland, Ohio.

2. Samuel, who is a Presbyterian minister in Marshall, Michigan ; he married Miss Rankin, of Newark.

7. Israel married Mary Lawrence, of Geneseo, New York, sister of the wife of Charles Hall, D. D.

8. Lydia married the Rev. Mr. —— Myers, of Geneva, New York.

9. Mariah married Foster Bernard, of Geneva, New York.

M

ROBERT HALL, (5th son of John Hall, 1st,) and Mary Hand, had children :

1. Catherine,, who married Samuel Rickey, son of John Rickey, Esq.
2. Sarah married Joshua Bullman, son of Joseph, of Long Hill.
3. Mary married Thomas Gibbs, of Illinois.
4. William married at Jacksonville, Illinois.
Robert Hall, with his family, removed to Illinois.

RICHARD HALL was a younger brother of John Hall, 1st; lived at Basking Ridge; married a Miss Compton, and had children :

1. John, who married Sarah Austin, daughter of Moses Austin, and sister of Moses Austin, many years deputy sheriff in Eliza-bethtown.
2. Joseph married Ruth Austin, sister of Sarah, John's wife; he lived between the Cayuga and Seneca Lakes, N. Y.
3. Samuel married Hannah Webster.
4. Jonathan married Rachel Austin, sister of Sarah and Ruth. He lived west of Seneca Lake, in Yates Co., N. Y.
5. Richard, Jun., married Peggy Rogers; lived in Lycoming Co., Penn.
6. Nathaniel married Nancy Jones, in Pennsylvania; removed to Ohio, and was there killed by lightning.
7. Margaret married, 1st, Jacob Howke; 2d, Enos Sillsby.
8. Polly married, 1st, Mr. Parker, and had a son, James Parker; Mr. Parker died, and she married George Chapin.

JOHN HALL, (1st child of Richard, brother of John Hall, 1st,) and Sarah Austin, had children :

1. Moses, born 25th August, 1776, married, 1st, Phebe Burrows, daughter of John, of Lycoming Co., Penn. She died, and he married, 2d, Mary Whitaker, daughter of Stephen. She died, 18th November, 1835, and he married, 3d, Phebe Whitaker, sister of his 2d wife. He lived at Geneva, N. Y.; carried on an iron foundry there.
2. Rachel married Jacob B. Hall, son of Jacob. (*See Jacob B. Hall.*)
3. John Hall, Jun., married Priscilla Fanning, daughter of Asher, of Canandaigua, and went to Zanesville, Ohio, and died 11th July, 1851.
4. Joseph married Polly Black, daughter of Archibald, and went to Michigan.
5. Mary married Stephen Whitaker, son of Stephen, and lived in Cleveland, Ohio. (*See Stephen Whitaker.*)
6. Jacob Burrows married, 1st, Abigail, daughter of Esq. Townsend; lived in Geneseo, and had children : 1. Sarah; 2. John; 3. Emily; 4. Abigail; 5. Elizabeth; 6. Catherine; 7. Wealthy Anne.
7. Catherine married Amzi Bruen, of Newark, New Jersey.

MOSES HALL, (1st child of John, son of Richard,) and Phebe Burrows, his 1st wife, had children:

4th Generation.

1. John Burrows, who married Agnes Millspaw, of Geneva; lives at Williamsport, on the Susquehannah River, and has a large iron foundry there.

2. Harriet married William C. Tighlman; and had children: 1. Burrows Tighlman; 2. Phebe Tighlman; and then Harriet died.

Moses Hall's wife Phebe then died, and by his 2d wife, Mary Whitaker, he had other children:

3. Jane, born 25th April, 1809, married John Humphrey, went to Michigan, and had children: 1. William Humphrey; 2. James Humphrey; 3. Charles Humphrey; 4. Henry Humphrey; 5. Mary Humphrey.

4. Phebe, born 5th November, 1810, married Nelson Rowley, went to Michigan, and had children: 1. Stephen Rowley.

5. Rachel, born 7th November, 1812.

6. Stephen Whitaker, born 5th August, 1815, married Nancy Graham; lives at Williamsport, with his brother John, and had children: 1. Sarah Jane; 2. Hetty Amelia.

7. Henry Axtell, born 9th February, 1817, married Susan Claghorn Babcock, daughter of Joseph M. Babcock, of Lenox, Massachusetts; lives in Geneva, and had children: 1. Lenox.

8. Mary, born 9th March, 1820, married, 30th September, 1847, the Rev. John Jermaine Porter, son of the Rev. Stephen Porter, of Geneva. He is pastor of the Presbyterian church, and settled first at Kingston, opposite Wilkesbarre, Pennsylvania.

9. Hetty, born 18th September, 1823, married Chauncey B. Ackley, son of Oliver Ackley, of New England; lives in Geneva, and had children: 1. Mary Ackley.

JOHN HALL, Jun., (3d child of John Hall, son of Richard,) and Priscilla Fanning, had children:

4th Generation.

1. Austin married Mary Mitchel.

2. Eveline married Mr. Harvy; had a daughter Jane, and then died; and the child died.

3. Elizabeth married Doct. John Scott; lives in Toledo, Ohio, and had a daughter Frances.

4. John married Kate Mitchel, sister of Austin's wife.

5. Mary married Mr. Throgmorton, of Zanesville, Ohio.

6. Jacob Burrows, who studied medicine, started for California, and died on the way.

7. Charles married Miss Withington, daughter of Daniel, who married Sarah Hall, daughter of Joseph, son of John.

8. Frances married Mr. Howard, who went with his brother-in-law, Jacob B. Hall, to California.

9. Jane, who died at 3 or 4 years.

10. Henry.

11. Sarah Jane married William Rogers, lived in New York, and had a daughter Molly.

JOSEPH HALL, (4th child of John, son of Richard Hall,) and Polly Black, lived in Michigan, and had children: 1. Elizabeth; 2. George; 3. Catherine; 4. John; 5. Charles; 6. Agnes; 7. Sarah married Daniel Withington, and had a daughter, who married Charles Hall, son of John, of Zanesville.

JACOB B. HALL, (6th child of John, son of Richard Hall,) and Abigail Townsend, lived at Geneseo, and had children: 1. Sarah; 2. Emily; 3. John; 4. Abigail; 5. Elizabeth; 6. Catherine; and by a 2d wife, 7. Wealthy Anne.

CATHERINE HALL, (7th child of John, son of Richard Hall,) and Amzi Bruen, had children:
1. John Bruen.
2. George Bruen.
3. Sarah Bruen.
4. Horace Bruen.
5. Eveline Bruen.
6. Austin Bruen. } twins.
7. Anson Bruen. }

JOSEPH HALL, (2d child of Richard, brother of John Hall, 1st,) and Ruth Austin, had children: 1. Richard; 2. David; 3. William; 4. Isaac; 5. Joseph, Jun.; 6. Susan; 7. Sarah; 8. Deborah; 9. Mary.

JONATHAN HALL, (4th child of Richard, brother of John Hall, 1st,) and Rachel Austin, had children:
1. Jonathan Austin married Anne Whitaker, daughter of Stephen; lived near Penn Yan, Yates county, New York, and had children: 1. Mary Anne; 2. Deborah married John Littell, son of John Littell, Esq.; 3. Moses; 4. Stephen Crosby.

JOSEPH HALL, (son of Jonathan, and brother of Jonathan Austin Hall,) married Sarah Flowers; lived in Michigan, and had children: 1. William; 2. Austin; 3. Charles; 4. Francis.

RICHARD HALL, Jun., (5th child of Richard, brother of John Hall,) and Peggy Rogers, had children:
1. Samuel.
2. Joseph.
3. William, and others to the number of fourteen.

MARGARET HALL, (7th child of Richard, brother of John Hall, 1st,) and Jacob Howke, had children: 1. Mary Howke; 2. Betsey Howke; 3. Margaret Howke; and by Enos Silsby, had children: 4. John Silsby; 5. James Silsby.

THOMAS HALLOCK.

THOMAS HALLOCK lived between the 1st and 2d mountains. He married Sarah Bedell, (daughter of Moses Bedell, and Elizabeth Littell, daughter of David Littell,) and had children :

1. David, who died unmarried.
2. Smith, who married Jane Raddin, daughter of Jeremiah Raddin, as her 3d husband.
3. John married Betsey, the widow of Moses Roff, and had a son, John.
4. Betsey married, 1st, Abraham Walker ; 2d, Jonathan Walker, sons of Asher. [*See Walker.*]
5. Polly married Hugh Davis, son of John Davis, of Washington Valley.
6. Catherine married Alexander Freeman, son of Henry, of Elizabethtown.
7. Susan married, 11th February, 1815, Thomas Mulligan, from Ireland ; lives in New York.
8. Thompson, who died a young man, unmarried.
9. William married Sarah Tucker, of New York ; lived there.
10. Fanny, born 20th June, 1804, married Joseph Pope, son of Samuel.
11. Caroline married John Van Buren ; lived in New York.
12. Sibbel, who died in infancy.

SMITH HALLOCK, (2d child of Thomas,) and Jane Raddin, had children :

1. Lewis, who died young.
2. Thompson, who died a young man, unmarried.
3. Catherine died at 13 years.
4. Jeremiah.

POLLY HALLOCK, (5th child of Thomas,) and Hugh Davis, lived in Newark, and had children :
1. Abraham Davis married Elizabeth ——— ; she died 1844.
2. Elizabeth Littell Davis married, 1st, David Higby, who died, and she married, 2d, Garret Skinner, and lived at Cleveland, Ohio.
3. Henrietta Davis married James Rogers ; lives in New York.
4. John Davis, (twin to Henrietta,) died a young man.
5. Hugh Littell Davis married Elizabeth Hicks, of Dover, and lives in Newark.
6. David Littell Davis.
7. Thomas H. Davis.
8. Sarah Davis married George Canuff ; lives at Cleveland, Ohio.
9. Catherine Ross Davis.

CATHERINE HALLOCK, (6th child of Thomas,) and Alexander Freeman, lived in Elizabethtown, and had children : 1. William Henry Freeman ; 2. Sarah Emeine Freeman ; 3. George Agustus Freeman. Mr. Freeman removed to Ohio, when his wife, and all his children, died.

SUSAN HALLOCK, (7th child of Thomas,) and Thomas Mulligan, lived in New York, and had children :
1. Bridget Mulligan, who married William Seaman.
2. Fanny Mulligan married Woodruff Crane.
3. William Mulligan married Anne ——.
4. John Mulligan.
5. Daniel Mulligan married —— ; lives in Rahway.
6. Harriet Mulligan.
7. Anne Mulligan.
8. Emma Mulligar.

FANNY HALLOCK, (10th child of Thomas,) and Joseph Pope, lived at Plainfield, and had children : 1. Lucinda Adaline Pope, born 3d October, 1827, married 28th February, 1848, John Stites, son of Samuel Stites, of Sussex, son of John Stites of Monnt Bethel ; lives in Sussex ; 2. James Nelson Pope ; 3. Amanda Walker Pope ; 4. William Lewis Pope ; 5. Frances Adelia Pope ; 6. Newton Hill Pope ; 7. Harriet Matilda Pope ; 8. ——.

JOSEPH HALSEY.

JOSEPH HALSEY lived near the Wheatsheaf Tavern, between Rahway and Elizabethtown. He married Elizabeth Haines, sister of Richard Valentine's wife ; he had children :

2d Generation.

1. Sarah, who married Joshua Conklin, of Williams Farms. [*See Conklin.*]
2. Abigail married James Miller, of Piscataway.
3. Rebecca married Thomas Williams, near Elizabethtown.
4. Joseph, Jun., married Mary Armstrong, daughter of John, from Ireland ; lived in Springfield.
5. Hannah married Benjamin Miller ; (their daughter married General William Crane, of Elizabethtown.)
6. Phebe married Benjamin Crane, of Westfield. [*See Benjamin Crane.*]
7. Daniel married Miss Williams, daughter of Samuel, and sister of John Williams.
8. Isaac married Rebecca Garthwaite, of Elizabethtown.
9. Rachel married Benjamin Magie, son of John, of Elizabethtown.
10. Deborah married, 1st, Jonathan Magie, brother of Benjamin ; 2d, Isaiah Meeker, of New Providence. [*See Meeker.*]
11. Nancy married John Hamilton ; lived in Westfield ; had no children.

3d Generation.

JOSEPH HALSEY, Jun., and Mary Armstrong, had children :
1. Joseph, 3d, who married, 1st, Mary Brookfield ; 2d, Miss Frazee.
2. Daniel married Miss Pierson, of Westfield.
3. Mary married Matthias Ross.
4. Hannah married Daniel Baker, of Westfield, son of Nathaniel.
5. John married Nancy Sayre, daughter of Isaac.

6. Abigail married Doct. John Condit, of Orange.

7. Isaac married Sally Smith, daughter of Walter, of Springfield.

8. Rhoda married the same Doct. John Condit.

JOSEPH HALSEY, 3d, (son of Joseph, Jun.,) and Mary Brookfield, had children:

1. Joseph, 4th, who married Sally Bryant, daughter of Samuel.

2. Mary married John Clarkson, son of John, and by Miss Frazee had other children.

DANIEL HALSEY, (2d child of Joseph, Jun.,) and Miss Pierson, had children: 1. Gitty; 2. Harriet, and others.

MARY HALSEY, (3d child of Joseph, Jun.,) and Matthias Ross, had children:

1. Ogden Ross, who married Lydia Ludlow, daughter of John, of Butler county, Ohio, and lives there. [See *Ludlow.*]

2. Abigail Ross married Capt. Jonathan Burnet, near Springfield.

3. Joseph Ross married, and lived near Springdale, Ohio.

HANNAH HALSEY, (4th child of Joseph Halsey, Jun.,) and Daniel Baker, had children:

1. Rhoda Baker, who married James DeCamp, son of James, of Rahway, and had children:

    1. Caleb DeCamp, who married Elizabeth Ward, of Urbana, Ohio.

    2. Mary DeCamp, who married Taylor Webster, of Hamilton, Ohio.

    3. Daniel DeCamp, who died at 18 years.

2. Mary Halsey Baker married Cornelius Ludlow, son of John, of Westfield, and had a daughter, Jane Ludlow, when Mr. Ludlow died. Jane Ludlow married the Rev. William Spencer; preaches at Sidney, Ohio.

3. Lewis Conklin Baker married Margaret Dunham, daughter of Joseph, and had an only daughter, Margaret.

4. Caleb Baker married Sarah Williams, daughter of Marsh Williams, and had children: 1. Daniel; 2. Marsh Williams; 3. John; 4. Hannah.

5. Nancy Baker married Jonathan Cory, son of Joseph, of Westfield, and had children: 1. Daniel Baker; 2. James; 3. Samuel; 4. William; 5. Sarah Jane.

6. Betsey Ryerson Baker married Samuel Young, of Butler Co., Ohio, and had children: 1. Josiah; 2. Hannah Elizabeth.

7. Hannah Baker married Andrew McClary, of Rossville, Ohio, and had children: 1. Mary McClary; 2. John McClary: 3. Andrew McClary.

JOHN HALSEY, (5th child of Joseph, Jun.,) and Nancy Sayre, had children:

1. John, who married, 1st, Hannah Pool, daughter of John, of Long Hill. [*See Pool.*] They removed to near Lebanon, Ohio, and had children:

    1. Caleb, who married Ruth Wood, and had children:
        1. Hannah, who married Edmund Monroe, son of Nathan; 2. Rosetta married Marsh Noe, son of Ellis; 3. Sarah Anne; 4. Mariah Josephine; 5. Joseph; 6. Eliza; 7 John Newel.
    2. Joseph, who died at about 22 years, unmarried.
    3. Rhoda married Rev. David Montfort, of Indiana, brother of the Rev. Francis Montfort.

John .Halsey married, 2d, the widow of Capt. Cushion, and daughter of the Rev. Mr. Vanhorn, and had,
    4. A daughter Eliza, who married, 1st, Asher Corlas; 2d, Doct. Elias Fisher.

2. Rhoda married Moses Ogden, of Elizabethtown, and had children:
    1. John Ogden; 2. William Ogden; 3. Joseph Ogden; 4. Moses Ogden.

3. Jane married David Miller, of Madison, son of Ichabod, of Rahway, and had children: 1. Caroline; 2. Matthias; 3. Sally Anne; 4. Charlotte; 5. David; 6. Ichabod. Mr. Miller died at Madison.

4. Joseph, 3d, married Mary Potter, daughter of Jacob Potter, of New Providence; removed to near Lebanon, Ohio, and had children:
    1. Mary, who married John Dynes, son of Chamber, and had children: 1. John Dynes; 2. William Dynes; 3. Abigail Dynes; 4. Mary Dynes; 5. Clarissa Dynes; 6. James Dynes; 7. Milton Dynes.
    2. Abigail married James Dynes, cousin of John, and had children: 1. Clarissa Dynes: 2. John Dynes; 3. James Dynes; 4. Sarah Dynes; 5. Martha Dynes.
    3. David.
    4. Joseph S.

5. Jacob Potter Halsey married Sally Banta, daughter of Daniel, from Jersey City, and had children: 1. John Russel Halsey; 2. William Henry Halsey.

ABIGAIL, (6th child of Joseph Halsey, Jun.,) and,
RHODA, (8th child of Joseph Halsey, Jun.,) and Doct. John Condit, had children:

1. Caleb Condit, who was killed by a fall of a horse.
2. Silas Condit, who lives in Newark; he has been clerk of the county, member of the legislature several times, and a member of congress; he had a son, Doct. John Condit; and by Rhoda, Doctor Condit had children:
3. Joseph Condit, who went to Canada.
4. Abigail Condit.
5. Smith Condit.

ISAAC HALSEY, (7th child of Joseph Halsey, Jun.,) and Sally Smith, had children:

1. Mary, who married David Bryant, son of Samuel, of Westfield.
2. Daniel married Jane Miller, daughter of ———, of Westfield.
3. Elizabeth married Samuel Meeker, of Springfield.
4. William married Abby Woodruff, daughter of Stites.
5. Smith married Betsey Miller, daughter of Nathaniel, of Springfield ; he lives in Newark.
6. Joseph A.
7. Samuel.

DANIEL HALSEY, (son of Joseph,) had a son, Ichabod, who went to Ohio, and married Mary Smith, daughter of John Smith, of Warren county, Ohio, and had children :

1. James Smith Halsey, who married Catherine Hinkle, of Springfield, Clark county, Ohio.
2. Ichabod Benton Halsey.
3. Martha married Doct. Jennings, of Warren county, Ohio, and went to Indiana.
4. Mary married Charles Anthony, of Springfield, Clark county, Ohio.
5. Cynthia married, 5th June, 1845, James K. Hurin, merchant, of Lebanon, Ohio, as his 3d wife. [*See Hurin.*]
6. Daniel, who is editor of a newspaper at Hamilton, Ohio.
Three daughters have died.

HEZEKIAH HAND.

HEZEKIAH HAND lived in Westfield; had three wives. By his 1st wife had five, by his 2d wife, five, and by his 3d wife, 12 children ; making 22 in all.

2d Generation.

1. John, who went and settled somewhere on the Mohawk river, in New York, and married there.
2. David, who married Abigail Osborn, daughter of Benjamin, of near Mount Bethel.
3. Sarah married ——, and removed to Philadelphia.
4. Elizabeth married Isaac Pack.
5. Charity married Job Gould, lived at Milford, Pennsylvania, and had children: 1. John Gould ; 2. Sarah Gould; 3. Rebecca Gould ; and by his 2d wife, had,
6. Hezekiah, who died unmarried.
7. Robert married Rachel Whitehead, daughter of Richard, of Short Hills.
8. Nehemiah, (twin to Robert,) born 6th September, 1764, married Sarah Clark, daughter of David, of Warren township, Somerset county.
9. Jacob married, 1st, Miss Lane ; 2d, Joanna Crane, a widow.
10. Nancy, who died young.

And by his 3d wife, Anna Ferrago, Hezekiah Hand had 12 children :
11. Martha, who married, 1st, John Tomer, and 2d, Joseph Stone.
12. Phebe married Henry Smalley, son of David Smalley, Esq., of Warren, Somerset county.
13. William married, 1st, Sarah Shaw, daughter of John, and had four children ; 2d, Elizabeth Richards, daughter of Samuel, of Springfield ; 3d, on 14th October, 1848, Elizabeth Littell, daughter of Doct. Anthony Littell. He was born 15th June, 1774; his 3d wife was born 22d May, 1790 ; had no children by 2d or 3d wives.
14. Mary married Azariah Dunham, of Plainfield.
15. Henry, born 19th November, 1779, and married Sarah Davis, daughter of Deacon Jacob Davis, and went to Ohio.
16. Charlotte married John Wayne.
17. Jotham married Jane Haviland.
18. Tabitha married Levi Thomas, son of William, and went to Western New York.
19. Jonathan married, for his 2d wife, Phebe Rino, daughter of Peter Rino.
20. Nancy married Levi Hetfield, son of Zophar, of Westfield, and had a pair of twins, who died in infancy.

ROBERT and NEHEMIAH, (sons of Hezekiah Hand,) removed from Westfield to Passaic Valley, about the year 1796.

3d Generation.

Robert Hand, and Rachel Whitehead, had children :
1. Fanny, who married, 5th March, 1807, John Stanley, of New York ; she had children :
    1. Matthias Stanley, who went to New Orleans, and died in 1846, unmarried.
    2. Eliza Anne Stanley, who married Sylvester Leonard, of

Rahway, and went to Ohio. John Stanley died, and his wife Fanny died 30th May, 1812, aged 27 years.

2. Margaret married William Bonnel, of Plainfield, and went to French Creek, Pennsylvania.

3. Robert married Hannah Crowel, daughter of Samuel, of New Vernon ; lives in Newark.

4. Uzel married Deborah Meeker, daughter of Daniel H., son of Isaiah ; lived in Newark.

5. Deborah married Abner Williams, son of Noah, of Long Hill ; lives in Morristown. [*See Williams.*]

6. Harriet married William Camp, Jun., son of William, of Livingston ; had one daughter, and then died.

7. Clarissa, born 30th October, 1799, married, 19th February, 1820, John Trowbridge, of Morris county.

8. Frances Everet, who went west to the Mississippi river.

ROBERT HAND, (son of Robert,) and Hannah Crowel, had children :

1. Salina, who married Henry Sugard, of Newark, and soon died.

2. Helen married Peter Sugard, cousin of Henry ; he died and she married, 2d, George Backus, of Newark.

3. Charles.

UZEL HAND, (son of Robert,) and Deborah Meeker, lived in Newark, and had children :

1. Caroline, who married Henry Low, son of Cornelius, of Cauldwell.

2. Robert married Elizabeth Hamilton, daughter of Jacob, of Millville, and had children : 1. Jane ; 2. Sarah Caroline ; 3. Henry Low.

3. Frances Everet married Charlotte Warlsie, and had children : 1. Gertrude Cook.

NOTE.— Robert Hand died 19th July, 1819, aged 54 years. Rachel, his wife, died 26th March, 1832, aged 73 years. Uzel Hand, (their son,) died 10th July, 1839, aged 47 years.

CLARISSA HAND, (daughter of Robert,) and John Trowbridge, had children :

1. Mary Jane, who married Francis Woodruff, son of John, of Elizabethtown.

2. Margaret, who married John Cooper, of Rahway.

3. Anna Mariah.

4. John Lewis.

5. Elizabeth Antoinette, born 14th February, 1831.

6. Henrietta, born 5th October, 1833.

7. Henry Augustine, born 17th July, 1836.

8. Uzel, born 7th June, 1839.

9. Frances, born 16th October, 1842.

10. Harriet, born 6th December, 1844.

NEHEMIAH HAND, (son of Hezekiah,) was born 6th Sept. 1764, and died 15th February, 1834. His wife, Sarah, died 26th Feb. 1844 ; they had children :

3d Generation.

1. Sarah, born 24th Dec. 1791, and died 24th Nov. 1793.

2. Matthias, born 9th Nov. 1793, married, 20th Nov. 1814, Miriam Foster, daughter of John W. Foster, of Westfield, and died 7th April, 1848.

3. David Clark, born 6th May, 1796, married, 24th Dec. 1814, Mary Badgley, daughter of Jonathan, and had no children.

4. Betsey, born 1st Nov. 1798, married, 24th Aug. 1814, John Combs, son of James, of Monmouth county, and had children : 1. Sally Anne Combs, born 17th Feb. 1815, and died 31st Aug. 1839, unmarried ; 2. David Hand Combs, born 13th Nov. 1818. John Combs left his wife and went to Middletown, Ohio ; David H., his son, when a young man, went to his father.

5. Benjamin, born 6th Feb. 1805, married Betsey Tice, daughter of John, of Westchester county, New Yrk.

6. John Winans, born 4th Dec. 1806, married Betsey Doty, daughter of Anthony ; has no children.

MATTHIAS HAND, (son of Nehemiah,) and Miriam Foster, had children :

4th Generation.

1. John Foster, born 18th August, 1815, and died 26th May, 1830.

2. Nehemiah, born 7th August, 1817, married, 10th August, 1837, Mary Marsh, of Westfield.

3. Mariah Clark, born 7th April, 1819, married William Ferris, son of Randolph, of Chatham.

4. Elizabeth, born 21st June, 1821, married William Fautoute, of Union township.

5. Martha, born 9th July, 1824, married Lewis Miller, son of William, of Westfield, whose wife was Sarah, daughter of Lewis Ludlow and Betsey Davis, daughter of Deacon Davis.

6. Abby, born 7th October, 1826.

7. William married Emma ——

8. Melissa.

BENJAMIN HAND, (son of Nehemiah,) and Betsey Tice, had children : 1. Caroline ; 2. Mahala Tice ; 3. Sarah Elizabeth.

WILLIAM HAND, (13th child of Hezekiah Hand,) and his first wife, Sarah Shaw, had children :

3d Generation.

1. Mary, who married Doct. Corra Osborn, son of Jonathan Hand Osborn.

2. Hannah, who married John Darby, Jun., son of John Darby of Scotch Plains.

3. William, Jun., who married Nancy Terry, daughter of Thomas Terry.

4. Sarah Anne married James Potter, son of Reuben Potter, of Westfield.

4th Generation.

MARY HAND, and Doct. Corra Osborn, had children :
1. Mahlon Osborn, who went to St. Louis, and married Mary Frothingham.
2. Mary Osborn married Samuel Hays, son of Doct. Samuel Hays, of Newark.
3 Letitia Osborn married David Miller, son of John, of Westfield.
4. Anne Osborn married Nathan Williams, son of Solomon, of Westfield.

HANNAH HAND, (2d daughter of William,) and John Darby, Jun., had children :
1. Ezra Darby, who married Mary Ludlow, was a lawyer, and ived in Elizabethtown. He died 1851.
2. Catherine Darby married Edward Hetfield, son of Zophar, of Westfield.
3. William Darby.
4. Mary Darby married John Hetfield, brother of Edward.
5. Sarah Darby.
6. John Darby.
7. Margaret Darby.
8. Elizabeth Darby.

WILLIAM HAND, Jun., and Nancy Terry, had children :
1. John ; 2. Mary ; 3. Charlotte ; 4. William ; 5. Henry 6. David ; 7. Thomas Terry.

SARAH HAND, and James Potter, had children : 1. Sarah Potter; 2. Reuben Potter ; 3. William Potter ; 4. Apollos Potter.

STEPHEN HAND, (brother of Hezekiah,) had 3 wives, the first of which was Eve ; by them had 23 children, among which were the following, viz. :

2d Generation.

1. Isaac.
2. Enoch.
3. Lydia, who married Thomas Baker, and went to Ohio.
4. Abigail.
5. Jane married John Baker, a brother of Thomas Baker.
6. Andrew.
7. Lewis.
8. Stephen.
9. Nathan.
10. Hannah married John McManners, son of Moses.
11. Mary married Alexander Smith ; lived in New York.
12. Sarah married Absalom Ladner.
13. Phebe.
14. James.
I know not that Benjamin is any way related to Hezekiah Hand.

BENJAMIN HAND.

BENJAMIN HAND lived on Long Hill, where Samuel Stanbury formerly lived, and owned the farm lately owned by John Littell, and now owned by Richard Ayre and his son William.

He married Phebe Wood, sister of Samuel Wood, who went to Dayton, Ohio. She was also a sister of the wife of George Brown, and of Esther, the wife of Jonathan Totten.

Benjamin Hand had children :

1. Daniel, who married Abigail Parrot, daughter of Samuel Parrot, and died. [*See Parrot.*]

2. Betsey married William Parrot, son of Thomas Parrot. [*See Parrot.*]

3. John married Anna S. Williams, son of John Williams, of Long Hill.

4. Dennis, who went to Ohio.

5. Polly married, 1st, Jeremiah Mott; 2d, Charles Layton, of New Vernon.

6. Electa married John Cauldwell, son of John, son of William, and went to Ohio. [*See Cauldwell.*]

7. Joseph. married ——.

JOHN HAND, and Anna S. Williams, had children :

1. Stites, who married Mary Anne Boyle.

2. John Eden.

3. Anna Mariah, who married Henry Frost, of New Vernon, and went to Ohio.

4. Harriet, who went to Ohio, and married there.

5. Emma, went to Ohio, and married there.

I know of no connection between the following families of Hand, with either the two foregoing by that name.

WILLIAM HAND.

WILLIAM HAND married Lois Ward ; they lived in Livingston township, and had children :

1. Mary, who married Captain Isaac Gillam.
2. Jonathan married Sarah Reed, daughter of Deacon William Reed, and removed to Basking Ridge.
3. Phebe married Joseph Ball, probably one of the nine sons of Thomas Ball. [*See Ball.*]
4. David married Patty Campbell, daughter of James Campbell, Esq.
5. Martha married Isaac Shipman, son of Abram, of Monroe, Morris county.
6. Moses married Mary Samson, daughter of David. [*See Samson.*]
7. Aaron married Phebe Smith, daughter of Walter Smith, of Springfield. He was a colonel in the Essex brigade of militia.

MARY HAND, (1st child of William,) and Capt. Isaac Gilliam, had children..

1. Lois Gillam, who married Cyrus Crane ; she died, and he married her cousin, Phebe Shipman, widow of John Tichenor.
2. Polly Gillam married Eleazer Baldwin.
3. Anna Gillam married Silas Baldwin, brother of Eleazer.
4. Isaac Gillam, Jun , married —— ——.
5. Phebe Gillam married Nathaniel Brown.
6. William Gillam married Polly Darling, daughter of Thomas.

JONATHAN HAND removed from Springfield to Basking Ridge ; he married Sarah Reeve, daughter of Deacon William Reeve, of Vauxhall ; they had children :

1. Aaron, who married Hannah Roy, daughter of William Roy and Elizabeth Whitaker, daughter of Eliphalet Whitaker. [*See E. Whitaker.*]
2. Polly married Robert Hall, brother of Richard. [*See Hall.*]
3. Sally, who died unmarried, nearly 50 years of age.
4. Gilbert married Eliza Howel, daughter of John, of Westfield, and went to Darke county, Ohio.
5. Esther married Hartman Vreeland, as his 2d wife ; has no children. She lives at Basking Ridge, a widow ; has adopted a son of her husband by his first wife, named Hartman Cornelius Vreeland.
6. Jonathan, Jun., married Anne Alward, daughter of Henry ; has no children. [*See Alward.*]

7. Caty married William Todd, son of James, and grandson of Alexander Martin.

8. Nancy married John Moore, son of Benjamin Moore, of Mount Bethel.

9. James married Betsey Pennington, daughter of John, of Dead River.

10. Betsey married Walter Smith Reeve, son of William, of Springfield.

AARON HAND, (1st child of Jonathan,) and Hannah Roy, lived at Basking Ridge, and had children :

1. William Roy Hand, who married Phebe M. Annin, daughter of William C. Annin ; he is a physician ; lives at Ringwood, Hunterdon county, and has children : 1. John Cooper Hand ; 2. William Milton Hand ; 3. Sarah Hand ; 4. Frances Hand.

2. Fanny.

3. Eliza Whitaker, who died at 9 months.

4. Sarah R., born 20th Dec. 1811, married Ebenezer Byram, son of Silas C., son of Naphtali Byram, of Morristown. [See Byram.]

5. Aaron Milton, born 1819, died 1820.

GILBERT HAND, (4th child of Jonathan Hand,) and Betsey Howel, had children :

1. Tyler, who died in infancy.

2. Tyler, 2d, who also died young.

3. Hannah, who married John Haas, son of Jacob, of Liberty Corner, N. J.

NOTE.–Jacob Haas's wife was Charity Cooper, daughter of Benjamin Cooper. John and Hannah Haas had children : 1. Lydia Haas ; 2. Sarah Elizabeth Haas ; 3. Job Lane Haas ; 4. Gilbert R. Haas ; 5. Charity Cooper Haas ; 6. John Calvin Haas.

4. Jonathan married, in Ohio, Ruth Roberts, and had children : 1. Eliza ; 2. William Reeve.

5. Eliza married John Sagebury, son of James Sagebury, of New York, whose wife was Sally Howel, sister of Eliza's mother.

6. William Reeve.

CATY HAND, (7th child of Jonathan Hand,) and William Todd, had children :

1. John Todd, who married ——.

2. Jane Todd married Ellis D. Baldwin, son of David. [See Baldwin.]

3. Sarepta Todd married George Bird.

4. Mary Todd.

5. Sarah Todd married William Gibson.

6. Jonathan Todd married ———.
7. William Todd.
8. Hugh Todd.
9. James Todd.

NANCY HAND, (8th child of Jonathan Hand,) and John Moore, had children :,
1. Elsie Moore, who married Joseph Coulter.
2. Sarah Moore married John Adams, of Mount Bethel.
3. Keziah Moore married Patterson Waldron, of Mount Bethel.
4. Benjamin Moore married Harriet Scofield.
5. Eliza Moore.
6. Jonathan Moore.
7. Esther Moore.
8. William Moore.
9. Catherine Moore.

DAVID HAND, (4th child of William,) and Patty Campbell, had children :
1. Sally, who did not marry.
2. Uriah married ———.
3. Lois married Mr. Winans, and went to Ohio.
4. Joseph B. married Mary Gardner, daughter of Moses.
5. Phebe married ——— ———, of Parcipany, and lived there.
6. Ira married Rhoda Crowel, daughter of Venus Crowel, of Livingston.
7. Prudence married Stephen Brown, son of Phinehas.

3d Generation.

IRA HAND, and Rhoda Crowel, had children :
1. Mary, who married Horace Vanhouten.
2. Isaac married Caroline Littell, daughter of James, son of Nathaniel, lives in Middletown, Ohio.
3. Phebe married Thomas A. Smith.
4. Lois married Enos Scott.
5. Matilda married Daniel Terril.
6. Caleb.
7. Luther.
8. James.
9. Francis.
10. Sarah.
11. Elizabeth.
12. Ira.

4th Generation.

MARTHA HAND, (5th child of William,) and Isaac Shipman, had children :
1. Phebe Shipman, who married, 1st, John Tichenor ; 2d, Cyrus Crane, as his 2d wife.

3d Gen.

N

2. Sally Shipman married —— ——.
3. Abraham Shipman married —— ——.
4. William Shipman married—— ——.
5. Nathaniel Gilliam Shipman married Amy Warner.

MOSES HAND, (6th child of William,) and Mary Samson, had children :
1. Daniel, who married Miss —— Winans.
2. Elias married —— —— and lives near West Point, N. Y.
3. Moses married —— ——.
4. Nathaniel, who did not marry.
5. Watson.
6. William.

COL. AARON HAND, (7th child of William,) and Phebe Smith, had children :

3d Generation.

1. Joseph Smith, born 7th June, 1784, married Lydia Buckbee, daughter of Thomas.
2. Isaac M., born 3d September, 1787, married. 1st, Mary Sands, of Long Island ; 2d, Jane, widow of John Barto.
3. Rebecca, born 12th December. 1789, and died at 3 years.
4. William, born 12th June, 1793, and died at 17 years.
5. John Smith, born 23d September, 1795, and died at 33 years, unmarried.
6. Mary P., born 25th August, 1798, married John Bond, son of Nathaniel, of Springfield, and had children: 1. Emma Bond, who married William Chatterton, of Elizabethtown ; 2. Eliza Bond.
7. Rebecca, born 18th February, 1802, and died at about 33 years, unmarried.
8. Hannah B., born 24th January, 1805, and died at about 33 years, unmarried.
9. Aaron A., born 11th November, 1807, and died at about 23 years, unmarried.
10. William, born 26th July, 1810, and died in infancy,

JOSEPH S. HAND, (son of Col. Aaron Hand,) lives where his father did. He and Sarah Buckbee had children :

4th Generation.

1. Louisa.
2. Mary, who married Asa B. Munn, son of Lewis, of Orange, and had children : 1. Joseph Lewis Munn.
3. William, who died at 35 years, unmarried.
4. Thomas married Mary Bruff, of Columbus, and lives in Cincinnati, Ohio, and had children : 1. Catherine.
5. Isaac S., who married two sisters. 1st, Sarah, 2d, Abby, daughters of Elias Thompson of Madison, lives on Long Island.
6. Catherine ; 7. Phebe.

ISAAC M. HAND, (son of Col. AaronHand,) owns the farm adjoining his brother Joseph's, and had children:

1. Edward.
2. Mariah Louisa, who died at 9 years.

JEREMIAH HART.

JEREMIAH HART lived on the south-east corner of the forks of the road at the Presbyterian church at New Providence. He was born 9th December, 1714, and died 17th November, 1749 ; his wife Sarah, born 11th June, 1718. They had children ;

1. Elizabeth, who married Jeremiah Ball, and had a daughter, Abigail Ball, who married Benjamin Samson, son of David. [*See Samson.*] Jerry Ball died, and Elizabeth married Nathan Baldwin, of South Orange, as his 2d wife.

2. Deborah, born 16th May, 1745, married Jonathan Howel Osborn, son of John, Sen. [*See Osborn.*]

3. Anna, born 25th April, 1747, married Lewis Baldwin, son of Nathan, above named.

4. Daniel, born 17th December, 1749, married, 1st, Hannah, daughter of Daniel Potter, 2d. She died 11th October, 1774, aged 23 years, and he married, 2d, June 6th, 1786, Prudence, daughter of Col. Samuel Potter, a cousin of his first wife. He died 7th December, 1832, aged 81 years ; his widow died 22d December, 1838, aged 87 years.

DANIEL HART, and Prudence Potter, had children :

1. Dency, born 14th January, 1792, married Frazee Noe, son of Lewis Noe.

2. Sally, born 3d April, 1796, is unmarried.

3. Daniel, who died young.

DENCY HART, and Frazee Noe, had children :

1. Daniel Hart Noe, who married 25th September, 1839, Mary Osborn, daughter of Stephen B., and has a son, Lewis Henry Noe.

2. John Noe, who married, 3d December, 1845, Martha C. Bonnel, daughter of Philemon ; she died 11th May, 1849, without children.

3. Emeline, who married John S. Dean, son of William, son of John, and had children :

    1. William Henry Dean; 2. Phebe Mundy Dean ; 3. Eliza Robison Dean ; she died at two and a half years; 4. Hannah Mariah Dean, 5. Eliza Jane Dean, twins ; 6. Sally Hart Dean ; 7 Dency Anne Dean ; 8. Martha Frances Dean.

DANIEL HEATH.

DANIEL HEATH lived at Mine Brook, Somerset county. He married Eleanor Runyon, and had children :

2d Generation.

1. John, who married Polly Kirkpatrick, daughter of Thomas. [See *Kirkpatrick*]
2. Hugh married Betsey Layton.
3. Elizabeth married Anthony Layton, son of John Layton.
4. Margaret, or Peggy, married Peter Layton, brother of Anthony.
5. Nancy married Samuel Dunham, son of David.
6. Daniel married Jane Wilson, daughter of Stafford, of Long Hill.
7. Polly married John Mooney.
8. Robert married Sally Coon, daughter of William, near Amboy.

JOHN HEATH, and Polly Kirkpatrick, had children :

3d Generation.

1. Elizabeth, who married, 1st, Nathaniel Lyon, son of Stephen, and had children : 1. John Lyon ; 2. David Lyon. Mr. Lyon then died, and she married, 2d, James Hill, and had children : 1. Phebe Hill, who married David Dunham, son of Amos ; 2. Margaret Hill.
2. Margaret, who married Lewis Douglas, son of Samuel, of Basking Ridge, lived in Newark, and had children : 1. Nathaniel Douglas ; 2. ———— Douglas.
3. Thomas married Eliza Brees, daughter of Col. John Brees, of Basking Ridge, and had children :
    1. William ; 2. Robert Finley ; 3. David ; 4. Crowel ; 5. Charlotte ; 6. John ; 7. Mary Kirkpatrick.
4. Anne married Silas Brees, son of Col. John Brees.
5. John married in New York, and lived and died there.

HUGH HEATH, (son of Daniel,) and Betsey Layton, had children :
1. Sally.
2. Nancy, who died at near 40 years of age, unmarried.
3. Fanny.
4. Eliza died a young woman.
5. John, who married Suffrona Umsted, at Stonehouse Village.
6. Margaret.
7. Martha, who died at about 25 years, unmarried.
8. Hugh Heath, Jun., who married Rachel Berry of Pompton, Morris county.
9. Robert married Sarah Mariah Campbell, of Plainfield.

DANIEL HEATH, (son of Daniel,) and Jane Wilson, lived at Long Hill, and had children :
1. Catherine Anne, who died at 29 years, unmarried.
2. Agnes, who married Samuel Southard, son of Lot, lived at Newark, and had children :

1. Sarah Jane Southard ; 2. Susan Southard, when she died.

3. Alphacene, who married the same Samuel Southard, as his 2d wife.

4. Jane married Barkley Dunham, son of Amos, of Liberty Corner, and had children :

    1. Oscar Wilson Dunham ; 2. Charles Dunham ; 3. Mary Jane Dunham ; 4. Daniel Heath Dunham.

5. Emeline married Willet T. Conklin, son of Stephen, of Somerville, and lived there. [*See Conklin.*]

6. Stafford Robert Wilson Heath, married, 24th January, 1843, Catherine Woodruff, daughter of Archibald Woodruff, of Newark. S. R. W. Heath is a merchant of Newark, and has children :

    1. Martha Crane ; 2. Jane.

7. Daniel, who died in Newark, aged 24½ years, unmarried.

8. Sarah Caroline, who married, 1st May, 1849, Elias Dayton, of Long Hill, son John Dayton, of Basking Ridge.

ROBERT HEATH, (son of Daniel, 1st,) and Sally Coon, lived at Mine Brook, where his father did, and have children :

1. Daniel, who married Matilda Johnson, daughter of Job Johnson

2. Sarah Anne married Cornelius Lane, son of Job Lane, of Peapack.

3. William married, December, 1849, Anne Voorhies, daughter of Garret Voorhies, Esq.

URIAH HEDGES.

URIAH HEDGES owned lot No. 39, of the Elizabethtown lots, and lived on it between the mountains. Joseph Doty owned part of the same lot afterwards.

Uriah Hedges married Betsey Badgley, sister of John and James Badgley, and had children :

1. Uriah Hedges. Jun., who married Phebe Dayton.
2. Stephen, who lived in Stony Hill Valley, east of William Robison's farm.
3. Joseph, who lived at Rockaway, Morris county.
4. Gilbert, who married Peggy Porterfield.

URIAH HEDGES, Jun., died 10th October, 1797, aged 72 years. He, and Phebe Dayton, had children :

1. Gilbert, who married, 1st March, 1773, Margaret McCarty.
2. Edward, who died 16th July, 1775, unmarried.
3. Dayton, who also died unmarried.
4. Benjamin, who married Polly Willcox, daughter of Peter Willcox, Jun.
5. James married, 3d April, 1788, Susannah, widow of Jonathan Elmen, Jun., and daughter of Benjamin Bedell, and had children :

   1. Polly Bedell, baptized 17th May, 1789 ; 2. Jane, baptized 1st July, 1792 ; 3. Sarah, baptized 8th January, 1797.

6. Farata, who died, an old woman, unmarried.
7. Betsey married 27th March, 1788, Thomas Martin. He died and she married, 2d, John Leonard.
8. Abigail married Anthony Badgley, Jun., son of Anthony.
9. Chloe married, 2d March, 1789, Timothy Bedell, son of Benjamin, and died 3d August, 1793.

GILBERT HEDGES, (son of Uriah Hedges, Jun.,) and Margaret McCarty, had children ;

1. John, who died 20th July, 1783.
2. Jane married, 12th May, 1793, Matthias Dean, son of John Dean, and went to Ohio.
3. Edward, who died 12th July, 1785.
4. Sally, who married Lewis Miller, of Westfield.
5. Polly married David Willcox, son of Noah Willcox, Sen. He died, and she married Nathaniel Roberts, of Green Village, Morris county.
6. Phebe, who died unmarried.
7. Catherine married Zophar Hetfield, of Westfield.
8. Betsey married Capt. Aaron Doty, son of Elder Joseph Doty.
9. Edward, 2d, born 1793, twin to Betsey, married, 24th December, 1815, Phebe Doty, born 1798, daughter of James Doty, and had children :

   1. Salina, who died at 4 years of age.
   2. Gilbert, who died at 14 years.
   3. Mary, who died at 21 years.
   4. Jenette, born 18—.

5. Nancy Mariah, born 18—.

6. Edward Locey, born 1833.

Gilbert Hedges, died ·5th August, 1822, aged 78 years. Margaret Hedges, his widow, died 18th March, 1838, aged 84 years.

JOHN HIGH.

JOHN HIGH lived in Westfield. He married Deborah' the widow of Mr. Brooks, and daughter of Mr. Crane, and had children :

1. Esther, who married Deacon William Sayre, and had no children.

2. Jacob, who married Hetty Dunham, daughter of John Dunham, Sen.

3. Sarah married John Dunham, Jun., brother of Jacob's wife. [*See Dunham.*]

4. Benjamin, who died unmarried.

5. John, Jr, married Rachel Squier, daughter of Benjamin Squier.

6. Eupheme married Robert Woodruff, of Westfield.

JACOB HIGH, (son of John,) removed from Westfield to Sterling Valley, (the great swamp.) about the year 1787. He and his wife, Hetty Dunham, had children :

1. Ephraim, who married, 1st, Abby Ross, daughter of Joseph Ross ; 2d, Polly Case, daughter of John Case.

2. William, born 19th December, 1777, who married Abigail Williams, daughter of Noah Williams.

3. Polly married Captain Benjamin Conklin, son of Joshua. [*See Conklin.*]

4. John married, 1st. Nelly Weir, daughter John Weir ; 2d, Jane Weir, sister of his first wife.

5. Jacob, Jr., who died at 22 years, unmarried.

6. Miriam, who married, 1st, Charles Wilson, son of James, of New Vernon ; 2d, Sylvester Andrews, a Yankee.

7. Hetty, who married Thomas D. Jones, son of Luther Jones. [*See Jones.*]

EPHRAIM HIGH, (1st child of Jacob,) and Abby Ross, had children :

1. Margaret, who married, 1st, Abraham Harman ; he died without children ; 2d, Isaac Denman, son of Philip, of Springfield.

2. Marsh, who married Anna Sutton, of Basking Ridge, and went to Ohio.

By his 2d wife, Ephraim High had children :

3. Eliza Anne married Peter Thomas, son of Griffin, of Logansville, and had 6 children.

4. Catherine married Simon Emmons, son of John, of Mendham, and had 5 children.

5. Esther married Henry Baird, son of William, of Logansville, and had 5 children.

6. Martha married James Colwell, son of John, son of Hugh Cauldwell, had 3 children, and went to Illinois.

7. Hannah married Byram Baird, brother of Henry.

8. Amadee married Lucinda Parcels, daughter of James, of Green Village.

WILLIAM HIGH, (2d child of Jacob,) and Abigail Williams, had children:

1. Eliza Marsh, who married Floyd Ferris, son of Randolph, went to Ohio, and had children:
   1. Margaret Jane Ferris, who died at 14 years.
   2. Anne Eliza Ferris, who married Cyrus R. Spencer, of Ohio.
   3. Walter Ferris.
   4. Emanuel Ferris.

2. Lucinda High, daughter of William, married William Douglas, son of Peter, and had children:
   1. Caroline, who died at 9 months.
   2. Abby Anne Douglas, married Daniel Willcox, son of Ezra.

JOHN HIGH, (4th child of Jacob, son of John High, 1st,) by his 1st wife, had a son, Ezra, and by his 2d wife had children: 2. William; 3. Jacob; 4. John.

MIRIAM HIGH, (6th child of Jacob, son of John High, 1st,) and Charles Wilson, had children:

1. Martha Wilson, who married James Darling, son of Thomas, of New Vernon, lives at Bloomfield, and has children: 1. Albert Darling.

2. John Wilson, who married Mary Bristol, of Connecticut, lives near Green Village, and had children: 1. Miriam; 2. Charles Wilson.

By her 2d husband,(Sylvester Andrews,) she had two children
1. Lorinda, who died 14th November, 1826, in infancy.
2. Harriet, who died 18th August, 1828, in infancy.

HETTY HIGH, (7th child of Jacob, son of John High, 1st,) and Thomas D. Jones, had 6 children:
1. Martha B.; 2. Matilda; 3. Margaret Jane; 4. Mary; 5 Wealthy Anne; 6. Emma. [See Jones.]

JOHN HIGH, Jr., (5th child of John High,) and Rachel Squier, lived in Westfield, and had children:
1. Rebecca, who married John Denman, son of Christopher, had no children:
2. Mary married Ezra Miller, son of Moses, son of John Miller. [See Miller.]
3. Linus married Anna Scudder, daughter of Ephraim, and sister of Smith, of Elizabethtown.

4. Rachel married James Mooney, son of Nicholas, of Westfield.

5. John, 3d, married Sarah Meeker, daughter of James Meeker, and sister of J. F. Meeker, of Elizabethtown.

LINUS HIGH, (son of John High, Jr.,) and Anna Scudder, had children :

1. Ephraim Scudder High, who became a Presbyterian minister, and went to Wisconsan.

2. John, who married Elizabeth Meeker, of Elizabethtown.

3. Martha Anne.

RACHEL HIGH, (daughter of John High, Jr.,) and James Mooney, had children :

1. Linus High Mooney.

2. Sarah Mooney, who married Jeremiah Price, son of Edward, of Elizabethtown, and had children :

    1. Elizabeth Price; 2. Linus Miller Price ; 3. Anna Price ; 4. Edward Price ; they live in Columbia, South Carolina.

3. James Mooney, who died at about 18 years.

JOHN HIGH, 3d, (5th child of John High, Jr., son of John High,) and Sarah Meeker, had children :

1. Hannah, who married John B. Oliver, son of Joseph, of Rahway, and had children : 1. Joseph Oliver ; 2. Augustus Oliver ; 3. Edward Oliver.

2. Rachel.

3. Mary.

4. Phebe married Amos Woodruff, and had children : 1. Sarah Meeker Woodruff.

5. Sarah Anne.

6. John James.

7. Linus.

WILLIAM HILL.

WILLIAM HILL came from Monmouth county, and settled at Mount Bethel, Somerset county, married Anna Layton, and had children :
1. Thomas, who married Susan Taynor.
2. William married Sarah Gunyer, and died soon after.
3. Lydia married John Bird, son of —— ——, of Mount Bethel.
4. John married Nancy Tilyou, born 25th December, 1780, daughter of John Tilyou, and grand-daughter of John Tucker, of Stony Hill. [*See Tilyou. See Tucker.*]

THOMAS HILL, and Susan Taynor, had children :
1. William, who married Anna Mundy.
2. Daniel.
3. Polly.

LYDIA HILL, (daughter of William,) and John Bird, had children :
1. William Bird.
2. Hervy Bird, who married Jane Moore, daughter of Henry.
3. David Bird married Janette Ruckman, daughter of Levi.
4. Rebecca Bird married Peter Moore, Esq., son of Henry.

JOHN HILL, (son of William,) and Nancy Tilyou, had but one child, Peter, who married Henrietta Klin . He was born 4th June, 1803. She was born 5th February, 1820. They had children :
1. Peter William, born 11th August, 1842 ; 2. Nancy, born 7th February, 1844 ; 3. Harriet, born 5th December, 1845 ; 4. John, born 31st May, 1847 ; 5. Mary Elizabeth, born 4th March, 1849.
John Hill died 31st January, 1846.

CHARLES HOLE.

CHARLES HOLE lived close by Blue Brook, between the mountains, and owned a tract of land between Uriah Hedges' and the large tract of John and James Badgley, and had children :
1. Rachel, who married Abraham Osborn, 23d July, 1769.
2. Zachariah married ——— ———.
3. Daniel married, 31st March, 1785, Mary Bedell, daughter of William Bedell, and went to Ohio. [See *William Bedell.*]
4. Charles, Jun., married Polly Scudder, and went to the Beech Woods, New York, and had a son, Daniel, and perhaps others.
5. John. (who was a doctor,) married, 1st, Hannah Clark ; 2d, Mercy Ludlow, daughter of Jeremy Ludlow, [see *Jeremy Ludlow,*] and went to Ohio, and by whom he had children :
    1. Jeremiah ; 2. Mary ; 3. Elizabeth ; 4. Jane, who married
        Jacob Mulford, son of Caleb, son of Job. [*See Job Mulford.*]
6. Betsey, who married ——— ———.
7. Polly.
8. William married, 5th July, 1785, Ruth Crane, daughter of Joseph. [See *Crane.*]

DANIEL HOLE, (son of Charles,) and Polly Scudder, had children :
1. Isaac, who went to the lakes, New York, and was there drowned.
2. Jacob married Phebe Leonard, daughter of David, in the Great Swamp.
3. Caleb married Betsey ———.
4. Charles married Abby Headley.
5. Polly went to the Beech Woods, and married there.
6. Daniel, Jun., married Polly Martin, daughter of Thomas, son of Alexander, and had children :
    1. Sally ; 2. Nancy ; 3. Thomas ; and went to the Beech Woods.

ZACHARIAH HOLE, (son of Charles,) had children :
1. Effa, who married Peter Banta, and had children :
    1. Christiana Banta, who married Isaac Roberts, son of
        Isaac.
    2. Albert Banta married Miss Brown.
    3. Hanna Banta married Martin Foutz.
    4. Peter Banta, a new-light preacher, married Keziah Bridge,
        daughter of John, of Wisconsan.
    5. Isaac Banta, also a preacher, married Miss Rica.
    6. Mary Banta married William De Groot.
    7. James Banta married ——— ———.
    8. Anna Banta married George Brewbaker.
    9. Rachel Banta married Samuel Johnson.
    10. Effa Anne Banta married, 1st, Thomas Wills, also a
        preacher ; 2d, Mr. Rusk.
    11. Henry Banta.

2. Polly Hole married John Auckerman, and had children :
  1. Lewis Auckerman, who married, 1st, Miss Wilson ; 2d Miss Brower.
  2. George Auckerman married Barbara Brewbaker, sister of George Brewbaker.
  3. David Auckerman was killed by lightning at 18 years.
  4. Zachariah Auckerman married —— ——.
  5. Elizabeth Auckerman married David Dillman.
  6. Fredrick Auckerman married —— ——.
  7. Solomon Auckerman married Miss Schenk.
  8. Catherine Auckerman.
  9. John Auckerman married Miss Schenk, sister of Solomon's wife.
3. Sarah Hole married William B. Wilson, from Kentucky, and had children :
  1. Henry Wilson, who married Margaret Sellers, daughter of William, from Kentucky.
  2. James Wilson married Catherine Shidler.
  3. William Wilson married Huldah Doty, daughter of John, son of Daniel Doty. She, with her child, was drowned in the canal, near Middletown.
  4. Mariah Wilson married Robert Swisher
  5. Madison Wilson married Margaret Neff
  6. Sarah Jane Wilson.
  7. Eliza Wilson married Joseph Hunt, lives in Illinois.
  8. John Wilson.
  9. Jackson Wilson.
  10. Washington Wilson married Anne Shippan.
4. James Hole married Miss Black.
5. William Hole.
6. Hannah Hole married Anthony Atkinson.
7. Lucretia Hole married Mr. Brandon.
8. Charles Hole married —— ——, and died.

SETH HURIN.

SETH HURIN married Mary Hazen, both born in New England, from whence they removed to Morris county, New Jersey, where all their children were born.

In 1787, they removed to Ulster county, New York, and from thence, in 1795, to Hamilton county, Ohio. He was born 22d November, 1729, and died in October, 1815. His wife was born 22d May, 1735, and died 30th June, 1794. They had children :

1. Hannah, born 4th July, 1754, married John Tharp, in Morris county, and died in Ohio, 29th November, 1841. They had children :

   1. Elizabeth Tharp, who married John Leming.

   2. Hurin Tharp, who died in infancy.

   3. Athalia Tharp, who married Robert Porter.

2. Elizabeth married Uzel Bates, of Morris, and had children :

   1. Othniel Bates ; 2. Catherine Bates.

3. Othniel married Bethia St. John, of New York, and went to Ohio.

4. Phebe, born 17th April, 1761, married Bethuel Norris, and had no children.

5. Mary, born 6th February, 1764, and died in infancy.

6. Enos, born 19th September, 1766, married, 1st, —— —— ; 2d, Lydia Marsh ; had no children.

7. Mary, 2d, born 11th October, 1769, married Jesse Genung and had children :

   1. Hurin ; 2. Rebecca ; 3. David Genung.

She died 4th July, 1844.

8. Eli, born 21st April, 1772, married Lucretia Martin, in Ohio, and died 21st January, 1828.

9. Silas, born 22d July, 1774, and married Agnes Ludlow, daughter of John, son of Col. Cornelius Ludlow. [See *Ludlow.*]

10. Catherine, born 22d March, 1777, married Mr. McHenry, and died 19th March, 1829.

SILAS HURIN, (9th child of Seth Hurin,) lived at Lebanon, Ohio. He and Agnes Ludlow had children :

1. Catherine C., who married Richard Skinner, lived at Delphos, in Van Wert county, Ohio, and had children :

   1. Myrilla Skinner, who married Dr. Guilford D. Coleman, and had children : 1. Catharine M. ; 2. Mary E. ; 3. Laura G. ; 4. Lyonel O. Coleman.

   2. Catherine Sophia Skinner.

   3. Edwin Skinner.

   4. Anna Maria Skinner married Riley O'Neil, and had children : 1. Laura Kate ; 2. Guilford K. O'Neil.

   5. Richard L. Skinner.

   6. James Hurin Skinner.

   7. Harriet Skinner.

   8. Mary Skinner.

   9. Agnes Skinner.

2. Mariah married George Pierson, and had children :
    1. Mary Agnes Pierson, who married, 24th March, 1851, Beniah E. Brower, of Lebanon.
    2. William Pierson.
    3. James Pierson.
3. Susan married Dr. Caleb Clements, lived in Labanon, and had children :
    1. Agnes Clements.
    2. Jane Clements.
    3. Sarah Bell Clements married, 3d January, 1851, James Monroe Smith, son of George J. Smith, of Lebanon.
    4. Alfred Clements.
4. Sarah Hurin married James M. Fisher, lives in Lebanon, and had children :
    1. Samuel Fisher ; 2. Eveline Fisher; 3. Amanda Fisher ; 4. Mary Fisher ; 5. Henry Fisher.
5. John Hurin, who died in infancy.
6. Amanda Hurin married John S. Weaver, and had children :
    1. Susan Weaver.
    2. James Weaver.
    3. Catherine Weaver.
    4. ——— Weaver.
    5. John Weaver.
7. Hannah Hurin, who died in infancy.
8. James Kemper Hurin, who married, 1st, Mary Foster. and had a child, Mary Foster. He married, 2d, Eliza Littell, daughter of John Littell, Esq., of New Jersey, and had a daughter, Eliza Littell Hurin, who died 27th July, 1843, aged 5 months and 6 days. Mrs. Eliza Hurin was born 16th December, 1815, and died 19th of May, 1843. He married, 3d, Cynthia Halsey, daughter of Daniel Halsey, of Ohio, and has children : 3. Alice ; 4. Ella Mariah ; 5. James.
9. Silas, who died at 17 years.
10. Agnes Hurin married William Logan, and had one daughter, Sarah Catherine, when Mr. Logan died.
11. William Hurin, who died in infancy.

DOCTOR JACOB JENNINGS.

DOCTOR JACOB JENNINGS built the "red house" that stood by the well west of Nathan Elmer's house, and lived there. He had children :
1. Sarah, baptized 28th January, 1770.
2. Samuel Kennedy, baptized 29th September, 1771.

He sold his house and farm to Thomas Sanders, of New York. I do not know that Sanders ever lived there. Nathaniel Littell lived there from April, 1784, until April, 1786.

JACOB JENNINGS.

JACOB JENNINGS, who married Phebe Ball, daughter of
Nathaniel Ball, [*see Ball*,] lived where William Parrot lately lived
and died, and had children :
1. Keziah, who married, 6th November, 1788, Jonathan Stevens,
Jun., son of Jonathan. [*See Stevens.*]
2. Esther married, 6th November. 1788, David Burnet.
3. Nathaniel married, 30th September, 1793, Sally Scudder,
daughter of Thomas. [*See Scudder.*]
4. Sally.
5. Salome.
6. Jeremiah, baptized 7th December, 1786.
7. Rebecca.

NOTE.— David Harris married one of the daughters. Jacob Jennings, Nathaniel Roff, and Jonathan Stevens, went to western Pennsylvania, the Redstone country, a little after 1800.

WILLIAM JENNINGS.

WILLIAM JENNINGS married the widow Bedell, who lived
where Jacob Davis Mulford now lives ; I have not learned with certainty her first husband's name, but probably it was Jeremiah Bedell,
who lived in this neighberhood iu 1768. She was the mother of
Gersh m Bedell ; Israel Bedell ; Chloe Bedell, who married, 8th
January. 1784, Joseph Ludlow, (son of Jeremy,) who afterwards
lived where his mother-in-law lived; and Sally Bedell, who
married 8th January, 1784, Seth Jewel, of Connecticut Farms.

DAVID JENNINGS was son of William Jennings, and married
Phebe Wood, daughter of Daniel, son of Joseph Wood, of Rockaway. She died 3d May, 1833, aged 63 years. They had children :
1. Catherine, who married John S. Bedford, son of Stephen.
[See *Bedford.*]
2. Daniel, who went to French Creek, Pennsylvania.
3. Henry married Rhoda Sayre, daughter of Benjamin Sayre, of
Connecticut Farms.
4. Eliza, (twin of Henry,) married Squier Parsons, son of
Samuel. [*See Parsons.*]
5. Mary married Amos S. Nichols, son of John, son of Jonathan
Nichols, of Madison, and had children: 1. Sarah Elizabeth Nichols ;
2. Rhece Nichols ; 3. John Henry Nichols ; 4. Albert Brant
Nichols ; 5. David Oscar Nichols ; 6. George Nichols.
6. Joanna married the same John S. Bedford, son of Stephen
Bedford.
7. Phebe married, 1st January, 1839, Albert Brant, son of Samuel, of Madison, and had children: 1. Samuel Brant ; 2. Daniel
Wood Brant.

JOHN JOHNSON.

JOHN JOHNSON lived in New-York, and did a large grocery business. He had several partners at different times, but became most extensively known as John Johnson & Sons. He married Betty Ward, daughter of David Ward, of Chatham, New Jersey, and had children : [See *Ward.*]

1. David Johnson, who married Laura Parmalee, and had no children. He retired from business to a farm on Long Island, and died 4th June, 1849, with cholera, without children.

2. John Johnson, who married Abigail ———.

3. Sarah Johnson married William M. Halsted, who was a large dry-goods merchant, in New York.

4. Mariah Johnson married Richard T. Haines, son of Benjamin, of Elizabethtown. [See *Townley.*]

5. Enos Ward Johnson married Harriet Morton, in England.

6. Philip Johnson married Mariah Freeman, of Bridgetown.

7. William Johnson married Sarah Freeman, sister of his brother Philip's wife, and had children : 1. William ; 2. Mariah Louisa 3. Augustus ; 4. Madora.

JOHN JOHNSON, (2d son of John Johnson,) was a dry-goods merchant in New York. He and Abigail ——— had children :

1. Laura ; 2. Elizabeth ; 3. Adaline ; 4. Mary ; 5. Augustus ; 6. Cornelia ; 7. ——— ; 8. William.

SARAH JOHNSON, (3d child of John Johnson,) and William M. Halsted, had children : 1. Mariah ; 2.David Johnson ; 3. Thaddeus ; 4. Enos ; 5. William M., Jun., who married, 20th February, 1851, his cousin, Mary L. Haines, daughter of Richard T. Haines ; 6. Sarah.

MARIAH JOHNSON, (4th child of John Johnson,) and Richard T. Haines, lived in Elizabethtown, and had children :

1. William A. Haines, who married Miss ——— Stagg.

2. Benjamin Haines.

3. Elizabeth Haines.

4. Sarah Halsted Haines, who married, 22d May, 1850, Samuel Knox, of New York.

5. John Johnson Haines.

6. Mary L. Haines married, 20th February, 1851, her cousin, William M. Halsted, Jun., son of William M. Halsted, of New York.

7. Stewart Haines.

ENOS W. JOHNSON, (5th child of John Johnson,) and Harriet Morton, had children : 1. Robert Morton Johnson ; 2. Edward Johnson.

PHILIP JOHNSON, (6th child of John Johnson,) and Mariah Freeman, had children :

1. Philip ; 2. Louisa ; 3. Elizabeth. His wife Mariah then died, and he married again, and went to Michigan.

UZEL JOHNSON.

UZEL JOHNSON came from Newark to Long Hill in 1767, lived where Abraham Clark now lives. He married, while in Newark, Phebe Wick, and had children:

2d Generation.

1. William, who married Phebe Bonnel, daughter of Captain Nathaniel Bonnel and had children: 1. Theodocia; 2. Abigail.

2. Theo locia, who died young, 29th November, 1772.

3. David, who also died young, 16th November, 1772.

4. Theodorus married Susan Brown, of Newark, removed to Franklin, Ohio, and died there.

5. Charles married Phebe Bedell, daughter of William Bedell, and died 2d June, 1787 leaving children, Charles and Betsey Johnson, who went to Ohio with their mother. [See *Bedell*.] Betsey Johnson married Boaz Murphy, he died, and she went to the Shakers.

6. Gabriel, who was born 8th December, 1768, married, 19th November, 1790, Lois Bonnel, daughter of —— Bonnel, of Connecticut Farms. She was born 6th April, 1772, and died 26th April, 1827, and he married, 19th July. 1829, Miss Fanny Smith, daughter of Doctor Peter Smith, of Flanders, Morris county. He died 16th March, 1850; had no children by his 2d wife.

7. David, 2d, who married, and had children:

3d Generation.

1. Lewis; 2. Charles; 3. Susan; 4. Phebe; 5. Daniel; 6 —— ; 7. David. And by his 2d wife, Polly Cauldwell, daughter of Dan Cauldwell, of Butler county, Ohio, he had children:

8. William, who married, and went down the Ohio river.

9. Betsey, who married Robert Cunningham, and had children: 1. Lucinda; 2. Zenas Henry Cunningham.

10. James married Jane Pierson, and lived in Montgomery.

11. John married, 1st, Harriet —— ; 2d, —— ——.

12. Mary Anne married, 1st, Mr. Everhard ; 2d, Francis Stevens.

8. Uzel married Phebe Woodruff, of Elizabethtown, and soon died.

Phebe, the wife of Uzel Johnson, Sen., died 18th Nov. 1788, aged 54 years, and he married, 15th October, 1789, Polly, the widow of Mr. Hole, and a sister of Capt. John Scudder, of Westfield, and had children by her:

9. John, who married, 22d June, 1811, Phebe Squier, daughter of Henry Squier, of Long Hill, and remov d to Ohio. [See *Walker*.]

10. Theodocia, who married William Kint, had one child, and he died, and she went to Ohio, and there married a Mr. Tharp.

11. Betsey married David Samson, son of Isaac. [See *Samson*.]

Uzel Johnson, Sen., died 10th September, 1804, aged 73 years. Mrs. Johnson, after the death of Mr. Uzel Johnson, married, on the 19th June, 1813, John Dean, of Springfield. She had by her first husband, Mr. Hole, children:

1. Sally Hole, who married Stephen G. Leonard.

2. Jane Hole, who married Elias Stanbury, of Rahway, and had children:

O

1. Frazee Stanbury, who died at 26 years, unmarried.
2. David F. Stanbury died at 28 years, unmarried.
3. Susan L. Stanbury, who married James M. Whitehead, and
   died 1846, at 26 years.
4. William Stanbury, who died 1833, at 21 years, unmarried.
5. John Stanbury, who died 1836, at 18 years.
  3. Rachel, who married Joseph Rutan, son of Abraham, as his
2d wife. [See *Rutan.*] He died, and she married Samuel Frazee,
son of Morris.

THEODORUS JOHNSON, (4th child of Uzel,) and Susan
Brown, had children :
1. Jesse, who married Elizabeth Baldwin, and had children :
   1. Frederick H. Johnson ; 2. William Baldwin Johnson ; 3. A
   daughter, who died young.
2. William, who died in Ohio, unmarried.
3. Phebe, who also died in Ohio, unmarried.
4. Daniel Brown was a Presbyterian minister, and died in Newark.
5. Mariah died, a young woman, in Ohio.
6. Cyrus married in Ohio.
7. Samuel.
8. Catherine.
9. Gabriel.

GABRIEL JOHNSON, Esq., (son of Uzel,) was a justice of the
peace twenty years in Morris county. He and Lois Bonnel had
children :
1. Sinesey, who was born 7th July, 1793, married, 1st, Anna
Crowel, born 27th March, 1816, daughter of Samuel Crowel, of
New Vernon, and removed to Dayton, Ohio, and had children :
   1. Matilda A., who married, 25th September, 1834, Jesse W.
   Harker, son of Jesse Harker, of Montgomery county, Pennsylvania, and died 1st July, 1836, leaving a daughter,
   Elizabeth Anne Harker, born 21st August, 1835.
   2. Augustus, born 27th February, 1820, married 5th January, 1847, Caroline Gilbert, daughter of James H. Gilbert,
   of the state of New York.
   3. Samuel Crowel, born 27th February, 1822, and died 20th
   December, 1842.
   4. Pamelia Elmer, born 27th March, 1824, and married 25th
   September, 1845, Nathan S. Lockwood, son of Jabez Lockwood, from Connecticut.
Mrs. Anne Johnson died 26th April, 1827, and Mr. Johnson
married, 2d, Anne Lindley, daughter of Joseph, son of Benjamin
Lindley, Esq, of Morristown ; has no children by her.
2. Charles, born 1st October, 1795, married Charlotte Ferris, of
Bridgeport, Connecticut, and had children : 1. Mary Charlotte ; 2.
Catherine Tichenor. His wife then died, and he married Jane
Hopping, of East Madison, and had children : 3. Virginia Bishop ;
4. Charles Emmet. His 2d wife then died, and he married, Sept.

3d Generation.

1849, Arabella Jones Floyd Nichol, youngest daughter of Benjamin Nichol, of Shelter Island, near Sag Harbor, Suffolk county,
Long Island.

3. Electa, born 25th December, 1797, married 26th April, 1815,
Abraham R. Colwell, son of John Cauldwell, and went to Urbana,
Ohio, and died 15th November, 1826. [*See Cauldwell.*]

4. Pamela, born 29th January, 1800, married, 8th December,
1822, Dr. Henry G. Elmer, son of Dr. Moses G. Elmer. He died
11th February, 1824, aged 25 years, and she married, 3d August,
1825, Sylvester Britton, son of Col. William Britton, of Madison.
He died soon after, and she died 3d June, 1826, without children.

6. Aaron, born 27th February, 1802, married, 18th February,
1828, Betsey Sayre, daughter of John Sayre, son of Isaac Sayre,
Jun., and had children:

1. William; 2. Rebecca; 3 Fanny Lois, who died at 5 years.

7. Uzel E., born 29th June, 1806, married, 4th April, 1833,
Catherine Tichenor, only daughter of Caleb Tichenor, of Livings-
ton, and lives there. His wife died, leaving children: 1. Mary
Tichenor; 2. Pamela; and he married 5th December, 1840,
Caroline Wood, daughter of Baldwin Wood, near Spring Valley,
and had other children: 3. Frances Henrietta; 4. Julia Day.

8. Mariah, born 14th May, 1809, went to Ohio, and married
Calvin Eddy, and soon returned to New Jersey. He died at
Stanhope. She died at her father's house, 31st August, 1845,
and left children: 1. William Eddy; 2. Anne Mariah Eddy.

9. William, born 20th October, 1812, and died 21st May, 1821.

JOEL JONES AND LUTHER JONES.

JOEL JONES came from Massachusetts, about the year 1787. He kept school on Long Hill, and married, 8th July, 1790, Jane Vance, daughter of Kennedy Vance. [See *Vance*.] He died 13th January, 1792, aged 29 years, leaving one child, Hannah, who died 27th March, 1792, aged 11 months, 11 days.

LUTHER JONES was brother of Joel. He came here the next year after his brother. He was a widower, and kept school near Littell's Tavern. He married, 15th November, 1789, Martha, the widow of John Bedell, and daughter of Peter Bebout. He had children by his 1st wife, in New England.

1. Silence. who married, 7th October, 1795, Gershom Mills, son of David Mills, in the Great Swamp.

Gershom Mills lived in New York, and had children:

    1. Harriet Mills, who married Abraham Demerest; 2. Luther Mills; 3. Isaac Mills; 4. Aaron Mills.

2. Erastus, who married Catherine Bedell, daughter of John Bedell, deceased, the only child of his father's wife, and had children:

    1. Elizabeth, born 21st March, 1817, and died 27th August, 1825.

    2. Caroline, who died 15th July, 1823, aged 5 months and 5 days.

    3. Mary M., who married Isaac L. Willcox, son of John Willcox. [See *Willcox*.]

Erastus Jones died suddenly, 23d September, 1834, aged 55 years.

3. Wealthy, who continued in New England, and there married Waite Albro, and had children:

    1. Jefferson Albro, who married Rachel Stewart.

    2. Erastus Albro married Amy Arnold.

    3. Minerva Albro married Nathan L. Robison.

    4. Betsey, who married Thomas T. Woodruff.

    5. Mary Albro, who married Joseph Sherman.

    6. Harriet Albro married Lyman S. Patchen.

    7. George Albro married ——— ———, in Brooklyn, and lives in Rochester.

    8. Martin, who died young.

    9. Solomon.

4. Ralph, who died 11th March, 1791, at about 10 years of age.

Luther Jones and Martha Bebout had children:

5. Peter Bebout, who went to Maysville, Kentucky, and married there, Elizabeth ———, and had children: 1. Luther; 2. John; 3. Alpheus; and others who died young. He died 16th October, 1830.

6. Joel, who died 6th October, 1818, aged 19 years.

7. Thomas Darling, who married, 18th August, 1821, Hetty High, daughter of Jacob.

3d Generation.

8. Hervy, twin to Abigail, died in infancy, with small pox.

9. Abigail married Joseph Parrot, son of Thomas Parrot, Esq. [See *Parrot.*]

THOMAS D. JONES, (son of Luther,) and Hetty High, lived in Sterling Valley, and had children :

1. Martha Bebout, who married Cornelius Totten, son of John, and had children :

1. Georgiana Totten ; 2. Matilda Totten, who died in infancy.

2. Matilda married James White, and had children :

1. William White ; 2. Anne Eliza White, and then they went to Savannah, Georgia.

3. Margaret married Jacob Leonard, son of Samuel, of Sterling Valley, and had children :

1. James Leonard ; 2. William Leonard.

4. Mary, who died of consumption, 28th September, 1850.

5. Wealthy Anne.

6. Emma.

NOTE —There was a family of Joneses who lived in a stone house, on Stony Hill, a little above where John Marshall now lives, on the opposite side of the road. I have only learned their names, or some of them : Isaac, Stephen, John, Edward, Justus, and Phebe.

I remember Phebe, an aged maiden woman.

DAVID KIRKPATRICK.

DAVID KIRKPATRICK came from Scotland, and settled at
Mine Brook, in Somerset county. He married in this country, Miss
McEowen, a sister of the father of Dr. Hugh McEowen, and had
children :

1. Elizabeth, who married Henry Sloan, son of William, of
Lamington.

2. Anne, who married Moses Esty, Esq., of Morristown.

3. Alexander, who was born 14th September, 1751, and married,
4th May, 1774, Sally Carle, daughter of Justice John Carle, of
Long Hill.

4. Andrew, who became chief justice of the supreme court of
New Jersey. He married Jane Bayard, daughter of Col. John
Bayard, of New Brunswick. She died 16th February, 1851.

5. Polly married Hugh Gaston, lived at Peapack, and had but
one child, Samuel Gaston, who married Nancy Cooper, daughter
of Henry Cooper, Esq., of Chester, in Morris county. He inherited
his father's farm of 300 acres, now owned by John Jeroloman.
Samuel Gaston had but one child, Henrietta Gaston.

6. Jennet, who married Dickinson Miller, son of Jonathan Miller,
of Basking Ridge, lived at Somerville. [*See Miller.*]

7. David, who lived on the homestead of his father. He married,
1st, Mary Farmer, of Parcipany, Morris county; 2d, Sarah, the
widow of his nephew, David Kirkpatrick, son of Alexander, and
sister of Peter Cooper, of Long Hill, by whom he had no children.

ELIZABETH KIRKPATRICK, (daughter of David,) and Henry
Sloan, lived at Lamington, and had children :

1. William Sloan, who was a Presbyterian minister, settled as
pastor of the Greenwich church, in Warren county, 40 years.

2. John Sloan was a physician, went to North Carolina, and died
there, unmarried.

3. Mary Sloan, who died young.

4. David Sloan was a physician, went to Ohio, and settled near
Hamilton, married a Miss Crane, and died about 1820, leaving two
children.

5. Elizabeth Sloan married Dr. Ebenezer K. Sherwood, and died,
leaving no children.

6. Henry Sloan married Phebe Suydam, was a major in the
militia, and lived where his father and grandfather did.

7. Samuel Sloan married Elizabeth Boylan, went to Raleigh,
North Carolina, as a merchant, and died there, leaving one son.

NOTE.—William Sloan, (the father of Henry Sloan, Sen.) and his wife, whose
maiden name was Mary Shields, emigrated from Ireland previous to 1750.
They had three sons and six daughters: (they may not be placed in the order
of their births.)

1. Henry, who married Elizabeth Kirkpatrick, daughter of David.
2. John, who died an old man, unmarried.
3. Samuel, who was an Episcopal minister, and settled in Maryland, and
married, and had but one child, a daughter, who married and died there.

4. A daughter, who married Samuel McCrea, a son of Parson McCrea, who was a long time the pastor of Lamington church ; he removed to Ballston, New York.

5 A daughter, who married David Chambers, a colonel in the Revolutionary War.

6. A daughter, who married Hugh Gaston, as his 1st wife, and died without children. Mr Gaston married, for his 2d wife, Polly daughter of David Kirkpatrick, and had a son, Samuel Gaston, who married Nancy Cooper, daughter of Henry Cooper, Esq.

7. A daughter, who married John Maxwell, Esq. She soon died without children, and he married Elizabeth Kirkpatrick, the widow of Henry Sloan, Sen., for his 3d wife.

8. A daughter, who married Robert Maxwell, (brother of John Maxwell, Esq. and also a brother of old General Maxwell, of Revolutionary memory,) and had children :

    1. John Maxwell, who married Mary Williams.
    2. William Maxwell, who did not marry.
    3, Mary Maxwell, who is unmarried.
    4. Anne married Adam Ramsey.
    5. Elizabeth Maxwell, who married Mr. Kennedy.

9. Mary Anne, who married John P. Bryan, of Peapack, and had children :
    1. Elizabeth Br an, who married the Rev. Mr. Grant, a Presbyterian minister, who settled near New Hope.
    2. Mary Bryan, who died young.
    3. Rachel Bryan, who married the Hon. George Maxwell, son of the above, named John Maxwell, Esq , by his 2d wife. George Maxwell was a member of congress, and had a son, John P. B. Maxwell, who was subsequently a member of congress.

ANNE KIRKPATRICK, (2d child of David,) and Moses Esty, Esq., had children :

1. David K Esty, who went to Cincinnati, was judge of the supreme court of Ohio. He married Lucy Harrison, daughter of General William Henry Harrison, subsequently president of the United States.

2. Charles Esty, who was surgeon in the Untited States Army, in the war of 1812, and died unmarried.

3. John Esty, who died in Philadelphia.

4. Sarah Esty, who married Lewis Mills, merchant, of Morristown.

5. Eliza Esty, who married Mr. Nottingham.

6. Hannah Esty married Mr. —— Burnet, son of Judge Jacob Burnet, of Cincinnati. He was president of Texas previous to the annexation of that state, to the United States.

7. Mary Esty married —— ——. She is principal matron of the female seminary at Cincinnati.

ALEXANDER KIRKPATRICK, (3d child of David,) and Sally Carle, lived in Passaic Valley, Somerset county, and had children :

1. David, who married Sarah Cooper, daughter of Daniel Cooper, 2d, and sister of Peter Cooper, and had a son, who died in infancy.

2. Mary, who married Lafferty Cross, son of Robert, and had children :

    1. David Cross, who died young.
    2. Carle Cross married Anne Barcalo, daughter of Stoffel, of Basking Ridge.

3. Martha Cross went to Illinois, and married there, 1st, Mr·
Wilson ; 2d, Mr. Baird.

4. Sarah Cross married Joel Cory, son of Parkhurst, and went
to Jerseyville, Jersey county, Illinois.

5. Bryant Cross went to Illinois, and thence to Missouri.

3. John married Mary Ayers, daughter of David Ayers, Esq., of
Liberty Corner. He was a captain of the militia ; removed to the
lakes, New York, and had children :
1. William ; 2. Elizabeth; 3. Sarah; 4. Hannah; 5. Samuel ;
6. Walter.

4. Jacob, who become the " Rev. Jacob Kirkpatrick, D. D."
He was settled at Amwell, Hunterdon county, over the Presbyterian
church, and had children :
1. Alexander, who married Miss Johnson, of Philadelphia, is
a merchant at Bridgeton, Cumberland county, New Jersey.
2. John, who died young.
3. David Bishop married Miss McNair, of Pennsylvania ; is a
farmer at Ringoes.
4. H. Augustus married Miss Quick, of Flemington ; is a physician at Redington.
5. Calvin is a merchant in New York.
6. Newton married Miss Sebring of Easton, Pennsylvania ; is
a teacher in Easton.
7. Charles W. is a harness-maker.
8. Jacob.
9. Lydia married Dr. ——— Lossey.
10. Anne.
11. Frances.
12. Elizabeth.
13. Sarah married Joseph G. Brown, a farmer.
14. Mary.

5. Sarah married William I. Annin, son of John, of Liberty Cor
ner, and had children :
1. Elizabeth Annin married Mr. ——— Locey, son of Jacob
Locey, Esq., of Pluckemin.
2. Sarah Annin married Joseph Annin, son of William C.
Annin, of Liberty Corner.
3. Martha Annin married Mr. Castner, son of Peter Castner.
4. Mary Annin, (twin to Martha,) married William Boyle, son
of Robert, and went to Illinois. [See Boyle.]
5. Lydia Annin married Ferdinand Boyle, son of Solomon,
son of Joseph. [See Boyle.]
6. John A. Annin graduated at Princeton college, studied
theology, and was ordained to the gospel ministry, by the
presbytery of Elizabethtown, 8th October, 1851 ; he preaches
at Franklin, Warren county, Ohio. He married, 25th
September, 1851, Elizabeth D. Fisher, daughter of the Rev.
Jesse Fisher, of Windham, Connecticut.
7. Antoinette Annin.

6. Elizabeth married Alexander Vail, son of James Vail, of Stone
house Village ; children :

1. Kerenhappuck Vail, who married Dr. William Cole, son of Elias, of Scotch Plains [See Cole.]
2. Thirza Vail married Clark Squier, son of Ludlow, of Plainfield. [See Squier.]

Mr. Vail then died, and she married William B. Gaston, Esq., son of Josep , and lives at Somerville, and has other children:

3. Alexander Gaston; 4. Joseph Gaston; 5. Hugh Gaston; 6. Frederick Gaston; 7. John Gaston; 8. William Gaston.

7. Lydia, who married Peter Demut, son of John Demut, lives at Peapack, and has children;

1. Sarah Demut; 2. Ida Demut; 3. John Demut; 4. Jacob Demut; 5. Vroom Demut; 6. Anne Demut.

8. Anne, who married John Stelle, son of Oliver, lived in Bernardstown, Somerset county, and had children:

1. Jephtha Stelle, who married Sarah Mandell, lives in Brooklyn, New York.
2. Jacob Stelle married Jane Compton, daughter of Moore Compton, and went to Illinois.
3. Freeman Stelle married Martha Runyon, daughter of David R. Runyon.
4. Lewis Stelle.
5. Provy Stelle.

9. Rebecca, who married Squier Terril, Esq , son of Thomas Terril, Esq., and had children:

1. Aula Terril; 2. Mary Terril; 3. Jane Terril; 4. Anne Terril; 5. Margaret Terril; 6. Thomas Terril; 7. Edward Terril; 8. Walter Terril; 9. George Terril.

10. Jane married John Cory, son of Parkhurst Cory, and went to Ohio, lived about 30 miles from Dayton, and had children:

1. Sarah Cory; 2. Johannah Cory; 3. David Cory; 4. Joel Cory.

11. Alexander married Eliza Tingley, daughter of Ebenezer Tingley. He lived and died on his father's farm, and left children

1. Ebenezer Tingley; 2. Hugh James; 3. Mary Elizabeth.

12. Martha married Israel Squier, son of Ludlow, and went to Illinois, and had children:

1. Harrison Squier; 2. Agnes Squier; 3. Caroline Squier; 4. John Squier; 5. Mary Squier; 6. Elizabeth Squier; 7. Ludlow Squier.

13. Robert Finley, who married Charity Terril, daughter of Thomas Terril, Esq. He lived on his father's homestead farm, and had children:

1. Lewis, who married Agnes Smalley, only daughter of Nathan, 1st January, 1851.
2. Amanda.
3. Lucinda.
4. Walter.

4th Generation.

CHIEF JUSTICE ANDREW KIRKPATRICK, (4th child of David,) lived in New Brunswick, and had children:

1. Bayard, who lived in Washington City, and had no children :

2. Littleton married in Philadelphia, and lived in New Bruns-wick.

3. Mary Anne married the Rev. Samuel B. Howe, D. D.

4. Jane married the Rev. Mr. Cogswell, D. D.

5. A daughter, who died unmarried.

3d Generation

JENNET KIRKPATRICK, (6th child of David, 1st,) and Dickinson Miller, lived at Somerville, and had children :

1. John Miller, who married Rebecca Williamson, daughter of Matthew, of Somerville, and went to Ohio.

2. David K. Miller, who married Jane Quick, daughter of Abra-ham, of North Branch, lives at Plainfield, and had children :

1. Jennet Miller ; 2. Abraham Miller ; 3. Mary Miller.

3. Andrew Miller is a lawyer, married Eliza Chamberland, of Flemington, and lives in Philadelphia, and has no children.

4. Caleb Miller is unmarried ; lives on the homestead at Somer-ville.

5. Dickinson Miller is a lawyer, married Eliza Van Voorst, and lives in Jersey City, and has no children.

6. Samuel Miller is unmarried ; lives with Caleb.

3d Generation.

DAVID KIRKPATRICK, (7th child of David, 1st,) and Mary Farmer, lived on his father's homestead, and had children :

1. Walter, who married 1st, Maria Cobb, daughter of Lemuel Cobb, Esq. ; 2d, Elizabeth Howel, daughter of Benjamin Howel, and niece of his first wife. They were both of Parcipany.

2. Hugh was sheriff of Somerset county ; is unmarried ; lives on his father's homestead.

3. Elizabeth, who married Alexander Cobb.

WALTER KIRKPATRICK, (son of David,) was a lawyer; lived on the homestead ; represented Somerset county several years in the council and assembly of the state of New Jersey. He had children: 1. Walter ; 2. Mary.

NOTE. — I know of no connection between the families of David Kirkpatrick. and Thomas Kirkpatrick.

THOMAS KIRKPATRICK.

By tradition in the families of Thomas Kirkpatrick, and Hugh Gaston, William Logan, and James Cauldwell, I am led to believe that Elizabeth, the wife of Thomas Kirkpatrick, and the wife of Captain William Logan, of Peapack, were sisters of Hugh Gaston, and that the father, of Hugh Gaston, was brother of Mary, the wife of James Cauldwell. [*See Cauldwell.*]

THOMAS and ELIZABETH KIRKPATRICK lived about a mile westerly of Liberty Corner, and owned a farm of 300 acres, on which was a sawmill ; they had children, John and Jane. Jane died unmarried at some 60 years of age.

JOHN KIRKPATRICK, (son of Thomas,) inherited his father's property, married Anne Coriell, daughter of Elias Coriell, and had children :

1. Sally, who married John Layton, lives in Plainfield, and had children :
    1. Josiah Layton.
    2. John Layton, who married Deborah Melissa Bedell, of Green Village.
    3. James Finley Layton.
    4. Thomas Layton.
    5. Mary Anne Layton.
2. Elizabeth married John King, son of John, of Liberty Corner, and had children :
    1. James King ; 2. Elias King ; 3. Mary Anne King ; 4. David King ; 5. Jane Elizabeth King.
3. Thomas married Mariah Hurd, and had children :
    1. Anne Eliza, who died at 3 years old ; 2. Jacob Hurd ; 3. Manning Rutan ; 4. Eugene ; 5. Amanda Bausabin.
4. Elias married Jane Squier, daughter of Ludlow, lived at Plainfield, was a justice of the peace, and had children :
    1. Anne Amelia ; 2. William ; 3. Emily ; 4. Abby ; 5. Walter.
5. James married, 1st, Aletta Van Arsdale, daughter of Philip, and had children :
    1. Anna ; 2. Frederick.
He married, 2d, Mary Stout, and had other children :
    3. James Harris ; 4. Josiah Layton ; 5. Hugh.
6. Lydia married Stephen Woodard, son of Samuel, and went to Chicago, Illinois, and had children :
    1. Phebe Anne Woodard ; 2. William Woodard ; 3. John Woodard ; 4. Benjamin Franklin Woodard.

7. Jane married David Kline, and had children :
   1. Anne Eliza Kline ; 2. Phebe Kline ; 3. Peter Fisher Kline ; 4. John Cassedy Kline ; 5. Jacob Kline ; 6. Franklin Miller Kline ; 7. Ellen Taylor Kline ; 8. Mary Malvina Pohlman Kline ; 9. —— ——.

8. Mary married Tunis Vannest, son of John, of Martinville, and had children :
   1. John Vannest, who died young ; 2. Anna Mariah Vannest ; 3. William Vannest ; 4. John Vannest, 2d. 5. Sarah Elizabeth Vannest ; 6. Mary Jane Vannest.

9. John, who died in Newark, aged about 30 years, unmarried.

10 Anne married Philip Van Arsdale, son of Peter, and had children :
   1. Peter Van Arsdale ; 2. John Van Arsdale ; 3. Elizabeth Van Arsdale.

11. Hugh married Elizabeth King, of Bellville, and had children : 1. John Franklin.

DAVID LACY.

DAVID LACY lived in a house west of the parsonage house, nearly opposite to Doctor Kent's. He married Martha Parrot, and had children :

1. Jacob, who married, 1st, Mary Clawson; 2d, Betsey widow of Moses Headley, and daughter of Benjamin Parker.

2. Samuel married Charlotte Dove.

3. Daniel married, 1st, Polly Bedell, who died 24th January, 1783, aged 20 years ; and he married, 2d, Hannah Van Court, below Plainfield.

4. John married, 1st, Catherine ——, who died 23d October, 1794 ; and he married, 20th December, 1705, 2d, Rhoda Jennings, and had children : 1. Aaron ; 2. Caty, baptized 7th May, 1786.

5 Nancy married Master John Blair, a schoolmaster, and had an only son, John.

6 Patty married, 27th September, 1783, Henry Roff, brother of the wife of David Smalley Esq.

7 Polly married, 30th January, 1785, John Adams, and removed to western New York.

8. Sarah, who died 9th July, 1770, aged 21 years, unmarried.

JACOB LACY, (1st child of David,) and Mary Clawson, had children :
1. David, who died unmarried.
2. Sally, who married, 1st, Potter Mascho ; 2d, Israel Brant.

3 Nancy married Luther Lindsley, of New Vernon, and went to Ohio.

4 Mary married James Leonard.

5. Jacob married Hannah Badgley, daughter of George ; lived in Springfield.

6. Dilly ; 7. Lany, who both went to the lakes, N. Y.

8. Clawson. who married Phebe Force, daughter of Benjamin, son of Squier, Sen. Jacob Lacy died about 1846, nearly 100 years of age.

SAMUEL LACY, (2d child of David,) and Charlotte Dove, had children :

1. Daniel, who married Nancy Thompson, daughter of Hezekiah, and had children :

    1. John, who married Caroline Johnson, son of John, of Amboy.

    2. Hezekiah married Jane Lindsley, daughter of Luther Lindsley. above named, and had children : 1. Jesse Clark ; 2. Elihu ; 3. Nancy.

    3. Jane married Marcus Bonnel, of Elizabethtown.

    4. Washington married Elizabeth Rogers, of New York.

    5. Thompson married Hannah Kirkpatrick, daughter of Isaac.

    6. Daniel married Rebecca Johnson, of Pennsylvania.

    7. Caleb married Mariah Exon.

    8. Isaac Augustus.

2. Patty, who died in her 2d year.

3. John is a bachelor.

4. Eunice died unmarried ; she was lame

5. Patty married Squier Meeker, had 2 children, and died.

6. Betsey married, 12th December, 1814, Joel Canfield, of Hanover.

DANIEL LACY, (3d child of David,) and Polly Bedell, had one son :

1. Nathan, who died young.

And by his 2d wife. Hannah Van Court, had a son :

2. Silas, born 30th March, 1789, who married Nancy Parker, born 15th May, 1790, daughter of Gershom Parker, and lived in Yates county, New York, and had children :

    1. Mary S. Lacy, born 10th December, 1809, and married John Mallory. son of Ephraim, and had a daughter, Ruth Anne Mallory, born 1st March, 1845. [*See Stephen Whitaker.*]

    2. Elizabeth Lacy, born 20th August, 1811, and died in infancy.

    3. James P. Lacy, born 16th September, 1813, married Eliza Wells, of Penn Yan, and had children : 1. Julia; 2. James.

3d Generation.

4th Gen.

4. Agnes Van Court, born 27th August, 1815, married Clinton B Taylor lives at St. Paul's, Minesota, and had children : 1. Mary Taylor ;2. Nancy Taylor.

5. Sally P., born 19th February, 1817, married Jeremiah G. Lane, of Vermont, lives in Jamestown, and had children : 1. Cyrus Lane ; 2. Edwin Lane ; 3. Andrew Lane.

6. Abraham Hobart Lacy, born 20th April, 1819, married Sarah Anne Beck ; lives in Warren, Pennsylvania ; have a son, Andrew Francis.

7. David Van Court, born 25th December, 1820, married Deborah Middleton, lives in Penn Yan; have a son, Charles Silas.

8. Hannah Van Court, born 28th January, 1822, married William P. Gaylord, son of Amos, of Benton.

9. Alfred Elderlin Campbell Lacy, born 10th December, 1823, married Catherine Newman, of Beech Woods, Pennsylvania, and had children : 1. Mary Irene; 2. Jeremiah Newman ; 3. William.

10. Henry Axtel Lacy, born 28th August, 1825, married Lucinda Pickard ; lives in Warren, Pennsylvania ; has a son, Adelbert.

11. Fanny Lacy, born 6th March, 1828, married Orange Reese, son of John, near Warren, Pennsylvania, and have sons : 1. Azora Lestelle Reese ; 2. John Reese.

12. Betsey Lacy, born 21st February, 1833.

PATTY LACY, (6th child of David,) and Henry Roff, had children :

1. Philetus Roff, who married, 24th December, 1823, Catherine Yaty Crane.

2. Miriam Roff married Daniel Sayre, of Connecticut Farms, and had children :
   1. Clarissa, who died unmarried ; 2. Daniel Sayre ; 3. Mary died unmarried ; 4. Henry Sayre married ——.

3. Hannah Roff married John Stanbury, son of Col. Rec. Stanbury, of Scotch Plains.

4. Willson Roff.

5. Robert Roff died a young man, unmarried.

6. Henry Roff.

7. David Roff died 17th October, 1818, a young man, unmarried.

8. Hamsley Roff married —— ——, in New York.

9. Daniel Roff married Sally Pack.

POLLY LACY, (7th child of David,) and John Adams, had children :

1. David Adams.

2. Chloe Adams.
3. Charlotte Adams.

ABRAHAM LACY, (probably a brother of David,) whose wife was Susannah, had 5 children :
1. Mary, who was baptized 22d April, 1786.
2. David Broadwell ; 3. Hannah ; 4. Abigail ; 5. Rachel ; all baptized 21st May,. 1786.

JOHN LAMB.

JOHN LAMB lived in Westfield ; he married Mary Thompson, eldest daughter of Thomas Thompson, (*see* *Thomas Thompson,*) and had children :
1. Patience, who married, 11th June, 1769, Noah Clark.
2. Joseph, born 11th October, 1756, and married Ruth Scudder, daughter of Benjamin Scudder, of Springfield, and went to Labanon, Ohio.
3. Betsey married Ichabod Ross, son of John Ross. [*See Ross.*]

COL. JOSEPH LAMB, (2d child of John Lamb,) and Ruth Scudder, lived near Lebanon, Ohio, and had children :
1. Elizabeth, who was born 28th Sept. 1780, and married, 1st, Frazee Bishop ; 2d, Joseph Worth ; and died in 1844, leaving three children : 1. William Bishop ; 2. Ezra Bishop ; 3. Eliza Bishop.
2. Benjamin Scudder Lamb, born 19th Dec. 1782, and lives in New York.
3. Isaac, born 1st July, 1787, married ——, and has 8 children.
4. Sarah, born 13th Sept. 1789, married William Davis, in Ohio, son of Jonathan. They, soon after their marriage, both joined the Shaking Quakers ; had no children ; Davis died, and she is still with them in 1851.
5. Thompson, born 21st Sept. 1794, married Caroline Stevenson. She died, and he married, 2d, Anna Benham. He died 21st July, 1848, leaving four daughters.
6. Mary, born 10th Jan. 1798, married Joseph Banker, and she died 28th Nov. 1824.
7. Joseph Q., born 28th Jan. 1800, married Hester Davis, daughter of Jonathan Davis. [See *William Bedell.*] She died, and he married, 2d, Margaret J. Lowe ; he had children : 1. Thompson ; 2. Abraham ; 3. Hester ; 4. Isaac ; 5. Ruth ; 6. Jacob ; 7. Charles ; 8. Caroline.
8. Anne, born 10th March, 1802, married John Schenck, who died 1846, leaving one child.
9. Hannah, born 3d Aug. 1805, married Peter Williamson, and had children : 1. Ruth Williamson ; 2. Mary Williamson ; 3. Milton Williamson ; 4. Peter Williamson ; 5. Eliza Williamson ; 6. Ezra Williamson.

ROGER LAMBERT.

ROGER LAMBERT, of Wiltshire, in England, was the father of
John Lambert, who emigrated to' this country, settled in Westfield,
and was the father of James Lambert, the father of James Lambert,
who was born 14th July, 1755, and married Hannah Littell, the
eldest child of Moses Littell (son of Benjamin) and Abigail
Thompson, (daughter of Thomas Thompson, of Connecticut farms,
New Jersey.) [*See Littell and Thompson families. See also
Warner Tucker.*]

NOTE.—The name of Roger Lambert is in the first list of " the Elizabethtown
Associates."

JAMES LAMBERT.

JAMES LAMBERT married Hannah Littell, the 25th December, 1774. She was born 15th November, 1759. They had children :

1. Moses, born 29th July, 1776, and died young.
2. Mary, born 24th September, 1778, married William Perigo,
of New York, and lived there.
3. Moses, 2d, born 21st October, 1780, married Betsey Dunham,
daughter of John He died 11th October, 1803.
4. James, born 8th August, 1782, went to New Orleans, and
married Eliza Leslie.
5. Charlotte, born 11th May, 1784, married Andrew Rogers, a
native of Ireland.
6. Rachel, born 22d December, 1786, married Henry Roff, son
of Nathaniel, of New Providence, New Jersey ; lived in New York,
and are both dead. [*See Roff.*]
7. Phebe, born 27th January, 1788, married Simeon Coles.
She died 10th August, 1820.
8. Sarah Sayres, born 11th May, 1791. She died 12th March,
1796.
9. Hannah, born 10th July, 1793, married Benjamin Radley, son
of John.
10. ———, twin to Hannah, born 10th July, 1793, and died in
infancy.
11. Isaac, born 20th February, 1796, went to New Orleans, and
married Adelia ———, and died there, leaving 3 children. Some of
them are dead.
12. Simeon, born 2d May, 1798, married his cousin, Freelove
Littell, daughter of John.
13. Enoch, born 4th September, 1801, married, Adaline Force,
and died in 1828 or –9.
14. John, born 4th March, 1804, went to New Orleans, married
———, and resides there.
15. Susan, born 4th September, 1807, married Isaac Brokaw,
son of John, son of Isaac Brokaw, the clock-maker, of Rahway.

MARY LAMBERT, and William Perrigo, had 10 children:
1. Sarah Perrigo, who married George Coddington, of New York, and had 8 children:
   1. Sarah Coddington, who died young.
   2. George Coddington married ——, and had 2 children.
   3. Moses Coddington.
   4. Eliza Coddington.
   5. William Coddington.
   6. Abraham Coddington, who died young.
   7. Mary Coddington.
   8. Henry Coddington.
2. Lewis Perrigo married Mary Anne Cooper, had 3 children:
   1. William Perrigo; 2. —— Perrigo; 3. Hester Anne Perrigo.
3. Hannah Perrigo married James Leach, and had 3 children:
   1. John Leach; 2. Phebe Dingy Leach; 3. Mary Leach.
4. Moses Perrigo married 1. —— ——, had no children; 2. —— ——, in New Orleans.
5. Mary Perrigo married Samuel Champ, from England; had 2 children: 1. James Champ; 2. William Champ.
6. Rachel Perrigo married Anthony Austin, of New York, and had 10 children:
   1. Peter Austin; 2. William Austin; 3. Mary Austin; 4. Joanna Austin; 5. Eliza Austin; 6. Harriet Austin; 7. Anne Louisa Austin.
7. William Perrigo married Hannah Eliza Littell, daughter of Jonas, and had one child, Susan Louisa Perrigo.
8. Anne Louisa Perrigo married James Noe, son of Peter, and had children:
   1. Mary Louisa Noe; 2. Josephine Noe; 3. James Noe.
9. Phebe Perrigo.
10. James Perrigo.

MOSES LAMBERT, and Betsey Dunham, had one child, Moses, who at about 17 or 18 years of age, was killed by the explosion of a steamboat boiler, at Whitehall, New York.

JAMES LAMBERT, 4th, and Eliza Leslie, had 3 children. He lived and died in New Orleans.
1. James, 5th.
2. Mary.
3. Elizabeth, who married George Roselias.

CHARLOTTE LAMBERT, and Andrew Rogers, had 10 children:
1. David Rogers married Eliza Miller, daughter of David Miller, son of Clark, son of Samuel, son of Alderman William Miller.
2. Mary Anne Rogers married George Moore, of Woodbridge. They went to Michigan, and had 7 children:
   1. William Moore; 2. Mary Moore, who died young; 3.

P

Andrew Moore; 4. Albert Moore; 5. John Hervy Moore; 6. Eliza Jane Moore; 7. —— ——.

3. James Rogers died young.

4. Henry Rogers married Mary Curtis, and went to Ohio.

5. Hannah Rogers married William Coward, of Plainfield ; had children:

    1. William Henry Harrison Coward.

    2. Eliza Coward.

6. Rachel Rogers married James Bailey, an Englishman ; went to Canada, and died, leaving 3 children.

7. Charlotte Rogers married Jeremiah Clark, of Rahway, and died, leaving 2 children :

    1. James Andrew Clark ; 2. Matilda Clark.

8. Eliza Rogers married Abraham Cobb ; had 3 children:

    1. John Livingston Cobb; 2. George Washington Cobb ; 3. —— Cobb.

9. James Rogers married Catherine Dunham ; had 3 children:

    1. George Rogers; 2. —— Rogers ; 3. Eliza Rogers.

10. John Rogers, who died 1848, aged about 24 years, unmarried.

RACHEL LAMBERT, and Henry Roff. [*For their descendants, see Henry Roff, 5th child of Nathaniel Roff.*]

PHEBE LAMBERT, and Simeon Coles, both died, leaving 2 children:

1. Sarah Coles, born 14th September, 1811.

2. James Coles, who went to Matanzas, and married there, and had 3 children:

    1. James Coles ; 2. Annette Coles ; 3. —— Coles.

HANNAH LAMBERT, and Benjamin Radley, had 4 children :

1. Squier Radley, born 5th September, 1812, married Susan Woodruff, daughter of Benjamin, of Westfield, and had 6 children :

    1. Charlotte Radley ; 2. Mary Radley; 3. Anna Radley ; 4. Alfred Radley; 5. Priscilla Radley ; 6. Hannah Radley.

2. Phebe Radley married her cousin, Isaac Littell, son of John and Deborah Littell ; had children:

    1. Norman Leslie Littell, born 10th December, 1839.

    2. Courtland Baker Littell, born 25th September, 1841.

    3. Augusta Littell, born 3d October, 1844.

    4. George M. Dallas Littell, born 27th January, 1847.

3. Hannah Radley married George Force, and had children :

    1. Georgiana Force.

    2. Walter Force.

4. Anne Elizabeth Radley.

SIMEON LAMBERT, and Freelove Littell, lived where his father did, at the old windmill, and had 10 children :

1. John Lambert, born 20th December, 1824.

2. Freelove Lambert, born 23d February, 1827.
3. Rachel Lambert, born 15th June, 1830.
4. Julia Lambert, born 8th June, 1832.
5. James Lambert, born 26th April, 1834.
6. Martha Anne Lambert, born 19th December, 1837.
7. Isaac Lambert, born 2d April, 1839.
8. Sarah Elizabeth Lambert, born 16th December, 1842.
9. Matilda Lambert, born 9th November, 1844.
10. Irene Lambert, born 19th January, 1848.

ENOCH LAMBERT, and Adaline Force, had 2 children:
1. Mary, who married Wickliff Williams, and had children:
    1. Lewis Williams: 2. Susan Radley Williams.
2. Susan married John Newman, son of Jeremiah, of Woodbridge; children:
    1. Mary Newman; 2. —— ——.

JOHN LAMBERT went to New Orleans, married, and lives there.

SUSAN LAMBERT, and Isaac Brokaw, had children:
1. Isaac Brokaw, born 17th September, 1842.

JOHN LEONARD.

JOHN LEONARD lived on Stony Hill, and married, 1st, ——
——, and had a son, Stephen Leonard, who lived in Rahway. His
first wife then died, and he married, 2d, Betsey, the widow of
Thomas Martin, and daughter of Uriah Hedges, Jun., by whom he
had children :

2. Lockey, who married Noah Willcox, Jun., son of Noah.
[See *Willcox.*]

3. Chloe married Jacob Bosworth.

4. Charles, who died a young man, unmarried.

5. Benjamin, who went to the lakes, and married there.

6. Phebe, who married William Brower, of Monmouth county.

7. Betsey, who married Benjamin Sanford, son of Samuel, of
Monmouth county.

WILLIAM LINE.

WILLIAM LINE was a captain of the militia, and lived
between the mountains near Blue Brook, the east branch of Green
Brook, and had children :

1. Sarah, who married, 5th Jan. 1769, Martin Day.

2. Isaac, who married, 23d Feb. 1774, Mary Maxwell, daughter
of William, and had but one child, Isaac, who went to the West.
His widow married John Willcox, Jun. [See *Willcox.*]

3. Isaiah married Sarah Pearce, daughter of Melvin Pearce, of
Scotch Plains, and had children : William, &c. (See page 148.)

4. John.

5. Margaret married, 7th March, 1783, Elihu Woodruff.

6. Joseph married Phebe Wood, of Morris county.

JOSEPH LINE, (son of Capt. William Line,) lived where his
father did. He and Phebe Wood had children :

1. Polly, who married Moses Willcox, son of John Willcox,
Jun. (See *Willcox.*)

2. Deborah married, 30th March, 1791, Joseph Tucker, son of
John. (See *Tucker.*)

3. Nancy married Noah Cory, of Scotch Plains.

4. Sarah married John Willcox 3d, son of John Willcox, Jun.
[See *Willcox.*]

NANCY LINE, and Noah Cory, had children:

1. Joseph Line Cory married Abigail Littell, daughter of Master
Benjamin Littell, and went to Indiana.

2. Aaron Cory, who married Betsey Parker, daughter of
Benjamin, of Scotch Plains.

Ezra Cory married Phebe Lee, daughter of Thomas, of Short
Hills.

4. Mary Cory died at about 20 years of age, unmarried.

5. Eliza Anne Cory.

6. Phebe Cory married Benhu McCoy, son of Goin, of Basking
Ridge.

7. Hannah Cory married Benjamin Cory, son of Daniel, Jun.,
of Long Hill, and had but one child, Albinos Cory.

GEORGE LITTLE.

1st Gen. GEORGE LITTLE and BENJAMIN LITTLE, brothers, were merchants of London, and emigrated from that city about the year 1630, or between that year and 1640, to Newbury, Essex county, Massachusetts. Benjamin's children settled in West Newbury, at Craneneck Hill, and many of his descendants are there in that vicinity to this day.

George Little had sons, Benjamin, Silas, and John.

A grandson of George Little, by the name of Nathaniel Little, had two sons, Tristram and Henry, who were still living (in 1848) on the old homestead of George and Benjamin Little, in Newbury. Tristram married Sally Little, daughter of David, son of Samuel Little, of New Hampshire. Henry also married a Little.

George Little's son Benjamin settled in the vicinity of Newbury, and his family spread out into New Hampshire.

He had a son Samuel Little, who married, and had six sons and four daughters, viz.: Abner, Stephen, Joshua, David, Jonathan, and Jacob; and daughters, Elizabeth, Polly, Abigail, and Sally, Sally married John Webster.

JONATHAN LITTLE, (son of Samuel,) married Dolly, a granddaughter of Benjamin Little, 2d, and had five sons, but no daughters, viz.:

Joseph, born 26th July, 1789, lived at Atkinson, Rockingham county, New Hampshire. He married Rebecca Webster, daughter of John Webster and Sally Little.

2. Stephen married Betsey ——.

3. John married Louisa Caleff, grand-daughter of Silas Little.

4. Jonathan studied physic, and died at 28 years.

5. David married Louisa Peasley.

JOSEPH LITTLE, (son of Jonathan,) and Rebecca Webster, had children:

1. John.

2. Jonathan.

3. Elbridge Gerry, born 11th Nov. 1817, graduated at college, studied theology at Princeton. He married Sarah E. Coleman, daughter of Daniel Coleman, Esq., of Newburyport; she died 28th March, 1851, aged 27 years. He is preaching in New England.

4. David.

5. Joseph Francis.

6. Laurana.

JOHN LITTLE, (son of George,) left home to seek his fortune, and went to Barnstable or Martha's Vineyard, and thence to Long Island, and from thence the family knew not where. But soon after 1665, Philip Carteret, Governor of New Jersey, sent messengers through all the adjoining provinces to invite settlers. These came in considerable numbers from New England and

Long Island. And in 1676, we find John Little in Elizabethtown, a purchaser of land of the proprietors.

George Little patented 100 acres in Woodbridge, 18th March, 1669, and John Little, of Elizabethtown, obtained " a warrant, survey, and patent for 134 acres of land bounded o n Staten Island Sound, or Great River," of the New Jersey proprietors, dated the 9th day of December, 1676.

John Little, as one of the freeholders of Elizabethtown, also obtained lot No. 6 of Corson's survey of the Elizabethtown lots above the first mountain, containing 196 acres, adjoining and lying directly north of Peter Willcocks's 400-acre tract, surveyed 6th January, 1736--7.

I have assumed that John Little, the son of George Little, is the ancestor of the large number of the descendants of Samuel Little in New Jersey. One fact I will adduce as almost conclusive evidence of it. It is the similarity of names in their descendants.

GENERATIONS OF GEORGE LITTLE.

1st Generation, GEORGE LITTLE.
2d, Benjamin Little, Silas Little, John Little.

3d, Samuel Little, of New Hampshire, and Nathaniel Little, grand-grandson of George.	3d, Samuel Littell, of New Jersey.
4th, Abner, Stephen, Joshua, *David*, *Jonathan*, Jacob, *Elizabeth*, *Polly*, *Abigail*, and *Sally*. (10)	4th, *John*, *Samuel*, *Joseph*, James, *Benjamin*, Daniel, *David*, *Jonathan*, *Sarah*, *Abigail*, *Catherine*, *Elizabeth*, Martha, Nathaniel. (14)
5th, *Joseph*, Stephen, *John*, *Jonathan*, *David*. (5)	5th, Andrew, *David*, *Nathaniel*, Samuel, *Catherine*, *Elizabeth*. (6)
6th, *John*, *Jonathan*, Elbridge Gerry, *David*, *Joseph*, Laurana. (7)	6th, *John*, Hugh, *Polly*, Luther, Nancy, *Betsey*, Huldah, and *David*. (8)

I have italicised the names common to both branches of the family for six generations, in one line, which I think will be strong evidence of being descended from the same ancestor. John or Samuel, of New Jersey, may have changed the spelling of the surname to Littell.

NOTE.—The Rev. Mr. Hunting, in his general history of Westfield, says that Andrew, Anthony, Abraham, Absalom, Moses, and John Littell, resided at the Willow Grove, in Westfield.

JOHN LITTLE, (son of George,) was most probably the father of SAMUEL LITTELL, of Essex county, who was born about the year 1780, and married Lydia Bonnel, and had children :

4th Gen.

1. Elizabeth.
2. Martha.
3. John.
4. Samuel, Jun., it is said, died a bachelor.
5. Joseph.
6. James.
7. Benjamin married Susan Tucker, of Elizabethtown.
8. Daniel married Miss Acorn.
9. David married Susannah Craig, daughter of Alderman Andrew Craig. [See *Craig*.]
10. Jonathan.
11. Sarah.
12. Abigail.
13. Catherine.
14. Nathaniel ; and two others, who died young.

1 have not ascertained with certainty whether Anthony Littell was son or brother of Samuel Littell, or whether the Andrew Littell, the father of Polly, William, and Ephraim, was son of John or of Anthony. This I remember, that the families of Andrew and Doct. Anthony Littell, both claimed kindred with the family of David Littell, son of Samuel.

5th Gen.

ANDREW LITTELL, a grandson of Samuel, and I suppose, from his age, son of John Littell, the eldest son of Samuel, he having died in 1784, an old man. His wife's name was Molly, who lived several years a widow, and died a very old woman ; or he may have been a son of Anthony Littell, who was probably a son or brother of Samuel. They lived in Stony Hill Valley, where James Bryson now lives.

They had five children, Polly, William, Ephraim, Sophia, and Temperance.

6th, 7th Gen.

1. Polly married Zachariah Sickle, 30th October, 1763, and had children :
    1. Huldah Sickle.
    2. Elias Sickle.
    3. Sarah Sickle.
    4. David Sickle.
    5. Zachariah Sickle, Jun.
2. William married, 1st, Sarah Baker, 23d July, 1769, daughter of Thomas Baker, Jun. ; 2d, Sarah Drake, daughter of Andrew Drake. He removed to Sussex, and had children :
    1. Mary, who married Henry Ayers, of Sussex, and had children :
        1. John Ayers.
        2. William Ayers.
    2. Levi married Betsey Clark, of Sussex, and had a daughter, Sarah, who married William Barkman, and had children : 1. Levi Barkman ; 2. Anne Barkman.

3. **Andrew Littell,** (3d child of William, son of Andrew, son of John Littell,) married Eve Snyder, of Sussex, and had children :

1. William, who married Christine McCurdy.
2. Joseph, who married ——— ———.
3. Margaret married John Coss, Jun., and had children : 1. Andrew Coss; 2. A daughter.
4. Temperance.
5. Catherine married Abraham Washer.
6. Eliza married ——— ———.
7. Caroline married Philip Simmons.
8. Mary married ——— ———.
9. Esther married ——— ———.
10. Amos.
11. John.

4. **Amos** married Catherine Wire, of Sussex, and had children :

1. Aaron, who married Betsey Harden.
2. Mary married Joseph Reed, and soon after died.
3. Clarissa married John B. Gustin.
4. Matilda married the same Joseph Reed.
5. Sally married Noadiah Shannon, and went to the lakes, N. Y.

3. **Ephraim Littell,** (son of Andrew, son of John Littell,) married ——— ———, in New England, and went to Ohio. He had a son, Elias, who married Rebecca Mulford, daughter of Caleb, son of Job. [See *Job Mulford.*]

4. **Temperance** married Joseph Valentine, son of Jonathan, and went to Ohio.

5. **Sophia,** who married, 25th June, 1775, Asa Frazee, son of Joseph Frazee, of Connecticut Farms. [See *Joseph* and *Asa Frazee.*]

ANTHONY LITTELL lived at the head spring of the west branch of Green Brook, in Stony Hill Valley. In looking over old deeds, one was found, dated 20th May, 1708, from Henry Norris, and Joanna, his wife, to Anthony Littell, for a first lot-right of land, formerly of Benjamin Homan, conveyed by said Homan to Henry Norris, and by Henry Norris, of the first part, to Anthony Littell.

Another conveyance intended to convey a moiety or half part of that 100-acre lot, No. 88 additional, taken up on the right of Joseph Thompson, son of Aaron Thompson, from Absalom Littell, millwright, to Andrew Littell, weaver, dated Feb. 1st, 1743-4, Lot No. 88 additional lies at the head of the west branch of Green Brook. Also a quit-claim from Abraham Littell, carpenter, and Andrew Littell, weaver, to Absalom Littell, millwright, dated April 2d, 1843, for a lot of land, &c., devised to said Abraham Littell and Andrew Littell, parties of the first part, by the will of their father, Anthony Littell, deceased, dated 9th Oct. 1731, excepting therefrom a certain lot of land the parties of the first part had previously conveyed to Robert Littell. This last conveyance was only executed by Abraham Littell, and was cancelled by Absalom Littell 19th Feb. 1750.

Thus it seems that Anthony Littell had sons, Abraham and Andrew, and perhaps Absalom and Robert, and may have had a son Anthony, the father of Doct. Anthony Littell, who lived where his father, Anthony Littell, lived.

DOCT. ANTHONY LITTELL lived at the head of the west branch of Green Brook. He died May, 1798. His mother died 13th Jan. 1784. Doct. Anthony Littell married Anna Maxwell, daughter of Caleb Maxwell, son of Samuel Maxwell, of Boston, and had children:

1. Caleb M. Littell, who married Mary Clark, daughter of Joshua Clark, of Westfield.

2. Elizabeth, born 22d May, 1790, who married, 14th Oct. 1848, William Hand, son of Hezekiah. [See *Hand.*]

3. Amos, who inherited his father's farm of 257 acres, and sold it to Ezra Miller, of Westfield. He died at 28 years, unmarried.

CALEB M. LITTELL, (son of Doct. Anthony Littell,) and Mary Clark, daughter of Joshua, lived in New York, was a grocer, and had children:

1. Thomas Picton Littell, who married Mary Archer.

2. Anne Elizabeth married William Archer, cousin of Mary.

3. Amos Clark Littell married Emeline ——.

4. George W. Littell married Mary Aikin, daughter of John.

5. Marcus.

6. Irene.

7. Mary Clark Littell married Mr. Briggs; he went to California, and died.

8. Sarah Anne Littell married, 5th Feb. 1851, Frederick Tappen, of New York.

9. Josephine.

Caleb M. Littell died 28th May, 1848, aged 57 years.

The widow of Doct. Anthony Littell married, 2d, Jonathan Acken, son of Deacon Joseph Acken, whose wife was Rebecea Crane, daughter of Jonathan Crane.

Jonathan and Anna Acken had children:

1. Rachel Acken, who married Ezekiel Ross, son of David, of Westfield.

2. William Acken married, 1st, Elizabeth Miller, daughter of Benjamin; 2d, Hannah Squier, daughter of John.

3. John Acken married Margaret Vail, daughter of William, of Piscataway.

4. Sarah Anne Acken married Matthias A. Brown, of Titusville, and had children: 1. Ellen Louisa Anna Brown; 2. Amos Littell Brown; 3. Caroline Elmer Brown.

Mrs. Brown lives in New York, and keeps a select school for young ladies.

I will remark here that Anthony Littell may have been a brother of Samuel, and Andrew son of Anthony.

JOSEPH LITTELL, (5th child of Samuel Littell, of New Jersey,) had children :

1. John, who had children:
    1. Enos was killed at the battle of Germantown, fighting by the side of his uncle Eliakim.
    2. Lewis, a sea-faring man, died at sea.
    3. A daughter, who married a tory, and went to the enemy.
2. Elias, who lived in Newark, and removed to Duck Creek, Pennsylvania.
3. Prudence, who died unmarried in Philadelphia, aged some 45 or 50 years.
4. Phebe, who married Elisha Parker, of Philadelphia, and had a son, a painter, in Philadelphia, and a daughter Sarah, who married —— ——, and had 3 or 4 children.
5. Simeon, who died in the time ofthe old French war.
6. Stephen, who died about the same time.
7. Jane.
8. Eliakim, who married, 1st, Hannah Jewel ; 2d, Mary Gillam. He distinguished himself in the war of the Revolution, and in the war with the Indians, as a partisan officer, and attained a captaincy in the army.

CAPTAIN ELIAKIM LITTELL lived on the hill called Hobart's Hill, between Chatham and Springfield, and died about 1805. By his wife Hannah Jewel, he had children :

1. Hobart, who married Matilda Ball, daughter of Doctor Stephen Ball. [See *Ball.*] He was born 2d March, 1767, and died 17th Jan. 1849, in Newark ; she was born 1774, and died 7th April, 1851, in Newark, aged 77 years.
2. Simeon married Susan Toy, removed from Burlington, New Jersey, to near Milton, Ohio, and had children : Eliakim, Mary, Rhoda, Fanny, and Stephen.
3. Stephen, born 3d Jan. 1772, and married Susan Gardner, born 6th Jan. 1777, daughter of Thomas Gardner, of Burlington, whose wife was Susan Elton.
4. Hannah, who died young.

And by his 2d wife, Mary Gillam, he had children :

5. Eliakim, who died at 8 years.
6. Squier, born 1st Dec. 1776, became a physician, went to Butler county, Ohio, and had a large practice. He was also a justice of the peace, and judge of the court. He married Mary Pearce, daughter of Michael Pearce, formerly of Scotch Plains, but went to Ohio about 1800. Doct. Littell had no children, and died 16th Nov. 1849.

HOBART LITTELL, (1st child of Capt. Eliakim, son of Joseph,) and Matilda Ball, had children :

1. Mariah Seabury, who married Morris Christy, son of Capt. Thomas Christy, of Newark, and died without children.
2. Sarah, who lives in Newark.
3. Elizabeth married Richmond Ward, of Newark, and lives there ; has but one son, Mortimer Seabring Ward.

STEPHEN LITTELL, (3d child of Capt. Eliakim Littell,) and Susan Gardner, were married 24th March, 1796. She died 15th March, 1813. He died 6th June, 1818. They removed from Burlington, N. J., in 1806, to Philadelphia, and had children:

1. Eliakim, born 2d Jan. 1797, married 12th Feb. 1828, Mary Frazee Smith, born 28th Oct. 1800, daughter of John and Mary Anne Smith, and sister of Gen. Persifor F. Smith, first governor of California, under the U. S. government. Gen. Smith's mother was daughter of Col. Persifor Frazee, of Chester county, Pennsylvania.

2. Susan Elton, born 22d March, 1799, and went to Ohio, and there married in 1821, James Urmston, had five children, and died 7th August, 1837.

3. Squier, born 9th Dec. 1803, graduated in Philadelphia, and studied physic. He married, about 1834, Mary Graff Emlin, daughter of Caleb Emlin, of Philadelphia; he died in 1838, leaving two children: 1. Rosalie, born 1835, and 2. Emlin, 1838. He went to his uncle Squier, in Ohio, and practised physic with him.

4. John Stockton, born 11th April, 1806, married, 1832, Susan Sophia Morris, daughter of Luke Morris and Anne Willing, of Philadelphia. He published the "Law Library," in Philadelphia, some years. He subsequently removed to Germantown, Penn., retired from business.

ELIAKIM LITTELL, (1st son of Stephen, son of Capt. Eliakim,) and Mary Frazee Smith, lived in Philadelphia, and Germantown, till 1844. He published for 20 years " The Museum of Foreign Literature," and then removed to Boston, Mass., and is publishing "Littell's Living Age," a weekly magazine. They had children:

1. Susan Gardner, born 8th January, 1830.
2. Robert Smith, born 5th May, 1831.
3. Mary Frazee, born 12th December, 1834.
4. Margaret Smith, born 30th November, 1837.

SUSAN ELTON LITTELL, (2d child of Stephen,) and John Urmston, in Ohio, had children:

1. Caroline Elton Urmston, born 1821, married Jacob Beard.
2. Eliakim Littell Urmston, born 1825.
3. Stephen Littell Urmston, born 1829.
4. Mary Enyart Urmston.
5. John Newton Urmston.
Mrs. Urmston died in 1837, and he married Anna Pearce, and live near Philanthropy, Ohio.

JOHN STOCKTON LITTELL, (4th child of Stephen,) and Susan Sophia Morris, had children:
1. Charles Walling, born 1832; 2. Harriet Hare; 3. Thomas Gardner; 4. Meta Morris, who died 1848.

BENJAMIN LITTELL

BENJAMIN LITTELL, (7th child of Samuel, 1st,) and Susan Tucker, lived in Westfield, on the farm on which his grandson, John Littell, now lives ; they had children :

1. Moses, who married Abigail Thompson, 5th child of Thomas Thompson, of Connecticut Farms, had 4 children : Hannah, Mary, Isaac and Betsey. He died 9th October 1773, aged 35 years.

2. Isaac, born 10th March, 1764, married Jemima Frazee, daughter of Gershom ; had 3 children : Jemima, Susannah, and Benjamin.

3. John married Phebe Thompson, 8th child of Thomas Thompson ; had 6 children : Gershom, Sarah, Abigail, Moses, John, and Isaac. He died 1st April, 1781, in his 35th year, and his widow married Benjamin Frazee, son of Samuel Frazee and Sarah Littell.

4. Sarah married, 1st, Samuel Frazee, by whom she had 4 children : Benjamin, Jonas, Betsey and Samuel Frazee ; 2d Benjamin Sayre, by whom she had 3 children : Sarah, Mary, and Moses Sayre.

5. Susan married William Ridgeway, and had 3 or more children : Rachel Rouse, John, and Phebe Ridgeway.

6. Mary married Thomas Terry, of Westfield ; she died 21st January, 1768, in her 17th year, and left a daughter, Mary Terry, who marrried Moses Frazee, born about 1768.

MOSES LITTELL, (1st child of Benjamin, 7th son of Samuel,) and Abigail Thompson, had children :

1. Hannah, born 15th November, 1759, married James Lambert. [See Lambert.]

2. Mary, born 13th March, 1762, married Jacob Davis. [See Davis.]

3. Isaac, (called Capt. Isaac,) born 10th March, 1764, and married Hannah Frazee, born 20th May, 1766, daughter of Jonas Frazee, (who was brother of Samuel Frazee, who married Sarah Littell.) He died 25th February, 1825 ; his widow died 16th February, 1834.

4. Betsey married Talmage Ross, son of Ichabod, son of John Ross ; they removed to Ohio, about 12 miles N. E. of Chilicothe. [See Ross.]

CAPTAIN ISAAC LITTELL, (son of Moses,) and Hannah Frazee, lived in Union Township, and had 6 children :

1. Jonas Frazee Littell ; born 27th April, 178–, married Susan Halsey, daughter of Joseph Halsey, of Springfield, lived in Elizabethtown, and had 4 children :

1. Louisa, born 17th September. 1809, married William P. Denman, and had 5 children:
    1. Charles Wallis Denman, born January, 1835.
    2. George Henry Denman. born January, 1838
    3. William Denman, born June, 1840.
    4. Hannah Louisa Denman, born April, 1842.
    5. Edward Denman, born May, 1846

2. Isaac, born 8th December, 1810, married, 1st, Emeline Slawson; had a son, George Washington, born 11th March, 1836.

His wife Emeline then died, and he married, 2d, Adaline Gibson, and had children:
    2. Harriet Arnfeldt, born 18th March, 1844.
    3. Emeline Littell, born 18th November, 1846.

3. Hannah Eliza, born 25th November, 1814, married William Perrigo, son of William Perrigo, and had a daughter, 1. Susan Louisa Perrigo, born 2d March, 1844.

4. George Washington, born 4th July, 1817, married Catherine Slawson; live in Providence, Rhode Island, and had children:
    1. William, born October, 1841.
    2. George, born February, 1848.

2. Abby Littell, (2d child of Capt. Isaac Littell,) born 20th July, 1787, and died 4th November, 1825. She married Ephraim Bolles, of Newark, and had 7 children:
    1. Hannah Elizabeth Bolles, born 1808, married Moses G. Baldwin, and had children:
        1. Helen Baldwin, born 1834.
        2. Elizabeth Baldwin.
        3. William Baldwin.
    2. Eliakim Bolles, born about 1811, married Mary Tucker, daughter of Gideon Tucker, of N. Y., and had children:
        1. William Bolles ; 2. —— ——, a daughter ; 3. Abby Bolles ; 4 and 5, twin daughters.
    3. Mary Frances Bolles married Rev. James Bolles.
    4. Jesse Nicholson Bolles married —— ——.
    5. Constance Bolles married Mr. Redfield, a lawyer ; lived in western N. Y.
    6. Alexander Bolles.
    7. Nathan T. Bolles married, 8th May, 1850, Mary Matilda Burnet, eldest daughter of Lewis M. Burnet, of Newark.

3. Moses Littell, (3d child of Captain Isaac Littell, son of Moses,) born 2d June, 1789, became a physician, went to Opelousas, Louisiana, married Constance Collins, had 6 children, and died 4th November, 1837 ; one of them named Theophilus Collins Littell.

4. Eliakim Littell, (4th child of Captain Isaac Littell,) born 11th July, 1791, married, 1st, Anne Findley, in the West Indies, removed to Opelousas, where his wife died, leaving 3 children:

1. David Findley Littell, born 1821.
2 Hart Littell.
3. Louisa Littell, who married Mr. Mudd.

Eliakim Littell then married, 2d, Henrietta Wagerhecker, and had children:

4. Augustus Littell.
5. Mary or Elizabeth Littell.

5. Mary Littell, (5th child of Capt. Isaac Littell,) born 15th July, 1799, married Henry Hodge of N. Y., and had children:

    1. Hannah Hodge, born 1818 or 1819, married Elisha Phinney, son of Gould Phinney, of Dundaff, Pennsylvania, and had children: 1. Mary Phinney; 2. Robert Phinney.
    2. Henry Hodge.

6. Isaac William Littell, (6th child of Captain Isaac Littell,) born 20th October, 1807, and died 22d May, 1837; he married Mary Crane, daughter of Esther, who was daughter of Benjamin, son of Benjamin Crane of Westfield, and had children:

1. Mary H., born 4th December, 1829.
2. William, born 8th August, 1831.
3. Theodore, born 1st January, 1834.
4. Sarah, born 14th December, 1835.

ISAAC LITTELL, (2d son of Benjamin Littell, son of Samuel, 1st,) and Jemima Frazee, had 6 children; viz.: Jemima, Susannah, Benjamin, Abby, Desire, and Sarah.

1. Jemima, who married David Mills, of Westfield, and removed to Sterlings Valley, in Morris county, and had children:

    1. Moses Mills, who married —— ——, a daughter of Daniel Terril, of Rahway.
    2. Gershom Mills married Silence Jones, daughter of Luther, of New Providence, and had children: 1. Harriet Mills, who married Abraham Demerest, of N. Y.; 2. Luther Mills; 3. Isaac Mills; 4. Aaron Mills.
    3. Aaron Mills.
    4. Abigail Mills.
    5. Benjamin Mills.

2. Susannah, (2d child of Isaac Littell,) married Jeremiah Jenkins, and had several children, one of whom was Jeremiah, Jun.

3. Benjamin, (3d child of Isaac Littell,) was a schoolmaster called Master Ben. Littell; he married Catherine Littell, daughter of Daniel, 8th son of Samuel, 1st, and had children:

    1. Jemima, who married Moses Whitehead.

(margin notes:) 8th Generation. 7th Generation. 8th Generation. 5th, 6th, 7th Generation. 6th Generation. 7th Gen.

2. Sophia married Charles Whitehead, brother of Moses.
3. Moses S. married Nancy French, daughter of David French, Sen.
4. Rebecca.
5. Isaac D.
6. Sally.
7. Abby married Joseph L. Cory, son of Noah, of Scotch Plains, and went to Indiana.

NOTE.—Moses S., Rebecca, Isaac D., and Sally went to French Creek.

4. Abby Littell, (4th child of Isaac Littell,) married Henry Burnet, and removed to Redstone, in Western Pennsylvania.

5. Desire Littell, (5th child of Isaac Littell,) married Elijah Davis, and removed to Shemokin, Pennsylvania.

6. Sarah Littell, (6th child of Isaac Littell,) married Thomas Lee, and died, leaving one son,
    1. Gershom Lee, who married Sarah Hetfield, daughter of Daniel, who died, leaving his widow, Sarah, and two sons : 1. Frazee Lee ; 2 Daniel Lee.

JOHN LITTELL, (3d son of Benjamin, son of Samuel 1st,) and Phebe Thompson, (8th child of Thomas,) had 6 children;

1. Gershom, born 21st December, 1766, married, 25th February, 1788, Phebe Terry, daughter of Thomas Terry, they had 13 children. (She still lives, 1850.)
2. Sarah married Joseph Sayre, lived in Westfield ; had 9 children.
3. Abigail, born 15th March, 1771, married, 28th February, 1793, Ebenezer Ludlow, born 13th January, 1770, son of Matthias Ludlow, of Westfield ; he died in N. Y., 23d December, 1833.
4. Moses married Betsey Terry, sister of Gershom's wife, who, after the death of Moses, went to Fulton county, Illinois, and died there, 19th April, 1843 ; they had 3 children :
5. John, born 29th November, 1774, married Deborah Dunham, born 19th August, 1779, a daughter of David Dunham and Freelove Decamp, (who was a daughter of John Decamp, and sister of Doctor Gideon Decamp.) They had 6 children.
6. Isaac married, 1st, Mary Ludlum, (now Ludow,) a daughter of William Ludlow, and brother of Matthias Ludlow, and had 4 children. He married, 2d, Rebecca McLane, of Staten Island, and had 2 other children.

GERSHOM LITTELL, (1st child of John Littell, son of Benjamin,) and Phebe Terry, lived in Westfield, and had children :

1. Sarah, born 11th September, 1789, married Hezekiah Pack, and died January. 1811 ; had no children.

2. Hannah, born 6th May, 1791, and died 3d September, 1828, and left one son. John Osborn, who married, 1st, Harriet Stites, daughter of Benjamin L. Stites, and died, leaving 2 children : 1. Benjamin Franklin Osborn ; 2. Mary Stites Osborn. John Osborn married, 2d, Llizabeth Anne Peck, a widow. and died ; had no other children.

3. Elizabeth, born 25th August, 1792, married William Marsh ; she died 25th October, 1826, leaving 8 children :

1. Miriam Marsh, born 5th March, 1809.
2. Charles Volney Marsh, born. July, 1812, married Catherine Storms, and had children : 1. Edward Marsh ; 2. Julia Marsh.
3. Eliza Marsh, born 18th August, 1815, married William Noe, and had children : 1. William Harrison Noe, born 1841 ; 2. Anne Elizabeth Noe, born 1846.
4. William Henry Harrison Marsh, twin to Eliza, went to Chicago.
5. David Marsh, born March, 1820, married Anne Conley.
6. Phebe Marsh.
7. Hannah Marsh.
8. Philetta Marsh, who died 7th October, 1848, aged 23 years, unmarried.

4. Thomas Terry Littell, born 28th June, 1794, married Mary Moore, of Woodbridge, and had 10 children :

1. Phebe, born 1820, married William Clawson.
2. William Moore Littell, born 1822, married Elizabeth Hulse, and had a son, Thomas.
3. Margaret, born 1824, married Shotwell Frazee, and had children : 1. Mary Frazee, born 1847 ; 2. Phebe Frazee.
4. Marietta married Squier Willcox, son of Benjamin Willcox, Jun. [See *Willcox*.]
5. John, born 1829.
6. Joseph, born 1831.
7. Agnes, born 1833.
8. Rachel, born 1836.
9. Althea, born 1839.
10. Abby, born 1842.

5. Abigail, born 6th May, 1796, married John Peny, who died in 1826 ; left children :

1. Sarah Peny, born about 1822, married William Baldwin.
2. Joseph Peny, born 1825.

Mrs. Abigail Peny died 7th May, 1847.

6. Mary, born 27th April, 1798.

7. Philetta, born 20th May, 1800, married John Moore, of Woodbridge. who was drowned in New York Bay, in 1824, and left one child :

1. Mary Moore, born about 1822, and married Joseph Hotton.

8. John, born 28th October, 1802, married Susan Webster, and died 26th January, 1825 ; left no children.

9. Carman, born 24th September, 1804, and died 23d September, 1822, unmarried.

10. Susan, born 3d October, 1806, married Abraham Denman, of Springfield, and had children:

    1. Almira Denman, born 1833.

    2. Carman Denman, born 1836.

    3. Hannah Denman, born 1841.

11. Gershom, Jun., born 5th July, [1808, and died 30th August, 1808.

12. Moses, born 1st September, 1809, married Magdalen Storms, of Brooklyn, N. Y., and had children:

    1. Anna Sanford, born about 1841.

    2. Gershom, born 1844.

13. Gershom, Jun., (2d,) born 4th June, 1812, married Anne Stites, daughter of Henry, of Scotch Plains, and had children:

    1 Henry Stites Littell, born 1839.

    2. Theresa Littell, born 1844.

SARAH LITTELL, (2d child of John Littell, son of Benjamin,) and Joseph Sayre, had children:

1. Abigail Sayre, who married, 1st, Isaac Acken, and had one child, who died young. Mr. Acken died, and she married, 2d, Hezekiah Pack, and had 4 children.

2. Rhoda Sayre, who married Thomas Terrill, son of Enoch of Scotch Plains; had 11 children, or more.

3. John Sayre married Catherine Thorp, daughter of James and Sarah Thorp, of Woodbridge; had many children.

4. Daniel Sayre married, and went to Crawford county, Pennsylvania.

5. Sarah Sayre married Archer Miller, son of Lewis, of Westfield, and had 5 children.

6. Isaac Sayre, who died at about 23 years, unmarried.

7. Hannah Sayre married John Burliew, of Rahway, and had 5 children.

8. Betsey Sayre married Elias T. Higgins of Rahway, and had 3 children.

9. Mary Sayre married James Tailor, of New York, a cartman; had no children.

Abigail Sayre, and Hezekiah Pack, had children:

    1. Joseph Sayre Pack, who married in New York.

    2. Hiram Pack married in New York.

    3. Abby Pack married Mr. Trump.

    4. Sarah Pack married Levi Shattuck, now an agent of the Central Rail Road, N. J.

Rhoda Sayre, and Thomas Terrill, removed to Crawford county, Pennsylvania, and had many children:

    1. Arabella Terrill; 2. Sarah Terrill; 3. John Terrill; 4. Albert Terrill; 5. Halsey Terrill; 6. Erastus Terrill; 7. Enoch Terrill; 8. —— ——; 9. Thomas

Q

Terrill; 10. Mary Terrill; 11. Eliza Terrill; and
perhaps more.

John Sayre, and Catherine Thorp, removed to Crawford
county, Pennsylvania, and had many children; among them
are John Sayre and Susan Sayre.

Sarah Sayre, and Archer Miller, lived in Rahway, and
had children:

1. Margaret Miller, who married Hiram Brooks, and
had children: 1. John Brooks; 2. Mary Brooks.
2. Sarah Miller married Thomas Lawrence, and had
children: 1. Franklin Lawrence; 2. Mary Lawrence.
3. Isaac Miller.
4. Mary Miller, who died young.
5. William Miller.

Hannah Sayre, and John Burliew, had children:

1. Alexander Burliew; 2. Mary Burliew; 3. Sarah
Burliew; 4. John Burliew; 5. ——, a daughter.

Mrs. Burliew then died.

Betsey Sayre, and Elias Higgins, had children:

1. Isaac Higgins.
2. Mary Higgins, who married John T. Conklin, son of
Stephen, of Somerville. [*See Conklin.*].
3. Jane Higgins.

ABIGAIL LITTELL, (3d child of John Littell, son of Benjamin,) and Ebenezer Ludlow, of Westfield, had children:

1. Phebe Ludlow, born 13th Jan. 1794, married, 24th July,
1815, Samuel Whitlock, of New York, and lives there. He was
son of Capt. William Whitlock.
2 Mary Ross Ludlow, born 24th March, 1796, married, Nov.
1815, to Jacob M. Vreland; lives in New York; has no children.
3. Sarah Ludlow, born 23d Jan. 1798, and died at about 8 years.
4. Matthias Ludlow born 23d Oct. 1801, married, April, 1836,
Sarah Anne Todd, and lives on Long Island; has 3 children.
5. Eliza Ludlow, born 23d Oct. 1805, married, June, 1823,
Jacob Day, a locksmith, of New York. She died, leaving 3
children.
6. Abby Ludlow, born 14th April, 1809, married, 25th Dec.
1829, Peter Rogers, from Scotland; lives in Philadelphia, and
has 8 children

Mr. Ebenezer Ludlow was born 13th Jan. 1770, and died in
New York, 23d Dec. 1833.

Phebe Ludlow, (daughter of Abigail Littell and Ebenezer Ludlow,) and Samuel Whitlock, had 8 children:

1. Samuel S. Whitlock, born 5th Feb. 1817, married, Feb.
1838, Esther Nixon, and had children: 1. Jennette Blair
Whitlock, born 2d Nov. 1840; 2. Phebe Anne Whitlock,
born 28th March, 1844; 3. William Whitlock, born July,
1846

2. William Whitlock, born 16th June, 1819, is a merchant in New Orleans.

3. Matthias Ludlow Whitlock, born 5th Oct. 1820, married Lucy Chew, of Brooklyn, in 1848; has gone to reside in Havre, France.

4. Catherine Eliza Whitlock, born 5th Sept. 1822, married, 11th Aug. 1846, Daniel Denice Conover, of New Jersey; he is now a flour-merchant in New York. They have children: 1. Augustus Whitlock Conover, born 8th April, 1848.

5. George W. Whitlock, born 28th June, 1824, went to San Francisco in 1846.

6 Daniel Bonnett Whitlock, born 25th April, 1828.

7. Mary Ross Whitlock, born 23d Aug. 1831.

8. Pamela Wigton Whitlock, born 16th Nov. 1833.

Matthias Ludlow, (son of Abigail Littell and Ebenezer Ludlow,) and Sarah Anne Todd, lived on Long Island, and had children:

1. Sarah Ludlow, born Nov. 1837.

2. Eliza Day Ludlow.

3. William Todd Ludlow.

Eliza Ludlow, and Jacob Day, had children:

1. Jacob Gardner Day, born 9th June, 1824.

2. Isaac Day, who died in Oct. 1846, aged 16 years.

3. John Day, born 15th March, 1833.

Abby Ludlow, and Peter Rogers, in Philadelphia, had children:

1. Peter Wallace Rogers, born 22d Sept. 1830.

3. Walter Rogers.

2. Abigail Marion Rogers, born ———, 1832

4. James Rogers.

5. Jacob Day Rogers.

6. George Cadwallader Rogers.

7. William Ludlow Rogers.

8. Julia Anne Rogers.

MOSES LITTELL, (4th child of John Littell, son of Benjamin,) and Betsey Terry, had 3 children:

1. William Littell, who married, 1st, Sarah Dunham, daughter of Joseph, of Westfield; removed to Cincinnati; had 2 children: 1. Asa, who married ——— ———; 2. Eliza married ——— ———. His wife Sarah then died, and he married, 2d, Sarah Legge, who bore him 2 daughters, twins, viz.: 3. Catherine, who married ——— ———; 4. Caroline, who married ——— ———.

2. Freeman Morris Littell, who married Charlotte F. Randolph, daughter of Benjamin F. Randolph, and died in Newark, 9th Mar. 1841, leaving children: 1. William; 2. Juliette, who died in 1848.

3. Charlotte Littell, who married Benjamin Williams Crane, son of Stephen Crane, of Westfield; removed to Fulton county, Illinois, and had 4 sons.

JOHN LITTELL, (5th child of John Littell, son of Benjamin,) and Deborah Dunham, lived where his grandfather Benjamin did, and had children :

1. Freelove, born 29th April, 1804, married Simeon Lambert, son of James. [See *Lambert.*]

2. Thompson, born 20th Dec. 1806, married, in Mobile, Anne Collins, a native of New Jersey. He is in mercantile business at Milwaukie, Wisconsan ; has no children.

3. Elizabeth, born 23d Aug. 1808.

4. Sarah, born 4th June, 1813, and died 6th July, 1823.

5. Isaac, born 19th Jan. 1816, married Phebe Radley, daughter of Benjamin Radley and Hannah Lambert, and had children : 1. Norman Leslie Littell, born 10th Dec. 1839 ; 2. Courtland Baker Littell, born 19th Sept. 1841; 3. Augusta Littell, born 3d Oct. 1844 ; 4. George M. Dallas Littell, born 27th June, 1847.

6. Eliakim, born 29th May, 1819, and died 25th Oct. following.

ISAAC LITTELL, (6th child of John Littell and Phebe Thompson,) and his 1st wife, Mary Ludlow, had children :

1. Margaret, who married Rev. Erastus Nichols, lived in Clinton, Michigan; had no children.

2. William married Susan Jane Randolph, of New York ; removed to Mobile, where he died, leaving one child, William Randolph Littell.

3. John went to Mobile, and died unmarried.

4. Mary married Stephen Woods, of New York ; had no children.

By his 2d wife, Rebecca McLane, Isaac Littell had children :

5. Anne Mariah, who married Mr. Oakes, and went to Nova Scotia.

6. Cornelia, who lives with her mother in New York.

SARAH LITTELL, (4th child of Benjamin Littell and Susan Tucker,) and Samuel Frazee, had 4 children :

NOTE.--This Samuel Frazee was brother of Jonas Frazee, the father of Hannah, wife of Capt. Isaac Littell, 3d son of Moses, son of Benjamin.

1. Benjamin Frazee, who married Phebe (Thompson) widow of John Littell, son of Benjamin, and had a son, Carman Frazee, who went to Mobile, married, and died there, leaving one son, Carman Frazee.

2. Jonas Frazee married Nancy Corwin, daughter of Stephen, Corwin, and went to Ohio.

3. Betsey Frazee had 3 husbands, but no children ;
　　1st, Simeon F. Randolph ;
　　2d, The Hon. Charles Clark ;
　　3d, Doct. Philemon Elmer. [See *Elmer.*]

4, Samuel Frazee, Jun., married Letitia Squier.

Samuel Frazee died, and his widow, Sarah Littell, married Benjamin Sayre, and had 3 other children :

5. Sarah Sayre, who married Eliakim Cory, son of Daniel, removed to Ballston, New York.

6. Mary Sayre married —— ——.

7. Moses Sayre.

Samuel Frazee, Jun., (4th child of Samuel Frazee and Sarah Littell,) and Letitia Squier, lived in Westfield, and had children:

1. Eliza Frazee, who married Samuel Cory, son of Benjamin, of Westfield.

2. Squier Frazee, who went to Ohio, and married there.

3. Simeon Frazee, who lives in Westfield, unmarried.

4. Moses Frazee, who went to Mobile, and died there, unmarried.

5. Sarah Frazee married Francis Pease; lives in Westfield; has no children.

SUSAN LITTELL, (5th child of Benjamin Littell and Susan Tucker,) and William Ridgeway, had children:

1. Rachel Rouse Ridgeway, who married Noah Ludlum, son of Cornelius Ludlum and Mary Ross, daughter of John Ross. [See *Ross.*]

2. John Ridgeway.

3. Phebe Ridgeway.

Rachel R. Ridgeway, and Noah Ludlum, had children:

1. Eliakim Ludlow, who married, 5th Sept. 1813, Polly Walker, daughter of Asher. [See *Walker.*]

2. Henry Ludlow.

Eliakim Ludlow, and Polly Walker, had children:

1. Emeline Ludlow.

2. Phebe, who married Alonzo Johnson.

3. Jane married Isaac Egbert, and had a son, William Henry Ludlow Egbert.

4. William, who went to Cincinnati, Ohio.

MARY LITTELL, (6th child of Benjamin Littell and Susan Tucker,) and Thomas Terry, had one child, Mary Terry, and died.

Mary Terry married Moses Frazee, and had 6 children:

1. John Frazee, who died at about 18 years.

2. Sarah Frazee, who married Moses Frazee, son of Gershom Frazee.

3. Mary Frazee married Moses Ross, son of Talmage Ross; lives in Ohio.

4. Catherine Frazee married, 1st, Abraham Woodruff, son of Jonathan, at the Two Bridges; 2d, Noe Clarkson, of Woodbridge.

5. Phebe Frazee married Jeremiah Newman.

6. Susan Frazee married Samuel Lee, son of Thomas Lee.

Mr. Moses Frazee lately died, over 80 years of age.

Sarah Frazee, (daughter of Mary Terry, daughter of Mary Littell and Thomas Terry,) and Moses Frazee, son of Gershom Frazee, had children:

1. John W. Frazee, who married Mary Rogers, daughter of John Rogers, lives at Plainfield, and had children: 1. Smith

Frazee ; 2. George Frazee ; 3. Amanda Malvina Fitz Allen
Frazee ; 4. Sarah Elizabeth Frazee.
2. Gershom Frazee.
3. Moses Frazee, who married —— ——, went to Ohio,
and had children : 1. Sarah Elizabeth Frazee ; 2. William
Henry Frazee.
4. Abraham Frazee married —— ——, and went to Illinois.
5. Matthias Frazee married Harriet Laing, daughter of Benjamin, son of John Laing, and had children : 1. Sarah Frances
Frazee ; 2. Mary Margaret Frazee.
6. Margaret Frazee married Frazee Terry, son of Thomas
Terry.
7. Phebe Frazee.
8. Mary Catherine Frazee.

Mary Frazee, (daughter of Mary Terry, daughter of Mary
Littell and Thomas Terry,) and Moses Ross, son of Talmage Ross,
had children :
1. Pamelia Ross, who married James Gay, and has 5 children.
2. Jacob Davis Ross married —— ——, and has 2 children.
3. Frazee Ross married —— ——, and has 2 childrn.
4. Talmage Ross.
5. John Ross.
6. Resin Ross.
7. Abby Eliza Ross married —— ——.
8. James Ross.
9. William Ross.

Catherine Frazee, (daughter of Mary Terry, daughter of Mary
Littell and Thomas Terry,) and Abraham Woodruff, had children :
1. Jonathan Woodruff, who married Anne Stanbury, daughter of Joshua.
2. Samuel Woodruff married Martha Thom, of Plainfield.
3. Mary Woodruff married William Rogers, son of John, and
died without children.
And by her 2d husband, Noe Clarkson, had other children :
4. Ephraim Clarkson.
5. Phebe Clarkson.
6. Ellen Clarkson.
7. Susan Lee Clarkson.
8. Sarah Clarkson.

Jonathan Woodruff, (son of Abraham Woodruff, and Catherine
Frazee,) and Anne Stanbury, had children : 1. Abraham Woodruff;
2. Susan Ellen Woodruff.

Samuel Woodruff, (son of Abraham,) and Martha Thom, had chil
dren : 1. Samuel Ross Woodruff; 2. Eupheme Catherine Woodruff.

Phebe Frazee, (daughter of Mary Terry, daughter of Mary
Littell and Thomas Terry,) and Jeremiah Newman, had children :
1. Clementina Newman, who married Morris Force, now-
deceased.
2. Mary Newman married Ezra Hand, son of John Meeker

Hand, and had children: 1. Phebe Hand ; 2. John Meeker Hand.

3. Thomas Newman, who went to Missouri.

4. John Newman married Susan Lambert, daughter of Enoch, and had children : 1. Mary Anne Newman; 2. —— ——.

5. Susan Newman married John Boylan, and had children : 1. Jesse Boylan ; 2. Jonathan Boylan.

6. Jesse Newman, who lives in Brooklyn.

Susan Frazee, (daughter of Mary Terry, daughter of Mary Littell and Thomas Terry,) and Samuel Lee, had children :

1. Frazee Lee, born 26th March, 1823, married Mary Hetfield, daughter of Isaac, son of Zophar.

2. Anne Lee, born 7th Jan. 1830, married Aaron Hetfield, brother of Frazee's wife.

3. Thomas Lee, born 14th Nov. 1832.

DANIEL LITTELL.

DANIEL LITTELL, (8th child of Samuel Littell, 1st,) had children :

1. James, who died a soldier in the Revolutionary war, unmarried.

2. Robert, who married Rebecca Casad, daughter of William ; lived at, and kept the Blueball Tavern, in Washington Valley, and subsequently removed to Sterling Valley, and died there, an old man,

3. Polly married Capt. Samuel Stanbury, and lived on Long Hill. He was brother of Col. Recompense and Capt. Jacob Stanbury, of Scotch Plains.

4. Abby married Charles Munroe ; lived in Wyoming, Penn., and had children, Amos Munroe and Sarah Munroe.

5. Catherine married Master Ben. Littell, son of Isaac, son of Benjamin. (*See page* 222.)

6. Martha married Thomas Perry, of Sussex county, and lived there, and had children: 1. Daniel Perry, who married his cousin Esther, 6th child of Robert, and widow of Thomas Roland ; 2. Joseph Perry married, 1st, Sally Martin ; 2. his cousin Elizabeth, daughter of Robert, and widow of Edmund Chamberlain.

ROBERT LITTELL, (son of Daniel,) and Rebecca Casad, had children :

1. Patty, who married Abraham Hathaway, son of Jacob, above New Vernon.

2. James went to sea, and did not return.

3. Catherine married William Sheldon, of Sussex county, and lived there. I know nothing of their descendants.

4. Sarah, born 10th March, 1779, married, 1st, Thomas Martin, from Ireland ; Alexander Clark Blair.

5. Elizabeth married, 1st, Edmund Chamberlain, of Sussex county, and lived there; 2d, her cousin Joseph Perry, son of Thomas.

6. Esther, who married, 1st, Thomas Roland ; he died, and she married, 2d, her cousin, Daniel Perry, son of Thomas.

7. Eunice married John Rose, of Sussex county, son of Jacob.

8. John Robert married Patty Totten, daughter of David Totten, Sen., and removed to the lakes, New York.

9. Isaac, who died at Greenbush, New York, a soldier in the war of 1812, aged 21 years.

10. Daniel married Mariah Hoagland, daughter of Isaac, of Newburgh, New York.

PATTY LITTELL, (1st daughter of Robert, son of Daniel,) and Abraham Hathaway, had children :

1. Elias Hathaway, who married Caroline Dewit, of Sussex Co.

2. Isaac Hathaway.

3. Rebecca Hathaway.

SARAH LITTELL, (4th daughter of Robert, son of Daniel,) and Thomas Martin, had children :

7th Generation.

1. Robert Martin, who died at about 23 years, unmarried.
2. James Martin, who died at about 32 years, unmarried.
Sarah had no children by her 2d husband.

ELIZABETH LITTELL, (5th child of Robert, son of Daniel,) and Edmund Chamberlain, had children :
1. Elias Chamberlain.
2. Phebe Chamberlain, who married Moses Kimbal.
3. Eliza Chamberlain married Jonathan Hambel.
4. Sally Chamberlain married —— ——.
5. Mary Chamberlain married George Beatty.

ESTHER LITTELL, (6th child of Robert, son of Daniel,) and Thomas Roland, had children :
1. Thomas Roland, Jun., who married Phebe Babbit.
2. Eliza Roland married William McClure.

EUNICE LITTELL, (7th child of Robert, son of Daniel,) and John Rose, had children :
1. Mary Rose, who married Samuel Johnson, and died, leaving 5 children :
2. Jacob Rose married —— ——.
3. Andrew Rose married —— , a sister of Jacob's wife.
4. Amanda Rose married John Leporte.
5. George Rose, who died a young man, unmarried.
6. Abraham Rose.
7. Charles Rose.
8. Anthony Rose.
9. William Rose.

JOHN ROBERT LITTELL, (son of Robert, son of Daniel,) and Patty Totten, had children :
1. Eliza, who married Charles Reed, and died, leaving 2 children :
2. Sally married Moses Johnson.
3. Isaac married —— ——.
4. Daniel.

DANIEL LITTELL, (son of Robert, son of Daniel,) and Mariah Hoagland, had children :
1. Elmira ; 2. Rebecca ; 3. George.

POLLY LITTELL, (3d child of Daniel,) and Capt. Samuel Stanbury, had children :
1. Phebe Stanbury, who married Daniel Potter, son of Daniel Potter, 2d. [*See Potter.*]
2. Recompense Stanbury married Eunice Ogden, daugh-

6th Gen.

ter of John Ogden, of Monroe, and had an only child, Phebe, and went to Worthington, Ohio. His daughter Phebe married there, —— ——, a physician.

3. Jonas Stanbury married Catherine Rague, daughter of Doctor John Rague, of Passaic Valley.

4. Samuel Stanbury, Jun., married, and went to Ohio.

5. John Stanbury married Mary Miller, daughter of Benjamin, of Morris county.

6. Peggy Stanbury married —— ——.

7. Amos Stanbury.

Captain Stanbury went to Ohio without his family. When there, he sent for his wife, who went, and took her son Amos with her.

DAVID LITTELL.

DAVID LITTELL, (9th child of Samuel Littell and Lydia Bonnel,) was born in January, 1718, and died August 2d, 1790. He married Susannah Craig, daughter of Alderman Andrew Craig, of Westfield. She died 5th June, 1753, aged about 37 years. They had 7 children :

1. Esther, born 19th February, 1739, married William Bedell. He died 30th January, 1814. She died 18th October 1828. [See *William Bedell.*]

2. Lydia, born 16th November, 1741, married, 1st, Andrew Prior. He died February, 1768, and she married, 2d, the 14th May, 1769, David Flinn, as his 2d wife. [See *Prior.*] She died 4th December, 1826.

3. Catherine, born November, 1743, married, 1st, Jabez Rogers. He died 1774, and she married, 2d, Moses Crane, of Parcipany, and lived there.

4. Elizabeth, born 27th October, 1745, married, 1st Oct. 1784, Moses Bedell. He died, and she married, 2d, David Van Sickle, brother of Zachariah. [*For her descendants, see Moses Bedell, Thomas Hallock, and Isaac Moore.*]

5. Andrew, born January, 1749, married Miss Runyon, sister of Daniel Heath's wife, [see *Heath,*] and went to western New York.

6. David, born January, 1751, married Hannah Miller, daughter of Enoch Miller, of Westfield.

7. Nathaniel, born 26th January, 1753, married Mary Cauldwell, daughter of William. [See *Cauldwell.*]

David Littell married a 2d wife, and had children :

8. Samuel, who most probably married his cousin, Sarah Littell, daughter of Jonathan. [See *Jonathan Littell.*]

9. Susannah married, 28th February, 1784, David Ruckman, probably a brother of Jonathan, [*which see.*]

Note.—I have not ascertained any of the descendants of Andrew, Samuel, or Susannah.

ESTHER LITTELL, (1st child of David Littell, son of Samuel,) and William Bedell, had children. [See *Bedell.*]

1. Susannah, born 27th November, 1761, married Jonathan Davis, son of Isaac Davis, whose wife was Sarah Palmer. After the death of Isaac Davis, his widow, Sarah, married Sylvanus Oakley, Sen. [See *Oakley.*] Susannah died 20th September, 1836.

2. Phebe, born 7th July, 1763, and died January, 1847. She married, 1st, Charles Johnson, son of Uzel ; 2d, Caleb Mulford, son of Job. [See *Bedell and Mulford.*]

3. Lydia, born 3d August, 1765, died 19th January, 1840. She married Elijah Davis, brother of Jonathan.

4. Polly, or Mary, born 7th July, 1767, married Daniel Hole, son of Charles, and died about 1826 or 7 [*See Bedell.*]

5. James, born 1769, married Nancy Oakley, and died in 1840.

Susannah Bedell, (1st child of William Bedell and Esther Littell,) and Jonathan Davis, who was born 30th January, 1760,) had children :

1. William Davis, born 13th December, 1781, married, 1805, Sarah Lamb, daughter of Col. Joseph Lamb. They both went to the Shakers in about one year after. He died 10th January, 1846, and she continues with them.

2. John Davis, born 20th November, 1783, and married Elizabeth Sering, and removed to Texas.

3. Polly Davis, born 19th August, 1789, and is with the Shakers.

4. Rufus Davis, born 18th June, 1792.

5. Jonathan Davis, born 18th July, 1795.

6. Huldah Davis, born 9th June, 1800, married John Monger.

7. Hetty Davis, born 29th October, 1805, married Joseph Q. Lamb, son of Col. Joseph Lamb, of Warren county, Ohio.

Lydia Bedell, and Elijah Davis, had children :

1. Esther Davis, who is with the Shaking Quakers, called Shakers, at Union or Shaker Town, Warren county, Ohio.

2. William Davis is also with the Shakers.

3. James Davis went to Indiana.

4. Daniel Davis is with the Shakers.

5. Jonathan Davis.

6. Samuel and Hannah, twins ; these two died young.

Mary Bedell and Daniel Hole, had children. [*See Bedell.*]

James Bedell, and Nancy Oakley, had children :

1. John married —— —— ; lives in Indiana.

2. Susan is with the Shakers.

3. David.

4. Sally is with the Shakers.

5. William married —— —— ; lives in Indiana.

6. Esther married —— —— ; lives in Indiana.

LYDIA LITTELL, (2d child of David, son of Samuel,) married 1st, Andrew Prior, as his 2d wife, (*see Prior ;*) 2d, David Flinn, born 22d March, 1731, and died 4th March, 1815. By David Flinn she had children :

1. Stephen Flinn, who married Sally ——, and had children. [*See Flinn.*]

2. Lydia Flinn, born 10th February, 1774, married Edmund

Buxton, born 24th January, 1768, lived east of Reading, in Hamilton county, Ohio, (he came from New England,) and had children :

7th Generation.

1. Charles Buxton, born 29th March, 1793, married, 25th June, 1812, Rebecca Ferguson, daughter of Hudson.
2. David Buxton, born 28th February, 1795, married Joanna Conklin, born 22d November, 1798, daughter of Stephen, son of Joseph Conklin, who married Mary Cory, sister of Elder Benjamin Cory, of Elizabethtown. [See *Conklin.*]
3. Anne Buxton married William Ferguson, a cousin of Charles's wife ; lives in Floyd county, Indiana. [See *page* 94.]
4. Moses Buxton, born 5th July, 1798, married, 28th January, 1818, Prudence E. Bacon, born 29th April, 1799, daughter of Nathan Bacon, of Cape May, N. J.
5. Jane Buxton, born 16th December, 1799, married, 20th May, 1819, Nathan Monroe, only son of Jehu, of Pennsylvania ; lives near Lebanon, Ohio.
6. John Buxton married Hannah Willey.
7. Aaron Buxton, born 13th March, 1804, married Hannah Lambern, daughter of Josiah Lambern.
8. William Buxton, born 10th March, 1806, married Catherine W. Terry, born 23d December, 1808, daughter of William Terry.

Mr. Edmund Buxton died 20th July, 1806.

Charles Buxton, (son of Edmund,) and Rebecca Ferguson, had children :

1. Edmund, born 4th August, 1813, and married Eliza Cortleyou, daughter of Albert, and had children : 1. Margaret; 2. Henry ; 3. Rebecca ; 4. Gennette ; 5. Charles.
2. William, born 22d October, 1815, married Elizabeth, Larew, lives in Madison, Indiana.
3. Jane, born 4th July, 1817, married Hezekiah Bonham and had children: 1. John Bonham ; 2. Ellis Bonham ; 3. Eliza Jane Bonham ; 4. Tyler Bonham.
4. John M., born 15th December, 1821.
5. Aaron, born 27th May, 1824, married Rebecca Pierson, daughter of Jesse, and had a daughter, Harriet.
6. Eliza Anne, born 26th May, 1826, and died about 1834.
7. Susan, born 13th January, 1829, married, August, 1850, James Conover.
8. Catherine, born 3d March, 1833.

David Buxton, (2d son of Edmund,) and Joanna Conklin, had children :

1. Lydia, born 11th June, 1818, and died 26th June, 1818.
2. Mary Jane, born 10th July, 1819, and died 26th April, 1843.
3. John, born 15th October, 1821.
4. Joseph, born 4th January, 1824, married 28th March, 1850, Hannah Cornell.

5. Sarah Anne, born 24th October, 1826, married, 8th October, 1849, Isaac Ferris, son of Rev. Isaac Ferris, a Baptist minister.
6. William, born 28th October, 1828.
7. Susan, born 20th March, 1831.
8. Emeline, born 3d December, 1833.
9. Freelove, born 9th January, 1837.
10. David, born 19th December, 1839.
11. Amos, born 16th January, 1841.
12. Olive, born 29th January, 1844, and died 6th December, 1844.

Anne Buxton, (3d child of Edmund,) and William Ferguson, live near New Albany, Floyd county, Indiana, and had children:
1. Enoch Ferguson, who married Nancy Brown, and lives at New Albany.
2. Nancy Ferguson married John Wood, and went to Missouri.
3. Isaac Ferguson married, 1st, Nancy Karr, daughter of Samuel, of Hamilton county, Ohio; 2d, Martha Breedlove.
4. William Ferguson married —— ——, and lives in Hancock county, Illinois.
5. John Ferguson.

Moses Buxton, (4th child of Edmund,) and Prudence E. Bacon, lived on his father's farm, near Reading, Hamilton county, Ohio, and had children:
1. Edmund Buxton, born 16th May, 1819, married Harriet Larew, daughter of Isaac, and lives at Madison, Indiana.
2. Lydia Buxton, born 25th April, 1821, married Peter Black, son of Peter, and died, 18th August, 1850, leaving a daughter, Louisa Black.
3. Nancy L. Buxton, born 18th September, 1823, married Henry Moody, lives in Carthage, Ohio, and had children: 1. Harriet Jane Moody; 2. Joseph Moody; 3. Henry Moses Moody.
4. Nathan B. Buxton, born 17th October, 1825, married Sarah Jane Mann, daughter of Col. Joseph Mann.
5. James B. Buxton, born 27th June, 1827, married Rebecca Parkhill.
6. David F. Buxton, born 29th April, 1831.
7. William W. Buxton, born 23d July, 1833.
8. Eliza Anne Buxton, born 12th May, 1836.
9. Isaac Newton Buxton, born 22d August, 1838.
10. George W. Buxton, born 3d March, 1841.

Mr. Moses Buxton died 13th October, 1850, with schirrous tumor in the stomach, which stopped the passage from the stomach to the bowels.

Jane Buxton, (5th child of Edmund,) and Nathan Monroe, had children:
1. Edmund Monroe, born 26th May, 1820, married, 3d December, 1842, Hannah Jane Halsey, daughter of Caleb, son of John Halsey and Hannah Pool, (see *Halsey* and

Pool,) and had children : 1. Nathan, who died young; 2. Oscar; 3. Hudson ; 4, Lewis Ridgeway, who died young. Mrs. Monroe died August, 1851.

2. John Monroe, born 18th February, 1823, married, 21st May, 1846, Martha Jane Maple, daughter of Elias Maple, from New Jersey, and had children : 1. Mary Jane ; 2. James Walter Monroe.

3. Aaron Monroe, born 6th May, 1825.

4. Charles Monroe, born 7th August, 1827, married. 10th Oct, 1849, Mary Pence, daughter of John, and had children : 1. Mary Jane.

5. Lydia Anne Monroe, born 16th September, 1829.

6. William Monroe, born 30th August, 1832.

John Buxton, (6th child of Edmund,) and Hannah Willey, had children :

1. Eliza ; 2. Lydia ; 3. Mary, who died at 7 years ; 4. Deborah ; 5. John, Jun. ; 6. Charlotte or Amanda.

Aaron Buxton, (7th child of Edmund,) and Hannah Lambern, had children :

1. Anne C., born 29th June, 1826.

2. Lydia, born 15th October, 1827.

3. Josiah L., born 29th October, 1830.

4. Emeline, born 17th March, 1834.

5. Laura, born 6th August, 1836.

6. Augusta, born 20th February, 1845.

William Buxton, (8th child of Edmund,) and Catherine W. Terry, had children :

1. Phebe Anne, born 15th April, 1827.

2. Charles, born 30th October, 1830.

3. Caroline, born 11th December, 1832.

4. Eliza Jane, born 15th August, 1836.

5. Charlotte, born 30th March, 1839.

6. Newton Stites, born 2d April, 1843.

3. Susannah Flinn, youngest daughter of Lydia Littell and David Flinn, married John Miller, in Warren county, Ohio, and had children, Daniel, David, Moses, and Lucy Jane Miller. Mr. Miller, and his wife and children, all went to the Shakers. Mr. Miller died in 1850, aged 79 years, and Susannah, his wife, in 1840, aged 62 years. The children are there still in 1851. Moses is the principal dealer about the country for the association, and Lucy Jane is conspicuous in the house.

CATHERINE LITTELL, (3d child of David,) and Jabez Rogers, lived at Parcipany. He was born 3d November, 1739, and died 1774, aged 35 years. She was born 19th October, 1743, and died 1794, aged 51 years. They had children :

1. Nathaniel Rogers, born 4th February, 1761, and died 1845, aged 84 years. He married Rachel McDaniels, daughter of Elkanah ; she was still living in 1848. They

lived near Lake Champlain, and had children; Moses and
John Rogers.

2. Sarah Rogers, born 30th June, 1764, married Robert
Templeton, of Parcipany, and died at 34 years.

3. Lydia Rogers, born 5th April, 1766, married Ebenezer
Burnet.

4. Elizabeth Rogers, born 30th March, 1768, and died at
13 years.

5. Jemima Rogers, born 5th February, 1770, and died at
7 years.

6. Joanna Rogers, born 22d December, 1771, married
Noah Estile, of Parcipany. He was born 16th December,
1766, and died 11th December, 1848. They lived near
Dover.

7. Stephen Rogers, born 28th August, 1773, married Phebe
Baldwin, daughter of Job.

8. Susan Rogers, born 28th April, 1775, married, 16th November, 1795, Jacob Hinds, of Hanover, who was born 14th
January. 1774, and removed to Bristol, Vermont.

Mr. Jabez Rogers died 1774, and his widow, Catherine, married Moses Crane, of Parcipany, and had 3 other children :

9. Josiah Crane, who went to 'Seneca Falls, New York,
and married Rachel ——, but had no children.

10. Phebe Crane, who married Edmund Compson, of Parcipany, and removed to Montezuma, New York, and had a
large family of children.

11. Elizabeth Crane married Caleb Woodworth, and had
10 children. She died, and Mr. Woodworth married a widow
with 10 children. Mr. Woodworth's 2d wife died, and he
married, 3d, Hannah Compson, daughter of Edmund Compson, his first wife's niece.

Sarah Rogers, (2d child of Catherine Littell and Jabez
Rogers,) and Robert Templeton, had children :

1. Elizabeth Templeton, who married Ashbel Cory, of
Troy, and had children : 1. Caroline Cory ; 2. Mary
Cory ; 3. Julianne Cory ; 4. Archibald Cory.

2. Mary Templeton, who married Freeman Ford, (son of
Samuel, son of William Odell Ford, son of Jonathan
Ford,) and had children : 1. Eveline Ford ; 2. William
Ford.

3. Catharine Templeton, who married Alexander Lawrence, and had children : 1 Alexander Lawrence.

Lydia Rogers, (3d child of Catharine Littell and Jabez
Rogers,) and Ebenezer Burnet, had children ;

1. Sarah Burnet, who married John Tichenor, son of
Jabez, and had one son and two daughters, when Mr.
Tichenor died, and she married William Churchill,
and went to Ohio.

2. Stephen Burnet, who died at 2 years.
3. James Burnet went to Georgia, and married there Sarah Wilson, of Powlington, and has one daughter and three sons living at Sparta, Georgia.
4. Ralph Burnet married Phebe Lindsley, of Morristown, had three sons and two daughters, and went to Sidney, Ohio, and died at about 54 years.
5. Hiram Burnet married Adeline Burrows, had one daughter, and died in 1813.
6. Ebenezer Burnet married Mariah Debow, of Morris Co., and went to Sidney, Ohio, and had 13 children.
7. Catharine Burnet married Joseph Warren, of Ramapo, N. Y., and went to Sidney, Ohio, and had 11 children.
8. Joanna Estile Burnet married David Norris, a blacksmith, a son of Lebbeus Norris, of Morristown; lives at Millville, Essex county, and has eight children.
9. John Seward Burnet married Mary Harrison, of Orange, had one daughter, and died at 22 years.
10. Phebe Burnet married Robert Fields, of Paterson; lived there, and has three sons.
11. Charles Burnet married Frances Tichenor, daughter of Jabez, and sister of Sarah's husband; had seven children, all of whom have died except one daughter.

Joanna E. Burnet, (8th child of Lydia Rogers and Ebenezer Burnet,) was born 7th Jan. 1801, and married David Norris, born 10th April, 1791, and had children:

1. James Burnet Norris, born 26th Nov. 1823, is a blacksmith; lives at Springfield; he married Mary Elizabeth Tailor, daughter of John, of Powerville, Morris county.
2. David Alonzo Norris is a blacksmith; went to Bridgeport, and married Sarah Anne Seely, daughter of Henry Seely, of that place, and lives there.
3. Harriet Louisa Norris, born 29th Nov. 1829, and died 3d February, 1840.
4. Sarah Frances Norris, born 1st January, 1831.
5. Mary Josephine Norris, born 16th February, 1833.
6. John Hunter Norris, born 20th April, 1834.
7. Phebe Martha Norris, born 24th October, 1836.
8. Harriet Jane Norris, born 26th April, 1840.

Joanna Rogers, (6th child of Catharine Littell and Jabez Rogers,) and Noah Estile, lived near Dover, Morris Co., and had children:

1. Jabez Lewis Estile, who married Dency M. Ross, daughter of David, of Rockaway; had children: 1. Martha Estile, who married, 7th April, 1850, Rev. Enoch Green, of the New Jersey Conference; 2. Mary Estile. Mr. Jabez L. Estile died of cholera at Rock-

R

away, 24th June, 1849, aged 55 years.

2. John Rogers Estile married Rebecca Bruen, daughter of Samuel, of Newark ; had children: 1. Noah Estile ; 2. Mary Estile ; 3. Joseph Estile.

3. Almira Estile married her second cousin, David Littell, son of Enos, son of David. [See *Enos Littell.*]

4. Stephen Rogers Estile married Margaret Shauger, of Rockaway, and had children : 1. Jane Estile ; 2. Eliza Estile ; 3. Melinda Estile ; 4. Melissa Estile.

5. William Estile married Anne Mariah Lyon, daughter of John Lyon, of Rockaway, and had children : 1. William Henry Estile.

Stephen Rogers, (7th child of Catharine Littell and Jabez Rogers,) and Phebe Baldwin, removed to a farm about four miles north of Seneca Falls, N. Y. He died 1813, aged 40 years, and left children : 1. Jabez ; 2. John.

Susan Rogers, (8th child of Catharine Littell and Jabez Rogers,) and Jacob Hinds, removed to Bristol, Vermont, and had children :

1. Stephen Lewis Hinds, born 28th October, 1796, married, 1st, Weathy Johnson, 2d, Phebe Hoit, and had children : 1. Miriam Johnson Hinds ; 2. Rachel Hinds ; 3. Isaiah Bower Johnson Hinds ; 4. Adelaide Hinds ; 5. Margaret Hinds.

2. Sally Hinds, born 7th October, 1798, and married Miron Sturtevant ; lives near Buffalo, New York, and had five children.

3. Joanna Hinds, born 8th Feb. 1800, married her cousin, Parson Hinds, son of Aaron Hinds, 31st December, 1818, and had one daughter, and died 3d March, 1820.

4. Jacob Hinds, born 28th January, 1804, and died the next day.

5. Moses Rogers Hinds, born 11th May, 1806, and died 25th October following.

6. Persis Urania Hinds, born 12th February, 1812, married, in 1828, William Delony, of Vermont : removed to Piqua, Ohio, and died in November, 1835, leaving two children.

ELIZABETH LITTELL, (4th child of David, son of Samuel,) and Moses Bedell, had children :

1. Sarah Bedell, who married Thomas Hallock. [See *Hallock.*]

2. Lyd'a Bedell, who married Isaac Moore, son of John. [See *Moore.*] By her second husband, David Van Sickle, she had no children.

6th Gen. DAVID LITTELL, (6th child of David,) was a blacksmith, and lived at Cheapside, in Livingston township ; was a justice of the peace, and an elder in the Hanover church many years. He was born January, 1751, and died 28th December, 1812. His wife, Hannah Miller, was born 6th October, 1750, and died 2d July, 1832, aged 81 years. They had children :

6th Gen. 1. Enos, born 19th May, 1774, and died 19th June, 1848, aged 74 years and 1 month. He married Mary Morehouse, daughter of David, at Canoe Brook.

2. Josiah ; 3. David—who both died young.

4. William, born 29th January, 1778, and died in a fit in his bed, 7th May, 1840. He married Mary Ward, daughter of Joseph, of Northfield, in Livingston ; she died 24th April, 1843, aged 62 years.

5. Andrew, who died 13th August, 1795, aged 23 years, 6 months, and 9 days, unmarried.

6. Rhoda, born 1st December, 1781, and married John Humes ; lives in Newark.

7. Elizabeth, born 30th March, 1784, and married David Whitehead, son of David, son of Deacon David Whitehead, of Elizabethtown ; he was a chairmaker. Mr. Whitehead had a cancer on the side of his nose, by which he suffered greatly many years, and which eventually caused his death.

8. Luther, who married Margaret Wade, daughter of Henry and Dolly Wade, of Livingston.

9. Hannah ; 10. Calvin, who both died young.

6th, 7th Gen. ENOS LITTELL, and Mary Morehouse, had children :

1. Hannah, who married, 16th May, 1821, Enos B. Morehouse, son of Jephtha, and died childless.

2. Esther Bedell married, 16th May, 1821, Aaron Morehouse, son of John, of Livngston, and removed to Delaware county, Ohio, and died 23d September, 1846, leaving chl'ren : 1. Elizabeth Morehouse, who married George McMasters ; 2. John Morehouse ; 3. Cornelia Morehouse ; 4. William Morehouse ; 5. Sarah Anne Morehouse ; and six others, making eleven.

3. William, who married, 26th October, 1825, Mary Baldwin, daughter of David, of Livingston ; lives in Newark ; had no children.

4. David, who married his 2d cousin, Almira Estile, daughter of Noah, of near Dover, and had children :
  1. Hannah Mariah, born 10th May, 1830 ; 2. Elizabeth Higgins ; 3. William Estile ; 4. Joanna Estile ; 5. Emma ; 6. David ; 7. Almira.

5. Stephen Morehouse Littell married, 23d Sept. 1832, Cornelia A. Baldwin, daughter of Isaac, son of David Baldwin, of Canoe Brook ; lives in Delaware, Ohio, and had children :

1. William Goldy Littell; 2. Sarah Frances; 3. Mary Elizabeth; 4. Eliza; 5. Isaac. [1]

6. Enos Whitehead Littell married Sarah Anne Foote, daughter of Capt. Foote, of Connecticut, and had one son, John Foote
Littell.

7. Betsey married, 19th June, 1833, Isaac Oakley Higgins, of
Newark, and lives there, and had children :
    1. Edward Payson Higgins; 2. Cornelia Littell Higgins; 3.
    Mary Elizabeth Higgins.

8. Aaron Condit Littell married, 20th Nov. 1838, Mary Birt,
daughter of Abraham Birt, of Morris county, and had a son, 1.
Enos Birt Littell. His wife died 25th Nov. 1839, and he married, 4th April, 1841, her sister, Elizabeth Birt, and had children :
2. James Higgins Littell; 3. William Littell; 4. John Wood
Littell.

9. Mary married, 22d Nov. 1838, John Wood, an Englishman,
lives in Newark, and had children :
    1. Frederick Augustus Wood; 2. Henrietta Wood; 3. John
    Wood; 4. Charles Wood.

WILLIAM LITTELL, and Mary Ward, lived at Northfield, and
had children :
1. Joseph Ward Littell, born 3d Oct. 1804, and married Locky
Force, daughter of Jonathan Force, of Livingston, and had children :
    1. Sarah Margaret, born 16th Dec. 1828 ; 2. George Ben-
    edict, born 19th June, 1832; 3. Josephine, born 11th Sept.
    1835.

2. Andrew, who married Locky Harrison, daughter of Capt.
Benjamin Harrison, of Hanover, and had 3 children, who all died
young.

3. Sarah married Samuel Lynch, of Orange county, New York,
and lives there.

4. Charles, who died at 20 years of age.

RHODA LITTELL, (daughter of David,) and John Humes,
live in Newark. He is a justice of the peace. They had children :

1. David Littell Humes. He married, and he and his wife both
died, and left no children.

2. William Humes, who married Jerusha Thompson, grand-
daughter of Judge Thompson, of Mendham, and had children :
    1. Charles Humes ; 2. Mary Elizabeth Humes ; 3. John
    Humes.

ELIZABETH LITTELL, (daughter of David,) and David
Whitehead, lived in Elizabethtown, and had children :

1. Enos Littell Whitehead, who married Joanna Coleman, of
Rahway ; lived in Elizabethtown, and had children :
    1. Elizabeth Whitehead, who married John Jones Vanhouten,
    of Elizabethtown.

2. Mary M. Whitehead married Israel Townley, son of Edward, of Westfield.

3. William M. Whitehead married —— ——.

4. Theodore F. Whitehead.

5. David Whitehead.

6. Francis L. Whitehead.

7. Julianne Whitehead.

2. John Miller Whitehead married Caroline Parker, of New York, and had children :

1. Louisa M. Whitehead.

2. Hannah F. Whitehead.

3. Eliza T. Whitehead.

4. Alphonso Timolat Whitehead.

3. Susan Brant Whitehead married William R. Todd ; lives in Newark, and had children :

1. David M. Todd.

2. Mariah Jane Todd.

3. Margaret Plum Todd.

4. Hannah Littell Whitehead, who married Victor Fleury, who is a baker at Morristown, and had children :

1. John W. Fleury ; 2. Victor Augustus Fleury ; 3. David Whitehead Fleury ; 4. George Wood Fleury.

5. Rhoda Humes Whitehead married Simeon D. Hoagland, son of Cornelius Hoagland, of Elizabethtown, and had children :

1. David Whitehead Hoagland ; 2. Adelaide Smith Hoagland.

LUTHER LITTELL, (son of David,) and Margaret Wade, had children :

1. Abbi Louisa, who married Isaac Rogers, and lives in New York, and had children :

1. James Henry Rogers ; 2. Mary Eliza Rogers ; 3. Valentine Eustace Rogers.

2. Rhoda Anne married David Ayers, son of William, son of David Ayers, Esq., of Liberty Corner, lives at Morristown, and had children :

1. Sarah Louisa Ayers ; 2. Malvina Thompson Ayers ; 3. David Humes Ayers ; 4. Anne Eliza Ayers ; 5. John Littell Ayers.

3. John, who went to the south, and was there drowned ; did not marry.

NATHANIEL LITTELL.

NATHANIEL LITTELL was son of David, son of Samuel, son of John, son of George Littell, who emigrated from London about 1635. Nathaniel Littell, Esq., married Mary Cauldwell, daughter of William Cauldwell, son of James, who emigrated from Ireland in 1732. He bought the lot of land, in 1786, of John Bedell, on which he built the house in 1787, where his son John now lives, and where he kept a store till he died, the 18th of February, 1811, aged 58 years. He was a justice of the peace, and an elder in the Presbyterian church. Mary, his wife, was born 14th Feb. 1757, and died 8th January, 1823. They had children :

1. John, born 28th November, 1779, married, 6th May, 1809, Mary Conklin, dau hter of William Conklin, Esq., of Basking Ridge. [See *Conklin.*]

2. Hugh, born 3d September, 1781, married 22 l January, 1814, Susan W. Scudder, daughter of Doctor Benjamin R. Scudder, son of Richard Scudder. [See *Scudder.*] He was a master mason in New York, was engaged in the erection of ten brick houses, when, on the 9th of November, 1822, he was ascending a ladder to the upper story of one of them, lost his balance, and fell to the curbstone of the street, broke in his skull, and died immediately. He had no children.

3. Polly, born 10th May, 1783, married, 22d March, 1800, Ebenezer Byram, born 29th April, 1778, son of Naphtali Byram, of Morristown. [See *Byram.*]

Ebenezer Byram, in 1803, removed to Warren Co., Ohio ; had 12 children, and died 12th October, 1821, and she married, 12th April, 1824, Samuel Robison, Esq., and had two other children. They live at New Harrison, Darke county, Ohio.

4. Aaron, born 17th January, 1786, and died 11th February, 1786.

5. Luther, born 20th April, 1787, and died 19th February, 1833, with consumption. He did not marry. He was elected a member of the legislature in 1829, held several of the most important town offices, and was, when he died, a colonel of the militia.

6. Nancy, born 13th April, 1789, married, 23d November, 1811, Peter Rounsavelle, born 7th July, 1791.

7. Betsey Thompson, born 16th August, 1791, married, 11th March, 1810, Dr. William F. Piatt, born 9th October, 1788, son of Capt. William Piatt, of Scotch Plains. They removed to New York, where she died 29th Nov. 1827 ; and he died 7th May, 1848. [See *Sarah Shotwell.*]

8. Huldah, born 16th December, 1794, married, 21st February, 1822, Daniel Price, now of Newark, son of Daniel Price. At the time she married, and some time before, she was a teacher of a school in Elizabethtown. She was taken with fever, and died 15th November, 1822, without children, aged nearly 28 years.

Mr. Price married again a niece of Rev Lewis Bond, of Plainfield, is a varnish manufacturer of Newark, and has no living children.

9. David Cauldwell, born 28th January, 1799, and died 12th November, 1810.

6th Gen. JOHN LITTELL, (1st son of Nathaniel, son of David.) lives where his father did, in Passaic Valley, near Littell's Bridge, and with his brother Luther, kept a store from 1811 to 1828, when they dissolved partnership, and he continued the store alone till 1838. when he sold out the goods to Jonathan Valentine, who continued it till 1839.

He was twice elected to the legislature, viz. 1837 and 1838 ; was appointed a justice of the peace and judge of the court in 1814, and again appointed justice of the peace in 1828, and continued by reappointments till 1848 ; was then again elected under the new Constitution and was in 1829 appointed by the legislature a commissioner of deeds, and by successive appointments continued in that office to the present time.

He was elected and installed an elder in the Presbyterian church in 1835, and was appointed one of the delegates of the Presbytery of Elizabethtown to the general assembly of the Presbyterian, church, in 1835 at Pittsburgh, and in 1840 and 1846 at Philadelphia and 1851 at St. Louis.

John Littell, (1st child of Nathaniel,) and Mary Conklin, had children :

1. William Conklin, born 15th April, 1810, and died 27th Sept. 1813.

2. Mary, born 29th February, 1812, married 25th July, 1838, Jonathan Valentine, son of Peter D. Valentine, and had children :
   1. Samuel Rutan ; 2 Luther Littell ; 3. Eliza Littell ; 4. William, who died in infancy ; 5. John, who died in infancy ; 6. Mary Abigail. [See *Valentine.*]

3. William, born 10th October, 1815, married, 26th October, 1836, Mehetabel Bonnel, daughter of Jonathan C. Bonnel, son of Nathaniel Bonnel, 3d. [See *Bonnel.*]

He keeps a store at the summit of the Morris and Essex Railroad, and is Postmaster there.

4. Eliza, born 16th December, 1815, married, 9th March, 1842 James K. Hurin, a merchant of Lebanon, Ohio, and went there,, and died 19th May, 1843, leaving a young child, named Eliza, who died at three months old. and he again married, 5th June, 1845, Cynthia Halsey. [See *Hurin.*]

5 Harriet, born 14th November, 1817, married, 16th May, 1848, John T. Willcox, son of Jonathan M. Willcox, son of Levi, and had a son, George. He kept a store in New Providence Village.

6. Susan, born 27th February, 1820, and married, 1st November, 1851, Charles Whitaker, son of Deacon Stephen Whitaker, of Cleveland, Ohio, and lives there.

7. John, born 30th January, 1822, married, 24th September, 1851, Deborah Hall, born 24th December, 1821, daughter of Jonathan A. Hall, of Penn Yan, N. Y.

8. Luther, born 21st April, 1824 ; graduated at Princeton College 25th June, 1844, studied theology at the Princeton theologi-

cal seminary, and was licensed to preach 4th October, 1849, by the Elizabethtown Presbytery, and was ordained to preach the gospel, and installed over the church at Mount Hope, Orange county, N. York, the 25th September, 1850, by the Presbytery of Hudson.

9. Huldah Rebecca, born 3d June, 1826, married, 2d May, 1850, to John Thomas, of Hamilton, Butler county, Ohio, and went there. Mr. Thomas was born 20th July, 1822, i- a lawyer, a son of the Rev. Thomas Thomas, a native of Wales, who graduated at Oxford, England.

10. A daughter not named, born 16th January, 1830, and died the same day.

WILLIAM LITTELL, (son of John, son of Nathaniel,) and Mehetabel Bonnel, lived at Summit, and had children :

1. William Henry, born 2d May, 1840.
2. Theodore, born 14th May, 1844.
3. Frederick Rose, born 12th April, 1847.
4. Julia Smith, born 3d April, 1851.

POLLY LITTELL, (3d child of Nathaniel, son of David,) and Ebenezer Byram, lived in Darke county, Ohio, and had children :

1. Mary Littell Byram, born 22d Dec. 1800, married, 12th March, 1818, James Gregory, and died 16th July, 1827, leaving children :

    1. Samuel Gregory, who married Jane Roll, daughter of John and Polly Roll, lives in Montgomery county, Indiana, and had children :

        1. —— ——, who died young.
        2. Sarah Gregory, who married John McClure ; lives in Montgomery county, Indiana, and has 4 children.
        3. Esther Gregory married William Smith ; lived in Tippecanoe county, Indiana. She died March, 1849, leaving a child 10 days old, named Will Esther.
        4. Martha Jane Gregory, born 24th Nov. 1825, married Silas Thomas, son of Samuel Thomas ; lives near Troy, Miami county, Ohio.

2. Abby Hedges Byram, born 19th August, 1802, and died 12th April, 1805.

3. Eliza Ogden Byram, born 25th Nov. 1804, married, 27th Dec. 1824, Thomas Barnes, son of Jared, and had children :

    1. Mary Elizabeth Barnes married, 8th May, 1845, Derick Lamer. She had a child the 8th Jan. 1847, and died the 9th, and the child the 10th, and both buried in one grave.
    2. Sarah Jane Barnes, born 1827, and died at about 5 years.
    3. Ebenezer Byram Barnes, born August, 1831.
    4. Huldah Anne Barnes, born August, 1832, married, March, 1850, James Custons, an Englishman by birth, brought up near Poughkeepsie, New York.
    5. Harriet Barnes died in childhood.
    6. Rachel Barnes died in infancy.
    7. Susan Barnes died in infancy.

8. Martha Barnes, born 1837.

9. James Barnes.

10. Harriet Barnes.

11. Caroline Barnes.

4. Nancy Littell Byram, born 8th Oct. 1806, and died 25th of the same month.

5. Amy Hedges Byram, born 16th Sept. 1807, married, 17th March, 1830, Amos Barnes, brother of Thomas, and died 1st Oct. 1847, leaving 4 children :

1. Jared Barnes, born 1st Jan. 1833.

2. Lewis Byram Barnes, born July, 1835.

3. John Barnes, born Jnly, 1837.

4. Elizabeth Barnes, born July, 1839.

9. Silas Condit Byram, born 2d Sept. 1809, married 7th April, 1831, Mary Clark, daughter of John, son of Thomas Clark and Rebecca Lyon, danghter of Joseph Lyon. [*See Joseph Lyon.*] He lives near Hill Grove, Darke County, Ohio, and had children :

1. Sarah Byram, born 7th Feb. 1832.

2. Mary Elizabeth Byram, born 49th Aug. 1834

3. Amy Jane Byram, born 8th March, 1837.

4. Anne Byram, born 19th April, 1839.

5. Eliza Mariah Byram, born 10th Sept. 1841, and died 9th Jan. 1843.

6. Harriet Byram, born 8th Feb. 1844.

7. Susan Byram, born 17th Sept. 1847.

7. Lewis Naphtali Byram, born 9th Nov. 1811, married, 3d March, 1836, Elizabeth McAnulty; lives in Randolph county, Indiana, and had children :

1. Martha Jane Byram, born 17th July, 1837.

2. James Byram, born 9th Dec. 1838.

3. David Byram, born 19th July, 1840.

4. William Courtney Byram, born June, 1842, and died in infancy.

5. John Littell Byram, born 20 h Jan. 1848.

6. Mary Ellen Byram, born 5th Augu t, 1849.

8. Nathaniel Littell Byram, born 3d Jan. 1814, married, 24th April, 1837, his cousin, Mary Byram. daughter of Silas C. Byram, son of Naphtali, and had a daughter, Harriet Byram, who lives with her relative, the Rev. David Holliday, at Peekskill, New York, [*see Byram,*] and also a son, William Nathaniel Byram, who died Nov. 1841, aged 4 months. He died 8th Sept. 1841, of consumption. His wife, Mary, died 20th July, 1847.

9. John Littell Byram, born 25th May, 1816, married, 9th Nov. 1839, Lucinda Manuel, daughter of Philip ; lives in Marion, Grant county, Indiana, and had children :

1. Silas Byram, born 15th June, 1841.

2. Mary Jane Byram, born 3d June, 1845.

3. John Franklin Byram, born 9th July, 1848.

10. James Gregory Byram, twin to David Clark, born 18th August, 1818, and died by accident, 10th May, 1822. (He fell off the fence, and pulled a rail down upon him.)

11. David Clark Byram, born 18th August, 1818, married, April, 1836, Eliza Law; lives near Hill Grove, Darke Co., Ohio, and had children:

    1. Milton Wesley Byram; 2. Ezra Potter Byram; 3. Clark Greenwood Byram; 4. Newton Byram; 5. Mary Byram; 6. Mariah Byram.

NOTE.— Eliza Law was daughter of Francis Law, who married Catherine Simpson, daughter of James, who married Jane Vansickle, sister of John and Abraham Vansickle, of Trenton, Ohio. [*See Joseph Crane, page 108.*]

12 Susan Littell Byram, born 25th April, 1821, and died 17th May, 1823.

And by Samuel Robison, Esq., Polly Littell had children:

13. Robert Luther Robison, born 16th December, 1824, and married, 6th May, 1845, Lavina Frybarger, daughter of John Jacob Frybarger, and had children:

    1. Sarah Anne Robison, born 13th May, 1846.

    2. Mary Ellen Robison, born 5th September, 1849.

14. Samuel Hervy Robison, born 10th May, 1827.

6th Gen. NANCY LITTELL, (6th child of Nathaniel, son of David,) and Peter Rounsavelle, had children:

1. David Cauldwell Littell Rounsavelle, born 5th December, 1812, and married Mary Parsons, born 16th April, 1807, daughter of Jonathan, and had children:

    1. Dayton Rounsavelle, born 18th October, 1834.

    2. Charles Rounsavelle, born 21st June, 1837, and died 10th March, 1838. His wife Mary died 20th October, 1840, and he married, 15th April, 1841, Sarah S. Whitson, born 19th June, 1814, daughter of David Whitson, of Baltimore, and had children:

    3. David Whitson Rounsavelle, born 11th July, 1843.

    4. William Littell Rounsavelle, born 7th May, 1845.

    5. Charles Emory Rounsavelle, born 28th April, 1849.

David C. L. Rounsavelle lives in Baltimore.

2. Hugh Rounsavelle, who died in infancy.

3. Mary, born 3d September, 1820, and died 22d March, 1822. Mrs. Nancy Rounsavelle died 23d December, 1822, and Peter immediately left this region of country.

BETSEY T. LITTELL, (7th child of Nathaniel, son of David,) and Doctor William F. Piatt, lived in New York, and had children:

1. Mariah Milnor Piatt, born 9th July, 1811, married, 13th November, 1827, Joel Wilson, son of John Wilson, Esq., of Plainfield, and had children:

    1. William Piatt Wilson, born 13th February, 1829.

    2. Mercy Wilson, born 24th March, 1831.

3. Eliza Wilson, born 26th November, 1833.

Mrs. Mariah M. Wilson died 4th August, 1834, and Joel Wilson married again, and lives in Rahway.

2. James Mortimer Piatt, born 17th July, 1814, went to sea and did not return

Mrs. Betsev T or Eliza T. Piatt died, and Docter Piatt married, 2d, Caroline Kempton, widow of Captain Kempton, and had a daughter Eliza or Lizzy C. K. Piatt, who is now teaching in a private family in New York. Dr. W. F. Piatt died 7th May, 1848. His 2d wife died previous to his death.

JONATHAN LITTELL.

4th Gen. JONATHAN LITTELL, (10th child of Samue, 1st, of N. J,) had 4 sons.

1. Henry, who it is said married, and lived in the northern part of Morris county.

2. Jonathan, who married Phebe Clark, sister or daughter of Isaac Clark, of Scotch Plains.

3. Cornelius, who married, 1st. Susannah Tucker, daughter of John Tucker, of Stony Hill, and had 2 children ; 2d, Martha Drake, and had 3 other children : Keziah, James, and Martha.

4. William, who married Phebe Meeker, daughter of John Meeker, of Scotch Plains, and had 7 children.

5th Gen. JONATHAN LITTELL, (son of Jonathan,) and Phebe Clark, had 5 children, viz :

1. Hannah, who married Hugh Drake, son of Andrew, of Plainfield.

2. Henry married Betsey Hedges, daughter of Benjamin, of Stony Hill

3. Nancy married Charles Rino, who lived north of Green Brook, near Scotch Plains.

4 Phebe married Bruen Brown, a Baptist minister, and went to Washington city.

5. Joanna, who went with her sister to Washington city.

6th Gen. HANNAH LITTELL, (1st child of Jonathan and Phebe Clark,) and Hugh Drake, lived at Plainfield, and had children :

1. Nancy Drake, who married Jonathan Randolph, son of Barzilla, of Plainfield.

2. Jacob Drake, who married Eliza Maloy.

3. Phebe Drake married Elkana Randolph.

4. Aaron Drake married Phebe Frazee, daughter of Moses, son of Henry Frazee.

5. John Drake married Henrietta Martin, daughter of Jonathan.

6. Mary Drake married John Briant, of Springfield.
7. Eliza.
Nancy Drake, (1st child of Hugh Drake and Hannah Littell,) and Jonathan Randolph, had children:

    1. Barzilla Randolph, who married Mary Dunn, of Piscataway.
    2. Hannah Anne Randolph married James Ayres, of New Market.
    3. Emeline D. Randolph married David Dunham, of Piscataway.
    4. Daniel Randolph.

Jacob Drake, (2d child of Hugh Drake and Hannah Littell,) and Eliza Maloy, had children:
    1. Mary Drake; 2. Caroline Drake.

Aaron Drake, (4th child of Hugh Drake and Hannah Littell,) and Phebe Frazee, had children:
    1. Adelia Drake; 2. Randolph Drake; 3. Sarah Drake; 4. Louisa Drake; 5. Henry Drake.

HENRY LITTELL, (2d child of Jonathan Littell and Phebe Clark,) and Betsey Hedges, had children:
    1. William, who married Nancy Willcox, daughter of William, son of Noah.
    2. Hedges, who went to the Genesee Valley, N. Y. and married, and had one child. He and his wife and child all died near together, with fever, in 1847.

WILLIAM LITTELL, (son of Henry,) and Nancy Willcox, lived in Westfield, near the Branch Mill, and had children:
    1. Mary, who married Rev. Reuben Porter, a Baptist minister, son of Reuben.
    2. Fanny.
    3. Henry married Sarah Rino, daughter of Ephraim.
    4. Charlotte, born 3d September, 1829.
    5. Catherine.
    6. Elizabeth.
    7. Abigail.
    8. Amos.
    9. Harriet.
    10. Aaron.

NANCY LITTELL, (3d child of Jonathan Littell and Phebe Clark,) and Charles Rino, had children:
    1. Betsey Rino.
    2. Dunham Rino.
    3. Hugh Rino, who married, and lives in Rahway.
    4. Amos Rino.

5. Phebe Rino.
6. Mary Rino.
7. Sarah Rino.
8. Rebecca Rino.
9. John Rino married and went to Albany, and died.
10. Charles Rino, who died in infancy.

Charles Rino's wife Nancy then died, and he married, 2d, Mary Marsh, daughter of Isaac Marsh, of Scotch Plains, and had 11 other children, viz. :

11. Charles Rino, 2d, who married Mary Van Sickle, of Elizabethtown.
12. Ephraim Rino, who went to New Orleans.
13. Anson Rino married Nancy ——, of New York.
14. Jedediah Rino married Georgiana Webber, of New York.
15. George Rino mrried Anne Darlin, of New York.
16. Hannah Rino married Amos Willcox, son of Cornelius, and had children : 1. Benjamin Sayre Willcox ; 2. Irene Willcox.
17. Thomas Rino.
18. William Henry Rino.
19. Alva Rino.
20. Abigail Rino.
21. Abilear Rino.

CORNELIUS LITTELL, (3d son of Jonathan, son of Samuel,) by his first wife, Susannah Tucker, had children :
1. Catherine, who married Samuel Frazee in Ohio, and had 10 children.
2. Rebecca married John Murdock in Ohio, and had 4 children.

NOTE.—Rebecca Murdock was drowned about 1820, in crossing a creek near Cincinnati, and Mr. Murdock removed, I have not learned where.

And by his second wife, Martha Drake, Cornelius Littell had 3 children :
3. Keziah married Moses Larew, and lived near West Chester, Ohio. He died about 1830, leaving 6 children, Amos, Mahlon, and Moses Larew, and Martha, Rebecca, and Jane Larew.
4. James Manning, who married Betsey Larew, sister of Moses Larew, Keziah's husband.
5. Martha, who married Jacob Rudasille.

CATHERINE LITTELL, (daughter of Cornelius,) and Samuel Frazee, had children :
1. Hannah Frazee, who married John Spivey ; lives at Connersville, Indiana.

2. Rebecca Frazee, born 23d August, 1805, married Garret Vleit, from Sussex; lives near Milwaukie, Wisconsan. He has been considerably engaged in government surveying. They had children:

    1. John B. Vleit, born 26th April, 1822, married, July, 1846, Manica Caroline Coon; has no children. His business is engineering in Milwaukie.

    2. Jasper Vleit, born 3d April, 1824. He is engineer on the Milwaukie and Mississippi Railroad

    3. William Vleit, born 29th May, 1827, is a farmer.

    4. Abraham Vleit, born 5th August, 1829, is with John, engineering.

3. Susan Frazee married, 1st, David Place, and removed to De Witt Clinton county, Michigan. Mr. Place died about 1832, leaving 4 children:

    1. Catherine Place married, October, 1846, George Sercomb, and had children: 1. George Orville Sercomb; 2. Caroline Vleit Sercomb.

    2. Caroline Place. twin to Catherine.

    3. Mary Anne P ace.

    4. Rebecca Place.

After the death of Mr. Place, Susan Frazee married, 2d, Henry Moore, and had children:

    5. Harriet Moore; 6. John Moore; 7. Charles Moore; and 3 others.

4. Cornelius Frazee married Rosannah Spivey; lives at Rossville, Ohio.

5. William Frazee married Fanny Boid, and soon after died, without children

6. Samuel Frazee died in Indiana, unmarried.

7. Catherine Frazee married William Boice, lives at Hartford, Blackford county, Indiana, and had 7 children.

8. Keziah Frazee married John Petro, lives in Shelby county, Illinois, and has children: 1. Cynthia Jane Petro; 2. Catherine Petro.

9. John T. Frazee married Julianne Conover, lives in Fayette county, Illinois, and had children: 1. Catherine Frazee; 2. Harrison Frelinghuysen Frazee; 3. Jasper Frazee; 4. Rebecca Frazee.

10. Martha Jane Frazee married Stephen Riggs, lives in Fayette county, Illinois, and had children: 1. Elbridge Riggs; 2. Alfred Riggs; 3. Albert Riggs.

KEZIAH LITTELL, (3d child of Cornelius,) and Moses Larew, had children:

1. Amos Larew, who married Rosannah Huffman, had but one son, Henry Marion Larew.

2. Mahlon Larew married Bridget Humes, and had children:
1. John Larew; 2. Lauretta Larew; 3. Augustus Larew.

3. Moses Larew married Amy Anne Morris, and has no children.

4. Martha Larew married Joseph Gorman, and had 8 children:
1. Elizabeth Gorman; 2. Keziah Gorman; 3. Sophronia Gorman; 4. William Gorman; 5. Amanda Gorman; 6. Matilda Gorman; 7. Amos Gorman; 8. Joseph Wilson Gorman.

Keziah Gorman, daughter of Joseph, married Andrew Norris, and had children: 1. Hannah Norris; 2. William Henry Norris; 3. Martha Anne Norris; 4. Robert Benjamin Norris.

5. Rebecca Larew married William Voorhees, and had children:
1. Decamp Voorhees; 2. John Voorhees; 3. Harriet Voorhees.

6. Jane Larew married Thomas Gaffner, and had children:
1. Owen Larew Gaffner; 2. Thomas Martin Gaffner.

WILLIAM LITTELL, (4th son of Jonathan, son of Samuel, 1st,) and Phebe Meeker, had children; he removed to Sussex county in 1800.

1 John Meeker, who married, 1st, Catherine Bedell, daughter of Abraham, son of Jacob Bedell; 2d, Betsey Polhemus, of Sussex.

2. Polly married Jacob B. Maxwell, son of John, son of John Maxwell

3. Elias married, 1st, Mary Collins, of Sussex; 2d, Lydia, a widow, whose maiden name was Lydia Doremus. She died 6th July, 1850, aged 62 years

4 Hiram married Peggy Stanbury, daughter of Capt. Jacob Stanbury, of Scotch Plains.

5. Nancy married, 1st, James McPeek, son of Jonathan McPeek, of Sussex; 2d. John Osborn Maxwell, brother of Jacob B. Maxwell, above named.

6. Sally married Benjamin McPeek, brother of James, above named.

7. Linus married, 1st, Miss —— Stites, of Elizabethtown; 2. Joanna Crane, of Lyons Farms.

JOHN MEEKER LITTELL, (son of William, son of Jonathan,) and Catherine Bedell, had children:
1. Lucinda, who died a young woman, unmarried.
2. Betsey, who married Alexander Hamilton Davis, of Newark.
3. Rachel went to the lakes, N. Y., and married there.
4. Phebe went also to the lakes, N. Y., and married there.
5. Elias married —— ——; lives in New York.
6 Hiram married Phebe and Mary ——, sisters; lives in N Y.
And by his 2d wife, Betsey Polhemus, he had other children:
7. Catherine, who married —— ——; lives in Newark.
8. John.

9. Cornelius, who died in infancy.

10. Cornelius, 2d, born after his father's death.

John M. Littell died of the cholera at Patterson, in 1832.

ELIAS LITTELL, (3d child of William Littell, son of Jonathan,) and Mary Collins, lived in Bloomfield, and had children :

1. Mary, who married John Doremus, brother of his father's 2d wife.

2. John Collins Littell married Lucetta Woodruff, daughter of Flavel, of Madison. He is a tailor in Newark, and had children :
  1. William Britton Littell ; 2. Mary Collins Littell ; 3. John Collins Littell ; 4. Rhoda Woodruff Littell.

3. William, who married Emma Hedenburg, daughter of Edward L. Hedenburg, of Newark. He is a carriage maker of Newark, and had children : 1. William ; 2. Emma S.

And by his 2d wife, Lydia, Elias Littell had a son, —— ——.

HIRAM LITTELL, (4th child of William, son of Jonathan,) and Peggy Stanbury, had one daughter.

1. Margaret, who married Mr. Balies, of Newark.

NANCY LITTELL, (5th child of William, son of Jonathan,) and James McPeek, lives at Lafayette, Sussex county, and had but one child, 1. William McPeek.

SALLY LITTELL, (6th child of William, son of Jonathan,) and Benjamin McPeek, had children :

1. Mary McPeek ; 2. Catherine McPeek ; 3. Phebe McPeek : 4. Sarah Elizabeth McPeek ; 5. Whitefield McPeek ; 6. Margaret McPeek ; and three others who died young, two of them 1st Aug. 844.

LINUS LITTELL, (7th child of William, son of Jonathan,) had children :

1. William ; 2. Stiles ; 3. Elizabeth.

NATHANIEL LITTELL.

NATHANIEL LITTELL is said by John Littell, his grandson, to be brother of Benjamin Littell; or rath·r that Nathaniel Littell, Jun., was cousin to John Littell, of Westfield; therefore Nathaniel Littell, Sen., was son of Samuel.

Nathaniel Littell, son of Samuel, married Susan Colie, of Springfield, thought to be a sister of Daniel Colie; he had children:

1. Henry.
2. William, who died a soldier in the Revolutionary war.
3. James married Jane Dumont, of Somerset county; lived near Green Brook, Piscataway.
4. John, who went to near Cherry Valley, New York, and settled there.
5. Benjamin married and had but one child, Susan, who married and went to French Creek.
6. Noah married Jane Gildersleeve, and lived at Jefferson Village, Essex county.
7. Nathaniel married Catherine Corsner, of Monmouth county.
8. Aaron married Sarah Dickerson, and lived in Elizabethtown, and died without children.
9. Mary, who married Hobart Jewel, of Sodom, Essex county.

HENRY LITTELL, (1st child of Nathaniel, son of Samuel, 1st,) had children:

1. Jonathan, who married Susan Steinbeck, daughter of Jacob, a German, and lived at Cheapside.
2. William, who had a large red·mark on the side of his face. He married Jan Smith, daughter of Uriah, of Cauldwell, and had children: 1. Mary; 2. John; and then removed to Indiana.
3. Abby married Samuel Lyon, son of Moses, of Short Hills.
4. Hannah married John Smith.
5. Susan married John Tailor, son of William, of Springfield.
6. Polly married John Sip, lived in Newark, and both died there, leaving two children: 1. William Sip; 2. Matilda Sip.
7. Nancy married Richard Swain, of Springfield.

JONATHAN LITTELL, (1st child of Henry, son of Nathaniel,) and Susan Steinbeck, lived at Cheapside, and had children:

1. Betsey, who died a young woman, unmarried.
2. Phebe, who married John Drew, Jun., son of John Drew, of W. O. Ridge, and had children:
      1. Charlotte Drew; 2. Teresse Drew; 3. Elizabeth Drew; 4. John Drew; 5. Phebe Drew.
3 Mary married Noah Stiles, Jun., son of Noah, of Connecticut, and had children;
      1. Emma Stiles; 2. Edward Stiles; 3. Adolphus Stiles.
4. Sally married Mervin Stiles, brother of Noah, Jun., and had children:

S

1. Laban Stiles; 2. Walter Stiles; 3. Montgomery Stiles;
4. Sarah Jane Stiles.

5. John, who died at 3 years.

6. Jane married William Stiles, brother of Noah and Mervin,
and had children:
    1. Mary Stiles; 2. John Lyon Stiles; 3. Cornelia Stiles;
4. Susan Stiles; 5. Louisa Stiles; 6. William Stiles.

7. Susan married Daniel Van Wert, from Connecticut, and had
children:
    1. Caleb Van Wert; 2. John Van Wert.

8. Vashti Budd Littell married Aaron S. Ross, son of Aaron F.
Ross, of White Oak Ridge, and had a son, William Augustus
Ross.

9. Frances, who married Baldwin Townley, of Livingston, and
had a daughter, Elizabeth Townley.

ABBY LITTELL, (3d child of Henry,) and Samuel Lyon, had
children:
    1. John Lyon; 2. Mary Lyon; 3. Sally Lyon; 4. William
Lyon; 5. Esther Lyon; 6. Caroline Lyon.

HANNAH LITTELL, (4th child of Henry,) and John Smith,
had children:
    1. Charlotte Smith; 2. David Smith; 3. Caleb Smith; 4. Caroline Smith; 5. Matilda Smith.

JAMES LITTELL, (3d child of Nathaniel, son of Samuel, 1st,)
and Jane Dumont, lived near Green Brook, in Middlesex county,
and had children:
    1. Richard Dumont Littell, who married three sisters, 1st,
Margaret Eliza Dunn; 2d, Anne Mariah Dunn; 3d, Rebecca
Dunn, daughters of Judge Dunn, of Staten Island, and lives there,
and by his first wife has children:
    1. Jane Johannah Dumont Littell.
    2. John Dumont Littell, who is a lawyer; lives at Hoboken,
       and married the only daughter of Smith Bloomfield, and has
       a daughter, born 1849.

By his 2d wife, Anne Mariah, he had no living children.

By his 3d wife, Rebecca, he had 7 children:
    3. Margaret Eliza.
    4. Mary Louisa.
    5. Emma.
    6. Richard Dumont Littell, born 1849; and 3 others, who
       have died.

2. William, who lived on Staten Island, and married a Miss
Farmer, near New Brunswick, New Jersey, and soon after his
marriage, in attempting to cross the Freshkill Creek, on his way
to visit his wife, was drowned. After his death, his widow had a
son, William, born about 1828 or 1830.

3. Margaret married Mr. Broadhead, and both died, leaving no children.

4. Rachel married Edward Sprague, from Long Island, and had a son, William Sprague, born about 1840.

NOAH LITTELL, (6th son of Nathaniel, son of Samuel, 1st,) and Jane Gildersleeve, lived at Jefferson Village, and had children :

1. Nathaniel B., who married Hannah Crowel, daughter of Sylvanus.

2. David married Mary Anne McDonald, daughter of John, from Ireland.

3. Polly married Richard Crowel, son of Daniel, of W. O. Ridge

4. Phebe married, 1st, Abraham Baker; 2d, Gilbert Rindell.

5. Smith, who was accidentally hung on a ladder in his father's barn, at about 17 years of age.

NATHANIEL B. LITTELL, (son of Noah,) and Hannah Crowel, lived at Jefferson Village, and had children :

1. Smith, who married Abby Neely, of Cherry Valley, Essex Co., and had children :

    1. Smith ; 2. Andrew.

2. Mary Jane married Baxter Wilkison, son of Crowel, and had children :

    1. Hannah Frances Wilkison ; 2. Joseph Wilkison ; 3. Samuel Wilkison.

3. Noah, who died, at about 24 years, unmarried.

4. Moses, born 6th Aug. 1829, married, 1850, Eliza Kinnan.

DAVID LITTELL, (son of Noah,) and Mary Anne McDonald, had children :

1. John Smith Littell, who married Amanda Miller, and had a daughter, Adaline Littell.

2. Levi Clark Littell.

3. Abraham Baker Littell.

4. Frances Denman Littell, who died Oct. 1847, aged 14 years.

POLLY LITTELL, (daughter of Noah,) and Richard Crowel, lives in Ohio, and has children :

1. Rebecca Crowel, who married Isaac Ross, of South Orange,

2. Louisa Crowel married —— ——.

3. Daniel Crowel married —— ——.

4. Moses Crowel.

5. Aaron Crowel.

6. Phebe Crowel.

PHEBE LITTELL, (daughter of Noah,) and Abraham Baker. had a daughter,

1. Mary Baker, who married David Mitchel.

And by Gilbert Rindell she had children :

2. Susan Brant Rindell.

3. Sarah Pierson Rindell.
4. Gilbert Rindell.
5. Robert Rindell.
6. Phebe Jane Rindell.

NATHANIEL LITTELL, Jun., (7th son of Nathaniel, son of Samuel, 1st,) and Catherine Corsner, lived at Green Brook, and had children:

1. John, born 14th May, 1781, and married Mercy Williamson, daughter of James, of Plainfield, and lived on the first mountain, above Bound Brook.
2. James married Mary Winans, daughter of Winant Winans, and went to Middletown, Ohio, and died there.
3. Griffin was a soldier in the war of 1812; taken prisoner at Hull's surrender, and never returned. He did not marry.
4. William went to Illinois; married Nancy Glasgow, and died there in Sept. 1850, leaving children: 1. Mary, who married Willard W. How; lives at Toledo; 2. Elizabeth Littell.
5. Benjamin married Mary Compton, daughter of James Compton, of Liberty Corner.
6. Aaron married Jane Brown, daughter of Stephen, of Washington Valley, and had children, Stephen and others, and removed to Mason county, Illinois.
7. Hannah married Henry Jemison, of Spottswood; lives near John Littell, her brother.

JOHN LITTELL, (son of Nathaniel, Jun., son of Nathaniel,) and Mercy Williamson, had children:

1. Nancy, who married Benjamin Willcox, son of Benjamin. [See *Willcox.*]
2. Susan married Joseph B. Morrison, and had children; 1. Mary Elizabeth Morrison; 2. William Henry Morrison; 3. Gilbert Morrison; 4. George Morrison.
3. Caty married James Watts, son of Robert, of Middlebrook, and had children:
    1. Mary Anne Watts; 2. James Runyon Watts; 3. Mary Watts; 4. George Watts.
4. Mary married Isaac Clark, of Rahway, and had children:
    1. James Henry Clark; 2. Jane Emily Clark; 3. Mary Elizabeth Clark; 4. Charlotte Clark.
5. Benjamin married Martha Millegan, daughter of William. He lived on the first mountain, above Bound Brook, and had children:
    1. Jane Anne; 2. Margaret Ellen; 3. Mary Louisa.
6. Israel married Sarah Sickles, daughter of Isaac, of Rahway, and had children:
    1. Lewis Edward.
7. Nathaniel.
8. Abby Eliza.

JAMES LITTELL, (2d son of Nathaniel, Jun.,) and Mary Winans, lived in Middletown, Ohio, and had children:

1. William, who married Sarah Burge, daughter of Anthony, and had children:
   1. Drusilla; 2. Francis; 3. Theodore.
2. Winans married Huldah Noble, daughter of Anthony, and had children:
   1. William; 2. Mary.
   He lives in Lafayette.
3. Catherine, or Kate.
4. Caroline married Isaac Hand, son of Ira, son of Daniel, a brother of Col. Aaron Hand, of Springfield, and had children:
   1. Mary Hand; 2. Ellen Hand. [See *Hand.*]
5. Sarah married William Mitchel, and had a daughter, Emma.

BENJAMIN LITTELL, (5th son of Nathaniel, Jun.,) and Mary Compton, had children:
   1. James; 2. Catherine; 3. Margaret Anne; 4. Edith; 5. Hannah; 6. Harriet, twin to Hannah; 7. William.

HANNAH LITTELL, (7th child of Nathaniel, Jun.,) and Henry Jemison, had children:
   1. Nathaniel Jemison; 2. Catherine Jemison; 3. Rebecca Anne Jemison; 4. Henry Jemison; 5. John Jemison; 6. Aaron Jemison; 7. Mary Jane Jemison; 8. Sarah Jemison; 9. Albert Jemison.

JOHN LONG.

1st Gen. JOHN LONG was a saddler, lived on Stony Hill, married Susannah Valentine, daughter of Jonah Valentine, and had children:

1. Levi, who married Abby Bond, daughter of Thomas, of Lyons Farms.

2. Catherine married Benjamin Swain, son of Jacob, of Wolf Hill. [See *Swain.*]

3. Susannah married, 1st, John Caffrey, from Ireland; 2d, Enoch Vreeland.

4. Michael married. 25th Dec. 1810, Lockey Stewart.

5. Joseph married Betsey Wilkison, daughter of Nathan.

6. Israel B., born 1803, married, 21st August, 1822, Polly Brown, daughter of William.

2d Gen. LEVI LONG, and Abby Bond, had children:
1. Marcus; 2. William; 3. Mary; 4. Hetty.

CATHERINE LONG, and Benjamin Swain, had children:

1. Hannah Swain, who married William McDonald, of Monmouth county, and had children:
    1. Joseph McDonald; 2. William McDonald, Jun.; 3. Thompson McDonald; 4. Benjamin McDonald; 5. Elizabeth McDonald.

2. John Swain married ——— ———, at Rahway, and went to the lakes.

3. Polly Swain married Abraham Simonson, and had children:
    1. William Simonson; 2. Joseph Simonson; and others who died.
And Abraham Simonson died, and she married Ephraim Howard, and lives at Scotch Plains.

4. Eliza Swain married James Curtis, son of John. [See *Betsey Frazee* and *John Curtis.*]

5. Jonah Swain married Jane Ward, daughter of Israel, son of Joshua. He left her and went to the South, and died at 21 or 22 years.

6. Joel Swain, who married a daughter of Charles Rino.

7. William Swain married in Pennsylvania.

SUSANNAH LONG, and John Caffrey, had children:
1. Lucy Caffrey, who married David Edwards.
2. Barnabas Caffrey, who married in Hanover.
3. Edward Caffrey.
4. Philip Caffrey.

5. John Caffrey.
6. James Caffrey.
7. Mary Caffrey.
8. Jane Caffrey, who died at 18 years.

MICHAEL LONG, and Lockey Stewart, had children:
1. Susan, who went to Ohio.
2. Phebe, who married Elias Clark, son of David, son of Elias, Sen. She was accidentally shot, and died of the wound.
3. Hetty married Mr. Vreeland, of Newark.
4. John married Hetty Vreeland, daughter of Charles, of Springfield.
Mr. Michael Long died 5th March, 1833.

JOSEPH LONG, and Harriet Wilkison, had children:
1. Harriet, born 15th June, 1828, married John Meeker, son of Aaron, of Springfield.
2. William Henry, born 16th March, 1830.
3. Mary Elizabeth, born 25th Jan. 1832, married William Burnet, son of Timothy, of Union.
Mr. Joseph Long died 3d March, 1831.

ISRAEL B. LONG, and Polly Brown, had children:
1. Sally, who married Alexander Baker, son of Samuel, of Elizabethtown.
2. Catherine married David Curtis, son of John. [See *Asa Frazee* and *Curtis*.]
3. William.
4. Samuel, born 1830.
5. George, born 8th Sept. 1832, and died 15th Aug. 1849.
6. Jacob, born 1835.
7. Lydia Anne, born 1837.
8. Susan, born 1839.
9. Hetty, born 1843.
10. Caroline, born 1845.
11. Mary Frances, born 28th June, 1847, and died 8th August, 1849.

JEREMIAH LUDLOW.

JEREMIAH LUDLOW lived in New Providence, where James M. Morehouse now lives. He died 1st August, 1764, aged 67 years. His widow died 12th March, 1790, aged 91 years. They had two children :

1. Jeremy, who married Elizabeth Doty, daughter of Joseph Doty, 1st. He lived where Jacob Davis Mulford now lives, in Passaic Valley, Morris county, and had children :

    1. Deborah, who married Jonathan Mulford, son of Captain Jonathan. [See *Mulford.*]

    2. Joseph, who married, 8th January, 1784, Chloe Bedell, [see *Jennings,*] lived where his father did, and subsequently removed to Western New York.

    3. Mercy, who married Dr. John Hole, son of Charles, [see *Hole,*] and removed to Ohio, a few miles below Dayton.

    4. A daughter, who had a daughter, who married Samuel Muchmore, of Madison.

2. Cornelius, who lived on Long Hill, and became a Colonel of the militia in Morris county. He married, 1st, Catherine Cooper, daughter of Daniel Cooper, Sen., and had one son; 2d, Martha Lyon, and had six other children—she died 9th October, 1790 ; 3d, Polly Wall. He died 27th April, 1812, aged 84 years.

COL. CORNELIUS LUDLOW, (son of Jeremiah,) and his 1st wife, Catherine Cooper, had but one child :

1. John, who married, 19th October, 1772, 1st, Catherine Cooper, his cousin, daughter of Daniel Cooper, Jun., and had five children ; 2d, Susan Demun, daughter of John, and had six other children.

2. Agnes, who married, 15th Oct. 1774, Jonathan Pierson.

3. Patty, who married William Remsen, of Elizabethtown.

4. Benjamin, who became Major General of the militia of New Jersey. He married Eleanor Harris, daughter of Benjamin Harris, of Morris county, and sister of the wife of John McCarter.

5. Israel, who married Charlotte Chambers, of Chambersburgh, Penn. He went to Cincinnati, Ohio, and was one of the surveyors of Symmes' Purchase, between the two Miami rivers, before 1800.

6. Elizabeth, who married Col. Israel Day, son of Timothy, of Chatham. [See *Day.*]

7. William, who married Betsey Haines, daughter of Samuel Haines, of Vealtown, and sister of Ruth, 2d wife of Nathaniel Whitaker ; and removed to Mill Creek, Ohio ; had six

or more children; removed to Oxford, Butler county, and was superintendent of the building of the college there. His children were named: 1. Israel; 2. Samuel; 3. Betsey; and others.

JOHN LUDLOW, (1st child of Col. Cornelius Ludlow,) and Catherine Cooper, had children, who all married in Ohio:

1. Sarah married John Lyon, and had no children.
2. Agnes married Silas Hurin, son of Seth. [See *Hurin.*]
3. Stephen married, 1st, Jane Porter; 2d, Le Anne Bell.
4. Cooper married, 1st, Elizabeth Reeder, daughter of Jacob; 2d, Elizabeth Layton, daughter of Judge Layton, of Mad River.
5. Lydia married Ogden Ross, son of Matthias, formerly of Springfield.

His wife Catherine then died, and by his 2d wife, Susan Demun, he had other children:

6. William married Charlotte Hand, daughter of John Hand, from Morris county.
7. Betsey married Matthew Patten, of Dayton.
8. Mary married Alexander Pendery.
9. Martha died at 15 years.
10. Susan married, 1st, Stephen Cummings; 2d, David Bingham, son of David.
11. John married Hetty Niles.
12. Ruth married James Baxter.
13. Catherine married John Long.

John Ludlow removed to Ohio about 1790, or shortly after, with his family, and lived near White's Station, on Mill Creek, in Hamilton county.

STEPHEN LUDLOW, (1st son of John, son of Col. Cornelius,) and Jane Porter, had children:

1. Oliver, who married Miss —— Conwell.
2. Mary Anne, who died at 14 years.
3. Catherine, who died at 13 years.
4. John is unmarried.

COOPER LUDLOW, (2d son of John, son of Cornelius,) had children:

1. Ellen, who married ——; 2. Stephen married ——; 3. John married Elmira ——; 4. Mary Anne.

LYDIA LUDLOW, (5th child of John, son of Col. Cornelius,) and Ogden Ross, had children:

1. Mary Ross, who married Joseph Gaston, had a son, John Gaston, and died.

2. Martha Catherine Ross married William Bigham, son of David, and had children: 1. Lydia Bigham ; 2. John R. Bigham ; 3. Caroline Bigham ; 4. Ross Bigham ; 5. Darwin Bigham ; 6. George Bigham.

3. Caroline Ross married Chamberlain Andrew, and had a son, John Andrew.

4. Sarah Ross married James Andrew.

5. John Ross lives at Lowell, Mass., and married Fanny Waldron, of Boston.

6. Charlotte Ross married John Matthews, and had children: 1. Louisa Matthews ; 2. Jenny Matthews.

7. Harriet Ross.

8. Denman Ross lives at Lowell, Mass. ; married Mary Waldron, of Boston.

9. Jane Ross married Holland Smith, and had a daughter, Jenny Smith, who died young.

10. Lydia Ross married Cyrus Warren.

WILLIAM LUDLOW, (6th child of John, son of Col. Cornelius,) and Charlotte Hand, had children : 1. Israel, who married Eliza McMullen ; 2. Jonn ; 3. Harriet ; 4. Caroline ; 5. Elizabeth ; 6. George.

BETSEY LUDLOW, (7th child of John,) and Matthew Patten, lived at Dayton, and had children :

1. Margaret Patten, who married James Douglass.

2. Susan Patten married William Wilson, merchant at Hamilton, and had children: 1. Charles Wilson ; 2. Elizabeth Wilson ; 3. William Wilson ; 4. James Hurin Wilson ; 5. Ebenezer Thomas Wilson.

3. Anne Patten married Hugh Wilson, brother of William, and went to Indiana.

4. Eliza Patten married Rev. David Reed ; lives in Jefferson county, Indiana.

5. Mary Patten.

6. Amanda Patten married —— ——.

7. William Patten married Mary Anne Duffield, daughter of Robert.

8. Sarah Bell Patten.

9. Martha Jane Patten.

10. Sophia Patten, who died of cholera, 21st July, 1850, at Hamilton.

MARY LUDLOW, (8th child of John,) married Alexander Pendery, and had children :

1. Ludlow Pendery ; 2. Goodlow Pendery ; 3. Martha Pendery ; 4. Ralph Pendery ; 5. William Pendery ; 6. Finley Pendery ; 7. Susan Jane Pendery ; 8. Israel Pendery.

SUSAN LUDLOW, (daughter of John,) and Stephen Cummings, had one daughter, Martha Jane Cummings, who married John W. Owens ; and by David Bingham had children: 1. Mary Judith Bingham ; 2. George Bingham ; 3. William Douglass Bingham ; 4. Susan Frances Bingham ; 5. David Bingham.

JOHN LUDLOW, (son of John,) and Hetty Niles, had children : 1. Harriet, who married Dr. —— Freeman ; 2. Stephen married —— —— ; 3. John.

RUTH LUDLOW, (daughter of John,) and James Baxter, had children : 1. Susan Jane married, and died ; 2. Martha Jane married J. H. Harper ; 3. Andrew James Baxter ; 4. John Ludlow Baxter.

CHARLOTTE LUDLOW, (daughter of John,) and John Long, had children : 1. Susan Long ; 2. Josephine Long ; 3. John Ludlow Long.

3d Gen.

AGNES LUDLOW. (2d child of Col. Cornelius Ludlow,) and Jonathan Pierson, had children :

1. Jonathan Pierson, Jun. who married Matilda Davis, lived at Hamilton, Ohio, was a judge of the court there, and had children :

5th Gen.

  1. Nancy Pierson, who married Moses Kline, and had children : 1. James Kline ; 2. Matilda Kline ; 3. Samuel Kline.
  2. Theodore Pierson.
  3. Ellen Pierson, who married —— ——.
  4. Isabella Pierson, who married William Kain.
  5. Joseph Pierson.

2. Polly Pierson married Gen. Solomon Doughty, son of Joshua Doty, of Long Hill, and had children :

  1. Agnes Doughty, who married Doctor John D. Jackson, of Rockaway, and had children : 1. Edward E. Jackson, who married Miss Osborn ; 2. Charlotte Jackson married Mr. —— Robison, son of Sheriff Collin Robison, of Morristown ; 3. Mary Jackson married Mr. —— Chandler ; 4. John Jackson, Jun., is a physician ; 5. Agnes Jackson ; 6. Laura Jackson.
  2. Joshua Doughty, who married Susan Southard, daughter of Col. Isaac Southard, of Somerville, is a merchant, and president of the Somerville Bank there, and had children : 1. Louisa Doughty ; 2. Sarah Doughty ; 3. Mary Doughty ; 4. John Rolan Doughty ; 5. Joshua Doughty ; 6. Susan Doughty.

3. Elizabeth Pierson Doughty was born 1803, married
Doct. Charles H. Jackson, and died 28th July, 1838,
without children:

4. Sineus Pierson Doughty, born 1808, and died 20th
October, 1832, unmarried.

5. Sarah Mariah Doughty, born 13th July, 1814, and
died 25th July, 1838, three days before her sister
Elizabeth, unmarried.

6. Eugene S. Doughty, who married Elizabeth Underdunk, a widow, of Somerville, is a lumber merchant
there, and had a son, Eugene. He was elected a
member of the legislature in 1850 and 1851.

3. Betsey Pierson, daughter of Jonathan Pierson married
Col. Solomon Boyle, of Long Hill, son of Solomon Boyle,
Jun. [*See Col. Boyle.*]

4. Sineus Pierson, who died in Ohio, a young man, unmarried.

GENERAL BENJAMIN LUDLOW, (son of Col. Cornelius Ludlow,) lived on Long Hill, where his father did.
He was major-general of militia, judge of the court of Morris
county, and was several times elected to the legislature, as
member of the general assembly, and member of the legisla-
tive council.

General Benjamin Ludlow, (4th child of Col. Cornelius
Ludlow,) and Eleanor Harris, had children:

1. Cornelius, who married Julia Anne Disborough, of New
Brunswick, and had children: 1. George; 2. Jane; and three
others. He was a justice of the peace, and judge of court of
Morris county. He died 24th November, 1836.

2. Israel, born 1796, and died 21st Dec. 1819, unmarried.

3. Mary, who married Dr. John W. Craig, now of Plainfield, and died 1846, without children.

4. Martha, born 1801, and died 17th November, 1802.

5. Susan, born 1803, and died 27th March, 1823, unmarried.

6. George Harris, born 1805. He was successively a justice of the peace, sheriff, and clerk of Morris county, and is
now in the lunatic asylum at Trenton, on account of insanity.

7. Martha, 2d, who married her cousin, George H.
McCarter, 17th November, 1840, and died about 1845, without
children.

8. Eliza, born 1809, and died 19th March, 1838, unmarried.

9. Charlotte Chambers, born 1810, died 22d July, 1830,
unmarried.

10. Eleanor, born 181-, and died 4th March, 1849, unmarried.

11. Benjamin, born 8th August, 1817, and died 17th November following.

General Ben. Ludlow born 1763, and died 27th January, 1817. His wife Eleanor born 1771, and died 4th September, 1819, aged 48 years.

ISRAEL LUDLOW, (5th child of Col Cornelius Ludlow,) and Charlotte Chambers, of Ci·.cinnati, had children :

1. James C. Ludlow, who lived on Mill Creek, a farmer, married Miss —— Clarkson, and had children :
>   1. Sarah Bella, who married Salmon B Chase, who was in 1850, a senator of the United States.
>   2. James Dunlop.
>   3. Charlotte Chambers married Charles A. Jones, a lawyer of New Orleans, La.
>   4. Reuhama.
>   5. Benjamin.
>   6. Hadassa.

2. Sarah Bella married Jephtha D. Garrard, a lawyer in Cincinnati, and son of Governor Garrard, of Kentucky, and had children :
>   1. Israel Garrard, a lawyer in Cincinnati.
>   2. Kenner Garrard.
>   3. Lewis Garrard.
>   4. Jephtha D. Garrard.

Mr. Garrard died in 1836, and his widow Sarah Bella married John McLean, one of the judges of the United States supreme court, and had a son, Ludlow McLean, who died young.

3. A daughter, who married Col. Ambrose Dudley, of Cincinnati, and had a daughter, Louisa Dudley, who married John G. D. Burrows, a merchant of Cincinnati.

4. Israel, who married in Kentucky, and died 184—.

OBADIAH LUDLUM.

OBADIAH LUDLUM, and Sarah his wife, came from
Long Island, and settled in Westfield, they had but one child
that grew up to manhood, who was named Obadiah, who
married Phebe Marsh, of Westfield, and had children:

1. Jacob, who married Margaret Pool, of Elizabethtown,
daughter of William Pool, and had children:
    1. Phebe, who married Jacob Woodruff.
    2 Jacob married Miss Lydia Clark.
    3. Caroline, who died unmarried.
    4. John married Margaret Emerson, and had children:
        1. Margaret, who married Isaac Scudder, son of
        Israel; 2. Sarah; 3. Gideon; 4. Mary Elizabeth.
2. Sarah married David Crane, of Elizabethtown.
3. Watson, who went to the South, and died unmarried.
4. Samuel, who married —— ——.
5. Smith married Ruth Badgley.
6. Patty married Daniel Munson, of New York.
7. Betsey married Ebenezer Stevenson, of New York.
8. Joseph, born 17th December, 1779, married Betsey
Morehouse, daughter of Simeon.
9. Joanna, born 26th September, 1781, married Daniel
Cory, son of Elder Daniel Cory, of Long Hill. [*See Cory.*]
10. Ezra married Rachel Segoine, of New York, and lived
and died there.

Obadiah Ludlum, Jun, died, and his widow married Elder
Daniel Cory, of Long Hill.

The family now spell the name *Ludlow.*

JOSEPH LUDLOW, (son of Obadiah Ludlum, Jun.,) and
Betsey Morehouse, lived on Stony Hill, he was an elder in the
Presbyterian church there, and had children:

1. Aaron M., who married, 1st, Eliza DeHart; she died,
and he married, 2d, Jane Osborn, daughter of John.
2. Ezra married Deborah Crane, daughter of John, of
New Providence; 2d, Mary Crane, daughter of John Crane,
of Newark.
3. Amos married Catherine W. Hart, daughter of John, of
New York, and went to Lebanon, Ohio; his wife died, and he
married there, 2d, Rosanna Simonton; she died, and he married, 3d, Hannah Smith, daughter of Samuel Smith, late of
Salem county, New Jersey.
4. Smith, who died an infant.
5. Hannah died 1st January, 1832, aged 22 years.
6. Joseph Marsh married Phebe Anne Dunham, of Westfield, had one son, when she died, and he married Jane Maxwell, of Connecticut Farms.

7. Israel, who died an infant.

8. Nancy married John M. Kindall, son of Joshua. [*See Kindall.*]

9. Jacob, who married Deborah T. Ruckman, daughter of Levi, born 18th January, 1818, and who died 20th February, 1847, leaving two children, Watson and Phebe, and he died 24th October, 1850.

10. Eliza, who died an infant.

11. Watson went to Lebanon, Ohio, and married Mary Smith, sister of Amos's 3d wife.

12. John, who died 20th February, 1845, aged 21 years.

Mr. Joseph Ludlow died 10th October, 1849, aged nearly 70 years.

AARON M. LUDLOW, by his 1st wife, had no children. By his 2d wife, Jane Osborn, he had children :

1. Jeremiah Osborn, born 9th January, 1840.
2. Henry Martin, born 19 h March, 1841.
3. Horace Judson, born 7th January, 1843.
4. Will'am Munson, born 1st. August, 1844.
5. Eliza Dellart, born 11th February, 1846.
7. John Clark, born 19th October, 1847.

EZRA LUDLOW, and Deborah Crane, had children :

1. Levi Mulford, who went to California.
2. Francis, who died at 9 months.
3. John Joseph.
4. Erastus, who died young.
5. Erastus, 2d.
6. John Edgar.
7. George.
8. James F. Meeker.

AMOS LUDLOW, and Catherine Hart, had children:

1. John Howe Darg.
2. Martha Anne Eliza died at 2½ years.
3. Henrietta, who died at 16 days.
4. Deborah Jane, who died at 2½ years.

And by his 2d, wife, Rosanna had, 5. Phebe Anne, who died at 1½ years.

And by his 3d wife, Hannah, had, 6. Catherine Wheeler.

7. Joseph LeRoy ; 8. Josephine ; 9. Mary Elizabeth.

WATSON LUDLOW, and Mary Smith, had children :

1. Samuel Joseph ; 2. Elizabeth Anne ; 3. Semantha Jane ; 4. Sarah M.

MATTHIAS LUDLOW.

MATTHIAS LUDLOW married Sarah Williams, daughter of Benjamin, lived in Wesfield, and had children:
1. Ebenezer, who married Abigail Littell, daughter of John, son of Benjamin. [*See Littell*]
2. Benjamin married Keziah Clark, of Westfield.
3. Cornelius married Abby Pierson, daughter of William, of Westfield.
4. William married, as his 2d wife, Sarah Martin, daughter of Alexander, of Long Hill.
5. Sally married William Lane, of Woodbridge.
6. Lewis married Betsey Davis, daughter of Deacon Jacob Davis, of Westfield.
7. Isaac was a physician, married Nancy Cutter, daughter of Camp Cutter.

LEWIS LUDLOW, and Betsey Davis, had children:
1. Malancton, who died a young man. unmarried.
2. Sarah, who married succesively William Miller, son of Lewis, Caleb Miller, son of Nathaniel, and William Day, an Englishman. By William Miller she had a son, 1. Lewis Miller, who married Martha Hand. daughter of Matthias, son of Nehemiah. By Caleb Miller she had children: 2. Israel M. Miller; 3. Mary Miller. And by William Day. an Englishman, she had children: 4. Catherine Day; 5. William Day; and two others.
3. Benjamin, who married Fanny Smalley, daughter of Abner, son of James Smalley, and had a daughter,
1. Elizabeth Ludlow, who married John Badgley, a grandson of Jonathan.
His wife Fanny died, and he went to Buffalo, New York, and there married again.

STEPHEN LUM.

STEPHEN LUM married in Connecticut Farms, and removed from thence to the farm he bought of Moses Miller, south of John M. Stites's bark-mill, and had children :

1. Moses, born February, 1780, and married, 13th May, 1810, Nancy Morehouse. daughter of Simeon, and removed to Newark, and died 18th October, 1819.

2. Amos married Fanny Morehouse, sister of Moses's wife.

3. John married a widow Osborn, lived in Newark.

4. Betsey did not marry.

5. Stephen M. married Betsey Frazee, and had children :
   1. Jane ; 2. Hannah.

6. Oba married —— ——, and died about 1830, leaving 4 children.

MOSES LUM, and Nancy Morehouse, had children :

1. Isaac, who died an infant.

2. Amos, who married Amanda Walker, daughter of Abraham, and had children :
   1. Louisa Eveline; 2. Lavina Parsons; 3. Martin Luther;
   4. Adaline Woodhull; 5. Amanda Walker.

3. Stephen married Catherine Conklin, daughter of Nicholas, of Newark, and had children:
   1. Sarah Seely ; 2. Elizabeth.

4. Rebecca M. married Sidney B. Day, of Orange.

5. Elias Riggs, who died at 4 years.

6. David, who died at 2 years.

AMOS LUM, (son of Stephen,) and Fanny Morehouse, had children :

1. Samuel Y. Lum graduated at college, studied theology, and was licensed to preach the gospel by the presbytery of Newark.

2. Jane, who married Elias D. Hughson, son of Peter, of Newark.

3. Hannah, who married, 20th September, 1848, Charles H. Freeman, of Macon, Georgia.

T

PETER LYON.

1st Gen.
PETER LYON was probably the son of Ebenezer Lyon, or Nathaniel Lyon, who are named in the list of the 2d generation of "the Elizabeth Town Associates," admitted in 1699.

Peter Lyon lived on Stony Hill nearly south of Littell's Bridge. He was born 1722, and died 23d Sept. 1784, aged 62 years. He married Joanna Clark, half sister of Elias Clark, of Stony Hill. She was born 28th Dec 1726, old style. They had children:

2d Gen.
1. Ebenezer, born 29th April, 1746, and married, 1st, Sarah Willcox, daughter of John Willcox, Sen. She died 1st June, 1795, aged 45 years. He married, 2d, Caty Drake, daughter of Edward Dra e; 3d, Fanny, the mother of William Titus [See *Titus*.]

2. David, who went to Virginia.

3. Joanna married John Blackford, and died 12th Oct. 1783, aged 21 years.

4. Benjamin married, 8th March, 1776, Joanna Willcox, daughter of Peter, Jun. He was a carpenter; built the house on Stony Hill, east of his father's, where John Marshall lately lived. He sold out, and removed to Green county. Pennsylvania, and there married, as his 2d wife, the widow Gertrude Rogers.

5. Bethiah married, 2d May, 1770, John Potter, son of Amos Potter, Sen. [See *Potter*]

6. Nathaniel married Mercy Willcox, sister of Ebenezer's first wife.

7. Susan married, 15th April, 1790, John Cory, brother of Noah and Parkhurst Cory, and had a daughter, Phebe Cory, who married Cornelius Miller, son of Noah, of Westfield, and removed to Indiana, and had a daughter, Anne Miller, who married her cousin Peter Lyon, son of Ebenezer.

8. Phebe married Jonas Clark, son of Jeremiah, of Rahway, brother of Elias Clark, Sen., and had children, Peter, Jeremiah, and Polly Clark.

2d Gen.
EBENEZER LYON, (son of Peter,) lived where his father did, and by his 1st wife, Sarah, had children:

1. Elizabeth, born 28th April, 1774, and married, 27th April, 1791, Moses Tucker, son of John. [See *Tucker*.]

2. Mary, born 16th May, 1776, and married James Brown, son of John. [See *Brown*.]

3. John, born 7th Oct. 1778, and died 11th Feb. 1842. He married Tabitha Moore, daughter of Isaac Moore, and had a daughter, Sarah, born 15th May, 1809, and married Dayton Badgley, son of Anthony. [See *Badgley*.]

4. Rachel, born 21st August, 1781, married Henry Moore, son of Joseph, of Mount Bethel.

5. Sally, (twin to Rachel,) married Jonathan Roff, son of Nathaniel. [See *Roff*.]

6. Peter, born 27th Feb. 1787, married his cousin Anne Miller, daughter of Cornelius, of Indiana, and grand-daughter of Susan Lyon (sister of Ebenezer) and John Cory.

Peter Lyon left his wife, and returned to this place, and died the 25th Aug. 1851.

7. Pnebe, born July 23J, 1789, and died in infancy.

8. Phebe, 2d, born 14th Dec. 1791, married William Alward, son of Benjamin, and went to French Creek. [See *Alward.*]

6. Mercy, born 21st May, 179), married, 5th Feb. 1815, Squier Pope, son of Samuel, of Mount Bethel.

10. Susan, twin to Mercy, is not married. Her mind is partially alienated.

RACHEL LYON, and Henry Moore, had children :

1. Henry More, Jun., who married Sally Allen, daughter of Gideon. [See *Allen.*]

2. Amos Moore married Charity Compton, daughter of James.

3. Peter Moore married Rebecca Bird, daughter of John. He was a justice of the peace.

4. Sarah Moore married Benjamin Coddington, son of Archibald.

5. John Moore married Eliza Frazee.

6. Jane Moore married Henry Bird, brother of Peter's wife.

7. Harriet Moore married George Coddington, son of William.

BENJAMIN LYON, (son of Peter,) and Joanna Willcox, had children :

1. Betsey, who married Thomas Parmer.

2. Phebe married George Cook.

3. Sheba married John Kinney.

4. Nancy married John Kauffman.

5. Noah did not marry.

6. Peter married ——— ———.

And by his 2d wife, widow Gertrude Rogers, had,

7. William married Betsey Hathaway.

8. Joanna married Ira French.

NATHANIEL LYON, (son of Peter) and Mary Willcox, had children :

1. Jotham, who lives on the Wabash River, in Indiana.

2. Mary, who married ——— ——— ; is now a widow in Indiana.

3. Phebe married Joshua Miller, in Ohio, son of Jacob. [See *Jacob Miller.*]

NOTE.—I know of no connection between Peter Lyon and Joseph Lyon.

JOSEPH LYON.

JOSEPH LYON married Rebecca Littell, **daughter of David,** and had children :
  1. Joseph, who married Barbara ——.
  2. James married Susan Smith.
  3. Samuel married Hannah ——.
  4. Thomas married Anna ——, in Philadelphia.
  5. John married Sarah Hetfield, daughter of John, of Elizabethtown, N. J.
  6. William married Hannah ——.
  7. Rebecca married Thomas Clark.
  8. Abigail married ——.
  9. Sarah married John Straun.
  10. Mary married Abraham Kimberland.

REBECCA LYON, (7th child of Joseph,) and **Thomas** Clark, had children :
  1. Joseph Clark, who married Mary Smith.
  2. William Clark married Hannah Smith, cousin of **Mary.**
  3. James Clark married Susan Smith, a Dutch girl.
  4. Thomas Clark married Anna Stout.
  5. John Clark married Sarah Hetfield, daughter of **Thomas,** of Elizabethtown.
  6. Samuel Clark married Mary ——.
  7. Abigail Clark married William Stoner.
  8. Sarah Clark married John Straw.
  9. Betsey Clark married —— ——.
  10. Mary Clark married William Moore.
  11. Rebecca Clark married James Thomas.

John Clark, (5th child of Thomas,) and Sarah **Hetfield,** had children :
  1. Hiram Clark, who married Elizabeth Long, daughter of Gideon.
  2. Elizabeth Clark married William Weaver, **son of** Judge Henry Weaver.
  3. Mary Clark married Silas C. Byram, son of Ebenezer, son of Naphtali, and lives near Hill Grove, Darke county, Ohio. [See *Naphtali Byram.*]
  4. Stephen Clark married Elizabeth Hamilton, daughter of Andrew.
  5. Susan Clark married Robert Law, son of Francis, and brother of David C. Byram's wife. [See *Byram.*]
  6. John Clark lives on the St. Joseph's river, **Michigan.**
  7. George Clark married —— ——.

JAMES MARSHALL.

JAMES MARSHALL was son of James Marshall, of Rahway. He married Phebe Marsh, sister of Daniel, Christopher, and Ralph Marsh, of Rahway. He lived in Stony Hill Valley, and had children:

1. Mary, who married Peter Allen, son of Joseph Allen, Jun., of Washington Valley. [See *Joseph Allen, Jun.*]

2. Nancy married, 10th March, 1790, William Allen, brother of Peter.

3. James married Mary Moore, daughter of Isaac Moore, of Passaic Valley; lived and died at Patterson.

4. Daniel married Polly Frazee, daughter of Jacob, on the first mountain, and went to Ohio.

5. Jane married David Brant, of Morris county. He left her, and went to Ohio, and she lived and died in New York.

6. John, born 1789, married Hannah Willcox, born 1795, daughter of Daniel Willcox. He lived on Stony Hill, and had children:

    1. Stephen, who married Amanda Smalley, daughter of Samuel, son of David, and had children: 1. Hutchings; 2. Samuel; 3. Mary Augusta; and then went to Illinois.

    2. Deborah, born 1816, married William Brant, son of Matthias, of Union, and had a daughter, Mary Alice, born 30th June, 1842, and then parted by consent.

    3. Mary Jane, born 1822.

JAMES MARSHALL, (3d child of James,) and Mary Moore, lived at Patterson, and had children:

1. John.

2. David, who died unmarried.

3. Sally married William Hadley, and removed west.

4. Daniel.

5. Rachel married William Walker; lives at Morristown.

6. Betsey, twin to Rachel, married Henry Crane, of Bloomfield.

7. Garret.

8. James.

9. Calvin, who died young.

JOHN MASCHO.

JOHN MASCHO married Catharine Potter, daughter of Daniel Potter, 2d. He lived on Long Hill, and had children:

1. Polly. [See *Potter.*]

2. David, who went to Western N. Y.

3. Sarah, who died young.

4. Daniel Potter Mascho, who married Sally Lacy, daughter of Jacob, son of David.

ALEXANDER MARTIN.

ALEXANDER MARTIN lived on the south side of Long Hill, below Henry Jennings' and the Washington schoolhouse.

His wife's name was Sarah. He was born 1730, and died 14th March. 1785, aged 55 years. She was born 1737, and died 20th December, 1797, aged 60 years; they had children :

1. Jane, who married James Todd, son of Alexander, of Bedminster, Somerset county. [See Todd.]

2. Sarah married William Ludlow, son of Matthias, of Westfield. [See Matthias Ludlow.]

3. Alexander, Jun., married, 26th Oct.1788, Mary Darling, sister of Thomas Darling.

4. David married Susannah Shotwell, daughter of John Smith Shotwell, and sister of William Shotwell, of Plainfield, and had no children.

5. Thomas married, 27th March, 1788, Betsey Hedges, daughter of Uriah. [See Hedges]

6. Anne, who married George Noble, and had a daughter Jane, who married Sylvanus Oakley, son of Ephraim Oakley. [See Oakley.]

7. Samuel married —— ——, and went to the West.

JANE MARTIN, (daughter of Alexander,) and James Todd, had children :

1. Alexander Todd, who died in 1849, aged 64 years.

2. Sally married John Norton.

3. William married Catherine Hand, daughter of Jonathan Hand, of Basking Ridge. [See Hand.]

4. James is not married.

5. Anne married John Nesbit, son of James, of Basking Ridge.

THOMAS MARTIN, and Betsey Hedges, had children :

1. Thomas, who married, 14th February, 1822, Rebecca Spinning, daughter of Benjamin, and had children :

    1. Jnette.

    2. John Dayton, who married. 18th July, 1850, Nancy Pierson, daughter of James H. Pierson.

2. Dayton, who married Sally Crowel, daughter of Silas Crowel, of Green Village, and had children : 1. Harriet Roberts Martin ; 2. William R. Martin.

NOTE.— Silas Crowel's wife was Agnes Roberts, daughter of Samuel, son of Samuel Roberts, Sen.

3. Polly married Daniel Hole, son of Charles Hole, Jun., and had children : 1. Sally Hole ; 2. Nancy Hole ; 3. Thomas Hole. They went to the lakes, N. Y. [See Hole.]

JOHN MAXWELL.

JOHN MAXWELL lived in Westfield, and had children :

1. William, who married, 1st, Abigail Day, daughter of David Day, Esq.; 2d, Elizabeth Baker, daughter of Thomas Baker, Jun.
2. John, 2d.
3. David.
4. Esther, who married Moses Miller, son of John Miller, Jun. [See *Miller.*]

WILLIAM MAXWELL, (son of John Maxwell, Sen.,) owned the farm of 99 acres, adjoining on the west that of John Bedell, and probably he, or his father-in-law, David Day, Esq., built the house where Peter Hill now lives.

He also owned a tract south of it, extending to the top of Stony Hill. He sold the farm of 99 acres, on the 11th of April, 1761, to Thomas Baker, and removed to or built a house on the north side of Stony Hill, on the other tract now owned in part by John W. Hand, lying east of T. O. Scudder's wood lot.

William Maxwell had children :

1. Sarah, who married Henry Frazee, son of Joseph. [See *Frazee.*]
2. David Day Maxwell, baptized 13th May, 1764, married Nelly ——, and removed to Canada.
3. William, Jun., who married Polly Badgley, 28th February, 1792, daughter of Anthony.
4. Polly married, 1st, Isaac Line, son of Capt. William Line, had a son, Isaac Line. Her husband then died, and she married John Willcox, son of John Willcox, Sen.
5. Abigail, who died 12th February, 1846, unmarried, an aged woman.
6. Samuel, who died a young man, unmarried.
7. Elizabeth married, 10th May, 1775, John Prior, son of Andrew. [See *Prior*]
8. John, who married near Pluckemin.
9. Jemima, who married —— ——.

JOHN MAXWELL, 2d, (son of John, 1st,) had children :

1. Nathaniel, who died unmarried, during the revolutionary war.
2. John, 3d, was a mason, learned his trade of Jacob Brittin, of Long Hill, was a captain of the militia, married Eunice Osborn, daughter of John, and in April, 1800, removed to Sussex county,
3. Daniel, who married Abby Potter, daughter of Caleb Potter.
4. Hannah married Aaron Baker, son of Daniel, son of Thomas Baker, 3d. [See *Baker.*]

CAPT. JOHN MAXWELL, (son of John, son of John, 1st, of Westfield,) and Eunice Osborn, had children :

1. Jacob Brittin Maxwell, born 5th August, 1786, and married

1st, Phebe T. Russel, born 18th March, 1790, daughter of James Russel, of Sussex ; 2d, Polly Littell, daughter of William, son of Jonathan Littell.

2. Elizabeth married Luke VanBuskirk, Jun., son of Luke, of Sussex.

3. John Osborn Maxwell married Betsey Carey, daughter of Jacob, of Sussex.

4. Esther married James C. Hagaman, son of Barna Hagaman.

5. Israel Baker Maxwell married Mary Anne Onsted, daughter of John.

JACOB B. MAXWELL, (1st child of Capt. John Maxwell,) now lives in New Providence, and by Phebe T. Russel had a son:

1. John T. Baker Maxwell, who married Abigail Higgins, daughter of Davis Higgins.

And by Polly Littell had children :

2. William Newton Maxwell, who died at 25 years, unmarried.

3. Nancy, born 17th February, 1817, who married Samuel Duryee, born 16th November, 1814, son of David, of Newark, and had children :

    1. William Brittin Duryee, born 17th March, 1840.

    2. John David Duryee, born 4th May, 1841.

    3. Phebe Ellen Duryee, born 25th March, 1844, and died 1st October, 1844.

    4. Mary Emma Duryee, born 7th October, 1846.

    5. Charlotte Elizabeth Duryee, born 28th August, 1848.

4. Israel Osborn Maxwell, born 5th August, 1820, and married Charlotte Catherine Strong, born 1826, daughter of Davis Strong, and had children :

    1. Jacob Brittin Maxwell, born 28th November, 1843.

    2. Clara Madora Maxwell, born 21st June, 1848.

5. Esther, who died young.

JOHN T. BAKER MAXWELL, (son of Jacob B. Maxwell,) and Abigail Higgins, live in New York, and had children :

    1. Phebe Anne; 2. Louisa ; 3. Charlotte ; 4. Harriet; 5. Margaret Davis ; 6. Addison Weld ; 7. Mary.

ELIZABETH MAXWELL, (2d child of Capt. John Maxwell, and Eunice Osborn,) and Luke VanBuskirk, Jun., of Sussex, had children :

1. Eunice VanBuskirk, who married Horace Cooper, of Morris county.

2. Mary Anne VanBuskirk married Charles Mackerly, son of Michael, and had children: 1. Michael Mackerly ; 2. Jacob B. Mackerly ; 3. Harriet Mackerly ; 4. Elizabeh Mackerly.

3. John M. VanBuskirk married Mary Anne Reed, daughter of Andrew Reed, and has a son William VanBuskirk.

Mr. Luke VanBuskirk, Jun., was accidentally killed by the fall of a tree, and his widow Elizabeth married Mr. Montague, and had a son: 4. Joseph Montague.

JOHN O. MAXWELL, (3d child of Capt. John Maxwell,) and Betsey Carey had children :
1. Phebe married Lansing Predmore, son of Joshua, of Sussex, and removed to Michigan.
2. Jacob Carey married, and removed to Beech Woods, N. Y.
3. Daniel ; 4. Rhoda ; 5. James ; 6. John Maxwell.

ESTHER MAXWELL. (4th child of Capt. John Maxwell,) and James C. Hagaman, had children :
1. Hannah Hagaman. who married Mr. Masker, from Patterson.
2. Jacob Brittin Hagaman married Telitha Predmore, daughter of Joseph, and cousin of Lansing Predmore, before named.
3. Eliza Hagaman married Daniel Gunderman, son of Peter, of Sussex county.
4. Sarah Ann Hagaman married Mr. Ross, of Sussex.
5. Catherine Hagaman, who died at about 25 years.
6. Margaret Hagaman, who died at about 23 years.
7. Rebecca Frances Hagaman.
8. James Hagaman.
9 and 10. Daniel and Mary Hagaman, twins.

ISRAEL B. MAXWELL, (5th child of Capt John Maxwell,) and Mary Anne Onsted. had children: 1. Nancy ; 2. Esther ; 3. John Jacob Maxwell ; and then removed to Michigan.

DANIEL MAXWELL, (son of John Maxwell, 2d.) and Abby Potter, were married 5th November, 1789, and had children :
1. Phebe. who married Mr. Bishop, near the Scotch Plains.
2. Esther, who married Ephraim Terril, of Westfield.
Abby, the wife of Daniel Maxwell, was drowned in January, 1800, in New York bay, by the upsetting of a sailboat of Elizabethtown, when several others were drowned.

DAVID MAXWELL, (3d child of John, 1st.) lived in Union, and had children :
1. John, who married Anna Hubbel, and lived in Union township.
2. Samuel married Ruth Ross, daughter of Daniel Ross, and sister of Phebe, the wife of John Crane, [see *Crane page* 104,] and removed to Ballston Springs.
3. Isaac married a daughter of George Scudder, and lived near Union Village, in Passaic Valley, and had children, David and Susan, who went to near Lake Ontario, in Western N. Y.
4. Ruth married Ezekiel Ross, brother of Samuel's wife.

JOHN MAXWELL, (son of David,) and Anna Hubbel, had children :
1. Susan, who married Stephen Foster, of Lyons Farms.
2. David, who died at about 58 years, unmarried.
3. Abner, who married Sally Allen, daughter of John, of Union.
4. Nancy, who died at about 64 years, unmarried.
5. Mary, who married Denman Meeker, of Lyons Farms.
6. Esther married Elias Crane, son of John, 4th. [*See Crane.*]

ROBERT MEEKER.

JOSEPH MEEKER, was in the first list of eighty associates, called " the Elizabethtown Associates," and was probably the father of Robert Meeker, Stephen Meeker, and David M. eker, who were brotners, and all settled in or near Elizabet .town.

The name of Benjamin Meeker is in the list of the 2d generation of associates, admitted in 1699.

ROBERT MEEKER had sons, James, Robert, Stephen, and David.

JAMES MEEKER, (son of Robert,) married Mary Crocheron, and had children :

 1. Mary, who married Ephriam Sayre, of Elizabethtown, and had children : 1. Betsey Sayre ; 2. Polly Sayre ; 3. Nancy Sayre ; 4. Ephraim Sayre, Jun.

 2. Isaiah married Deborah, the widow of Jonathan Magie, and daughter of Joseph Halsey.

 3. Francis married Walters Burrows. [See Burrows.]

 4. Anna, who died a young woman.

 5. Hannah married Edward Hill, of Basking Ridge.

 6. Rebecca married Simeon Morehouse. [See Morehouse.]

 7. James married Hannah Foster, of Lyons Farms.

 8. Aaron.

 9. Hetty, who married Samuel Foster of Lyons Farms.

ISAIAH MEEKER, (son of James,) came up to Turkey, in 1775, and settled on No. 18, of the Elizabethtown lots, first owned by William Broadwell, where Abraham Kent now lives, and died there, 23d February, 1814, aged 73 years. He married Deborah, the widow of Jonathan Magie. She was the daughter of Joseph Halsey, who lived near the Wheatsheaf Tavern, between Elizabethtown and Rahway. She died 6th March, 1886.

Isaiah Meeker, (2d child of James Meeker,) and Deborah Halsey, had children :

 1. Abigail, who was born 1767, and married, 9th Sept. 1824, Thomas Parrot, Esq, as his 2d wife. She died 1st July, 1846, aged 79 years. She had no children.

 2. Daniel Halsey married, 19th Dec. 1790, Sally Wood, daughter of Capt. Daniel S. Wood. He died 27th May, 1798, aged 30 years.

 3. Nancy, born 1771, married, 23d Dec. 1790, John Roberts son of Samuel Rob rts. She died 30th July, 1842, aged 71 years. He died 22d April, 1842, aged 75 years.

 4. Caleb, born 1772, married Charity Frost, daughter of John M. Frost, of Morris county. He died 8th Jan. 1815, aged 43. She died 10th Feb. 1850, aged 72 years. [See *Ward.*]

 5. Jonathan Magie, born 2d April, 1776, and married Elizabeth Townley, born 22d August, 1780, daughter of Richard Townley, son of Effingham, and had no children.

 6. Mary married Arauna Muir, of New Vernon.

 She died ———. He died 27th Aug. 1838, aged 60 years.

7. Isaac, born 1778, married, 5th March, 1808, Betsey Willcox, daughter of Daniel.

DANIEL H. MEEKER, (son of Isaiah,) and Sally Wood, had children :

1. John M, who married Mary C. Budd, daughter of Doct. John C. Budd.
2. Deborah married Uzel Hand, son of Robert. [See *Hand*]
3. Daniel, who went to Connecticut.

NANCY MEEKER, (daughter of Isaiah,) and John Roberts, had children :

1. Phebe, born 1791, and died unmarried.
2. Abigail, who married Nathan Firman Pierson, and had children : 1. John Roberts Pierson ; 2. George Pierson ; 3. Elizabeth Pierson ; 4. Daniel Pierson ; 5. Elias Pierson ; 6. Jonathan Meeker Pierson.

Charlotte H, who died 2d March, 1838, aged 36 years.

JOHN M. MEEKER, (son of Daniel H., son of Isaiah,) and Mary C. Budd, had children :

1. Gertrude, who married Jabez Cook, son of Ellis Cook, of Hanover, and had children: 1. Anne Cook ; 2. William Cook ; 3. Mary Cook.
2. John ; 3. Sarah ; 4. Mary ; 5. George ; 6. Henrietta Meeker.

CALEB MEEKER, (son of Isaiah,) and Charity Frost, had children :

1. Polly, who married Amos Willcox, son of John Willcox, Jun., and died 27th Nov. 1831, leaving a son, Theodore, who married —— ——, and lives in N. Y.
2. Nancy ; 3. Betsey Townley ; 4. Charity Frost, who all three died young.
5. Caleb Halsey Meeker, who married Hannah Gillam, daughter of John, son of James Gillam, and had children :
   1. Albert, 2. Harriet ; 3. Almira ; 4. Mary ; 5. Emma.
6. Jonathan Magie Meeker married, 1st, Almira Voder ; 2d, Mary Elizabeth Delliger, of N. Y., and had children :
   1. Frederick ; 2. Mary ; 3. Alvin ; 4 William ; 5. Theodore ; 6. Ellis.
7. Isaac, born 8th Dec. 1811, married Mehetabel Barnet Willcox, daughter of John, 3d, and had children :
   1. Sarah Anne, who married, 27th Feb. 1850, Benjamin Spinning, son of John, [see *Spinning ;*] 2. John Lewis Meeker ; 3. Charity Frost Meeker ; 4. Isaac Henry Meeker ; 5. William Francis Meeker.

MARY MEEKER, (daughter of Isaiah,) and Arauna Muir, had children :

1. David Austin Muir, who is a dry goods merchant in Broadway, New York. He married Mary Jaques, daughter of Isaac Jaques, New York, and had children :

1. Elizabeth J. Muir, who married, 10th Nov. 1851, David G Tappen, of Morristown ; 2. Frances Muir ; 3. Lewis Muir ; 4. Austin Muir ; 5. Harry Muir.

2. Jonathan M. Muir.

3. Josiah Frost Muir, who is a paper manufacturer at Chatham. He married Almira Parkhurst, daughter of Ezra, and had children:
   1. Harriet Muir ; 2. James Muir.

4. Deborah Halsey Muir.

5. Caleb Meeker Muir, who married, May, 1849, Abigail Brown, daughter of Benjamin, of Chatham.

6. Mary Caroline Muir.

7. Isaac Newton Muir, who died at 6 years.

ISAAC MEEKER, (son of Isaiah,) and Betsey Willcox, lived east of Sterling's Valley, and had children :

1. Mariah, who married Lewis Noe, Jun., son of Lewis, and had children :
   1. Jonathan Meeker Noe ; 2. Isaac Meeker Noe ; 3. Lewis Mulford Noe.

2. Harriet, who married, 12th May, 1840, Abraham Valentine, son of Peter D. Valentine. She died 16th June, 1843, aged 31 years, without children.

3. Eliza Anne, who married, 3d April, 1841, Daniel Noe, of Woodbridge, and died without children.

JAMES MEEKER, (son of James, son of Robert Meeker,) and Hannah Foster, lived at Connecticut Farms, and had children :

1. Nancy, who married John Brewster, son of Timothy, and had but one child, James M. Brewster.

2. Nathan, who married Nancy Watkins, daughter of Trembly Watkins, and had children :
   1. James Trembly Meeker, who married Joanna B. Munn, daughter of Doct Jephtha B. Munn, of Chatham.
   2. Elizabeth W. Meeker.

3. James F. Meeker, who married Rebecca Bloomfield ; is a merchant in Elizabethtown, and had children.
   1. James R. Meeker, who married Anna Halsey, daughter of John T. Halsey.
   2. William Bloomfield Meeker.

4. Stephen J. Meeker, who married, 1st, Phebe Magie ; 2d, Eliza Woodruff, daughter of Flave, and had children :
   1. David Magie Meeker, who married Olivia Gardner, daughter of Samuel Gardner, of Clinton.
   2. Phebe H. Meeker, who married Charles Brown.
   3. Jane H. Meeker.
   4. Hannah Meeker, who married Mr. —— Harrison, of Orange.

5. Sally Meeker, who married John High 3d, son of John, Jun., of Westfield. [See *High.*]

JOHN MILLER.

1st Gen. JOHN MILLER lived in Westfield, and had children:
1. Enoch, who married Hannah Baker, who was born 1702, and lived in Westfield.
2. John, Jun. also lived in Westfield.

2d Gen. ENOCH MILLER, (son of John,) and Hannah Baker, had children:
1. Enoch, Jun., who married Eliza Ross.
2. Andrew married Sarah Ross.
3. Moses married, 1st, Azuba Meeker, of Elizabethtown; 2d, Molly Riley, an Irish girl; 3d, Hannah, widow of Benjamin Bonnel, son of Benjamin Bonnel, Esq. He lived at Union Village, in Passaic Valley, and was an elder in the Presbyterian church of New Providence.
4. Jacob, born March, 1747, married Lucretia Marsh, daughter of Joshua, of Westfield, lived on Long Hill, and removed to Butler county, Ohio.
5. Jedediah.
6. Lydia married Robert Goble, and went to Ohio, and then to Indiana. They had children: 1. Robert Goble; 2. Abby Goble married Robert Shafer; 3. Hannah Goble; 4. —— Goble.
7. Elizabeth married William Scrawfoot; lived at Springfield, N. J.
8. Josiah married Jemima Ward, of Cheapside; lived in Westfield.
9. Hannah, twin to Josiah, married David Littell, Esq., son of David, and lived at Cheapside, in Livingston township. [See *David Littell.*]

3d Gen. ELDER MOSES MILLER, (3d son of Enoch,) and Azuba Meeker, had children:
1. Rhoda, who married, 20th Feb. 1787, Enos Potter, son of Col. Samuel Potter. [See *Potter.*]
2. Sally married Nathaniel Crane, son of Caleb Crane and Elizabeth Townley, of Elizabethtown.
3. Rachel married Smith Miller, 8th Jan. 1792, son of Moses, son of John Miller, Jun., son of John. [See *Moses Miller.*]
4. Lewis married Betsey Noe, daughter of John, of Long Hill. She died 15th June, 1811, aged 59 years, and he married again. He died 8th Feb. 1850.
5. Charity married, 1st, Noah Meeker, of Union; 2d, Thomas Conn, from Ireland, 31st March, 1811.

6. Elizabeth married Zophar Williams, son of John, of Livingston.

Elder Miller died —— ——. Azuba his wife died 13th April, 18)9, aged 68 years. Zophar Williams died 23d Sept. 1847.

LEWIS MILLER, (son of Elder Moses, son of Enoch Miller,) and Betsey Noe, lived in Warren, Somerset county, and had children:

1. Phebe, who married James C. Lyon, son of John. She died 28th Aug. 1835, aged 32 years

2. Mary married Samuel Osborn, son of Nehemiah. [See Osborn.] She died.

3. Charlotte married Mr. —— Badgley.

4. Lewis Noe Miller married, 1st, Anne Pennington, and had a son; he married, 2d, Harriet Ruckman, daughter of Levi, and had a son, Levi; 3d, Lockey Moore, daughter of Jesse.

5. Rhoda Anne married John Adams, of Martinville.

6. Eliza married Stephen Haff, and has a daughter, Mary Elizabeth Haff.

7. Meeker married —— ——.

SALLY MILLER, (daughter of Elder Moses,) and Nathaniel Crane, lived in Elizabethtown, and had children:

1. Elihu Crane, who married Eliza Miller, daughter of Kennedy Miller, of Elizabethtown, and had children: 1. Sarah Crane, who died 1850, aged 20 years; 2. Nathaniel Martin Crane.

2. Moses Miller Crane married Phebe Williams, daughter of John, of Long Hill, and had children: 1. Annar Crane, who married Mr. —— Miller; 2. Jane Crane; 3. John Williams Crane.

3. Betsey Crane married Parmer Kenyon, and had children: 1. Henry Kenyon; 2. Sarah Kenyon; 3. John Kenyon.

4. Mary Crane.

5. Abigail Crane married Henry Kiggins, of Elizabethtown, and had children: 1. Charles Kiggins; 2. Symmes Crane Kiggins; 3. Theodore Kiggins, who died young.

CHARITY MILLER, (daughter of Elder Moses,) and Noah Meeker, had children:

1. William Meeker, who married Eliza Osborn, daughter of Nehemiah, and had children: 1. John W. Meeker; 2. Theodore Meeker.

2. Allen Meeker married Aletta Woodruff, daughter of Benjamin, of Union.

3. Nathaniel Crane Meeker married Electa Dove. She died, and left one child, Mary Elizabeth Hortensia Meeker, and he went to Brazos, Texas.

4. Job Meeker married Patty Pangborn, daughter of Stephen, of Plainfield.

Noah Meeker died, and she married, 31st March, 1811, Thomas Conn, and had children:

5. George Conn, who went to the South, and married Charlotte Newman.

6. Benjamin Ludlow Conn.

7. Charlotte Conn married Edwin Castner; she died, leaving 2 children:

1. Sarah Elizabeth Castner; 2. Charlotte Castner.

8. Sarah Conn.

9. Mary Conn, who married John Peters, from England, lives in Elizabethtown.

10. Elizabeth Conn.

ELIZABETH MILLER, (daughter of Elder Moses,) and Zophar Williams, had children:

1. John Williams, who died at 20 years of age.

2. Polly Williams, who married Ezra Drake, son of Noah, and had one child, Elizabeth Drake, who married Freeman Tucker, son of Lines, and had two sons: 1. Williams Tucker; 2. Lines Ezra Tucker; and she died Dec. 5th, 1847.

JACOB MILLER.

₂ᵈ Gen. JACOB MILLER, (4th son of Enoch,) and Lucretia Marsh, lived near Trenton. Ohio, and had children:

1. Sarah, who married Moses Crane, son of Noah, in N. J., and had children:

    1. Lucretia Crane, who married Michael Culver, and had children: 1. Moses Culver; 2. Sarah Culver; 3. Huldah Culver.

    2. Noah Crane married Mary Hamilton, daughter of Andrew Hamilton, from Ireland, and had children: 1. Stephen; 2. Catherine.

    3. Stephen Crane married Betsey Simpson, daughter of Aaron, and had a daughter, Huldah. [See *Simpson.*]

Sarah Miller married, 2d, John Martin, in Ohio, and had a daughter.

    4. Huldah Martin, who married David Randolph.

2. Joanna, born July, 1787, and married, 1st, Stephen Clark, son of Samuel Clark, Esq., [*see Clark,*] and had children:

    1. Jonas Clark, who married Susan Flenner, daughter of David, and had children: 1. Jane Clark, who married ―― ――; 2. Stephen Clark married ―― ――; 3. Elizabeth Clark; 4. Susanna Clark; 5. David Clark.

    2. David Clark married Mary Slypher, and had a son, Augustus Clark.

    3. Jane Clark married John Hamilton, brother of Noah Crane's wife.

Joanna Miller married, 2d, Jacob Morris, in Ohio, and had children:

    4. Mary Morris, who married William Jordan.

    5. Hannah Morris married Charles Porter.

4th Gen. 3. Jacob Miller married Mary Thompson, daughter of Price; lives, near Reading, and had an only child, Jacob Miller.

4 Joshua Miller married, 1st, Sally Miller, his 2d cousin, daughter of Enoch, of N. J., and had an only child by her, Matilda, who married Moses Davis, son of Moody Davis, and lives in Indiana.

Joshua Miller married, 2d, Phebe Lyon, daughter of Nathaniel, son of Peter, and had children:

    2. Eliza Anne, who married ―― ――.

    3. Charlotte, twin of Eliza Anne, married Rev. William Davis.

    4. Jotham, who died unmarried, at 24 years.

    5. Jacob married ―― ――, and lives in Indiana.

    6. John.

    7. and 8. Martha and Lucretia, twins.

5. Elias Miller married Catherine Moore, daughter of Gershom, and had children:

    1. Rebecca Anne, who married Joshua Bruce.
    2. Ellis married Miss Johnson.
    3. Lucretia.
    4. Philetha married ―― ――.
    5. Mary married ―― ――.
    6. Hannah married Solomon Winters.
    7. John.
    8. Elias.

  6. Hannah Miller married her cousin, Nathan Potter, son of Enos, and had 5 children. They and all their children have died.

  7. Huldah Miller married Solomon Flenner, brother of Jonas Clark's wife, and had children:

    1. William Flenner, who married Lany Flenner, daughter of Daniel, brother of David Flenner.
    2. John Flenner.

  8. Ellis Miller, born 17th August, 1800, married Rosanna Hamilton, born 5th January, 1805, is sister of Noah Crane's wife. He is a lumber merchant of Hamilton, Ohio; they had children:

    1. William Hamilton Miller, born 16th July, 1823, and is a lawyer.
    2. Jacob Miller, born 28th September, 1825.
    3. Catherine Miller, born 30th August, 1827, married Ezra Potter, son of Samuel M. Potter, son of Russel, and had a daughter, Mary Potter. [*See Potter.*]
    4. Mary Anna Miller, born 28th December, 1829, married Abner C. Campbell, son of Samuel, near Franklin; lives in Hamilton. He is a partner of his father-in-law, Ellis Miller, and has a daughter Catherine.
    5. Charles Marsh Miller, born 30th October, 1839.

JOHN MILLER, JUN.

JOHN MILLER, Jun., (2d son of John Miller, of Westfield,) had children :

1. Moses, who married Esther Maxwell, daughter of John Maxwell, Sen., of Westfield.
2. Maline, who was a seafaring man ; know not what became of him.
3. John, 3d, who married Phebe Valentine, daughter of Richard, of Stony Hill. [See *Valentine.*]
4. Jonathan married —— ——, daughter of Samuel Williams, of William's Farms, and lived between Basking Ridge and Liberty Corner.
5. Mary, who married Isaac Crane, of New Providence. [*See Isaac Crane.*]
6. Ruth married Joseph Crane, brother of Isaac. [*See Joseph Crane.*]
7. Abigail married Mr. —— Haines.
8. Abner.

MOSES MILLER, (son of John Miller, Jun.,) and Esther Maxwell, had children :

1. Smith, who married, 8th January, 1792, Rachel Miller, daughter of Elder Moses Miller, son of Enoch.
2. Betsey married Samuel Headly, of North Farms, towards Newark.
3. Sally married Moses Williams, son of Samuel, of Williams' Farms. [See *Williams.*]
4. Ezra married Mary High, daughter of John High, Jun., of Westfield.

SMITH MILLER, (son of Moses, son of John, Jun.,) and Rachel Miller, daughter of Elder Moses Miller, had children :

1. Joseph, who died at 16 years.
2. Betsey, who married John Fisher, son of George, of Fox Hill, Hunterdon county.
3. Ezra, who went to Ohio, married —— ——, and had 3 children, one of which was Smith.
4. Smith Maxwell Miller, born 16th February, 1799, married Catherine Coddington, daughter of Benjamin, of Mount Bethel.
5. Mary married Daniel Alward, son of Benjamin, Sen., at Dead River.
6. Sally married Joseph Magie, son of Michael, of Elizabethtown.

7. Esther married old Minard Farley, of Hunterdon county; he died, and she married Peter Green; lives in Surgeonsville, in Hunterdon county, and has a daughter, Josephine Green.

8. Abby married William Lyon, son of Aaron, of Lyon's Farms, and has children: 1. William Lyon; 2. Baker Lyon; 3. Adelaide Lyon.

9. Azuba married Henry P. Webb, of Cauldwell, and has a son.

10. Phebe married William Bowen, of Springfield, and has children: 1. William Frederick Bowen; 2. John Joseph Bowen.

11. John Wesley married Margaret Collins, at Elizabethport, and had children: 1. William Henry; 2. Emily.

BETSEY MILLER, (daughter of Smith,) and John Fisher, had children: 1. Miller Fisher; 2. William Fisher; 3. Hannah Fisher; 4. Daniel Fisher; 5. Rachel Fisher; 6. John Fisher.

SMITH M. MILLER, (son of Smith,) and Catherine Coddington, had children:

1. Joseph, who married Mary Kinner, daughter of Alexander, of Piscataway.

2. Jane married William Wetmore, son of Samuel, of Springfield.

3. Hannah; 4. Martha; 5. Mary; 6. Caroline; 7. Minard Farley; 8. William; 9. Edward.

MARY MILLER, (daughter of Smith, son of Moses,) and Daniel Alward, lived near Dead River, and had children:

1. Benjamin Alward, who married his cousin, Amanda Lawrence, daughter of Stephen, who married Esther Alward, sister of Daniel. [See *Alward.*]

2. Moses Miller Alward married Sarah Drake, daughter of Abraham J. Drake, son of William.

3. Elizabeth Alward.

4. Elisha Alward, born 29th April, 1826, married, 31st August, 1847, Rachel Drake, daughter of said William Drake, of Schoolie's Mountain; 5. Daniel Alward, Jun.; 6. William Alward; 7. Esther Alward; 8. Smith M. Alward; 9. Rachel Alward

SALLY MILLER, (6th child of Smith,) and Joseph Magie, had children:

1. Joseph Magie; 2. Phebe Anne Magie; 3. Minard Farley Magie; 4. Hester Magie.

EZRA MILLER, (son of Moses, son of John, Jun.,) and Mary High, lived in Westfield, and had children :

1. Eliza, who married Charles Williams, son of Nathaniel, went to Racine, Wisconsin, and had children :

    1. Jane Williams, who married William Vandeveer ; 2. Rebecca Williams, who died at about 20 years ; 3. Alexander Williams ; 4. Mary Williams ; 5. Margaret Williams ; 6. Anna Williams ; 7. Belden Williams.

2. Rachel, who married John Drake, son of Nathaniel, of Scotch Plains, and had children :

    1. Harriet Drake ; 2. Ezra Drake : 3. Sarah Drake ; 4. Huldah Drake ; 5. Emma Augusta Drake.

3. Esther married David B. Crane, of Newark, (son of John, son of Prince, son of Moses Crane, of Parcipany, Morris county,) and had children :

    1. Mary Crane ; 2. Mentor Crane ; 3. Asenath Crane ; 4. Moses Crane ; 5. William Crane.

4. Linus High Miller married Abigail Price, daughter of Elihu, of Elizabethtown, and had children :

    1. Sarah ; 2. Anna ; 3. Moses ; 4. William.

5. Moses married Frances Durand, of Racine, and lived there, and had children :

    1. William ; 2. —— ——.

6. Ezra married, 17th Dec. 1849, Evelina Pierson, daughter of Deacon Squier Pierson.

7. William, who went to Racine, Wisconsin.

8. Mary Anne married Aaron H. Verselas, son of George Verselas, Esq., of Germantown, Hunterdon county, and had children :

    1. Mary Helen Verselas; 2. Rebecca Frances Verselas.

9. Rebecca.

JONATHAN MILLER, (son of John, Jun.,) and Miss —— Williams had children :

1. Dickerson, who married Jane Kirkpatrick, daughter of David, Sen., [See Kirkpatrick.] and had children : 1. John, who went to Ohio ; 2. David, who married —— ——— ; 3. Andrew, a lawyer ; 4. Dickerson, a lawyer ; 5. Caleb ; 6. Samuel.

2. Phebe, who married William C. Annin, of Liberty Corner.

3. Polly, who married Capt. William Tuttle, of Morris county, and had no children.

4. Williams, who married Polly Boyle, daughter of Joseph, of, Long Hill ; lived where his father did and had children : 1. Joseph, who married two sisters ; 2. Jonathan ; 3. Elizabeth, who married Jacob Stultz Haas, son of Jacob Haas, near Liberty Corner; lives in Darke county, Ohio, near Hill Grove, and keeps a tavern ; 4. George.

EPHRAIM MILLER.

EPHRAIM MILLER lived at Smalley's Bridge, in Somerset county, and had children :

1. Eliphalet who married ———, daughte r of Col. Seely, of Chatham.
2. Elizabeth married Jacob Stevens, son of Jonathan. [See *Stevens.*] And by a 2d wife ———, Ephraim Miller had children.
3. Ephraim, who was partially insane.
4. Conklin married Mary Reel, of Virginia ; lived near Dayton, Ohio, and had children :
1. John, who died at about, 16 years.
2. Hannah.
3. Sarah.
4. William married Anne Eliza Sourby, daughter of William, of Dayton.
5. Samuel.
6. Martha married the Rev. Mr. Griffith, a Presbyterian Minister, from Wales.
7. Ephraim married Margaret Howey, daughter of Albert.
8. Henry married.
9. Emily.
10. Margaret, died at 4 years.
5. Sabra.
6. Hannah married Jacob Kautz, near Cincinnati, and had children:
1. Emily Kautz.
2. Jacob Kautz married Mary Walker.
3. Sarah Kautz married William Gallagher.
4. Margaret Kautz.
7. Meeker Miller

JOHN MOORE.

1st Gen.

JOHN MOORE lived near Patterson, and had children :

1. Tabitha, who married Jacob Smalley, son of John Smalley, Sen. [See *Smalley*.]

2. Isaac married, 1st, Sally Smalley, daughter of John Smalley, Sen., 2d, Lydia Bedell, daughter of Moses, and grand-daughter of David Littell.

3. John, Jun., married and lived near Patterson, and from thence removed to the Lakes. He had children : 1. Charles ; 2. Rachel, who married her cousin, William Moore, son of Benjamin ; 3. Anne married David Pier ; 4. Sarah ; 5. Ruth ; 6. Abraham ; 7. Harriet.

2d Gen.

ISAAC MOORE, (son of John,) and Sally Smalley, lived in Passaic Valley, in Warren Township, Somerset county, and had children :

1. David, who married Betsey Boyle, daugher of Solomon, and sister of Col. Solomon.

2. Daniel married, 16th July, 1793, Betsey Rolph, daughter of Jonathan. [See *Rolph*]

3. Rachel married Garret Vreeland, of Acquackanak.

4. Mary married James Marshall, son of James ; lived at Patterson. [See *Marshall*.]

5. John married Chloe Tucker, daughter of Samuel, and went to Cincinnati, Ohio.

6. Tabitha married John Lyon, son of Ebenezer. [See *Lyon*.]

7. Sally married Samuel Evans, of Hanover, Morris county. Isaac Moore, by his 2d wife, Lydia Bedell, had children :

8. Isaac married Mary Davis, daughter of John, of Washington Valley, and had children :

    1. Mary ; 2. Abraham ; 3. Louisa ; 4. John ; 5. Isaac ; 6. Rachel ; 7. Martha ; 8. Sarah.

9. Moses married Phebe French, daughter of David French, Sen. They both died and left children :

    1. Emeline, who died at 3 years ; 2. Lydia lives at Brooklyn ; 3. Israel, who married Sally Anne Allen, daughter of David ; 4. Harriet married Mr. Force, a blacksmith ; lives at Madison ; 5. David married Catherine Drake, daughter of Mary Drake ; 6. Isaac, went to California, in Apail, 1849.

10. Betsey married, 22d Jan. 1808, Daniel Parker, son of Judah.

11. Samuel married Mary Ludlow, daughter of Joseph, son of Jeremiah.

12. Ruth married, 2d Aug. 1821, Garret Brown, of Acquackanak.

13. Nancy married Robert Anderson, son of James, had children :

    1. Lydia ; 2. Aaron ; 3. Phebe ; 4. Eliza ; 5. Sarah ; 6. Charlotte, and wentto Indiana.

14. Rhoda married Reuben Smalley, son of James, [*See Smalley,*] and went to the Lakes.

15. Phebe, who died a young woman.

16. William I. married Eleanor Falls, lives where his father did, and had children: 1. Delia Anne; 2. Charles Wesley; 3. Lewis Craig.

17. Susan married William Stevens, son of James Stevens, lives on Wolf Hill, near Union Village, and had children:

4th Gen.

 1. Mary Jane Stevens, who married John McIntire, and went to Seneca Falls, N. Y.

 2. Phebe Anne Stevens married John G. McCord, son of Nathaniel, of Martinville, and went to Jacksonville, Illinois.

 3. Sarah Louisa Stevens; 4. Elizabeth Stevens; 5. Almira Stevens; 6. Ellen Stevens; 7. William Stevens; 8. Harriet Stevens; 9. Moses Stevens; 10. Susan Stevens.

Mrs Susan Stevens died at the birth of her last child, 28th May, 1845.

SIMEON MOREHOUSE.

SIMEON MOREHOUSE came up from Elizabethtown, in the time of the Revolutionary war, and lived some time back of Long Hill, North of Peter Rutan's. He then removed to near the Franklin Mill, and subsequently bought of Jeremiah Ludlow, or his heirs, the farm on which his son Amos now lives. He married Rebecca Meeker, daughter of James Meeker, of Elizabethtown, [*see Meeker,*] and had children:

3d Gen.

1. James, who died 12th October, 1784, aged 6 years.

2. Betsey, born Jan. 1780, and married Joseph Ludlow, son of Obadiah, Jun. [*See Ludlow.*]

3. Hannah, who died 13th October, 1784, aged 3 years.

4. David, born 1st April, 1783, and married Sally Walker, daughter of Asher. [*See Walker.*]

5. Samuel, who died in infancy.

6. Amos, born 15th April, 1786, married, 9th May, 1811, Phebe Noe, born 13th May, 1790, daughter of John.

7. Hannah 2d, who died at 17 years.

8. Nancy married, 13th May, 1810, Moses Lum, son of Stephen, [*see Lum,*] lived in Newark.

9. Fanny married, 18th September, 1815, Amos Lum, brother of Moses, [*see Lum,*] lived in Newark.

10. Polly married John Marsh Parsons, son of David. [*See Parsons.*] Simeon Morehouse died 4th May, 1836, aged 81 years; his wife died 16th December, 1839, aged 86 years.

DAVID MOREHOUSE, (son of Simeon,) and Sally Walker, lived on Long Hill, and had children :

1. Asher Woodruff Morehouse, who married Eliza Anne Whitehead, daughter of Samuel, of Morristown.

2. Jonathan Walker Morehouse married Mary Anne Tyack, daughter of John, of New York, lives in Elizabethtown.

3. Arnon, who went to Mobile, and married Mary ——, and lives there.

4. Rebecca.

5. David Jun., married Mary Condit, daughter of Haines Condit, of Morristown, and lives there.

6. Sally Anne.

AMOS MOREHOUSE, (son of Simeon,) and Phebe Noe, lives where his father did, and had children :

1. David Noe Morehouse, who died a young man, unmarried.

2. John A. Morehouse, who married Julia Anne Wilber, of Brooklyn.

3. Mary, born 23d March, 1817.

4. James M., born 2d Feb. 1820, married, 1st, Susan M. Kinney, daughter of John, and had a son, Horace Beach, born 10th October, 1844 ; his wife Susan died 30th March, 1848, and he married, 2d, 20th March, 1850, Henrietta Van Kirk, daughter of Nathan.

5. Elias Riggs Morehouse, born 4th December, 1824.

JAMES MOREHOUSE.

JAMES MOREHOUSE, was son of David Morehouse, of Canoe Brook, near Cheapside, in Livingston township. He married, 1st, —— ——, a daughter of Capt. Enos Baldwin, of Cheapside, and had a son, Baldwin Morehouse, who married Polly Potter, daughter of Noadiah, of Ohio. The first wife of James Morehouse, died ; and he married, 26th Nov. 1788, Mary Potter, daughter of John, [see *Potter*,] and had other children :

2. Joanna.

3. Esther, who married Joel Kennedy, and lived at Hamilton, Ohio ; he died ——.

4. Amos ; 5. Betsey ; 6. Aaron ; 7. Moses ; 8. Nancy.

Mr. Morehouse removed to Warren county, Ohio.

CAPTAIN JONATHAN MULFORD.

EZEKIEL MULFORD, DAVID MULFORD, THO-
MAS MULFORD, and two other brothers, with their father,
whose name is not now (1810) known, lived at East Hampton, Long Island. Ezekiel Mulford married Abia, whose
mother was Deborah Mulford, a daughter of John Mulford,
probably a relation of her husband. He removed, about the
year 1700, to Cape May, in New Jersey, and had two sons,
Ezekiel and Jonathan.

Jonathan, at four years old, at the request of his uncle
David, who was a bachelor, was sent back to East Hampton.
But his uncle David died four days before he arrived, making his nephew, Jonathan, his sole heir. The child lived with
his grandfather, who at a proper age bound him an appren-
tice to Thomas Osborn, a tanner and shoemaker. His father
also died before he arrived at 21 years of age. Soon after
he came of age, he went to Cape May, and received his
share of his father's estate, amounting to £170, and returned
to East Hampton. Soon after his return, he married Esther,
a daughter of Cornelius Conklin, and shortly afterwards removed to Passaic Valley, and, by deed bearing date the 26th
of April, 1740, bought of John Pierson a tract of land "containing fourscore acres," lying adjoining and west of Nathaniel Smith's tract, and adjoining the river, and having
John Bedell, Jun. on the west, on which he lived till his
death. He was born 29th September, 1718, and died 16th
October, 1789, aged 71 years. His wife, Esther Conklin,
was born 27th August, 1715, and died 22d October, 1776,
aged 61 years.

3d Gen.

CAPT. JONATHAN MULFORD, and Esther Conklin,
had children:

1. Mary, born 18th December, 1741, and married Obadiah
Valentine, son of Richard. [See *Valentine.*]

2. Deborah, born 30th Jan. 1744, married John Bedell,
son of Henry. [See *Henry Bedell.*]

3. Ezekiel, born 24th June, 1746, and died 3d July, 1768,
aged 22 years, unmarried.

4. Jonathan, Jun., born 6th Nov. 1748, married, 27th Nov.
1771, Deborah Ludlow, daughter of Jeremy Ludlow. He
died 5th Dec. 1792; she died 28th April, 1801, aged 50½
years.

5. David, born 5th October, 1750, and died October, 1768,
unmarried.

6. Isaac, born 9th July, 1753, and died 25th October,
1759, aged 6 years.

7. Cornelius, born 18th April, 1757, and died 14th May, 1823, aged 66 years. He married Nancy Bryant, of Springfield, who died 16th March, 1837, aged 77 years.

8. Esther, twin to Cornelius, who married Edward Ball. [See *Ball*.] Esther Ball died January, 1819, aged 62 years.

9. Mary B., who died young.

Capt. Jonathan Mulford, after the death of his 1st wife, married Eleanor or Aula Bedell, widow of Jacob Bedell, (her maiden name was Aula Powers,) and had a son, Isaac 2d, who died Jan. 29th, 1783, aged 1 year and 4 months.

JONATHAN MULFORD, (son of Capt. Jonathan,) and Deborah Ludlow, had children :

1. Jane, who died in infancy.

2. Elizabeth married John Crane, son of Joseph. [See *Crane*.] She died 9th March, 1828, aged 53 years.

3. David, who married Polly, daughter of Elder Benjamin Cory, of Elizabethtown. They both died without children.

4. Mary, who died 28th Sept. 1781, aged 2 years.

5. Daniel, who graduated at Princeton College, about 1805, studied law, commenced practice, and bid fair to become eminent in his profession; but consumption seized upon him, and he died 26th Oct. 1811, aged 30 years.

6. Jane, (2d) who died in infancy.

7. Mary, (2d) twin to Jane, 2d, who died 3d Dec. 1796, aged 11 years.

8. Levi, who died 7th Sept. 1814, aged 26 years, unmarried.

CORNELIUS, MULFORD, (son of Capt. Jonathan,) and Nancy Bryant, had children:

1. Sally, who married Capt. Stephen Day, son of Benjamin, and had a son, Mulford Day, and died 7th April, 1801, aged 20 years. [See *Stephen Day*.]

2. Polly, who married, 31st Jan. 1824, Elias Coles, son of Master William Coles, and had children, Mulford and Mary, and died 4th May, 1843, aged 56 years. [See *Cole*.]

ESTHER MULFORD, (daughter of Capt. Jonathan,) and Edward Ball, lived in Clinton, and had children :

1. Prussia Ball, who married, 1st, Jacob, Peshine, 2d, John Gardner, both of Newark.

2. Sally Ball married, 1st, Edward Bruen, 2d, David Doremus, both of Newark.

3. Nancy Ball married, 1st, Caleb Pierson, of Newark, 2d Smith Burnet, Esq., as his 2d wife.

4. Jane Ball married Edward Gruet.

5. Hetty Ball married Mr. Robison, of Newark.

EZEKIEL MULFORD, (brother of Capt. Jonathan Mulford,) came to this valley from Cape May. His first wife's name was Jane, who died 6th Aug. 1759, aged 40 years, and he married Jemima Marsh, 6th Sept. 1767. He had children :

1. John.
2. Deborah. Mr. Ezekiel Mulford, with his son, John, returned to Cape May. soon after his 2d marriage, leaving his daughter here, who married Daniel Willcox, son of John, Sen. [See *Willcox.*]

JOB MULFORD.

JOB MULFORD, came from Long Island, and settled at Connecticut Farms. He lived a little east of Scudder's Mills, in Union Township.

He married Sarah Hampton, sister of Jonathan. Hampton, of Elizabethtown, and had children :

1. John, who married Esthei Ball, daughter of Nathaniel Ball. [See *Ball.*]
2. Abigail married Mr. Harrison.
3. Abraham married, for a 2d wife, Hannah Sickle.
4. Davis married Hannah, widow of Mr. Willis.
5. Caleb married, 13th Oct. 1786, Sarah Stevens, daughter of Jonathan Stevens.

His wife Sarah, died 30th Dec. 1787, and he married. 23d June, 1788, Phebe, the widow, of Charles Johnson, and daughter of William Bedell, and removed to Warren county, Ohio.

6. Hannah, who married John Allen.
7. David married ———, and had a son, Job, who married Effa Thompson, daughter of Daniel Thompson, of Ohio. [See *Thompson.*]

JOHN MULFORD, (son of Job,) and Esther Ball, had children :

1. Mary, who married Andrew Drake, of Staten Island, and lived there.
2. William married Hannah Durand, daughter of Bryant Durand, and brother of John Durand, of Jefferson's Village.

His wife Hannah died, and he married, 2d, Betsey, the widow of Lewis Ludlow, and daughter of Deacon Jacob Davis, of Westfield.

CALEB MULFORD, (son of Job,) had children :

1. Jacob. who married Jene Hole, daughter of Doct. John Hole, of Montgomery county, Ohio. [See *Hole.*]
2. Rebecca married Elias Littell, son of Ephraim, son of Andrew Littell. [See *Littell.*]

3. William married Martha Meek, and died without children:

4. Job married Mary Dudley. They all lived in Ohio.

3d Gen.

WILLIAM MULFORD, (son of John, son of Job Mulford,) lived where Thomas Squier formerly lived, in Passaic Valley, Morris county, and by his wife Hannah, had children :

1. Mary, who married Henry Clearman, of New York, and had 6 children, who all died young.

2. Esther, who died at 16 years.

3. Sarah, married John Cameron, of New York, and had children: 1. Mary Cameron ; 2. William Cameron ; 3. George Cameron ; 4. Isabel Cameron ; 5. Hannah Cameron ; 6. John Cameron.

4. John, who married Phebe Lodowiska Davis, and went to Ohio. Mr. Mulford's wife. Hannah, then died, and he by his wife Betsey, had other children :

5. Hannah Eliza who married David E. Townley, son of Enos B. [see *Townley*,] and had children :

1. Sarah Elizabeth Townley ; 2. Hannah Jane Townley ; 3. Laura Townley ; 4. Phebe Jaques Floride.

6. Harriet.

7. Mary married her cousin Joseph Davis, son of John, [see *Davis*,] and had children :

1. Phebe Lodowiska Davis.

8. Esther, 2d.

9. William, who died a young man, unmarried.

10. Paulina married Joel D. Thompson, son of Aaron. [See *Thompson*.]

11. Jacob Davis married 17th Oct. 1849, Sarah Valentine, daughter of P. D. Valentine.

12. Isaac Newton.

NOTE.—There was also a Jeremiah Mulford, in this place. In the Rev. Mr. Elmer's record of baptisms is recorded Abigail, daughter of Jeremiah Mulford, Jun., baptized 29th Feb. 1769. Deborah, daughter of widow Mulford, baptized 26th March, 1769. Hannah, daughter of widow Mulford, baptized 17th Feb. 1772.

JOHN NOE.

1s Gen. JOHN NOE, was son of Daniel Noe, of Woodbridge. He married Mary Ayres, of Woodbridge, and came up and bought the farm formerly owned by William Darling, at the east end of Sterling Valley, where Isaac Meeker now lives, and lived there till his death. He died 26th April, 1828, aged 71 years. His wife Mary died 31st Oct. 1823, aged 64 years. They had children:

1. Ellis, who married, 1st, Esther Osborn, daughter of Smith S. Osborn. She died 15th Oct. 1805, aged 23 years, and he married, 2d, Rachel, the widow of David Cole, of Westfield, and daughter of Noah Williams, of Long Hill. She died 27th Dec. 1827, aged 51 years, and he married, 3d, Jane Crane, of Elizabethtown. He lived in Elizabethtown, and kept the Hotel there several years.

2. Betsey, who married Lewis Miller, son of Elder Moses Miller. [See *Miller.*]

3. Rachel married Philemon Bonnel, son of Nathaniel Bonnel, 3d. [See *Bonnel.*]

4. Phebe married Amos Morehouse, son of Isaiah Morehouse. [See *Morehouse.*]

5. David married, 10th April, 1810, Huldah, widow of Timothy D. Pettit, and daughter of Nathaniel Bonnel, 3d.

6. Sally married Israel Doty, son of James Doty, and died 3d Oct. 1828, aged 31 years. [See *Doty.*]

7. Matthias Freeman married Martha Howel, daughter of Calvin Howel, of Madison.

2d Gen. ELLIS NOE, by his wife Esther Osborn, had children:

1. John, who died in Western New York.

2. Ketura, who married James McGinnis, and had children: 1. Elmira, who married, 6th Dec. 1849, Nicholas Dellicker, of Newark; 2. John McGinnis; 3. Uzel McGinnis, and by his 2d wife Rachel, Ellis Noe, had children:

3. Hester, who married David Sanderson. They live above Somerville; had no children.

4. Eliza married William Starkweather, and had a son, Augustus Starkweather.

5. Isaac married Mariah Miller, of Elizabethtown; lives in New York, and had children:
1. Ellis; 2. Augustus; 3. Samuel D. Burchard; 4. Henry Martin; 5. Francis; 6. Daniel.

6. Daniel W. Noe married Mary Mulford, daughter of Jonathan, of Pluckemin. He died 18th Feb. 1846, and had children:
1. Daniel, who died young; 2. Esther.

7. David married Mary ——, at Patterson, and had a son

Albert. And by his 3d wife, Jane Crane, Ellis Noe had children :

8. Rachel, who married, 7th June, 1849, her cousin, Matthias Doty, son of Israel, and had children :
1. John Henry ; 2. Eliza Mundy.
9. Ellis.

DAVID NOE, (son of John,) and Huldah Bonnel, had children :

1. Joseph Crane, born 25th Sept. 1811.
2. Mary, born 12th Jan. 1814, and married Samuel Clark, son of Daniel S. Clark, Esq., and had children :
    1. Arthur Berry Clark ; 2. Samuel Clark.
3. Martha Bonnel, born 24th Aug. 1816, who married George B. Ayres, son of David, of Metuchen, and had children :
    1. Anna Mariah Ayres, who died 14th May, 1840, aged 2 years ; 2. David Ellis Ayres, born 18th Oct. 1840 ; 3. Ezra Fairchild Ayres, born 17th Oct. 1742 ; 4. George Wallas Ayres, born 7th Feb. 1845 ; 5. Hellen Mundy Ayres, born 4th Nov. 1847 ; 6. Huldah Noe Ayres, born 10th March, 1849.
4. Ellis Frazee, born 1st Dec. 1818 ; went to Illinois, and died there 17th Oct. 1844.
5. David, born 3d March, 1821.
6. Jane Bonnel, born 19th Aug. 1823.
7. Huldah, born 1st Feb. 1826, and died 12th March, 1833.

Mr. David Noe was ordained an elder in the Presbyterian church, 22d July, 1822.

MATTHIAS F. NOE, (son of John,) and Martha Howel, lived at Morristown, and had children :
1. Ellis ; 2. Stephen ; 3. David ; 4. Mary Eliza ; 5. Hannah ; 6. John.

LEWIS NOE.

LEWIS NOE was brother of John, he came up from Woodbridge, and bought the farm formerly owned by Thomas Darling, where Smith M. Miller now lives. He married Phebe Mundy, daughter of Henry Mundy, of Metuchen. He died 5th April, 1838, aged 73 years. She died 11th May, 1814, aged 54 years; they had children:

1. Henry lives in Brooklyn, New York.
2. Frazee, who married 3d November, 1810, Dency Hart, daughter of David, and died 11th April, 1832.
3. Margaret married David French, Jun., son of David, lives in Stony Hill Valley. [*See French.*]
4. Lewis married 7th April, 1834, Mariah Meeker, daughter of Isaac. [*See Isaac Meeker.*]
5. Huma married Ellis Coddington, of Woodbridge.
6. Phebe, married 21st January, 1815, Joel Drake, son of Jeremiah.

FRAZEE NOE, (son of Lewis,) and Dency Hart had children :

1. Daniel Hart Noe, who married 25th September, 1839, Mary Osborn, daughter of Stephen B. Osborn, and had children: 1. Lewis Henry.
2. Phebe Mundy Noe, who died 5th June, 1832, aged 17 years.
3. John Noe, married 3d December, 1845, Martha Bonnel, daughter of Philemon Bonnel, she died without children.
4. Sarah Emeline Noe, born 1811, married John S. Dean, born 1806, son of William, and had children :

1. William Henry Dean, born 1831 ; 2. Phebe Mundy Dean, born 1834; 3. Eliza Robison Dean, who died at 2 years old; 4. Hannah Mariah Dean; 5. Eliza Jane D ean, born 1st, April. 1839, twins. 6. Sally Hart Dean, who died 6th February, 1849, aged about 7 years ; 7. Dency Anne Dean, born 1846 ; 8. Martha Frances Dean, born November, 1849.

DAVID OAKLEY.

DAVID OAKLEY of Long Island, had sons:

1. David, Jun., who continued at Long Island.

2. Ephriam, who was born 1700, and married Sarah, who died 9th April, 1761, aged 52 years; he died 3d April, 1761; they were buried in the New Providence church yard. I have no account of their children.

3. Thomas came to New Jersey, § lived in Morris county, near Passaic river, above Jonathan C. Bonnel's factory and paper mill.

He married Betsey French of Westfield, and had three children, who all died, and his wife also died, and he married her sister, Nancy French, and had three children, and his 2d wife died, and he married Nancy Clark, of Long Island, and had 8 other children.

4. Sylvanus came to New Jersey, and lived where John Willcox now lives. His 1st wife's name was Martha, who died 23d August, 1768, aged 43 years, and he married 2d, 8th December, 1768, Sarah Davis, widow of Isaac, and mother of Jonathan and Elijah Davis. [*See Bedell.*] And he married, 3d, Mary, the widow of Henry Clark, of Westfield, and daughter of Richard Valentine. He died 23d May, 1787, aged 63 years.

SYLVANUS OAKLEY, (4th child of David, 1st,) had children:

1. Ephriam, married 5th July, 1774, Susanah Raimond.

2. Matthew, baptized 24th February, 1765.

3. David, baptized 1st November, 1767.

4. Isaac, who died 23d September, 1768. And by his 2d wife Sarah, widow, of Isaac Davis, he had other children:

5. Esther, baptized 21st, January, 1770.

6. Nancy married, 1791, James Bedell, son of William, and went to Ohio. [*See Bedell.*]

7. John, who did not marry; he was lame, had a wooden leg.

8. Polly married John Abel, and went to Ohio. (His daughter Nancy went to the Shakers.)

9. Elzabeth, who died 11th October, 1791, aged 11 years.

EPHRAIM OAKLEY, (eldest son of Sylvanus,) and Susannah Raimond, had children:

1. Rachel, who married her cousin, Sylvanus Oakley, son of Thomas.

2. Isaac, who went to the Beech Woods, Wayne Co., Penn.

3. Peter Raimond Oakley, who went to Ohio.

4. Hannah, who married Cooper Osborn.

5. Patty married, 1st, David Miller ; 2d, David Goble, 31st October, 1787.

6. Sylvanus married Jane Noble, daughter of George Noble.

7. David, who went to the Beech Woods, with Col. Seely, of Chatham.

THOMAS OAKLEY, (3d son of David,) by his 2d, wife, Nancy French, had children:

1. Sylvanus, who married Rachel Oakley, eldest daughter of Ephraim.

2. Dorcas, married 2d July, 1795, Josiah Day, son of Nathaniel Day, of Chatham. [*See Day.*]

3. David, who went to the south.

Thomas Oakley, by his 3d, wife, Nancy Clark, had other children :

4. Jonathan, married at Haverstraw, New York, and lived and died there.

5. Phebe married Elijah Day, brother of Josiah, and went to Ohio.

6. Aaron, born 15th August, 1783, married, 9th November, 1804, Sarah Doty, born 20th August, 1788, daughter of Joseph Doty, 3d, and lived on Stony Hill.

7. Johannah married Richard Minthorn, and went to the Lakes, New York.

8. Jeremiah, who went to the south.

9. Daniel, married 10th September, 1814, Lockey Cory, daughter of George ; lives at Franklin Place.

10. Clark married Lucy Wood, of Spotswood; lives on Staten Island.

11. Lot, who died young.

AARON OAKLEY, (son of Thomas,) and Sarah Doty, had children :

1. Ira, who died at 19 years.

2. David Austin, who married Eliza Douglas, daughter of Peter, of New Vernon.

3. Elias Runyon Oakley went to Cincinnati, Ohio, and there married Mary Anne Turner. She died April, 1847, and he removed to Iowa.

4. Rosetta D. married Ebenezer Sturges, son of Benjamin, of Green Village.

5. Edward H. A. Oakley.

6. Aaron Doty Oakley married, 1st, Sarah J. Housey. She died, and he married, 2d, Sarah A. Minnick, daughter of Jacob, of Lancaster county, Pennsylvania.

7. Sarah E. married, 7th Feb. 1847, John G. Hovey, of Worcester, Massachusetts.

8. Nancy C. Oakley.

v

DANIEL OAKLEY, (son of Thomas,) and Lockey Cory, had children:

1. William.
2. Julianne, who married Daniel Paxton, and had children: 1. Eliza Anne; 2. Lewis.
3. Electa married Charles R. Morehouse; has no children.
4. Nancy; 5. Sarah; 6. Ezra; 7. Daniel Thomas.

SMITH STRATTON OSBORN.

SMITH S. OSBORN was son of Jacob Osborn, of Long Island. He married Sarah Burnet, daughter of Stephen or Jonathan Burnet, of Long Island. She was a cousin to Col. Israel Day; he lived where George Cory now lives. He died 25th April, 1816, aged 58 years. She died 15th Sept. 1841, aged 81 years. He was a shoemaker. They had children:

1. Esther, who married Ellis Noe, son of John Noe, [see John Noe.] She died 15th Oct. 1805, aged 23 years.
2. Stephen Burnet Osborn married, 21st Feb. 1808, Sally Potter, daughter of Amos Potter, Esq., and died 22d Oct. 1844.
3. Hannah married 15th Oct. 1817, Richard Holloway, son of Elijah. They lived at the east end of Sterling Valley. She died Jan. 1848, leaving but one child, Smith S. Osborn Holloway.
4. Jacob; 5. Stratton. They went to Western New York, and both died there.
6. Ellis, who went Ohio, and died there.
7. Israel Day Osborn, who married Charlotte Vreeland, daughter of Daniel, and have no children. They live near the Franklin Mill, on the east side of the river.

STEPHEN BURNET OSBORN, (son of Smith S. Osborn,) and Sally Potter, had children: (They lived where David Flinn once lived.)

1. Esther, who married Joel Faurette, son of James Faurette, of New Brunswick. They lived near the Summit, where Col. Samuel Potter formerly lived, and have no children.
2. Mary married Daniel H. Noe, Esq., son of Frazee, son of Lewis Noe, and had a son, Lewis Henry Noe.
3. Elias married Meribah Osborn, daughter of Daniel Osborn, of Plainfield; they lived where his father did; she died 16th Feb. 848, leaving a daughter, Sarah B. Osborn, and he married, 16th Nov. 1848, Eliza Anne Pierson, daughter of John M. Parsons, and had a daughter, Harriet Newel Osborn.
4. Charlotte Potter married, 14th Feb. 1844, Ellis Bonnel, (as his 2d wife,) son of Philemon. [See Bonnel.]
5. Elizabeth, born 1830.
6. Hannah, who died 27th March, 1833, aged 13 years.
7. Phebe P., who died 16th Sept. 1834, aged 11 years.
8. Sarah Burnet, who died 21st Sept. 1834, aged 8 years.

THOMAS OSBORN.

THOMAS OSBORN was a son of Jacob, and brother of Smith S. Osborn. He came from Long Island to this Valley about 1780, and lived where Jonathan Meeker, Esq , now does.

His 1st wife's name was Lois Ellison. They had children:

1. Elizabeth, who married Stites Scudder, son of Richard. [See *Scudder*.]

2. Smith S. Osborn, who was a physician. He married Kitty Howel, widow of Joseph Howel, of Burlington county. Her maiden name was Kitty Reynolds. They had but one daughter, Eliza S. Osborn, who married Samuel Willcox, Esq., son of John, Jun., and lives in Newark. [See *Willcox*.]

Thomas Osborn's wife Lois died 18th Jan. 1783, aged 37 years, and he married, 13th May, 1783, Rachel, the widow of David Sayre, brother of Deacon William Sayre. Her maiden name was Rachel Roff. After Mr. Osborn's death, which occurred 5th of April, 1804, she married Col. Jedediah Swan, of Scotch Plains. Doct. Smith S. Osborn died 29th Sept. 1806, and his sister, Mrs. Elizabeth Scudder, died 22d Nov. 1848.

JOHN OSBORN.

JOHN OSBORN, who is named in the 2d generation of the Elizabethtown Associates, admitted in 1699, and is said to have come from Long Island, and probably the father of John Osborn, who married Puah Howel, who died 15th April, 1785, aged 60 years. They lived where Doc. Ridley Kent now does, and owned also the Lacy farm opposite to it, extending north to the river. He was born 1718, and died 1st Sept. 1776, in consequence of a kick by a horse. They had children:

1. Esther, who married, 25th Dec. 1767, Joseph Abbot, of Newark.

2. Puah, who married, 25th Oct. 1770, Joseph Marsh, of Morris county.

3. Jonathan Howel married, 5th Jan. 1766, Deborah Hart, daughter of Jeremiah ; she died 11th March, 1782, aged 37 years, and he married, 2d, in the winter of 1783, Margaret Simpson, daughter of John.

4. Rachel, who married, 3d Sept. 1771, Jonathan Bailey, of Morris county. [See *Bailey*.] He died and she married, 2d, Andrew Wade, of Morris county, [See *Brown*.] He died and she married, 3d, Dec. 7th, 1787, Isaac Clark, (a blind .man ;) lived in this valley. He died, and she married, 4th, Samuel Tucker, son of Abner Tucker. [See *Tucker*.] Mr. Tucker died ; left her a widow again, and she lived several years, till Feb. 1840.

5. Polly married brrham Bedell, son of Jacob Bedell. [See *Bedell*.]

6. Eunice, who married, 6th Nov. 1785, Capt. John Maxwell, son of John. [See *Jacob Bedell and John Maxwell*.]

7. John, Jun., married, 28th Dec. 1785, Mary Bebout, daughter of Peter Bebout.

8. Jane married Samuel Clark. Esq., son of elder John Clark, [See *Clark*.]

ESTHER OSBORN, (daughter of John,) and Joseph Abbot, had children:

1. Mary Abbot, who married David Hays, merchant of Newark, and had children:
   1. Esther Hays, who married Ira Tichenor, of Camptown: lives in Richmond, Virginia, and had an only child, Mary Tichenor, who married Lewis Lyman, of New York.
   2. Nancy Hays, who married Henry King, of Morristown, and had children: 1. Caroline King; 2. Oliver King.
   3. David Hays, who is a lawyer, and married the widow Caroline Hays, of Burlington, N. J.
2. Rebecca married William Badgley, of Elizabethtown, and had children: 1. Joseph Badgley, who went to Indiana; 2. Cornelius Badgley, who lives in N. York; 3. Mary Anne Badgley, who married Henry Donnington, of Elizabethtown, and had children: 1. William Donnington; 2. John Donnington; 3. Joseph Donnington; 4. Sarah Donnington; 5. Caroline Donnington; 6. Mary Donnington.

PUAH OSBORN, (daughter of John,) and Joseph Marsh, removed to Sussex, and had children:

1. Polly Marsh, who married John Day, son of George Day, Jun., of Long Hill. [See *Day.*] He died and she married Thomas Higby, of Sussex.
2. Howel Marsh married Miss Russel, daughter of James, of Sussex, and sister of Jacob B. Maxwell's wife, and lives on Long Island.

JONATHAN HOWEL OSBORN, (son of John Osborn,) and Deborah Hart, had children:

1. Jeremiah Hart Osborn, who married 1st, 23d December, 1789, Polly Squier, daughter of Ellis Squier. [*See Ellis Squier.*] She died 21st Nov. 1793, aged 25 years, and he married, 2d, 3d March, 1795, Polly Clark, daughter of Stephanus, and went to Ohio. [See *Stephanus Clark.*]
2. Jane, born 16th July, 1770, married David Parsons, son of William. [*See Parsons.*]
3. Rhoda married Moses Potter, son of Amos Potter, Sen., and went to Ohio. [*See Potter.*]
4. Sarah, who died 12th April, 1792, aged 9 months.
5. Jonathan, who died 8th January, 1789, aged 4 years.
6. Puah, who went to Ohio, and married William Squier, son of Meeker, son of Benjamin Squier. [*See Squier.*]
7. Sarah; 2d, who died young.

And by his 2d, wife, Margaret Simpson, J. H. Osborn had children:

8. Deborah, who married George Doty Clark, son of John, son of Elder John Clark. [*See Clark.*]
9. Esther, who died 12th February, 1794, aged 5 years.
10. John, born 20th April, 1787, married, 2d July, 1809, Sally

Clark, born 1789, daughter of John Clark, son of Elder John Clark, and lives where his father did.

Mr. Jonathan Howel Osborn died 2d December, 1792, aged 49 years, by accident in the woods. His widow Margaret, died 7th September, 1832, aged 82 years.

3d Gen.

JOHN OSBORN, (son of Jonathan Howel Osborn,) and Sally Clark, had children:

1. Jane, who married Aaron M. Ludlow, son of Joseph. [*See Ludlow.*]

2. Aaron C., who died 15th October, 1826, aged 14 years, 2 mo.

3. Jonathan H., who died 18th October, 1826, aged 12 years, 1 month, and 21 days.

4. Jeremiah, who died 11th July, 1838, at Carlisle, Penn., aged 21 years, 8 months, and 12 days.

5. Margaret, born 20th August, 1809, married, 12th September, 1838, Samuel Kent, a carpenter, son of Abraham, and had children: 1. Mary Emily Kent, born 1840; 2. Sarah Anne Kent, born 1844.

6. Sarah H., who died 23d January, 1823, aged 1 year, 4 mo. 11 days.

7. Sarah Anne, who married 16th May, 1844, Samuel Totten, son of Jeremiah. [See *Totten.*]

8. Deborah, born June, 1826.

9. Sibbel, born 23d August, 1828, and married 24th September, 1851, Albert Pierson, son of James H. Pierson, son of Jacob S. Parsons. [*See Parsons.*]

10. John Clark Osborn, who died at 8 months.

RACHEL OSBORN, (daughter of John, Sen.,) married, first, Jonathan Bailey, of Morris county; [see *Bailey;*] 2d, Andrew Wade, of Morris county, and had a daughter, Patty, who married Thompson Brown, son of George; [see *Brown;*] 3d, Isaac Clark, of Morris county, in this Valley; [see *Isaac Clark;*] 4th, Samuel Tucker, (as his second wife,) son of Abner Tucker.] [See *Tucker.*]

4th Gen.

JOHN OSBORN, Jun. (son of John,) and Mary Bebout, had children:

1. Puah, who married Burrows Vanwy, of Sussex county, and had children: Jane Vanwy, who married William Completon, of Guernsey county, Ohio, and lives there.

2. Lewis married, 16th Nov. 1811, Mary Anne Cory, daughter of George, and went to Ohio.

3. Nancy married, 3d April, 1813, Daniel Wilson, son of Samuel, and went to the Lakes, New-York, and had children: 1. Jane Wilson; ————,

4. Jane married, 15th April, 1815, Isaac Denman, son of Joseph, of Springfield, and had children:

1. Runyon Denman, who married ————.

2. Elizabeth Denman married Theodore Hill

3. John Denman married ———.
4. Mary Denman, born —— ——, 1823.
5. William Denman, born —— ——, 1828.
6. Jonathan Howel Denman, born —— ——, 1830.
7. George Denman, born —— ——, 1832.

5. Jonathan Howel Osborn married Phebe M. Sturgis, daughter of Eleazer Sturgis, of Green Village; lives at the Saw Mill on Passaic River, near Baskingridge, and had children:

   1. Mary Jane, who married William M. Corbit, and had a son, Lewis Corbit.

   2. Lewis F., who married Anne Eliza Armstrong, daughter of Lewis, of Pleasant Valley, and had children: 1. William Osborn ; —— ——.

   3. Sarah Roberts Osborn.

NEHEMIAH OSBORN.

NEHEMIAH OSBORN came from Connecticut Farms to Long Hill; he married Mary Baldwin, daughter of Gabriel Baldwin ; he died 14th March, 1846, in his 85th year. They had children:

1. David L., born 4th January, 1787, and married Phebe Ward, daughter of Joshua, of Cheapside, and had children:

   1. Joshua Ward ; 2. David Nelson ; 3. Albert H., who married Adaline Boyle, daughter of Dr. William Boyle; [see *Boyle* ;] 4. William Sanford ; 5. Edwin ; 6. Phebe Anne.

2. Rachel, born 30th October, 1788, and died 20th July, 1808, unmarried.

3. Ezra, born 27th March, 1790, and died at about 30 years, unmarried.

4. Asa, born 19th Dec. 1795, married, 20th May, 1824, Jane L. Bennet, and had a daughter, Mary Jane. His wife Jane died 1827, aged 20 years, and he married Hannah Wood, daughter of Daniel S. Wood, Jun and had a daughter, Anne Eliza, born 18th January, 1831, and married, 24th Sept. 1850, Philemon Tomkins, son of A. A. Tomkins.

5. Matthias, born 20th Sept. 1797, married Elizabeth Bonnel, born 11th February, 1797, daughter of Nathaniel Bonnel 3d, and had children :

   1. Mary Elizabeth, born 29th Nov. 1829.

   2. Martha Jane, born 28th Sept. 1833.

   3. Sarah Anne, who died in infancy.

Matthias Osborn was ordained, 30th November, 1828, an elder in the church at New Providence.

6. Nehemiah, born 8th February, 1799, lives at Sparta, in Sussex county ; he married, first, Miss Hunt ; 2d, the widow Coursen.

7. Samuel B., born 16th February, 1804, married, 1st March, 1824, Mary N. Miller, daughter of Lewis. She died 23d February,

1844, in her 40th year, and left children : 1. Eliza ; 2. Martha ; 3. David ; and had several others, who died young.

8. Eliza, born 3d October, 1807, and married William Meeker, son of Noah. He lives near Succasunna Plains, Morris county [See *Charity Miller*, daughter of Elder Moses.]

BENJAMIN PARKER.

BENJAMIN PARKER lived on the north side of Long Hill, about a mile west of the Washington School-house. He married Lydia Osborn. He died 7th April, 1794, aged 60 years. She died 3d November, 1822, aged 85 years. They had children :

1. Stephen, born 29th May, 1759, and died 27th March, 1787, unmarried.

2. Abraham, born 16th Jan. 1762, and died at middle age, unmarried.

3. Calvin, born 13th Feb. 1768, married, 11th June, 1788, Sarah Badgley, daughter of Moses Badgley, and had a son, Moses Badgley Parker, who died a young man unmarried. Calvin's wife died 6th December, 1796, aged 27 years, and he married Rhoda Mascho, daughter of John Mascho.

4. Betsey, born 8th Feb. 1770, and married, 12th Nov. 1796, Moses Headley ; he died, and she married Jacob Lacy, son of David Lacy. He died about 1844, nearly 100 years old, and she still lives (1850) a widow, where her father did.

CALVIN PARKER and Rhoda Mascho had children :

1. Archibald, who died a young man, unmarried.

2. Jane, who married Maxwell Badgley, son of Samuel Badgley. [See *Badgley*.]

3. Sally, who married John Hampson, grand-son of John Smith Shotwell. [See *Shotwell*.]

4. Betsey married William Lariew, of Sussex, and lives there.

5. Benjamin married Phebe Bedford, daughter of John S. Bedford. 6. Nancy married ——. 7. Hetty, who died young.

WILLIAM PARROT.

WILLIAM PARROT lived where Ezra Wilcox now does, and owned 200 acres of land, including that now owned by Ezra Wilcox, Abraham Valentine and David A. French, extending from the River to the Stony Hill Road. It was divided between his sons William and Thomas. He married the widow of Daniel Clark, and had children:

1. William, Jun. who married Catherine Williams, daughter of John Williams, of Northfield, in Livingston Township, and sister of Zophar Williams.

2. Thomas, who married, 20th December 1786, Rosannah Rutan, daughter of Abraham Rutan ; she died, and he married, 2d. September 9th, 1824, Abigail Meeker, daughter of Isaiah Meeker. He lived on Long Hill, and was a Justice of the Peace of Morris county. He died 21st September, 1840. His 2d wife died 1st July, 1846, aged 79 years.

3. Samuel, who married, 18th August, 1783, Polly Thompson, daughter of Thomas, of Long Hill. He with his family, removed to the Lakes, New York.

WILLIAM PARROT, Jun. (son of William,) and Catherine Williams, lived where his father did, and had children:

1. Abraham, who married Mary Frazee, daughter of Abraham Frazee, and lived in New York.

2. Betsey, who married, 1st January, 1816, Mahlon Smalley, son of David Smalley, Esq. [*See Smalley.*]

3. Abigail married, first, Samuel C. Parsons, son of Jonathan Parsons, and had a son John Parsons. Mr. Parsons died, and she married, second, Israel Stevens, son of John, and had a daughter, Angeline Stevens. They live in New York.

4. Squier, born 27th April, 1790, and married, 3d December, 1816, Martha Townley, daughter of David, son of George Townley.

5. Polly married, 5th April, 1817, William Williamson, of Westfield, and had children:

   1. James Williamson, who married Margaret Anne Lyon, daughter of William Lyon, of Lyons' Farms, and had children; 1. Amanda Jenette Williamson ; 2. Sally Anne Williamson; 3. Amelia Williamson.
   2. Sally Anne Williamson, who married Isaac Cole, son of Freeman Cole, Esq. of Plainfield, and had children: 1. Hannah Eliza Cole; 2. Mary Cole; 3. Freeman Cole.

NOTE.—Freeman, Esq. only son of Joseph Cole, [see *Cole,*]

and Hannah Drake had children:

1. Mary who died at 16 years.
2. Joseph who died at 13 years.
3. William D. who married Catherine Smalley, daughter of Mahlon. [*See Mahlon Smalley.*]
4. Betsey married Moses Hetfield French, son of Willis. [*See Willis French.*
5. Isaac married Sally Anne Williamson, daughter of William Williamson and Polly Parrot. [*See Polly, daughter of William Parrot, Jun.*]
6. Elias, who died a young man.

ABRAHAM PARROT (son of William Parrot, Jun.) and Mary Frazee, lived in New York, and had but one child Emeline, who married, first, Frederick Manchester, second, Samuel Miller. By her first husband she had children:

1. Mary Anne Manchester; 2. Henrietta Manchester; 3. Sarah Manchester. And by Samuel Miller she had children: 4. Abraham Miller; 5. Emeline Miller; 6. Catherine Miller; 7. Elizabeth Miller.

SQUIER PARROT (son of William Parrot Jun.) and Martha Townley, had children;

1. Mary, who died at 13 years of age.
2. Elizabeth married Vincent Frazee, son of James Frazee, of Scotch Plains, and had children: 1. William Frazee; 2. Rosetta Frazee; 3. Isabel Frazee; 4. Mary Ellen Frazee;
3. Abraham who married Sarah Anne Burrows danghter of Rev. Waters Burrows, and had children: 1. George; 2. Mary Francis.
4. Caroline married, 17th November, 1847 Daniel W. Day, son of Capt. Stephen Day. [*See Day.*]
5. Margaret.
6. Abigail married, 31st December, 1849, Alexander Cooper, son of Peter. [*See Cooper.*]
7. William, who died yonng; 8. Catherine; 9. George Townley; 10. Mary 2d; 11. Martha.

THOMAS PARROT, Esq. (son of William,) and Rosannah Rutan, had children:

1. William, who married Betsey Hand, daughter of Benjamin, went to Ohio, and had children:

1. Abraham, who married Margaret Birdsal; 2. Sylvester married Henrietta Ogden; 3. Abigail married Daniel Hoffman; 4. Electa married ———; 5. Thomas married ———; 6. Anne married Jonah Marlow; 7. Simeon; 8. Daniel.

2. Anna, who married Isaac Crane, son of Norris, as his 2d wife. [See *Norris Crane.*]

3. Peter, who married Sally Crane, daughter of Norris, and had children :

    1. Jane, who married William Force, son of Squier Force, Jun. live in Morristown.

    2. Hetty married Sylvester Force, son of Squier Force, Jun. ; 3. Mary.

    4. Phebe married William High, Jun. son of William. [See *William High.*]

    5. Hannah; 6. John.

4. Polly married Isaac Crane, son of Norris, as his first wife. [See *Crane.*]

5. Joseph, born 23d March, 1800, married, 30th August, 1820, Martha Cory, daughter of Daniel Cory, Jun. son of Elder Daniel Cory, of Long Hill, and had a daughter, Phebe M. who married, 15th Feb. 1838, Augustine Trowbridge, and had two daughters ; and she died. Martha Cory, wife of Joseph Parrot, died, and he married, second, May 27th, 1824, Abigail Jones, born 26th January, 1804, daughter of Luther Jones, and had children : 2. Erastus; 3. Thomas; 4. Elizabeth, born 10th April, 1828.

SAMUEL PARROT (son of William) and Polly Thompson had children :

1. Abigail, who married Daniel Hand, son of Benjamin Hand. He died without children, and she married William Reynalds, of Livingston, and had a son, Parrot Reynalds, who married Joanna Vashti Budd, daughter of Dr. John C. Budd, and died without children.

2. Thompson.

3. Johannah.

4. Mary, who died young.

5. Joseph.

6. Cornelia, who married Sears Smalley, son of Abner Smalley.

7. Samuel, Jun.

8. Nancy.

WILLIAM PARSONS, Esq.

WILLIAM PARSONS, Esq. came to Passaic Valley from Long Island, and settled on lot No. 13 of the Elizabethtown lots, first owned by William Broadwell, where J. H. Parsons lived. He was born 1710, and died 4th October, 1765, aged 55 years. His wife's name was Deborah, who died 5th Feb. 1792, very aged. They had children:

1. Deborah, who married David Potter, son of Daniel Potter, as a first wife.

2. William, Jun. who married Mary Searing, of Connecticut Farms. He died 10th Nov. 1792. She was born 2d Sept. 1734, and died 16th August, 1815. They had children:

    1. Samuel, born 21st February, 1757, and married Polly Crane, daughter of Isaac. He died 25th Dec. 1822. She died 12th Nov. 1850, aged 90 years.

    2. Sally, born 10th Dec. 1758, and died 17th Aug. 1831, aged 73 years. She married Capt. Samuel Potter, son of Col. Samuel Potter, and removed to Lamington. [See *Capt. Samuel Potter.*]

    3. Jacob Searing, born 7th Jan. 1761, and married, 21st March, 1785, Sally Bonnel, daughter of Benjamin Bonnel, Esq.

    4. Daniel, born 10th Nov. 1762, married, 21st March, 1785, Sarah Woodruff, daughter of Matthias Woodruff, of Chatham, and went to Ohio.

    5. Jonathan, born 7th Nov. 1764, married, 30th December, 1790, Elizabeth Allen, daughter of Daniel Allen. He died 9th Sept. 1821, aged 57 years. She died 4th July, 1844.

    6. Elizabeth, born 14th Feb. 1767, married, 17th Feb. 1786, Samuel Cory, of Westfield. He died 1st March, 1810, and she married George Townley. She died 6th May, 1847, without children.

    7. David, born 28th Nov. 1768, married, 23d Dec. 1789, Jane Osborn, daughter of Jonathan Howel Osborn. She died, and he married, second, Hannah Sturgis, of Green Village. She died, and he married, third, Deborah Mott, who died 18th July, 1829, aged 52 years. He died 10th Nov. 1849, aged nearly 81 years. He had no children by his third wife.

SAMUEL PARSONS, (son of William, Jun.) and Polly Crane, had children:

1. Chloe, who died 7th April, 1788, when young.

2. Polly married, 1st Dec. 1811, Parker Parcel, of Springfield, and had children:
  1. Chloe Parcel who married Chauncy Canfield, of Con-
     necticut, and had a daughter Chloe, and then died.
  2. Matthias Parcel married ——— ; 3. Elizabeth Parcel
  4. Phebe Parcel married Augustus Garrison; went to Il
     linois. 5. William Parcel married ——— ; 6. Catherine
     Parcel; 7. Huldah Parcel; 8. Mary Parcel married
     Moses Vail, and had children, Mary Elizabeth and
     Harriet Vail, twins.
3. Lewis, who died 6th April, 1789, aged 5 years.
4. Isaac Crane Parsons died 24th March, 1849, unmarried.
5. Sally, who married John Coddington, and had a daughter, 1. Mary Coddington, who married Samuel Baldwin, son
of David. Mr. Coddington then died, and she married Wm.
Petty, and had children:
       2. Samuel Petty; 3. Sarah Anne Petty; 4. Charlotte
       Petty; 5. David Petty.
6. Chloe, who married Aaron McKinstry, son of John, of
Lamington, and had children:
  1. Mary McKinstry; 2. Elizabeth McKinstry; 3. Matilda
     McKinstry; 4. Thankful McKinstry; 5. Jonathan Mc-
     Kinstry; 6. Sarah McKinstry.
7. Betsey, who married Jonathan Ketchum, lived in Newark, and had children:
  1. David Ketchum, who married ——— ; 2. Elmira Ketch-.
     um; 3. Margaret Ketchum married ——— ; 4. Hyla
     Anne Ketchum.
8. Squier, who married Eliza Jennings, daughter of David,
and had children:
  1. Samuel; 2. Caroline; 3. Phebe Lucretia married Geo.
     Stanford, son of John, of Boundbrook; 4. Betsey; 5.
     Aaron; 6. Mary. Mrs. Eliza Parsons died January
     5th, 1852.

JACOB SEARING PARSONS, (son of William, Jun.,)
lived where his father did. He and Sally Bonnel had children:
  1. William, who died a young man, unmarried.
  2. Benjamin, who married Fanny Willcox, daughter of
William, son of Noah Willcox; lived in New-York.
  3. Nancy married John Anderson; lived in New- York.
  4. James Hervey married, 20th Sept 1812, Betsey Doty,
daughter of James; lived where his father did. He died
1st March, 1846; his wife died 10th Dec. 1832, aged 42
years; they had children:
  1. William, who died at 27 years.

3th Gen.

2. Pamelia, who married Lyman Meeker, son of Zadoc Meeker, of Clinton.
3. Israel married Harriet Pierson, daughter of Charles,
4. Albert married, 24th Sept. 1851, Sibel ₁ Osborn, daughter of John Osborn.
5. Nancy married, 18th July, 1850, John D. Martin, son of Thomas. [See *Martin.*]
6. Lewis married —— ——.
7. Betsey, who died at Clinton, of cholera, 24th August, 1849.
  5. Mariah married David Howel of Morris county. He was Elder of the church of New Providence.
  6. Electa, who did not marry.

JONATHAN PARSONS, (son of William, Jun.,) lived where his son, Luke, now does ; he and Elizabeth Allen, had children :

4th 5th Gen.

1. Eliphalet, who married Nancy Parcel; removed to Baltimore, and has children : 1. Ira, born 1812, and died at 3 years ; 2. Ira, 2d, who died at 23 years ; 3. Elizabeth, who died at 5 years ; 4. Lewis ; 5. Francis Asbury ; 6. Harriet, who died at 3 years; 7. Joseph ; 8. Stephen ; 9. Harriet, 2d ; 10. Anna ; 11. John, who died at 1 year.
2. Samuel Cory, who married Abigail Parrot, daughter of William, Jun.; had a son, John Parsons, and died.
3. Charlotte married Thomas Squier, son of Stephen. [See *Squier.*]
4. Luke, who lives where his father did ; he married, 1st, Eliza Halsey, daughter of John Halsey, of Morristown, and had children :

5th Gen

1. Emily Eugenia, who died 8th Jan. 1841, aged 9 years.
2. Henry Halsey Parsons, born 22d Jan. 1824.
3. George Searing Parsons, born 26th Sept. 1825. His wife Eliza, died 27th June, 1827, aged 25 years, and he married, 2d, Eliza Halsey, daughter of Henry Halsey, 3 miles east of Morristown, a cousin of his first wife, and had a son.
4. William Edgar Parsons, born 23d Sept. 1829. His 2d wife, Eliza, died 9th Feb. 1838, aged 40 years, and he married, 3d, Eliza Walker, daughter of Miller, by whom he had no children.
  5. Anne, born 16th Dec. 1805, and married, 10th March, 1827, David Coddington, son of Archibald, of Mount Horeb ; lived at Plainfield, and had children :
  1. Jonathan P. Coddington, born 20th Oct. 1829 ; 2. Mary Louisa Coddington ; 3. Edward James Codding-

ton, born 23d Sept. 1834 ; 4. Ira Coddington, died at 3
weeks : 5 Charles Emory Coddington, who died at
5½ months.

6. Mary, who married David C. L. Rounsavelle, son of
Peter, and grandson of Nathaniel Littell, Esq. and had one
son, Daton Rounsavelle, and died in Baltimore, 20th October,
1840, where they lived. [See *Nancy Littell, daughter of Nathaniel Littell, Esq.*]

7. Jonathan, who went to Baltimore; he was born 12th
January, 1812, and married Mary Anne Marr, born 7th Nov.
1813, daughter of Thomas Marr, and half sister of D. C. L.
Rounsavelle's 2d wife, and had children :
    1. Eliphalet, born 18th July, 1834 ; 2. George Francis,
born 12th August, 1836 ; 3. William, born 25th Nov.
1838, and died at 3½ years ; 4. Charles Emory, born
28th May. 1841 ; 5. David Essex, born 30th June,
1843 ; 6. Emma Eliza, born 12th November, 1846 ;
7. John, 8th July, 1848.

DAVID PARSONS, (son of William, Jun.) had children :
1. Lewis, born 23d March, 1790, and went to Ohio.

2. John Marsh, born 30th June, 1791, and married, 12th
March, 1820, Polly Morehouse, daughter of Simeon; live on
Stony Hill, and had children :
    1. William ; 2. Eliza Anne, who married, 16th Novem-
ber, 1848 Elias Osborn son of Stephen B. Osborn'
[see *Osborn ;*] 3. John L. ; 4. Nancy M. who married, 16th November, 1848, Ezra Reeve, of Newark ;
5. Rebecca.

3 Polly, born 25th May, 1794, and married Samuel Marsh,
of Westfield.

4. Rhoda, born 24th March, 1796, and died young.

5 Esther, born 18th March, 1798, is not married.

6. Deborah, born 15th July, 1800, is not married, she lives
with Maj. J. Potter.

7. Howel, born 4th July, 1803; he went away, they know
not where.

8. William, born 9th March, 1807, and died young.

MATTHIAS PARSONS.

MATTHIAS PARSONS lived in this Valley. I know
not that he was of kin to William Parsons or his family. He
married Mercy Shaw, sister of Richard Shaw, and had children : 1. John, baptized 25th May, 1788 ; 2. Abigail, baptized
25th May, 1788 ; 3. Phebe, baptized 25th May, 1788 ; 4.
Mary, baptized 26th June, 1791. Mr Parsons, with his family, removed to the Big Miami River, Ohio.

JOHN POOL.

JOHN POOL lived on Long Hill, near where David Morehouse now lives. He married, 13th January, 1773, Jemima Mulford, daughter of Jeremy, and had children :

1. Elizabeth, and Joan, twins, baptized 4th Dec. 1774, and both died young.

3. Polly, who married Noah Williams, son of Noah, of Long Hill, and went to Ohio, and was there drowned.

4. Hannah, who married, 25th February, 1797, John Halsey, and went to near Lebanon, Warren Co. Ohio. [See *Halsey.*]

BENJAMIN PETTIT, ESQ.

BENJAMIN PETTIT, ESQ came from New Rochelle, in the State of New York, to Passaic Valley, and by deed dated 31st December, 1729, purchased 105 acres of land of Jona. Carle ; he also purchased in 1737, of the Committee of the Freeholders of Elizabethtown, 100 acres adjoining and lying west of the other tract, and between that and Nathaniel Smith's tract, and both adjoining the River, which are in possesion of his desendants to this day, on which Major Jotham Potter now lives. Benjamin Pettit, Esq. died 30th January, 1771, aged 72 years, and left children, Mary, Abigail and Benjamin Pettit, Jun.

BENJAMIN PETTIT, Jun. married Phebe Potter, daughter of Joseph Potter, and died 7th October, 1757, aged 35 years ; they had children :

1. Elizabeth, born 5th March, 1753, and married, 1st, John Parker, an Uncle of the wife of Hugh Cauldwell, and 2d, John Smith, and went to Western New York.

2. Phebe, born 26th February, 1756, and married 15th June, 1772, John Brittin son of William, [see *Brittin,*] and had children, Pettit and Betsey Brittin.

Pettit Brittin married for his 2d wife Betsey Rorback, and had children : 1. John Brittin ; 2. George Brittin ; 3. Sarah Brittin.

Betsey Brittin married James Primrose, and had children : 1. John Primrose ; 2. Pettit Primrose ; 3. Sarah Primrose ; 4. Phebe Primrose ; 5. Hannah Primrose ; 6. George Washington Primrose.

3. Benjamin 3d, born 17th December, 1757 ; he was Capt. in the militia. He married in the winter of 1783 Elizabeth Day, daughter of Timothy, of Chatham, and died 25th Oct. 1794, aged 37 years. After the death of Benjamin Pettit, Jun. his widow Phebe married Kennedy Vance, of Longhill. [See *Vance.*]

3d Gen.   4th Gen.   5th Gen.

CAPTAIN BENJAMIN PETTIT and Elizabeth Day, had children:

1. Timothy Day Pettit, who married 22d November, 1806 Huldah Bonnel, daughter of Nathaniel Bonnel 3d, and died 4th August, 1808, aged 25 years, leaving a son.

    1. Timothy Day Pettit, who died 25th December, 1842, aged 35 years, unmarried.

2. Benjamin Pettit 4th, who died 20th September, 1806, aged 21 years, unmarried.

3. Betsey Pettit, who died 16th January, 1795, 6½ years.

4. Phebe Pettit, born 23d December, 1795, and married 6th May 1810, Jotham Potter, son of Amos Potter Esq. [See *Potter.*] On the death of Timothy D. Pettit 2d, in 1842, the name of Pettit became extinct, and the farm is in possession of and owned by Major Jotham Potter, and his wife Phebe Pettit.

SAMUEL POTTER.

SAMUEL POTTER, the ancestor of the Potter family, in this region of county, came from Wales, in England ; he had childr n :

1. Hannah, who was born 1691 ; 2. Daniel, born 1692.

3. Sarah, born 1696 ; 4. Samuel, Jun., bo n 1699.

5. Joseph, born 1702; 6. Elizabeth, twin to Joseph, born 1702.

7. Noadiah, born 1704, and lived at Vauxhall, in Clinton township; 8. Mary, born 1708.

DANIEL POTTER 1st, (2d child of Samuel 1st,) lived in Connecticut Farms, and had children :

1. Daniel 2d, born 1723: he died by accident, 15th Oct. 1774.

2. Amos 1st, born 1725.

3. Samel 3d, born 1727 ; he was a Col. in the Revolutionary War.

These three brothers came up from Connecticut Farms, and took charge and possession of Lots No. 6. No. 26 and No. 27, of the Elizabethtown Lots, drawn by their father, Daniel Potter, and also Lot No. 22, drawn by David Potter, at the Summit of the Morris and Essex Rail Road.

Daniel Potter 2d, lived where his son Amos Potter, Esq., afterwards lived. Amos Potter, lived in a house opposite to that built by John Blackburn.

Samuel Potter, (the Col.,) lived at the Cross Roads, a little west of the Summit.

DANIEL POTTER 2d, (son of Daniel, son of Samuel Potter 1st,) by a first wife, had a son, David Potter, who married Deborah Parsons, daughter of William Parsons, Esq. She became crazy Deb, and died childless. And for a second wife, Daniel Potter 2d married Catherine Lacy, sister of David Lacy. They had children:

1. Hannah, who married Daniel Hart, son of Jeremiah. [See Hart,]

2. Catherine married John Mascho. [See Mascho.]

3. Sally married Silas Howel, of Hanover, Morris county, and lived there.

4. Jacob married, 14th May, 1775, Susannah, daughter of elder John Clark. He was ordained an elder in the presbyterian church, 4th November, 1794, and was an efficient member of the church and a useful member of society.

5. Amos married, first Sarah Clark, sister of Jacob's wife ; second, Elizabeth, the widow of Capt. Benjamin Pettit, by whom he had no children.

W

6. Phebe married John Stevens, son of Jonathan. [See *Stevens.*]

7. Noadiah married Polly Clark, daughter of Abraham, of Westfield, and went to Ohio.

8. Jotham, who died 21st August, 1777, aged 13 years.

9. Daniel 3d married, 28th April, 1791, Phebe Stanbury, daughter of Capt. Samuel Stanbury, of Long Hill, and had children :

1. Recompence Stanbury Potter, who married ———.
2. Phebe married Mr. Martin, of Plainfield.

Daniel Potter 3d lost his wife, and he married Agnes Van Court, below Plainfield, who after Mr. Potter's death married Stephen Whitaker, of Yates county, N. Y. [See *Whitaker.*]

JACOB POTTER, (4th child of Daniel 2d,) and Susannah Clark, had children : (he died 30th April, 1841, aged 86 ; she died 23d March, 1841, aged 84 years, both ripe for heaven)

1. Jerusha, who died September, 1777, aged 1 year.
2. Jerusha 2d, born 3d Jan. 1788, and died 7th March, 1796.
3. Susannah born, ——— 1780, and died 26th March, 1795.
4. Jonas, born 23d Dec. 1782, and died 9th April, 1800.
5. Nathan, who married Elizabeth Day, daughter of Moses Day, of Chatham.
6. Mary married Joseph Halsey, and went to Ohio, near Lebanon, and had children :

1. Mary Halsey, who married John Dynes.
2. Abby Halsey married James Dynes, cousin of John.
3. David Halsey ; 4. Joseph Halsey ; 5. Jacob Halsey.

7. Amos married, 1st September, 1814, Phebe Denman, daughter of Joseph, of Springfield, and had children :

1, Caroline, born 14th November, 1815, married James F. Kent, of the state of New York.
2. Mary married Sidney A. Lyon, son of Lewis Lyon, of Springfield.
3. Sarah Willis Potter.
4. James Miller Potter married Jane Elizabeth Ramsey, of Rahway.
5. Charlotte Denman Potter, who died at 19 years, unmarried.
6. William Clark Potter.
7. Eliza, who died 21st October, 1839, aged 2 years.
8. Phebe Anne.
9. Israel Milton Potter, born 8th January, 1835.

8. David married in Ohio, Rhoda Potter, daughter of Russel, son of Amos Potter 1st. He lived near Middletown, Ohio.

9. Moses M. Potter, who died 10th October, 1815, aged 16 years, 5 months and 4 days.

10. Jacob M. Potter, who died at 18 years.

DAVID POTTER (son of Jacob) had children: 1. Jacob, who died young; 2. Mary Elizabeth, who married Hervy Hathaway; 3. Russel; 4. Louisa; 5. Susan. David Potter's wife Rhoda then died, and he married Elizabeth Starr.

AMOS POTTER, Esq. (5th child of Daniel Potter 2d,) and Sarah Clark had children:

1. Hannah, who married Moses Thompson, son of Thomas, of Long Hill. [See *Thompson.*]

2. Jotham, born 3d Oct. 1781, married, 6th May, 1810, Phebe Pettit, daughter of Capt. Benjamin Pettit.

3. Elizabeth, who died 25th Jan. 1796, aged 12 years and 2 months.

4. Sally married, 21st Feb. 1808, Stephen B. Osborn, son of Smith S. [See *Osborn.*]

5. Charlotte married, 14th November, 1816, Jotham Meeker Baldwin, and had children:

1. Jotham Baldwin.

2. Elizabeth Baldwin, who married Isaac H. Labaugh, of New York.

3. James Baldwin, who went to Illinois.

4. Rowena Baldwin.

5. Sarah Baldwin.

They lived in N. Y. Mr. Baldwin died 16th June, 1845. Amos Potter's wife Sarah died 15th January, 1796, aged 36 years, and he married Elizabeth, the widow of Capt. Benjamin Pettit. [See *Pettit.*] He was a Justice of the Peace, and died 8th July, 1834, aged 77 years. His widow died 19th January, 1835, aged 73 years.

JOTHAM POTTER, (2d child of Amos Potter, Esq.) was a major in the militia, a Justice of the Peace, and an elder in the presbyterian church, ordained 30th November, 1828. He and Phebe Pettit had children:

1. Benjamin Pettit Potter, who married, 7th December, 1742, Elizabeth Griffin, and had children:

1. Emily; 2. Edward Griffin; 3. Ludlow, who died at 2 months.

2. Betsey Day, who married, 11th November, 1835, Ellis Bonnel, son of Philemon. [See *Bonnel.*]

3. Sarah C. who married, 5th January, 1837, Daniel L. Bonnel, son of William. [See *Bonnel.*]

4. Amos, born 1820.

5. Ludlow Day married, 4th June, 1850, Henrietta Malvina. Ketchum, daughter of Enoch Ketchum, of Pennington,
Mercer county, New Jersey. He graduated at Princeton
College, studied theology at the seminary there, was licenced
to preach, by the presbytery of Elizabethtown, in October,
1846, and went to Brookville, Indiana, and was ordained and
installed over the presbyterian church there.

6. Mahetabel Merry.

7. Phebe Pettit.

8. Harriet Newel.

NOADIAH POTTER, (7th child of Daniel Potter 2d,)
and Polly Clark, lived below Franklin, Ohio, and had children:

1. David, who married in Baltimore ; lived at Hill Grove,
Darke county, Ohio, and had children :

    1. Mary ; 2. —— —— ; 3. Noadiah ; 4. Sidney ; 5.
    Clayton.

2. Abraham.

3. John Clark Potter married Sally Gard, daughter of the
Rev. Stephen Gard, of Trenton, Ohio ; lived at Greenville,
Darke county, Ohio, and had children :

    1. Cecelia, who died a young woman in August, 1849, of
    cholera,

    2. Thaddeus.

3. Polly married Baldwin Morehouse, son of James. [See
Morehouse.]

5. Hiram married Hetty Fort; was a merchant in Greenville, ; had no children.

6. Moses married Margaret Ainsworth, of Franklin; lived
near Greenville.

AMOS POTTER.

AMOS POTTER 2d, (son of Daniel Potter 1st,) had children:
1. Elizabeth, who was baptized, 25th Jan. 1767, married Daniel Doty, son of John Doty. [See *Daniel Doty.*]
2. Joanna, who died 23d Dec. 1767.
3. Daniel, who died 18th Feb. 1768.
4. John, who married, 2d May, 1770, Bethiah Lyon, daughter of Peter Lyon, and went to Ohio.
5. Russel married Rhoda Maxwell, sister of Caleb Maxwell, and went to Ohio. [See *Maxwell*]
6. Moses married, 29th April. 1792, Rhoda Osborn, daughter of Jonathan Howel Osborn, and went to Ohio. [See *Osborn.*]
7. Rebecca married Ellis Squier, son of Benjamin, son of John, of Westfield, and went to Ohio. [See *Squier.*]
8. Rachel, (by a 2d wife,) married Dan Cauldwell, son of William Cauldwell, and went to Ohio. [See *Cauldwell.*]
Amos Potter's wife died 13th Feb. 1768.

JOHN POTTER, (son of Amos, son of Daniel 1st,) and Bethiah Lyon had children:
1. Phebe, baptized 20th Nov. 1775, and married Ezekiel Wright, Jun., son of Ezekiel.
2. Rachel married Nathaniel Bond; lived near Ellis Squier's in Ohio.
3. Johannah married, 26th April, 1790, Allen Woodruff; went to Ohio, and there joined the Shakers.
4. Polly married James Morehouse, son of David, of Cheapside. [See *Morehouse.*]
5. Daniel married, 1st, Abby Morehouse; 2d, Betsey Drew, daughter of John Drew, both of Cheapside.
6. Benjamin married Miss Dean, daughter of Thomas Dean.
7. John married Christiana Potter, daughter of Isaac, son of Col. Samuel, and removed to Sussex, and had children:
1. John Chatfield; 2. Samuel Bebout; 3. Benjamin; 4. Jonathan; 5. Isaac Warren; 6. Henrietta Amanda.

RACHEL POTTER, (2d child of John Potter, son of Amos,) and Nathaniel Bond, had children;
1. John Bond, who married Eliza Crowel, daughter of Moses Crowel, of N. Jersey, and had children: 1. Julia Anne; 2. Elias; 3. Nathaniel; 4. Crowel; 5. Mary Jane; 6. Henry; 7. Ezra Bond.
2. Joseph Bond, who married Lavisy Osborn, daughter of Jeremiah H. Osborn, [see *Osborn,*] and had children: 1. Caroline; 2. Benjamin; 3. Alfred; 4. Edwin; 5. Squier; 6. Milton.
3. Anna Bond married Squier Osborn, brother of Joseph Bond's wife, and had children: 1. Rachel Osborn; 2. Sarah Osborn.
4. Martha. 5. Mary.

RUSSEL POTTER, (5th child of Amos, son of Daniel Potter 1st,) and Rhoda Maxwell had children:

1. Anna, who married Samuel Martin, son of Joseph, of Penn-sylvania, and had children : 1. Daniel Martin ; 2. Russel Martin ; 3. Rachel Martin; 4. Mary Martin; 5. Sarah Martin; 6. Ezra Martin; 7. Maxwell Martin.

2. Maxwell, who married, 1st, Elizabeth Coddington, daughter of William, of Maryland, a native of New Jersey, and had a son, Benjamin, who married Phebe Squier, daughter of David, son of Ellis Squier. Maxwell Potter married, 2d, Sally, the widow of David, son of Ellis Squier, [see *Squier*,] and had a daughter, Sarah Anne Potter, who married John Martin, and had a son, Edwin.

3. Levi, who married Chloe Potter, daughter of John, of Mary-land, formerly of New Jersey, (not son of Amos,) and had chil-dren : 1. Rachel; 2. Charlotte ; 3. Russel, and John, twins; 5. Julia Anne; 6. Elizabeth; 7. Thompson.

4. Betsey, who married Josiah Kerr, son of Josiah, of Penn-sylvania, and had children : 1. Margaret Kerr ; 2. Elizabeth Kerr.

5. Rhoda married David Potter, son of Jacob. [See *Jacob Potter.*]

BENJAMIN POTTER. (son of Maxwell,) and Phebe Squier had children :

1. Samuel Maxwell Potter, who married Elizabeth Moore, daughter of Abraham ; 2. George ; 3. William ; 4. Philip Landis ; 5. Anne Eliza ; 6. Sarah Bell.

2. Hannah Potter, who married 1st, Samuel Lee, son of Elder James Lee, a baptist minister; 2d, James Emmons, and had chil-dren : 1. Maxwell Potter Lee, who married, 1851, Margaret Moore ; 2. James Lee ; 3. Elizabeth Lee, who married 1st, Joseph Banker, and had children : Jacob, and Franklin Banker ; 2d, William Hart-ley. 4. Mary, who married Dudley Jones, and had 4 children. And by James Emmons, Hannah had a son, Ezra Emmons.

3. Rhoda Potter, who married Moses Morehouse, son of James Morehouse, and had children: 1. Emeline Morehouse, who married John Emmons, and had 3 children. 2. Ezra Morehouse ; 3. Rhoda Anne Morehonse ; 4. Mary Morehouse; 5. James Morehouse; 6. Sarah Morehouse.

4. Mary Potter married William Lucas, and had children : 1. Samuel Lucas ; 2. Joel Lucas ; 3. Eliza Lucas ; 4. Nelson Lucas ; 5. Mary Anne Lucas ; 6. William Lucas ; 7. Benjamin Lucas; 8. John Lucas ; 9. Lucinda Lucas.

5. Ezra Potter married 1st, Mary Gard, daughter of the Rev. Ste-phen Gard, and had children : 1. Ann Eliza ; 2. Laura ; Ezra married 2d, Catherine Miller, daughter of Ellis, and had other children : 3. Frank ; 4. Mary.

6. William Potter married Rachel Taylor, daughter of Joseph, and had children : 1. Charles ; 2. Sarah ; 3. Oscar; 4. Juliette ; 5. Samuel.

7. Eliza Potter, who married John Hartley, and has children : 1. Elizabeth Hartley; 2. Augustus Hartley; 3. Newton Hartley ; 4. John Leland Hartley. And by his 2d wife, Levi Potter had one daughter.

MOSES POTTER, (son of Amos, son of Daniel Potter 2d.) and Rhoda Osborn, went to Ohio, and had children:

5th Gen.

1. Levi, who married Sally Sutphen, from Monmouth Co. New Jersey, daughter of Abraham, and had children:
    1. John Johnson Potter, who married Catherine Burge, daughter of Anthony.
    2. Mariah Sutphen Potter. 3. Francis Marion Potter.

2. Rhoda married Samuel Wood; lived in Dayton, and had children: 1. Betsey, who married John Robb; 2. Jonas Wood; 3. Jerry Wood.

3. Sally married Stephen Paine, of New York; he died leaving three sons.
    1. Moses Potter Paine, who married Mary Robison.
    2. Daniel Paine married Elizabeth Young
    3. Jonathan Paine married Hannah Barnet.

4. Jane, born 2d April, 1794, married John Sutphen, born 28th Sept. 1794, brother of Levi's wife.

5. Amos, who married Eleanor Denny, from Pennsylvania, and had children: 1. James; 2. Mary Magdalen; 3. Rhoda.

6. Jonathan Howel Potter, who married 3 wives, and died in 1849, of cholera. He married, 1st, Charlotte Van Scoyke, and had children: 1. Amos Van Scoyke Potter; 2. Levi Potter; he married, 2d, Elizabeth Conover, and had a son, 3. Carleton Sutphen Potter. He married, 3d, Sarah Anne Bond, and had no children by her.

JANE POTTER, (4th child of Moses,) and John Sutphen lived at Middletown, and had children:

6th Gen.

1. Abraham Sutphen, who married Eliza Brown, daughter of Christopher, of Virginia, and had children: 1. Levina Anne Sutphen; 2. Mariah Louisa Sutphen; 3. Sarah Lucinda Sutphen; 4. Rhoda Magdalen Sutphen.

2. Joseph Sutphen married Caroline Johnson, and had children: 1. Charles Sutphen; 2. Harriet Jane Sutphen; 3. Mary Bell Sutphen.

3. Moses Sutphen married Lucy Van Ness, and had a son, Isaac Sutphen, and died at just 30 years of age.

4. Sally Mariah Sutphen married Andrew Brown, brother of Abraham's wife, and had a daughter, Eliza Caroline Brown.

5. Carleton Waldo Sutphen married Elizabeth Cochran, daughter of Thomas, and had children: 1. John Thomas Sutphen; 2. Ruth Jane Sutphen.

    6. Rhoda Jane Sutphen. 7. John Sutphen.
    8. Martha Anne Sutphen. 9. Levi Potter Sutphen.
    10. James Heaton Sutphen. 11. Darias Lapham Sutphen.
    12. Eliza Caroline Sutphen, who died at 4 years.

COL. SAMUEL POTTER.

COL. SAMUEL POTTER, (son of Daniel, son of Samuel Potter 1st) married Jemima Baldwin, 5th child of John Baldwin. [See *John Baldwin.*]

Col. Potter died 11th July, 1802, aged 76 ; his wife Jemima died. 25th November, 1819, aged 89 years. He was an officer in the militia, in the revolutionary war, and an elder, and one of the principal supporters of the church of New Providence, and a justice of the peace ; they had children :

1. Caleb, who married 1st, on the 23d April, 1770, Phebe Parrot ; 2d, a widow Hinds.
2. Lydia married Joseph Allen, brother of Daniel. [See *Allen.*]
3. Samuel, who married Sarah Parsons, daughter of William Parsons, Jun., and settled on Lamington river, Bedminster township, Somerset county.
4. Isaac married 1st, Abigail Bebout, daughter of Peter, of Long Hill ; 2d, Abigail Swain, daughter of John Swain, of Cheapside.
5. Enos, born 28th March, 1762, married 20th February, 1787, Rhoda Miller, daughter of Elder Moses Miller, and went to Ohio.
6. Jemima married Mr. —— Cory, and went up the North River.
7. Prudence married Daniel Hart, son of Jeremiah, as his 2d wife. [See *Hart.*]
8. Mary, baptized 5th March, 1769, married 2d December, 1787, James Thomas, of Hanover,, Morris county.
9. Bethuel, baptized 27th March, 1774, and died 10th October, 1776.

CALEB POTTER, (son of Col. Samuel,) and Phebe Parrot lived where Noah Frazee now does, and had children :

1. Abigail, who married, 5th November, 1789, Daniel Maxwell, son of John 2d. [See *Maxwell.*] She was drowned in January, 1800, in N. Y. Bay, by the upsetting of a ferry boat.
2. Samuel, who married, 25th March, 1797, Betsey Dunham, daughter of John Dunham, and had children :
    1. Abigail, who married Peter Bebout, son of Stephen. [See *Bebout*]
    2. Nancy married William B. Crane, son of Joseph, Jun. [see *Crane,*] and removed to Middletown, Ohio.
Mr. Caleb Potter died 27th May, 1799, aged 49 years. His first wife died 25th April, 1771, aged 31 years.

CAPT. SAMUEL POTTER, (3d child of Col. Samuel Potter,) and Sarah Parsons, lived at Lamington, and had children :

1. Jonathan, who married Hannah Woolverton, of Canada ; he died in 1831, aged 53 years. He became Colonel of the militia.
2. Searing, who died at 17 years.
3. Elizabeth, who married Thomas Mulford, near Pluckemin.

4. Sarah married Hugh Bartley, son of John, and grand son of Capt. William Logan, of Peapack ; he lives in Morris county.

5. Samuel, who died at 20 years.

Capt. Potter died 17th August, 1831.

COL. JONATHAN POTTER, (son of Capt. Samuel,) and Hannah Woolverton had children :

1. Serring, who married Elizabeth Smith.

2. Dennis married Mary Anne Hyler, daughter of Philip, and had a daughter, Margaret, who married William Bonnel, and died in 1831, aged 27 years.

3. Mariah, who died in 1809, aged 3 years.

4. Sarah married Col. John McKinstry.

5. Samuel married Jane Rue, daughter of John, of Lamington.

6. Thankful married Benjamin Dunham, son of David, at the Cross Roads.

7. Jonathan W. married Gertrude Craig, daughter of William, of New Germantown.

8. Mary married David Dunham, brother of Benjamin.

SERRING POTTER, (son of Col. Jonathan,) and Elizabeth Smith had children :

1. Joseph ; 2. Jonathan ; 3. Serring ; 4. Edmund ; 5. Hervy ; 6. Elizabeth ; 7. Sarah.

SARAH POTTER, (4th child of Col. Jonathan,) and Col. John McKinstry had children:

1. Jonathan McKinstry ; 2. Emily McKinstry ; 3. John Mc Kinstry ; 4. Samuel McKinstry ; 5. William McKinstry ; 6. Hannah McKinstry.

SAMUEL POTTER, (5th child of Col. Jonathan,) and Jane Rue had 8 children, 5 of which are living :

1. William ; 2. Jonathan ; 3. Mary ; 4. Hannah ; 5. Emma Jane.

THANKFUL POTTER, (6th child of Col. Jonathan,) and Benjamin Dunham, had children :

1. Mary Dunham, who married, April, 1851, Philip Philhower.

2. Hannah Dunham ; 3. David Halsey Dunham ; 4. Jonathan Dunham ; 5. Warren Dunham ; 6. William Dunham ; 7. Martha Dunham ; 8. Sarah Dunham.

JONATHAN W. POTTER, (7th child of Col. Jonathan,) has a grist mill and a store at Morristown, and lives there. He and Gertrude Craig had children :

1. Samuel, born 1841.

2. Elizabeth, born 1844.

3. Hannah, born December, 1850.

MARY POTTER, (8th child of Col. Jonathan,) and David Dunham had children:

1. Martha Dunham; 2. Serring Dunham; 3. David Dunham; 4. William Blauvelt Dunham, and two others, who died young.

ELIZABETH POTTER, (3d child of Capt. Samuel Potter,) and Thomas Mulford had children:

1. Samuel Mulford, who died at 28 years, unmarried.

2. William P. Mulford, who married Henrietta Britton, daughter of Col. Elihu Britton, of Elizabethtown. [See *Elihu Britton.*]

3. Barnabas Mulford married Margaret Todd, daughter of Major William Todd, of Bedminster, and had 6 children.

4. Eleazer Mulford married Miss Campbell, near Somerville.

5. Mahlon Mulford married Anna Price, of Elizabethtown.

6. Mary Mulford, who died in infancy.

7. Mary Elizabeth Mulford married Daniel W. Noe, son of Ellis, and had children: 1. Daniel, who died young; 2. Esther Noe. Daniel W. Noe died, and she married Mr. Farrington.

SARAH POTTER, (4th child of Capt. Samuel,) and Hugh Bartley had children:

1. Caroline Bartley, who married John Salmon, and had 3 children:

    1. Searing Salmon, who married Angeline Salmon, daughter of Joshua.

    2. Harlan Page Salmon; 3d child died young.

2. Jonathan P. Bartley married Dorothy Caskey, and had 7 children. He was elected to the legislature, for the county of Morris, in 1850, and was accidently killed, in his saw-mill, in June, 1851.

3. Samuel P. Bartley married Eliza Ewalt, in Ohio; had three children, and removed to Ohio in 1850.

4. Sarah Elizabeth Bartley married Aaron Salmon, of Flanders, and had 4 children.

5. Hannah Bartley died at 18 years, unmarried.

6. A son, who died young.

7. William Bartley married Elmira Wolf, of Flanders.

8. Hugh Bartley, Jun. married Elizabeth Vroom, of German Valley.

ISAAC POTTER, (4th child of Col. Samuel Potter,) and his first wife, Abigail Bebout lived where his father did, and had children:

1. Nancy, who married Philemon Elmer, son of Jonathan., Jun. [See *Elmer.*]

2. Christiana married John Potter, son of John, son of Amos, 1st. [See *John Potter.*]

3. Polly, married, 1st April, 1809, Daniel Vreland, of Springfield, and had children:

    1. William Alanson Vreland; 2. Eliza Vreland; 3. Caroline Vreland; 4. Abigail Bebout Vreland; 5. Lewis Vreland; 6. John Vreland.

4. Nathan 'married Betsey Notrip, of Sussex, and had children :
1. Israel; 2. Charlotte; 3. Mary Melvina.
5. Israel, who died young.
6. Louisa, married 28th May, 1814, Samuel S. White, Esq., of
Sussex, lived there, and had children :
    1. Job Sanford White ; 2. Sylvester Russel White ; 3
    Abigail Caroline White ; 4. Nathan Potter White ; 5.
    Thomas Gordon White : 6. Amanda White.
7. Lydia married Mr. —— Digit, in New York, and died without children.
Mrs. Abigail Potter died 6th February, 1804, and he married
2d, Abigail Swain, daughter of John Swain, of Cheapside, and had
other children:
8. Isaac Newton married Mary Ayers, daughter of David Ayers,
of Union township.
9. Amanda married Benjamin Lord, a dentist, of New York.
10. Malvina married Caleb Baldwin, son of Noah, of Bloomfield.
11. Jemima, who went to Lawrenceburgh, Indiana, with her
brother Samuel.
12. Samuel Sanford Potter, who graduated at college, in New
York, studied theology, was licensed to preach the gospel. He
preached some time in Newark. He married, 8th September, 1845,
Phebe Riggs, daughter of Rev. Elias Riggs, and had children :
    1. Margaret Riggs Potter ; 2. Joseph Lewis Potter ; and in
November, 1850, removed to Lawrenceburgh, Indiana, and is settled over the Prebyterian congregation there.
Mr. Isaac Potter died 20th April, 1832, aged 73 years.

ENOS POTTER, (5th child of Col. Samuel,) and Rhoda
Miller removed to Columbia, Ohio, at the mouth, of the Little Miami river, in company with Ludlow and Stites, in 1788, and from
thence to Fort Washington, now Cincinnati, in 1789, and from
thence, in 1793, to a section of land near Middletown, which he
purchased of John Cleeves Symmes, before leaving New Jersey.
They had children :
1. Azuba, born in N. Jersey, 25th January, 1788, and died 19th
March, 1794.
2. Nathan, born 28th June, 1791, and married, 28th June, 1822,
his cousin, Hannah Miller, daughter of Jacob ; had 5 children, who
all died young, and his wife died 17th April, 1834, and Nathan
Potter died near Trenton, Ohio, 17th June, 1836.
3. Jonathan, born 18th December, 1793, and died 24th February, 1823, unmarried.
4. Bethuel, born 22d September, 1796, married Fanny Rogers,
and had a son, Jonathan, who married —— ——, and has 4 children ; Bethuel died 23d December, 1819; his wife died previously.
5. Jemima, born 25th March, 1799, married 14th November,
1816, Aaron Flowers.
6. Samuel, born 25th October, 1801, married 18th January,
1825, Nancy Baker. She died 30th November, 1829, leaving a

daughter, Elizabeth, born 31st August, 1826, who married John
Stewart, of Cincinnati. Samuel married, 2d, Fanny Bryant,
daughter of Nathaniel. May, 27th 1S30, and had children:

6th Gen.

2. Mary, born 6th March, 1831, married James Lane; 3.
Martha Anne, born 17th August, 1833; 4. Mariah, born
9th October, 1835; 5. Emeline, born 25th August, 1838;
6. Margaret, born 3d February, 1841; 7. Rhoda, born
27th April, 1844; 8 Abby Ellen, born 11th May, 1846,
died 5th October, 1846; 9. William B., born 30th August,
1847.

7. Mary, born 5th April, 1804, and married, 18th May, 1826,
David Bryant, brother of Fanny, and had a son Enos Bryant, and
she soon after died.

8. Enos Baldwin Potter, born 24th August, 1806, married 26th
February, 1829, Abigail Bryant, sister of David and Fanny, and
had children: 1. Harriet; 2. James; 3. Lewis, who died young;
4. Samuel. Enos B. Potter died in Dayton.

5th Gen.

9. Aaron, born 31st March, 1809, lives in Hamilton, Ohio; is an
extensive marble manufacturer. He married, 23d September, 1830,
Emeline Ramsdale, who was born in Boston, Mass. 19th July,
1813. They had children:

6th Gen.

1. A daughter, born and died in Cincinnati, 22d December,
1831.
2. Charlotte A. born in Cincinnati. 9th January, 1833.
3. Amos, born 20th February, 1834, and died 8th July, 1834.
4. Nathan, born 2d December, 1835, and died 13th Jan 1838.
5. Laura, born in Hamilton 28th April, 1839, died 28th February, 1841.
6. Georgetta, born 16th May, 1846, died 8th December, 1849.
Mr. Enos Potter died 9th January, 1814. His widow Rhoda
died 2d April, 1825.

JOSEPH POTTER.

3d Gen. JOSEPH POTTER, (5th child of Samuel Potter, 1st,) and Elizabeth Woodruff had 10 children:

I have learned nothing of the 6th, 7th, 8th, and 9th of them ; the first was,

3d Gen. 1. John, who married Hannah Beach, of Jefferson Village.
2. Sarah married John Wade, of Connecticut Farms.
3. Betsey married Henry Woodruff, of Elizabethtown.
4. A daughter, who married Mr. Hallock.
5. Phebe married Benjamin Pettit, Jun., son of Benjamin, of New Providence. [See *Pettit.*]
10. Matthias married Mary Day, daughter of David Day, Esq., of New Providence. [See *Day.*]

3d, 4th, 5th Gens. JOHN POTTER, (son of Joseph,) and Hannah Beach had three sons, two of which died young, the other whose name was,
1. John married Hannah Wade, daughter of Benjamin, and had children:
2. Elias, who died at about 25 years, unmarried.
2. Susan, who died at about 18 years, unmarried.
3. Jotham, who married Rebecca Crane, daughter of John, son of John Crane, of Westfield. Jotham was a major in the militia.
4. Benjamin married Phebe Crane, sister of Jotham's wife.
5. John married Huldah Crane, also sister of Jotham's wife, and had but one child, Mary Hannah.

MAJOR JOTHAM POTTER, (son of John, son of John,) and Rebecca Crane had children:
6th Gen. 1. Susan, who married Joseph Potter, son of William B. Potter, son of Matthias, and had no children.
2. Betsey married David Crane, son of Oliver, of Elizabethtown, and had a son, Oliver Crane.
3. Elias married Mariah Crane, daughter of Stephen, of Elizabethtown, son of Elijah, and had children:
7th Gen. 1. Susan Elizabeth ; 2. Emeline ; 3. Catherine ; 4. Louisa, and went to Peoria, Illinois.

5th Gen. BENJAMIN POTTER, (4th child of John, son of John, son of Joseph,) and Phebe Crane, daughter of John Crane, had children:
6th Gen. 1. Rebecca, who married Israel Rowland, of Woodbridge.
2. John married Phebe Ball, daughter of David, and had children: 1. Anna ; 2. Caroline Burnet.
3. Alpheus.
4. Hannah married Mr. Fornote, and went to the South, and died.
5. Phebe married David Bird, of Woodbridge.

MATTHIAS POTTER, (10th child of Joseph Potter 1st,) and Mary Day, had children:

1. Philetta, born 16th December, 1763, and married Benjamin Brookfield, son of Benjamin, of Rahway.

2. Aletta, born 11th October, 1767, and married Aaron Thompson, 12th child of Thomas. [See *Thompson.*]

3. Sally, born 20th February, 1771, married John Meeker, of Springfield.

4. Polly, born 6th April, 1773, married John Crane, son of John, of Westfield, [see *Crane,*] and had no children.

5. Joseph, born 20th October, 1775, married Polly Horton, daughter of Joshua, of Springfield.

6. William Broadwell, born 11th April, 1781, married Catherine Magie, daughter of Michael, and sister of the Rev. David Magie, D. D. of Elizabethtown.

7. Emily, born 6th January, 1784, married Clark Townley, son of Richard Townley, [see *Townley,*] and had children: Jonathan and Sally Anne Townley.

PHILETTA POTTER, (1st child of Matthias,) and Benjamin Brookfield, had children:

1. Mary Brookfield, who married Mr. Davis, of Ohio.

2. Amelia Brookfield married Enoch Scudder, son of Jesse, son of Benjamin.

3. Fanny Brookfield married Seth Bowden, of Newark.

4. Aletta Brookfield married Mr. —— Ellive, of Ohio.

SALLY POTTER, (3d child of Matthias,) and John Meeker had children:

1. Cornelia Meeker, who married William Clark, son of James, of Springfield.

2. Eliza Meeker married John Clawson, of Morris Co.

3. Susan Meeker married Jacob Mulford, son of Jeremiah, son of Jeremiah Mulford, of Cheapside.

JOSEPH POTTER, (5th child of Matthias,) and Polly Horton, removed to Tomkins county, New York, and had children:

1. Matthias, who married —— ——, a daughter of Thomas Dean, North of Springfield.

2. Mary married Jarvis Beach, from New England.

WILLIAM B. POTTER, (6th child of Matthias,) and Catherine Magie, lived in Connecticut Farms. He was an Elder in the Presbyterian Church there. They had children:

1. Joseph, born 22d March, 1803, married Susan Potter, daughter of Major Jotham, and had no children.

2. Samuel Smith Potter, born 26th January, 1806, and married Ellen Johnson, daughter of James, of New York, and had children :

  1. Margaret; 2. William B.; 3. James Johnson; 4. Samuel; 5. Joseph; 6. Charles Pitman.

3. Jane Magie Potter, born 24th April, 1810, married William Darby, Jun., son of William, of Rahway, and had children: 1. Catherine Darby; 2. Sarah Darby; 3. William Darby 3d.

4. Catherine Haines Potter, born 5th October, 1812, married John Davis Crane, son of John Grant Crane, and had children: 1. Anne Nesbitt Crane; 2. Sarah Catherine Crane; 3. Albert Grant Crane; 4. John Joseph Crane.

5. David Magie Potter, born 18th September, 1815, and married Eliza Sherwood, daughter of William, son of Moses Sherwood, of New York, and had children: 1. William; 2. Charles Henry; 3. Hannah Anne, who died at about 3 years; 4. Sarah Catherine; 5. Anne Elizabeth.

6. Matthias Day Potter, born 26th September, 1818, married Harriet Hedden, of New York, and had a son:

  1. Joseph Matthias Potter, and died in his 26th year.

ABRAHAM PRICE.

ABRAHAM PRICE married Mary Anne Miller, daughter of Matthias Miller, of Elizabethtown, and removed to the farm on Stony Hill, lately owned by Levi Willcox, deceased, and had sons. Matthias, David, Abraham, and Benjamin, who all removed to the western country; they had daughters:

5. Rachel, born 14th July, 1774, and married George Cory, son of Ebenezer Cory. [*See Cory.*]

6. Sarah, who married, 11th Jan. 1785, John Hand, of Long Hill, brother of Benjamin, and went to Ohio.

7. Phebe, who married Nathan Wilkison, 30th Sept. 1795. They had children:

    1. Sally Wilkison, who married Benjamin, Willcox, son of Benjamin. [*See Willcox.*]

    2. Harriet Wilkison married David Badgley, son of Anthony. [*See Badgley.*]

    3. Abraham Price Wilkison, born 2d Sept. 1800, married Jane Nafie, and had children: 1. Theodore: 2. William; 3. Mariah; 4. Sarah Anne 5. Adaline; 6. David L.

    4. Betsey Wilkison married Joseph Long, son of John. [*See Long.*]

    5. Squier Wilkison, born, 1808; is unmarried.

    6. David Wilkison.

    7. William Wilkison, who married Mary Reeve, of Springfield, and lived there, and had a daughter, Sarah Caroline Wilkison.

    8. Emeline Wilkison married Asa Baldwin, son of David C. Baldwin. [*See Gabriel Baldwin.*]

8. Abigail, who married John Atkins, and lived in New York. He died of cholera, 28th July, 1832, aged 53 years.

Mr. Abraham Price, died 27th Sept. 1784, and his widow, Mary Anne, married John Stevens, half brother of Jonathan Stevens, but had no other children.

RICE PRICE was son of Samuel Price, of Warren Co. He married Phebe Clark, daughter of Jacob Clark, on the first mountain; lived about Stony Hill, and had children:

1. Jonas, who married Jane Raddin, daughter of Jeremy, and died at 24 years. [*See Raddin.*]

2. Samuel married Anne Corwin, daughter of Stephen. [*See Corwin.*]

3. Jacob married Jemima Badgley, daughter of Anthony Badgley, Jun.

4. Phinehas married Susan Evans; became a Methodist Preacher, and went to Delaware county, Pennsylvania.

5. Rhoda married John W. Foster, of Westfield, as his 2d wife, and had children:

    1. Susannah Foster, who married Martin Hulbert, son of Joshua, of Mendham, and had children: 1. Ira Marcus Hulbert; 2. James Hulbert · 3. Levisa Hulbert; 4. William Hervy Hulbert, who died at 3 years; 5. Martin Hervy Hulbert, who also died at 3 years; 6. Harriet Hulbert; 7. Martin Hulbert; 8. a daughter.

    2. Levisa Foster, who married David Dunham, son of Amos Dunham, of Liberty Corner, and had children: 1. Oliver Dunham; 2. Anna Mariah Dunham; 3. Susan Francis Dunham; 4. Catherine Dunham; 5. Caroline Amanda Dunham; 6. Louisa Dunham.

    3. Marcus Foster, who died at 10 months.

6. Mary married Abraham Kent, in May, 1790, and lives where Isaiah Meeker formerly lived.

7. William married Sally Badgley, daughter of Samuel Badgley, and removed to Chemung county, New York.

8. Hannah married Jeremiah Totten, son of Jonathan. [*See Totten.*]

MARY PRICE, (6th child of Rice Price,) and Abraham Kent, had children:

1. Jane Kent who died at 3½ months.

2. Samuel Kent, who married, 12th September, 1838, Margaret Osborn, daughter of John, and had children: 1. Mary Emily Kent; 2. Sarah Anne Kent.

3. Rhoda Anne Kent, who died in her 10th year.

4. Mary Kent, born 1818.

5. Phebe Kent married, 30th November, 1837, Joseph Hastings, son of James, of Elizabethtown, and had children:
    1. Theodore Hastings; 2. John Hastings; 3. Louisa Hastings; 4. Mary Hastings; 5. Joseph Hastings.

6. Catherine E. Kent, who married, 4th November, 1842, George Scofield, son of ——, and had a daughter, Anne Eliza Scofield.

7. Abraham Kent, who died at 15 months.

8. Abraham Kent, 2d, born ——, 1829.

9. Christopher Kent, born ——, 1833.

WILLIAM PRICE, (son of Rice Price,) and Sally Badgley, had children.

1. Jacob, who married Eliza ——.

2. William Henry married Hetty Brown, daughter of William. son of John Brown.

3. Samuel married —— ——.

4. Phebe Anne, who died at 14 years.

5. George; 6. Davison Day; 7. Jesse.

8. Sarah Jane, who died at 4 years.

9. Martin Hulbert.

ANDREW PRIOR.

ANDREW PRIOR lived where Elias Osborn now lives. He had children, by his 1st wife Polly ——:

1. Simeon.
2. Sarah, who married, 12th July, 1770, John Winans.
3 John married, 10th May, 1775, Elizabeth Maxwell, daughter of William Maxwell.
4. Betsey married William Maxwell, Jun, brother of John Prior's wife.
5. Jane, who died young.

By his 2d wife, Lydia Littell, daughter of David Littell, he had children:

6. Andrew, Jun., who went to Ohio with his step-father, David Flinn. [See *Flinn.*]
7. Moses, who also went to Ohio, and was killed by the Indians, in 1794.

Mr. Prior died 5th February, 1768, and his widow Lydia married, 14th May, 1769, David Flinn, and had children:

1. Lydia, who married in Ohio, Edmund Buxton, and lived in Hamilton county, Ohio.
2. Susannah married John Miller, in Ohio, had a family, and all went to the Shakers.

ANDREW PRIOR, Jun., married, 1st, Polly Marsh, and had by her 9, and by his 2d wife, 3 children:

1. Nancy, who married Samuel Littell, son of ——, of Cincinnati, and had children: 1. Moses Littell; 2. William Littell; 3. James Littell.
2. Lydia married James Centre; had a child Nancy, who died at 9 years.
3. Sally married William Wilson; had 4 children.
4. Huldah married Edward Price; live in Indiana; had children: 1. William; 2. Hester Anne.
5. Phebe married, 1st, William Bowman; 2. Henry Myers.
6. Charlotte married —— ——.
7. Mary Anne.
8 Moses married Sarah Ferguson, a niece of Charles Buxton's wife.
9. Aaron married Abigail Clark, daughter of Joseph.

And by his 2d wife Polly, Andrew Prior, Jun., had

10. William; 11. John; 12. ——.

JEREMIAH RADDIN.

JEREMIAH RADDIN lived near Blue Brook, above Feltville. He married, 13th July, 1775, Lucretia Willcox, daughter of William Willcox, Sen., and had children:

1. Betsey, who married William Willcox, son of Noah Willcox, Sen. [See *Willcox.*]

2 William married, 6th February, 1807, Hannah Clark, daughter of Elias Clark, Sen., on Stony Hill.

3. Jane married, 1st, Jonas Price, son of Rice Price ; 2d, Samuel Clark, son of Ichabod Clark, of Westfield ; 3d, Smith Hallock, son of Thomas Hallock. [See *Hallock.*]

4. Susan married John Clark, son of Ichabod, son of Elias Clark, Sen.

WILLIAM RADDIN, (son of Jeremiah,) and Hannah Clark, lived where his father did, and had children :

1. Jeremy, born April. 1806, married Abby Frazee, born 27th August, 1806, daughter of Reuben Frazee and Joanna Willcox.

2. Freeman married Fanny Anderson, daughter of Robert, son of James.

3. Susan married Samuel Heady, of Clinton.

4. Ellis, who went to Chicago. ·

5. David. born February, 1818, married Phebe Morehouse, born 29th July, 1824, daughter of John Morehouse. of Elizabethtown, and had children : 1. John, born 29th Nov. 1846 ; 2. Hetty Amelia, born 29th Nov.1849.

6. Eliza married John C. Hays, son of Oliver Hays, of Union Township.

7. John ; 8. Samuel.

William Raddin died, and his widow married Anthony Badgley, son of Anthony.

JEREMY RADDIN, (son of William, son of Jeremiah,) and Abby Frazee, had children :

1. Reuben, born 27th July, 1824. and married Phebe Atkins, daughter of John.

2. Mary, born 5th April, 1830, and married Henry Burrel, of Newark.

3. William, ——, married ——, lives in Newark.

4. Ellis, born 30th December. 1834.

5. Hervy, born 24th March. 1837.

6. Eliza Jane, born 9th May, 1839.

7. Abby, born 7th February, 1846.

DOCTOR JOHN RAGUE.

DR. JOHN RAGUE was a Frenchman, he married Miss —— Bonnel, the aunt of Lois, wife of Gabriel Johnson, Esq., and lived in Passaic Valley. They had children:

1. Betsey, who was brought up by her cousin, Lois Johnson, and married —— ——.

2. Catherine married Jonas Stanbury, son of Capt. Samuel Stanbury, and lived on Long Island.

3. James went to Urbana, Ohio, and married Polly, a widow, and daughter of Coats Thornton, of Champaign Co. Ohio, and had children:

    1. Lemuel, who married Harriet Samples, daughter of Bethuel, of Urbana.

    2. Llewelen, who was a Lieut. in the U. S. Army.

    3. John F. married in New York, and lives in Iowa City.

GILBERT RANDOLPH.

GILBERT RANDOLPH married —— ——, lived at Stone House Village, and had children:

1. Elizabeth, who married Matthias Lyon; went to the Lakes, New York; had 8 children.

2. James, who died at home, unmarried.

3. Rhoda married Moses Parcel, brother of Capt. John Parcel, of Liberty Corner, and went to Western New York, and had 13 children.

4. Peter married Harriet Steele, daughter of Oliver Steele, lived at Stone House Village.

5. David married Sally Smally, daughter of Jacob, and lived at Stone House Village.

6. Justus married Sally Strimple, of Rahway, and went to Ohio.

7. Isaac married Sally Steele, sister of Peter's wife and lived in the Stone House.

RODA RANDOLPH, (daughter of Gilbert,) and Moses Parcel had children:

1. John Parcel, who married —— ——, a daughter of Henry Smally, son of David, Esq.

2. Randolph Parcel; 3. Enos Parcel; 4. Isaac Parcel; 5. Albert Parcel; 6. Lewis Parcel; 7. Mary Parcel; 8. Elizabeth Parcel; 9. Squier Parcel. They then removed to Western New York, and had 4 others.

PETER RANDOLPH, (son of Gilbert,) and Harriet Steele, had children:

1. Steele, who married Margaret Smalley, daughter of Andrew, and had children: 1. Peter; 2. George.

2. Lewis married Mary Compton, daughter of Moore Compton, of Long Hill, and had children:

    1. Almira; 2. Abel Steele; 3. Moore Compton; 4. Harriet; 5. Ruth; 6. Catharine Anne; 7. Peter; and removed to Illinois.

3. Anne; 4. Mary.

DAVID RANDOLPH, (son of Gilbert,) and Sally Smalley, had children:

1. Mary Anne, who married Jacob Cole, son of Elias. [See *Cole.*]

2. Gilbert.

ISAAC RANDOLPH, (son of Gilbert,) and Sally Steele, had children:

1. Isaac, Jun., who married Eliza Jane Ayers, of Cumberland county, and live there, and had children:

    1. Asa; 2. David; 3. Oliver.

2. Oliver.

3. Lewis married Nancy Hiscox, of Rhode Island, live at Green Brook, and had children: 1. Isaac; 2. Julia; 3. Gilbert.

4. Christian; 5. Jeptha; 6. Mary; 7. William.

ZEBULON RIGGS.

Three brothers by the name of Riggs lived in Massachusetts, and removed from there to Connecticut. Edward Riggs, one of the three, removed from Connecticut to Newark, N. J. and had a son Joseph Riggs, who lived and died in Orange, and he was the father of Zebulon Riggs, the father of

PRESERVE RIGGS, of Mendham, who married Puah Hudson, and had children:

1. Elias, born 1st April, 1770, who was a presbyterian minister, and preached a few years at Perth Amboy, and came to New Providence in October, 1806, and was installed the 16th June, 1807, and continued in the ministry there till his death, which occurred the 25th February, 1825, aged 54 years, respected and beloved by all his people,

2. Silas, who married Harriet Rose, of Long Island, and lived at Succasunna Plains.

3. Mary married Mr. Blachley, of Mendham, and had a son, Moses Blachley.

4. Hannah married David Cook, brother of the Rev. Henry Cook, of Metuchen; lived at Geneva, New York, and had children:

1. Elias Cook.
2. William Cook.
3. Charles Cook, who married his cousin Anna Mariah Cook, daughter of the Rev. Henry Cook, of Metuchen.
4. Caroline Cook, who married Herman Camp, lived at Truman-burg, Tomkins county, New York.
5. Sarah Cook, who died unmarried.

5. Elizabeth married Dr. Absalom Woodruff, son of Dr. Absalom Woodruff, of Mendham; she died without children. He married Matilda Jones, of Morristown, and lives there.

6. Nancy married William Camp Gildersleeve, son of the Rev. Mr. Gildersleeve, of Wilkesbarre, Pennsylvania. She died at Wilkesbarre, and left children:

1. Elizabeth Gildersleeve.
2. Mary Gildersleeve.
3. Norman Gildersleeve, who at about 17 years.

7. Sarah, who married Robert Stoddart, Esq. a lawyer, of Geneva, and had children:

1. John Stoddart; 2. Elizabeth Stoddart; 3. Anne Stoddart; 4. Luther Stoddart; 5. George Stoddart; 6. Sarah Stoddart; 7. Elias Stoddart.

REV. ELIAS RIGGS, (son of Preserve,) married Margaret Congar, daughter of David Congar, of New Windsor, Orange county, New York, and widow of David Hudson, of Newark, who was son of David Hudson, of Mendham, brother of the wife of Preserve Riggs, and had children:

1. Joseph Lewis, who is a presbyterian minister, and married Elizabeth Anne Roosa, daughter of Egbert Roosa, of Wells, Bradford county, Penn. where he is settled as a pastor. He had children:

1. Edward Hinman; 2. William Congar.

2. Elias, who married Martha Jane Dalzel, of Mendham. He became a presbyterian minister, and with his wife went in October, 1832, as missionaries to Greece, and from thence to Smyrna, in Asia; they had children:

1. Elizabeth; 2. Margaret; 3. Edward; 4. Emma Louisa.

3. Margaret married, 1st Oct. 1834, James Mitchel Ray, a native of Cauldwell, Essex county, N. J. now a resident of Indianapolis, Indiana, and is cashier of the state bank of Indiana. They had children:

1. Anna Axtel Ray; 2. Harriet Martha Ray; 3. Louisa Montfort Ray; and have lost six children.

4. Hannah married the Rev. Joseph Y. Montfort, of Greensburgh, Indiana, son of Rev. Francis Montfort, of Ohio. They had children:

1. Elias Riggs Montfort.
2. Francis Cosat Montfort.
3. Margaret Congar Montfort.

5. Phebe married, 8th Sept. 1845, Rev. Samuel S. Potter, son of Isaac. He is a presbyterian minister, settled in 1850, in Lawrenceburgh, Indiana. They had children:
    1. Margaret Riggs Potter.
    2. Joseph Lewis Pot'er.

6. Elizabeth married, 25th Aug. 1842, Antrim Robbins Forsyth, merchant of Greensburgh Indiana, son of John Forsyth, of Trenton, N. J. and had chidren:
    1. Elias Riggs Forsyth.
    2. William Congar Forsyth, who died in infancy.

Mrs. Elizabeth Forsyth died 7th Sept. 1848. Mrs Margaret Riggs, widow of the Rev. Elias Riggs, died at the house of her son Joseph, in Wells, Bradford county, Penn. on the 28th March, 1851, aged 69 years and 4 days, and was buried April 2d, by the side of her husband in the New Providence church yard.

SILAS RIGGS, (son of Preserve Riggs,) and Harriet Rose, had children:
    1. Peter.
    2. Nancy, who married Caleb Wheeler.
    3. Alexander married —— ——, in Pennsylvania.
    4. Albert married Nancy Stansborough.
    5. Edward, who died at Louisville, Kentucky, in 1846.
    6. Elizabeth married Alpha Durham, and live at Tunkhannock.
    7. Harriet married Erastus W. Ripley, and went to Iowa. He is at the head of the college at Davenport, Iowa.
    8. Charles Warren, who died February, 1848, at about 21 years.

WILLIAM ROBISON.

WILLIAM ROBISON married Betsey Robison, 2d Dec. 1772. They lived on Stony Hill, where Andrew Hyslop now lives. They had children:

1. David, who married 24th Dec. 1795, Agnes Vance, daughter of Kennedy, of Long Hill.
2. Phebe married 5th November, 1794, Henry Mooney, live in Morris County.
3. John married Lydia Wilson, of Maryland, was a methodist preacher of some celebrity.
4. William married Nancy Roll, daughter of John, son of Isaac, of Springfield.

REV. JOHN ROBISON, and Lydia Wilson, had children:
1. William, who married Anne Mariah Lafoucherie, and had children:
   1. John Lafoucherie; 2. James Edwards; 3. Susan.
2. Elizabeth married Alexander Gilmore, a methodist preacher; (preaching in 1850, in Springfield.)
3. Catherine is unmarried, she lives in Springfield.

WILLIAM ROBISON, (son of William,) and Nancy Roll, had children:
1. John, who went away, the family knows not where.
2. Wesley, who became a methodist preacher, and married Margaret Worth, of Rahway.
3. Caroline married, 1st, Oliver Rowland; 2d, William Mawby, and had children:
   1. Victoria Mawby; 2. William Mawby: 3. Frederick Mawby.
4. James, who is crazed.
5. Isaac. who died at about 18 years, unmarried.
William Robison, Sen., died 6th August, 1815, aged 71 years. His wife Betsey died 11th October, 1799, aged 47 years.

NATHANIEL ROFF.

NATHANIEL ROFF, lived near Union Village. in **Essex** County. He married. 7th November, 1773, Jemima Shipman, daughter of Jabez, and had children:

1. Jane, who married James Craig, son of James, son of James, son of Alderman Andrew Craig. [See *Craig.*]

2. Betsey married 16th July, 1773, Daniel Moore, son of Isaac. [See *Moore.*]

3. Deborah married Daniel Smalley, son of David Smalley Esq. [See *Smalley.*]

4. Phebe married William Stevens, son of Jonathan. [See *Stevens.*]

5. Jonathan married Sally Lyon, daughter of Ebenezer, and had children:

    1. Betsey; 2. Peter; 3. John; 4. David; 5. James; 6. William; 7. Mary; 8. Phebe.

6. David married a daughter of John Shadwell, of Mayslick, Kentucky.

7. Henry married Rachel Lambert, daughter of James, of Westfield. [See *Lambert.*]

8. James.

HENRY ROFF, (son of Nathaniel,) and Rachel Lambert, lived in New York, and had children:

1. Phebe, who married Lewis Dingy, and had children:

    1. Charles Dingy; 2. Louisa Dingy; 3. Phebe Eliza Dingy; 4. Lewis Dingy.

2. Anne Eliza married John M. Force, of New York, and had children: 1. Mary Force, and others.

3. Mary Jane married James Hope, of New York, both died, leaving 3 children:

    1. Phebe Anne Hope; 2. Josephine Hope; 3. Mary Jane Hope, who died young.

4. Charles married Mariah Dunlap, of New York, and had a son, Henry.

Nathaniel Roff may have been brother of Richard Roff, Sen. He with his sons, Jonathan, David, James, and William Stevens, removed to Kentucky, before A. D. 1800.

RICHARD ROFF.

RICHARD ROFF lived where Oliver Steele lately lived ; he was some years sheriff of Somerset county. He had children:

2d Gen

1. Ebenezer, who married Abby Roberts, and lived near Mount Bethel.
2. Nelly married Simeon Millham, and had no children.
3. Betsey married Isaac Vail, and lived at Green Brook.
And by a 2d wife, he had children :
4. Richard married Amy Allen, daughter of David Allen, Sen.
5. Nathaniel married, 1st, Johannah Rogers, daughter of Simeon; 2d, Lydia Tainor ; 3. Sally, the widow of Zacheus Day.
6. Moses married Betsey Ludlow, lived near Mount Bethel.
7. Nancy married, 1st, Mr. Wright ; 2d, Moses Rogers, son of Nathaniel ; 3d, Jotham Loree.
8. Jonathan married Phebe Ludlow, sister of Moses' wife, and left no children.
9. Francis, a son, who died at about 24 or 25 years, unmarried.

EBENEZER ROFF, and Abby Roberts had children :

3d Gen

1. Mary, who married William Stites, son of Isaac. [See *Stites.*]
2. Israel married, 1st, Abby Smalley, daughter of John, son of James Smalley ; 2d, Rhoda Drake ; and by his first wife, he had a daughter :
   1. Keziah, who married George Giles, son of Samuel, of New Market.
And by his 2d wife, Rhoda Drake, had children :
   2. Phebe ; 3. Abby ; 4. William ; 5. Watson.
3. Anne married James Moore, 14th December, 1813, son of Joseph, and had children :
   1. Ruth Moore, who married Cornelius Van Ness.
   2. Betsey Moore married James Hancock.
   3. Julia Anne Moore married —— ——.
   4. Mary Moore married Theodore Housal.
4. Hiram, who died at about 22 years.
5. Betsey, who married Allen Willet, son of Thomas Willet, and had a son, Runyon Willet, and she died.
6. William, who died at about 20 years.
7. Sally, who married, after her her sister Betsey died, the same Allen Willlet, and had children :
   1. Harrison Willet, who married Rachel Stites, daughter of Amos ; 2. Lewis Willet.

BETSEY ROFF, (3d child of Richard,) and Isaac Vail had children :

3d Gen

1. Joel Vail, who married Phebe Webster, of Plainfield.
2. Lydia Vail married Mr. —— Vandyke.

RICHARD ROFF, (son of Richard,) and Amy Allen, had children:

1. Sally, who married Alvan Morse, from New England, and went to the Lakes, New York.
2. David, who went to Wheeling, and married, and lives there.
3. John married, 1st, Lavina Cheeseman ; 2d, Sally Hamilton, daughter of David, son of John ; had no children.
4. Mary married John Morris, of Metuchen.
5. Aaron married Polly ——, of Lamington, and lived there.
6. Eliza went to Ohio, with her uncle Col. John Allen.
7. Caroline married Christopher Lefevre ; lived at Jersey City.

NATHANIEL ROFF, (5th child of ᵗRichard,) and Johannah Rogers had but one child :

1. Phebe, who married Isaac Bird, and had children :
 1. Margaret Bird. who married Jacob Van Ness; 2. Mary Bird married —— ——; 3. Roff Bird married —— ——; 4. George Bird married —— ——; 5. Anne Bird ; 6. ——; 7. Isaac Bird, Jun.

And by his 2d, wife, Lydia Tainor, he had children :

2. Johannah, who married Israel Wilson, son of Hopewell, and had children : 1. Caroline Wilson, who married 1st, William Coon ; 2d, Moses Hughes.
3. Sally married Samuel Leonard, of New Vernon ; live in Morristown, and had children : 1. William Leonard ; 2d, Lydia Leonard, who married Cornelius Mesler, of Morristown ; 3. Levi Leonard, who died at 24 years ; 4. Isaac Leonard, who enlisted, and went to Mexico and did not return ; 5. Jane Leonard.
4. Mary, who died unmarried
5 Anne, who married 1st, Elijah Day, son of Zacheus, by his first wife, and had children : 1. Nathaniel Day ; 2. Erastus Day ; 3. Mary Day ; 4. Henry Day ; 5. Sarah Day ; 6 Abby Anne Day. Elijah Day then died, and she married Nathaniel Edgar, as his 2d wife, and had children : 7. Theodore Edgar ; 8. Elizabeth Edgar ; 9. Jane Edgar.
6. Jane. born 10th August, 1809, married William Hoit, son of John, from Connecticut, and had children :
 1. William Hoit, born 1st January, 1846.
 2. Anne Augusta Hoit, born 26th April, 1840; when her husband, William Hoit, died, and she married Clarkson Wilson, born 4th June, 1817, son of Zachariah, son of Hopewell. and had children :
 3. Harriet Wilson, born 10th July, 1840.
 4. Clarkson Wilson, born 6th February, 1844.
 NOTE.—Clarkson Wilson, by his first wife, Prudence Anne Lincoln, had children : 1. Sarah Wilson ; 2. Elizabeth Wilson.
7. Nathaniel Roff, Jun.
8. **Agar Lindley Roff, married Julia Scudder, of Westfield,**

and had children: 1. Firman; 2. Albert; 3. ——; 4. Cornelia; and by his 3d wife, Sally, Nathaniel Roff had a son,
 9. Elias.

MOSES ROFF, (6th child of Richard,) and Betsey Ludlow, had children :
 1. Deborah, who married Mr. Mundy, and went to Ohio.
 2. Mariah married David Loree, nephew of Jonathan, before named.
 3. Phebe married —— ——.
 4. Jonathan married —— ——, and went to Sussex.

NANCY ROFF, (7th child of Richard,) and Mr. Wright, had a daughter,
 1. Sarah Wright. And by Moses Rogers, had children :
 2. Mariah Rogers.
 3. Samuel Rogers.
 4. Jacob Rogers.
They removed to Redstone, Pennsylvania.

JOHN ROLL.

JOHN ROLL, (called in German Johonis Mongle,) came
from Germany and settled between Springfield and Westfield,
near the mountain, and had children :

1. Isaac. who married Sarah Cauldwell, daughter of James,
of Long Hill.

2. John married, 1st, Rachel, who died 21st May, 1768,
aged 30 years, and he married, 2d, Edith Wick, in 1769.

3. Abraham married, 1st, Mary Brooks, 2d, Caty Vreeland.

4. Molly, who married Mr. Woolley.

5. Jane, who married Thomas Cory, son of Elnathan. [See
Cory.]

ISAAC ROLL, (son of John 1st,) and Sarah Cauldwell,
lived and kept a tavern, in Springfield, many years ; they had
children :

1. John, born 28th August, 1765, married, 13th December,
1785, Mary Earl, who was born 21st August, 1768, daughter
of John Earl, near Middleville.

2. Mary, baptized 14th June, 1767, and died young.

3. James, who married, 1st, Joanna Earl, sister of John's
wife ; 2d, Abby Meeker, daughter of Benjamin Meeker.

4. Elizabeth, baptized 21st July, 1771, and died young.

5. Abraham, who went to the west and died there.

6. Jacob married Sarah Pierson, daughter of Samuel Pierson, of Springfield, and went to Cincinnati, Ohio, and had
an only child, Pierson Roll.

7. Catherine married Abner Woodruff, of Springfield, and
removed to Redstone, Pennsylvania. He was brother of
Caty Woodruff, the wife of Col. Abraham Woolley, of
Springfield.

8. Abigail.

9. Betsey married Daniel Ayers, of Springfield, son of Benjamin Ayers, of Long Island.

10. Sally married Jacob Thompson.

JOHN ROLL, (son of Isaac Roll, son of John,) and Mary Earl
had children :

1. William, who was born 16th October, 1786, and married Mary
Eddy, daughter of William Eddy, of Green Village.

2. Nancy, born 10th March, 1788, and married William Robison,
son of William, of New Providence, and died 9th May, 1819. [See
Robison.]

3. James, born 10th October, 1789, married, 1st, Mary Clark,
daughter of Abraham ; 2d, Julia Shipman, daughter of Jacob, son
of Abraham, of Monroe, Morris county ; 3d, Charity Hedges, by
whom he had no children.

4. Isaac, born 14th October, 1791, and married 1st, Rebecca Higgins, daughter of James; 2d, Mary Clark, widow of Henry Stites, of Scotch Plains, and by her had no children.

5. John, born 14th October, 1793, and died 2d April, 1794.

6 John 2d, born 11th July, 1795, and married, 20th May, 1818, Phebe Sutton, daughter of Joseph Sutton, of Hacketstown; lived in Newark.

7. Luther, born 29th July, 1797. married, 1st, Susan ———; she died, and he married, 2d, Elizabeth Brant, and removed to Georgia.

8. Charles, born 5th May, 1799, married, 1st, Phebe Terril, daughter of Enoch; 2d, Nancy Cory, daughter of Andrew, of Westfield.

9. Wesley, born 10th October, 1801, married Anne Smith, born 6th December, 1802, daughter of Jonathan Smith, of Scotch Plains.

10. Mary, born 21st January, 1804, married, 1st. David Camp; 2d, Charles Roll, son of Peter, son of Abraham Roll.

11. Jacob, born 11th January, 1808, went to Georgia, and married three times, but had no children.

WILLIAM ROLL, (son of John, son of Isaac, son of John 1st,) and Mary Eddy had children: (he removed to Illinois)

4th Gen

1. Mary Anne; 2. John; 3. Phebe; 4. Caroline; 5. Elizabeth; 6. William died young; 7. Sarah, twin to William; 8. James; 9. Nancy; 10. Alfred.

JAMES ROLL, (3d child of John, son of Isaac Roll,) by his 1st wife Mary, had a son:

1. John, who died at about 22 or 23 years.

And by his 2d wife, Julia Shipman, had other children:

2. James Madison, who was drowned on his way to Illinois, aged 21 years.

3. Stephen Buckley, who married ——— ———.

4. Chancellor Livingston.

5. Philetta Hicks, (twin to Chancellor,) married William ———, of Plainfield.

6. Henrietta.

7. Manning Rutan.

ISAAC ROLL, (4th child of John, son of Isaac,) and Rebecca Higgins had children:

1. Hannah Eliza, who married David J. Crane, son of Benjamin 3d. [See *Crane.*]

2. James Higgins married Hannah Mariah Smith, daughter of Joseph, of Springfield.

3. Mary Earl married, 1st, Oliver DeCamp; 2d, Philemon Dickerson. son of Philemon Dickerson, Esq., of Springfield.

4. Ellen married John Dickerson, also son of Philemon Dickerson, Esq.

5. John married Elizabeth Bond, daughter of Elihu Bond, brother of the Rev. Lewis Bond, of Plainfield.

6. Nancy Jane married Isaac Brokaw, son of Caleb, of Bound Brook.

7. David Elmer.

JOHN ROLL, (6th child of John, son of Isaac,) and Phebe Sutton had children:

1. Jacob; 2. Joseph; 3. Luther; 4. Archibald; 5. George Van; 6. Albert.

LUTHER ROLL, (7th child of John, son of Isaac,) and Susan —— had children:

1. William; 2. Mary Frances; 3. Luther; 4. ——, who was drowned. 5. Sarah Anne; 6. Robert.

His wife Susan then died, and he married Elizabeth Brant, and removed to Georgia.

CHARLES ROLL, (8th child of John, son of Isaac,) and Phebe Terril had children:

1. Albert; 2. James Hervy, who died at about 6 years.

3. Anne Eliza; 4. Cecelia. And by his 2d wife, Nancy Cory, had other children:

5. Parkhurst Cory; 6. Lucy Jane.

7. A son, who died in infancy.

WESLEY ROLL, (9th child of John, son of Isaac,) and Anne Smith had children:

1. Eliza Jane, who married Edward Tailor, son of James, of Springfield, and had children:

1. James Maro Tailor; 2. Wilber Denman Tailor.

2. Martin Luther; 3. Jonathan Smith; 4. Mary Louisa.

5. William Henry; 6. Eccell Anne; 7. Susan Almira.

8. Jacob Earl; 9. Sarah Emily; 10. John James.

11. Josephine, who died at $2\frac{1}{2}$ years; 12. Charles Wesley.

13. Anna Elizabeth.

MARY ROLL, (10th child of John, son of Isaac,) and David Camp had children:

1. David Wheeler Camp; 2. Caroline Camp, who died at 6 yrs. And by Charles Roll had children:

3. Mary Augusta Roll; 4. Caroline Virginia Roll.

5. Charles Roll; 6. Sidney Roll.

JAMES ROLL.

JAMES ROLL, (son of Isaac, son of John 1st,) and Joanna Earl had an only daughter :

1. Joanna, who married George Frazee, son of George Frazee, of Westfield.

And by his 2d wife, Abby Meeker, had other children :

2. Phebe, who married Clark Baldwin, son of Stephen, of Cheapside, and had children: 1. Sarah Baldwin ; 2. Emily Baldwin ; 3. Mariah Baldwin ; 4. Abby Baldwin ; 5. Stephen Baldwin.

3. Sally married Walter Smith, son of William, of Springfield,· and had children : 1. Mary A. Smith; 2. Abby L. Smith; 3. Edward C. Smith ; 4. Albert Smith ; 5. Ellen Smith.

BETSEY ROLL, (daughter of Isaac, son of John 1st,) and Daniel Ayers had children :

1. James Ayers, who went to Cincinnati, and married.

2. Isaac Ayers married Elsie Allen, of Millville, and went to Michigan.

Betsey Roll then died, and Daniel Ayers married Abby Denman, (daughter of Jacob Denman, by a first wife,) and had other children :

3. Jacob Denman Ayers, who married Mary Anne Denfer, daughter of Stephen Denfer, from France.

4. William Ayers married Phebe Bedell, of New Vernon.

5. Eliza Ayers, born 1803, married Samuel C Smith, a tailor, son of Moses Smith, of Springfield, and had children :

    1. Mary Elizabeth Smith, who married William Wade.

    2. Emma Smith ; 3. Henry C. Smith.

6. Phebe Ayers, married Jacob Thompson, son of Moses, son of Hezekiah Thompson. [See *Jacob Thompson*.]

7. Daniel Ayers, who died at 9 years.

8. Mariah Ayers married Nathan Robbins, and went to Oswego, New York.

9. Benjamin Ayers, who died in youth.

NOTE—Jacob Denman's 2d wife, was Elizabeth, daughter of Robert] Cauldwell. [*See Cauldwell.*]

JOHN ROLL, son of John, and brother of Isaac, lived on the north side of Long Hill; sold his farm to John Williams, and went to Ohio ; he had children :

1. Matthias, who married, 7th April, 1785, Mary Rutan, daughter of Abraham, and went to Ohio.

2. John, Jun., who married Patty Force, fo Horse Neck, Cauldwell Township, Essex county.

3. Abraham married Patty Vance, of Mendham.

4. Isaac, who died 11th March, 1787, aged 21 years.

5. Isaac 2d, who married Prudence Vance, of Mendham. sister of Abraham's wife.

6. Abigail, who married, 7th April, 1785, Samuel Miller, grandson of James Cauldwell 1st.

And by his 2d wife, Edith Wick, John Roll had children:

7. Wick, who died 8th January, 1790, aged 20 years.

8. Jacob, who was killed by lightning, 14th August, 1793, near the house, at about 18 years.

9. Edward.

MATTHIAS ROLL, (1st child of John Roll, son of John,) and Mary Rutan, had children :

1. Charity, who married, 1st, Samuel Trousdale, and had children : 1. Jane Trousdale ; 2. Polly Trousdale ; 3. Lydia Trousdale. Charity married, 2d, John Ayers.

2 Joseph married Rebecca ——.

3. Abigail married Reuben Blackford.

4. Rachel married William Stewart.

5. Isaac married Hannah De Camp.

6. Anna married Christopher Lintner.

7. John married —— ——.

8. Israel married —— ——.

9. Polly married David Baker.

10. Matthias married —— ——.

11. Samuel married —— ——.

12. Silas was a physician, and married —— ——.

ABRAHAM ROLL.

ABRAHAM ROLL, (son of John 1st,) was born 29th Aug.
1739, and died 20th October, 1813. He married, 1st, Mary
Brooks, born 5th February, 1742; 2d, Caty Vreeland, sister
of Daniel. She was daughter of Jacob Brooks, who lived on
the Coriell place, in Westfield. He became blind before he
died. By his first wife he had children:

1. Elizabeth, born 29th August, 1759, and died 26th September, 1850. She married Isaac Sayre, son of Isaac, from
New England. [See *Sayre.*]

2. Jacob, born 8th November, 1761, and married Betsey
Mills. He owned the grist mill in New Providence several
years, and sold out, and went to Ohio. They had children:
 1. Sally; 2. Mary; 3. Philemon; 4. Moses; 5. Abraham.

3. Brooks, born 9th February, 1763, married Phebe Ross,
daughter of James, a shoemaker, of Westfield.

4. Hannah, born 2d September, 1766, married Moses Parmalee, of Westfield.

5. Baltus, born 3d May, 1769, married Susan Jennings, of
Elizabethtown; had no children. He lived on the top of the
first mountain in Westfield, and was murdered in his own
house about 1833, by some persons unknown.

6. Peter, born 7th May, 1773, married Polly Belton, of
Short Hills.

7. Jephtha, born 3d Dec. 1776, married Abby Brookfield,
of Rahway..

8. Abraham, born 28th Sept. 1779, married Betsey Dunham, daughter of David; had two daughters, and removed
to Ohio.

9. Mary, born 12th March, 1783, married Abner Smalley,
son of James. [See *Smalley.*]

And by his 2d wife, Caty Vreeland, Abraham Roll had children:

10. Isaac, who married Susan ——; lives in Rahway.
11. Abby married Mr. Trembly.
12. David.
13. Jane married ———.

BROOKS ROLL, (son of Abraham,) and Phebe Ross, had
children:

1. Abby, who married a son of John Dunham.
2. Mary married Isaac Baldwin, son of David, of Canoe
Brook. [See *Baldwin.*]
3. Sally married Aaron Bailey, son of Samuel, of Springfield.

4. James married Caty Dunham, daughter of David, and half sister of his uncle Abraham Roll's wife.

Mr. Brooks Roll died 19th Jan. 1833.

HANNAH ROLL, (4th child of Abraham,) and Moses Parmalee, had children :

1. Mary Parmalee.
2. Betsey Parmalee married Henry Howard, of N. York.
3. Abby Parmalee married Aura Wilson, as his 2d wife, near Poughkeepsie.
4. Rebecca Parmalee married, 1st, Mr. Manning, of Plainfield ; 2d, Aaron Coe, Esq., of Westfield.
5. Brooks Parmalee married Miss Wilson, daughter of Aura Wilson, by his 1st wife.
6. Nancy Parmalee died unmarried.
7. Lockey Parmalee married James Stafford, and went west, where he died, and she returned with 3 children, Isaac, Abby, and James Stafford.
8. Sally married Mr. Parmalee, a distant relation.

PETER ROLL, (6th child of Abraham,) and Polly Belton, had children :

1. Charles, who married his second cousin, Mary Roll, 10th child of of John, son of Isaac Roll, and had children : 1. Mary Augusta ; 2. Caroline Virginia ; 3. Charles ; 4. Sidney.
2. Baltus.
3. A daughter.

JEPHTHA ROLL, (7th child of Abraham,) and Abby Brookfield had children :

1. Sarah, who married Thomas J. Blanck ; lives in New York.
2. William married Susan ——.

ISAAC ROLL, (10th child of Abraham,) had children :

1. George Washington, who married Sally Wood, daughter of John, son of John Wood.
2. Samuel Oliver married ———, a sister of Caroline's husband.
3. Catherine married, 1st, Mr. Shotwell, 2d, John Wilson.
4 Caroline married ———, a brother of Samuel's wife.
5. Isaac Clawson.
6. Sanford Vreeland.
7. William Stone.
8. Johila Marsh.

JOHN ROSS.

JOHN ROSS, of Westfield, was born 24th Dec. 1715, and died 7th April, 1798. He was, in 1748, Alderman of the borough of Elizabeth; he married, 1st, June, 11th 1736, Hannah Talmadge, who was born 6th July, 1715; 2d, Joannah Crane, a widow, and daughter of Alderman William Miller. She was born 15th Sept. 1728. married Mr. Ross, 22d Jan. 1754, and died 13th Sept. 1779, without children by him, and he married, 27th Feb. 1780, 3d, Susannah, the widow of another Mr. Crane, his 2d wife's aunt, and sister of the same Alderman Miller, and she died Nov. 1797, without children by him. By his first wife, Hannah Talmadge, he had children:

1. John Ross, Jun., born 26th August. 1737, married Sarah Scudder, sister of Corbet Scudder.

2. Rebecca, born 14th June, 1739, married Cornelius Ludlow, of Westfield.

3. Timothy, born 26th Aug. 1741, married Polly Briant, daughter of John. [*See Lamb.*]

4. Sarah, born 11th July, 1743, married Andrew Miller, and died 4th Aug. 1817, in her 75th year.

5. Ichabod, born 24th Sept. 1745, married, 1st, Miss Davis; 2d, Betsey Lamb, daughter of John. [*See Lamb.*]

6. James, born 9th Nov. 1751, married 1st Hannah Thompson, daughter of Thomas, of Union Township; 2d, Sarah Thompson, elder sister of his first wife. [*See Thompson.*]

JOHN ROSS, Jun., (son of John) and Sarah Scudder had children:

1. Hannah, who married Samuel Freeman.

2. Sarah married Mr. Tucker.

3. Polly married John Stevens, of Rahway.

REBECCA ROSS, (2d child of John 1st,) and Cornelius Ludlow had children:

1. Noah Ludlow married Rachel Rouse Ridgeway, and had children:
   1. Eliakim Ludlow, who married Polly Walker, daughter, of Asher, of Passaic Valley. [*See Walker.*]
   2. Henry Ludlow.

2. Rebecca Ludlow.

3. John Ludlow.

TIMOTHY ROSS, (3d child of John,) and Pol'y Briant had one child:

1. Samuel Ross, who married Huldah Randolph, daughter' of Thomas, and had children :
   1. Timothy, who married Sarah Laing, daughter of John and had children : 1. William, who died young ; 2. Charles : 3. Mary, who married Mr. Decker, and died without children ; 4. Harriet ; 5. Daniel, who married his cousin, Susan Ross, daughter of Milan ; 6. Clark ; 7 Milan.
   2. Milan married Susan Force, and had children ; 1. Samuel ; 2. Randolph ; 3. John ; 4. William ; 5. Susan, who married her cousin, Daniel Ross, son of Timothy.
   3. John, who married, and died without children.
   4. Sally married Mr. Coon, who died and left her a widow. And by a 2d wife, a daughter of Ezekiel Day, Samuel Ross had two children :
   5. James ; 6. —— a daughter, who married **Peter Houseman.**

2d Gen SARAH ROSS, (4th child of John Ross 1st,) and Andrew Miller. had children :
1. Hannah Miller, who married Thomas Parcel, of Chatham.
2. Rebecca Miller married John Brokaw, of Rahway.
3. Enoch Miller married Johannah Garthwaite.
4. John Miller married Abigail Stites, daughter of Richard. [See *Stites.*]
5. Abner Miller married Bethiah Tryon, of Orange county, New York.
6. Timothy Miller.
7. Sarah Miller, who married James Tharp.
8. Andrew Miller.
9. Susan Miller, who married Capt. John Scudder.

3d Gen JOHN MILLER, (4th child of Andrew Miller, and Sarah Ross,) and Abigail Stites, had children :
1. Cornelia Miller, who married Gideon Ross, son of James, son of John Ross 1st.
2. Hezekiah Stites Miller, who married Elizabeth Burnet, sister of Samuel Burnet, of Livingston, and had children :
   1. Lucinda Miller ; 2. Joseph Augustus Miller ; 3. Elizabeth Jenette Miller ; 4. Cornelia Miller ; 5. Julia Anne Miller ; 6. John Stites Miller ; 7. James Ross Miller ; 8. Ophelia Miller ; 9. George W. Miller.

2d Gen ICHABOD ROSS, (5th child of John,) and Miss — Davis, had children :

1. Talmadge, who married Betsey Littell, daughter of Moses. [See *Littell.*]

2. John, who married Anna Keyt, daughter of James.

By his 2d wife, Betsey Lamb, Ichabod Ross had children:

3. Mary, who died unmarried at about 17 or 18 years.

4. Elizabeth married, 1st, Joshua Clark, son of Robert; 2d, Sanford Hicks.

5. Ichabod, Jun. married Phebe Miller, daughter of Abner Miller.

6. Hannah married Henderson Williams.

TALMADGE ROSS, (son of Ichabod, son of John,) and Betsey Littell, daughter of Moses, son of Benjamin Littell, removed to Ohio, about 12 miles north of Chilicothe, and had children;

1. Moses, who married Mary Frazee, 2d child of Moses Frazee, and Mary Terry.

2. John married Sarah Lee, daughter of Thomas Lee. He died 12th May, 1844, aged 57 years, 8 months, and 4 days.

3. Abby, born 12th July, 1791, married Charles Marsh, son of Charles, of Westfield.

4. Jacob died in 1814, unmarried, aged 22 years

5. Talmadge died in 1814, unmarried, aged 20 years.

6. Eliza, who also died unmarried.

7. Linus H. Ross married —— ——, and lived near Sandusky, Ohio.

8. Abraham.

9. Thompson Seabury Ross.

MOSES ROSS, (son of Talmadge,) and Mary Frazee, lived near Chilicothe, and had children:

1. Pamela, who married James Gay, and had five children.

2. Jacob Davis Ross married —— ——; had two children.

3. Frazee Ross married —— ——; had two children.

4. Talmadge Ross; 5. John Ross.

6. Resin Ross married —— ——,

7. Abby Eliza Ross married —— ——.

8. James Ross.

9. William Ross.

JOHN ROSS, (2d son of Talmadge,) and Sarah Lee, had ten children:

1. Talmadge Ross, born 1810, and married Eliza Stites, daughter of Henry, of Scotch Plains, and had children:

    1. Anne Eliza, born 1st Jan. 1836; 2. Mary Jane, born 1839; 3. John Henry Ross, born 18th May, 1845.

2. Joseph Ross, born 4th Jan. 1813, married Nancy Squier, daughter of John Squier, son of Aaron Squier, of Long Hill, and had a child, Charles Gideon Ross.

3. Eliza Ross, born 11th Feb. 1815, and married John Frazee, son of Levi Frazee, of Westfield. and had children:
1. Caleb Maxwell Frazee, born 5th Oct. 1838.
2. Susan Frazee, born 11th March, 1840.
3. Preston Frazee, born 17th August, 1842.
4 John Ross Frazee, born 1st October, 1845.
5. Henry Martin Frazee, born 6th September, 1847.

4. Susan Ross, born 23d February, 1817, and married Isaac Thom, son of James Thom, of New Market, and had children:
1. James Thom, born 24th February, 1838.
2. Sarah Anne Thom born 14th October, 1839.
3. Mary Augusta Thom, born 26th Feb. 1845.

5. John Ross, born 5th March, 1820, married Harriet Bullman. He died 22d April, 1848; she died 20th Feb. 1848, leaving no children.

6. Mary Ross, born 27th March 1822, married Clarkson Shotwell, son of Daniel Shotwell, of Plainfield, and had one child. Susan Shotwell, born 29th April, 1847.

7. James Ross, born 27th August, 1826, and married Mary Freeman, daughter of Caleb of Plainfield.

8. Moses Lee Ross, born 18th November 1828.

9. Seth Williston Ross, born 31st March, 1832.

10. Cornelia Ross, born November, 1834.

JOHN ROSS, (2d son of Ichabod,) and Anna Keyt, had children:
1. Elizabeth, who married John Miller, son of Enoch. and had children; 1. John R. Miller; 2. Catherine Miller; 3. Keziah Miller; 4. David Miller; 5. James Miller.

2. Electa married Josiah Crane, son of John 4th, and had children:
1. John Grant Crane married Abby Miller, daughter of John O. Miller. He lives on the old-John-Crane homestead.
2. Mary Crane married Hampton Cutter, son of William, of Woodbridge.
3. Anne Elizabeth Crane married Job Williams, son of Moses, of Union.
4. Josiah Crane, Jun, married Sarah Jane Miller, daughter of Jacob.

3. Mary married Miller Williams, son of Moses, and went to Ohio, where she died.

4. Anne married Benjamin Williams, son of Nathaniel, and had one daughter, Anne Williams, who married John Norris.

ELIZABETH ROSS, (4th child of Ichabod,) and her first husband, Joshua Clark, had children:
1. Mary Clark, who married Caleb M. Littell, son of Doctor Anthony. [See *Littell*.]

2. Amos Clark married Sarah Meeker, daughter of Samuel, of Springfield.

And by her 2d husband Sanford Hicks, Elizabeth Ross, had

3. A daughter, who married John Chatterton, of Elizabethtown.

ICHABOD ROSS Jun, (5th child of Ichabod, son of John,) and Phebe Miller, had children:
1. John, who married —— ——.
2. Betsey.
3. Ichabod 3d.
4. Abner married —— ——.

HANNAH ROSS, (6th child of Ichabod Ross, Sen.) and Henderson Williams, had children:
1. Sarah Williams, who married Peter Messier, and had a daughter, Eliza Anne Messier, who married Augustus Howel.
2. Mary Williams, who married Asa D. Vandergrift.
3. Phebe Anne Williams married John Dunham, son of John, son of John, of Passaic Valley, and had a daughter, Ellen Dunham, and then died.
4. Benjamin Williams.
5. Theodore Williams married Miss —— Mulford.
6. Emeline Williams, who died.

JAMES ROSS, Esq. (6th son of John Ross 1st,) by his first wife, Hannah Thompson, had children:
1. Betsey, who married John Marsh Clark.
2. Sarah, born 6th May, 1777, and married Doctor Joseph Quinby, of Westfield, and died 1803, without children.

James Ross, Esq. by his 2d wife, Sarah Thompson, had children:
3. James Thompson Ross, who died unmarried.
4. Hannah married, January, 1807, Henry Baker, son of William. [See *Baker*.]
5. Gideon, married, 20th April, 1829, Cornelia Miller, born 8th May, 1793, daughter of John Miller, son of Andrew Miller, and Sarah Ross, daughter of John Ross 1st.

BETSEY ROSS, (daughter of James Ross, Esq.) and John Marsh Clark, had children:
1. Betsey M. Clark, who married Benjamin T. Clark, son of Charles Clark, Esq.
2. James Ross Clark, born 20th June, 1793, and married Catherine Tucker, daughter of Joseph Tucker, and had children:
1. James Ross Clark, Jun. born 12th May, 1827.
2. John Joseph Clark, born 16th July, 1832.

4th Gen BETSEY M. CLARK, and Benjamin T. Clark, had children :
1. James Marsh Clark, who married Miss Maxwell.
2. Sarah Anne Clark married Edwin Keyt.
3. Eveline Clark married Mr. Bryer.
4. Susan Clark married Mr. Maxwell.
5. Charles Augustus Clark married Ruth Sanford.
6. Lockey Clark married Mr. Bryer.
7. Benjamin Clark ; 8. Catherine Clark ; 9. Hannah Clark.
10. Gideon Clark ; 11. Henry Clay Clark ; 12. A daughter.

2d Gen HANNAH ROSS, (4th child of James Ross, Esq.) and Henry Baker had children :
1. James Ross Baker, who died September, 1820, aged about 12 years.
2. William T. Baker, who married Elizabeth Anne Miller, daughter of Abner, and had children :
  1. Catherine Baker, born 1839 ; 2. Elizabeth Baker.
3. Sarah Eliza Baker, who married William Radford, of New York, and had children :
  1. William Henry Radford ; 2. James Radford ; 3. Edwin Radford.
4. James Ross Baker 2d, who married Catherine Mundy, and had children : 1. Eliza Radford Baker.
5. Phebe Webb Baker married John Squier, son of John, son of John Squier, and had children : 1. James Wade Squier.

GIDEON ROSS, Esq. (5th child of James Ross, Esq.) was a surveyor, a justice of the peace, a major in the militia, and was several times elected a member of the legislature. He and Cornelia Miller had children :
1. James, born 17th June, 1732, and died 21st, July, 1739.
2. Cornelia, born 20th December, 1835.

JONATHAN RUCKMAN.

JONATHAN RUCKMAN lived on Stony Hill, south of David Smalley, Esq. He married Sarah Allen, daughter of Joseph Allen, Jun and had children:

1. Stephen, who married, 12th March, 1794, Esther Dobbin, of Cauldwell.

2. Nathan, born 1777, married Hannah Alward, daughter of Benjamin Alward.

3. David married Betsey Coon, daughter of Capt. Israel Coon, and had no children.

4. Levi married Jane Leforge, daughter of Abraham, and died 16th October, 1844.

5. Jonathan, who died a young man, unmarried.

6. Phebe married John Cory; lived on the 2d mountain, south east of Mount Bethel.

7. Joseph, married, 1st, Mary Alward, sister of Nathan's wife; 2d, Sally Kelly, of Mount Horeb. He had children: 1. John; 2. Josiah; 3. Elisha; 4. Joseph; 5. Eliza. And by his 2d wife, 6. Jonathan; 7. David.

STEPHEN RUCKMAN, (son of Jonathan,) and Esther Dobbin, had children:

1. Sally, who married Samuel Dixon, of Washington Valley.

2. Betsey married Isaac Morehouse, of Livingston, and went to Indiana.

3. Phebe married Isaac Coddington, son of Achibald, of Mount Horeb.

4. Hetty, who went to Indiana with Isaac Morehouse, and died.

5. Isaac married Nancy Winans, of Washington Valley.

6. Stephen, Jun. went to Indiana, and married there.

7. Jane married William Buck, near Germantown, Hunterdon county.

8. Thirza married John Buck, of the same place.

9. Ellen married Abraham Bryant, of the same place.

NATHAN RUCKMAN, (2d child of Jonathan,) and Hannah Alward had children:

1. William, who died at about 24 years, unmarried.

2. David N., born 21st April, 1804, who married 1st, Jane Stevens, daughter of James Stevens, and had 1, a son James; his wife then died, and he married, 2d, Hannah P. Bonnel, daughter of Stephen C. Bonnel, son of James, and had children: 2. William.
3. Nancy; 4. Hannah; 5. David; 6. Bern; 7. Lemuel.
8. Stephen C. Bonnel. [See *Bonnel*.]

3. Rachel married Francis Vaughn, and went to North Western Pennsylvania.

4. Hannah, who died at 18 or 19 years, unmarried.

5. Sarah married Charles Foster, son of Silas Foster, of Chatham.

LEVI RUCKMAN, (4th child of Jonathan,) and Jane Leforge, had children:

1. Martin, born 27th October, 1811, married Jane Dow, of Bedminster, born May, 1806. They had children :
   1. Lucy Anne, born 20th December, 1833.
   2. Enoch, born 20th February, 1835.
   3. Jonathan Lewis, born 2d March, 1836.
   4. Benjamin F., born 25th October, 1837.
   5. Phebe, born 25th March, 1839.
   6. Phinehas, born 26th April, 1842.
   7. David Martin, born 14th November, 1843.
   8. William Henry, born 7th December, 1845.
   9. Levi, born 8th August, 1848.
2. Sarah married Joseph F. Tilyou, and obtained a divorce from him.
3. Eliza married Jefferson Moore, son of Jesse, of Mount Bethel, and had children : 1. Harriet Moore ; 2. Wesley Moore ; 3. Mary Jane Moore ; 4. Jacob Moore ; 5. Jonathan Moore.
4. Deborah married Jacob Ludlow, son of Joseph. [See *Ludlow*.]
5. Harriet married Lewis Noe Miller, son of Lewis. [See *Miller*] She had one son, Levi Miller, and died.
6. Jenette married David Bird, son of John, of Mount Bethel, and had children : 1. Harriet Bird ; 2. Jacob Bird ; 3. Levi Bird.
7. Mary married, 23d June, 1849, Watson Bird, son of Elias, and had children: 1. John Henry Bird ; 2. ———.
8. Atwood.
9. Rebecca.
10. Hannah.

PHEBE RUCKMAN, (6th child of Jonathan,) and John Cory, had children :

1. Daniel Cory, who married Rachel Willet, daughter of Jonathan, of Warren, and had several children.
2. Jonathan Cory, who married Mary Titus, daughter of William, and had children: 1. Elizabeth Cory ; 2. Maryette Cory ; 3. Phebe Cory ; 4. Anne Jane Cory. Both Daniel and Jonathan Cory have been members of the legislature, from Somerset county.

RICHARD RUNYON.

RICHARD RUNYON, (whose ancestors were French,) was born 14th April, 1719. He had a sister, who married a Mr. Layton, and had children.

Peter Layton, who was called Capt. Layton, lived at Long Hill, did not marry.

Provy Layton, who married Justice John Carle, of Long Hill. [See *Carle.*]

A Mr. John Runyon married, 10th September, 1765, Violet Layton.

1st Gen. RICHARD RUNYON married Jane Van Court, born 13th August, 1727, and had children:

1. Sarah, born 30th March, 1746, and married Elias Coriell, son of Abraham, of Piscataway, and died in 1820, aged 74 years. [See *Coriell.*]

2. Anna, born 27th October, 1747, and married Daniel Sayre, brother of Ephraim Sayre, of Madison, and had children:

    1. James Sayre, who married Deborah Dunham, daughter of John, son of John.

    2. Elias Sayre married Miss Hetfield, of Elizabethtown, and had a son, Thomas O. Sayre.

3. Elias, born 7th June, 1749, married, 9th January, 1771, Deborah Clark, born 27th July, 1749, daughter of Daniel Clark. Elias Runyon died 8th March, 1793.

4. Elizabeth, born 11th December, 1750, married Moses Carpenter, of Goshen, New York; had an only daughter, Elizabeth Carpenter, and soon after died.

5. Jean, born 6th December, 1752, and died of consumption, at about 20 years.

6. Rosannah, born 3d November, 1754, and died unmarried.

7. John, born 26th November, 1756, married Polly Conklin, daughter of Stephen, of Basking Ridge, and went to Ohio, and settled near the head of the Little Miami river. He died in 1836, and she died in 1842. They had children:

    1. Stephen, who died in 1813, unmarried; 2. Richard; 3. John; 4. Elias; 5. Betsey, who married Joseph McLain; 6. Debby married James McLain, brother of Joseph; 7. Polly married Mr. —— Vance: 8. Anna, and three other daughters.

2d Gen. ELIAS RUNYON, (son of Richard,) and Deborah Clark lived at Long Hill, where their father did, and had children:

1. Richard, born 26th November, 1771, married Phebe Lewis, daughter of Isaac, of Sussex.

2. Anna, born 24th September, 1773, married Ludlow Squier, son of Thomas. [See *Squier.*]

3. Daniel, born 23d March, 1776, married 1st, Hope Lewis, sister of Richard's wife ; she soon died, and he married 2d, Polly Squier, daughter of Thomas, of Livingston.

4. John, born 17th August, 1778, married his 2d cousin, Margaret Runyon, daughter of Richard, of Piscataway.

5. Jean, born 16th January, 1781, and died 4th February, 1781, in infancy.

6. Israel, born 16th March, 1782, married Polly Deeds, daughter of Michael, of Springfield, and died 28th September, 1813.

7. Elias, born 5th November, 1784, was a physician, married Agnes Day, daughter of Col. Israel Day, of Chatham ; had no children.

8. Peter P., born 19th May, 1787, married Phebe Tenyck, daughter of Tunis Tenyck, of New Brunswick. Is a justice of the peace, and judge of the court in Middlesex county.

9. Jane, born 29th December, 1790, married Savage Wright, from Virginia, and lives in Piscataway.

RICHARD RUNYON, (son of Elias,) and Phebe Lewis lived in New Brunswick, and had children :

1. Sally, born November, 1797, married John Dunham Martin, son of Arauna, of New Brunswick, and had children :

   1. Mary Martin, who married Charles Martin, son of Still Martin, of New York.

   2. Richard Runyon Martin; 3. Arauna Martin ; 4. Isaac Lewis Martin.

2. Debby, born February, 1799, married Ambrose F. Randolph, son of Still F. Randolph, and had children :

   1. Still Randolph ; 2. Richard Runyon Randolph; 3. Howard Malcom Randolph.

3. Jane, born ——, 1802, married James Boyce, son of George and had children : 1. Susan Hankinson Boyce married Dr. Sears, of N. Y.; 2. Charles Decilding Boyce ; 3. Peter Boyce ; 4. Albert Boyce ; 5. Henry Boyce.

DANIEL RUNYON, (son of Elias,) owns his father's farm at Long Hill ; was appointed a Justice of the Peace in 1834, and acted in that office fifteen years. He and Polly Squier had children :

1. Caroline, who is unmarried.

2. Phebe, who married Augustus Stewart, son of Christopher, of Plainfield ; went to Illinois, and had children :

   1. John Runyon Stewart; 2. Mary Ellen Stewart; 3. Edward Stewart.

3. George married Mary Giles, daughter of John Giles ; lives in Plainfield, and had children : 1. William Henry ; 2. Alfred ; 3. John.

PETER P. RUNYON, (son of Elias,) and Phebe Tenyck had children:

    1. Trembly, who died young.
    2. Debby.
    3. Mary, who married Peter C. Onderdonk, son of John.
    4. John, twin to Mary, died at about 6 or 7 years.
    5. Elias married Emily Fitz Randolph, daughter of David, editor of the N. B Fredonian.
    6. Susan married Mahlon Runyon, son of Abel.
    7. Virginia.

PETER RUTAN.

PETER RUTAN owned two 100 acre lots, Nos. 28 and 29 addition of the Elizabethtown lots. and now owned by the heirs of Nicholas Van Winkle, Joseph H.. Patten, and others. He had a son, Abraham, that survived him; who owned the eastern half of the 200 acre tract, and lived on it near the spring.

ABRAHAM RUTAN was an Elder in the Presbyterian Church of New Providence. He married, ———; she died 15th Dec. 1788,; they had 5 sons and 8 daughters:

    1. John, who married, 20th March, 1774, Catherine Jones, and went to the west.
    2. Samuel married Eleanor Bedell, daughter of Jacob, and went west. [*See Bedell.*]
    3. Peter, born 1757, and died 12th April, 1802, aged 45 years, unmarried.
    4. Joseph, born 1769, married, 14th June, 1791, Hannah Baker, daughter of Thomas Baker, Jun. She died 26th July, 1804, aged 34 years, and he married, 2d, Rachel Hole, daughter of Uzel Johnson's 2d wife. He died 19th March, 1809, aged 40 years.
    5. Abraham married Hannah Shipman, daughter of Abraham, of Munroe, Morris county. He died 25th Dec. 1804, aged 30 years, and left two children. Manning and Eliza; Eliza died young; Manning married Miss Hurd, and lived at Dover, Morris county, and subsequently removed to Greenville. Montcalm county, Michigan.
    6. Sally, who married, 6th June, 1775, Simeon Simpson, son of Alexander, as his 2d wife. [*See Simpson.*]
    7. Hannah married John Cauldwell, son of William. [*See Cauldwell*]
    8. Mary married, 7th April, 1785, Matthias Roll, and went to Ohio. [*See Roll.*]

9. Rosannah married, 20th Dec. 1786, Thomas Parrot, son of William. [*See Parrot.*]

10. Martha married, 17th Oct. 1787, Moses Camp, son of Aaron. [*See Camp*]

11. Charity married John Miller, and had a son, James Miller, who lived at New Vernon, and a daughter, Anna, who married in Pennsylvania, Samuel Ayers, and lived near Rossville, Ohio.

12. Anna married. 29th April, 1790, Moses Squier, son of Thomas. [*See Squier.*]

13 Elizabeth married, 14th June, 1791, Abraham Cauldwell, son of William. [*See Cauldwell*]

James Miller, son of Charity Rutan, and John Miller, married Anna Collard, and had children : 1. John Miller; 2. Charity Miller, who married Nathaniel Bonnel, of Green Village, as his 2d wife ; 3. Ebenezer Miller married Hannah Winters, of N. Y. ; 4. Mary Miller ; 5. Joseph Miller married Sarah Messler, daughter of John Vleit Messler; 6. James Miller ; 7. Margaret Miller married Mr. Logan.

JOSEPH RUTAN, (son of Abraham, son of Peter,) lived where his father did. He and Hannah Baker had children :

1. Daniel, who married Jane Cauldwell, daughter of Hugh, and had children :

    1. Hugh, who died in Newark, unmarried, aged about 24 years.

    2. Hannah, also died in Newark, unmarried, about 24 years.

Daniel Rutan died 6th Feb. 1820, aged 28 years. His widow, Jane, died 2d Feb. 1849, aged 61 years.

2. Abigail, born 19th March, 1795, and married Peter D. Valentine, son of Jonathan. [*See Valentine*]

3. Abraham, who died 9th May, 1811, aged 15 years

4. Samuel married Lockey Meeker, daughter of Joseph O. Meeker, of Scotch Plains, and died 1st April, 1827, aged 28 years. [*See Dunham.*] And by his 2d wife, Rachel Hole, Joseph Rutan had children :

5. Eliza, who married Barnabas Earl, and went to Kalamazoo county, Michigan.

6. Joseph married Sally Anne Fornote, daughter of William, of Rahway.

JOSEPH RUTAN, (son of Joseph,) and Sally Anne Fornote, lived in Rahway, and had children :

1. Mary Elizabeth, who married, 4th August, 1844, William Harris Smith, son of Adam Smith, of Bound Brook. He died in Feb. 1848, leaving a daughter, Mary Williams Smith.

2. Henrietta Adams ; 3. Jane Anne; 4. Francis Adelia; 5. Hannah Baker. Joseph Rutan, Jun, died in April, 1844.

DAVID SAMSON.

DAVID SAMSON lived on the north side of Long Hill, where Philemon Dickerson now lives; he married Hannah Bonnel, sister of Nathaniel Bonnel 1st, and had children:

1. Stephen, who died, at about 23 years.
2. Jacob, who died, at about 21 years.
3. Sebra, who married Mr. Armstrong, and removed to Pennsylvania.
4. Mary married Moses Hand, son of William. [*See Hand.*]
5. Isaac married Mary Day, daughter of Stephen Day, Esq., of Chatham. He lived and died in Springfield.
6. Moses is unmarried; lives with the widow of Peter Dickerson.
7. Aaron went to sea on board a vessel of war, and did not return.
8. Abraham married Chloe Bonnel, daughter of Capt. Nathaniel Bonnel.
9. Benjamin married Abigail Ball, daughter of Jeremiah Ball, and grand-daughter of Jeremiah Hart. [*See Ball and Hart.*]

ISAAC SAMSON, (son of David,) and Mary Day had children:

1. Nancy, who married Aaron Dean, son of John, of Springfield.
2. Joanna married Mr. Freeman, of Union Township.
3. David, born May, 1791, married Betsey Johnson, daughter of Uzel, by his 2d wife.
4. Mariah married, 11th Jan. 1809, David Nafie, of Springfield.
5. Nathan, who died in Springfield.
6. Charlotte married and went to Western New York.
7. Julia Anne, who died young.

DAVID SAMSON, (son of Isaac,) and Betsey Johnson had children:

1. Isaac Johnson Samson, who married Hannah, the widow of William Potter, of Rahway, and daughter of Mr. Garthrite. She had a son, William Potter, and they had children: 1. David Samson, born Jan. 1840; 2. John Wesley, born 14th July, 1843. Isaac Johnson Samson died 6th Dec. 1846.
2. Nathan Scudder Samson, who married Catherine Anne Rino, daughter of Wilson Rino, of Piscataway.
3. William Edgar Samson, born 11th February, 1822, married Caroline, widow of Edward Tornsee, and daughter of Mr. Powel, of Brooklyn, New York; have no children.

4. Stephen, born 11th October, 1825.
5. Mary Jane, born 27th November, 1830.
6. Mariah, born 1st June, 1833.
7. Elizabeth Day, born 13th February, 1838.

ABRAHAM SAMSON, (son of David. Sen..) and Chloe Bonnel, lived at Madison, Morris county, and had children

1. Julia, who married Wickliff Condit, son of Ebenezer ——, and soon died.
2. Sally married Christopher Seely Miller, son of Eliphalet, of Chatham, and went to Ohio.
3. Aaron Smith, who died at 5 years.
4. Nancy Bonnel Samson.
5. Zebra
6. Amanda married James B. Condit, brother of Wickliff; live in Licking county, Ohio.
7. Elizabeth Shaver married Oswald Joseph Burnet, son of William, of Morris county.
8. Mary Malvina married John Radley, son of William, of Ohio, and live there.
9. Enoch Nelson ; 10. Anne Mariah ; 11. Wickliff Condit.
Mr. Abraham Samson died about the 1st July, 1851.

NOTE —Nancy, wife of Sylvanus Bonnel, and sister of Chloe, wife of Abraham Samson died 4th July, 1851, and her 2d son Calvin married Julia Anne Crowel, from near Philadelphia, and had children : 1. Mary ; 2. William ; 3. John ; 4. Emma ; 5. George Washington Bonnel ; he lives in Iowa.

BENJAMIN SAMSON, (son of David. Sen) and Abigail Ball, removed to Knox county, Ohio ; they had children :
1. Benjamin Pettit, who married Mary Jones, of Union ; live in Newark.
2. Harriet married Mulford W. Casterline, son of Mrs. John Marshall. [See *Daniel Willcox*]
3. Bonnel married in Newark.
4. Eliza, who died at about 15 years.
5. Hervy, who died in Newark.
6 Abeline, who married Mr. Tailor, in Ohio.
7. Hannah married Mr. Lennel, in Ohio.
8. Vashti married in Ohio.

ISAAC SAYRE.

ISAAC SAYRE came from New England; he married Jane Swaine, daughter of Matthias Swaine. They lived between the mountains, south west of Springfield, and had children :

1. Elizabeth. who married Enoch Vreeland, son of Brown Vreeland, and lived where Jonathan Gillam now lives.

2. Matthias married, 27th September, 1767, Patience Thompson, daughter of Aaron, of Long Hill. [See *Aaron Thompson.*]

3. Catherine married Timothy Griffin, ot New Providence. [See *Griffin.*]

4 Isaac married, 22d February, 1774, Elizabeth Roll, daughter of John Roll, Sen. [See *Roll.*] She died, 26th September, 1850, in her 92d year, after being a long time a widow.

2d Gen

MATTHIAS SAYRE, (son of Isaac,) and Patience Thompson, had children :

1. Caleb, who went to the west, unmarried.

2. Chloe, who married John Scudder, of Westfield, and went to the west.

3. Noah married Rachel Hubbel, and went to the west.

4. Matthias Swaine Sayre went to sea, and died unmarried.

ISAAC SAYRE. Jun. (son of Isaac,) and Elizabeth Roll lived where his father did, and had children :

1. John, who married Abby Brown, of Connecticut, sister of Jonathan Brown, of Chatham ; he lived in Passaic Valley, in Chatham township, opposite the Methodist church. He was horribly shot through the window of his house, about 1835, the ball passing through his mouth, and knocking out several of his teeth ; he died the 2d day after.

2 Mary Brooks Sayre married Noah Ross, son of James Ross, and brother of Brooks Roll's wife. [See *Brooks Roll.*]

3. Brooks married Polly Conklin, daughter of Joshua Conklin. [See *Conklin.*]

4. Jane married Ralph Eltsone, went to Ohio, and had an only son, Cornelius Elstone.

5. Catherine married Moses Thompson.

6. Betsey married Aaron Briant, son of Cornelius ; he died he 2d March, 1850.

7. Anthony Swaine Sayre married Mariah Armstrong, of Long Island.

8. Hannah married Israel Ward, son of Joshua, and had a daughter, Jane Anne Ward, who married 1st, Jona Swaine, son of Benjamin ; and 2d, George W. Ogden, son of Richard, and had a daughter, Susan Ogden.

JOHN SAYRE, (son of Isaac Sayre, Jun.,) and Abby Brown, had children :

4th Gen²
1. William, who married Nancy D. Bonnel, daughter of William Bonnel, son of Capt. Nathaniel, and had children :
>   1. Elizabeth Bonnel Sayre ; 2. John Francis Sayre ; 3. George Sayre ; 4. Emily Brown Sayre ; 5. Sarah Doty Sayre ; 6. Daniel Brown Sayre.

2. Betsey, who married Aaron Johnson, son of Gabriel Johnson Esq. and had children : 1. William C. ; 2. Rebecca. [See *Johnson*.]

BROOKS SAYRE, (son of Isaac Sayre, Jun.,) and Polly Conklin, had children :

4th Gen
1. Elizabeth, who married Henry Faitoute, son of Moses, of Union ; 2. William ; 3. Mary married Joseph Kain, a carpenter, of Somerville ; 4. Isaac ; 5. Hannah ; 6. Brooks Sayre, Jun.

CATHERINE SAYRE, (5th child of Isaac Sayre, Jun.) and Moses Thompson, had children :
1. Sarah Thompson, who married Elias Morgan, son of Elias, of Elizabethtown, and had children :
>   1. Mary Elizabeth Morgan, who married William Day, son of Josiah Day, of Chatham ; 2. John Sayre Morgan ; 3. Sarah Catherine Morgan ; 4. Abby Mariah Morgan ; 5. Elias Allen Morgan ; 6. James Henry Morgan.

2. Aaron Ogden Thompson, who married Eliza Wood, from Newburgh, and had a son, William Thompson.

3. Eliza Ogden Thompson married John H. Jaques, and had a son, David Jaques, when she died.

4. Isaac Moses Thompson married Mary Smalley, daughter of Abner Smalley, and Mary Roll, 9th child of Abraham Roll, and have children : 1. Abner Thompson ; 2. ———.

BETSEY SAYRE, (6th child of Isaac Sayre, Jun.) and Aaron Briant, had children :
1. Mary Briant, who married Daniel Kissam, son of Richard, and had children :
>   1. Samuel Kissam, born 1827 ; 2. John R. Kissam, born 1829 ; 3. Franklin Kissam, born 1840 ; 4. Nancy Kissam, born 1845.

2. Isaac Briant ; 3. Hannah Briant married William Kent, son of Nathaniel ; 4. Abby Briant married Lewis Denman, son of John, of Canoe Brook ; 5. William H. Briant ; 6. Emily Briant.

ANTHONY S. SAYRE, (7th child of Isaac Sayre, Jun.)
and Mariah Armstrong, lived where his father did, and had
children:
1 Etheniel, a daughter, born 1827; 2. Allavosto, a son,
born 1829; 3. Vezifri, a son, born 1830; 4. Vinelia, a daughter, born 1833; 5. Fla Alva, a daughter, born 1838.

EPHRAIM SAYRE.

EPHRAIM SAYRE lived on and owned Lot No. 51, Addition
of the Elizabethtown lots, where Squier Par.ot now lives. He
had a son David, who married, 20th December, 1766, Rachel
Roffe. He died 3d October, 1781, aged 42 years, and his widow
married, 2d, Thomas Osborn, [see *Osborn.*] and after his death she
married, 3d, Col. Jedediah Swan, of Scotch Plains. He also had
a son Daniel, who married Anna Runyon, daughter of Richard
Runyon, Sen., and had children: 1. James, who married 30th January, 1796, Deborah Dunham, daughter of John, Jun. and lived
at Madison; 2. Elias, a clock maker, of Elizabethtown, who
married —— ——, and had a son, Thomas O. Sayre.
Ephraim Sayre had a son, —— ——, who went to Virginia,
whose son William came from thence to this Valley, and married
Miss Canfield, of Monroe, Morris county, and died 15th December, 1820, leaving several children.
And still another son, William, who lived where his father
did. He married Esther High, daughter of John High 1st, of
Westfield, and had no children. He was an elder in the presbyterian church in New Providence. His wife Esther died,
and he married, 2d, Anna, the widow of Jonathan Acken, of
Scotch Plains, and removed to Plainfield, where he died. [See
Dr. Anthony Littell]

EZEKIEL SAYRE.

EZEKIEL SAYRE lived in 1788, on Stony Hill, where
John Marshall now lives. He had children:
1. Levi, who was baptized 31st January, 1768.
2. John, who was baptized 29th October, 1771.
3. Huldah, who married in Ohio, Col. John Wallace.
4. Pierson married in New Jersey.
5. Benjamin. 6. Rachel.
Mr. Ezekiel Sayre removed to Ohio before 1800, and lived
near Reading, Hamilton county.

NOTE.—See another Ezekiel Sayre, son-in-law of John
Bonnel, page 50.

RICHARD SCUDDER.

RICHARD SCUDDER owned and lived on the farm of 100 acres now owned by John Littell, adjoining the river. He also owned about 100 acres of the farm now owned by Thomas O. Scudder. He married Rebecca Stites, daughter of Elijah Stites, of Scotch Plains. [See *Stites.*] He died 24th December, 1785, and left children :

2d Gen

1. Dr. Benjamin R. Scudder, who married Sally Wade, of Connecticut Farms ; they lived at Paterson Landing, where he died.

2. Nancy married, 3d Jan. 1785, Alexander Steele, of Somerset county.

3. Stites married Elizabeth Osborn, daughter of Thomas Osborn, [*see Osborn.*] and died 1st April, 1812 : she died 22d November, 1848.

4. Mary married James Bishop, of New Market, Middlesex county.

5. Thomas married 1st, Elizabeth Ayers, daughter of David Ayers, Esq. of Liberty Corner ; and 2d, Rebecca Auten, 18th Dec. 1811 ; and he died in March, 1812, of typhus fever.

6. Sally married Zebulon Ayers, of Middlesex county, and lived several years where Lines Tucker now does, and finally removed to Seneca county, New-York.

DR. BENJAMIN R. SCUDDER, (son of Richard,) and Sally Wade had children :

3d Gen

1. Susan, who married, 1st, 22d Jan. 1814, Hugh Littell, son of Nathaniel Littell, Esq. He died 9th November, 1822, without children ; and she married, 2d, the Rev. Peter Ditmus Freliegh, of Acquackanac, and had a son, Peter D. Freliegh, who is a lawyer, and married Caroline A. Wilkin, daughter of John C. Wilkin, of Orange county, New York. The Rev. Mr. Freliegh died, and she married, 3d, John Conklin.

2. Rhoda married Mr. —— McRea, and had no children.

3. Nancy married Benjamin Servin, and had children : 1. Benjamin Servin ; 2. Oliver Servin.

4. Sally married Jacob Van Riper, and had four children.

NANCY SCUDDER, (daughter of Richard,) and Alexander Steele, had children :

3d Gen

1. John Steele, who is unmarried.

2. Richard Steele is unmarried.

3. Polly Steele is unmarried.

4. Stites Steele married —— ——, and had children : 1. Alexander Steele ; 2. Mary Anne Steele, who died young. And then he died.

5. Rebecca Steele married Peter L. Die, had 3 children, and then died ; her children were :

    1. David Die, who married Emma Sayre, daughter of Coe Sayre, and had children : Warrren Die ; Anne Eliza Die.

    2. Anne Mariah Die, who married James Gosman.

    3. John Die married Eliza Coles.

6. Thomas Steele, who died at about 30 years.

7. Peggy Steele.

8. Ross Steele married Amanda Tailor ; he is a merchant in Somerset county, New Jersey.

9 Hetty Steele.

Mr. A. Steele and family removed to Seneca county, N. York.

MARY SCUDDER, (daughter of Richard,) and James Bishop removed to Seneca county, New York, and had children :

    1. Aury Bishop, who married Miss McDuffy, daughter of James McDuffy.

    2. Letty Bishop married Samuel Miller.

    3. Caty Bishop married Titus Philips, and went to Michigan.

STITES SCUDDER, (son of Richard,) and Elizabeth Osborn, had children :

    1. Richard, who died 3d March, 1812, aged 15 years.

    2. Thomas Osborn, born 24th Dec. 1799, and married Martha Vail, daughter of Daniel Vail, of Stonehouse Village; lives where his father did, and has no children.

    3. Lois married Jotham Willcox, son of Daniel, and went to Seneca county, New York. [See *Willcox*.]

THOMAS SCUDDER, (son of Richard,) and Elizabeth Ayers lived where his father did, and had children :

    1. Rosetta, who married Joseph Miller, of Hunterdon county, and had children : 1. Alexander Miller ; 2. William Miller.

    She died 1821, aged 25 years.

    2. Sally, born 11th September, 1801, and married Samuel Schureman, born 20th February, 1795, son of John Schureman ; they had children :

        1. Eliza Schureman, born 14th April, 1819, and married Abraham Melick, and went to Illinois.

        2. Mariah Schureman, born 22d January, 1821, and married 22d July, 1843, Jonathan Totten, son of Jeremiah Totten, and had no children.

        3. Thomas Schureman, born 16th July, 1823, and married Catherine Colie, born 8th August, 1824, daughter of Smith Colie, of Springfield, and had children :

            1. George Allein ; 2. Albert Monroe ; 3. William Eugene, born 4th October, 1851.

        4. John Nelson Schureman, born 10th December, 1825.

        5. George Bangheart Schureman, born 23d February, 1827.

        6. Henry Schureman, born 16th June, 1830.

        7. William Mulford Schureman, born 3d December, 1835.

8. Harriet Louisa Schureman, born 23d August, 1838.

9. Joseph Perry Schureman, born 30th October, 1840.

10. Sarah Catherine Schureman, born 2d October, 1842.

Samuel Schureman died 9th September, 1849.

3. Mary, who married Godfrey C. Kline, of Hunterdon county, and had children : 1. Elizabeth Kline ; 2. Rosetta Kline ; 3. Isaac Kline ; 4. William Kline ; 5. Sarah Catherine Kline ; 6. Mary Frances Kline.

4. Elizabeth, who married William B. Fisher, of Hunterdon county, and had children : 1. Jonathan Fisher ; 2. Elizabeth Fisher ; 3. Ellen Fisher ; 4. Josephine Fisher.

SALLY SCUDDER, (daughter of Richard,) and Zebulon Ayers, had children :

1. Decator Ayers.

2. Sally Mariah Ayers, who died at about 17 years.

3. Richard S. Ayers, who married his cousin Mary Willcox, daughter of Jotham, [see *Willcox*,] and died without children.

4. Louisa Ayers married Denton Gurnee, and had children :

    1. Francis Gurnee ; 2. Augusta Gurnee.

5. Rebecca Ayers.

6. Anson Ayers.

7. Nancy Ayers.

THOMAS SCUDDER.

THOMAS SCUDDER, brother of Richard, lived where George Townley lately lived and owned that farm of 100 acres, sold to Mr. Townley, and with his family removed to the west. He married, 5th April, 1773, Abigail Clark, daughter of Daniel Clark, [see *Daniel Clark*,] and had children :

1. Sarah, who married, 10th September, 1793, Nathaniel Jennings, son of Jacob. [See *Jennings*.]

2. Jotham ; 3. Abigail, who married ———— ; 4. Ruth ; 5. Clark ; 6. Jane baptized 24th September, 1789 ; 7. Daniel Clark.

Old Mrs. Scudder, the mother of Richard and Thomas Scudder, died 10th April, 1784.

3d Gen

JABESH SHIPMAN.

JABESH SHIPMAN married Agnes Rogers. lived and owned the farm next west of Thomas Squier's, now occupied mostly by Jacob Grisinger and Thomas Conn.   They had children:

1. Abigail. who married, 17th September, 1772; John Shadwell, and went to Kentucky.

2. Jemima married, 7th November, 1773, Nathaniel Roff, and went to Kentucky.   [See *Roff*]

3. David married Betsey Tingley.   He died 12th October, 1787.

4. John married, 15th May, 1792, Betsey Stevens, daughter of Jonathan Stevens, Sen.

5. Jabesh, Jun. married the widow Phebe Bryant; she died 16th November, 1792.

6. Sarah married, 14th November, 1785, Jasper Dove, who died 18th October, 1789, and left one son, Jasper Dove, Jun. who died about 1818, unmarried.

7. Esther married, 16th February, 1793, John Frazee.

8. Phebe, who died 16th March, 1784. unmarried.

9. Leonard, who died 4th January, 1793.

JOHN SHIPMAN and Betsey Stevens, had children:

1. David, who married Nancy, the widow of Caleb Putney, and died without children.

2. Abigail married, 14th June, 1817, Isaac Doty, son of Henry, of Washington Valley.

3. Anne married Nathan Smalley, son of Isaac.   [See *Smalley*].

ABIGAIL SHIPMAN, (daughter of John,) and Isaac Doty, had children :

1. Henry Doty.

2. Phebe Anne Doty. who married John Drake, son of Elkanah, and had children: 1. Horace Jones Drake ; 2. Emily Drake.

3. John Shipman Doty, who married Bridgetta Kaverson. daughter of Michael, and had children: 1. Nelson Doty: 2. Eugene Doty.

4. Marquis Doty, who married Henrietta Williamson.

5. Elizabeth Doty.

JOHN SHOTWELL.

JOHN SHOTWELL came from England, and settled on the road between Scotch Plains and Plainfield ; he married, 1st, Miss Smith, daughter of Shubal Smith ; 2d, Mary Webster ; he had children :

1. John Smith Shotwell, who married 1st, Miss Webster, sister of his father's 2d, wife ; 2d, Phebe Shotwell, daughter of Joseph Shotwell, of Woodbridge.

2. Jacob married Bersheba Pound, daughter of Elijah Pound, of Piscataway.

3. William married Elizabeth Pound, sister of Jacob's wife.

4. Isaiah married Constant Lippencott, of Shrewsbury, Monmouth county.

5. James married Elsee, widow of William Runyon, and daugh- of Andrew Smalley, of Harris's Lane.

6. Hugh married Rosetta Arrison, of Sussex, daughter of John Arrison, who lived at Wyoming, and was driven out from there by the Indians, in time of the war.

7. Mary married John Stevens, and had a son, John Stevens.

8. Sarah married, 1st, Ralph Smith, son of Ralph Smith, of Hanover, and had no children by him ; 2d, Capt. William Piatt, son of John Piatt, from France.

9. Martha married Jonathan Hand Osborn, son of Jonathan Osborn, of Scotch Plains.

JOHN SMITH SHOTWELL, (1st son of John,) by his first wife, Miss Webster, had children :

1. John, who died unmarried.

2. William, who lived at Long Hill, near Franklin Place, and died unmarried.

3. Samuel married Hetty Davison, a widow, and daughter of Nathan Cooper, of Chester, Morris county.

4. Susannah married David Martin, son of Alexander, of Long Hill. [See *Martin*]

5. Elizabeth married Dennis Hughes, from Ireland.

6. Sarah married Mr. Hamson, and had 2 children and died, viz.

    1. Henry Hamson ; 2 John Hamson, who married Sally Parker, daughter of Calvin, of Long Hill.

7. Mary married her cousin, Daniel Shotwell, son of Jacob, as his 1st wife.

8. Joseph Smith Shotwell married Deborah Fox, daughter of George Fox.

9. Nathan, who died unmarried.

JACOB SHOTWELL, (2d son of John,) and Bersheba Pound had children :

1. Sarah, who died at 29 years, unmarried.
2. Ralph, who married, 1st, Betsey Marsh, daughter of William Marsh, of Ash Swamp ; 2d, Osee Tingley, daughter of Jacob Tingley, of Washington Valley.
3. Daniel married, 1st, his cousin Mary Shotwell, daughter of Smith Shotwell ; 2d, Phebe Cole, daughter of Master William Cole.
4 Elijah, born October, 1779, married his cousin Jemima Piatt, daughter of Capt. William Piatt.
5. John, (twin to Elijah,) married Massy Smith, daughter of Samuel Smith, of Newark, and had no children.

RALPH SHOTWELL, (son of Jacob,) and his first wife, Betsey Marsh, had children :

1. Jacob, who married Dorcas Drake, daughter of Noah Drake.
2. Sarah married Richard Manning, son of Isaac Manning, of Plainfield.
3. Bersheba married Isaac Line, son of Amos Line, and went to French Creek, New York.
4. Mary married Smith Line, brother of Isaac. And by his 2d wife, Osee Tingley had other children :
5. John.
6. Betsey married James Bullman, near Rahway.
7. Anne married Alfred Berry, of Dover ; lives in Plainfield.
8. David married Amelia Clark, daughter of David Clark, of Westfield.

DANIEL SHOTWELL, (3d child of Jacob,) and his first wife, Mary Shotwell, had but one son :

1. John Smith Shotwell, who lives in New York. And by his 2d wife, Phebe Cole, had children :
2. Mary, who married James Bruen, and had children : 1. Margaret Bruen, who married Patrick De Corsey, from Ireland ; 2. Phebe Bruen ; 3. Philip Bruen ; 4. Catherine Bruen ; 5. George W. Bruen ; 6. Mary Bruen.
3. Elizabeth married Daniel Hatfield, son of Daniel, and had children : 1. Jacob Shotwell Hatfield ; 2. Sarah Hatfield ; 3. William Hatfield.
4. William, who went to Illinois.
5. Sarah, who married Corra Meeker, son of Jotham Meeker, and had children : 1. Phebe Meeker ; 2. John Meeker ; 3. Jotham Meeker
6. Rachel married William Williamson, son of Piatt Williamson, and had children : 1. Piatt Williamson ; 2. Rebecca Anne Williamson.

7. Jemima married, 25th Sep. 1849, Silas Cole, son of Elias Cole.

8. Emeline Davis Cole married Mulford Cole, son of Elias, and had children: 1. Elias Cole; 2 Phebe Cole; 3. Jemima. Daniel Shotwell died 8th August, 1851.

ELIJAH SHOTWELL, (4th child of Jacob,) and Jemima Piatt, had but one child:

1. William Piatt Shotwell, who was a Justice of the Peace; married Harriet Pearce, daughter of Noah Pearce, and had children: 1. Greenleaf Shotwell, married Elizabeth Cleveland, daughter of Ezra Cleveland, of Elizabethtown, and died 30th May, 1849; 2. Caroline Piatt Shotwell; 3. Ellen Jemima Shotwell; 4. William Piatt Shotwell.

WILLIAM SHOTWELL, (3d child of John 1st,) and Elizabeth Pound had children:

1. Rachel, who married Richard Dell, at Dover, and lives there.

2. Catherine.

3. Anne married Jesse Wilson, of Sussex.

4. Phebe married Isaac Wilson, of Sussex.

5. Elizabeth married Joseph Adams, of Sussex.

6. Elijah married Miss Birdsal, in Canada.

7. John married Miss Marsh, in Canada.

8. Smith; 9. Sarah.

William Shotwell with all his family, excepting Rachel, removed to Canada.

ISAIAH SHOTWELL, (4th child of John,) and Constant Lippencott, had children:

1. Mary, who married Thomas Lane, near Rahway.

2. Jedediah married Anna Pound, daughter of Samuel, of Piscataway.

3. Abel married Betsey Vail, daughter of Abraham, of Green Brook.

4. Peter married Phebe Vail, sister of Abel's wife.

5. Thomas married Elizabeth Satterthwaite, daughter of Joshua, of Shrewsbury, and lived there.

6. William died unmarried at about 60 years; he was crazy.

7. Joseph L. married Christain Vail, sister of Betsey and Phebe.

8. Samuel married Sarah Rich, daughter of Joseph, of Pennsylvania, and lived there.

9. Edmund married Sarah Shepperd, of Philadelphia, and lived there.

10. Hugh married Hannah Cole, and lived at Morestown, Pennsylvania.

JAMES SHOTWELL, (5th child of John,) and Elsee
Smalley, lived in Sussex, and had children:

　　1. William.
　　2. Jonathan lived in Warren county, and died 14th Jan.
1850, aged 55 years.
　　3. Charles.
　　4. Nancy married, 1st, Mr. Vleit ; 2d, Mr. Smuch, of Sussex.
　　5.Clarissa.

HUGH SHOTWELL, (6th son of John,) and Rosetta
Arrison, removed to Harrison co. Ohio, and had children :
　　1. John, who married Sarah Shanklin, and had children :
　　　　1. Catherine : 2. Rosetta ; 3. Susannah ; 4. Emily ; 5.
　　　　Caroline.
　　2. Esther married, 1st, Timothy Smith, and had children :
　　　　1. John Smith ; 2. Rosetta Smith ; 3. James Smith ; 4.
　　　　Hugh S. Smith ; 5. Timothy Smith.   Esther marri-
　　　　ed, 2d, George Seaton, and had other children : 6
　　　　Jonathan Seaton ; 7. Charlotte Anne Seaton.
　　3. Susannah married Charles Wintermute, and had children ;
　　　　1 William ; 2. Joseph ; 3. Rosetta.
　　4. Esther Wintermute ; they lived in Sussex.
　　4. Charlotte married Ephraim Sayre, and had children :
　　　　1. Hugh ; 2. William ; 3. Wesley ; 4. Nancy Sayre.
　　5. Nancy married, 1st, Peter Van Dolah, and had children :
　　　　1. William Van Dolah, who married Julia Walton.
　　　　2. John Van Dolah married Amelia —— ——.
　　Nancy married, 2d, Jacob Ebert ; live in Hamilton Ohio,
and had children :
　　　　3 Margaret Ebert.
　　　　4. Rosetta Ebert.
　　　　5. Sarah Ebert, who married, 22d July, 1851, Mr. Lewis,
　　　　a lawyer, of Hamilton.
　　　　6. Jerome Ebert.
　　6. William lives in Cadiz Ohio ; married Rhoda Beebe and
had children :
　　　　1. Stewart Beebe ; 2. William. who died at 25 years.
　　　　3. Theodore ; 4. Walter, who died at 16 years.
　　　　5. Loretta ; 6. Joseph.
　　7. Joseph lives in Lima, Allen county, Ohio.   He married
his cousin Mary Allison, and had children :
　　　　1. Jeptha, who married Nancy Cooper.
　　　　2. George ; 3. Louisa.
　　8. Arrison Shotwell lives in Harrison county, Ohio.   He
married Mary Dickerson, and had children :
　　　　1. Elizabeth ; 2. Victoria ; 3. Judson, and others.

SARAH SHOTWELL, (8th child of John,) and Capt. William Piatt had children :

1. James Piatt, who married Rachel Baird.

2. Jemima Piatt married Elijah Shotwell, son of Jacob.[See *Elijah Shotwell*]

3. William F. Piatt, born 9th October, 1788, and married, 1st Eliza T. Litte l, daughter of Nathaniel Littell, Esq. and had children :

> 1. Mariah M. Piat, who married Joel Wilson, son of John Wilson, Esq and had children : 1. William Piatt Wilson ; 2 Mercy Wilson ; 3. Eliza Wilson.
>
> 2. James Mortimer Piatt, who went to sea and was lost.

His wife Eliza died 29th November, 1827, and he married Caroline Kempton. widow of Capt. Kempton of N. Y. where they both lived, and had a daughter, Eliza C. Kempton Piatt.

Capt William Piatt was a Capt. in the U. S. service, and was killed by the Indians, in 1794 : his widow died in 1850, aged about 94 years.

William F. Piatt was a physician in New-York, and died 7th May, 1848 ; his 2d wife Caroline had died previous to his death. [See *Nathaniel Littell, son of David*]

MARTHA SHOTWELL, (9th child of John,) and Jonathan Hand Osborn, had children :

1. Corra Osborn, who is a physician and lives in Westfeld. He married, 1st, Mary Hand, daughter of William Hand ; 2d, Hannah Downer, daughter of Samuel Downer, of Westfield.

2. John Osborn married Nelly Tunison, daughter of Maj. Tunison, of Somerville.

3. Amos Osborn married Lockey Woodruff, daughter of Reuben, of Westfield ; 4. Letitia King Osborn married Dennis Vail, son of Wm. Vail.

DR. CORRA OSBORN, and his 1st wife, Mary Hand, had children : 1. Mahlon Osborn, who went to St. Louis, and married Mary Frothingham.

2 Mary Osborn married Samuel Hays, son of Dr. Samuel Hays, of Newark.

3. Letitia Osborn married David Miller, son of John Miller, of Westfield

4. Anne Osborn married Nathan Williams, son of Solomon. And by his 2d wife, Hannah Downer, he had children :

5. Corra Osborn, born —— ——, 1830.

6. Jonathan Osborn. born —— ——, 1832.

SAMUEL VAN SICKLE.

SAMUEL VAN SICKLE lived in Sterling Valley, a little
east of William High's house ; he had a brother, David Van
Sickle, who married Elizabeth, the widow of Moses Bedell,
and daughter of David Littell. [*See David Littell, son of
Samuel* 1st]

NOTE.—Sarah Thompson, daughter of Thomas Thompson, married, 1st, Mr.
Van Sickle, of Long Hill, and had a daughter, Elzabeth, who married Jacob Britton, son of W liam. [*See Britton*] She married, 2d, Mr. Rutan, who had a
son, Peter, who lived in Albany, N. Y ; 3d, James Enos, or Innes, of Long Hill.

SAMUEL VAN SICKLE had children:
1. Zachariah, who married, 30th Oct. 1763, Mary Littell,
born 4th March, 1749, daughter of Andrew Littell, a grandson of Samuel 1st.
2. John.
3. Anthony.
4. Elizabeth.   (Is not this Elizabeth the wife of Jacob Britton.)
5. Christian.
6. Caty, who married Jabez Clark, son of Daniel. [*See
Clark*]

NOTE.—Andrew Littell was born 15th Dec. 1718, and died
1784; his wife's name was Mary, or Molly, born 5th Jan.
1725, and died very old. They had children :
1. William Littell, born 12th April, 1745. (*See page* 215.)
2. Sophia Littell, born 27th March, 1747.
3. Mary Littell, born 4th March, 1749, married Zachariah Van Sickle.
4. Rachel Littell, born 6th Jan. 1751.
5. Ephraim Littell, born 13th Dec. 1760.
6. Hannah Littell, born 5th Oct. 1762.
7. Temperance Littell, born 30th May, 1769.

ZACHARIAH VAN SICKLE, and Mary Littell had children :
1. Huldah, who married Jonathan Terry, son of William,
of Short Hills.
2. Elias ; 3. Sarah ; 4. David.
5. Zachariah, Jun., who married, 20th October, 1789,
Rosannah Bowman.
Zachariah Van Sickle, with his family, excepting Huldah,
removed to Western Pennsylvania.

HULDAH VAN SICKLE, and Jonathan Terry had children :
1. Hannah Terry, who died in her 24th year.

2. Mary Terry, who married Asa French, son of Anderson.

3. William Terry went to the west and married there, Phebe ———.

4. Lewis Terry married Phebe Hedden, daughter of Edward.

5. Martha Terry married, 1st, David Miller; 2. Cornelius Brokaw.

6. Ruth Terry married Jeremiah Valentine, son of Joseph. [See *Valentine*]

7. Sally Terry who died at 1½ years.

8. Sarah Anne Terry, who is unmarried.

9. Abba Terry, who married Cutter Dollbeer, son of Samuel.

MARY TERRY, (2d child of Huldah Van Sickle and Jonathan Terry,) and Asa French had children: 1. Caroline Elmer French; 2. Mary French; 3. Noah Terry French; 4. Huldah Anne French; 5. Ezra French.

LEWIS TERRY, (4th child of Huldah Van Sickle, and Jonathan Terry,) and Phebe Hedden had children: 1. William Terry; 2. Mary Terry, who married Caleb Conklin, and went to Missouri; 3. Harriet Terry, who died in 1844, at about 25 years; 4. Jonathan Terry; 5. Edward Terry; 6. Lewis Terry, who died in 1846, at about 17 years; 7. Caroline Terry, who died in 1848, at 16 years.

MARTHA TERRY, (5th child of Huldah Van Sickle and Jonathan Terry,) and David Miller had children:

1. Carlisle Brown Miller, who married Mary Badgley, daughter of Ahijah.

2. Erastus Miller, who married Eliza Anne Badgley, daughter of Ahijah.

And by Cornelius Brokaw, Mary Terry had,

3. William Terry Brokaw, who married Sarah Mariah Manning, daughter of Squier Manning. [See *Bailey, page* 17.]

ABBA TERRY, (9th child of Huldah Van Sickle and Jonathan Terry,) and Cutter Dollbeer had children:

1. Huldah Anne Dollbeer, who married Thomas Richards, son of William Richards, of Springfield.

2. Erastus Miller Dollbeer; 3. Martha Elizabeth Dollbeer.

4. Lewis Faitoute Dollbeer, who died in infancy.

5. Jonathan Woodruff Dollbeer, who died in infancy.

6. John Terry Dollbeer.

JOHN SIMPSON.

JOHN SIMPSON came from Long Island, and settled on No. 27 of the Elizabethtown lots, above the 1st mountain, drawn by Daniel Potter, where John M. Parsons, now lives; he had children, Alexander and John, and died 10th July, 1773.

ALEXANDER SIMPSON, (son of John,) married Elizabeth ———; she died 2d April, 1768, and he died 1st May, 1768; he was an elder in the presbyterian church; they had children:

1. Simeon, who married, 1st, Mary ———; she died 21st January. 1774, and he married, 2d, 6th June, 1775, Sally Rutan, daughter of Abraham, and removed to Washington county, Pennsylvania, and died there.

2. Abraham, who died 29th March, 1770.

3. Stephen, who went west with Simeon.

4. Nancy married, 1st. Mr. Ayers; 2d, Mr. Rhodes.

5. Mary married, 14th November, 1775, Capt. Nathaniel Bonnel, as his 2d wife. [*See Bonnel.*]

JOHN SIMPSON, (son of John,) lived where his father did; he married Sarah Carle, of Millstone; and died 9th May, 1786, aged 60 years; they had children:

1. Margaret, who married Jonathan Howel Osborn, son of John, Sen. [*See Osborn.*]

2. Lynche, called also Magdalen, who married, 26th March, 1774, Samuel Waldron, and went to French Creek, Pennsylvania.

3. John 3d, married Susan Drake, near Scotch Plains.

4. Abraham married Jane Pierson, had a son Jacob, and went to Ohio.

5. Isaac married Rachel Drake, sister of John's wife.

6. Jacob married Sally Turner, of Morristown; lived at Hanover, and had no children.

7. Anna married 13th May, 1789, as a 2d wife, Samuel Miller, and had children:

   1. John Miller; 2. Abigail Miller, who married Mr. Pew, lives in Green county, Ohio. Samuel Miller died 3d July, 1793, and she married, 2d, Sept. 20th, 1795, Moses Badgley, as his 2d wife, and went to Ohio; and had children:

   3. Ephraim Badgley; 4. Hugh Badgley. Moses Badgley had by his first wife, 1. Benjamin, who married Miss Street; 2. Sally married Ephraim Simpson.

8. Sally married Enoch Badgley; had a daughter Sarah Badgley, who died 23d April, 1784.

9. Alexander, born 2d May, 1763, married 8th May, 1788, Elizabeth Cauldwell, daughter of William, and in 1815, went to Dayton, Ohio; he died in March, 1833. She died 3d February, 1829.

10. Ephriam went to Ohio, lives in Green county, and married Sally, a daughter of the above named Moses Badgley, by his first wife, and had an only daughter, Cynthia, who married William Thegley ; lives in Indiana, and had several children.

11. William married, 6th April, 1796, Betsey Woodruff.

JOHN SIMPSON 3d, (son of John, son of John,) and Susan Drake lived where his father did, and had children :

1. William, who married Sally Brown, daughter of John, of Stony Hill, and had children : 1. Jane; 2. John; 3. Pamela, and then removed to the west.

2. Effa, who married Ephraim Griffin, son of Timothy, [See *Griffin.*]

3. John 4th, who married his cousin —— ——, a daughter of Samuel Waldron.

4. Sally married, 18th March, 1809, Stephen Whitehead Beach, son of James Beach, of Livingston, and went to French Creek.

5. Israel married Jane Heuston, daughter of Henry Heuston, of Belleville, and lived there.

ISAAC SIMPSON, (son of John, son of John,) and Rachel Drake lived by Salt Brook, where Ambrose Tailor now lives. He died 14th July, 1829, aged 72 ; she died 25th June, 1838, aged 78 years. They had children :

1. Susannah, who married James Beach, of Livingston, above named.

2. Catherine married Elias Bonnel, son of James, son of John. [See *Bonnel*]

3. Sally married Stephen C. Bonnel, brother of Elias.

4. Ephraim, who went to Ohio.

5. Jonathan Drake married Hannah Spinning, daughter of Benjamin. He left her, went to Honesdale, Pennsylvania, obtained a divorce, and married again.

6. Jacob married —— ——.

7. Rachel married, 1st, Simeon Hanford, from Connecticut, and had children :

    1. Jonathan Hanford, who married Catherine Griffin, daughter of William M. Griffin.

    2. Hetty Hanford married Samuel Badgley, son of David.

    3. Henrietta Hanford.

She married, 2d, Ambrose Tailor, and had other children :

    4. Mary Elizabeth Tailor, born June, 1835.

    5. Nancy Caroline Tailor ; 6. Almond Dunbar Tailor.

    7. Catherine Bonnel Tailor.

Mr. Tailor died 15th January, 1852.

ALEXANDER SIMPSON, (son of John, son of John,) and Elizabeth Cauldwell lived where David A. Oakley now lives, and had children :

1. Aaron, born 19th February, 1792, married Jemima Scudder, daughter of Jesse Scudder, of Springfield.

2. Moses, born 5th September, 1793, married Eliza Baker, daughter of Aaron Baker, Esq. of Dayton, Ohio.

3. Polly, born 22d March, 1795, married Benjamin Spinning, Jun. son of Benjamin. [See *Spinning.*]

4. Electa, born 3d June, 1800, married David Stout, an iron monger, of Dayton.

5. Betsey, born 8th April, 1803, and died 27th September, 1818.

AARON SIMPSON, (son of Alexander,) and Jemima Scudder lived near Hamilton, Ohio, and had children : 1. Benjamin.

2. Elizabeth, who married Stephen Crane, son of Moses Crane and Sarah Miller, daughter of Jacob. [See *Jacob Miller.*]

3. John ; 4. Mariah.

MOSES SIMPSON, (2d son of Alexander,) and Eliza Baker, lived in Dayton, Ohio, and had children :

1. Electa Emeline, who married Seth Crowel, of Dayton, and had children : 1. Charles Elmore Crowel ; 2. Moses Simpson Crowel ; 3. David Baker Crowel ; 4. Florence Eliza Crowel ; 5. Silas Simpson Crowel.

2. Elizabeth, who married Robert Allen, of Dayton, and had children : 1. William Rutan Allen ; 2. Aaron Baker Allen.

3. Henry Allen, who died January, 1849 ; 4. Emeline Allen.

5. Theodore Allen ; 6. Robert Allen, Jun.

3. Jane Mariah Fuller, who married George W. Morris, and had children : 1. Amelia Morris ; 2. Charles Morris ; 3. Ira Morris ; 4. Mahlon Morris.

4. Silas Maxwell Baker.

5. Aaron Baker Alexander, who died 20th July, 1839.

ELECTA SIMPSON, (4th child of Alexander,) and David Stout, had children :

1. Elias Riggs Stout, who married Lydia Britton.

2. Atlas Lacock Stout, who married Virginia Crane.

3. Phebe Stout, who died at 5 years.

4. Moses Simpson Stout, who died at 24 years.

5. Elizabeth Stout ; 6. Henry Stout ; 7. Orin Stout.

8. Ira Stout.

WILLIAM SIMPSON, (11th child of John, son of John,) and Betsey Woodruff, had children :

1. Nancy, who married Robert Ball, of Hanover, Morris county.

2. Eliza, who married Samuel Woodruff, of Hanover.

3. Mahlon, who married Hannah LeHomedeau, of Warren Co. and had children : Alexander and Israel ; Mahlon died, and his widow married William D. Bedford. [See *Bedford.*] 4. Chilion.

JOHN SMALLEY.

JOHN SMALLEY lived in Passaic Valley, Warren township, Somerset county ; he married Anne Randolph, and had children :

1. James, who married Abigail Jennings, sister of Jacob Jennings.

2. Isaac married Rachel Stewart, daughter of Joseph Stewart, of Washington Valley.

3. Jacob, twin to Isaac, married 1st, Tabitha Moore, daughter of John Moore ; 2d, Betsey Willet, daughter of Jonathan, by whom he had no children.

4. David married Hannah Roff, sister of Henry Roff. [See *Lacy*.] He was a justice of the peace, and a practical surveyor.

5 Sally married Isaac Moore, brother of Jacob's 1st wife. [See *Moore*.]

JAMES SMALLEY, (son of John,) lived near Passaic river, where his father did, on the farm of 130 acres, now owned by John Littell ; he and Abigail Jennings had children :

1. Jonas, who married, 30th September, 1793, Rebecca Wise, and went to Western Pennsylvania.

2. Abner married Mary Roll, daughter of blind Abraham Roll. [See *Roll*]

3. David I. married Nancy Tucker, daughter of Jacob Tucker, son of Warner.

4. John marreid Sally Moore, daughter of Benjamin Moore, of Acquackanac.

5. Keziah married Derrick Thomas, son of William Thomas, of Stony Hill.

6. Reuben married Rhoda Moore, daughter of Isaac Moore, Sen. and removed to the Lakes, New York.

7. Jacob I. married his cousin Anne Smalley, daughter of Jacob Smalley ; lived at Paterson.

8. Benjamin married Keziah Thomas, sister of Derrick.

9. Mary married Samuel Compton, of Dead River, in Somerset county.

10. Rachel married Jacob Moore, son of John Moore, Jun. of Paterson.

11. Catherine married Mr. Brown, in the Lake country, New York.

ABNER SMALLEY, (2d son of James,) and Mary Roll, had children :

1. Sayre, who married, 13th February, 1823, Cornelia Parrot, daughter of Samuel.

2. Fanny married Benjamin Ludlow, son of Lewis, of Westfield, and had an only child, Elizabeth D. Ludlow, who married 26th September, 1850, John Badgley, son of Squier, son of Jonathan Badgley.

3. Mary married Isaac M. Thompson, son of Moses Thompson, and Catherine Sayre, daughter of Isaac, Jun.

DAVID I. SMALLEY, (3d son of James,) and Nancy Tucker went to the Lakes New York, and had children:
1. Abner, who married Rachel Caterline.
2. Hannah married her cousin Matthias Townley, son of William. [See *Townley*.]
3. Margaret married Matthew Benjamin.
4. Huldah.
5. Charlotte married Elias Parker, son of Samuel.
6. Abby married Mr. —— Coriell,
7. Joel married Harriet Armsbury.

JACOB I. SMALLEY, (7th child of James,) and Anne, his wife, had children:
1. Louisa, who married Joseph Corley.
2. Betsey married Horace Betawnia.
3. Abraham married Betsey Bower.
4. Squier; 5. Phebe; 6. Sally Anne; 7. John; 8. Andrew Jackson.

ISAAC SMALLEY, (son of John,) and Rachel Stewart, lived on Stony Hill, where Mahlon Smalley now does, and had children:
1. Elias, who married Hannah Compton, daughter of Reuben Compton, and went to the Lakes, N. Y.
2. Lewis married Miss Ayers, near Liberty Corner, and went to the Lakes N. Y.
3. Nathan married Anne Shipman, daughter of John Shipman. [*See Shipman.*]
4. William married Caty Jobs, sister of Nicholas Jobs, Esq., of Liberty Corner.
5. Polly married Benjamin Coon, son of Levi Coon, near Mount Bethel.
6. Deborah married Samuel Martin, of Martinville.
7. Rachel married Andrew Putnam, son of Mills, of Green Vally.

NATHAN SMALLEY, (son of Isaac,) and Anne Shipman had children:
1. Nelson, who went to East Florida, and died there.
2. Cornelius, who become insane when a young man.
3. Agnes, who married, 1st Jan. 1851, Lewis Kirkpatrick, son of R. Finley Kirkpatrick, son of Alexander. [*See Kirkpatrick.*]

JACOB SMALLEY.

JACOB SMALLEY, (son of John,) and Tabitha Moore had children :

1. Sally, who married David Randolph, son of Gilbert. [*See Randolph.*]
2. Anne married her cousin, Jacob T. Smalley, son of James. [*See James Smalley.*]
3. Phebe married Moses Ayers, son of Jonathan, of Stone House Village.
4. Ruth married Squier Tingley, son of Jacob Tingley, of Washington Valley.
5. Electa married Restors Cox, from New England ; lives in Washington Valley.
6. Elizabeth, who died at 17 years, unmarried.
7. Isaac I. married Nancy, widow of James Pope, and daughter of Jonathan Drake.
8. Jacob, Jun., married Mariah Bullman, daughter of Joseph, of Long Hill, and went to Illinois.
9. Mary married Jacob Drake, brother of Isaac's wife.
10. Tabitha, who died at 6 years.

PHEBE SMALLEY, (3d child of Jacob,) and Moses Ayers had children:

1. Julia Anne Ayers, who married Israel Coddington, son of Archibald.
2. Sylvanus Ayers married Eliza Fisher.
3. Ezekiel Ayers married Miss Lockerman, daughter of Vincent E. Lockerman.
4. Jonathan Ayers married Mary Coddington, daughter of Jerry.

RUTH SMALLEY. (4th child of Jacob,) and Squier Tingley had children:

1. Ira Tingley, who married Mary Coulter, daughter of Lafferty.
2. Jacob S. Tingley is a carriage maker, at Plainfield.
3. Sally Tingley married Nathaniel Drake, son of Noah. [*See Drake.*]
4. Tabitha Tingley married Benjamin Fisher, son of Jerry.
5. Isaac S. Tingley is a carriage maker, at Plainfield.

ELECTA SMALLEY, (5th child of Jacob,) and Restors Cox had children :

1. Julia Anne Cox, who married Jackson Smalley, son of Samuel.

2. Marietta Cox married —— ——.

3. James Hartwell Cox married Elizabeth Tucker, daughter of Lines. [*See Tucker.*]

4. Freelove Cox married Archibald Baird ; 5. Martha Cox.

ISAAC I. SMALLEY, (7th chil l of Jacob,) and Nancy Drake had children : 1. Tabitha ; 2. Jacob.

JACOB SMALLEY, (8th child of Jacob,) and Mariah Bullman had children : 1. Oscar, who married Mary Crosby, in Illinois ; 2. Helen Finley married Mr. Classby, in Illinois.

MARY SMALLEY, (9th child of Jacob,) and Jacob Drake had children : 1. Theodore Drake ; 2. James Drake ; 3. Isaac S. Drake ; 4. Francis Marion Drake ; 5. Sally Anne Drake ; 6. Elizabeth Drake.

DAVID SMALLEY, Esq., (son of John Smalley 1st,) and Hannah Roff had children :

1. Henry. who married Phebe Hand, daughter of Hezekiah, of Short Hills.

2. Daniel married Deborah Roff, daughter of Jonathan Roff. [*See Roff.*]

3. Hannah married Samuel Casad, of Warren Township.

4. Samuel married, 1st Rhoda Moore, daughter of Benjamin of Mount Bethel; 2d, Mary Pennington, daughter of John, of Dead River.

5. Prudence married John Geddis.

6. David D. married, 1st, Polly Blackford, and was a justice of the peace ; 2d, Betsey Allen, daughter of William Allen.

7. Patty married John Dunham, Jun., son of John ; had a daughter Hannah, when he died, and she went to Michigan.

8. Mahlon married, 1st Jan. 1816, Betsey Parrot, daughter of William.

9. Hannah married, 10th Sept. 1809, John Dunn, son of Francis Dunn, of Washington Valley.

HENRY SMALLEY (1st son of David Smalley, Esq.) and Phebe Hand, had children :

1. Chilion, who married Caroline Allen ; 2. Rhoda married Mr. Latrop ; 3. Henry, who married —— ; 4. Noah.

DANIEL SMALLEY, (2d son of David Smalley, Esq.) and Deborah Roff had children :

1. Pamela, who married Levi Coon, Jun.

2. Elizabeth, who married Henry Doty, Jun. ; 3. Letta married George Lavzalier ; 4. Hannah married Piatt Drake, son

of Andrew; 5. Roff, who went to Indiana; 6. Mahlon, who went to Lancaster, Ohio.

SAMUEL SMALLEY, (4th child of David Smalley, Esq.) and Rhoda Moore had children:

1. Keziah, who married Isaac Titus, of Washington Valley, son of John. [See Titus.]

2. David married Docia Wood, daughter of Dael S. Wood, Jun, [see Wood,] and went to Western New York, near Lake Ontario.

And by his 2d wife, Mary Pennington, he had children:

3. John, who married Phebe Wooden, daughter of Gideon Wooden.

4. Rhoda married David Weir, son of William, of Sterling Valley.

5. Amanda married Stephen Marshall, son of John. [See Marshall.]

6. Henry married Hannah Townsend, of Brooklyn, N. Y.

7. Jackson married Julia Anne Cox, daughter of Restors Cox; 8. Samuel; 9. Mary.

NOTE.—Samuel Smalley and wife and their six younger children, with their families, removed to Illinois.

DAVID D. SMALLEY, Esq. (son of David, Esq.) and Polly Blackford, had children:

1. Blackford, who went to Illinois, and married there.

2. Sally married Aaron Carter, son of Gabriel, of Madison.

3. Hannah married John Linberger, of Washington Valley.

4. Samuel.

5. Rachel married John Knapp.

6. Mary married, in Illinois, Mr. Wilson.

All the above six went to Illinois, with their families. And by his 2d wife, Betsey Allen, he had children:

7. Phebe married Peter P. Voorheis, son of Peter, near Paterson.

8. Nancy married Edward Sea, and live up the North river.

9. David D. married, 1st November, 1849, Caroline Titus, daughter of William.

MAHLON SMALLEY and Betsey Parrot, had children:

1. Catherine, who married William Cole, son of Freeman Cole, Esq. and had children:
   1. Mary Cole; 2. Elizabeth Cole; 3. David Cole; 4. Adeline Cole.

2. Adeline.

3. Harriet married Elias Drake, son of Nathaniel, of Scotch Plains, and had children:
   1. George Drake; 2. Augusta Drake; 4. Julia Anne.

RICHARD SMITH.

RICHARD SMITH lived on Long Island, and had children:

1. Richard Smith, Jun. who married, and removed to Herkimer county, New York.

2. Thomas married Lois Sutton, sister of Abner and Jeremy Sutton; he lived where Ephraim Stelle does, at Stonehouse Village.

3. Cornelius married Dorcas Tingley, and lived near Pluckemin

4. Elijah married Mary Sutton, sister of Lois, wife of Thomas, and lived on the west end of Long Hill, where his son Abner now lives.

5. John, who lived near Lake Champlain, New York.

6. Sally; 7. Hannah.

THOMAS SMITH, (2d son of Richard,) and Lois Sutton, had children:

1. Richard, who married Jemima Hayden.

2. Thomas is unmarried.

3. Rhoda married Jacob Van Ness, and lived near the Sterling farm.

4. Sarah married her cousin Abner Smith, son of Elijah.

CORNELIUS SMITH, (3d son of Richard,) and Dorcas Tingley, had children:

1. Ebenezer.

2. John, who married Mrs. Coon.

3. Mary married Mr. Bateman.

4. Betsey married Andrew Compton.

ELIJAH SMITH, (4th son of Richard,) and Mary Sutton, had children:

1. Richard, who married Rachel Worth, daughter of Benjamin, and went to Nova Scotia.

2. Betsey, who died at the age of 16 or 17 years.

3. Laura married Clark Winans, near Rahway.

4. Abner married his cousin Sarah Smith, daughter of Thomas.

5. Elijah, Jun. married Sarah McCoy, daughter of James McCoy, of Basking Ridge, and had a daughter Rachel, when he died. His daughter Rachel married Elias Dayton, son of John, of Basking Ridge, and had several children, when she died, and Mr. Dayton married Sarah Caroline Heath, daughter of Daniel Heath. [See Heath, page 181.]

6. Jacamiah married, 1st, Catherine Wilson, daughter of Samuel Wilson; 2d, Mary Sickle, daughter of George Sickle, of Stanhope, Sussex county.

7. Anne married George Collyer, son of John Collyer, of Basking Ridge, and had a son, James Collyer, when she died.

8. Silas, who was drowned at about 16 years of age.

RICHARD SMITH, (1st son of Elijah,) and Rachel Worth had children :
4th Gen
1. Grace, who married William Wright.
2. John went to Western New York.
3. Madison married Sarah Trane.
4. Mary, who died at 19 or 20 years.
5. Eliza married Mr. Woodard, in Western N. Y.
6. Aretta married Asa Merrel.
7. Harrison.
8. Richard.
9. Jane married her sousin, Elijah Smith, son of Abner.
10. Annitia, who went to Illinois.

LAURA SMITH, (3d child of Elijah,) and Clark Winans had children : 1. Elijah Smith Winans, who married Miss Quick, daughter of John Quick ; 2. Betsey Winans ; 3. Benjamin Winans ; 4. David Winans, ; 5. William Winans.

ABNER SMITH, (4th child of Elijah,) and Sarah Smith had children :
1. Sophia Anne.
2. John Sutton, who married Julia Bonnel, daughter of Jonathan C. Bonnel. He was a physician, and died 16th Aug. 1841, without children.
3. Elijah married his cousin, Jane Smith, daughter of Richard Smith. She died at about 20 years, without children, and he went to Illinois.
4. Sarah married Nathaniel Gillam, son of Peter, of Mendham.
5. Mary Elizabeth married Adolphus Cone, and went to Illinois ; 6. Cornelia.

JACAMIAH SMITH, (6th child of Elijah,) and Catherine Wilson had children :
1. Phinehas, who married Susan White, of Brooklyn, N. Y. and had children : 1. Walter ; 2. George ; 3. Howard ; and died 4th February, 1848.
2. Silas, who died at 18 months.
3. Samuel lives in Brooklyn, N. Y.
4. Laura Anne, born 13th January, 1820, and married James C. Blazier, born 28th April, 1810, son of Philip Blazier, and had children :
1. Catherine Blazier, born 27th June, 1842.
2. Silas Blazier, born 3d October, 1843.
3. Philip Ira Blazier, born 27th August, 1845.
4. Susan Blazier, born 16th February, 1848.
5. Martha married Asa F. Curtis, son of John Curtis, and

had children: 1. Cornelia and Caroline Curtis, twins; **3.** George Curtis. Caroline died young.

6. Richard; 7. Daniel; 8. John.

And by his 2d wife, Mary Sickle, had other children:
9. Catherine; 10. Andrew; 11. Dayton; 12. **George.** 13. Abner; 14. Sarah.

Jacamiah Smith died 8th September, 1847.

WILLIAM SPENCER, ESQ.

WILLIAM SPENCER, Esq. merchant of Chatham, was son of Henry Spencer of Elizabethtown; he was born July, 1765, and died suddenly, in his chair, 29th July, 1848.

He married Alpha Genuing, born 1768, daughter of Thomas Genuing; he was justice of the peace, and kept a store in Chatham some 50 years: they had children:

1. Polly, who married Jonathan Walker, son of Asher, of Long Hill. [*See Walker*]

2. Sally married Thomas Bond, the younger.

3. Charles married Amelia Bruen, daughter of Jonathan Bruen, of Madison.

4. Hannah married, 1st, Miller Squier, son of Henry Squier, of Long Hill; 2d, James Ba'entine.

5. Samuel married Prudence Mulford, daughter of Jeremiah, of Livingston.

6. Phebe married Stephen Young.

7. William Hervy married, 1st, Jane Clark, daughter of D. S. Clark, Esq. of New Providence; 2d, Nancy Baker, daughter of Jeremiah Baker, of Dover.

8. Eliza married Thomas Phipps.

9. James Lyman married Caroline Willcox, daughter of John Willcox 3d.

10. Julia Anne married William Ashley.

SALLY SPENCER, and Thomas Bond had children:

1. Sanford Bond, who died young.

2. Hervy Bond, who died in infancy.

3. Hervy Bond 2d, who married Margaret Beach, daughter of William Duane Beach, and had children:
1. Hellen Bond. 2. Emma Bond.

4. Sarah Bond married James Wood, of Newark, and had children: 1. Elizabeth Wood; 2. Francis Wood.

5. Charles Bond; 6. Lewis Bond; 7. Thomas Bond.

8. Elizabeth Bond.

(margin left: 3d Gen)

(margin left: 4th Gen)

CHARLES SPENCER and Amelia Bruen, had children:
1. Eliza; 2. Matilda; 3. Lewis; 4. Albert; 5. Charles.
6. Joseph Ogden.

HANNAH SPENCER and Miller Squier, had children:
1. Eliza Squior, who married Mills Day, and had children:
    1. Henry Day; 2. Helen Day; 3. Mary Day; 4. Electa
    Day.
2. Henry Squier married Catherine Garret, of Cauldwell,
and had children : 1. Albert Squier, and others.
3. Phebe Anne Squier; 2. Juliette Squier.
And by James Balentine, Hannah Spencer had children:
5. Mary Balentine ; 6. Sarah Balentine.

SAMUEL SPENCER and Prudence Mulford, had children:
1. Mary, who married David Sayre, son of Ezekiel, and had
children : 1. Fredrick Sayre, and others.
2. Mulford married, 1st, Caroline Mills ; 2d, Elizabeth Day.
3. William ; 4. Julia Anne ; 5. Harriet ; 6. George.

PHEBE SPENCER and Stephen Young, had children :
1. Mary Young ; 2. William Young; 3. Lyman Young;
4. Caroline Young.

WILLIAM HERVY SPENCER and Jane Clark, had
children :
1. William Nelson ; 2. John Morris.
And by his 2d, wife Nancy Baker, had children:
3. Alpha Jane; 4. Margaret; 5. Mary ; 6. Phebe.

ELIZA SPENCER and Thomas Phipps, had children :
1. Eliza Phipps; 2. William Phipps ; 3. Thomas Phipps ;
4. Emma Phipps.

JAMES L. SPENCER and Caroline Willcox, had children:
1. Elizabeth Caroline, who married Elias Allen, son of
David Allen, had children : 1. Cornelia Allen, and others.
2. John Lyman, who married, 13th January, 1852, Mary
Allen, daughter of David.
3. Emily Arno ; 4. Lewis Craig ; 5. William Francis.
6. Henry Newton ; 7. Georgiana and Josephine, twins.

JULIA ANNE SPENCER and William Ashley, had
children :
1. George Ashley; 2. John Hervy Ashley ; 3. William
Ashley ; 4. Amelia Ashley ; 5. Lyman Ashley.

BENJAMIN SPINNING.

BENJAMIN SPINNING was probably one of the descendants of Humphrey Spinning, who was among the first
of the Elizabethtown Associates.   He married Charity ——,
and came up from Elizabethtown and lived where his son
John Spinning now lives. He died 11th March, 1814, aged
46 years. His widow died 30th November, 1823, aged 56
years. They had children :
1. Benjamin, Jun. who married Polly Simpson, daughter of
Alexander, and went to Dayton Ohio, and had children ;
    1. Anne, who married Caleb Burchard, live in Spring-
    field, Illinois, and had children : 1. Cornelia Burchard ;
    2. Elizabeth Burchard ; 3. Florence Burchard.
    2. Eliza Jane married Nathan Allen, of Dayton, and
    had children : 1. George William Allen; 2. Almira
    Allen.
    3. Alexander Simpson married Miss Piew ; live in Green
    county, Ohio.
    4. De Witt Clintonm arried Hannah Wright, daughter of
    John.
2. Rebecca married, 14th Feb. 1822, Thomas Martin, Jun.
son of Thomas. [See *Martin.*]
3. Hannah married Jonathan D. Simpson, son of Isaac, and
died 13th December, 1838, aged 38 years, without children.
4. John, born 19th August 1793, and married Phebe Winters, of Fishkill, New York, and had children :
    1. Benjamin, who married, 27th Feb. 1850, Sarah Anne
    Meeker, daughter of Isaac, son of Caleb.
    2. Charles ; 3. Mary ; 4. Jane ; 5. Julia ; 6. John.
5. Solomon married Margaret Winters, sister of John's
wife, and had children :
    1. George ; 2. Catherine ; 3. John; 4. Dayton.
6. Prudence married, 20th Feb. 1819, Solomon Dean, son
of John, and had children :
    1. Benjamin S. Dean, who married Phebe Badgley,
    daughter of Squier ; 2. John Dean ; 3. Sylvester Dean ;
    4. Mary Cohoon Dean, who died young·

BENJAMIN SQUIER.

BENJAMIN SQUIER lived in .Westfield, and had sons :
1. Ellis, who married, 23d January, 1769, Rebecca, daughter of Amos Potter 1st. [See *Potter.*]
2. Meeker, who married Rachel, daughter of Stephen Meeker, of Essex county, New Jersey.
3. William, who married Sarah Conklin.

ELLIS SQUIER, son of Benjamin Squier, of Westfield, lived in New Providence, where the Franklin school-house now stands. He and Rebecca Potter had children :
1. Mary, who married Jeremiah H. Osborn, son of Jonathan H. Osborn, [*see Osborn,*] she died without children, and he married 2d, Polly Clark, daughter of Stephanus, and had children :
   1. Squier Osborn who married Anne Bond, daughter of Nathaniel
   2. Louisa Osborn, who married Joseph Bond, son of Nathaniel.
   3. Sarah Osborn, who married Peter Hendrickson, and had a daughter, Mariah, who married George Potts.
   4. Moses Osborn, who did not marry.
2. Rhoda was baptized, 8th August, 1773, and died young.
3. Johannah married, 13th March, 1794, Samuel Baldwin, son of Gabriel. [See *Baldwin.*]
4. David, born 1777, who married, November, 1805, in Ohio, Sally Gard, born 11th Feb. 1778, daughter of Daniel, and sister of the Rev. Stephen Gard, and had three daughters ; when he died, and his widow Sally married Maxwell Potter, son of Russel Potter, and had a daughter Sarah Anne Potter.
5. Timothy married in Ohio, 1st, a widow Briggs ; 2d, Rebecca Tucker, daughter of John, of Springdale. (not of Henry Tucker's family,) and had three daughters.
6. Mary 2d, baptized 19th Feb. ҭ794, and married in Ohio, David Sergeant, son of Sampson Sergeant. By his 1st wife had three sons :
   1. Ellis Sergeant ; 2. Sampson Sergeant ; 3. Timothy Sergeant. They lived and both died at Leport, Ind.
Ellis Squier and family, and Jeremiah H. Osborn, removed to Ohio, about the year 1798, and lived near the Blue Ball between the Miamis.

JOHANNAH SQUIER, (daughter of Ellis,) and Samuel Baldwin, had children :

1. Squier Baldwin, who married Sally Crowel, daughter of Samuel, of Dayton, whose wife was Elizabeth Gard.

2. Amos Baldwin, married Miss Keziah Tucker, daughter of John, and sister of Timothy Squier's second wife.

3. Sarah married Uriah Sawyer, from New England.

DAVID SQUIER, (son of Ellis,) and Sally Gard, had children:

1. Phebe, who married Benjamin Potter, son of Maxwell, son of Russel Potter. [*See Russel Potter.*]

2. Eliza married Philip Landis, son of Philip, and had children:

1. Elizabeth R. Landis ; 2. Mary G. Landis ; 3. Sarah G. Landis ; 4. John Leland Landis ; 5. Charles Landis ; 6. David Landis ; 7. Phebe Anne Landis ; 8. Juliette Landis ; 9. Harriet Landis ; 10. Susannah Landis.

3. Juliette married Sutton Van Pelt, and had children:

1. Alexander Van Pelt ; 2. David Squier Van Pelt ; 3. Camilla Van Pelt. Mr. David Squier died in 1814, aged 38 years, and his widow Sally married Maxwell Potter, son of Russel Potter. [*See Russel Potter.*]

TIMOTHY SQUIER, (5th child of Ellis,) and Rebecca Tucker, had children:

1. Harriet Anne, who married David Benedict Groat, live in the state of New-York.

2. Samantha, who married William Stone, had two children, and he died.

3. Mary married Mr. Winters, of Logansport, Indiana.

MEEKER SQUIER, (son of Benjamin,) and Rachel Meeker lived near the Blue Ball, Warren county, Ohio, and had children:

1. Rebecca, who married, 1st, Thomas Morton, and had children: 1. Rachel Morton ; 2. Samuel Morton ; 3. Meeker Morton. Rebecca married, 2d, Samuel Sergeant, (as his 2d wife,) and had other children: 4. Ivy Sergeant ; 5. Eliza Sergeant ; 6. Thomas Sergeant ; 7. Rebecca Sergeant ; 8. Phebe Anne Sergeant.

2. Anna, who married David Johnson, and had children : 1. Ithaman Johnson ; 2. Phebe Johnson ; 3. Rachel Johnson ; 4. John Johnson.

3. William, who married Puah Osborn, daughter of Jonathan H. Osborn. [*See Osborn.*]

4. John, who married Mary Potter, daughter of Russel, son of Levi. [*see Russel Potter,*] and had children : 1. Levi ; 2.

Joanna; 3. Russel; 4. Rachel; 5. Rhoda Anne; 6. Mary
Jane; 7. Ezekiel; 8. Ivy; 9. Adeline.

5. Ezekiel, who is not married.

6. Phebe, who married John Squier, son of Thomas, of
New Jersey.

7. Stephen, who married Sarah Bond, daughter of Caleb,
and had children: 1. Levi; 2. Caleb; 3. Rachel; 4. Charlotte.

WILLIAM SQUIER, (3d child of Meeker Squier,) and
Puah Osborn had children:

1. Jeremiah, who married Caroline Bond, a daughter of
Caleb, and had children: 1. Charlotte; 2. Emmazetta; 3.
Edward.

2. Ezekiel, who married 1st, Anne Conover, who had no
children; 2d, Mary Martin, in 1851, daughter of Samuel and
Anna Martin.

3. Deborah, who married David Eagle, and had a son,
William Eagle.

4. Meeker, who married —— ——.

WILLIAM SQUIER, (son of Benjamin,) and Sarah Conklin lived near the Blue Ball, Ohio, and had children:

1. Caleb, who married Elizabeth Wells; 2. Abraham, who
married Polly Ball, daughter of Ezekiel, of Middletown. [See
Ball.]; 3. David; 4. Ellis; 5. William; 6. Mary, who married John Shuckman; 7. Abigail, who married Jeremiah Mas-
terson; 8. Sarah married Henry Row; 9. Daniel married
Miss —— Case; 10 Rebecca.

THOMAS SQUIER.

THOMAS SQUIER lived where William Mulford, now lives, in Morris connty. He married, 1st, Jemima Camp, daughter of Aaron Camp, Sen , and had children :
1. Sarah, who married Jacob Tingley, and lived in Washington Valley.
2. Aaron married Nancy Vance, daughter of Kennedy Vance, of Long Hill.
3. Stephen married Hannah Littell, daughter of Samuel, of Rockaway, Morris county.
4. Moses married, 29th April, 1790, Anna Rutan, daughter of Abraham, and went to Western Pennsylvania.
5. Ludlow married Anna Runyon, daughter of Elias, of Long Hill. He lived at Plainfield, By a second wife, Thomas Squier had a daughter.
6. Anna, who married David Coriell, son of Elias, of Long Hill. [See Coriell.]

SARAH SQUIER and Jacob Tingley had children :
1. Jemima Tingley, who married Elias Cole, son of Master William Cole. [See Cole.]
2. Anna Tingley married William D. Stewart, son of David. [See Stewart.]
3. Osee Tingley married Ralph Shotwell, son of Jacob. [See Shotwell.]
4. Squier Tingley married Ruth Smalley, daughter of Jacob, and had children :
    1. Ira Tingley, who married Mary Coulter, daughter of Leffert, and lives at Martinville.
    2. Sarah Tingley married Nathaniel Drake, son of Noah. [See Drake.]
    3. Jacob Smalley Tingley is a carriage maker of Plainfield.
    4. Isaac S. Tingley.
    5. Tabitha Tingley married Benjamin Fisher, son of Jerry Fisher, and removed to Jefferson county, N. Y.
5. George Hacket Tingley, who lives in New York.

AARON SQUIER and Nancy Vance had children :
1. Betsey, who married Noah Frazee, son of Maxwell. [See Frazee.]
2. Samuel, who is not married. He lives and owns the farm on which his father and grand-father Vance lived.
3. John married Mary Meeker, daughter of Joseph Ogden Meeker, of Westfield, and had children :

1. Nancy. who married Joseph Ross. son of John Ross, of Westfield.
2. Mary married Isaac H. Potter. son of Recompense, of Plainfield. and died June, 1850, and left 3 children.
3. Ogden, who died at 16 years.
4. Agnes who died at 9 months.

4. Thomas married Catherine Tate, of New York, and had children : 1. John ; 2 Catherine, and then removed to Geneva, New York.

5 Horatio married Elizabeth Crocker. of New York, and had children : 1. Mary : 2. Caroline ; 3. Horatio ; 4. Samuel.

Aaron Squier died 9th Aug. 1818, aged 57 years. His wife died 15th June, 1801, aged 30 years. His son John d.ed 2d April, 1834, aged 39 years.

STEPHEN SQUIER and Hannah Littell lived on Staten Island, N. Y.. and had children :

1. William, who married Sally Merrel, daughter of John Merrel, and had children :
    1. Fanny, who is unmarried.
    2. John, who was drowned, at 17 or 18 years of age.
    3. Stephen married Barbara Van Name, daughter of Simon.
    4. Caty married —— ——. 5. Eliza married —— ——.
2. Sally married Samuel Sharp, son of William, and had children :
    1. Charles Snowden Sharp.
    2. Elizabeth Sharp, who married, 1st, Mr. Chandler ; 2d Mr. Sayre.
    3. William Sharp.
    4. Priscilla Sharp. Mr. Sharp removed to Western New York.
3. Thomas married Charlotte Parsons, daughter of Jonathan. He is a tailor ; lives in Madison, and had children :
    1. Anna ; 2. Mary Elizabeth married Effingham Townley, son of Enos B. [see *Townley ;*] 3. Israel Rickey ; 4. Hannah Mariah ; 5. Harriet ; 6. Helen Coriell ; 7. Horace Sheldon ; 8. Emily Parsons, who died at 17 months old.
4. Betsey married Abel Van Camp, and had children :
    1. Hannah Mariah Van Camp, who married William Wilson, and had children : 1. Julia Helen Wilson, and others.
    2. Sally Anne Van Camp married Mr. Thompson, and had children :
        1. Mary Thompson : 2. Elizabeth Thompon ; 3. William Thompson ; 4 Charlotte Thompson.
    3. Charlotte Van Camp married James Coburn.
    4. Helen Rebecca Van Camp married Drake Benjamin.
    5. Gilbert Van Camp ; 6. Eliza Jane Van Camp.
    7. Ludlow Squier Van Camp.

5. Samuel married Anne Merrel, daughter of Frederick, and had children :

    1. Anne Eliza, who married Mr. Eddy.

    2. John, who was drowned at about 19 years.

    3. Mercereau, who died at about 20 years.

    4. Sarah ; 5. Mary Louisa ; 6. George.

LUDLOW SQUIER, (son of Thomas,) and Anna Runyon, had children :

    1. Abby, who married Richard Coriell, son of Peter. [See *Coriell.*]

    2 Clark married Thirza Vail. daughter of Alexander Vail. son of Daniel, and had children : 1. Elizabeth ; 2. William ; 3. Joseph.

        4. Kerenhappuck ; 5. Alexander.

    3. Israel married Martha Kirkpatrick, daughter of Alexander, and had children :

        1. Harrison ; 2 Agnes ; 3. Caroline ; 4. John ; 5. Mary.

        6. Elizabeth ; 7. Ludlow. and then removed to Illirois.

    4. Deborah married William Darby, son of John, of Scotch Plains.

    5. Jane married Elias Kirpatrick, Esq. son of John. [See *Kirkpatrick.*]

    6. Ludlow married Mary Wright, daughter of Savage Wright.

OLIVER STELLE.

OLIVER STELLE was son of Isaac Stelle, of Piscataway, Middlesex county. He was born 1st August 1756, and married 21st January, 1778, Mary Ryno, and removed to Bernard's Township, Somerset county, in April, 1794. They had children:

1. Christiana, who is unmarried.
2. Ephraim, who married Anna Manning, daughter of Isaac.
3. Isaac married Rachel Clawson, daughter of Correlius.
4. Harriet married Peter Randolph, son of Gilbert. [See *Randolph*]
5. Ruth married John Worth ; have no children.
6. Sarah married Isaac Randolph, brother of Peter. [See *Randolph*]
7. John married Anne Kirkpatrick, daughter of Alexander; he went on a visit to his son Jacob, in Illinois, and died there 24th April, 1850, with three days illness.
8. Anne who died in youth.
9. Mary, who died a young woman.
10. Clarkson married Lucinda Terril, daughter of Thomas, Esq. He died 13th July, 1850, suddenly without sickness.
11. Rachel, who died a young woman.

EPHRAIM STELLE and Anna Manning, had children :
1. Elizabeth, who married Drake Terril, son of Thomas, Esq. [See *Terril*]
2. Sally married, 23th December, 1819, William Coddington, Esq of Bound Brook.
3. Margaret married Charles Smalley, son of Andrew, Esq lives on Mine Brook, and had children :
    1. Anne Smalley ; 2. Theodore Smalley ; 3. Manning Smalley.
    4. Daniel Smalley, who died young.
4 Isaac, who died at 4 years old : 5 Mary.
6. Jane married David Tingley, son of Ebenezer, and lives in Newark ; 7. Oliver.

ISAAC STELLE and Rachel Clawson, had children :
1. Mary, who married Madison Terril, son of Thomas, Esq. [See *Terril*] 2 Clarissy.

JOHN STELLE and Anne Kirkpatrick, had children :
1. Jeptha, who married Sarah Mandell, and lives in Brooklyn, New York.
2. Jacob married Jane Compton, daughter of Moore Compton, and went to Illinois.
3. Freeman married Martha Runyon, daughter of David R.
4. Lewis, who died young ; 5. Provy.

CLARKSON STELLE and Lucinda Terrel, had children :
1. Rachel, who married Isaac Runyon, son of David R.
2. Mary Anne; 3. Mercy; 4. Lewis; 5. Thomas Terril.
6. Adeline.

JONATHAN STEVENS.

JONATHAN STEVENS lived near where Samuel Squier now lives; he had children:

1. John. who married Phebe Potter, daughter of Daniel, and sister of Amos Potter, Esq.
2. Sarah married Caleb Melford, son of Job. [See *Job Mulford.*]
3. Betsey married John Shipman, son of Jabesh. [See *Shipman.*]
4. Jane, who died an old woman, unmarried.
5. Christopher married Rachel Dunham, daughter of John Dunham, Jun.
6. Jonathan married, 6th November, 1788, Keziah Jennings, daughter of Jacob, and had no children.
7. James married Rhoda Garthwaite, of Connecticut Farms. She died 28th July, 1850, at Union Village, over 80 years of age.
8. William married Phebe Roff, daughter of Nathaniel Roff, and went to Ohio.
9. Jacob married Betsey Miller, daughter of Ephraim Miller. [See *Miller.*]
10. Frazee married Charlotte Headley, of Connecticut Farms.

JOHN STEVENS, (1st son of Jonathan,) and Phebe Potter had children:

1. Philemon, who died young.
2. Israel, who married 3d December, 1816, Abby Littell, daughter of Ebenezer; lived in New York, and had children:
   1. Squier, who married Margaret Jones, of New York.
   2. John married Caroline Conkrite, of New York.
   3 William married Mary Woolsey.
   4. Harriet, who died young.

His wife Abby then died, and he married Abigail, the widow of Samuel C Parsons, and daughter of William Parrot, Jun. and had a daughter, 5. Angeline.

3. Gershom Manning, who died a young man.
4. Sarah, who died a young woman.
5. Amos, who married, 22d January, 1820, Rachel Totten, daughter of David, and had children: 1. Miller; 2. Elizabeth.

CHRISTOPHER STEVENS, (5th child of Jonathan,) and Rachel Dunham had children:

1. Mulford Cory, who married Mary Willet, daughter of Thomas, and had children: 1. Aura Bennet; 2. Sarah; 3. Eugene; 4 Rachel; 5. Gennet; 6. Linus; 7. Thomas, and then removed to Ohio.
2. Linus High married Ruth Crane, daughter of Joseph, son of Joseph, and had children: 1. Hannah Jane; 2. Phebe Anne; 3. Joseph Crane, and then removed to Bloomfield.

JAMES STEVENS, (7th child of Jonathan,) and Rhoda Garthwaite had children:

1. Jonathan, who married Miss Baldwin, of Bloomfield, and live in Newark.
2. Phebe is unmarried; lives in Plainfield.
3. Daniel Meeker went to Baltimore, and married there.
4. Sarah lives in New York.
5. William married, 22d Sept. 1823, Susan Moore, daughter of Isaac, and had children: 1. Mary Jane; 2. Phebe Anne; 3. Sarah Louisa; 4. Elizabeth; 5. Almira; 6 Ellen; 7. William; 8. Harriet; 9. Moses; 10. Susan. [*See Moore.*]
6. Eliza lives in New York.
7. James Hervy married ———, and lives in New York.
8. Jane married David N. Ruckman, son of Nathan, and had a son, James Ruckman, and then died.

JACOB STEVENS, (9th child of Jonathan,) and Betsey Miller, had children:

1. Miller, who married Asenath Mayhew, daughter of Joseph, near Cincinnati.
2. Jonathan married Harriet Day, in Delhi, near Cincinnati.
3. William married ———, and went to Indiana.
4. Hannah married Alexander Stewart; lives in Cincinnati.
5. Jacob.
6. Eliphalet married Margaret Day, sister of Jonathan's wife.

JOSEPH STEWART.,

JOSEPH STEWART married Mary, the widow of Samuel Doty ; lived in Washington Valley, and had children :
1 Enoch.
2. Rachel, who married Isaac Smalley, son of John. [*See Smalley.*]
3. David married Rachel Doty, daughter of the above named Samuel Doty. and sister of Henry Doty.
4. Mary married John Drake, son of Jeremiah.

DAVID STEWART and Rachel Doty had children :
1. Samuel. who died at about 24 years, unmarried.
2. Mary married Ezekiel Decamp, son of Ezekiel, and went to the Lakes.
3 Isaac married Sally Parker, daughter of Gershom.
4. Phebe married Abner Rino, son of John. of Piscataway.
5. Sarah married Lewis Willet. son of Thomas.
6, William Doty, born 1st Oct. 1794, and married Anne Tingley, daughter of Jacob. She died 1st March, 1848.
7. David, Jun., went to Georgia ; married Sophia Rise, and died there.
8. Rachel married Michael O'Conner ; she soon died.
9. Rhoda married the same Michael O'Conner
10. Margaret married Aaron Bennet, son of Aaron, of Long Island.
11. Anne married Jacob Wambold, son of Jacob, of Elizabethtown.
12. Eliza married Joel Pangborn, son of Richard, of Plainfield.

WILLIAM D. STEWART and Anne Tingley had children :
1. Abel, who married Abby Totten, daughter of John, son of David.
2. Thirza Shotwell married John Q. Drake. son of Noah.
3. Andrew Jackson married Phebe Frazee, daughter of Gershom.
4. Esther married Lias Wilson, son of James.
5. Anne married John Doty, son of Henry.
6. George married Elizabeth Ogden, an English girl.
7. William.
8. Joseph Warren.

JOHN STITES.

JOHN STITES was born in England, in the year A. D. 1595. Tradition says that he emigrated from London to New England in the time of Oliver Cromwell. He finally settled on Long Island, and died there in 1717, aged 122 years.

RICHARD STITES, son of John, was born 1640. He lived at Hempstead, L. I. and died 1702, aged 62 years.

WILLIAM STITES, son of Richard, was born at Hempstead, in 1676. He removed to Springfield, N. J. and died there in 1727, aged 51 years. William Stites had children :

1. John, born 1706 at Hempstead ; died at Springfield, 1782.
2. Hezekiah, born 1708,   "   "   "   "   1728.
3. Richard, born 1715,   "   "   "   "   1727.
4. Rebecca, born 1717, and married Jacob Carle. [See *Carle*.
5. William, Jun. died at Mount Bethel, aged 91 years.
6. Elijah, born 1721, and died at Scotch Plains, 1765.
7. Benjamin married Betsey Willcox, daughter of Peter Willcox, Jun. and lived and died at Scotch Plains.

JOHN STITES, eldest son of William, was an Alderman of the borough of Elizabeth, lived near Scudder's Mills, on Rahway River. He married Miss Rushmore, of Long Island, a sister of the wife of Thomas Thompson, Sen. [See *Thompson.*] They had children :

1. Hezekiah, who became a physician, and settled at Cranbury, Middlesex county.
2. Sarah. His wife then died, and he married Miss Hampton, and had other children :
3. A daughter, who married the Rev. Mr. Gano, of New York.
4. A daughter, who married the Rev. Mr. Manning, and went to Rhode Island.
5. Abigail married Isaac Woodruff, Esq. of Elizabethtown.
6. John married. in New York, returned to Elizabethtown, and after a time went to the West.
7. Richard married Sarah Thompson, daughter of the above named Thomas Thompson, [*see Thompson*,] and had children.
    1. Abby, who married John, son of Andrew Miller, and Sarah Ross, she is the mother of Cornelia, the wife of Gideon Ross, Esq. and lives with him.
    2. Richard, born 1777, and died in Savannah, Georgia, in 1813 leaving a son, Richard W. Stites, now, (1850,) living in Morristown.

WILLIAM STITES, Jun. (5th child of William,) lived at Mount Bethel, Somerset county ; he married Miss Searing, and had children :

1. John ; 2. William 3d.

3. Isaac married Anna Butler, daughter of Amos, and died 7th August, 1830, aged 76 years.

William Stites. Jun. married, 2d, Sarah, widow of Amos Butler, by whom he had no children.

ISAAC STITES, (son of William, Jun.) and Anna But'er, had children :

    1. Elijah, who married Phebe Bird, daughter of George, and had children :
        1. Searing ; 2. Ellis ; 3. Rosannah ; 4. Elijah : 5. Hezekiah ; 6. Isaac.

    2. Samuel married Patty Martin, daughter of Ephraim Martin ; they removed to Illinois, and had 14 children.

    3. John married Ruth Moore, daughter of Joseph, and had children :
        1. Jacob ; 2. Samuel ; 3. Phebe ; 4. John ; 5. Joseph ; 6. Peter ; 7. Susan ; 8. Eliza : 9. William ; 10. Benjamin ; 11. Harriet.

    4. Sarah married John Jennings, son of Benjamin.

    5. William married, 1st, Mary Roff, daughter of Ebenezer, and had children :
        1. Mahala, who married David Simmons lives in Elizabethtown
        2. Mary Anne married William Bonnel, of Elizabethtown.
        3. Israel, who went to Michigan.
        4 Amy, who married Charles Whitmore.
        5. Martha Jane married —— ——.
        He married, 2d, the widow Lydia Garrison, and had a son Joel, and died in New Providence.

    6. Amos, who married Agnes Kelly, daughter of Samuel, and had children :
        1. Samuel Kelly ; 2. Anna ; 3. Rachel ; 4. Debby ; 5. William Harrison ; 6. Amos Butler ; 7. Isaac A.

ELIJAH STITES, (son of William Stites, Sen.) lived at Scotch Plains He married —— ——, and had children :

    1. Rebecca, who married Richard Scudder. [*See Scudder.*]
    2. Elijah.
    3 Nancy, who married David Ross.
    4. Prudence married John R no. of Piscataway.
    5. Chloe married Elias Miller, of Westfield.
    6. Hannah married Peter Kino, brother of John.
    7 Abner married, 18th Feb. 1786, Huldah Crane, daughter of Isaac, of New Providence.

ABNER STITES lived in New Providence, was a Capt. of the Militia, and an elder in the Presbyterian church. He died 29th August, 1831, his wife died 24th June 1835, aged 71 years. He and Huldah Crane had children:

1. Elijah is a merchant in Springfield. He married Jane Wade, daughter of Jonas Wade, Esq. of Springfield, and has no living children.

2. William is a paper manufacturer of Springfield; was a Justice of the Peace, and Judge of the court; has been several times a member of the legislature. He married Hannah B. Smith, daughter of Capt. John Smith; had an only daughter, Jane Robison, who married Dr. John C. Elmer, of Mendham, son of Dr. Horace Elmer.

3 Huldah Grant married John Thompson, son of Jabez. [*See Thompson.*]

4. John M. Stites is a tanner and currier in New Providence. He is an elder in the presbyterian church. He married his cousin Jane Bonnel, daughter of Nathaniel 3d. He was born 2d Sept 1797, she was born 3d July, 1795; they had children:

1. William Crane, born 16th Nov. 1829.
2. Huldah, born 24th July, 1833.

5. Chloe married Ezra Fairchild, of Mendham. He is principal of a classical school on Long Island; they had children: 1. Emily Fairchild.
   2. Elias Fairchild, who married, 16th March, 1850, Agnes Anderson, daughter of Robert Anderson, Esq. of Plainfield, she died about 9 months thereafter.

6. Abner, born 24th Sep. 1803, is a merchant in Springfield; married Charlotte Bonnel, born 27th Aug. 1814, daughter of Sylvanus, son of John Bonnel, and have children: 1. Edward Morris born 12th October, 1847; 2. Charlotte Morrell, born March, 1850.

7. Apollos married Mary Bryant, daughter of Simeon Bryant, of Springfield; lives in New York, and has two children, Theodore and Matilda.

BENJAMIN STITES, (son of William Stites, Sen.) and Betsey Willcox, had children:

1. Henry, who died at Redstone, on his way to Cincinnati.
2. Benjamin, Jun married, and went to Cincinnati.
3. Elijah went to Cincinnati.
4. Hezekiah went also to Cincinnati.
5. Isaiah married Mary Foster, daughter of Jacob Foster, of Lyons Farms.

NOTE—The wife of Benjamin Stites, Jun. was said to be the first white woman that ever landed at Cincinnati.

410

ISAIAH STITES, (son of Benjamin,) and Mary Foster lived at Scotch Plains, and had children:

1 Jacob Foster, who married Sarah Frazee, daughter of Henry, and sister of Maxwell.

2. Henry married Mary Clark. of Westfield.

3. Benjamin married Eliza Anne Drake, daughter of Nathaniel Drake, of Scotch Plains; he is a grocer in Newark.

JACOB F. STITES, (son of Isaiah,) and Sarah Frazee, had children:

1. Isaiah, who married, 1st, Miss Drake; 2d, Sarah ——, and has no children.

2. Mary, who died at 14 or 15 years.

3. Charlotte married Philemon Dunn, and had a son, Albert Dunn; 4. Henry.

HENRY STITES, (son of Isaiah,) and Mary Clark, had children:

1. Eliza, who married Talmadge Ross, son of John, son of Talmadge.

2. John, who married and lives in New York.

3 Anne married Gershom Littell, son of Gershom.

4. Aaron married and lives in New York.

BENJAMIN STITES, (son of Isaiah,) and Eliza Anne Drake, had children:

1 Huldah, who married James Cleaver, son of William H. Cleaver; 2. Julia; 3. Mary; 4. Caroline; 5. Benjamin.

EPHRAIM SUTTON.

EPHRIAM SUTTON lived on Sutton's Hill, (2d mountain,) west of William Allen's, and married, and had children:

1. Jesse.

2. William, who married Lavina, a Dutch girl. had children:

1. James; 2. Enoch, who married Betsey Clark, daughter of Elias. [See *Clark.*]

3. Henry; 4. Mary, who married John Sibbens.

5. David married Sally Parker, daughter of Judah; 6. William Jun. 7. Catherine; 8. Sally; 9. John.

The family all removed to Ohio together.

JACOB SWAIN.

JACOB SWAIN lived on Wolf Hill, near Union Village: his wife was Hannah ——; they had children:

1. Sarah, who married Elias Clark, Jun. son of Elias.

2. Benjamin, who married Caty Long, daughter of John, and had children:

1. Hannah married William McDonald, of Monmouth, and had children: 1. Joseph McDonald; 2. William McDonald.

3. Thompson McDonald; 4. Benjamin McDonald.

5. Elizabeth McDonald; the others died young.

2. John, who married at Rahway, and went to the Lakes.
3. Polly married Abraham Simonson, and had children :
    1 William Simonson ; 2. Joseph Simonson, and others
    who died young. She married 2d, Ephraim Howard,
    and lives at Scotch Plains
4. Eliza married James Curtis, son of John. [See *Asa Frazee*]
5. Joaa married an only daughter of Israel Ward, son of
Joshua ; he left her, and went south, and she married
George W. Ogden, son of Richard.
6 Joel, who married a daughter of Charles Rino.
7. William married in Pennsylvania.

THOMAS TERRIL.

THOMAS TERRIL came up from Rahway, and settled on
Stony Hill, about one mile east of Mount Bethel Church ; he married Mary Dunn, daughter of Philemon Dunn, of Piscataway ; he
was a justice of the peace, and had children :
    1. Lewis, who married Aula Van Lew, of New York, and lived,
and died there, without children
    2. Squier married Rebecca Kirkpatrick, daughter of Alexander ;
he was justice of the peace, and judge of the court of Somerset
county.
    3. Gertrude, who died at 42 years, unmarried.
    4. Lucinda married Clarkson Stelle, son of Oliver. [See *Stelle.*]
    5. Charity married Robert F. Kirkpatrick, son of Alexander,
[See *Kirkpatrick*]
    6. Harriet married David Coon, son of Capt. Israel Coon ; she
died, and left three chidren: 1. George Coon ; 2. Walter Coon ;
3. Firman Coon.
    7. John, who died at about 13 years.
    8 Drake married Elizabeth Stelle, daughter of Ephraim, son of
Oliver. He died 1842. aged 37 years.
    9. Madison married Mary Stelle, daughter of Isaac, son of Oliver.

SQUIER TERRIL, Esq. and Rebecca Kirkpatrick had children :
    1. Aula, who married Budgley Gottra. son of James Gottra, Esq.
    2 Mary married Silas Smalley. son of Andrew Smalley, Esq.
    3. Jane married John Ross, son of John of Bound Brook.
    4. Anne ; 5. Thomas ; 6. Margaret ; 7. Edward ; 8. Walter.
    9. George.

DRAKE TERRIL and Elizabeth Stelle, had children :
1. Harriet ; 2. Mary Anne ; 3. Ephraim ; 4. Sarah Jane.
5. Elizabeth ; 6. Margaret.

MADISON TERRIL and Mary Stelle had children :
1. Lewis ; 2. Clarissa, who died at 9 years ; 3. Rachel.
4. Jason ; 5. Isaac ; 6. George.

WILLIAM THOMAS.

WILLIAM THOMAS lived on Stony Hill, was a half bushel maker; he had children :

1. Derrick, who married Keziah Smalley, daughter of James. [See *Smalley.*]

2. Keziah married Benjamin Smalley, son of James [See *Smalley.*]

3. Esther married Stephen Crane, son of Joseph. [See *Joseph Crane*]

4 Peggy.

5. Levi married Tabitha Hand, 18th child of Hezekiah Hand, and went to western New York.

THOMAS THOMAS.

THOMAS THOMAS was born 1777, in a house which stood on the line between Wales and England After his father's death, a nobleman of London conceived a favorable opinion of him, took him under his care, educated and sent him to Oxford college, where he graduated ; he then studied theology, was licensed, and ordained to the gospel ministry ; he married Elizabeth Robison, daughter of Thomas Robison of London, and emigrated to America in 1818 ; went to Cincinnati, and preached in the first church there, some time.   He thence removed to Paddy's Run, in Butler county; thence to Venice, in the same county, and was installed over the presbyterian church there ; and died 9th October, 1831 ; they had children :

1. Mary, who married Nelson Gelpin, from Connecticut.

2. Elizabeth, who died in infancy.

3. Thomas Ebenezer, who graduated at Miami University, Oxford, Ohio, studied theology, was licensed, preached at Harrison, below Cincinnati, and removed from thence to Hamilton, and was pastor of the presbyterian church there, till he was appointed, in 1849, president of Hanover college, Jefferson county, Indiana. He married Lydia Fisher, daughter of Nathaniel Fisher, of Boston.

4. Elizabeth married Charles Burrows, son of Eden, of Franklin, Ohio, formerly of Elizabethtown, in N. J.

5. Alfred is a lawyer, of Hamilton, Ohio ; he married Mary Eliza Fisher, sister of Thomas E 's wife.

6. Sarah Robison is unmarried.

7. Anne married David Linton, son of David, a quaker.

8. John, born 20th July, 1822, *is* a lawyer of Hamilton, Ohio: he married 23d May, 1850, Huldah R. Littell, daughter of John Littell, Esq. of Essex county, N. J.

MARY THOMAS, and Nelson Gelpin had children:

1. Sarah Gelpin married, 15th May, 1850, Rev. Mr. Crow, pastor of the church at South Hanover, Jefferson county, Indiana.

2. Thomas Gelpin; 3. Huldah Gelpin: 4. Alfred Gelpin.
5. John Gelpin: 6. Sarah Robison Gelpin
7. Mary Spencer Gelpin; 8. David Gelpin.

REV. THOMAS E. THOMAS and Lydia Fisher had
children :
1. Ebenezer; 2. Mary May; 3. Elizabeth ; 4. Alfred.
5. John.

ELIZABETH THOMAS and Charles Burrows had children :
1. Richard Burrows; 2. Mary Burrows.
3. Sarah Burrows, who died in infancy.
4. Thomas Burrows; 5. Jane Burrows.

ALFRED THOMAS and Mary Eliza Fisher had children :
1. Eliza Lillie ; 2. Anne.

ANNE THOMAS and David Linton had children :
1. Anna Linton; 2. —— ——; 3. —— ——.

JOHN THOMAS and Huldah R. Littell, had children :
1. Clara Linton, and others.

HUR THOMPSON.

Tradition in the Thompson family says that three brothers, Moses. Aaron. and Hur Thompson, emigrated from Scotland to America: that one of them, (probably Moses,) settled in Pennsylvania; one in Connecticut, and that Hur settled in Elizabethtown.

Moses, Thomas and Hur Thompson were among the first settlers of Elizabethtown and their names are in the first list of the "Elizabethtown Associates," respecting their tract of land, of some 500,000 acres, purchased of the Indians, as recorded in the "Old Book of Records" in Elizabethtown.

In the year 1699, there was a town meeting held in Elizabethtown. of all the Associates then living, and ' those holding under them, or some of them." and among these is the name of John Thompson, who is the only Thompson therein named.

And in the same "Old Book" John Thompson and Samuel Thompson are said to be sons of Hur Thompson. It may reasonably be inferred then that Hur Thompson was the father of John Thompson, who was probably the father of Thomas Thompson. who was born 25th Jan 1712, and died 2d Nov. 1803, aged 91 years, 9 months and 8 days. He survived his 2d wife just one week. Tradition also says that Thomas had a brother, John Thompson.

JOHN THOMPSON. (son of Hur Thompson,) had seven children. He lived a short distance east of the residence of the late General William Crane. about two miles west of Elizabethtown. The seven children were :

1. Thomas, who married 1st. Hannah Rushmore, of Hempstead, Long Island ; 2d, Rachel Shotwell, widow of Benjamin, of Piscataway.

2. Moses, who settled near the Church, in Connecticut Farms, and died there.

3. Aaron, who settled on Long Hill, in Morris county, and died in the time of the French war.

4. Hannah, who married Thomas Baker, and with him removed to Turkey, now New Providence, Essex county. [*See Baker.*]

5. Sarah married 1st, Mr. Van Sickle, of Long Hill, and had a daughter, Elizabeth, who married Jacob Britton, son of William. [*See Britton.*] Sarah married 2d, Mr. Rutan. who had a son. Peter, who lived in Albany, N. Y. She married 3d, James Enos, or Innes, of Long Hill.

6. Patience married Mr. Willis. of Short Hills, in Westfield township, and had children, but her descendants are not now known.

7. Betsey married William Cauldwell, son of James, of Long Hill. [*See Cauldwell.*]

THOMAS THOMPSON.

THOMAS THOMPSON, (son of John,) lived in Union Township, near Rahway River, and owned the mills below Springfield. He and Hannah Rushmore had children :

1. Mary, who married, 1st. John Lamb. [*see Lamb ;*] 2d, Matthias Hetfield, by whom she had no children.
2. Lavina, born 6th July. 1731, and died young.
3. John married Lucy Woolcott, of Connecticut.
4. Abigail, who died in infancy.
5. Abigail 2d. married 1st, Moses Littell. [*See Moses Littell, son of Benjamin ;*] 2d, John Seabring.
6. Hezekiah married 1st. Jane Ross ; 2d, Jane Woodruff.
7. Abner married Mary Ross and died July, 1815.
8. Phebe, born April, 1748, and died 29th October, 1836. She married first, John Littell, son of Benjamin. [*See Littell ;*] 2d, Benjamin Frazee, a grand-son of Benjamin Littell.
9. Sarah, born 9th Nov. 1750, and died 28th Jan 1812 ; she married, 1783, James Ross, Esq. son of John, as his 2d wife.
10. Hannah, born 23d Nov. 1753, and died 27th Feb. 1778. She married James Ross, Esq., son of John, as his 1st wife. [*See Ross.*]
11. Carman married Patience Headley.

Thomas Thompson, by his 2d wife Rachel, had,

12. Aaron, born 19th Dec. 1760, and died 3d July, 1792. He married Aletta Potter, daughter of Matthias Potter.
13. Rachel, born 31st Jan. 1763, married 1st, Noah Marsh ; 2d, John Potter, and removed to Redstone.
14. Chloe, who married Ephraim Price, of Elizabethtown.
15. Hur, born 9th July, 1767 ; died at about 18 or 19 years.

JOHN THOMPSON, (son of Thomas,) and Lucy Woolcott had children :

1. Caleb, who married 1st, Mary Jennings ; 2d, Phebe Blake.
2. Phebe married Anthony Fountain, son of Vincent, of Staten Island.
3. John married Martha, daughter of David, and widow of Carman Thompson.
4. Abby, who died in 1833, aged 64 years, unmarried.
5. Hepsibah married Ephraim Marsh, son of Ephraim, of Westfield.
6 Josiah Woolcott married Hetty Merrel, of Staten Island, and lived there.

7. Lucy married 1st, Andrew Hennel; 2d, Jacob Burbank, had no children.

8. Chloe married James Hallet, of Westfield.

9. Julia, born 22d Aug. 1784, married Caleb Jeffreys, son of Caleb, of Union.

10. Asa Lay married Hannah Sayre, daughter of Benjamin, of Union.

11. Thomas Rushmore married Joan Quigley, daughter of Capt. Aaron Quigley.

CALEB THOMPSON, (1st child of John.) and Mary Jennings, had children:

1. Sarah, who married Stephen Woodruff son of Gabriel.

2. William, who went to sea when about 22 years old, and did not return.

3. John; 4. Aaron; 5 David Smith; 6. Asa Woodruff.

PHEBE THOMPSON, (2d child of John,) and Anthony Fountain, had children:

1. Amy Fountain, who married Mr. Houseman as his 2d wife.

2. John Fountain married Keziah ———, and had four children.

3 Charles Fountain married Jane Van Pelt; had eight children.

4 Mary Fountain died at about 30 years, unmarried.

5. George Fountain died at about 10 years.

JOHN THOMPSON, (3d child of John,) and Martha Thompson, had children:

1. Phebe Anne; 2. Elizabeth, and others.

HEPZIBAH THOMPSON, (5th child of John,) and Ephraim Marsh, had children:

1. Betsey Marsh, who married Jacob Stein.

2. Lucy Marsh married Joseph Christie.

3. Abigail Marsh married Mr. Schrever, of New York.

4. Caroline Marsh married Jesse Wood, of New York.

5. Edwin Marsh.

JOSIAH W. THOMPSON, (6th child of John,) and Hetty Merril live on Staten Island, and had children:

1. William, who married ——— ———.

2. Mariah; 3. John married twice.

4. Josiah married Miss Pool.

5. George married Sophia ———.

CHLOE THOMPSON, (8th child of John,) and James Hallet had children:
1. Aaron Gilbert Hallet, who died at about 21 years.
2. Polly Hallet, who married Adonijah Holbrook.
3. Susan Hallet married Philander Webb.
4. John Hallet married —— ——.
5. Lcuy Anne Hallet married William Fowler, and had a daughter, Elizabeth Fowler.
6. Catherine Hallet.
7. James Hallet married —— ——.

JULIA THOMPSON, (9th child of John,) and Caleb Jeffervs, had children:
1. Isaac Morse Jefferys, who married Sarah Potter, daughter of John.
2. Jane Eliza Jefferys married Jeremy Jagger, son of Stephen, and had no children.
3. Henrietta Jefferys married David C. Baldwin, son of Phinehas.
4. Lucy Anne Jefferys married Josiah Miller, son of Enoch, of Westfield.
5. Sarah Thompson Jefferys married Abraham W. Baldwin, son of David C., son of elder Thomas Baldwin.
6. Rachel Reeve Jefferys married Samuel Ketchum, son of Samuel.
7. Caleb Henry Jefferys left home in 1834, and did not return.

ASA L. THOMPSON, (10th son of John,) and Hannah Sayre, had children:
1. Julia Anne. 2. Hepzibah, who died at 12 years.
3. Elizabeth. 4. Asa Ferdinand.
5. William Baldwin, who died at 17 years.
6. Josiah, who married Catherine —— ——, of New-York.
7. Hannah, who died at about 18 years.
8. Thomas, who died at about 3 years.

THOMAS R. THOMPSON, (11th son of John,) and Joan Quigley, had children:
1. Betsey Anne.
2. Aaron Quigley, who married Theodocia Sayre, daughter of James, son of Ephraim, of Madison; 3. John; 4. Charity; 5. Thomas; 6. Henry Radley; 7. Mary.

AARON QUIGLEY THOMPSON, (2d child of Thomas R.,) and Theodocia Sayre, had children: 1. Joan Elizabeth; 2. Theodocia; 3. Sidney; 4. Mary Kate.

HEZEKIAH THOMPSON, (6th child of Thomas,) and Jane Ross, lived on Rahway River, in Union Township, and had children:

1. Mary, who married Benjamin Gardner.
2. Sarah married Benjamin Crane 3d. (*See Crane.*)
3. Moses married, 1st, Esther Bonnel, daughter of Henry; 2d, Polly Winans, daughter of Joshua.
4. Jacob, who died young.
And by his second wife, Jane Woodruff, had,
5 Jacob 2d, 6 Thomas, 7. Isaac, who all three died young.
8. Jane, who had a daughter Mary Anne, who married David Totten, son of John. [*See Totten.*]
9. Nancy married Daniel Lacy, son of Samuel. [*See Lacy.*]
10. Betsey married Jesse C. Baker, son of Jonathan I. [*See Baker.*]
11. Phebe married Robert Earl; he died 15th May, 1848. and left children:
1. John Earl. 2. Mary Elizabeth Earl.

MARY THOMPSON, (1st child of Hezekiah,) and Benjamin Gardner, had children:
1. Hezekiah Thompson Gardner married in Baltimore and died in Alabama.
2. Jane Ross Gardner married Ephraim Broadwell, son of Simeon, and lived in Dayton, Ohio. He died 13th Feb. 1849. [*See Appendix.*]
3. Phebe Gardner married Theophilus Eaglesfield, brother of Wooldridge Eaglesfield, and has children:
1. Thomas Eaglesfield.
2. Jane married William Railsback.
3. Sarah. 4. Mary Anne. 5. William Eaglesfield.
4. Noah Gardner married Sarah Baker.
5. Polly Gardner married Caleb Scudder.
6. Jacob Gardner married Sarah Miller, of Black River.
7. Moses Gardner married Phebe ——, and had children:
1. Benjamin. 2. Mary. 3. John. 4. Hezekiah T.
8. Sally Gardner married Wm. Hall, and had children:
1. Hampton Hall. 2. Julia Hall. 3. George Hall.
9. Thomas Gardner.
10. Carman Gardner.

MOSES THOMPSON, (3d child of Hezekiah,) and Esther Bonnel, had children:
1. Nancy, who married John Searing.
2. Jane married Wm. Baker, son of William. [*See Baker.*]
And by his 2d wife, Moses Thompson had children:
3. Sally, who married James Anderson, son of Andrew, of Springfield, and had children:

1. Aaron Anderson. 2. Eliza Anderson. 3. Caroline Anderson. 4. Henrietta T. Anderson. 5. Mary W. Anderson. 6. Sarah E. Anderson. 7. Jane B. Anderson. 8. James H. Anderson, born 1837.

4. Hezekiah married Mary Birt, daughter of Jacob, and had children:
1. Henrietta. 2. Ellen Louisa. 3. Hezekiah.

5. Jacob married Phebe Ayers, daughter of Daniel, and had children :
1. William Ayers. 2. Moses. 3 Mary Ayers.

6. Mary married Mitchel Anderson, brother of James, and had children :
1. George Anderson. 2. Moses Thompson Anderson.

7. Hetty, born 27th June, 1810, married Oliver Wade, born 23d April, 1804, son of Uzel, and had children :
1. John P. Wade, born 28th January, 1829.
2. Mary Wade. 3. Hezekiah T. Wade. 4. Emily Hart Wade.

8. Aaron married Phebe Marsh, and had children :
1. Mary. 2. William Henry.

ABNER THOMPSON, (7th child of Thomas,) and Mary Ross, had children :
1. Joseph. 2. Smith. 3. Daniel.

4. Hannah, who married Jacob Woolley, Sen. of Springfield, and had children :
1. Polly Woolley, who married Charles Thompson Day, son of Thaddeus. [*See Day.*]
2. Abner Woolley, who was killed by the fall of a tree in Michigan, aged 27 years.
3. Jacob Woolley, Jun. married Mary Burnet, daughter of Capt. Jonathan, and had children : 1. George W. Woolley. who married his cousin Delia ——. He is a shoe manufacturer, of Springfield. 2. Hervey Woolley. who married —— ——, a daughter of Augustus Richards. 3. Jonathan B. Woolley ; 4. Mary Woolley.
4. Betsey Woolley married Jacob Miller, son of Enoch, of Westfield.
5. Thompson Woolley married Elizabeth Dean, daughter of William. son of John, and had children : 1. Mary Woolley ; 2. Hannah Woolley ; 3. George Woolley.
6. Hannah Woolley married Squier Woodruff, son of Reuben.
7. Charlotte Woolley married Samuel Mooney, son of Nicholas.
8. Abraham Woolley married ——.

4th Gen

CARMAN THOMPSON, (11th child of Thomas,) and Patience Headley, had children:

1. Mary, who married Peter Bennet, of New Brunswick.
2. Sarah married Mr. Pettenger, of New Brunswick.
3. Carman married ———, and died in Albany.

AARON THOMPSON, (12th child of Thomas,) and Aletta Potter, had children:

1. Martin E. who married Mary Kitchel, daughter of the Hon. Aaron Kitchel, of Morris county, and lived in New York.
2. Aaron married Eliza Ryerson, daughter of Judge Ryerson, of Pompton, lived in New York, and had no children.

MARTIN E. THOMPSON, (son of Aaron,) and Mary Kitchel, had children:

1. Elizabeth, who married Henry Beach, of Hanover, had no children.
2. Susan married her cousin James Price, son of Thompson.
3. Matilda married Mr. E. Tomkins.
4. Aaron.
5. William, who went to California.
6 Mary Emma married Henry Munson, of Long Island.
7. Charles; 8. Edwin; 9. Henrietta.

RACHEL THOMPSON, (13th child of Thomas,) and Noah Marsh, of Westfield, had one daughter, Harriet, who married Mr. Leonard, of Bound Brook. And by John Potter, she had two daughters. Mr. Potter removed to Redstone, Pennsylvania, and there his daughters married two brothers, by the name of Potter, from New Providence, and removed to Ohio.

CHLOE THOMPSON (14th child of Thomas,) and Ephraim Price, had children:

1. Thompson Price, who married Miss James; lived in New York.
2. David Price, who was murdered about 1826, on his way from Texas to Mexico.
3. Rachel Price married Mr. Belknap, of New York.
4. Mary Price married Mr. Condit, son of the Rev. Aaron Condit, late of Hanover, and soon after died.

AARON THOMPSON.

3d Gen AARON THOMPSON, (brother of Thomas and Moses Thompson,) came up, and settled on Long Hill, on lot No. 31 addition of the Elizabethtown lots. He had children:

1. Joseph. (See remarks under Anthony Littell.)
2. Thomas, who married, 1st December, 1763, Abigail Ross.
3. Patience married, 27th September, 1767, Matthias Sayre, son of Isaac Sayre, of Springfield. [*See Sayre.*]

THOMAS THOMPSON, (son of Aaron,) and Abigail Ross lived on Long Hill, where Joel D. Thompson now does, and had children:

1. Polly, who married Samuel Parrot, son of William, Sen. [*See Parrot.*]
2. Aaron married, 20th June, 1807, Keziah Dunham, daughter of John Dunham, Jun.
3. Joanna married, 3d July, 1791, Noah Beach, of Hanover Morris county.
4. Patience married, 20th October, 1795, Phinehas Beach, brother of Noah.
5. Moses married Hannah Potter, daughter of Amos, Esq.

AARON THOMPSON, (son of Thomas, son of Aaron,) and Keziah Dunham, had children:

1. Joel Dunham, born 7th April, 1808, and married Paulina Mulford, daughter of William Mulford, and had children:
   1. Mary and Esther, twins; 3. Aaron.
2. Hester, died 17th Aug. 1844, in her 33d year, unmarried.
3. William, who married, and went to Louisville, Kentucky.
4. Aaron married Lavina Smith, and went to Louisville.

Aaron Thompson died 15th November, 1737, aged 71 years. Keziah, his widow, died 5th December, 1748, aged 68 years, 5 months.

MOSES THOMPSON, (son of Thomas,) lived on part of his father's farm; he and Hannah Potter had children:

1. Elizabeth, who died 12th November, 1823, aged 24 yrs.
2. Jotham Potter, died 12th Sept. 1828, aged 25 years.
3. Thomas, who married in New York, Martha Baker, and removed to Peoria county, Illinois.
4. Hannah married John K. Swift, of Sing Sing, N. Y. and live there.
5. Sarah C. who died 28th February, 1846, aged 36 years.
6. Mary; 7. Susan.
8. Amos married, 19th May, 1850, Catherine Doty, daughter of Sylvester Doty.

The three latter went in May, 1847, to Peoria.

Moses Thompson died 10th June, 1844, aged 69 years.

His wife Hannah died 3d January, 1838, aged 60 years.

TIMOTHY THOMPSON.

1st Gen

TIMOTHY THOMPSON was born in 1709, and was son of Thomas Thompson, and probably the same Thomas Thompson, named as one of the " Elizabethtown Associates."

It is not known that he was of kin to Hur Thompson.

Timothy Thompson married Sarah Sallee, lived in Connecticut Farms, and had children :

Daniel, Benjamin and Jabez. He died 27th September, 1780, aged 71 years.

DANIEL THOMPSON, (son of Timothy,) married Euphemia Badgley, lived in Passaic Valley, and had children :

1. Timothy, who married Sarah Enyart, daughter of Benjamin.

2. Benjamin married Betsey Lewis, daughter of Isaac, and sister of Richard Runyon's wife.

3. William, who died 27th March, 1789.

4. Sally married Rufus Enyart, brother of Timothy's wife.

5. Effa married Job Mulford, son of Davis, son of Job. [See Mulford.]

6. Betsey married William Barrack, of Licking Co. Ohio.

7. John, who died in youth.

These last three were twin-born.

8. Polly married Mr. McFane, in Licking county, Ohio.

9. David, who died in Ohio, a young man.

Daniel Thompson and his family, and Benjamin Enyart's family, went to Ohio, about 1800.

BENJAMIN THOMPSON, (son of Timothy,) married Hannah ——, who died 15th April, 1790, aged 26 years, leaving children, Henry and Nancy. He removed to Ohio, and married as his 2d wife, Rachel Enyart, daughter of Benjamin.

JABEZ THOMPSON, (son of Timothy,) was born 19th November, 1759, married Mary Jones, of Lyons Farms, and had children :

1. John, born in May, 1788, and married 16th July, 1816, Huldah G. Stites, daughter of Capt. Abner Stites.

2. Elias I. married, 6th June, 1811, Nancy Lewis, daughter of Isaac Lewis, and sister of Richard Runyon's wife ; they live in Newark.

Jabez Thompson died 31st March, 1835.

JOHN THOMPSON, (son of Jabez, son of Timothy,) and Huldah G. Stites, had children : 1. Jabez, who died a young man ; 2. Silas Stites ; 3. Jane Stites ; 4. Caroline Elmer ; 5. Ezra Fairchild.

Mr. Thompson's wife, Huldah, died 21st Aug. 1832, aged 36 years, and he married Hannah Cooper, sister of the Rev. William H. Cooper, son-in-law of Elias I. Thompson. He lives in Madison county, New York.

ELIAS I. THOMPSON, (son of Jabez,) and Nancy Lewis had children:

1. Mary, born 16th March, 1812, and married, 20th July, 1831, the Rev. William H. Cooper, now pastor of the Presbyterian Church in Wampsville, Madison county, New York, and had children: 1. Harriet Augusta Cooper; 2. Emma Josephine Cooper; 3. Elias Thompson Cooper; 4. Edward Payson Cooper.

2. Martha, born 4th Dec. 1813, and married, 8th May, 1839, Jacob F. Reemer; lives in Newark, N. J., and had children: 1. Harriet Thompson Reemer; 2. Charles Henry Reemer; 3. Anna Matilda Reemer; 4. John Reemer.

3. Harriet Newel, born 8th March, 1816, married, 3d Aug. 1842, the Rev. William W. Holloway, who is now pastor of the Reformed Dutch Church at Amity, Saratoga county, N. York, and had children: 1. William Whiteman Holloway; 2. Harriet Newel Holloway.

4. George Washington, born 10th Oct. 1819. He graduated at Rutgers' College, New Brunswick; studied theology; married, 6th Oct. 1845, Mary Anne Stilwell, daughter of James Stilwell, of New Berlin, Union county, Pennsylvania, and is pastor of the Presbyterian church at ——, in Juniatta county, Pennsylvania, and has a child, Charles.

PETER TILYOU.

PETER TILYOU came from France. His son, Vincent Tilyou, married, 1st, Nancy Tiebout; 2d, Jane Freeman, daughter of Joseph. He lived in New York, and by his first wife had children:

1. John, who married Elizabeth Tucker, daughter of John, of New Jersey. [*See Tucker.*]

2. Peter Vincent, who married, 1st, Lucy Bigelow; 2d, Sally Field.

3. Nancy, who married Mr. Spencer.

And by his 2d wife, Jane Freeman, he had children:

4. Vincent, born 24th May, 1788, and married Catherine Curry, born 25th Aug 1791, who had an only sister, Jane Curry, and were daughters of Francis Curry.

5. Hetty married Francis Curry, brother of Vincent's wife.

6. Joseph F. married as his 2d wife, Sarah Ruckman, daughter of Levi, who obtained a divorce from him, and he married again; lives near Basking Ridge, and has several children.

JOHN TILYOU, and Elizabeth Tucker lived on Stony Hill, in New Providence, N. J., and had children:

1. Nancy, who married John Hill, son of William. [*See Hill.*]

2. Mary married Cornelius Frazee, son of Cornelius. [*See Frazee.*]

PETER V. TILYOU lived in New York. He by his 1st wife, Lucy, had a son:

1. John, who married Betsey Field, and had children: 1. Peter V.; 2. Eliza; 3. Lucy; 4. Catherine; 5. Caroline; 6. Evelina; 7. John V.; 8. Emma; 9. Thaddeus; 10. Josephine; 11. Adelaide; 12. Oscar.

And by his 2d wife, Sally Field, Peter V. Tilyou had children:

2. Christian married Mary ——.

3. Louisa, who married Chandler Ingersoll, and had children: 1. Adeline; 2. Chandler; 3. Lucy; 4. Francina Ingersoll.

VINCENT TILYOU was a sea-captain, and traversed the seas many years. Capt. Vincent Tilyou and Catherine Curry lived in New York, and had children:

1. Jane, who married Stephen Decator Morrison, in June, 1845, and died 19th March, 1846.

2. Catherine married James D. Morrison, brother of Stephen D., and had children: 1. Catherine Morrison: 2. Vincent Morrison; 3. Mary Jane Morrison; 4. Harriet Morrison; 5. John Francis Morrison; 6. Margaret.

3. Esther.

4. Harriet Newel, who married the Rev. Shubal Stiles Parker, a Baptist Minister, who first settled in Burlington, and subsequently in New Brunswick, N. J., and had children: 1. Franklin Wheelock Parker; 2. Jane Tilyou Parker.

5. Vincentine S.

6. Vincent.

NOTE.— Jane Curry, sister of Capt. Vincent Tilyou's wife, married John B. Halsted, of New York, and had children:

1. Sarah Halsted.

2. Susan Halsted, who married Mr. Brush.

3. Jane Halsted died 17th Feb. 1849, aged 32 years, unmarried.

4. Francis Halsted; 5. Benjamin Halsted; 6. John Halstead; 7. Catherine Halsted.

HETTY TILYOU, (daughter of Vincent, Sen.,) and Francis Curry had children:

1. Jane Curry, who married Lothrip L. Sturges, and had children:

1. Mary Jane Sturges, who married Jeremiah Wardwell, and has children: 1. William Wardwell; 2. Theodore Wardwell.

2. William Sturges married Jenette Smith.

3. Charles Sturges.

4. Theodore Sturges; 5. Catherine Sturges; 6. Wallace Sturges; 7. Edwin Sturges.

2. Esther Curry married John Laws, and had children: 1. Janet Laws; 2. William Laws.

3. William Curry married Julia Washburn, and had children: 1. William Curry; 2. Richard Curry; 3. George Curry; 4. Theodore Curry.

4. Catherine Curry married George M. Clearman, and had children: 1. Lewis Clearman; 2. Mariah Clearman; 3. Mary Augusta Clearman; 4. Isaac Clearman; 5. Emma Clearman; 6. Frederick Clearman; 7. Catherine Clearman;

SILAS TITUS.

SILAS TITUS had children:
1. Polly, who married David Van Norton, and lives at Bound Brook.
2. Josiah married —— ——, and lives up the North River.
3. John married, 1st, Hannah Manning, daughter of Jerry Manning, and lived in Washington Valley. He married, 2d, the widow Rachel Boice.
4. William married Jane Squier, daughter of Thomas, of Livingston. He lived in Passaic Valley, in Warren, and died 4th April, 1848, aged 73 years; 5. Isaac.
6. Nelly, who died a young woman.

JOHN TITUS, (son of Silas,) and Hannah Manning had children:
1. Isaac, who married Keziah Smalley, daughter of Samuel, and lives in Washington Valley.
2. Sarah. And by his 2d wife, Rachel, had children:
3. John, who married —— ——.
4. Rachel married William Reed, son of Kelly Reed.

ISAAC TITUS, (son of John,) and Keziah Smalley, had children:
1. Martha, who married Amos Giddis, son of Jacob, of Washington Valley.
2. Hannah married Philip Winans, son of John, of do.
3. David, who died at about 10 years.
4. Rhoda, who married Israel Moore, son of Isaac, of Mount Bethel.
5. Manning; 6. Samuel; 7. Lewis; 8. William Henry; 9. David 2d, who died at 3 years; 10. Madison; 11. Amanda; 12. Mahlon.

WILLIAM TITUS, (son of Silas,) and Jane Squier had children: 1. Betsey.
2. Mary, who married Jonathan Cory, son of John, and had children: 1. Elizabeth Cory; 2. Marietta Cory; 3. Phebe Cory; 4. Anne Jane Cory.
3. Phebe married Mr. Brewster.
4. Anne married Isaac C. Allen, son of Daniel. [*See Allen.*]
5. Charlotte married William Freeman, son of Caleb, of Plainfield, and had children: 1. George Freeman; 2. John Freeman; and they, Charlotte and William, both died.
6. Jennette married Thomas Vail, son of Joel, of Plainfield.
7. William is a baker, in Newark.
8. Caroline married, 1st Nov. 1849, David Smalley, son of David D., Esq. 9. Thomas Squier; 10. George.

ALEXANDER TODD.

ALEXANDER TODD lived near Liberty Corner, and had children : David and James Todd

James Todd, who married, 23d March, 1784, Jane Martin, daughter of Alexander Martin, of Long Hill, [see Martin,] and had children :

1. Alexander, who died suddenly, 6th May, 1849, aged 64 years, unmarried.
2. William married Catherine Hand, daughter of Jonathan, of Basking Ridge. [See Hand.]
3. Sally married John Norton, from Ireland, and had a son, Thomas Norton.
4. James Todd, Jun. is unmarried,
5. Anne married John Nesbitt, son of James, and had children : 1. Augustus Nesbitt ; 2. Andrew Jackson Nesbitt.

WILLIAM TODD, (son of James,) and Catherine Hand had children :

1. John, who married Elizabeth Pouleson, daughter of Cornelius.
2. Jane married Ellis D, Baldwin, son of David, [see Baldwin,] and had children : 1. David ; 2. Catherine ; 3. John ; 4. Emily Baldwin.
3. Sarah married George Bird, son of Isaac, of Mount Bethel.
4. Mary married James Waldron, son of John, of Washington Valley, and had children : 1. John ; 2. Catherine ; 3. Hester Sylvenia Waldron.
5. Sally married James Gibson, son of William; lives in New York, and had children : 1. James Gibson ; 2. Sarah Gibson.
6. Jonathan married Hannah Vatican ; lives in the Beach Woods, Pennsylvania, and had a son : 1. Milton Ira.
7. William ; 8. Hugh ; 9. James.

JOSEPH TOMKINS.

JOSEPH TOMKINS married Martha Campbell, of Orange.
They lived at Cauldwell, and had children :
1. Sarah, who died a young woman.
2. Hannah, who married, 25th Feb. 1809, Jacob Marcell,
of Newark, and had children : 1. Benjamin Marcell ; 2. Alfred
Marcell ; 3. David Marcell ; 4. Stephen Marcell ; they then
removed to Illinois.
3. David Bonnel, who died unmarried, at about 35 years.
4. Nathaniel, who married Nancy Bedford, daughter of
David, of Columbia, Morris county, and had children :
    1. William Allen, who married Rebecca Vaughn, and
       had children : 1. Anne Bedford ; 2. Mary Elizabeth ;
       3. John ; 4. Martha Jane.
    2. David Bonnel, who went to Illinois, and died unmar-
       ried.
Joseph Tomkins married for his 2d wife, Jerusha, a widow,
the daughter of David Bonnel, of Union, who removed to
Passaic Valley, and had a son.
5. Ashbel Allen, born 22d Aug. 1806, and married, 11th
June, 1828, Mary N. Bonnel, daughter of Philemon Bonnel,
and had children :
    1. Philemon Bonnel, born 19th April, 1829, and married
       Anne Eliza Osborn, daughter of Asa, 24th Sept. 1850.
    2. Huldah Bonnel, born 5th June, 1837 ; 3. and 4.
       Martha Bonnel and Mary Esther, twins, born 22d
       April, 1841.
Mr. A. A. Tomkins lives in New Providence village ; is engaged in blacksmithing.
Mr. Nathaniel Tomkins lived on Stony Hill, in Warren,
where his wife died, and he and his son William and family,
removed to Illinois.
Jerusha, the 2d wife of Joseph Tomkins, married, 1st, John
Beach, [see Beach ;] had 8 children, when he died, and she
married, 2d, David Muchmore, of Livingston, by whom she
had no children. She married, 3d, Joseph Tomkins, who
died 23d Oct. 1832, at 75 years, and she was again left a widow ; and after several years she went with one of her sons to
Lexington, Kentucky, where she died 19th July, 1843, in
the midst of her children :

JAMES TOTTEN.

JAMES TOTTEN was probably the son of Sylvanus Totten, who lived in this neighborhood in 1765.

He lived on the north side of Long Hill, where Noah Williams lately lived; he married Hester Propo, who died 7th June, 1773; he died 7th May, 1774; they had children:

1. Sarah, who married, 16th March, 1767, Moses Blancher.
2. David married, 25th January, 1775, Sarah Pierson.
3. John married Rhoda Marsh, of Rahway, sister of Daniel Marsh.

John Totten died 11th September, 1810, aged 56 years.

Rhoda his widow died 20th January, 1835, aged 82 years.

DAVID TOTTEN, (son of James,) and Sarah Pierson lived in Sterling's Valley, and had children:

1. Mary, who married Israel Brant.
2. Elizabeth married Mr. Boylan.
3. John married Tempe Conklin, daughter of Joshua. [*See Conklin.*]
4. Joseph married, 17th June, 1820, Mariah Hathaway, of Morristown.
5 James married Sally Freeman, daughter of Philip.
6. Martha married John Robert Littell, son of Robert. [*See Littell.*]
7. Rachel married Amos Stevens, son of John. [*See Stevens.*]

JOHN TOTTEN, (son of David,) and Tempe Conklin, had children:

1. Betsey, who married John Putnam, son of Miles, live in Green Valley, near Plainfield, and had children:
    1. Andrew Jackson Putnam; 2. Miles Putnam; 3. John Davis Putnam; 4. Randolph Putnam; 5. Lewis Craig Putnam, twin to Randolph; 6. Mary Putnam; 7. Harriet Putnam.
2. David married Mary Anne Thompson, daughter of Jane, daughter of Hezekiah Thompson, and had children:
    1. Jane; 2. Elias; 3. David.
3. Anne married Samuel Pangborn, of Green Valley, and had children:
    1. Eli Pangborn; 2. Benjamin Pangborn; 3. John Pangborn; 4. Drake Pangborn; 5. Mary Adeline Pangborn; 6. Abel Stewart Pangborn.
4. James married Eliza Wood, daughter of Silas, of Logansville, and had children: 1. Phebe; 2. Mary Anne, 3. William; 4. Abby; 5. Ellen; 6. Catherine Elizabeth; 7. Carter; 8. Fanny.

5. Abby married Abel Stewart, son of William D. Stewart, Esq. [*See Stewart.*]

6. Eunice married Alexander Cameron, son of Elisha, of Sterling's Valley.

7. Joshua married, 1st, Emeline Foster; 2d, Caroline Spinning, daughter of John, of Elizabethtown, and had children:
1. Henry Francis; 2. John Spinning Totten.

8. Cornelius married Martha Jones, daughter of Thomas D. Jones, and had children: 1. Georgiana; 2. a daughter, who died young.

JAMES TOTTEN. (son of David,) and Sally Freeman, had children:

1. Nancy, who married William Ayers, son of David, of Union, and had children:
1. Lewis Ayers, born 1835; 2. Mary Jane Ayers, born 1838.

2. Silas married Adeline Mc Cormic.

3. Freeman married Jane Whitenack, and had children:
1. Eugene; 2 Sarah Elizabeth; 3. Thomas; 4. Linus.

4. Linus, who died at about 17 years.

5. Jane married William Fulkerson.

6. William married Eliza Squier, daughter of John.

7. Hervey; 8. George Washington, 9. John Henry, twins.

10. Jackson.

JOHN TOTTEN, (son of James 1st,) and Rhoda Marsh, lived in Passaic Valley, and had children:

1. Benjamin, who died in infancy.

2. Betsey, born 1785, and married 29th March, 1798, Joshua Kindall, son of Job Kindall, of Burlington county, and had children:
1. John Marsh Kindall, who married, 8th March, 1838, Nancy Ludlow, daughter of Joseph, and had children:
1. Joshua; 2. Hannah Ludlow; 3. John Ludlow.
4. Sarah Anne.
2. Anne Doty Kindall married Ezra Wooden, son of Gideon, of Green Valley, and had children: 1. Elizabeth Wooden; 2. William Wooden; 3. Sarah Wooden; 4. Mariah Wooden; 5. Ludlow Wooden; 6. Martin Wooden; 7. Susan Wooden.
3. Margaret Kindall.
4. William Kindall, born 1823, has a daughter Frances, born March, 1843.
5. Elihu Kindall, who died of cholera, 10th July, 1849.
6. Eliza Kindall; 7. Mariah Kindall.

Mr. Joshua Kindall died 6th December, 1831, aged 51 yrs.

SAMUEL TOTTEN.

SAMUEL TOTTEN, (brother of James Totten 1st) lived a little south of the corner store south of the church, and kept a tavern there. He died 25th June, 1775; his widow died 17th March, 1790 ; they had children :

1. Samuel Totten, Jun. who married 9th June, 1785, Martha Tuttle.

2. Martha married, 31st July, 1788, Joseph Day, [*See Day.*]

3 Jonathan married, 15th October, 1792, Esther Wood, daughter of Jeremiah Wood.

Mr. Jonathan Totten died 24th February, 1837, aged 68 years.

JONATHAN TOTTEN, (son of Samuel,) and Esther Wood, had children :

1. Jane, who ma ried John McClasky Schureman, son of John, and had children: 1. Jonathan Schureman, who married Keziah ; 2. Samuel Schureman married Cornelia Dickerson, daughter of Philemon ; 3. Henrietta.

Jane then died, and Mr. Schureman married again, Mrs. Melick, who had a son, Abraham Melick, who married Eliza Schureman, daughter of Samuel Schureman, brother of John McClasky. By this 2d wife, J. McC. Schureman had a son, Leonard Schureman, who is a stone cutter, in Morristown.

2. Nancy, who married Jacob Nixon, and had children :
    1. Pamelia Nixon, who married Mr. Dunn ; lives in Morristown, and keeps a large milliners' shop.
    2. Harriet Jane Nixon married Aaron Hedden, son of Thomas.

3. Jeremiah married Hannah Price, daughter of Rice Price : live in Roxbury, Morris county.

4. Betsey, who lived in New-York, and died 31st Jan. 1852, unmarried.

5. Esther, who married Ezra Williams, son of Noah ; lives in New-York, and have no children

6. Abraham Morrel, who died 20th Dec. 1827, aged 27 years.

7. Joseph Wood married, 31st July 1823, Jemima Douglas, daughter of Jesse V. Douglas, of Springfield.

JEREMIAH TOTTEN, (son of Jonathan,) and Hannah Price, had children :

1. Samuel, who married Sarah Anne Osborn, daughter of John, and had children: 1. John Osborn, and others.

2. Jonathan, born 1st Sept. 1821, married, 22d July 1843, Mariah Schureman, daughter of Samuel, have no children. [*See Scudder.*]

3. William ; 4. Jane ; 5. Benjamin ; 6. Abigail; 7 Agnes. 8. Hannah ; 9. Anne; 10. Edwin.

JOSEPH W. TOTTEN, (son of Jonathan,) and Jemima Douglas, had children :

1. Abraham Morrel.
2. William Pierson.
3. Mary Elizabeth.
4. Hetty Mariah, who married ——, and died at 19 years.
5. Charles Jackson ; 6. John ; 7. Jonathan.

BENONI TREMBLY.

BENONI TREMBLY lived on lot No. 61 of the Elizabethtown lots south of Aaron M. Ludlow's house. He was a wagon maker, was an elder in the New Providence church, and had children :

1. Benjamin, baptized 19th June, 1763.
2. Jonathan, baptized 16th December, 1764.
3. Abraham, baptized 15th August, 1766.
4. Becca, baptized 14th October, 1770.

I have not learned from whence he came, nor who were his family connections. He died 6th October, 1788.

JOHN TOWNLEY.

JOHN TOWNLEY, Esq. was born in England, in the year 1400

2d Gen Nicholas Townley, the third son of John Townley, Esq. lived in the county of Palatine, of Lancaster. His wife was Elizabeth, daughter of Richard Catteral, Esq. of Catteral, relict of William Tempest, son of Roger Tempest, Esq. Lord of the Manor of Broughton.

3d Gen Richard Townley, Esq. son of Nicholas Townley, was reader of Grays Inn, in the fourth year of the reign of Henry VIII. His wife was Margaret, the daughter of John Clark, of Wazley, by which marriage royalty came into the Townley family.

4th Gen Nicholas Townley, Esq. of Royall, county of Palatine, was son and heir of Richard Townley. He married Anne, daughter of Sir Hugh Vaughan, of Littleton Place, Middlesex, Privy Councillor of Henry VII and VIII.

5th Gen Francis Townley, 3d son of Nicholas Townley, was of Littleton Place, being left heir of his great uncle, Francis Vaughan, Esq. He married Catherine, daughter of Thomas Foster, Knight, one of the Justices of the Court of Common Pleas at Westminster, in the reign of James 1st.

6th Gen Nicholas Townley, Esq. of Littleton, son of Francis Townley, died June 3d, 1687. He married Joanna, daughter of William White, Esq. of Northaim, county of Sussex, and squandered his fortune.

7th Gen Col. Richard Townley, 8th son of Richard Townley, went to America in the suite of Lord Effingham Howard, governor of Virginia, in the year 1683. He settled in Elizabethtown, New Jersey.

The foregoing account of the Townley family was sent to this country in 1769, by Charles Townley Clarence, of London, Knight York Herald and King of Arms.

Col. Richard Townley was one of the Privy Council of deputy governor Lord Neil Campbell, in 1686. He left two sons, Charles and Effingham Townley.

CHARLES TOWNLEY.

8th Gen

CHARLES TOWNLEY, Esq. (son of Col. Richard Townley,) was born 1686, and died, 2d September, 1756, in his 70th year. Abigail, his widow, died 31st December, 1759. They were both buried in St John's church yard, in Elizabethtown; they had children:

1. Effingham, who married Miss Rebecca Crane; he was born about 1710, married in 1735, and died about 1789.
2. Sarah or Abigail, who married John Herriman; their only daughter married Moses Hetfield.
3. Mary married Stephen Burrows; their only daughter married Anthony Morss.
4. Anne married Joseph Tooker, and had four sons, Charles, Joseph, Abner, and John Tooker.
5. Elizabeth married, 27th August, 1760, Caleb Crane, and left children:
    1. Nathaniel Crane, who married Sally Miller, daughter of Moses. [*See Crane.*]
    2. Abby, who married Amos Clark.

9th Gen

EFFINGHAM TOWNLEY, (son of Charles,) and Rebecca Crane had children:

1. Richard, who was born 22d or 27th August, 1736, and died 4th August, 1801; he married 1st, Rachel Carpenter, born 15th December, 1733, and died 1764; 2d, Rhoda Clark, born 4th December, 1743, and died 21st July, 1823.
2. Catherine married Joseph Denman, of Springfield.
3. Joanna, who died in infancy.
4. Abigail married Mr. Pendergrass, of Philadelphia.
5. Peggy married Stephen Baker, and died in 1802.
6. George, who died in infancy.
7. Sarah married John Sayre, son of Joseph Sayre, of Elizabethtown, and died in 1815.
8. Mary married Jeremiah Jaggers.
9. Charles married 1st, Hannah Thompson, and died in 1802; 2d, Sarah Thompson, the widow of Moses Earl; 3d, —— ——, the widow of Timothy Miller.
10. George 2d married Martha Baldwin, daughter of Capt. Enos Baldwin.
11. Joanna 2d married John Donahoe, of Philadelphia, and died in 1804.
12. John married Phebe Bonnel, and died in 1801.
13. Jane married Daniel Osborn.

10th Gen

RICHARD TOWNLEY, (1st son of Effingham, son of Charles,) and Rachel Carpenter, had children:

1. James, born 29th June, 1760, and was killed with a scythe, in 1772.

2. Rachel, born 12th December, 1763, married Henry Norris, and died 16th November, 1824 ; she had three children, who all died young.

Richard Townley by his 2d wife, Rhoda Clark, had children :

3. Jonathan, born 13th October, 1766, married, 11th December, 1787, Phebe Magie, daughter of John.

4. Phebe, born 20th October, 1768, married 28th January, 1788, Elder David Magie, son of John.

5. Clark, born 26th November, 1770, married 1st, Phebe Sale, daughter of Daniel Sale, Sen. ; 2d, Emily Potter, daughter of Matthias Potter.

6. Rebecca, born 22d May, 1772, married Benjamin Haines, of Elizabethtown.

7. Rhoda, born 12th April, 1774, and died in 1776.

8. Sarah, born 26th October, 1776, married William Crane, Esq. son of Joseph. [*See Crane.*]

9. Elizabeth, born 22d August, 1780, married Jonathan M. Meeker, Esq. son of Isaiah Meeker, of New Providence, and had no children.

JONATHAN TOWNLEY, (3d child of Richard, son of Effingham, son of Charles,) and Phebe Magie were married 11th December, 1787 ; he died 29th September, 1827 ; they had children :

1. Richard, who married Hannah Wade, daughter of Jonas Wade, Esq. of Springfield.

2. Jonathan, Jun. married his cousin Rhoda Magie, daughter of elder David Magie, of Elizabethtown, and had no children.

3. Phebe, twin to Jonathan, married Col. William Brown, of Elizabethtown.

4. Mary married Samuel Pierson, son of Deacon Pierson, of Union.

5. John married Eveline Nutman, daughter of Daniel, of Elizabethtown.

6. Rebecca married Ichabod Ogden, son of Ezekiel, of Elizabethtown, and had children :

1. Jonathan Townley Ogden; 2. John Joseph Ogden.

3. James Hervey Ogden; 4. Robert Townley Ogden.

5. Phebe Rebecca Ogden.

RICHARD TOWNLEY, (son of Jonathan,) and Hannah Wade, had children :

1. Robert, who married Miss Baldwin, daughter of Johnson Baldwin.

2. Jonas Wade.

3. Phebe O. married, 20th November, 1851, Henry Meeker.

4. Harriet married Alexander Ball, son of David, of Newark.

5. James.

6. Richard, who died in February, 1848, aged about 16 years.

NOTE.—Robert, Jonas, and James went to Fort Wayne, in Indiana, and are merchants there.

PHEBE TOWNLEY, (4th child of Richard, son of Effingham, son of Charles,) and Elder David Magie had children:

1. Rhoda Magie, who married her cousin Jonathan Townley, Jun. [See *Townley*]

2. David Magie married, 1st, Margaret Van Vechten, of Somerville, and had children: 1. Elizabeth Magie, who died at 18 months; 2. Phebe Magie.

His wife then died, and he married, 2d, Gertrude Frelinghuysen, daughter of General John Frelinghuysen, of Somerville, she died without children, and he married, 3d, Margaret Delneau, and had children: 3. Gertrude Frelinghuysen Magie; 4. David Magie.

3. Betsey Magie.

4. Phebe Ogden Magie married Lewis F. Day, son of Foster Day, of Elizabethtown, and had children:
1. David Magie Day; 2. Eliza Bonnel Day.

5. Mary Meeker Magie married Rev. Joseph Cory, son of Mulford, son of Elder Benjamin Cory, of Elizabethtown; he is a presbyterian minister, settled in New Vernon; they had children, David Magie Cory, and others.

CLARK TOWNLEY, (5th child of Richard, son of Effingham, son of Charles,) and Phebe Sale, had children:

1. Susan, who married Robert Meeker.

2. Daniel married Sarah Headley.

3. Richard; 4. Edward; 5. Mary.

And by his 2d wife, Emily Potter, had other children:

6. Jonathan; 7. Sally Anne.

REBECCA TOWNLEY, (6th child of Richard, son of Effingham, son of Charles Townley,) and Benjamin Haines had but one son, Richard T. Haines, who married Mariah Johnson, daughter of John Johnson, grocer, of New York; lived in Elizabethtown, and had children:

1. William A. Haines, who married Miss Stagg.

2. Benjamin Haines.

3. Elizabeth Haines.

4. Sarah Halsted Haines married, 22d May, 1850, Samuel Knox, of New York.

5. John Johnson Haines.

6 Mary L. Haines married, 20th February, 1851, her cousin William M. Halsted, Jun son of William M. Halsted, merchant, New York.

7. Stewart Haines.

SARAH TOWNLEY, (8th child of Richard, son of Effingham, son of Charles Townley,) and William Crane, Esq. had children :

1. David R. Crane, who married Phebe Anne Hallam, daughter of Lewis, of New York.

2. Agnes Crane married Rev. Curtis Tally, a methodist minister, and had a daughter, Helen Williams Tally.

3. Richard T. Crane married June T. Dollbeer, of Union. and had children : 1. Theodore T. 2. Frederick T.

4. Joseph W. Crane married 1st, Harriet J. Willcox, daughter of Ezekiel, and had a daughter, Harriet Jemima Crane ; his wife died, and he married 2d, Emma S. Brookfield, daughter of Lewis P. Brookfield, of Spring Valley, and had children : 2. Lewis W. Crane ; 3. Charles Augustus Crane.

5. Jonathan T. Crane, who graduated at Princeton college, and became a methodist minister, is principal of the Pennington male seminary, at Pennington, N. J. He married Mary Helen Peck, daughter of George Peck, D. D. of New York, and had children : 1. Mary Helen Peck, and others.

SARAH TOWNLEY, (7th child of Effingham, son of Charles,) and John Sayre had children :

1. Samuel Sayre, who married Polly Parker.

2. Joseph Sayre married Betsey Alesworth.

3. John Sayre married Mary Jewel.

4. Job Sayre, who died in infancy.

5. Ezekiel Sayre married Sally Bonnel, daughter of John, near Chatham [*See Bonnel.*]

6. Abigail Sayre married William Reid.

7. Nathan Sayre married Abigail Southwell.

SAMUEL SAYRE, (1st son of John Sayre and Sarah Townley,) and Polly Parker had children :

1. Joanna Sayre, who married Daniel Pierson, of Newark, and had an only daughter, who married and lives in N. York.

2. Job Sayre married Phebe Crane ; have no children.

3. Sally Sayre married Aaron Crane, and has one son.

4. Polly Sayre married Granville Tower. and had children :
   1. Job S. Tower, who married Miss Crane : lives in Elizabethtown, and had two children.
   2. Ezra Tower, who married in Morris county, and has several children.

5. Joseph Sayre, who married in Cincinnati ; lives there, and has several children.

6. Nathan Sayre, who married a Mrs. Watkins, formerly Miss Gillam ; has four children, all married, and live in N. Y.

7. John Sayre, who died unmarried.

8. Phebe Sayre married Benjamin Coe : lives in Connecticut, and has many children.

JOSEPH SAYRE, (2d son of John Sayre, and Sarah Townley,) and Betsey Alesworth had 8 children, only one of whom is living, Samuel Sayre, who married Elizabeth Telfair, and had 7 children.

JOHN SAYRE, (3d son of John Sayre and Sarah Townley,) and Mary Jewel had ten children, only two of them are living :

1. James Hervey Sayre, who married Hannah Williams, and have 5 children.

2. Walter F. Sayre, who married Rachel Luster, and had 3 daughters.

EZKEIEL SAYRE, (5th son of John Sayre and Sarah Townley,) and Sally Bonnel had children :

1. Electa Sayre, who married Stephen Bowers, son of Daniel.

2. Catherine Sayre, who died at about 35 years, unmarried.

3. David Sayre married Mary Spencer, daughter of Samuel, son of William Spencer, Esq.

4 John Edgar Sayre.

5. Lewis Sayre.

ABIGAIL SAYRE, (6th child of John Sayre and Sarah Townley,) and William Reid had children :

1. Margaret Reid, who married William Bonnel, of Union, and had several children.

2. Isabella Reid, who married Joel Searing.

3. John Joseph Reid.

4. Sarah Reid.

NATHAN SAYRE, (7th child of John Sayre, and Sarah Townley,) and Abigail Southwell lived in Elizabethtown, and had children :

1. Joanna, who married Wickliff G. Broadwell, son of Jacob G. Broadwell, son of Hezekiah. [See *Broadwell.*] They have no children.

2. George T. Sayre married Eliza Bonnel, daughter of Sylvanus, son of John. He is a merchant of Madison, Morris county ; has two children.

3. Sally Sayre. 4. Caroline Sayre.

5. Edward Sayre married Miss Rosette; had one child. His wife died, and he went to Illinois, and married again, and has other children.

6. Jane Sayre.

7. Francis Sayre married Susan Price, daughter of Edward, of Elizabethtown.

8. Albert Sayre married a Miss Sayre, of Newark, and lives there.

CHARLES TOWNLEY.

10th Gen

CHARLES TOWNLEY, (9th child of Effingham, son of Charles Townley,) and Hannah Thompson had but one son:

1. Stephen, who married Elizabeth Bryant, daughter of Simeon Bryant, of Springfield.

And by his 2d wife, Sarah Thompson, had children:

2. Rebecca, who married Jacob Denman, son of Jacob, of Springfield.

3. Moses married Jane Lum, daughter of Clark Lum, of Union. And by his 3d wife, Mrs. Miller, had children:

4. Charles, who went to Washington, and married and died there.

5. George, who went away and has not returned.

6. Fanny married William Sanders, and lives at Mendham.

STEPHEN TOWNLEY, (1st son of Charles,) and Elizabeth Bryant had children:

1. William, who became a Presbyterian minister. He married Eliza Barton, daughter of John Barton, of Elizabethtown, and sister of the Rev. William B. Barton, of Woodbridge; is settled in Indiana, and has no children.

2. Charles, who died at about 20 or 21 years.

GEORGE TOWNLEY, (10th child of Effingham, son of Charles Townley,) and Martha Baldwin, removed from Connecticut Farms, in March, 1797, and bought of Thomas Scudder, a farm of 100 acres, near Union Village, in Passaic Valley, where they lived and died.

He was born 20th June, 1755, and died 28th September, 1840 She was born 30th November, 1755, and died 22d May, 1810, and Mr. Townley married, 2d, Elizabeth, the widow of Samuel Cory, and daughter of Williiam Parsons. She died 6th May, 1847, without children. [*See Parsons.*] They had children:

1. Joanna, born 23d Nov. 1774, and married Samuel Headley, of Union.

2. David, born 20th March, 1777, married, 1st, Mary Tucker, daughter of James Tucker, 2d, Mary Marsh, daughter of Joseph Marsh, of Morristown.

3. George, who died 30th March, 1808, aged 24 years.

4. Effingham, who died 26th July, 1807, aged 21 years.

5. Phebe. born 14th January, 1789, married, 30th June, 1808. David Jaques, of New-York.

6. Martha, who died 25th April, 1812, at 18 years of age, unmarried.

7. Enos Baldwin, who married, first, Sally Bonnel, daughter of Bellows Ben. Bonnel ; second, Abigail Deforest, of Connecticut. [*See Bonnel.*]

JOANNA TOWNLEY, (1st child of George,) and Samuel Headley, had children :

11th Gen

1. Phebe Headley married Richard Merrel, and had no children.

2. Hannah Headley married William S. Headley, son of Cary Headley. and had children :

    1. Joanna Headley, who married William S. Burnet. son of Capt. Jonathan Burnet. and had children : 1. Mary Burnet : 2. Martha Burnet ; 3. Levi Burnet.

    2. Phebe Headley married Silas Burnet, brother of William S., and had children : 1. Roxanna Burnet ; and others.

    3. Caroline Headley.

    4. John Headley married Sarah Courter, daughter of John E. Courter.

    5. Jane Headley married George Baker, of Hempstead, Long Island.

    6. Wicklyff Headley.

3. Samuel Headley died a young man, unmarried.

4. Martha Headley married Caleb Miller, son of Nathaniel, and had children :

    1. Isaac S. Miller, who married and lives in Newark.

    2. Davis Miller married and lives in Newark.

    3. Anne Miller.

5. George I. Headley died a young man, unmarried.

6. Davis Headley married Susan Ball. daughter of Ezekiel, son of Timothy, and had children :

    1. Sears Headley ; 2. Wheeler Headley ; 3. Andrew Headley ; 4. Olivia Headley ; 5. Laura Headley.

7. Mary Headley married Ewel Freeman, of Westfield, and died soon after, aged 18 years, without children.

DAVID TOWNLEY, (2d child of George,) and his first wife, Mary Tucker, had children :

1. Mary, who died a young woman, unmarried.

2. Martha married Squier Parrot. son of William. [*See Parrot.*] And by his second wife, Mary Marsh. had a son.

3. George. who married Mary Stuchfield, an English girl, and lives in New-York.

PHEBE TOWNLEY, (5th child of George,) and David Jaques, lived in New York, and had children:

1. William Jaques.
2. Phebe Jaques, who married John W. Lewis, and had children: 1. Charlotte Augusta Lewis; 2. Philo Lewis; 3. Francis Lewis; 4. Edward Lewis.

ENOS B. TOWNLEY, (7th child of George,) and Sally Bonnel, had children:

1. Joanna, who married Mr. Noe, went to Ohio, and died.
2. David E., born 5th April, 1815, who married Hannah Eliza Mulford, born 5th January, 1812, daughter of William, and had children:
   1. Sarah Elizabeth, born 10th July, 1840; 2. Hannah Jane, who died at 4 years; 3. Laura, born 30th March, 1846; 4. Phebe Jaques Floride, born 9th October, 1848; 5. Isabel.
3. Hannah Mariah married Jacob Jeroloman, of Newark,
4. Effingham married Mary Elizabeth Squier, daughter of Thomas, son of Stephen Squier, and had children:
   1. Emily Parsons; 2. Montery Tailor; 3. Helen Flora.
5. Elizabeth married William Stevens, above Morristown.
6. Enos married Jane Wilson, of New York.

Enos B. Townley, by his 2d wife, Abigail Deforest, had children:

7. Mary; 8. Moses B.; 9. Susan; 10. Martha; 11. George; 12. Joanna 2d.

EFFINGHAM TOWNLEY.

EFFINGHAM TOWNLEY, (son of Col. Richard Townley,) left two sons:

1. Richard; 2. Effingham, Jun.

RICHARD TOWNLEY, (son of Effingham,) was born 18th December, 1720, and married Catherine Anderson, 14th April, 1747, and had children:

1. William, born 21st January, 1748, died 2d May, 1749.
2. William 2d, born 15th May, 1750.
3. Rebecca, born 13th July, 1751, and died 13th Aug. 1751.
4. Walter, born 28th June, 1752.
5. Rebecca 2d, born 11th August. 1754.
6. Sarah, born 10th January, 1757.
7. Effingham, born 1st August, 1759.

EFFINGHAM TOWNLEY, JUN., (son of Effingham.) was born 11th December, 1729, and married in 1750, Jemima Earl, and had children:

1. Evetts, born 8th August, 1751.
2. **Henry, born 1st February, 1754.**

3. Joshua, born 24th August, 1757.
4. James, born 7th July, 1760.
5. Charles, born 30th March, 1762.
6. Richard, born 31st January, 1764.
7. John, born 9th September, 1766.

EVETTS TOWNLEY, (1st son of Effingham, Jun.,) had a son Isaac, who had a son Clark, whose wife was Rachel, and lived near Jeffersons Village, and had children :

1. Margaret, born 1826.
2. Ezra, born 1830.
3. George, born 1834.

10th Gen

JAMES TOWNLEY, (4th son of Effingham Townley, Jun,) had children :

1. Matthias married, 1st, Nancy Searing, daughter of John, of Union ; 2d, Johannah Smith, daughter of Walter, of Springfield.
2. Edward married, 1st, Miss Burrows ; 2d, Abigail Price.
3. William married —— ——.
4. Else married Cornelius Badgley.
5. Sally married William Higgins.

10th Gen

MATTHIAS TOWNLEY, (1st son of James,) and Nancy Searing had children :

1. William, born 17th Dec 1775, married Margaret Tucker, daughter of Jacob, born 30th Oct. 1780.
2. Sally, who died unmarried.
3. Nancy married Ephraim Rino, of Short Hills.
4. Betsey married Elias Morgan, of Elizabethtown.
5. Sarah married David Allen, son of David. [*See Allen.*]
6. Edward married Anna Hamilton, daughter of David.
Matthias Townley, by his 2d wife, Johannah Smith, had children:
7. Isaac married Mary Collins.
8. Keziah married Mr. Evans, of Newark.
9. John Clark, who died at 25 years, unmarried.
10. Abby married Daniel Clark, son of Ichabod.
11. Smith, who did not marry.

11th Gen

WILLIAM TOWNLEY, (son of Matthias,) and Margaret Tucker had children:

1. Matthias, born 20th Jan. 1798, married Hannah Smalley, daughter of David I., and had four children: 1. William ; 2. David ; 3. Huldah ; 4. Harriet.
2. Alfred married Mary, widow of Cornelius Frazee, and daughter of John Tilyou ; had no children.
3. Sally, who died Dec. 1st 1805, aged 3½ years.

12th Gen

4. Piatt, born 6th May, 1804, married Sophia Mollidore, of Philadelphia, and had children: 1. Margaret; 2. Hannah: 3. George; 4. Susan; 5. Alonzo.

5. David, born 12th Oct. 1806, married Susan Clark, daughter of Stephen, of Westfield.

6. Sarah, born 12th Nov. 1808, married John McIntire,. son of James, of New Brunswick, and had children: 1. William McIntire; 2. Ellen McIntire; 3. John Henry McIntire; 4. James McIntire.

7. Alexander, born 11th May, 1811, married Mary Samos, daughter of Charles, of Dover, Morris county, and had children: 1. William; 2. Anne; and died at about 24 years.

8. Amos, born 8th Aug. 1813, married Mary Tunison, near Somerville, and had a daughter, Mary.

9. William Mills, born 24th Jan. 1816, married his cousin. Joanna, daughter of Edward Townley, and had a son, George. His wife, Joannah, died and he married, 2d, Martha Scudder, daughter of Abraham, and had a son, Silas Crane.

10. Anne, born 28th Jan. 1818, married Josiah G. Winn, from Connecticut, and had children: 1. Isaac Newton Winn; 2. Susan Emeline Winn; 3. Mary Elizabeth Winn; 4. Matilda Fairchild Winn; 5. Ellen Mansville Winn; 6. George Henry Winn.

11. Hannah, born 9th March, 1820, married Thomas Seaman, son of Joshua, and had children: 1. Thomas Jefferson Seaman; 2. Margaret Anne Seaman; 3. Hannah Mariah Seaman; 4. Stephen Franklin Seaman; 5. Harriet Newe Seaman.

EDWARD TOWNLEY, (6th child of Matthias,) son of James, and Anna Hamilton lived in Westfield, and had children :

1. John Hamilton Townley, who became a Presbyterian Minister; settled in Morristown. He married Cornelia Searing, daughter of James Searing, of Newark.

2. Joanna, who married her cousin William Townley, son of William.

3. David, who died at the age of 24 years.

4. Anne Elizabeth married Lewis Bunn.

5. William, who died 20th Dec. 1848, aged 23 years.

6. Israel married Mary Whitehead, daughter of Enos Littell Whitehead, of Elizabethtown.

7. Matthias.

8. Mary Louisa.

9. Harriet.

10. Almira, who died at 4 years.

11. Gertrude, who died at 2 years.

WARNER TUCKER.

WARNER TUCKER married Elizabeth Lambert, sister of James Lambert ; lived in Westfield, and had children :

1. Jacob, who married Hannah Lines, daughter of Henry, and lived on the north side of the first mountain, above the Scotch Plains.

2. Ephraim married, first, Sarah Miller, of Westfield ; 2d, Rhoda, the widow of Ephraim Valentine, and sister of Abraham Price.

3. Samuel married, first, Patty Tucker, daughter of John, of Stony Hill Valley.

His 2d wife, I have not learned her name. His 3d wife was Rachel, the widow of Isaac Clark, and daughter of John Osborn. [See Osborn]

4. Isaac married Joanna Cory, sister of Parkhurst Cory, of Warren Township.

5. Moses married Mary Masters, daughter of Gideon, on the first Mountain.

6. Mary married Moses Masters, son of Gideon, above named. The two latter removed to Ohio.

JACOB TUCKER, (son of Warner) and Hannah Lines had children :

1. Abner, who married Jemima Frazee, daughter of Asa, of Stony Hill Valley.

2. Alfred. He with Abner, enlisted in the army, and did not return.

3 Nancy married David I. Smalley, son of James. [See Smalley]

4. Margaret married William Townley, son of Matthias. [See Townley.]

5. Samuel married Polly Tucker, his cousin, daughter of Ephraim ; had a daughter, Rhoda, and then removed to Indiana.

6 Jacob married Polly Soper, of Pennsylvania, and had children, Jacob 3d, Benjamin, and Harriet.

EPHRAIM TUCKER, (son of Warner,) by his first wife, Sarah Miller, had children :

1. Hannah, who married John Miller, son of William, of Westfield.

2. Ephraim, Jun. married Phebe Hand, daughter of Daniel, on the first mountain, whose wife was sister of Master William Cole. [See Cole.]

3. Sally married Benjamin Tucker, son of James, (no relation.)

And by his 2d wife Rhoda, Ephriam Tucker had children :

4. Polly, who married her cousin Samuel, son of Jacob.

5. Benjamin.

SAMUEL TUCKER, (son of Warner,) and Patty Tucker, his first wife, had children:

1. Sally, who married Jonathan Parker, son of Judah, and had children:

> 1. Allen Parker; 2. Samuel Parker; 3. Judah Parker;
> 4. Harriet Parker, who married Perry Sutton; 5.
> Patty Parker.

2. Nancy, who married Joseph Brooks, and had a son, Samuel Brooks.

3. Chloe married John Moore, son of Isaac, and went to Cincinnati. [*See Moore.*]

4. Polly married Samuel Parker, brother of Jonathan

And by his 2d wife, had a son.

5. Moses. By his 3d wife, Rachel, he had no children.

ISAAC TUCKER, (son of Warner,) and Joanna Cory, had children:

1. Polly, who married in Ohio, Mr. Enochs.

2. Hannah, who married in Ohio.

Isaac Tucker then died, and his widow married David Woodruff, and went to Ohio, and took her children with her.

I know of no relation between Warner Tucker and John Tucker.

JOHN TUCKER.

JOHN TUCKER married Catherine Line. He lived on Stoney Hill Valley, and had children :

1. Henry, who married Polly Mc Daniels, and went to Ohio.

2. Mary married 7th January, 1790, Job Camp, son of Aaron, and went to Ohio. [See Camp.]

3. Susannah married Cornelius Littell, son of Jonathan, and went to Ohio. [See Littell.]

4. Nancy married Joseph Morse, and removed to Ohio, in 1795.

5. Chloe married William Ryan, 17th December, 1786, and went to Ohio.

6. Moses married 27th April, 1791, Betsey Lyon, daughter of Ebenezer, and died 24th August, 1837.

7. Joseph married 30th March, 1791, Deborah Line, daughter of Joseph, she was born 22d March, 1777.

8. Elizabeth married John Tilyou, son of Vincent. [See Tilyou.]

9. John married Betsey Stewart, daughter of Joseph, and had no children.

10. Rebecca married Jacob Binge, and went to Ohio.

11. Patty married Samuel Tucker, son of Warner. [See Warner Tucker.]

2d Gen

HENRY TUCKER, (1st child of John Tucker,) and Polly Mc Daniels, removed to Hamilton county, Ohio, about 1793. He was born 30th June, 1760. She was born 3d December, 1760, married 17th December, 1780, and had childrn :

1. Elizabeth, born 11th September, 1782, and married Daniel Voorhies, son of Daniel. He was born 25th December, 1776 ; Elizabeth Voorhies died 11th June, 1849.

2. Sarah, born 17th Jan. 1785, married Oliver Voorhies, born 28th October, 1778 ; a brother of Daniel.

3. Catherine, born 30th December, 1786, married Providence White, son of Capt. Jacob White, of White's Station.

4. Mary, born 10th January, 1788, married, November, 1809, Nathan Smith, son of John, of Indiana.

5. Abigail, born 1st May, 1789, married Abraham Skillman, son of Jacob, of Springdale, near her father's farm.

6. Nancy, born 24th August, 1792, married Jacob Voorhies, son of Cornelius, a brother of Daniel and Oliver.

7. Henry, Jun., born 18th March, 1794, died 29th May, 1814, unmarried.

8. Fanny, born 28th March, 1797, married Arthur S. Sorter, born 3d March, 1793, son of Thomas.

9. Charlotte, born 4th March, 1799, married Jacob A. Riddle, son of John.

10. Manning Randolph, born 14th September, 1801, married Rebecca Perlee, born 21st Feb. 1800, daughter of Peter Perlee; they were married 5th May, 1824, and lived on his father's homestead farm of 253 acres, in the valley below Springdale.

ELIZABETH TUCKER, (1st child of Henry Tucker, son of John,) and Daniel Voorhies, had children :

1. Clarissa Voorhies, born 3d September, 1801, and married Samuel Beaty.

2. Henry Voorhies, born 4th July, 1803, married Mary Brandenburg.

3. Sarah Voorhies, born 1st September, 1805, married Joseph Brandenburgh.

4. Alfred Voorhies, born 26th August, 1807, married Lucinda Snuck.

5. Elevesta Voorhies, born 23d October, 1809, died 11th July, 1810.

6. Eliza Voorhies, born 9th August, 1811, married Joshua Thomas.

7. Mary Voorhies, born 23d August, 1813, married Isaac Littell.

8. Catherine Voorhies, born 10th August, 1815, died 31st December, 1833.

9. Caroline Voorhies, born 14th Aug. 1817, married David Stitt.

10. Charlotte Voorhies, born 14th March, 1820, died 24th May, 1822.

11. Manning Voorhies, born 14th March, 1820, married Rachel Shepherd.

12. Rebecca Voorhies, born 3d February, 1828.

SARAH TUCKER, (2d child of Henry Tucker, son of John,) and Oliver Voorhies, had children :

1. Abigail Voorhies, born 1st Oct. 1802, married Samuel Sharp.

2. Mariah Voorhies, born 4th Aug. 1804, married William Cotton.

3. Nancy Voorhies, born 18th Jan. 1807, married John Cotton.

4. Tucker Voorhies, born 7th Sept. 1808, married Nancy Carter.

5. Wilson Voorhies, born 1st June, 1810, married ——.

6. Elizabeth Voorhies, born 9th April, 1811, married Elihu Lyons.

7. Newton Voorhies, born 23d Feb. 1813, married Sarah Cotton

8. Catherine Voorhies, born, 30th August, 1817, married Richard Carter.

9. Smith Voorlies, born 26th Aug. 1819, married Rebecca Abrams.

10. Manning Voorhies, born 1st May, 1822, married Elizabeth Jennings.

11. Mason Voorhies, born 8th Dec. 1824, married Martha Jones.

12. Jahia Voorhies, born 20th Feb. 1827, married Sarah Clingham Smith.

13. Isabel Jane Voorhies, born 6th Feb. 1829, married Jacob Wilson.

CATHERINE TUCKER, (3d child of Henry, son of John,) and Providence White, had children:
1. Jacob White, who married Margaret Austin.
2. Eliza White married Robert Mc Neal
3. Nancy White.
4. Providence White.
5. Sarah White married Abraham Sanborn.
6. William White married Jane Cosner.
7. Catherine White.

MARY TUCKER. (4th child of Henry Tucker, son of John,) and Nathan Smith, had children:
1. Sarah Smith, born 11th Sept. 1810, married William L. Watkins.
2. Fanny Smith, born 17th Nov. 1812, married James Hunt.
3. Henry Dayton Smith, born Jan. 1815, married Margaret Conwell.
4. Caroline Smith, born 1817, married James W. Hunt.
5. Manning T. Smith, born 22d March, 1819, married Jane Wallace.

ABIGAIL TUCKER. (5th child of Henry Tucker, son of John,) and Abraham Skillman, had children:
1. Mary Anne Skillman, who married William P. Pendry, son of Alexander.
2. Isaac Newton Skillman married Drusilla Cheeseman, daughter of Richard.
3. Charlotte Skillman.
4. Jacob Skillman, who died at about 10 years.
5. Henry Manning Skillman.
6. Martha Anne Skillman.
7. Sarah Skillman.

NANCY TUCKER, (6th child of Henry Tucker, son of John,) and Jacob Voorhies ha   children:

1. Margaret Voorhies born 28th March, 1814, and married, 1st, Harrison Young ; 2d, Joseph McNamar.

2. Henry M. Voorhies, born 1st January, 1816, married Louisa Bennet.

3 Benjamin S. Voorhies, born 26th November, 1817, married Elizabeth Roach ; lives in Cincinnati.

4. Daniel J. Voorhies, born 11th October, 1819, married Margaret Roney, daughter of Silas, and have children:
  1. James Madison ; 2. Nancy Tucker.

5. William Fergison Voorhies, born 23d July, 1821, married Elsie Hervey.

6 John T. Voorhies, born 16th May, 1824; died 6th May, 1851.

7. Wilson G. Voorhies, born 15th May, 1826, and died at 23 years.

8. Lydia Mariah Voorhies, born 23d July, 1828, married James Taylor.

9, and 10 twins, born 22d December, 1829, and died in infancy.

11. Mary Frances Voorhies. born 17th May, 1830, died at 16 months.

FANNY TUCKER, (8th child of Henry Tucker, son of John,) and Arthur S. Sorter had children:

1. Mary Jane Sorter, born 14th August, 1821, married Lewis Morse, and died 3d March, 1851.

2. Martha Anne Sorter, born 6th September, 1825, married Levi Clark, and died 22d May, 1844.

3. Arthur Sorter, born 22d November, 1828, died 14th November, 1832.

4. Absalom Sorter, born 13th October, 1830, died 10th May, 1850.

5. Arthur S. Sorter, born 4th September, 1833.

CHARLOTTE TUCKER, (9th child of Henry Tucker, son of John,) and Jacob A Riddle had children:

1. Manning Riddle, who married Lydia Stilwell; live in Troy.

2. Nancy Jane Riddle married, 1st, Mr. Sayre ; 2d, Mr. Buckle ; live at Piqua.

3. Mary, who died young ; 4. Asenath.

MANNING R. TUCKER. (10th child of Henry Tucker, son of John,) and Rebecca Perlee, lives on his father's homestead farm, and had children:
E2

1. Harriet Mariah Newel, born 14th May, 1825, and married William R. Morse, son of Henry Morse, Esq. of Dayton.
2. Mary Smith, born 15th December, 1826.
3. Peter, born 14th February, 1828, died 21st October, 1833.
4. Martha Anne, born 19th October, 1829, died 14th November, 1832.
5. Henry, born 3d October, 1831.
6. Angeline, born 16th May, 1833.
7. Manning Perlee, born 14th March, 1835.
8 Fanny, born 26th March, 1837. died 23d April, 1842.
9. John Newton, born 22d November, 1839.

NANCY TUCKER, (4th child of John,) and Joseph Morse removed to Ohio, and settled in Hamilton county, 9 miles from Cincinnati. He died 1817; she died 1836; they had children:
1. John Morse, born 1792, married, successively, Elizabeth and Anne Swallow, sisters.
2. Isaac Morse, born 1794, and died 1817, unmarried.
3. Hetty Morse, born 1796, married William Murdock, and had children:
    1. Nancy Murdock; 2. John Murdock; 3. William Murdock; 4. Sarah Murdock; 5. Citizen Murdock; 6. Henry Murdock; 7. Lewis Murdock; 8. James Murdock.
Mr. Murdock died in 1835.
4. Lewis Morse, born 6th September, 1799, married 14th October, 1832, had no children.
5. Henry Morse, born 11th September, 1801, married, 1st, 28th December, 1820, Phebe Ryan half sister of Martin Ryan; 2d, Sarah K. Cheever, daughter of John M. Cheever.
6. Nancy Morse, born 1803, and married Daniel W. Turner.
7. Sarah Morse, born 1805, married Elisha Turner, brother of Daniel.
8. Joseph Morse, born 1807, and died at 2 or 3 years.

HENRY MORSE, (5th child of Joseph Morse, and Nancy Tucker,) was successively a merchant in Cincinnati; a member of the senate of Ohio, in 1834; a judge of the court of common pleas, and held other offices, civil and military; he has now retired to a farm near Dayton, Ohio. By his first wife, Phebe Ryan, he had chidren:
1. Mary Jane Morse, born 31st October, 1821, and married Mr. Dyer; lives in Arkansas.
2. Joseph Morse, born 11th January, 1825, and died 1849, unmarried.

3. William Ryan Morse, born 18th August, 1826, and married, 1851, Harriet M. N. Tucker, daughter of Manning R. Tucker, son of Henry, son of John.

4 Martha Ellen Morse, born 14th December, 1827.

5. Henry Morse, born 30th October, 1830, and died 22d December, 1832.

6. Caroline Morse, born 7th July, 1834, and died 22d July, 1834.

CHLOE TUCKER, (5th child of John,) and William Ryan had children:

1. Elizabeth Ryan, who married John T. Jones. in Ohio.

2. Martin Ryan married Hetty Price, daughter of Hezekiah.

3. Mary Ryan married Osborn Cooper.

4. William Ryan, Jun. married Sally Gray, and had children:

1. William H. Ryan; 2. Elizabeth Ryan; 3. John W. Ryan; 4. Malinda A. Ryan, who married Jacob R. Tingley.

MOSES TUCKER, (6th child of John,) and Betsey Lyon, had children:

1. Sally, who married Jonathan M. Willcox, son of Levi. [*See Willcox.*]

2. Clarissa married John Bryant, of Plainfield, and had children: 1. Joel Bryant; 2. Apollos Bryant; 3. Anne Eliza Bryant.

3. Abigail married David B. Jolley, son of Richard; he went to the south and died; his widow lives in New York, and has three children:

1. Richard Jolley, who married in New York, Margaret M. Fisher, daughter of Richard.

2. Robert Jolley married Martha ——.

3. John Jolley.

4. Elizabeth married Levi Clark, Esq. son of Daniel S. Esq. and had children. Frances and Emeline Clark.

5. Polly married David Cole, son of Joseph Cole, Jun. of Scotch Plains; had an only child Mary Cole, and died.

6. Susan married Asa W. Ridge, live at Plainfield, and have children:

1. Mary Abeline Ridge; 2. Susan Elizabeth Ridge; 3. Sarah Frances Ridge; 4. Theodore Ridge; 5. John Henry Ridge; 6. Moses William Ridge.

JOSEPH TUCKER, (7th child of John,) and Deborah Line lived near Union Village, and had children:

1. Lines, who married Phebe Allen, daughter of Gideon.

2. Hetty married Daniel Allen, brother of Lines' wife. [*See Allen.*]

3. Frances married Elisha Jolley, son of Richard, and had children :

    1. Henrietta Jolley, married Mr. Fisher, of New York.

    2. Phebe Jolley, who married —— ——.

    3. Mary Louisa Jolley married —— ——.

    4. Betsey Meeker Jolley, who died at about 18 years.

    5. Oscar Jolley ; 6. William Jolley died at about 3 yrs

    7. Frances Jolley, who died at 14 years.

4. Betsey married Elam Genung; they went to Indiana, where she died, leaving two children : 1. William Roy Genung ; 2. Phebe Elizabeth Genung.

LINES TUCKER, (son of Joseph, son of John,) and Phebe Allen lived where his father did, and had children :

    1. Susan, who married Benjamin Moor, son of Isaac B. Moor.

    2. Freeman married Eliza W. Drake, daughter of Ezra Drake, and only grand child of Zophar Williams ; she died 5th December. 1847, leaving children :

        1. Williams Tucker.

        2. Lines Ezra Tucker. who died at about 5 months.

And Freeman Tucker married. 2d, 30th June, 1850, Hannah Mariah Norman, daughter of Samuel Jolley's 2d wife, by a former husband.

    3. Amos. who died aged about 21 years.

    4. Debeline married. 1st January, 1849, Joseph S. Runyon, son of Richard, of Monmouth ; lives by Smalley's Bridge.

    5. Mary Elizabeth married T. Hartwell Cox, son of Restors Cox.

    6. Martha S.

REBECCA TUCKER, (10th child of John Tucker,) and Jacob Binge had children :

    1. Polly Binge, who married John Vernon.

    2. Caty Binge married Allen Parker, son of Jonathan, son of Judah.

    3. John Binge married Elizabeth Coonrod.

    4. Betsey Binge married Benjamin Chamberlain.

DANIEL VAIL.

DANIEL VAIL, who was the son of Isaac and Christiana Vail, removed from Green Brook, below Plainfield, to the west end of Long Hill, near Stonehouse Village, in Somerset Co. He married Mary McEowen, sister of William McEowen, Esq. of Pluckemin, and had children :

1. Anne, who married John Hill, (merchant,) son of William Hill, of Basking Ridge and had no children.

2. Daniel married Dinah Vandeveer, daughter of Jacobus Vandeveer, of Bedminster.

3. Catherine married Dr. Hugh McEowen, cousin of William McEowen. Esq She died 22d December, 1851.

4. Jacob married Sarah Fitz Randolph, daughter of Edward, of Green Brook, and live in Rahway Township.

5. Harriet married Frazee Cole, son of Joseph [*See Cole.*]

6. Alexander married Eliza Kirkpatrick, daughter of Alexander

7. Martha born 22d November, 1798, and married, May, 1823 Thomas O. Scudder, born 24th December, 1799, son of Stiles, son of Richard of New Providence, and had no children. [*See Scudder.*]

8. Israel married Mariah Barkalo, daughter of Stoffel, of the Sterling Farm, near Basking Ridge.

DANIEL VAIL, (2d child of Daniel,) and Dinah Vandeveer, had children :

1. Mariah, who married Abner Cory, son of Parkhurst, and had children : 1. Martha Jane Cory ; 2. Phebe Cory, who married Mr. Whitenack.

2. Catherine married Abraham Smith, below Plainfield.

3. Alexander married Nancy Southard, daughter of Lot, son of the Hon. Henry Southard.

4. Caroline married Cornelius Barkalo, son of Stoffel, of Basking Ridge, and had children : 1. Virginia Barkalo ; 2. Israel Barkalo.

CATHERINE VAIL, (3d child of Daniel,) and Dr. Hugh McEowen had children :

1. Mary McEowen, who married Dr. Edward A. Darcey ; removed to Illinois, and had children : 1. Caroline Darcey ; 2. Catherine Darcey.

2. Matilda McEowen married Rev Elias Fairchild, D. D. of Mendham ; he is secretary and agent of the Foreign Evangelical Society ; they live in Newark, and have no children.

3. Alexander McEowen married Margaret Brown, daughter of Elias Brown, Esq. of Pluckemin, whose wife was

daughter of William McEowen, Esq. above named; lives where his father did.

JACOB VAIL, (4th child of Daniel,) and Sarah Fitz Randolph had children:
1. Althea   2. Mary;   3. Nelson;   4. Eden;   5. Nerr; 6. Margaret;   7. Israel.

ALEXANDER VAIL, (6th child of Daniel,) and Eliza Kirkpatrick had children:
1. Kerenhappuc, who married Doct. William Cole, son of Elias, and had children: 1. Mary Cole ; 2. Martha Cole. [*See Cole.*]
2. Thirza, who married Clark Squier, son of Ludlow. [*See Squier.*]
Mr. Vail then died, and his widow married William B. Gaston, Esq., of Somerville. [*See Kirkpatrick.*]

ISRAEL VAIL, (8th child of Daniel,) and Mariah Barkalo had children:
1. William, who died at about 11 years: 2. Oscar; 3. Christopher Barkalo; 4. Anna Mariah; 5. Martha; 6. Daniel; 7. Melinda.

JAMES VAIL was a brother of Daniel Vail, Sen., and lived at the Stone House Village. He married Betsey Carle, eldest daughter of Jonas Carle, and had children:
1. Isaac, who married Agnes Cooper, daughter of Daniel, son of John, and had children: 1. John Cooper Vail ; 2. Lydia Anne, who married Charles Ross, merchant, of Elizabethtown.
2. Anna, who married Edward Vail, son of Joel, below Plainfield, and had no children.
3. James married Mary Simpson, daughter of James Simpson, of Mount Be hel, and had children : 1. Isabel ; 2. Isaac.
Jacob Vail, another son of Isaac Vail ; lived near Stone House Village ; he died an old man without children.

KENNEDY VANCE.

KENNEDY VANCE lived where Samuel Squier now does. He married Phebe, the widow of Benjamin Pettit, Jun, and daughter of Joseph Potter, [*See Pettit and Potter.*] She died 9th March, 1793; they had children :

1. Samuel, who was shot dead by the British, 8th June, 1780, aged 20 years, at the battle of Springfield.
2. Nancy, who married Aaron Squier, son of Thomas. [*See Squier.*]
3. Jane married, 8th July, 1790, Joel Jones. [*See Jones.*]
4. John, who went to Western New York, and married Eve Rope.
5. Agnes married David Robison, son of William. [*See Robison.*]

RICHARD VALENTINE.

RICHARD VALENTINE owned Nos. 35 and 44 of the Elizabethtown lots, and lived on No. 44, where Israel B. Long now lives. This lot contained 184 acres, and extended over the Mountain, and adjoined Peter Willcox's tract, lying west of it It also adjoined the Pettit tract, No. 45, lying west of Valentine's He married Phebe Haines, and died 10th March, 1766, aged 63 years; his widow, Phebe, then married William Miller, of Westfield; and after his death, she returned to her former homestead, on Stony Hill, and died there, 21st May, 1783, aged 76 years. Richard Valentine and Phebe Haines had children:

1. Jonah, who married Susannah Bedell, daughter of John Bedell, Jun.
2. Ephraim married Rhoda Price, sister of Abraham Price. [*See Ephraim Tucker.*]
3. Obadiah married, first, Mary Mulford, daughter of Capt. Jonathan Mulfo d ; 2d, Elizabeth, the widow of William Maxwell, and daughter of Thomas Baker, Jun. ; 3d, Elizabeth, 16th Feb. 1786, widow of Benjamin Day, Esq., and sister of Phebe, the wife of Peter Davison, the father of John R. Davison, of Newark, and also sister of Samuel Roberts, Sen., children of Daniel Roberts.
4. Phebe married John Miller 3d, of Westfield, son of John, Jun. [*See Miller.*]
5. Mary married, first, Henry Clark, of Westfield; 2d, Sylvanus Oakley, son of David. [*See Oakley.*] She married,

19th Jan. 1789, 3d, David Cammel, and died 7th March, 1795, aged 61 years.

6. Elizabeth married. 19th Sept. 1767, Benjamin North.

7. Rachel married William Baker. [*See Baker*]

8. Sarah, twin to Rachel, died 26th June, 1768, aged 26 years, unmarried.

JONAH VALENTINE, (1st child of Richard,) and Susannah Bedell had children :

1. Jemima, who married, 11th July, 1784, William Woodruff, of Westfield.

2. Samuel, who died in his 19th year.

3. Martha married Joseph Marsh, of Rahway.

4. Phebe married Andrew Joline.

5 Susannah married John Long. [*See Long.*]

6. Joseph married Temperance Littell, daughter of Andrew.

7. Benjamin, who died in his 14th year.

8. Lydia married Brown Brookfield ; lives on the north side of Long Hill ; is a widow ; she had no children.

9. Esther married John Bloomfield.

10. Sarah married, 2d Jan. 179), David Littell, from Ireland, and removed to Lebanon, Ohio.

JOSEPH VALENTINE, (6th child of Jonah,) and Temperance Littell, (daughter of Andrew,) had children :

1. William ; 2. Martha ; 3 Samuel ; 4. Jeremiah ; 5. Joseph, Jun.

JEREMIAH VALENTINE, (4th child of Joseph.) married Ruth Terry, daughter of Jonathan Terry and Huldah Van Sickle, and had children : [*See page 333*]

1. Lucy Anne ; 2. Abigail ; 3. Erastus Lewis ; 4. Temperance ; 5. Joseph ; 6. Andrew ; 7. Susan ; 8. Ruth.

EPHRAIM VALENTINE, (2d child of Richard,) and Rhoda Price had children :

1. Benjamin, who married Polly Briant.

2. David.

3. Richard.

4. Sarah married Israel Martin.

5. Abigail married Dennis Woodruff.

ELIZABETH VALENTINE, (6th child of Richard,) and Benjamin North had children :

1. Mahala North.

2. Ruth North, who married, 1st, Mr. McCloud, of Philadelphia ; 2d, Richard Ogden, son of Nathaniel. She had no children.

OBADIAH VALENTINE, (3d child of Richard,) lived on lot No 35 of the Elizabethtown lots, where Israel Doty now lives; he and his first wife, Mary Mulford, had children:

1. Esther, who married, 18th May, 1783, Levi Willcox, son of William. [See *Willcox.*]

2. William married, 1st April, 1787, Joanna Crane, daughter of Joseph, Sen. and went to Ohio.

3. Jonathan married, 10th April, 1791, Abigail Day, daughter of Benjamin Day, Esq. and daughter of his father's 3d wife.

4. David married, 23d September, 1792, Sarah Day, sister of Jonathan's wife, and went to Dayton, Ohio; [see *Aaron Baker.*] he had a daughter Nancy, who married Lewis Broadwell, son of Simeon, of Dayton, and had a son Jonathan, who married, and lives in Piqua, Ohio.

5. Levi, who died at 14 years of age.

6. Daniel married Miss Winans, of Union, and went to Dayton, Ohio.

Mary, the wife of Obadiah Valentine. died 9th June, 1777, aged 36 years. And by his 2d wife Elizabeth, the widow of William Maxwell, he had,

7. Mary, who went to Ohio, and there married John Craig, in 1805.

His 2d wife, Elizabeth died. 13th September, 1785, and he married Elizabeth, the widow of Benjamin Day, Esq. and daughter of Daniel Roberts, by whom he had no children

He died 19th May, 1788, aged 48 years; his widow died 4th October, 1830, aged 82 years.

JONATHAN VALENTINE, (son of Obadiah,) and Abigail Day, had chidren:

1. Benjamin, who died 29th July, 1787.

2. Betsey, born 1st December, 1791, and died 25th August, 1792

3. Peter Davison, born 20th October, 1793, married, 28th November, 1812, Abigail Rutan, daughter of Joseph Rutan; she was born 19th March, 1794.

4. Sarah; 5. Phebe; 6. William, who all three died in infancy.

Mr. Jonathan Valentine died 18th April, 1801, aged 35 years.

And his widow married John Schureman; she died 3d Sept. 1817, aged 47 years.

PETER D. VALENTINE, (son of Jonathan, son of Obadiah,) and Abigail Rutan, had children:

1. Jonathan, born 19th September, 1814, and married, 25th July, 1838, Mary Littell, daughter of John Littell, Esq.

He was elected a member of the legislature in 1849, and again in 1850; he has served 5 years as a justice of the peace.

2. Hannah, born 3d November, 1816, and died 6th July, 1820.

3. Abraham, born 4th October, 1818, married, 12th March, 1840, Harriet Meeker, daughter of Isaac Meeker; she died 16th June, 1843, aged 31 years, and he married Debby Anne Willcox, daughter of Ezra.

4. Elizabeth.

5. Daniel Rutan.

6. William married, 19th February, 1852, Caroline Amanda Stout, daughter of Elijah Stout, of Kingston, Somerset county.

7 Sarah, who married, 17th October, 1849, Jacob D. Mulford, son of William. [*See Job Mulford.*]

8. Harriet.

JONATHAN VALENTINE, Esq. (son of Peter D. Valentine.) and Mary Littell, had children:

1. Samuel Rutan, born 13th July, 1839.

2. Luther Littell, born 30th September, 1842.

3. Eliza Littell, born 13th November, 1845.

4. William, who died in infancy.

5. John, born 21st November, 1849, and died 22d January, 1850.

6. Mary Abigail, born 14th July, 1851.

RICHARD WALKER.

RICHARD WALKER had three wives, one of which was Sarah; he lived in Westfield, and had children:

1. Asher, who married Phebe Miller, daughter of Daniel Miller.

And by a 2d wife, he had other children:

2. Sarah, who married Elnathan Cory, son of Ebenezer.

3. Abraham, whose wife's name was Sarah.

4. John, who married Hannah Cory, daughter of Ebenezer.

5. David, and others.

Abraham and John Walker probably bought the tract of land where George Cory now lives, of Jacob Carle.

They lived on that place, between the years 1774 and 1784, and probably sold it to Smith S. Osborn, who lived there in 1784, and they removed to the west.

ASHER WALKER bought of Alexander Porter, the farm, part of which is now owned and occupied by Samuel Duryee, and lived there He died 19th November, 1805, aged 63 years; his wife Phebe died 8th December, 1798, aged 53 years; they had children:

1. Susan, who married Henry Squier, son of Eleazer Squier, of Westfield, and had children:

    1. Eli Squier, who married Matilda Johnson.

    2 Miller, who married Hannah Spencer, daughter of William Spencer, Esq. [See Spencer.]

    3. Phebe married John Johnson, son of Uzel, and went to Ohio.

Susan married, 2d, Joseph Ross, and had a son Jonas.

2. Miller, who married Theodocia Brittin, daughter of Jacob. [See Brittin.]

3. Sally married David Morehouse, son of Simeon. [See Morehouse.]

4. Abraham married, 1st, Electa Bonnel, daughter of James; 2d. Elizabeth Hallock, daughter of Thomas.

5. David married Roxy Miller, daughter of Ichabod, of Rahway.

6. Jonathan married, 1st, Polly Spencer, daughter of William Spencer, Esq. of Chatham; 2d, Electa Miller. daughter of Major Luke Miller, of Madison; 3d, Rhoda Johnson, of Chester, Morris county; 4th, Elizabeth, the widow of his brother Abraham.

7 Temperance, who died 19th August, 1794, aged 23 years, unmarried.

8. Phebe married, 14th May, 1808, Peter Van Horn, of Bergen county.

9 Polly married, 5th September. 1813, Eliakim Ludlow, son of Noah, son of Cornelius, of Westfield. [*See Noah Ludlow.*]

MILLER WALKER, (2d child of Asher, son of Richard,) and Theodocia Brittin, had children :

1. Abraham Brittin Walker, who married Hetty Crowel, daughter of David A. Crowel, of Chatham, and has an only child, Henry Hartstein.

2. Isaac Brittin, who died 4th February, 1836, aged 23 years, unmarried.

3. Jacob Brittin, who went to Mobile, and married Susan Youngblood, and lives there, and had children :
1. Eugene ; 2. Eugenia.

4. David, who died 27th May, 1827, aged 27 years, unmarried.

5. Eliza married, 30th August. 1838. Luke Parsons, son of Jonathan, as his 3d wife ; she has no children.

Mrs. Theodocia Walker died 16th September, 1834, aged 59½ years.

Mr. Miller Walker died 16th March, 1840.

ABRAHAM WALKER, (4th child of Asher,) and Electa Bonnel. his first wife, had but one child :

1. Rhoda, who married Dr. John L. Munn, son of Dr J. B. Munn, of Chatham, and had children :
1 Jephtha B. Munn ; 2. George Ludlow Munn.
3. Joanna Munn.

His wife Electa died 21st November, 1808 ; and by his 2d wife. Elizabeth, he had children :

2. Electa, who married Thomas Garrison, live in Newark, and have children :
1. Harriet Newel Garrison ; 2. Sarah Elizabeth Garrison ; 3. Theodocia Backus Garrison : 4. Aruna Garrison ; 5. Adelaide Garrison ; 6. Thomas John Garrison.

3. Amanda married Amos Lum, son of Moses, of Newark. [*See Lum.*]

4. Abraham married Jane Crane, daughter of John Crane, of Newark, and have children :
1. Mary Elizabeth ; 2. James Mahlon ; 3. Abraham Brittin Walker.

5. David Littell Walker.

6. Mary married John Price, spectacle maker, of Newark, and have children :
1. Henry Martin Price ; 2. Adelaide Price ; 3. Electa Price.

7. Eliza married Henry H. Soloman, of New Brunswick, as his 2d wife, and had children : 1. Lavenia ; 2. ——— ———.

8. Sarah Anne, who died 29th June, 1838, aged 15 years.

9. Louisa Emeline, who died 4th August, 1839, aged 13 years.

Mr. Abraham Walker died 19th April, 1827, aged 52 years. His widow married Jonathan Walker.

DAVID WALKER, (5th child of 'Asher,) and Roxy Miller, had children :

1. David, who died 12th August, 1817, aged 2½ years.

2. Chatfield, who went to Ohio, and married ———— ————.

David Walker died 25th July, 1828, aged 44 years, and his widow went to Cincinnati, Ohio, with her son.

JONATHAN WALKER, (6th child of Asher,) and Polly Spencer, had one daughter, Mary, who married Luke C. Dehart, of Madison, and had children :

1. William Dehart ; 2. George Dehart.

And by Electa Miller, he had children :

2. John Henry.

3. Sarah Anne.

4 George.

5. Caroline.

And by his third wife, Rhoda Johnson, had

6. William.   By his 4th wife he had no children.

PHEBE WALKER, (8th child of Asher,) and Peter Van Horn, had children :

1 Garret Van Horn ; 2. Burgher Van Horn.

Mr. Van Horn died 9th February, 1825, aged 37½ years ; his widow Phebe, died 28th May, 1830, aged 48 years.

POLLY WALKER, (9th child of Asher,) and Eliakim Ludlow, had children :

1. Emeline Ludlow.

2. Phebe, who married Alonzo Johnson.

3. Jane married Isaac Egbert, and had a son:

1. William Henry Ludlow Egbert.

4. William, who went to Cincinnati, Ohio.

DAVID WARD.

DAVID WARD married Hannah Farrand, of Newark.
They lived at Chatham, and had children:

1. Enos, (Captain,) who married Mahetabel Burnet, daughter of James, of Madison.

2. David, born 19th September, 1749, married Hamutal Ladner, born 15th December, 1750, of Madison; he died 19th July, 1814; she died 1830.

3. Hannah married, (bellows) Benjamin Bonnel, son of Benjamin, Esq. [See B nnel.]

4 Polly married Isaac Howard, and had no children.

5. Ichabod married, 1st, Johannah Day, daughter of Stephen Day, Esq., as her 2d husband.

Ichabod Ward married, 2d, June 21st, 1789, Esther, the widow of John Mills Frost, and daughter of Josiah Broadwell, Esq.

6. Phebe, who died at about 20 years, unmarried.

7. Betty married John Johnson, a wholesale grocer, of New York. [See John Johnson.]

8. Sarah married Philip Cockran, of New York; she died without children, and he married Hannah, the daughter of Capt. Enos Ward, his first wife's niece.

CAPTAIN ENOS WARD, (1st child of David,) and Mahetabel Burnet, had children:

1. Ruth, who married Gabriel Pierson, son of Benjamin.

2. Hannah married Philip Cockran, as his 2d wife, and had no children.

3. Matthias married Eleanor Bonnel, daughter of John, son of Nathaniel Bonnel 1st.

4. James married Sophia Seely, daughter of Col. Sylvanus Seely.

5. Hamutal married Paul Day, son of Thaddeus, and had no children.

RUTH WARD, (1st child of Capt. Enos Ward,) and Gabriel Pierson, had children:

1. Matthias Pierson, who married Charlotte Genung, daughter of David Genung.

2. Enos Pierson, who died at 25 years, unmarried.

3. Juliette Pierson, died at 18 years, unmarried.

4. Phebe Pierson is unmarried.

5. Sarah Pierson married Paul Day, son of Thaddeus, as his 2d wife, and had no children.

6. Mahetabel Pierson is unmarried.

7. Benjamin Pierson died at 13 years.

8. Hannah Mariah Pierson died at 3 months.

MATTHIAS PIERSON, (1st child of Gabriel,) and Charlotte Genung, had children:
1. Juliette Pierson, who married Thomas H. Skinner.
2. Ambrose Pierson, who died at about 18 years.
3. Nancy Jane Pierson married Henry Judson.
4. Charles Pierson married Emily Trowbridge, daughter of Shubal, of Brooklyn.
5 Matthias Ward Pierson married Drusilla Startup.
6. Sarah Pierson, who died young.

MATTHIAS WARD, (3d child of Capt. Enos,) and Eleanor Bonnel, had children :
1. Philip, who married Jane Garthwaite, of Elizabethtown.
2. Mahlon married Caroline Hunt.
3. Sarah, who died at about 18 years, unmarried.
4. Mahetabel died at about 19 years, unmarried.
5. Harriet married Robert Lackron, a European.
6. Louisa married Calvin Smith, son of Frederick, of Chatham.
7. Laura married David Bowers, son of David, of Newark.
8. Enos died at 25 years, unmarried.
9. Juliette is unmarried.

JAMES WARD, (4th child of Captain Enos,) and Sophia Seely, had children :
1. John, who died unmarried, upwards of 20 years old.
2 Jane, who died at about 20 years, unmarried.
3. Sylvanus, who married Abby ——, near Bethany, Pennsylvania, and lives there.

DAVID WARD 2d, (2d son of David Ward 1st,) and Hamutal Ladner had children :
1. Barnabas, born 17th Nov. 1771, and was drowned 1808. He did not marry.
2. Benjamin, born 16th May, 1774, and died 15th July,1803. He married, 5th Oct. 1796, Lydia Young, daughter of Moses and Rosannah Young.
3. Phebe, born 30th Oct 1781, and married, 3d April, 1802, the Rev. John Hancock, son of John and Mary Hancock, and live in East Madison.
4. John, born 4th June, 1786, married, 27th Nov. 1808, Melissa Bond, daughter of Thomas Bond, of Chatham, and died 27th March, 1837.
5. Philip, born 16th March, 1789, and died in youth.
6. Farrand, born 20th Oct. 1796, married Charlotte Bruen, daughter of Carter Bruen, and died 14th July, 1835.

BENJAMIN WARD, (2d child of David Ward 2d,) and Lydia Young had children:

1. Sylvesta, born 28th July. 1797, married, 28th Feb. 1818, John R. Mulford, son of Christopher, and had no children.

2. Menzies, a son, born 15th Sept. 1802, and died 6th Oct. 1815.

PHEBE WARD. (3d child of David Ward 2d,) and Rev. John Hancock had children:

1. Jane Hancock, born 8th Oct. 1803, married, 22d Feb. 1835, Vincent B. Budd, as his 2d wife, son of Doct. John C. Budd, and had children: 1 Jane Hancock Budd. born 21st June, 1836 ; 2. Benjamin Ward Budd, born 11th July. 1842.

2. John Wesley Hancock, born 30th Aug. 1805. He was a surveyor, and married, 17th Dec. 1828. Mary Anne C. Griswold, daughter of Chauncy, and Polly Griswold. She died 15th Feb. 1849 ; they had children : 1. Jane, born 9th Nov. 1829, died 20th July, 1833 ; 2. John Wesley, born 6th Jan. 1831, died 22d July, 1833 ; 3. Phebe, born 17th April, 1833 ; 4. John Emory, born 18th July, 1835 ; 5. Ellen, born 6th Nov. 1837, died 4th June, 1839 ; 6. Mervin Griswold, born 25th Dec. 1839 ; 7. Mary Anne, born 20th Dec. 1841 ; 8. Roswell, born 24th Sept. 1845 ; 9. Robert Harris, born 1st Feb. 1848.

3. Phebe Hancock, born 16th Oct. 1807. died 28th March, 1823.

4. Mary Graham Hancock, born 4th Nov 1814.

5. Monroe Hancock. born 26th Feb. 1817, married Sally Anne Cole, daughter of Henry. and had children : 1. George Hugh, born 25th June. 1843 ; 2. Fletcher, born 7th July, 1848, died 5th Sept. 1849 ; 3. William, born 16th June. 1850.

6. Emeline Hancock, born 8th March, 1819, died 23d Nov. 1836.

JOHN WARD, (3d child of David Ward 2d,) and Melissa Bond had children :

1. Nancy Ladner, born 26th Jan. 1810, married, 27th Jan. 1828, to Vincent B. Budd, as his 1st wife, son of Doct. John C. Budd, and died Feb. 16th 1834. They had children : 1. Thomas Bond Budd, born 10th Jan. 1829 ; 2. Melissa Ward Budd, born 14th June, 1831 ; 3. Nancy Ladner Budd, born 30th Sept. 1833, died 19th Aug. 1834.

2. Lydia Young, born 28th March, 1812, married, 1st Dec. 1830, to Moses L. Bruen, son of Ichabod and Damaris Bruen, and had children : 1. John Ward Bruen, born — Aug. 1833 ; 2. Laura Johnson Bruen, born June. 1838.

3. David Farrand. born 20th Nov. 1814, married. 20th Feb. 1839, to Charlotte B. Matthews, daughter of Charles, and had no children by her.

4. Julia Anne, born 27th April, 1817, married, 10th Jan. 1838, Benjamin B. Griswold, son of Chauncy Griswold, and had children : 1. Chauncy Griswold, born 1st April, 1839 ; 2. Mary Ward Griswold, born 31st May, 1841 ; 3. Anna Ladner Griswold, born 5th March, 1845 ; 4. Lydia Bruen Griswold, born 21st Feb. 1847.

5. Mary Bond, born 11th Nov. 1822, married, 8th Dec. 1847, to James Albright, son of Robert Albright, Esq., and had children: 1. Eliza Albright, born 1st Sept. 1848 ; 2. Julia Ward Albright, born 2d Sept. 1850.

FARRAND WARD, (6th child of David Ward 2d,) and Charlotte Bruen had children :

1. David Johnson, born 8th Sept. 1822.

2. Phebe Bruen, born 6th Jan. 1825, married Allen S. Felch.

3. Harriet Elenora, born 25th April, 1829, married George W. Felch. She died 23d Oct. 1849.

4. Benjamin Collins, born 2d Oct. 1832, died 4th April, 1834.

5. Benjamin Farrand, born 18th Sept. 1834.

David J. Ward married Catherine Tunis, daughter of Joseph M. and Charity Tunis, and had children : 1. Charlotte Augusta ; 2. Joseph Farrand.

ICHABOD WARD, (5th child of David,) and Johannah Day had children :

1. Elijah, who married Matilda Lindsley, daughter of Judge Lindsley, of Orange.

2. Moses married Jane Day, daughter of Stephen Day, Jun.

3. Damaris married Ichabod Bruen, of Madison.

4. Sally married Matthias Bonnel, son of Bellows Ben. Bonnel. [*See Bonnel.*]

Ichabod Ward, by his 2d wife, Esther, had children :

5. David, who died at about 17 years.

6. Phebe married Jonathan C. Bonnel, son of Nathaniel Bonnel 3d. [*See J. C. Bonnel.*]

NOTE.—Mrs. Esther Ward, by her first husband, John Mills Frost, had children :

1. Josiah Frost, who married Abigail Jones.

2. Charity Frost married Caleb Meeker, son of Isaiah. [*See Meeker.*]

JONATHAN WHITAKER.

Tradition in the Whitaker family says that three brothers embarked in England for America; that the ship in which they embarked was cast away, and but one of the three arrived; whose name was Jonathan Whitaker, who settled in New England; his wife's name was Elizabeth. They had children :

1. Nathaniel, who married Miss Smith.
2. Eliphalet married Ruth Bailey.
3 Elizabeth married Stephen Ogden, of Basking Ridge.
4. Mary married, 1st, Samuel Brown; 2d, Ebenezer White.
5. Jonathan, Jun. married Mary Miller.

Nathaniel Whitaker became a presbyterian minister, and settled in Norwich, Connecticut: he was sent in 1764 or 65, with Mr. Samuel Occum, an Indian preacher, to England, to collect funds for "Moore's Charity School," of Lebanon, an Indian school.

Jonathan Whitaker, Sen. removed with his family, (except Nathaniel,) from New England to New Jersey, and purchased of Thomas Penn and Richard Penn, proprietors of the Province of Pennsylvania, (by Richard Peters and Lynford Lardner, their attornies and agents,) for the sum of £225, lawful money of the State of New Jersey, a tract of land, lying on both sides of Mine Brook, in Somerset county, 407½ acres, by deed bearing date 19th December, 1752; and by writing of transfer on the back of said deed, bearing date 7th day of July, 1763, for the sum of £625, current money, of East New Jersey, at eight shillings per ounce, he conveyed to Jonathan Whitaker, Jun his eldest son, the whole of the aforesaid tract of 407½ acres, excepting about 163 acres previously sold and conveyed to his son Eliphalet.

ELIPHALET WHITAKER, (son of Jonathan,) married Ruth Bailey, and at length sold his farm, and removed to Georgia, and settled there, leaving two children, Samuel and Elizabeth, in New Jersey.

SAMUEL WHITAKER, (son of Eliphalet,) was born 26th November, 1756, and died 6th June, 1818, aged 61½ yrs. He married, 2d March, 1783, Mary, a widow, and daughter of John Rivers. She was born 15th March, 1754, and died 2d October, 1825, aged 71½ years; they had children :

1. Mary, born 20th Dec. 1784, and married, 24th Dec. 1804. John Taylor.
2. Benjamin, born 16th February, 1787, and died 27th Oct. 1827.

3. Samuel, born 11th June, 1789, and died 16th May, 1818.
4. Phebe, born 9th July, 1792, and died 22d April, 1810.
5. Elisha, born 21st February, 1795, married, 28th April, 1824, Anne M. Finley, daughter of Alexander, of Basking Ridge; she was born 14th December, 1799, and died 2d October, 1842.

MARY WHITAKER, (daughter of Samuel,) and John Taylor lived in New York, and had children:

5th Gen 1. Mary Antoinette Taylor, born 10th March, 1806, and married Jabez Hays.
2. Abigail Amelia Taylor, born 7th October, 1808, and married Mr. Chandler.
3. Samuel Taylor, born 16th August, 1811, and married Harriet Jackson.
4. Phebe Taylor, born 5th September, 1813, and died 15th August, 1815.
5. Horace Taylor, born 13th November, 1815; married, and soon died.
6. Phebe Taylor, born 21st November, 1818.
7. George Edwin Taylor, born 25th August, 1821, and married Martha Durkin.
8. John Romeyn Taylor, born 27th December, 1824.
9. Susan Taylor, born 4th November, 1827, and died young.

ELISHA WHITAKER, (son of Samuel,) and Anne M. Finley lived in Newark, and had children:
1. Phebe Amelia, born 24th March, 1826, and died 14th April, 1846.
2. Samuel Elisha, born 12th February, 1831.
3. Alexander Finley, born 10th May, 1832, and died 13th April, 1833.
4. Alexander Finley, born 6th June, 1834.
5. Mary Anne, born 7th June, 1840.
6. Elisha Samuel, born 23d January, 1842, and died 10th October, 1842.
Elisha Whitaker married for his 2d wife, 12th June, 1844, Eliza M. Kinsey, widow of Jonathan Kinsey, of Philadelphia, and daughter of Nathaniel Manning; she was born 14th February, 1808.

ELIZABETH WHITAKER, (daughter of Eliphalet,) married William Roy, son of Judge John Roy, of Basking Ridge, and had children:
1. Hannah Roy, who married Aaron Hand, son of Jonathan; she died 21st January, 1850. [*See Hand.*]
2. William Roy, Jun. married Deborah Whitaker, daugh-

ter of Stephen, son of Jonathan Whitaker, Jun.; he lived in Yates county, New York.

William Roy, Sen. died, and his widow Elizabeth married Richard Hall, son of John Hall. [See *John Hall.*]

ELIZABETH WHITAKER, (daughter of Jonathan Whitaker, Sen.) married Stephen Ogden, of Basking Ridge, lived where Patrick Matthews now does, and had children:

1. Jonathan Ogden, who lived near Morristown, was judge of the court.

2. Nathaniel Ogden.

3. Isaac Ogden was a physician, lived at Germantown, Hunterdon county, New Jersey, and had a son Oliver Wayne Ogden, who was several years Marshall of the state of New Jersey.

4. Sally Ogden, who married John Gaston, father of Joseph Gaston, of Pluckemin, who was the father of John Gaston and William B. Gaston, Esqs. of Somerville.

MARY WHITAKER, (daughter of Jonathan Whitaker, Sen.) married, 1st, Samuel Brown; 2d, Ebenezer White, and removed to Long Island.

Mrs. White, after the death of her husband, returned to Basking Ridge, and lived in the house where General Lee was taken prisoner, in the revolutionary war. She had a daughter, Susan White, who married her cousin, Stephen Whitaker, eldest son of Jonathan Whitaker, Jun. and had an only daughter, Susan Whitaker, who married Alexander Finley. [*See Finley.*]

JONATHAN WHITAKER JUN.

JONATHAN WHITAKER, Jun. (son of Jonathan,) and Mary Miller lived on part of the 407 acres of land purchased of his father, on Mine Brook, and had children :

1. Stephen, who married, 1st, his cousin, Susan White, daughter of Ebenezer White; she died 1st September, 1773; 2d, Ruth Conklin, daughter of Stephen Conklin, who was born in Suffolk county, Long Island, 22d December, 1753, and died in Somerset county, N. J. 21st October, 1797.

2. Phebe married Rev. Francis Peppard, and lived in Sussex. [*See Peppard.*]

3. Polly, who died 19th February, 1822, aged 68 years, unmarried.

4. Sally married Moses Allen, removed to Crawford county, Pennsylvania, 18 miles west of Meadville, and had children : 1. Stephen Whitaker Allen; 2. Jeremy Allen.

5. Rebecca, born 10th May, 1754, married William Conklin, Esq. son of Stephen. Mr. Conklin was an elder in the Presbyterian church at Basking Ridge. [*See Conklin.*]

6. Jonathan 3d married Mary Mitchel, had 13 children, and removed to Warren county, Ohio, about 1800.

7. Nathaniel, born June, 1758, and married, June, 1787, Hannah Drake, daughter of John Drake, of Mendham, and had a daughter, Sally, who married Garret Voorhies, Esq. His wife Hannah died December, 1794, and he married, 2d, Ruth Haines, daughter of Samuel Haines, near Vealtown, and had a daughter, Hannah, who married Nicholas Arrowsmith, Jun. Esq.

Nathaniel Whitaker died 27th October, 1841, and his widow Ruth died 10th November, 1844.

Jonathan Whitaker, Jun. died 1785, aged 73 years.

STEPHEN WHITAKER, (1st child of Jonathan Whitaker, Jun.,) was born 10th January, 1747, and died 4th November, 1827. He and Susan White had a daughter, Susan, who married Alexander Finley. And by his 2d wife, Ruth Conklin, had children :

2. Jonathan, who married Mary Bailey, daughter of Thaddeus Bailey, of Sussex county; and lives in Yates county, New York.

3. Mary married Moses Hall, son of John, son of Richard Hall. [*See Hall.*]

4. Deborah married William Roy, Jun., son of William, son of John Roy, and lived in Yates county, New York. Mr. Roy was an Elder in the Presbyterian Church. She died 20th July, 1851.

5. Stephen, born 21st July, 1784, and married Mary Hall, sister of Moses Hall, lives at Cleveland, Ohio; he was an Elder and Deacon in the Presbyterian Church there.

6. Ruth married, 1st, Ephraim Mallory, and had a son, John Mallory; 2d, Jacob Vandeventer, son of Jacob, of Peapack, lived in Yates county, New York. She died 16th Oct. 1850, of cancer in the breast.

7. Isaac married Acsah Cushman, of Benton, Yates Co., and went to Michigan.

8. Phebe married Moses Hall, after the death of her sister Mary, and has no children.

9. Anne married Jonathan A. Hall, son of Jonathan, and nephew of Moses, and lives near Penn Yan, New York. Mr. Hall died 24th January, 1852. [*See Hall.*]

Stephen Whitaker's 2d wife, Ruth, died, and he married, 3d, Polly, the widow of John Cross; she died, and he married, 4th, Agnes (Van Court,) the widow of Daniel Potter; [*See Potter,*] she was sister of Hannah Van Court, who married Daniel Lacy, son of David Lacy. [*See Lacy.*] His 4th wife Agnes died in Benton, Yates county, New York, 29th July, 1837.

JONATHAN WHITAKER, (2d child of Stephen, son of Jonathan, Jun.,) and Mary Bailey, live in Yates county, N. Y. He was an Elder and an efficient member of the Presbyterian Church at Benton; he was born 24th January, 1780; she was born 27th August, 1784. They had children:

1. Squier Bailey, born 29th May, 1807, and married, 1st, Mary Amsbury, daughter of Stephen; 2d, in 1832, Lydia C. Amsbury, sister of his first wife; she died in childbed, with her first child, 24th January, 1852, leaving an infant son.

2. Stephen Madison, born 3d June, 1809, and married Mary Anne Gage, daughter of Martin Gage, of Bellona, and is a merchant there. They had children:

    1. Ephraim Seward; 2 George Homer; 3 Mary Virginia; 4. Stephen Eddy.

3. Alexander Finley, born 7th August. 1811, married, 20th June, 1843, Louisa P. Torrence, daughter of Richard Torrence. He is a Major General of Militia, and a farmer. They had children:

    1. Hellen Lucinda, born 17th March, 1845.

    2. Charles, who died 25th February, 1850, aged 3 months and 19 days.

    3. Melville Torrence, born 26th April, 1851.

4. William Harlow, born 16th Aug. 1813, married Anne Eliza Mc Dowel, daughter of Jonathan, and had children:

    1. William Henry; 2. Jonathan; 3 Augustus; 4. Marietta; 5. Francis; 6. Alice Aurelia; and a daughter.

5. Ephraim Mallory, born 27th August, 1816, married 12th September, 1844, Eliza W. Bates, live in Ann Arbor, Michigan, is a merchant there, and has children: Grenville Adolbert, born 23d November, 1846, and Herbert Belletti, born October 6th, 1850.

6. Ruth Ann, born 15th November, 1818.

7. Marietta, born 21st December, 1820.

8. George W., born 27th November, 1823, and died at 20 months old.

MARY WHITAKER, (3d child of Stephen, son of Jonathan Whitaker, Jun.,) and Moses Hall, lived at Geneva, and had children :

5th Gen.

1. Jane Hall, born 25th April, 1809, and married John Humphry ; live in Michigan.

2. Phebe Hall, born 5th November, 1810, married Nelson Rowley ; live in Michigan.

3. Rachel Hall, born 7th November, 1812.

4. Stephen Whitaker Hall, born 5th August, 1815, married Nancy Graham, and live at Williamsport, Pennsylvania.

5. Henry Axtel Hall, born 9th February, 1817, married Susan C. Babcock ; live in Geneva.

6. Mary Hall, born 9th March, 1820, married 30th September, 1847, the Rev. John Jermain Porter, of Geneva.

7. Hetty Hall, born 18th September, 1823, married Chauncey B. Ackley ; live in Geneva.

DEBORAH WHITAKER, (4th child of Stephen, son of Jonathan Whitaker, Jun ,) and William Roy, had children :

1. Charles Roy, who married Elizabeth Tracy, and had children :

1. William Tracy Roy ; 2. Chester Roy.

2. Eliza Roy, who married Doctor Joel H. Ross, and live in New York.

DEACON STEPHEN WHITAKER, (5th child of Stephen, son of Jonathan Whitaker, Jun.,) and Mary Hall, had children :

1. John Hall Whitaker, born 6th May, 1813, and married Francis Elvina Grosvenor, daughter of Vine Grosvenor, of Pittsfield, Mass ; live at Toledo, Ohio ; is an iron monger. His wife died 2d September, 1849, aged 32 years, and left one child, Charles Henry, born 5th September, 1846.

2. Charles, born 13th March, 1817, and married, 1st November, 1851, Susan Littell, daughter of John Littell, Esq., son of Nathaniel, of New Providence, Essex county, New Jersey. [*See Nathaniel Littell, son of David.*]

3. Mary Catherine, born 13th January, 1820.

4. Stephen Conklin ———, died suddenly of erysipelas, November, 15th 1851, after 4 days illness.
5. Henry Axtel, who died at 5 years.
6. William Henry.
7. Helen Elizabeth, who died at 11 months.

RUTH WHITAKER, (6th child of Stephen, son of Jonathan Whitaker, Jun.,) and Ephraim Mallory, lived in Yates county, New York.

NOTE.—Ephraim Mallory was son of Meredith Mallory and Mary Barnum, of Connecticut; they had three children: 1. John; 2. Meredith; and 3. Ephraim Mallory.

Ruth Whitaker and Ephraim Mallory, had children:

1. John Mallory, who married Mary Lacy, daughter of Silas Lacy, son of Daniel Lacy [See Lacy] and Hannah Van Court, sister of Agnes Van Court, widow of Daniel Potter, [See Potter] the 4th wife of Stephen Whitaker, son of Jonathan, Jun. John Mallory had an only daughter, Ruth Anne, born March, 1845.

2. Deborah Mallory, born 9th November, 1811, who married Milton Curtis, son of Tracy Curtis, and had a son, Charles Curtis, born 28th November, 1833. Mr. Curtis died 17th October, 1839.

Ephraim Mallory died 1813, and his widow, Ruth, married Jacob Vandeventer, son of Jacob, of Peapack, and had children:

3. William Vandeventer, born 1819, who married Elizabeth Derry, daughter of John Derry, near Penn Yan, and had children: 1. Edward; 2. John Jacob; 3. Frank Derry Vandeventer.

4. Mary Vandeventer, born 9th November, 1820, married Doctor William Breck, born 14th November, 1818, son of Joseph Breck, and live at Springfield, Mass. and have a son, Theodore Frelinghuysen Breck.

5. Stephen Vandeventer, born 7th February, 1823, married Anne Eliza Andrews, daughter of Doctor Jerry Andrews, and have a son, William Bryant Vandeventer, born 7th December, 1843.

6. Elizabeth, who died in 1829, aged 11 months.

ISAAC WHITAKER, (7th child of Stephen, son of Jonathan, Jun.,) and Acsah Cushman, removed to Michigan. He was born 16th January, 1792; she was born 11th July, 1796. They had children:

1. Charles, born 16th November, 1818, married Laura Beach, 20th December, 1843, daughter of William Beach, and had chiildren:

    1. Finley Beach, born 2d December, 1846.
    2. Caroline Fidelia, born 8th May, 1849.

2. Stephen Deming, born 12th December, 1820, and married, 5th October, 1845, Caroline Kellogg, daughter of Judge Kellogg, of Sharon, Conn. and have a daughter, Adeline Matilda, born 10th August, 1848.

3. Phebe Caroline, born 24th December, 1824.

4. Isaac Milton, born 2d May, 1826.

5. Matilda Jane, born 19th July, 1828.

6. Sabrina, born 28th September, 1831, and died 15th June, 1836.

7. Byron Cushman, born 11th May, 1835.

PHEBE WHITAKER, (2d child of Jonathan Whitaker, Jun.,) and the Rev. Francis Peppard, lived in Sussex, and had children :

1. Phebe Peppard, who died in childhood.

2. Jonathan Peppard removed to Wheeling, Virginia, and from thence to Worcester, Ohio, and rendered much assistance in the establishment of the church in that new settlement. He had a numerous family.

3. Phebe Peppard 2d married John Caruthers, Esq., of Lycoming county, Pennsylvania, and had one daughter and six sons. She died about 1847, aged 80 years.

4. Elizabeth Peppard married Lewis Kerr, son of Joseph, and lived in Brook county, Virginia. She died about 1820, aged about 53 years. Lewis Kerr was many years an Elder in the Presbyterian church.

5. Nathaniel Peppard married Peggy Green, or Miss Freeman, and had a numerous family, living in Indianapolis. He has been many years a Ruling Elder in the Presbyterian church.

6. Sarah Peppard married Aaron Kerr, brother of Lewis, about the year 1800 ; they were both born in 1777 ; he was elected at the age of 22 years an Elder in the Presbyterian church, at Hardwich, Sussex county, New Jersey, and about the same time elected to a seat in the Legislature of New Jersey. He subsequently removed to Washington county, Pennsylvania, and continued to serve his country and the church in a public capacity.

7. Rebecca Peppard.

8. Isaac Peppard, who died in youth.

After the death of the Rev. Francis Peppard, his widow removed with her son-in-law, Aaron Kerr, to Pennsylvania, about 1810. She died at about 80 years of age, in the triumphs of the gospel.

ELIZABETH PEPPARD and Lewis Kerr removed to Washington county, Penn. about 1808, and had children :

1. Phebe Kerr, who married Doct. John Todd, from New

York, and had one son, John Todd. Doct. Todd died, and his
widow Phebe married Doct. Cebar. She died about 1846.

2. Lydia Kerr married William Gordon, of Western Pennsylvania, and had 7 children, viz. Hampton, Amanda, James,
and others.

3. Isaac Kerr married Miss Thompson, daughter of William, and had children, William, Amanda, Lydia, and two
others.

4. Elsie Kerr married James Carson, of Brook county,
Virginia, and had children, Harriet, Sarah, William, James,
and others.

Mr. Lewis Kerr married, 2d, Sarah Dawson, and had
other children.

NATHANIEL PEPPARD and his wife had children :

1. Elizabeth married Mr. Landis, and had a daughter,
Mary, who married the Rev. Lawrence G. Hay, of the
Allahabad mission, in Northern India.

2. Mary married Mr. Morris, and lives in Indianapolis,
Indiana.

3. Hampton ; 4. Phebe married —— ——, in Indianapolis.

5. James married —— ——, in Indianapolis.

6. Margaret married Mr. Demoss ; lives in Indianapolis.

7. Joseph married —— —— ; lives in New Orleans.

8. Phebe married Mr. Beabitt ; she is now a widow.

SARAH PEPPARD and Aaron Kerr had children :

1. Susan Kerr, who married Doct. Samuel Todd, brother
of Doct. John Todd, and had children :

    1. Barton Todd, who married —— ——, and lives in
        Washington county, Pennsylvania.

    2. Jane Todd.

    3. Stephen Todd married, —— ——, and lives in Mo-
        nongahela City.

    4. Andrew Oliphant Todd is a Presbyterian minister ;
        settled in Ohio. He married, 1851, —— ——.

    5. John Milton Todd ; 6. Elizabeth Todd ; 7. Hamilton
        Todd ; 8. Samuel Erskine Todd.

Doct. Todd died, and his widow, Susan, married Mr. Apple-
gate, near Monongahela City.

2. Francis P. Kerr, was a physician ; married Jane Fleming, daughter of Daniel. He died in 1825, aged 25 years,
leaving children, Daniel and Francis.

3. Elizabeth Green Kerr married Joseph Fleming, brother
of Jane, and had children : 1. Kerr Fleming ; 2. Alexander
Fleming ; 3. Susan Fleming ; 4. Hampton Fleming ; 5
Amanda Fleming ; 6. Joseph Fleming ; 7. Hervy Fleming.

4. Joseph Kerr, born 5th Feb. 1806, is a Presbyterian minister ; was ordained in 1833, and soon went as a missionary

to the Indians, west of Missouri, and subsequently settled in Poland, Ohio, near the west line of Pennsylvania. He married Mary Anne Caldwell, daughter of William Caldwell, of Pittsburg, and had children: 1. E. Byington; 2. Joseph Brainerd; 3. Clarissa; 4. Elliot; 5. Walter Lowry; 6. Anna Jane.

5. Phebe Kerr married James Hair, of Washington county, Pennsylvania, and have children: 1. Hamilton Hair, and others.

6. Hampton Kerr married Jane Lee, daughter of John Lee, of Washington county, Pennsylvania, and had children: 1. Lee Anne; 2. Aaron.

7. Amanda Kerr married, first, Rev. Joseph Reed, and had one child, Sarah Elizabeth Reed. Mr. Reed died, and she married, 2d, Henry Haman, of Pittsburg, and lives there.

8. Aaron Hervy Kerr is a Presbyterian minister in Ontario, Indiana; was licensed in 1847. He married, in 1848, Elizabeth Craig, daughter of the Hon. Walter Craig, of Penn.

Walter Ker, the ancestor of the Kerrs, before named, was banished from Scotland, in the time of the persecution, and was permitted to remove to America. He came to N. Jersey, and settled in Freehold, in the year 1685, and as a layman was eminently useful in the establishment of the gospel in that region; his descendants have been blessed as useful members of the church of Christ. He had a son, Samuel, who had two sons, Samuel and Joseph. Joseph had sons, Lewis and Aaron Kerr.

Samuel had a son Jacob, who was a minister of the gospel, and Pastor for thirty years over two churches near Salsbury, Maryland, and died in 1795.

Rev. Jacob Kerr had a son, Doct. Samuel Kerr, of Prince Anne, Somerset county, Maryland, who had a son, Rev. Jacob W. E. Kerr, Pastor of the Presbyterian church at Deerfield, West Jersey Presbytry

JONATHAN WHITAKER 3d, (6th child of Jonathan, Jun.) and Mary Mitchel lived in Warren county, Ohio. He died July, 1810, aged 79 years; his widow died November, 1850, aged 87 years; they had children:

1. Nathaniel, who married Nancy Hayden.

2. Abigail, who died young.

3. Jonathan M., who married, 1st, Jane Irvin; 2d, Anne McIntire; 3d, Polly Miller, daughter of John Miller, of Springdale; he removed to Centreville, Indiana.

4. William, twin to Jonathan M. married Sarah Skinner, sister of Richard Skinner, who married Catherine Hurin, [see *Hurin*,] and daughter of Daniel Skinner.

5. Sarah married David Reeder, son of Daniel, of Pleasant Ridge, and removed to Illinois,

6. Abigail married Daniel Skinner, son of Abraham, brother of Daniel.

7. Benjamin married, 1st, Catherine Felter; 2d, Hannah Miller, sister of Jonathan's 3d wife, and has living children:
    1. Jonathan, who married Nancy Cox.
    2. Mary.

8. Stephen married Huldah Skinner, sister of Daniel, Abigail's husband; lives near Mason, Hamilton county, Ohio.

9. James, born 22d October,1798, married Mary Abbot, daughter of John; he is a mason, lives in Huntsville, Ohio.

10. Polly Halsted married Joseph Runyon, of Lebanon, and had children, Courtland Runyon and Mary Runyon.

JONATHAN M. WHITAKER and Jane Irvin, had children:

1. James Irvin, who married Mary McClure.

2. Mary Halsted married Alexander Morrow, son of Richard.

3. Nancy Jane, who died at about 18 years.

4. William Mitchel married Sarah Jane McKannis, daughter of Robert.

5. Sarah lives in Piqua.

Jonathan M. Whitaker, by Anne McIntire, had children:

6. David Newton, who died at about 23 years.

7. Martha died at about 13 years.

8. Jonathan Milton, born 25th October, 1829, lives at Piqua.

9. Margaret Anne died at about one year.

10. Mary Jane lives at Reading.

By his 3d wife, Polly Miller, he had no children.

WILLIAM WHITAKER, (4th child of Jonathan 3d, 6th child of Jonathan, Jun.) and Sarah Skinner, had children:

1. Mary M. who married Daniel Morris, and went to Texas.

2. Jonathan Miller went to Texas, and married there, Cynthia Robins.

3. Martha Anne married David Enyart, son of David.

4. Sarah Skinner married Nelson Littleton, of Middletown.

5. Phebe Mills, twin to Sarah Skinner, married, 1st, Daniel Pauly: 2d, Ambrose Voorhies.

6 Isabel Skinner married Paulaski Whelan.

7. Amanda married Andrew May, Jun. lives in Indiana.

8. Rebecca Reeder ; 9. Richard.

10. William Pitt Skinner went to Texas.

11. Caroline.

JAMES WHITAKER. (9th child of Jonathan 3d,) and Mary Abbot lived at Huntsville, and had children :

1. John, who married Hannah Jane Clifton ; live in Rossville, and had children: 1. Laura ; 2. Clement.

2. Jonathan married, 1st, Elizabeth Jaques, who had no children ; 2d, Charlotte Harper, lived in Tennessee, and had children : 1. Austin ; 2. Mary Anne.

3. Stephen married Sarah Irvin ; live in Butler county, Ohio.

4. Joseph married Emily Jones ; live about 40 miles west of Hamilton, Ohio, in Indiana.

5. Benjamin ; 6. Ichabod ; 7. James.

8. Albert, born 10th June, 1842.

NOTE.—The widow Mitchel, mother of Jonathan Whitaker's wife, Mary Mitchel, married William Conklin, Sen. as his 2d wife.

NATHANIEL WHITAKER, (7th child of Jonathan Whitaker, Jun.,) and Hannah Drake had one daughter, Sally, who married Garret Voorhies, Esq. ; lives where her father did, and had children:

1. John Voorhies, born 14th June, 1817.

2. Matilda Voorhies married, 8th Jan. 1851, Charles Barker, an Englishman. She died in childbed, Sept. 28th 1851 ; had twins, born 21st Sept. and both died before her.

3. Anne Voorhies married, Dec. 1849, William Heath, son of Robert.

4. Hannah Voorhies married, 28th Oct. 1847, James Garritson Kline, son of John, son of David Kline, of Reddington, Somerset county, and had a daughter, Dorothy Kline, born 17th Nov. 1849.

5. Ellen Voorhies ; 6. Garret Voorhies.

7. Nathaniel Whitaker Voorhies.

8. Samuel Scott Voorhies ; 9. Mary Voorhies.

10. Ruth Elizabeth Voorhies; 11. Ralph Voorhies.

Nathaniel Whitaker, by his 2d wife, Ruth Haines, had but one daughter, Hannah, who married Nicholas Arrowsmith, Jun. Esq. son of Nicholas, Esq. of Peapack, and had children:

1. Theodore Arrowsmith.

2. Elizabeth Barnet Arrowsmith, who married Charles Dayton, of New Brunswick, merchant, son of Jesse Dayton, of Fort Plain, and had children: 1. Mary Elizabeth Dayton ; 2. Anna Whitaker Dayton ; 3. Emma Dayton ; 4. Charles Meredith Dayton ; 5. Frances Salina Dayton ; 6. James Dayton.

3. Henrietta Arrowsmith, who married, 22d November, 1848, Doctor Alexander N. Dougherty, of Newark, and had a son, Alexander Dougherty.

JOHN WILLIAMS.

JOHN WILLIAMS, brother of Samuel, lives in West-field, and had children:

1. Noah, who married Betsey Marsh, daughter of Joshua, of Westfield. He died 3d Jan. 1824, aged 73 years.
2. John, Jun., who died un married.
3. Cornelius married Betsey Reddin, of Westfield; lived in New York several years, and removed to New Providence, where he died 28th Aug. 1828, aged 76 years. His wife died 2d Nov. 1818, aged 55 years. and left no children.
4. Henry married Betsey Scudder.
5. Squier married Nancy Williams, daughter of Henry.
6. Smith married Betsey Hetfield, daughter of Deacon Hetfield, of Westfield.
7. David married, 3d Aug. 1788, Hannah Marsh.
8. Lewis married Chloe Campbell.
9. Ezekiel married —— ——; lived and died in N. York.
10. Abner went to the South, and died unmarried.

NOAH WILLIAMS, (1st son of John,) came from West-field, and purchased the farm now owned by Edward Price, on the north side of Long Hill, and died 3d January, 1824, age 73 years   He and Betsey Marsh had children:

1. Ezra, who married Margaret Faitout, and for several years kept a tavern and store in the village of New Provi-dence. His wife Margaret died, and he married, 2d, Hetty Totten, daughter of Jonathan Totten, and removed to New York, and is there a shoe maker; he has had no children.
2. Noah, who married Polly Pool, daughter of John Pool.
3. Rachel, who married, 1st, David Cole, of Westfield, had a son, John Cole; when Mr. Cole died, and she married Ellis Noe, son of John, and had children: 1. Hester Noe; 2. Eliza: 3 Isaac Noe; 4. Daniel W. Noe; 5. David Noe. [See Ellis Noe.]
4. Daniel, who died in New York.
5. Abigail, who married William High, son of Jacob. [See High.]
6. Abner married Deborah Hand, daughter of Robert Hand; live in Morristown, and had children:
   1. Frances.
   2. Mariah, who married William Crowel, of New York, and lives there.
   3. David, who married —— ——; 4. Robert.
   5. Margaret married Caleb Conklin, son of John John-son Conklin, of Spring Valley.
   6. Alfred married Elizabeth Wilson, of Morristown, and lives there.
   7. Abner Williams, Jun.; 8. Harriet; 9. Alvira.
   10. Charles; 11. Catherine.

SAMUEL WILLIAMS.

SAMUEL WILLIAMS, (brother of John,) lived at Williams' Farms, between Westfield and Elizabethtown. He had three wives, and seventeen children some of his children were, Joel, Samuel, Jedediah, David, Moses, Nathaniel, John, Polly, and another daughter, who married Jacob Searing.

Moses married Sally Miller, daughter of Moses Miller, of Westfield.

JOHN WILLIAMS, (son of Samuel,) came up and bought the farm of John Roll, on the north side of Long Hill ; he was born 10th August, 1768, and died 25th February, 1839, aged 70½ years. He married Anna Spinning, who was born 2d September, 1771, and died 6th March, 1828; they had children :

1. Anna Spinning, born 10th November, 1792 ; married, 3d December, 1808, John Hand, son of Benjamin, of Long Hill.

2. Ebenezer Spinning, born 28th October, 1794, and married, 17th March, 1819, 1st, Sarah Carle ; 2d, Lydia Carle, daughters of Jonas Carle.

3. Mariah, born 11th December, 1796, married, 10th Jan. 1816, John W. Stiles, son of Daniel Stiles, of Elizabethtown, and live there.

4. Phebe S. born 12th January, 1800 ; married, 24th Feb. 1825, Moses M. Crane, son of Nathaniel Crane, of Elizabethtown, and live there.

5. Stiles, born 19th August, 1802, married Annetta Rogers, daughter of Dr. John Rogers, the widow of Mr. VanWagener, of Luzerne county, Pennsylvania ; has no children.

6 Lockey, born 23d December, 1804, married, 23d March, 1826, Cornelius Winnie, son of Martin Winnie, and had 5 children, who all died young, and then she died.

7. Elias Riggs, born 2d July, 1807, married 16th February, 1832, Mary Vandervoort, daughter of Paul Vandervoort, of Lamington ; he lives where his father did.

8. Eliza Ellen, born 25th February, 1810, and married the above named Cornelius Winnie.

9. Harriet Edney. born 9th October, 1812, and married Jacob G. White, of New Vernon.

ANNA S. WILLIAMS, (daughter of John, son of Samuel,) and John Hand had children:

1. Stiles Williams Hand, who married Mary Anne Boyle.
2. John Eden Hand.

3. Anna Mariah Hand married Hervy Frost, of Green
Village, and went to Ohio.
4. Harriet Hand went to Ohio, and married.
5. Emma Hand went to Ohio, and married.

EBENEZER S. WILLIAMS, (son of John,) and Sarah
Carle, had children :
1. Daniel Carle ; 2. Theodore ; 3. Sarah Anne.
He had no children by his 2d wife Lydia.

MARIAH WILLIAMS, (daughter of John,) and John W.
Stiles had children :
1. David W. Stiles; 2. Henrietta Stiles; 3. Eliza Ellen
Stiles ; 4. Ebenezer Stiles ; 5. Harriet W. Stiles; 6. Lockey
Anne Stiles.

PHEBE S. WILLIAMS, (daughter of John,) and Moses
M. Crane had children :
1. Elias Spencer Crane, who died at 14 years.
2. Anna W. Crane, who married Abraham Miller, of
Union; 3. Jane Crane ; 4. John Williams Crane.
5. Charles Crane.

ELIAS R. WILLIAMS, (son of John,) and Mary Vandervoort, had children :
1. John ; 2. Paul Vandervoort ; 3. Elias Edwin ; 4. Mary
Anne.
ELIZA ELLEN WILLIAMS, (daughter of John,) and
Cornelius Winnie lives on the Sterling farm, and had children :
1. Jane Winnie; 2. Henry Winnie; 3. Spencer Winnie ;
4. Anna Winnie ; 5. Rachel Winnie ; 6. Harriet Annetta
Winnie.

HARRIET EDNEY, WILLIAMS, (daughter of John,)
and Jacob G. White had children :
1. Theodore White; 2. Eliza Ellen White; 3. William
White, who died at 5 years ; 4. Benjamin Franklin White;
5. A son.

PETER WILLCOCKSE.

PETER WILLCOCKSE came from England, and settled between the mountains, on a hill known to this day as "Peter's Hill," on the north side of Blue Brook, a little above Feltville, 6th January, 1736,–7. There was surveyed to him there, by Joseph Morss, surveyor for the "Elizabethtown Associates" 424 acres of land, lying along the east branch of Green Brook, called Blue Brook; Feltville is situated on this tract.

The Rev. Mr. Hunting, in his history of the Parish of Westfield, says that "this Parish was settled about the year 1720, by the English, and that James Badgley and Peter Willcox located on the mountain before any persons settled below, because it abounded in heavy timber."

Peter Willcockse married Phebe Badgley, sister of James and John Badgley, lately from Long Island, and had children:

1. Peter Willcox, Jun, who married Betsey Miller.
2. William, who married, 1st, Miss Howel: 2d, Betsey Hole, sister of Charles Hole.
3. John married Massy Ross; he died 22d November, 1776, aged 49 years.
4. Stephen married Polly Carter, and lived near Elizabethtown.
5. Sarah married Joseph Allen, Jun. of Washington Valey. [See Allen.]

2d Gen

PETER WILLCOX, Jun. and Betsey Miller, had children:

1. David, who died young.
2. Noah, who married his cousin, Rachel Willcox, daughter of William.
3. Betsey married Benjamin Stites, son of William. [See Stites]
4. Hannah married, 5th December, 1764, John Frazee, son of Joseph.
5. Sabera married her cousin, Ephriam Miller, of Westfield.
6. Polly married Benjamin Hedges, son of Uriah, Jun.
7. Joanna married Benjamin Lyon, son of Peter. [see Lyon.

3d Gen

NOAH WILLCOX, (2d son of Peter, Jun.) and Rachel Willcox, had children:

1. David, who married Polly Hedges, daughter of Gilbert, and had no children.
2. William married Betsey Raddin, daughter of Jeremy
3. Joanna, born 15th February, 1783, and married, 1st Reuben Frazee; 2d, Edward Page.

4th Gen

4. Cornelius marrie l Abby Corwin, daughter of Stephen.
5. Betty married Ahijah Badgley, son of Jonathan. [*See Badgley.*]
6. Noah, Jun. married Lockey Leonard, daughter of John.

WILLIAM WILLCOX, (2d son of Noah,) and Betsey Raddin, had children :

1. Fanny, who married Benjamin Parsons, son of Jacob Searing Parsons.
2. Nancy married William Littell, son of Henry, son of Jonathan Littell. [*See Littell*]
3. Charlotte, who died in infancy.

JOANNA WILLCOX, (3d child of Noah,) and Reuben Frazee had children :

1. Lockey Frazee, who had a son, Robert Dunlap, who married Joanna Whittlesey. of Plainfield.
2. Abby Frazee married Jeremy Raddin. son of William.
3. Eliza Frazee who died at about 7 years.
4. William Frazee married Margaret Roseboam, daughter of Garret Roseboam, of Plainfied.
5. Jane Frazee married Merton Osborn, of Clinton.
6. John Frazee, who died at about one year.
7. Mary Frazee died at about 7 years
8. John Frazee married Jane ——, of Long Island ; lives in Newark.
9. Andrew J. Frazee, who died in infancy.

CORNELIUS WILLCOX, (4th child of Noah,) and Abby Corwin, had children :

1. Harriet, who married Sears Hetfield.
2. Isaac married Sarah Dunham, daughter of Samuel, of Liberty Corner.
3. Ezra married Sarah Baker, of Elizabethtown.
4. Amos married Hannah Rino, daughter of Charles.
5. Mary married Edward Darcy Pennington, son of William, of Dead River.
6. Aaron ; 7. Anne.

BETSEY WILLCOX, (5th child of Noah,) and Ahijah Badgley had children :

1. Mary Badgley, who married Carlisle Miller.
2. Eliza Badgey married Erastus Miller, brother of Carlisle. 3. Noah Badgley.

NOAH WILLCOX, Jun, (6th child of Noah,) and Lockey Leonard, had children :

1 Eliza, who married Absalom Martin Moffett, and had children : 1. Bryan Moffett ; 2. Caroline Moffett ; 3. Mary Moffett ; 4. John Moffett ; 5. Lavisa Moffett ; 6. Emma Moffett.

2. Phebe married Byram Darlin, son of William, and had children : 1. John Darlin ; 2. Susan Darlin ; 3. Rachel Darlin ; 4. Clarence Darlin.

3. Charlotte married Dennis Moffett, son of Absalom Moffett, and had children ; 1. Elizabeth Moffett ; 2. Albert Moffett ; 3. Harriet M ffett ; 4. Henry Moffett.

4. Hervy.

5 Caroline married Samuel Ball, son of David, of Union, and had children : 1. Emma Ball, and others.

6. John ; 7. Albert ; 8. Noah, 3d. 9. Mary Anne.

10. Amanda.

WILLIAM WILLCOX, (2d child of Peter Willcockse,) and Miss Howel had children :

1. William, Jun., who married, 13th Sept. 1767, Phebe Osborn.

2. Levi married. 18th May, 1733, Hester Valentine, daughter Obadiah. He died 2d March, 184 She died 7th June 1833.

3. Benjamin married Mary Mills, of Westfield.

4. Cornelius, who died unmarried.

5. Sabera married, 9th Aug. 1770, David Broadwell, o Rahway

6 Elizabeth married, 26th Jan. 1767, James Hall.

7. Polly, who died young.

8. Phebe married, 3d May, 1770, Joseph Jennings, west of Mount Bethel.

9. Lucretia married Jeremy Raddin. [*See Raddin.*]

10. Sarah married, 30th May, 1776, David French. [*See French.*]

11. Rachel married her cousin Noah Willcox. [*See Noah Willcox.*]

LEVI WILLCOX, (son of William,) and Esther Valentine had children :

1. Mary, who married, 1st, Anthony Doty, son of Joseph Doty 3d : 2d, Joseph Wilson, brother of Jacob Wilson, of Morristown

2. Rachel married William Van Blarcum, of Paterson, and lives there.

3 Jonathan Mulford married Sally Tucker, daughter of Moses. She died 24th August, 1849.

4. Levi, Jun. married, 1st, Huldah Crane, daughter of John Crane, and removed to Covington, Indiana. He married, 2d, in Indiana, Clarissa Norris.

MARY WILLCOX, (daughter of Levi,) and Anthony
Doty had

1. Betsey, who married John W. Hand, son of Nehemiah,
and had no children.

By Joseph Wilson, she had children :

2. Robert Turner, who married, 1st, Mary Wood, daughter of Daniel S. Wood, Jun. ; 2d Harriet Brookfield,
daughter of Job Brookfield, Esq., of Morristown. He is
a marble cutter, and a Justice of the Peace, and Judge
of the court.

3. Rachel, who married William Boylan, of Newark.

JONATHAN M. WILLCOX, (son of Levi,) and Sally.
Tucker had children :

1. John Tucker, born 16th Nov. 1814, and married, 16th
May, 1848, Harriet Littell, daughter of John Littell, Esq.,
and had one child : 1 · George, born 21st Nov. 1849.

2. Silas married Sarah Anne Drake, daughter of Jonathan,
and had children : 1. Sarah Anne ; 2. Jonathan M.

3. Hetty is unmarried.

LEVI WILLCOX, Jun., (son of Levi,) and Huldah Crane
had children :

1. David Bartine, who died at about 20 years.
2. Annar married, 1st, —— —— ; 2d, Mr. Atkinson
3. Elias Crane married, 8th Feb. 1849, Rachel V. Field.
4. Orpha, who died at about 14 years.
5. Albert ; 6. Francis ; 7. Mulford ; 8. John ; 9. Mary.

BENJAMIN WILLCOX, (3d son of William,) and Mary
Mills had children .

1. Benjamin, Jun., who married, 1st, Sally the widow of
Moses F. Badgley, and daughter of Nathan Wilkison.

2. Eliza, who married Benjamin Cory, son of George, and
died without children.

3. Mary, who died young.

BENJAMIN WILLCOX, (son of Benjamin, son of William,) and Sally Wilkison had children :

1. Joseph, who married Phebe Bailey, daughter of John,
son of Samuel, of Springfield.

2. Squier married Maryetta Littell, daughter of Thomas
T. Littell, and had children : 1. Anne Elizabeth ; 2. Sarah.

3. Susan married Isaac Brant, son of James, of Rahway.

4. Marcus ; 5. John ; 6. David ; 7. Sarah Anne.

Sally, the wife of Benjamin Willcox, Jun. then died, and he
married, 2d, Nancy Littell, daughter of John, of Martinville,
who was son of Nathaniel Littell, Jun., son of Nathaniel, son

of Samuel Littell, and had children : 8. Mary Elizabeth ; 9.
Mercy ; 10. Benjamin; 11. James; 12. George.

PHEBE WILLCOX, (daughter of William,) and Joseph
Jennings had children :

1. Polly Jennings.
2. Henry Jennings, who married Sally Mulford, and had
children : 1. Phebe Jennings ; 2. Elizabeth Jennings ; 3.
Hannah Jennings ; 4. Mulford Jennings.
3. Rhoda Jennings, who married John Lacy, and had a
child, Mary Lacy.

JOHN WILLCOX, (3d child of Peter Willcockse,) and
Massy Ross had children :

1. John Willcox, Jun., who married Polly, the widow of
Isaac Line, and daughter of William Maxwell.

NOTE.—She had a son, Isaac Line, by her first husband.

2. Isaac, who married Polly Dunham.
3. Peter 3d, who married —— ——.
4. Daniel married, 19th Oct. 1783, Deborah Mulford,
daughter of Ezekiel Mulford, brother of Capt. Jonathan Mulford. [*See Mulford.*]
5. Stephen, who died young.
6. Moses married Polly Line, daughter of Joseph Line ;
lived in Middlesex county, below New Brunswick.
7. Sarah married Ebenezer Lyon, son of Peter. [*See Lyon.*]
8. Massy married Nathaniel Lyon, son of Peter. [*See
Lyon.*]
9. Polly married Isaac Garthrite.

JOHN WILLCOX, Jun., (son of John Willcox,) and Polly
Maxwell had children :

1. Abigail, who married, 2d July, 1795, Israel Brant. She
married, 2d, John Morris, of Newark, and 3d, Daniel Magie,
of Elizabethtown, and had no children.
2. Sarah married, 28th Feb. 1796, Daniel S. Clark, son of
Samuel Clark, Esq. [*See Clark.*]
3. Betsey married Aaron Ball, son of Aaron Ball, Esq.
[*See Ball.*]
4. William and John, twins ; William died young.
5. John 3d, born 15th Jan. 1788, and married Sarah Line,
born 1st Nov. 1793, daughter of Joseph Line.
6. Polly married her cousin, Ezekiel Willcox, son of
Daniel.
7. Samuel married Eliza S. Osborn, daughter of Dr. Smith
S. Osborn. He is a Justice of the Peace in Newark, and had
children : 1. Augustus; 2. Catherine ; 3. Samuel.

8. Amos married, 13th Jan 1818, Polly Meeker. daughter of Caleb, and had a son. Theodore His wife died and he married. 2d. Elza Nail, of New York ; he is a marble worker, in Newark, and has other children.

JOHN WILLCOX 3d, (son of John Willcox, Jun,) and Sarah Line, lives where his father did, and had children :

1. Caroline, who married James L. Spencer, son of William. [See Spencer.]
2. Hetty married Isaac Meeker, Jun., son of Caleb. [See Meeker.]
3. Isaac Line married, 19th September, 1838, Mary M. Jones, only daughter of Erastus Jones, and have children, Caroline and Erastus.
4. Henry, born 25th September, 1818.
5. Edmund Arnold.
6 Abigail, born 27th September, 1827, married Henry Jemison, son of Henry Jemison and Hannah Littell, daughter of Nathaniel Littell, Jun. (See page 261.)
7. John Morris, born 31st July, 1829, married, 12th Nov. 1851, Anna Mariah Vail.
8. Mary Louisa. born 23d April, 1831.

DANIEL WILLCOX, (4th child of John Willcox, Sen..) and Deborah Mulford, had children :

1. Hannah, who married Joseph Casterline, and had a son Mulford Casterline, who married, 26th May, 1823. Harrie, Samson. son of Benjamin. Mr. Casterline then died, and she married John Marshall, son of James [See Marshall.]
2. Ezekiel, born 13th Dec. 1780, and married, 1st, his cousin, Polly Willcox, daughter of John Willcox, Jun. ; she died, and he married, 2d, Betsey Brown, daughter of Matthew Brown. of Woodbridge. He married, 3d, the widow Drummond, of Monmouth Co. He lives between Westfield, and Rahway.
3. Jotham married Lois Scudder. daughter of Stites Scudder, and removed to Seneca county, New York, between the Lakes.
4. Jane married Isaac Meeker, son of Isaiah. [See Meeker.]
5. Mary married Marsh Allen. son of William. [See Allen.] She married, 2d, John Muchmore, of Madison.
6 Ezra married, 1st, Sarah Mizener, daughter of Isaac, of Kingston; she died, and he married, 2d, Rachel Jennings, daughter of Benjamin, of Washington Valley.
Mr. Daniel Willcox died 27th February, 1842.

EZEKIEL WILLCOX, (2d child of Daniel, son of John,) and his 1st wife, Polly Willcox, had children :

1. Abigail, who married Abraham Randolph, live in Cher-

ry Valley, Ashtabula county, Ohio, and had children : 1.
Amos ; 2. Eliza ; and others.

2. Eliza Anne married Madison Stone, of Connecticut,
and live in Cherry Valley.

3. Daniel Mulford married Susan Reed, daughter of John
Reed, of New York ; lives in Rahway, and had children :

    1. Mary ; 2. Anne Eliza ; 3. John ; 4. Ezekiel Morri-
son.

4. Mary Jane married Hiram Williams.

5. John, who died in his 20th year.

6. Harriet married Joseph W. Crane, son of William
Crane, Esq. [*See Crane.*]

Ezekiel Willcox, by his 2d wife, Betsey Brown, had

7 Emily, who married Mr. Frank, and had a daughter,
Emily Frank, when he died.

8. Matilda, who married John Emmick.

And by his third wife, Mr. Willcox had

9. Ezekiel Halsey.

JOTHAM WILLCOX, (3d child of Daniel, son of John,)
and Lois Scudder, had children :

1. Eliza Catherine, who married Benjamin Bartlet, and
had children : 1. Martha Bartlet ; 2. Mary Jane Bartlet; 3.
Eliza Anne Bartlet ; 4. Hudson Bartlet who died young.

2. Daniel, who married Eliza Ellen Fisher, and had children : 1 Louisa Catherine ; 2. Jotham Osborn; 3. Peter
Fisher ; 4. James Hamilton ; 5. Mary Helen.

3. Mary Jane married, 1st, her cousin Richard S. Ayers,
son of Zebulon ; he died without children, and she married,
2d, Edward T. Judd, and had children :

    1. Frances Judd ; 2. Richard W. Judd.

4 Stites married —— ——.

5. Richard.

EZRA WILLCOX, (6th child of Daniel, son of John,)
and Sarah Mizener, had children :

1. Daniel, who married Abby Anne Douglas, grand daughter of William High.

2. Deborah Anne, who married Abraham Valentine, son
of Peter D. Valentine. [*See Valentine.*]

Ezra Willcox, by his 2d wife, Rachel, had children :

3. Aaron D , who died 21st May, 1847, aged 20 years.

4. Jane ; 5. Patience

6. Fanny ; 7. Sarah ; 8. John ; 9. Benjamin.

MOSES WILLCOX, (6th child of John,) and Polly Line
had children :

1. Phebe, who married John Pennington.

2. Abigail married Mr. Farringsworth, and went to Illinois.

3. Anne married Henry W. Tuttle, of Morris county.

4. Joseph married —— ——.

5. Isaac married Miss Bastido.

6. Moses, Jun.

7. Eliza married Mr. Brees.

8. Cornelia married Mr. Brees, brother of Eliza's husband.

9. Catharine.

10. John.   Mr. Willcox died in the winter of 1850-1.

STEPHEN WILLCOX, (4th son of Peter Willcockse,)
and Polly Carter had children:

1. James, who married Betsey Jewel.

2. Peter.

3. Phebe married Abraham Mann.

3d Gen.

CAPT. DANIEL S. WOOD.

CAPT. DANIEL S. WOOD came from Long Island to
Passaic Valley, about the year 1754, and learned the blacksmith trade, with a Mr. Moore.   Mr Wood, when he became
of age, bought the farm of Mr. Moore, and set up the business himself, and lived on the farm till his death, which occurred the 8th February, 1832, aged 91 years.   The farm is part
of lot No. 20 of the Elizabethtown lots, surveyed in 1736-7,
above the first mountain.   He married Mary Potter, of
Hanover, and had two children, who died young, and his wife
died 18th February, 1768; he then married Sarah Johnson,
sister of Uzel Johnson; she died 12th April, 1806, in her 56th
year.   They had children:

1. John, who was baptized, 27th April, 1772, and died young.

2. Sally, who married, 19th December, 1790, Daniel Meeker, son of Isaiah.   [*See Meeker.*]

3. Docia is unmarried.

4. Daniel Smith married Nancy Baldwin, daughter of
Gabriel, and died 23d December, 1842.

5. Joseph, who was baptized 17th April, 1785, and died in
infancy.

6. Samuel, who is unmarried.

7. Elizabeth A. married Capt. Stephen Day, son of Benjamin Day, Esq as his 2d wife.   [*See Day.*]

8. Margaret Williston, who married the Rev. Waters Burrows, son of Waters Burrows.   [*See Burrows*]

9. David married Sarah Bonsal, of Spring Valley, Morris
county; he is a grocer in Newark, and has children:

1. Mary E.; 2. Samuel W.; 3. Mariah H.; 4. Francis
P. Wood.

DANIEL S. WOOD, Jun. (son of Capt. Daniel S. Wood,) and Nancy Baldwin, had children :

1. Docia, who married David Smalley, son of Samuel, and removed to Ohio.

2. Rachel married Major William M. Clark, son of D. S. Clark Esq. [*See Clark.*]

3. Lillis married Judah Phelps, of Connecticut; he died leaving children :

    1. Lemuel Cicero Phelps.

    2. Harriet Eliza Phelps, who married, 10th April, 1850, George Rawden, of Newark.

    3. William Phelps ; 4. Franklin Phelps. The family live in Newark.

4. Sally married Major William M. Clark, as his 2d wife. [*See Clark.*]

5. David Jones married Rhoda Brookfield, daughter of Job, of Spring Valley, and removed to New York, near Lake Ontario, and had children :

    1. Georgiana, 2. Smith Halsey, who both died young.

    3. Georgiana ; 4. David Franklin.

6. Daniel Halsey, born 19th September, 1809, and married Hannah Bell Lippencott, born 2d September, 1823, daughter of William Lippencott, of Allegany county, New York, and have children :

    1. Theodore Bell, born 11th August, 1841.

    2. Daniel S. born 21st September, 1843.

7. Hannah married Asa Osborn, son of Nehemiah, and has an only daughter, Anne Eliza, who married, 24th September, 1850, Philemon Tomkins, son of Ashbel A. Tomkins. [*See Tomkins.*]

8. Mary married Robert T. Wilson, Esq. grand-son of Levi Willcox. [*See Willcox.*] She died 14th February, 1842, leaving a daughter, Mary, who died in infancy.

9. Margaret married David A. French, son of Willis. [*See French.*]

10. Isaac L. born 10th August, 1821, married, 13th February, 1847, Sally Doty Bonnel, born 13th September, 1831, daughter of Philemon, and had children :

    1. John Bonnel Wood, born 19th December, 1848.

11. Samuel is unmarried.

12. John, born 25th September, 1818, married, 27th October, 1846, Charlotte A. Torboss, born 6th June, 1831, daughter of Peter Torboss, of Union Village, and had children :

    1. Mary Eliza, who died at 2 months ; 2. Peter Torboss, born 9th June, 1850.

APPENDIX.

LEWIS BAKER.

LEWIS BAKER, son of Daniel Baker, of Westfield, married Elizabeth Robison; lived at Littletown, Morris Co. and had children:

1. Catherine, who married David Wheeler, and had a son, Lewis B. Wheeler.

2. Abigail married Stephen Young, of Malapardis, Morris county.

3. Sarah married Mahlon Johnson.

4. Daniel married —— ——.

5. Abraham married ——; lived at Haverstraw, N. Y. and died about 1810, leaving children, Isaac and Jacob.

6. Mary married Jared Howel, of Parcipany, Morris Co. and had children: 1. Stephen Howel; 2. Abraham Howel; 3. Eveline Howel; 4. Mary Howel; 5. Sebel Howel; 6. James Howel.

7. Jane married Mr. Tomkins, son of Uzel Tomkins, of New Vernon, and had children: 1. Uzel Tomkins: 2. ——;

8. Sineus married Sally Conklin, daughter of Isaac son of Stephen 1st, and had children: Sineus, Harriet and Isaac Baker. [See page 87.]

9. Nathaniel married —— ——, and had children: Lewis and others.

10. Lewis married —— ——, lived where his father did, and had two children.

ABIGAIL BAKER, (2d child of Lewis) and Stephen Young, had children: 1. Ephraim Young, who married Mary Drennen; 2. Eliza Young; 3. Julia Young married Mr. Cock; lived at Dover.

SARAH BAKER, (3d child of Lewis,) and Mahlon Johnson, had children:

1. Jacob Johnson, who married Hetty Vail, daughter of Davis Vail

2. Chilion Johnson married Anne Woodruff; live at Crawfordsville, Indiana.

3. Baker Johnson, born 23d October, 1803, and married Electa King, daughter of the Rev Barnabas King, of Rockaway: he is a Presbyterian minister of Sussex county, and has children: 1. Susan H. Johnson; 2. Thomas S. Johnson; 3. Sarah E. Johnson; 4. William N. Johnson; 5. Barnabas B. Johnson.

4. Alfred Johnson married Sarah Baker, daughter of Jonathan, of Littletown, and has children:

1. Margaret Johnson ; 2. Lucilla Johnson ; 3. Hervy Johnson ; 4. Thomas Johnson ; 5. Mary Johnson.

DAVID C BAKER. (See page 19.)

DAVID C. BAKER, (son of Aaron Baker, Esq.) and Sophia Van Cleve, daughter of Benjamin Van Cleve, Esq. lived near Dayton. Ohio, and had children :
1. Mary Sophia 2. Clara ; 3. Charles, who died at 5 yrs.
4. David. And by his second wife, Sophia Sourby, David C. Baker had, 5. Harriet ; 6. Axia Green ; 7. Aaron ; 8. Hannah ; 9. Mahala.

NOTE.—Benjamin Van Cleve married, first, Mary Whiting, and had children :
1. John W. Van Cleve born 1800.
2. Henrietta Maria, who married Samuel Dover.
3. Mary married James Andrews.
4. William, who died at about 6 years.
5. Sarah Sophia, who married David C. Baker, son of Aaron Baker. Esq. Mr Van Cleve married, for his second wife, Mary Tamplin. He was a surveyor and clerk of Montgomery county, Ohio, and lived in Dayton.

EZEKIEL BALL. (See page 31.)

EZEKIEL BALL, of Middletown, Ohio, had children :
1. Stephen. who was a captain of militia, married Rebecca Irene, and had children :
1. Abby ; 2 William ; 3. Pierson ; 4. Peney ; 5. John ; 6. Nancy.
2. Abby married Matthew Nichols, and had children :
1. Ibbe Nichols ; 2. Joseph Nichols ; 3. William Nichols ; 4. Sally Nichols ; 5. Polly Nichols ; 6. Joanna Nichols.
3. Polly married Abraham Squier, son of William. [See *Squier.*]
4. Hannah married Joseph Hays,
5. Sally married Robert Fisher.
6. Phebe married Elias Spinning.

DAVIS BALL. (See page 31.)

DAVIS BALL, (10th child of Nathaniel Ball) married Mary Hetfield, daughter of Thomas Hetfield, of Elizabethtown.

NOTE.—Mary Hetfield was sister of Sarah Hetfield, the

wife of John Clark, son of Thomas Clark, and John Clark
was the father of Mary Clark, the wife of Silas C. Byram, son
of Ebenezer. (See page 249 and 276.)

Davis Ball went to Ohio previous to 1804, and kept a ferry
over the Great Miami river, near Trenton, Butler county, and
was there drowned. Davis Ball and Mary Hetfield had
children :

1. Stephen, who married Susan Berry, daughter of Thomas.
2. Abner married Rhoda Martin, daughter of Isaac.
3. Dr. Bonnel Ball married Rachel Denman, daughter of
Moses, on Elk Creek.
4. Aaron married Puah Thompson, daughter of Joseph, and
grand-daughter of John Sallee, who married Puah Ball, sister of Davis.
5. Eunice married William Carr, son of John.
6. Sarah married, 1st, Daniel Craig, son of John ; 2d, John
Huff, son of Isaac.

STEPHEN BALL, (1st child of Davis,) and Susan Berry,
lived in Michigan, and had children :

1. Sarah, who married Dr. John Pinkerton.
2. Israel married Terresa Wright, daughter of William, and
grand-daughter of John Potter.
3. Squier married, in Michigan, Mary Sergeant.
4. Eliza married in Michigan.
5. Mahala married William Perry, a Yankee.
6. Davis married Catharine Clark, daughter of Stephen,
brother of Mary, wife of Silas C. Byram, and son of John
Clark.
7. Thomas ; 8. Esther.

ABNER BALL, (2d child of Davis,) and Rhoda Martin,
had children :

1. Mary, who married Thomas Smiley.
2. Eunice married Isaac Martin.
3. Sarah married —— ——.
4. Phebe.

DR. BONNEL BALL, (3d child of Davis,) and Rachel
Denman, lived in Indiana, and had children :

1. Mariah, who married William Maxwell.
2. Prudence married John Stout.
3. Stephen married —— ——.
4. Sarah ; 5. Aaron ; 6. Mary ; 7. Wilson ; 8. Doctor.

AARON BALL, (4th child of Davis,) and Puah Thompson had children :

1. Abner.

2. Phebe, who married John Watson.
3. Daniel married Elizabeth Huff, daughter of Isaac.
4. Ellen ; 5. Stephen ; 6. Davis.

EUNICE BALL, (5th child of Davis,) and William Cárr had children :
1. Mary Carr, who married Joseph Van Hyse.
2. Sarah Carr married John Sykes.
3. Rhoda Carr married John Cornquit,
4. William Carr ; 5. Aaron Carr ; 6. Susan Carr.

SARAH BALL, (6th child of Davis.) and Daniel Craig, had children :
1. Melinda Craig, who married Joseph Van Sickle.
2. John Craig married Jane Berry.
And by John Huff, Sarah Ball had children :
3. William Huff married Catharine Wright, daughter of Joel Wright.
4. Wilson Huff; 5. Doctor Bonnel Huff; 6. Abner Huff.
7. Wesley Huff; 8. Ann Eliza Huff.

WILLIAM BROADWELL, JUN. (See page 59.)

WILLIAM BROADWELL, JUN. married, 1st, Mary, and had children :
1. William 3d, who died 5th May, 1761, in his 6th year.
2. David.
3. Nathaniel, who married Joanna Lindsley, daughter of John, and sister of Silas Lindsley, Esq. of Spring Valley.
William Broadwell married, 2d, Mary or Polly, and had children :
4. Silas ; 5. Ezra ; 6. Airy ; 7. William.
8. Jane, who married her cousin, Moses Broadwell, son of Josiah, Esq.
9. Elizabeth ; 10. Susan ; 11. Rebus ; 12. Joanna.

NATHANIEL BROADWELL, (3d child of William, Jun.) and Joanna Lindsley lived near Morristown, and had children :
1. John, who married Phebe Lindsley, daughter of Major Joseph Lindsley, and half sister of Abraham Conklin's wife, and had children :
  1. Mahlon, who married, 1st, Sarah Agnew ; 2d, Anne Goslin.
  2. Henry married Anne Eliza Wainwright.
2. Sally married Thomas Armstrong, son of Nathaniel, of Newtown, on the Little Miami, and had children :

1. Perrine Armstrong, who married William Harrison.
2. Eliza Armstrong, who died at 20 years, unmarried.
3. Sidney Armstrong married Elizabeth Waldron.
4. John Armstrong died at 28 years, unmarried.
5. Edwin Armstrong.
6. Milton Armstrong married Julia Deboldt.
7. Eliab Armstrong.

3. Ira, who married Deborah Conklin, daughter of Abraham, live near Madisonville, Hamilton county, Ohio; and had children:

1. Adelia, who died at 4 months.
2. Albert, born 7th December, 1815, and died 22d November, 1839.
3. Mary Eliza, born 1st May, 1818, and married William Smith, who died of cholera, in Cincinnati, 4th July, 1849, leaving two children: 1. Albert Broadwell Smith; 2. Ira Herbert Smith.
4. Sarah Anne, born 25th October, 1820, and died at 6 months.
5. Mariah, born 31st July, 1821, married, 5th September, 1846, Allen Cameron, and had children: 1. Ira Francis Cameron; 2. Catherine Isabel Cameron.
6. Julia Anne, born 13th March, 1828.
7. Nancy, born 21st August, 1831.
8. Cordelia, born 6th October, 1834.
9. Emma Elizabeth, born 10th October, 1838, and died 11th February, 1839.

4. Lindsley married Susan Carman, daughter of Joseph, of Monmouth county, N. J. (She was aunt of Isaac Conklin's wife.) They had children:

1 Jane, who married George Clark.
2. Joanna married Doctor Albert Essex.
3. Nathaniel.
4. and 5. Amazon and Missouri, twins, named after those two great rivers.
6. Harriet; 7. Clarissa; 8. Louisa.
9 Jackson; 10. Ferdinand.

5. Polly married Zimri Hale, and had children:

1. Albert Hale, who married Mary ——.
2. Elizabeth Hale married Nathaniel Van Zant, a Physician.
3. Joanna Hale.

6. Julia died in 1828, aged 27 years.

7. Eliab married Jane Nailor, and had children;
1. Joanna; 2. Jane

8. Henry, who died at about 7 years.

MOSES BROADWELL, (See page 79.)

MOSES BROADWELL, (son of Josiah Broadwell, Esq.) and Jane Broadwell, his wife, daughter of William Broad. well, owned four sections of Land near Springfield, Illinois and lived on one of those sections, and had chil ren :
1. Polly ; 2. William ; 3. David ; 4. John ; 5. Cynthia.
6. Jefferson ; 7. Sally ; 8. Euclid.

EPHRAIM BROADWWELL, (2d child of Simeon,) married Jane Ross Gardner, daughter of Samuel Gardner, (who married Mary, eldest daughter of Hezekiah Thompson, *see Thompson,*) lived in Dayton, Ohio, and had children :
1. Mary, who died at 16 months.
2. Harriet died at 9 months.
3. William married Avira Smith, and had children :
   1. Ellen ; 2. Mary ; 3. Julia ; 4. Eliza   And he died at 25 years.
4. Simeon married Mary Elliot, daughter of James, of Hamilton, Oh o.
5. John married Margaret Embra, and had children :
   1. Anna ; 2 Caleb ; 3. Sarah Jane ; 4. Harriet.
   5 Mary. And he died at 35 years.

WILLIAM CAULDWELL, (See page 71.)

DAN CAULDWELL, (9th child of William,) and Rachel Potter, had children :
1. Polly, who married David Johnson, son of Uzel. [*See Johnson*]
2. Betsey marrie Josiah Carter, and had children :
   1. Nancy Carter, who married David Lee.
   2. Sarah Carter, who died at about 15 years.
   3. Mary Catherine Carter.
   4. Dan Collins Carter.
3. Nancy was drowned in the Little Miami river, at about 18 years.
4. William married, 1st, Rebecca Stevenson, and had one child. He married, 2d, Mary Seward, and had children :
   2. John, who d ed young.
   3. Sarah Anne, who married William Givens, and had children : 1. Aula Anne ; 2 Sarah Anne Givens.
   4. Catherine married Joseph Horsley, editor of the Western Republic, at Delphi, Indiana.
5. John married Lydia Winans, and had children :
   1. Richard W.; 2. Sarah Elizabeth; 3. Anne Augusta.

6. Sally married Hugh Stevenson, brother of William's wife, and had children :
    1. William ; 2. James ; 3. Eliza Jane Stevenson.

7. Charlotte married Mr. Stone, and soon after died, at about 19 years.

8. Catherine married her cousin, 'Jerry Cauldwell, son of Abraham. [*See Abraham Cauldwell.*]

9. James Thompson Cauldwell married Lydia Anne Hillyer, and had children

    1. Catherine Amanda, who married Eli Jester, and had a son, Charles Wesley Jester.

    2. James Wesley married Eliza Voorheis.

    3. Sarah Jane married, 1st. John Pennington, 2d Enoch Thompson, and had children : 1. Aula Anne ; 2. America Genevieve, (a daughter.)

    4. William Nelson ; ·5. Mary Elizabeth ; 6. Minerva Anne ; 7. and 8. Angeline and Emeline, twins ; 9. Martha Epenetus ; 10. Margaret Emezetta.

10. Rachel Cauldwell married Benjamin Seward, and died without children, and Mr. Seward married. 2d, the widow, Anne Boyd, a daughter of Mr. Enyart, and had one child : Pamela Anne Boyd, who married John Stevenson, brother of Hugh and Rebecca, and had children :

    1. William Stevenson, who died at about one year.

    2. David Enyart ; 3. Mariah ; 4. James ; 5. Sarah.

    6. George Washington ; 7. Margaret Jane.

    8. Dan Taylor Stevenson.

ABRAHAM CAULDWELL, (10th child of William,) and Elizabeth Rutan, had children : (See page 72.)

NOTE.—Mrs. Elizabeth Cauldwell died 20th February, 1826, aged about 48 years.

1. Joseph, born 24th March, 1791, in N. J. and married, 1st, Isabel Linn. daughter of James Linn, of Butler Co. Ohio ; 2d, Betsey, the widow of James Stewart, and daughter of John Thompson, of Piqua ; Joseph lived in Piqua, and Isabel Linn, had children :

    1. William, born 31st March, 1817, married, Nancy Stewart, daughter of John, of Shelby Co., and had one child, Elizabeth, and died 19th September, 1850.

    2. James Thompson Cauldwell, born 12th May, 1820.

    3. Ella Jane, born 18th December, 1822, and died November, 1846, unmarried

    4. Catherine Elizabeth, born 20th June, 1825, and her mother died 2 days after. And she died of cholera, Oct. 1850. And by his 2d wife, Betsey had children :

    5. Freeborn Thompson, born 20th Nov. 1827, and died 28th April. 1850.

    6. Charlotte T., born 13th December, 1829, and died September, 1833.

7. Sarah Eleanor, born 9th August, 1833.

8. Minerva Gillespie, born 15th March, 1839.

NOTE.—Joseph Cauldwell's 2d wife, had children by Mr. James Stewart:

1. Jane T. Stewart, born 20th August, 1817, and married Azel Cauldwell, son of John, son of John, and had children :
    1. Dennis; 2. John; 3. James Mc Nabb; 4. Electa; 5. Martha; 6. Catherine.

2. John T. Stewart, born 31st December, 1819, married Jane Jeffers.

3. Thomas T. Stewart, born 26th November, 1823, and married Elizabeth Ullery.

2. Jerry Cauldwell married his cousin, Catherine Cauldwell, daughter of Dan, and had children :
    1. Abraham Simpson, who married Margaret Jeffers, daughter of Thomas ; he lives in Montgomery county, Indiana.
    2. Dan Bethuel; 3. Silas Roll; 4. James Milton.
    5. Mary Anne ; 6. Sarah Elizabeth; 7. William Christy.
    8. John Squier Potter.

3. Hannah married, 1st, Joseph A. Loyd, had one child, Jerry Loyd, who died, and then Mr. Loyd died, and she married, 2d, William Hultz, and had children:
    2. Elizabeth Hultz, who married James Van Hyse, a merchant in Chester, and had children : 1. Rachel Anne.
    2. Hannah Jane, who died at 2 years ; 3. Lewis C. Van Hyse.
    3. Hannah Hultz married, 1st, Jackson Van Gorder, who died two weeks after marriage, and she married, 2d, Frederick Acre, and had children: 1. William Wallace Acre ; 2. John Richmond Acre.
    4. Rebecca Jane Hultz married Josiah Jeffers, and had children : 1. Silas Jeffers ; 2. Olive Jane Jeffers, who died at 2 years ; 3. Hannah Matilda Jeffers.

4. Betsey married her cousin, Robert M. Cauldwell, son of John, son of William, and had children :
    1. Luther Littell, born 1st December, 1818, and died at about 19 years.
    2. Eliza Jane, who married Nathaniel Thompson, and had children : 1. James S. Cauldwell Thompson ; 2. Charles Swain Thompson.
    3. Abraham Cauldwell.
    4. Hannah Cauldwell died at 17 years.
    5. Jonathan Chaplin died at 19 years.
    6. Enos H. Harrison died at 16 years.
    7. David Cauldwell, born about 1838.

JOHN CAULDWELL, (1st child of John, son of William,) and Electa Hand, had children :

1. Abraham, who married Cornelia Fairchild, daughter of Henry.
2. Hannah married, 1st, Milton Rutan; 2d, Isaac Mars.
3. Ludlow married Matilda Plummer.
4. Azel married Jane Stewart, daughter of Joseph Cauldwell's 2d wife.
5. Phebe married Silas Dyer; 6. Mary; 7. John.
8. Peter married Lucinda Rutan, sister of Milton Rutan.

Note.—Abraham R. Colwell's daughter, Mariah, married her 2d husband, Mr. Foster, and live near Lacon, Magnolia county, Illinois, and his daughter, Anne Eliza, married, 1st May, 1851, Joseph M. Dana, of Athens, Ohio, and live there.

ABNER CRANE, (5th son of Joseph, see page 102.)

ABNER CRANE, (son of Joseph,) lived near Red Lyon, in Warren county, Ohio; he married in Ohio, Huldah Robison, and had children :

1. Lydia, who married George Lease.
2. Isaac.
3. Abby married Andrew Coffin.
4. Abraham married his cousin, Ruth Romaine, daughter of Isaac Romaine, who married Betsey Crane, daughter of Samuel.
5. Hannah married William Lease, brother of George.
6. Samuel married Ellen Jane Dearth, daughter of Samuel.
7. Huldah Anne married John Decker, son of Joseph.
8. Abner Edwin married Sarah Jones.
9. Ruth Jane.   Abner Crane died April, 1848.

MOSES CRANE, (7th son of Joseph,) lived near Red Lyon, and removed to Indiana; he married in Ohio, Susan Dilts, and had children :

1. Silas, who married Jane Romaine, daughter of Isaac, a sister of Abraham Crane's wife.
2. Whitley married Betsey Robison.
3. Nelson married Sarah Maloy.
4. Polly married Cornelius Bogart.
5. Alfred married Mary Anne Bogart, sister of Cornelius.
6. Davison married in Indiana.
7. Elias married in Indiana.
8. Joseph married Hannah Snorff.
9. Ruth Anne married in Indiana.
10. Rachel married in Indiana
11. Moses Miller.

SYLVESTER CRANE, (son of John Crane, son of Joseph,) married in Illinois, a 2d wife, Mary Brier, and had children : Huldah, Theodore ; his wife Mary then died, and he married Mary Jane Booe, and had a son, William Crane.

GENERAL WILLIAM CRANE, (page 108.)

JOSEPH H. CRANE, (3d son of Gen. William Crane,) lived in Dayton, Ohio, and was Judge of the Supreme Court. He married Julia Anne Elliot, daughter of Doctor John Elliot, and had children :

1. Mariah, who married Doctor Joshua Clements, and had a son, Joseph Clements, born in 1835.
2. Joseph married Sarah Schenck, daughter of Lieut. James Finley Schenck, of the Navy.
3. Joshua Clements, born in 1834 ; the other children have died.

Judge Crane died 12th November, 1851.

ABRAHAM CONKLIN, (See page 83.)

ABRAHAM CONKLIN, (8th child of Stephen Conklin,) and Jemima Lindsley lived on Indian Hill, Columbia township, Hamilton county, Ohio, and had children :

1. Anna, who died of fits, unmarried, at 40 years.
2. Mariah married, 1st, John Perry, and had children :
    1. Eveline Perry, who married Jefferson Arnet.
    2. Mary Anne Perry married Henry Palsey.
    3. Nancy Perry married Robert McMains.
    4. Margaret Perry.
    5. Deborah Perry married Sidney Mount.

Mr. Perry then died, and she married Noble Junkin, and had other children :

    6. Henry Junkin ; 7. Richard Junkin ; 8. Washington Junkin.

3. Deborah, born 6th March, 1795, and married Ira Broadwell, born 11th March, 1794, son of Nathaniel. [*See Broadwell*, in Appendix.]
4. Richard lives in Cincinnati, is a manufacturer of white lead ; he married, 1st, Margaret Van Zandt, daughter of Henry ; 2d, Lucy Renton ; 3d, Elizabeth, the widow of Sidney Armstrong.
5. Eliza married William Tingley, son of Jonathan, and had children: 1. Elizabeth Tingley ; 2. John Beers ; 3. Jonathan ; 4. Samuel ; 5. Jemima ; 6. William Benton. 7. Albert Lindsley Conklin.

6. Zela married, 1st, Sally Chapman, and removed to Missouri ; she died, and he married —— ——, in Missouri.

7. Joseph Lindsley lives in Cincinnati, is a manufacturer of lard oil ; he married, 1st, Elizabeth Ross ; 2d, Phebe Anne Allen ; 3d, her sister, Margaret Allen, and had children :
    1. Phebe Anne, by 2d wife, and by 3d wife, 2. Stephen Allen Conklin ; 3. Lafayette Conklin.

8. William married Sarah Flanagan, live in Cincinnati, and had children : 1. William Morton ; 2. Margaret : 3. Jemima.
    4. Sarah ; 5. Mary.

9. Willimina married William Morton, and had children :
    1. Jemima ; 2. Susannah ; 3. Sarah ; 4. Emily.
    5. Isaac Morton.

10. John Runyon Conklin married Amanda Connet, lives in Missouri, and had children :
    1. Albert ; 2. Ira ; 3. Charity ; 4. Ellen ; 5. Eliza.
    6. Mary ; 7. John ; 8. Charles ; 9. Deborah ; 10. Sarah.

RICHARD CONKLIN, (son of Abraham,) and Margaret Van Vandt had children :
    1. Jane, who married Henry J. Drake.
    2. Stephen married Mary Forgy.
    3. Isaac married Mary Carman, daughter of Benjamin, from Monmouth county, New Jersey.
    4. Rosalinda married Jesse Tumy.
    5. Mary Elizabeth ; 6. Margaret ; 7. Richard.
Richard Conklin by his 2d wife, Lucy Renton, had children :
    8. Flora ; 9. Kate Conklin.

ZELA CONKLIN and Sally Chapman, had children :
    1. William ; 2. John ; 3. Jemima ; 4. Joseph ; 5. Jefferson ; 6. Richard ; 7. Ira ; 8. Willimina ; 9. —— ——, and by his 2d wife, had three others.

JOSEPH CONKLIN.

JOSEPH CONKLIN was brother of John and of Joshua Conklin, of Williams Farms. (See page 87.)

Joseph Conklin married Mary Cory, sister of Elder Benjamin Cory, of Elizabethtown, (see page 94) and had children :
    1. Isaac, who married Joanna Williams, sister of Jonathan and Thomas Williams.
    2. Joseph, Jun. married Rebecca Ross, daughter of Daniel.
    3. Mary married William Pangborn.
    4 Moses married Margaret Woodruff.
    5. Benjamin married Hannah ——.
    6. Sally married Peter Martin.

7. Phebe married William Jones.

8. Stephen married Anna Crane, daughter of Jacob Crane, at Crane's Mills. (See page 104.) This Jacob Crane had a brother John, who lived on Rahway river, and a brother Isaac, who went to Ohio, lived on Bedell's Station, about 4 miles south of Union, or Shaker Village.

BENJAMIN CONKLIN, (5th child of Joseph,) and his wife, Hannah ——, had children :
1. Charity ; 2. Fanny.
3. Mariah married, as his 2d wife, Mulford Cory, son of Elder Benjamin. (See page 94.)

STEPHEN CONKLIN, (8th child of Joseph,) and Anna Crane had children :
1. Susan, who married Eli James, son of Thomas, he lives in Indiana, and had children : 1. Anna James ; 2. Conklin James ; 3. Martin James ; 4. Susan James.
2. Joseph married Sarah Kinnan, and had a daughter, Anna Mariah.
3. Stephen, Jun. married Sarah Mills, daughter of Abner, lived in Cleremont county, Ohio, and had children :
    1. Elizabeth ; 2. Henry ; 3. Caroline ; 4. Mary ; 5. Cher-lana.
4. Joanna married David Buxton, son of Edmund. [*See Lydia Littell, daughter of David, page 236.*]
5. Martin married Elizabeth Estel, and had a daughter, Sarah Anne Conklin.
6. Dayton married Catherine Woodruff, and had children :
    1. Amanda ; 2. Rebecca ; 3. Olive.
7. Mary married, first, Henry Philips, and had a daughter Angeline Philips. She married, second, Robert Kennedy, and had children : 2. Samuel Kennedy ; 3. David Kennedy ; 4. John Kennedy.
8. Sarah married, first, James Lee, and had a son James Lee. She married, second, David Smith, and had children :
    2. Sarah Anne Smith : 3. Mary Smith.
She married, third, Abraham Hopper, and had children :
    4. Joan Hopper ; 5. Susan Hopper ; 6. Angeline Hopper ; 7. Rebecca Hopper.
9. Spencer married Sarah Anne McFallen, live in Iowa.

STEPHANUS CLARK. (See page 75.)

STEPHANUS CLARK, (son of Daniel,) and Keziah Doty, had children :

1. Polly, who married Jeremiah H. Osborn, in Ohio, as his second wife. (See page 308.)

2. Debby married John Bridge, son of Benjamin.

3. Sally is unmarried; lives at the Wabash, Indiana.

4. David married Phebe Allen, daughter of Joseph. (See page 3.)

5. Israel married ———— ————.

6. Elmer, who is a new light preacher.

JONATHAN HALL. (See page 164.)

JONATHAN HALL, (4th child of Richard,) and Rachel Austin, had children :

1. Esther, who died in infancy.

2. James died in infancy.

3. Jonathan Austin married Anne Whitaker, daughter of Stephen.

4. Moses, who died a young man, by a kick of a horse.

5. David married Mary Hall, daughter of Joseph Hall, (2d child of Richard,) and Ruth Austin, and lived in Michigan, and had children :

    1. Ruth; 2. Susan; 3. Charles; 4. Margaret; 5. Rachel; 6. Reliance; 7. Richard; 8. John.

6. Aaron married Mary ————, and had 5 or 6 children.

7. Joseph married Sarah Flowers; lived in Yates county, New-York, and had children :

    1. William; 2. Austin; 3. Charles; 4. Francis.

JOHN STITES. (See page 408.)

JOHN STITES, (son of Isaac. son of William, Jun.,) and Rurh Moore, daughter of Joseph Moore, had children :

1. Isaac, who married Deborah Kelly, of Mount Bethel.

2. Jacob married Ada Anne Ayers, daughter of William, of Sparta.

3. Samuel married Amy Ayers, sister of Ada Anne.

4. Phebe married James T. Smalley.

5. John married, first, Betsey Ayers, sister of Ada Anne and Amy; second, Lanar Youngs.

6. Joseph married Harriet Ferrigo.

7. Peter married Margaret Dutton, daughter of Amos, of Sparta.

8. Susan married John J. Moffett, son of John.

9. Eliza married George Bady, son of Thomas, of Sparta.

10. William married Mary Nixon, daughter of Matthias, of Newfoundland, Morris county.

11. Benjamin married Phebe Nixon, sister of Mary.

12. Harriet married Daniel Wilson, son of Zachariah, of Mount Bethel.

The following named persons, residing in Passaic Valley, have held the offices attached to their names respectively:

First in Essex Co.—Samuel Potter was a Captain in the Revolutionary war, and after the war a Colonel of Miltia; Captains of Militia, Daniel S. Wood; Benjamin Pettet, John Maxwell, Amos Potter, John Bonnel, Moses G. Elmer, Jabez Thompson, Jotham Potter, David C. Clark, Stephen Day, Samuel Bailey, Luther Littell, of a unifom Company, Aaron Doty of Militia; Major Jotham Potter, Major Luther Littell; Col. Luther Littell.

Second in Morris Co.—Colonel Cornelius Ludlow, Major Benjamin Ludlow, Brigadier Gen. Benjamin Ludlow, Major Gen. Benjamin Ludlow, Brigadier Gen. Solomon Doughty, Major Gen. Solomon Doughty, Capt. Solomon Boyle, Major Solomon Boyle, Col. Solomon Boyle; Captains, Peter Layton, Samuel Stanbury, Benjamin Conklin, Henry W. Tuttle, William M. Clark, Major William M. Clark.

Judges of the court of Common Pleas of Morris Co.—John Carle, Esq., Benjamin Ludlow, Esq., John G. Cooper, Esq., Cornelius Ludlow, Esq., Sheriff George H. Ludlow, Clerk George H. Ludlow, of Essex Co. Samuel Clark, Esq. appointed 1809, John Littell, Esq., appointed 1814.

Justices of the Peace of Essex Co.—Benj. Pettit, Benj. Bonnel, Samuel Potter, Nathaniel Littell, Samuel Clark, Amos Potter, Jonathan M. Meeker, John Littell, appointed 1814, Jotham Potter, Samuel Willcox, Amos Willcox, Daniel S. Clark, Levi Clark, John Lyon, 1836, Apollos M. Elmer, 1837, Jonathan Valentine, Daniel H. Noe, John Wood, of Morris Co., John Carle, Esq., Aaron Ball, Benjamin Ludlow, John G. Cooper, Gabriel Johnson, Thomas Parrot, Cornelius Ludlow, George H. Ludlow, Daniel Runyon, William M. Clark.

The following have been members of the Legislature—Luther Littell, elected in 1829; John Littell, 1837 and 1838; Jotham Potter, 1842 and 1843; Jonathan Valentine, 1849 and 1850; John Carle member of Council in 1783; Benjamin Ludlow was several times member of Council, and member of the Assembly.

The names of the following persons, are found in the Records of the Presbyterian Church, and in deeds as the owners of land, and dwellers within the bounds of the Congregation of New Providence, of which we know nothing more of their history than is noted—John Pierson, William Johnson, Samuel Ross, William Jones, Timothy Whitehead, are named as Elders of the Presbyterian Church.

Abner Brown, Ezekiel Day, Jesse Osborn, Enos Osborn, Edward Jones, Henry Ross, Nathaniel Salmon, John Porterfield, Job Pierson, John Winans, William Crawford, Daniel Bedell, Thomas Cushman, Abraham Osborn, Eliakim Anderson, Zebulon Smith, Jesse Clark, Daniel Jones, Samuel Ross, Jun., Christopher Wamsley, Andrew Blanchard, John Howel, Josiah Frazee, are named, January 5th, 1768, as being members of the Church.

And the following are named under the dates perfixed as dwellers here, viz: 1760, Benjamin Clark ; 1762, Absalom Bedell ; 1763, Abraham Hendricks, Samuel Otter, John Haines, Henry Bonnel, Daniel Ogden ; 1764, Aaron French, Timothy Riggs, John Allen ; 1765, old M. Babcock died ; Richard French, Henry Parcels, Matthias Clark, Deacon Thompson, Mica Howel ; 1768, Stephen Ayers, Schoolmaster ; Jeremiah Bedell ; 1770, Moses Freeman, 1772, Nathaniel Tailor, James Winans, William Carle ; 1773, Andrew Blanchard was one of the Committee to build 16 feet addition to the Church ; 1773, Daniel Woodruff, Joseph Marsh, Samuel Hazel ; 1774, John Sayre ; 1776, Isaac Jones, John Line, Charles Townley, Lawyer Ogden, Deacon Morehouse, Elder Joseph Allen, Elder Daniel Day, Elder Samuel Rolfe, Stephen Morehouse, Stephen Morehouse, Jun., Benjamin Ross.

It is said that John Miller, page 285, was the ancestor of the Miller family in East New-Jersey, and that his sons William, Andrew, Enoch, John, and Aaron, and daughter Hannah, came to New-Jersey from Long Island, then called "Nassau Island."

There is the record of a deed in the Clerk's Office in Newark, N. J. from John Stanbrough and John Norris, of Southampton, in the county of Suffolk, in the Island of Nassau, Province of New-York, to William Miller, of Elizabethtown, N. J. for a hundred acre lot of land No. 55, dated August 30th, 1727. This was the second lot north west of the village of Westfield, and whereon Alderman William Miller lived and died. The next year, May 2d, 1728, William Miller purchased of his brother, Andrew Miller, of Smithtown, Nassau Island, the next lot north west of the above. Therefore it would seem that John Miller, the father, lived on Long Island, and not in Westfield.

JOHN MILLER, of Long Island, (see page 285,) had children :

1. William, who was an Alderman of the borough of Elizabeth, and his name is in the second list of Associates of 1699.

2. Andrew, who married Mary Andrus, of Newark.

3. Enoch, who married Hannah Baker. (See page 285.)

4. John, whose wife's name was Martha.

5. Aaron, who married and had sons, Aaron, Jun. a clock maker, Cornelius, and Robert, and a daughter Betsey, who married Isaac Brokaw, a clock maker, a son of John, near Somerville.

6. Hannah, who married, first, Nathaniel Bonnel 1st, (see page 46 ;) second, Deacon Whitehead.

7. Susannah, who married, first, Mr. Crane ; second, John Ross 1st, as his third wife. (See page 356.)

Alderman WILLIAM MILLER had two or three wives. His children were :

1. Noah, who married Miss Brooks, daughter of Samuel Brooks, who died about 1780.

2. William, Jun. married —— ——.

3. Samuel married —— ——.

4. Joanna, who married, first, Mr. Crane, and had a son, Noah Crane, who married his cousin, Nancy Miller, daughter of William, Jun. Joanna married, second, John Ross, as his second wife. (See page 356.)

5. ——, a daughter, who married Mr. Burnet, the father of the wife of James Wilkison, who lived near the Franklin Mill, New Providence township.

NOAH MILLER, (1st child of Ald. William Miller,) and Miss Brooks had children :

1. Noah, Jun. who married a daughter of Abraham Bonney, Esq. of Woodbridge.

2. Eli Miller, who married Betsey Bryant, daughter of John, of Westfield, and went to the west.

3. Samuel Brooks Miller, who represented the county of Essex several years in the legislature, was a justice of the peace, and judge of the court. He married ——, daughter of Amos Swan, and had children :

    1. Jedediah, who died at about 25 years, by a cut of a scythe.

    2. Eliza, who married Jonathan Osborn, late Sheriff of Essex, son of David, and had children : 1. Matilda, who married Mr. Silvers ; 2. Anne Osborn ; 3. Mary Osborn.

    3. Amos, who is a physician in New-York.

    4. Rhoda Anne, who married Wm. Phyfe, son of Dunican, a cabinet maker of New-York.

    5. Samuel Brooks, who died a lunatic in 1851, aged 30 yrs.

    6. Hannah. 7. Mary.

WILLIAM MILLER, Jun. (son of Alderman William,) had children :

1. Ephraim, who removed when an old man to Springdale, Ohio, and died there, at about 90 years. (See page 293.)

2, John, who married Hannah Tucker, daughter of Ephraim. (See page 444.)

3. Noah, who married Miss Ludlow, and had children :

    1. Sabra, who married Matthias Welsch, and removed to near New Albany, Indiana.

    2. Sarah, who married Elihu Meeker, of Union.

4. Ezra.

5. Nancy, who married her cousin Noah Crane, a grandson of Alderman Miller ; they removed to Ohio, and had children : 1. Levi Crane ; 2. Noah Crane, Jun. who set up the first prining press in Dayton, Ohio, and printed the first newspaper published in that town ; 3. Ephraim Crane ; 4. Wm. Crane ; 5. Ichabod Crane ; 6. Anna Crane ; and others.

SAMUEL MILLER, (3d son of Ald. William Miller,) had children :

1. William, who married Massy Raddin, sister of Jeremiah, (see page 339) and had children : 1. Phebe ; 2. Hannah.

2. Clark Miller, who married, first, Miss Cory, daughter of John Cory, and sister of Parkhurst Cory ; second, Sally Miller, daughter of Aaron, Jun. son of Aaron.

3. Mary, who married Charles Gillman, (he kept a tavern in Westfield,) and had no children.

4. Marsh, who married Betsey Cory, sister of Clark's first wife.

5. Phebe, who married Daniel Perrine, and had children :
1. Polly Perrine, who married Daniel Willis, of Elizabethtown;
2. Hannah Perrine.

6. Hannah, who married, first, Daniel Clark, and had one daughter, Sarah, who married Jonathan Woodruff, Esq. and had no children ; Hannah married, second, Col. Jacob Crane, and had two daughters, Joanna Crane and Hannah Crane, and removed to Canada.

PHEBE MILLER, (daughter of William, son of Samuel,) married John C. Clark, of Westfield, and had children :
1. Polly Clark, who married Jacob Keyser, of New-York.
2. Chloe Clark married Lewis Miller, of Westfield.
3. John M. Clark married Mariah Foster, daughter of John W. Foster, and had no children.
4. Asa Clark is not married,
5. Simeon Clark married ——— ———.
6. Hannah Clark married John H. Wessels, of New-York.

HANNAH MILLER, (daughter of William, son of Samuel,) married Moses Whitehead, and lived near Chatham, and had children :
1. Catherine M. Whitehead, who married John Bird, of Hunterdon County.
2. Nathaniel M. Whitehead married widow Betsey Price, a daughter of John Crane, of Springfield.
3. Phebe Whitehead married William Clark, a carpenter, son of Stephen.
4. William Wesley Whitehead, who died at about 26 yrs.
5. Mary Whitehead married David N. Osborn, son of David L., son of Nehemiah, (see page 310,) and went to Michigan.
6. Alanson Whitehead married Margaret Baker, daughter of Hedges, (see page 21,) and removed to Michigan.
7. Elizabeth married ———, and went to Michigan.

CLARK MILLER, (2d child of Samuel,) and Miss Cory, had children :
1. David, who married Hannah Aiken, daughter of John, son of Deacon Joseph Aiken, and had children :
  1. John, who married Miss Dolbeer, and had children :
    1. John, who went to the west and died unmarried.
    2. Eliza married David Rogers, son of Andrew Rogers and Charlotte Lambert. (See page 209.) 3. Mary, who married Mr. Stites, and died of colera, 1832.
2. Samuel, who went to Springdale, Ohio, and married the widow of a son of Noah Crane, probably Levi, and had a son Levi, and other children.

By his 2d wife, Sally Miller, Clark Miller had other children : William and Martha.

MARSH MILLER, (3d child of Samuel, son of Alderman William,) and Betsey Cory, had children :

1. Samuel, who married Jemima Woodruff, daughter of Noah and Sabra Winans (a daughter of Thomas Winans,) and had children :

 1. Eliza ; 2. Mary P., who married George W. Pierson, son of Moses, of Westfield ; 3. Samuel, who died young.

 4. Aaron, who married —— ——, in New-York.

2. Parkhurst, who died young.

3. Betsey married John Foster, son of John W. Foster, and had children :

 1. Theodore Miller Foster, who married ——, and live in Philadelphia.

 2. Marsh Miller Foster, who married Miss Fox, of Rahway.

 3. Mariah Foster, who married Talmage R. Marsh, son of Charles. She died leaving children : 1. John M. Clark Marsh ; 2. Mariah Marsh.

ANDREW MILLER, (2d child of John first,) and Mary Andrus lived about one mile west of Elizabethown, on the road to Westfield, and had children :

1. Andrew Miller, Jun., who lived in Newark.

2. Samuel, who lived about one mile west of his father's.

3. Hannah.

ENOCH MILLER, (son of John 1st,) and Hannah Baker had children: Enoch, Jr., Andrew, Moses, &c. (See page 285.)

ENOCH MILLER, Jun. (son of Enoch,) and Eliza Ross, (see page 285) had children :

1. Moses, who married Amy Tucker.

2. Enoch 3d, who married Keziah Ross, daughter of David and Nancy Ross.

3. Benjamin, who died an old man, unmarried.

4. Betsey, who married Peter Willcox, Jun. (see page 481) and removed to Ohio.

5. Hannah married Samuel Marsh, son of Moses, and removed to Ohio.

6. Polly married Joseph Dunham, removed to Ohio, and had children: 1. Moses Dunham ; 2. Ross Dunham, who lives in Westfield ; 3. Enoch Dunham ; 4. Asa Dunham ; 5. Benjamin Dunham ; 6. Sarah Dunham ; and others.

MOSES MILLER, (son of Enoch Milller, Jun.) and Amy Tucker had children :

1. Phebe, who married Elijah Ross, son of David Ross, above named, and removed to Butler county, Ohio, and had ten or twelve children.

2. Abby, who married Joseph Denman, son of William, of Springfield.

3. ————, a daughter, who married Elihu Campbell.

4. Samuel; 5. Amy. The three latter went to the west.

ENOCH MILLER 3d, (son of Enoch, Jun.) and Keziah Ross had children:

1. Rebecca, who married Andrew H. Clark, Esq.

2. David, who married Eunice Coriell, daughter of David, of New Market.

3. John married, first, Betsey Ross, daughter of John, (see page 359;) second, Penina Smith, daughter of Jonas Smith, of Orange.

4. Hannah married Dr. Isaac Hendricks Pearce.)P. 104.)

5, Jacob married, first, Betsey Woolley, daughter of Jacob, of Springfield; 2d, Eliza Lee, of Rahway.

6. Keziah, who married Silas Q. Tappen of Hanover.

7. Moses, who went to Ohio, and married there.

8. Stites married, first, Miss Cogswell, of New-York : 2d, ————, in New Orleans.

9. Elijah, who died unmarried.

10 Josiah, who married Lucy Ann Jefferys, daughter of Caleb. (See page 417.)

11. Abner married Miss Tappen, sister of Silas Q. Tappen.

12. Eliza married Mr. Blakely, of Union.

JEDEDIAH MILLER, (son of Enoch 1st,) (see page 285) married and removed to Wilkesbarre, Penn. One of his daughters married John Drew, of Springfield ; another married Mr. Crammer, and removed to Shemokin, Penn.

ANDREW MILLER, (son of Enoch 1st,) and Sarah Ross, daughter of John, (see page 357,) had children :

1. Hannah, who married Thomas Parcel, lived near Chatham, and had nine children.

2. Rebecca married John Brokaw, son of Isaac, the clock maker.

3. Enoch married Johannah Garthwaite, daughter of Jeremiah, of Elizabethtown, and had one son, and five daughters.

4. John married Abigail Stites, daughter of Richard. (See page 407.)

5. Timothy married, first, Susan Cory, daughter of Abner, second, Mary Denton ; lived in South Brunswick.

6. Abner married Bethiah Tryon, of Orange Co. New York, had one son and one daughter.

7. Sarah married James Tharp, of Rahway Neck.

8. Andrew married three times, had children by each ; he lived in Woodbridge.

9. Susan was second wife of John Scudder, cabinet maker ; they removed to Ohio. She died leaving three daughters.

JOHN MILLER, JUN. (son of John 1st,) and his wife Martha had children :
1. Moses, who married Esther Maxwell.
2. Maline.
3. John 3d, who married Phebe Valentine, daughter of Richard, and had but one son :
    Abner 1st, who married Betsey Keyt, daughter of James Keyt and Betsey Jessup, and had children :
    1. Phebe, who married Ichabod Ross, son of Ichabod.— (See page 360.)
    2. Abner 2d, who married Hannah Searing, daughter of Jacob, of Union.
    3. Anna married Israel R. Coriell, son of David, of New Market.
    4. John O. Miller married Sarah Ludlow, daughter of Benjamin and Keziah Ludlow ; he lives on the old Miller homestead.

ABNER MILLER 2d, (son of Abner 1st, son of John, Jun) and Hannah Searing, had children :
1. Phebe.
2. Charles, who married the widow of Stephen Marsh, and daughter of Joseph Morss, son of Doctor Isaac Morss, and lives at Trembly's Point, in Rahway.
3. Elizabeth, who married William T. Baker, son of Henry, (see page 22.) and removed to Chicago.
4. Hannah married William H. Pierson, merchant at Westfield, (as his 2d wife,) son of Sylvanus.
5. Abner 3d married Mary Clark, daughter of David W. Clark, and had a son Irvin.

ANNA MILLER, (3d child of Abner Miller and Betsey Keyt,) and Israel R. Coriell lives at New-Market, and had children :
1. Elizabeth M. Coriell, who married William H. Pierson, merchant, (as his 1st wife,) son of Sylvanus. She died leaving 4 children : Elizabeth, William, Israel and Sarah Pierson.
2. David Coriell, who married Miss Silvers, daughter of Noah, of Rahway, and had children :
    1. Ellen Coriell. 2. Theodore Coriell. 3. Israel Coriell. 4. Abner Coriell.

JOHN O. MILLER, (4th child of Abner Miller and Betsey Keyt,) and Sarah Ludlow had children :

1. Abigal Miller, who married John Grant Crane, son of Josiah, (see page 104) and has a daughter, Elizabeth Crane, who married Daniel Carle Williams, son of Ebenezer S. Williams, of Baskingridge. (See page 480.)

2. Louisa married Elias M. Crane, son of Elias, of Union. (See page 104.)

3. James married Sarah Jane Marsh, daughter of Eli, son of Charles.

4. John Alfred Miller, who went to Red River, Louisiana.

ROBERT MILLER, (son of Aaron, son of John 1st,) married Sarah Kennedy, daughter of Rev. Mr. Kennedy, of Baskingridge, and had children:

1. William Kennedy Miller, a clock maker, of Elizabethtown, married Miss Williams, of Union.

2. Aaron Miller, who married Rhoda Morris, daughter of John, and lived in Rahway.

3. Sarah Miller, who married William Dawes.

4. Phebe Miller married John Hoagland, near Elizabethtown.

BETSEY MILLER, (daughter of Aaron,) and Isaac Brokaw, the clock maker, 3d son of John, had children:

1. John Brokaw, who married Rebecca Miller, daughter of Andrew Miller and Sarah Ross. (See page 285.)

2. Aaron Brokaw, who married Betsey Tucker, daughter of the 3d wife of Capt. Enos Baldwin. (See page 26.)

3. Nancy Brokaw married, first, Solomon Marsh, son of John, of Woodbridge; second, Daniel Moore.

4. Cornelius, born 27th Sept. 1772, married 1st, Elizabeth Anne Tucker, daughter of Daniel; 2d Mary Miller, a widow and daughter of Jonathan Terry, son of William.

JOHN BROKAW, (son of Isaac,) and Rebecca Miller had children:

1. Isaac Brokaw married Susan Lambert, daughter of James. (See page 208.)

2. Betsey Brokaw married William P. Baldwin, of Orange, and had a daughter, Betsey Baldwin.

3. John Brokaw, who married Miss Brokaw, near Somerville.

4. Andrew Brokaw married Betsey Meeker.

5. Cornelius Brokaw married Miss Tichenor, of Canoe Brook.

6. Enoch Brokaw married ——, who died at about 30 yrs.

AARON BROKAW, (2d child of Isaac,) and Betsey Tucker, had children:

1. Cornelius Brokaw; 2. Isaac Augustus Brokaw.

3. Charles Brokaw, who married Susan Tharp, daughter of James Tharp and Susan Miller.

4. Phebe Eliza Brokaw married William Baker, who lives in Rahway.

CORNELIUS BROKAW, (4th child of Isaac,) and Elizabeth Anne Tucker had children :

1. Nancy Brokaw, who married Edmund M. Brown, son of William, of Rahway.

2. Daniel, who died in infancy; 3. Cornelius, who also died in infancy.

And by his 2d wife, Mary, had a son William Terry Brokaw, who marrried Sarah Manning, daughter of Squire. (See Bailey, page 17.)

NOTE.— JOHN BROKAW lived near Somerville, and had children :
1. John, who was killed by the enemy in the Revolutionary war.
2. Benjamin, who married ——.
3. Isaac, the clock maker, who married Betsey Miller.
4. Richard, who married ——.
5. Phebe, who married John Field, of Millstone.
6. Polly, who married Cornelius Van Dyke.
7. Bergun Brokaw.
8. ——, a daughter, who married Mr. Van Arsdale.
9. ——, a daughter, who married Capt. Cornelius Lott.

www.ingramcontent.com/pod-product-compliance
Lightning Source LLC
Chambersburg PA
CBHW072039020426
42334CB00017B/1322